MEDIEVAL NORWICH

Medieval Norwich

Edited by

Carole Rawcliffe and Richard Wilson

Hambledon and London

London and New York

Hambledon and London

102 Gloucester Avenue, London NW1 8HX

175 Fifth Avenue
New York, NY 10010
USA

First Published 2004

ISBN 1 85285 449 9

A description of this book is available from the
British Library and from the Library of Congress.

Typeset by Carnegie Publishing, Lancaster,
and printed in Great Britain by Cambridge University Press.

Distributed in the United States and Canada
exclusively by Palgrave Macmillan,
a division of St Martin's Press.

Contents

Illustrations

Plates
Between pages 58–59

Between pages 250–251

Text Illustrations

Maps

Tables

Preface

From the early 1500s until the mid-eighteenth century Norwich ranked as England's second city, and has since remained East Anglia's regional capital. Yet, surprisingly, given its standing in the urban hierarchy, it boasts no extended history to celebrate its eminence beyond Francis Blomefield's two-volume efforts of the 1740s, themselves part of an eleven-volume history of Norfolk. Ideally, it requires the largest Victoria County History tome or even a series, such as Sir Francis Hill's celebrated four-volume survey of Lincoln, to do justice to Norwich's long history, to capture the richness of its medieval life and to record its more recent achievements. In fact, the Wrst option has been twice seriously proposed in the last thirty years. On both occasions the enterprise stumbled on the rocks of finance. In these days of regular research assessment exercises no solitary academic can spend half a lifetime on one such demanding project, while gifted amateurs of Sir Francis's calibre have always been rare birds indeed.

Buoyed by the success of the publication of *Norwich Cathedral: Church, City and Diocese, 1096-1996* (1996), we decided to produce a similarly multi-authored history of Norwich. Although it could never achieve the unity a single scholar would bring to the task, a set of essays on the city's history seemed the only solution to balance hard economics and practicality. Besides, many historians and archaeologists have been working on various aspects of Norwich's history in recent years. These two volumes bring together the researches of no fewer than thirty-three such scholars. Even so, there are inevitable gaps: the most obvious being an account of the Norwich School of Painters. But we decided that a brief essay, with a limited number of illustrations, would be inadequate, especially as the subject already possesses an extensive literature. Nevertheless, we hope to have conveyed the extraordinary richness of the city's history and archaeology, the glory of its archival sources, and the sheer variety of work undertaken over the last few decades. We hope also to point the way forward to new vistas yet unexplored.

The project has enjoyed funding from a number of institutions. The life of Norwich during the past thirty years in all its aspects, cultural, sporting and educational, has been much enriched by the munificence of the

Norwich Town Close Estate Charity. It has provided generous support towards the publication of these volumes. To the Trust we dedicate our efforts as a small testimony to their important role in the city. We have also received grants from Thomas Anguish's Educational Foundation, the University of East Anglia and its Centre of East Anglian Studies, and from the City Council.

These funds have allowed us to employ Dr Christine Clark as senior research fellow on *The History of Norwich.* She has dealt efficiently and tactfully with our contributors, presenting to them the velvet glove that masked the iron fists of the editors. We are immensely grateful for her efforts, as indeed we are for those of our contributors, unpaid, largely uncomplaining in meeting our requests, constructive in reading each other's chapters and always enthusiastic about the undertaking as a whole. Professor Colin Davis played a notable part in getting the project started. To Professor Christopher Harper-Bill we owe an especial debt for answering an appeal for last minute copy with characteristic helpfulness and good humour.

Our thanks must also extend to Dr John Alban and the staff of the Norfolk Archive Centre. Whether in temporary accommodation after the Wre of 1994 or in the process of moving to their splendid new quarters at County Hall, they have provided the best and most efficient of services. In similar circumstances regarding changes of accommodation, Dr Clive Wilkins-Jones, Team Librarian of the Norfolk Heritage Centre, has offered friendly and patient help regarding the collections in his care. Norma Watt, Assistant Keeper of Art at the Castle Museum, proved, as always, an invaluable source of advice and guidance with illustrations. Most of the maps and diagrams have been drawn by Phillip Judge, the unsung hero of so many publications emanating from the University of East Anglia. Jenni Tanimoto of the Centre of East Anglian Studies and Dawn Goff of the School of History assisted in many, largely unseen, ways. We have drawn heavily upon the photographic skills of Sheila Davies and the expertise of Margery Rhodes, Slide Librarian in the School of World Art Studies at UEA. Matthew Martin, Clerk to the Norwich Town Close Estate Charity until 2003, ensured that all our dealings with its trustees ran smoothly. Brian Ayers, County Archaeologist and latterly chair of the Centre of East Anglian Studies Committee, with his unrivalled knowledge and infectious enthusiasm, made sure our account possessed a proper archaeological dimension. Professor Richard Britnell of the University of Durham generously read, and commented upon, the medieval chapters. Both volumes were indexed by Alisdair Hawkyard, to whom we also extend our thanks. Peter Martin read the entire manuscript with the eyes of both a seasoned author and general reader and the patience of Job. Unflagging support for the project and its editors has come from Professor John Charmley, Dean of the School of History. Martin Sheppard, publisher of this book, as well as histories of Norwich's cathedral and university, undertook the enterprise with a determination to produce the two volumes attractively both in appearance and price. We are most grateful to him for bringing this about.

Carole Rawcliffe Richard Wilson

University of East Anglia

Abbreviations

Blomefield, *Norfolk*	F. Blomefield, *An Essay Towards a Topographical History of the County of Norfolk* (11 vols, London, 1805–10)
BNP	*Bury and Norwich Post*
CCR	*Calendar of Close Rolls*
CChR	*Calendar of Charter Rolls*
CFR	*Calendar of Fine Rolls*
CLPFD	*Calendar of Letters and Papers Foreign and Domestic, Henry VIII*
Cotton, *HA*	Bartholomew de Cotton, *Historia Anglicana*, ed. H. R. Luard (RS, 1859)
CPR	*Calendar of Patent Rolls*
CSPD	*Calendar of State Papers Domestic*
CUL	Cambridge University Library
DCN	Dean and Chapter of Norwich
DNB	*Dictionary of National Biography*
EAA	East Anglian Archaeology
EconHR	*Economic History Review*
EDP	*Eastern Daily Press*
EEN	*Eastern Evening News*
EHR	*English Historical Review*
HC	Heritage Centre, Norfolk and Norwich Millennium Library
HMC	*Reports of the Royal Commission on Historical Manuscripts*
IJ	*Ipswich Journal*
NA	*Norfolk Archaeology*
NCC	Norwich Consistory Court
NCR	Norwich City Records
NC	*Norfolk Chronicle*
NCQS	Norwich Court of Quarter Sessions

NG	*Norwich Gazette*
NM	*Norwich Mercury*
Norwich Cathedral	I. Atherton and others, eds, *Norwich Cathedral: Church, City and Diocese 1096–1996* (London, 1996)
NPD	Norwich Private Deeds
NRO	Norfolk Record Office
NRS	Norfolk Record Society
Pelling, *Common Lot*	M. Pelling, *The Common Lot: Sickness, Medical Occupations and the Urban Poor in Early Modern England* (London, 1998)
Pound, *Census*	J. F. Pound, ed., *The Norwich Census of the Poor 1570* (NRS, xl, 1971)
PCC	Prorogative Court of Canterbury
PP	*Parliamentary Papers*
PRO	Public Record Office (National Archives)
RCN	W. Hudson and J. C. Tingey, eds, *The Records of the City of Norwich* (2 vols, Norwich, 1906–10)
reg.	register
RS	Rolls Series
SRS	Suffolk Record Society
Tanner, *CLMN*	N. Tanner, *The Church in Late Medieval Norwich* (Toronto, 1984)
TRHS	*Transactions of the Royal Historical Society*
UEA	University of East Anglia
VCH	*Victoria County History*

The Contributors

Carole Rawcliffe is Professor of Medieval History in the School of History at UEA, and has edited the first volume of *The History of Norwich*, as well as those chapters up to the 1660s in the second. She is a medical historian, with a particular interest in Norwich and its hospitals.

Richard Wilson is an Emeritus Professor of History at UEA, and has edited the chapters in *The History of Norwich* after the English Civil War. His research interests include the history of brewing, textiles and the English country house.

Christine Clark is a Senior Research Associate in the School of History at UEA, and has published on many aspects of the business, economic and social history of East Anglia in the modern period. She has worked as Research Assistant on *The History of Norwich.*

Brian Ayers is County Archaeologist for Norfolk. He has written extensively on the built environment of Norwich and is a Fellow of the Society of Antiquaries of London and of the Royal Society of Arts.

James Campbell has recently retired as Tutorial Fellow and Professor of Medieval History at Worcester College, Oxford. His many publications include work on medieval Norwich and East Anglia.

Penelope Dunn has recently completed a doctoral thesis at UEA on the social and economic history of Norwich in the aftermath of the Black Death. She previously held a Scouloudi Fellowship at the Institute of Historical Research, University of London.

Jonathan Finch is a Lecturer in Archaeology at the University of York. He has worked on the church monuments of Norwich and Norfolk and their role in the construction of identity and memory.

Ruth Frost completed a doctoral dissertation at Cambridge University on the aldermen of late fifteenth-century Norwich. She teaches at Okanagan University College in British Columbia, Canada.

Christopher Harper-Bill is Professor of Medieval History in the School of History and former Director of the Centre of East Anglian Studies, UEA. He has published widely on the Church in medieval East Anglia.

Ralph Houlbrooke is Professor of Early Modern History at the University of Reading. He has published on Tudor church courts, the early modern family and attitudes to death, as well as on Tudor Norfolk and Norwich.

David King is an Honorary Research Fellow in the School of History at UEA. He is preparing the *Corpus Vitrearum* of medieval stained glass in Norfolk and is window glass consultant to the Norfolk Archaeological Unit.

Philippa Maddern is Associate Professor of History at the University of Western Australia. She has published on many aspects of late medieval East Anglian society, including violence and disorder.

Muriel C. McClendon is Associate Professor of History at the University of California, Los Angeles. She has written on the Reformation in Norwich and on the Protestant sense of identity.

Elizabeth Rutledge trained as an archivist but has mainly worked freelance as a lecturer and researcher. She is a research fellow of the Centre of East Anglian Studies at UEA, and has published on medieval Norwich and Lynn.

Norman Tanner SJ was University Research Lecturer at Oxford University whence he has recently moved to become Professor of Church History at the Gregorian University of Rome. His publications include works on religion in medieval Norwich.

Andy Wood is a Reader in the School of History at UEA. He specialises in English social history in the early modern period, and has published widely in the fields of popular culture and social history.

Introduction

Carole Rawcliffe

> The inhabitants in general are remarkable for their urbanity, hospitality, and the readiness with which they contribute to all public and private charitable institutions. The better classes for their taste and munificence; and greatly to the credit of the lower classes, much less of that inclination to dissoluteness of manners prevails among them than is usually found in large and populous cities. So strict is the attention of the magistrates, in checking in its earliest existence the progress of vice and immorality, that the execution of a criminal in the city does not occur for many years together ... The walls are said to include a space of more than three miles in circumference, but the whole has never yet been built upon, large portions of ground in the extremities next the walls being laid out in gardens and orchards, which gives the city a more rural appearance than many towns of not one quarter its extent.[1]
>
> P. Browne, *The History of Norwich*, 1814

Thus the Norwich antiquary, Philip Browne, who is writing about his native city at the close of the Napoleonic wars. His demonstrable pride in this well-behaved and cultivated community, with its green space and strong sense of mutual obligation, would have struck an immediate chord with far earlier generations of citizens. In 1559, members of the ruling assembly reflected that, 'from tyme owte of mynde' there had been 'a comely and decent order used within this cittye', notably with regard to the paving of the streets. 'Whiche thing,' they observed, 'hath not only bene a great ease and helthefull commodyte to the inhabitauntes ... but also a goodly bewtefying and an occasion that dyuerse [diverse visitors] havyng accesse to the same cittye from ffarre and strange places haue moche commended and praysed.'[2] From the later middle ages onwards, when members of the governing elite sank a small fortune into rebuilding, cleansing and disciplining the urban environment, Norwich consciously projected itself as a model for others to follow. However 'wretchedly divided' its electorate may have been, however many 'bloody noses and

FIGURE 1. Prospect of Norwich, looking east across the city, from William Cuningham's *Cosmographical Glasse* of 1558. (*Norfolk Heritage Centre, photograph by Terry Burchell*)

broken heads' were nursed in private,[3] its public face remained – or did its best to appear – calm and confident.

In an unpublished history of the city, drafted in 1737 within months of his death, its librarian, Benjamin Mackerell, praised 'the painful industry of the common sort, the great humanity of the wealthy and the firm loyalty of the greatest number'. Norwich, he believed, must be 'the most healthful city in England', blessed as it had been for centuries by 'the goodness of its situation, the serenity of the air and the multitude of gardens in all parts'.[4] Such, indeed, is the image presented in the first perspective map of Norwich (and of any English provincial town) produced by the local physician, William Cuningham, in his *Cosmographical Glasse* of 1558 (Figure 1). With its open landscape, handsome buildings and general air of wellbeing, prosperity and peacefulness, it is in every respect 'a fine city'.[5] This phrase, long used as a slogan to promote local tourism, flowed easily from the pen of another resident, the author, George Borrow. His autobiography of 1851, *Lavengro: the Scholar, the Gypsy, the Priest,* dwells lovingly upon the 'venerable houses', the 'gray old castle upon the top of that mighty mound' and the 'old Norman master-work, that cloud-encircled cathedral spire'. Overtaken by the brash, booming and fiercely competitive industrial cities of the north, Norwich seemed to have entered its somnolent twilight years. To the average Victorian reader, obsessed with modernity, antiquity was hardly a term of praise. Yet at this stage in its history the city could do little more than reflect wistfully on the achievements of a more glorious past. Its principal claim to fame now lay, as Borrow observed, in being 'perhaps the most curious specimen at present extant of the genuine old English town'.[6]

The comments made by visitors to Norwich underscore the sharp contrast between the image assiduously cultivated by its rulers and the reality of life in a city beset by the vicissitudes of boom and slump, growth and decline. One of the first to pass judgement was the East Anglian versifier and agriculturalist, Thomas Tusser (d. 1580), who in his youth experienced the less attractive aspects of urban society as the aggressive Tudor poor laws began to bite. He was struck by Norwich's affluent and tidy appearance, but aware that a scholar down on his luck with a growing family to support could expect no warmer welcome on such clean streets than a sturdy beggar. The corporation was then still struggling to rehabilitate itself after the traumatic events of Kett's Rebellion (1549), in which several of its members had played an ambivalent part.[7] Allegations of double-dealing, ineffective leadership and even treason were all the harder to bear in view of the successful efforts previously made to live down Norwich's late medieval reputation as a notorious trouble spot.[8] During the late 1420s the mayor and aldermen already had cause to lament that 'Norwich in diuers parties of the Rewme of Ingelond is heuyly voysed for lak of good and vertuous gouernaunce'. The confiscation of the city's liberties by the crown, in 1437, because of dissension among the elite, placed only a temporary curb upon the warring factions.[9] Further disturbances in 1443, resulting in a longer period of royal rule and a hefty fine, were followed seven years later by demonstrations against the unpopular bishop, Walter Lyhart.[10] By the date of Queen Elizabeth's accession, there was clearly a great deal of ground to recover, as the city seemed to have lapsed into its old habits.

The salubrious, untroubled environment depicted in Cuningham's map, which was itself part of this propaganda campaign, had been bought at a price, as Thomas Tusser discovered. For him and others without work the much-vaunted 'ayer' of Norwich blew uncomfortably chill:

> At Norwich fyne, for me and myne, a Citie trim.
> Where straungers well may seeme to dwell,

That pytch and pay, or keepe their day,
But who that want shall find it scant so good for him.

From Norwich ayer, in great dispayer,
Away to flie, or els to die,
To seeke more health, to seeke more welth,
Then was I glad.

From thence so sent, away I went,
With sicknes worne, as one forlorne ...[11]

If Tusser was disillusioned by his experience of Norwich, some remained sceptical of the wholesome image projected by its rulers at every opportunity. As the courtier-poet, Sir John Harington (d. 1612), observed with characteristic asperity:

> whether it be the praise of the bishops, or the people, or both, I know not; or whether I have here a partiall relation; but by that I have heard, I should judge this city to be another Utopia. The people live so orderly, the streets kept so cleanly, the trades-men, younge and old, so industrious, the better sort so provident, and withal so charitable; that it is as rare to meet a beggar there as it is common to see them at Westminster.[12]

Yet there was more than empty rhetoric in these claims. Norwich had, indeed, staged a dramatic recovery in the face of disease, rebellion and recession. By the 1570s it was setting the national agenda for schemes of poor relief and urban regeneration: characteristics which already seemed to define the city centuries before Browne published his encomium. As late as 1790, the *Ipswich Journal*, in a rare tribute to a regional rival, observed that 'no place enters more warmly into acts of kindness towards the poorer part of their fellow citizens'.[13]

For many, including the poet, Michael Drayton (d. 1631), Norwich's admirable combination of sobriety, hygiene and productivity owed much to the Strangers, who had fled religious persecution in the Netherlands to a more congenial home. He commended

That hospitable place to the industrious Dutch,
Whose skill in making stuffs, and workmanship is such,
(For refuge hither come) as they our aid deserve,
By labour sore that live, whilst oft the English starve;
On roots and pulse that feed, on beef and mutton spare,
So frugally they live, not gluttons as we are.[14]

On his visit in 1650, John Taylor was overwhelmed by the sheer profusion of 'stuffs' cascading off the looms of Norwich's master weavers, 'either for wearing, or ornaments; to adorne houses with Hangings, Carpets, or Curtaines, of innumerable sorts, colours, varieties, and more hard names than any Apothecary hath upon his Boxes or Gallypots'. He also noted with surprise that over half the area within the walls remained undeveloped.[15] His reaction was typical. However else responses may have differed, everyone agreed that Norwich presented a veritable *rus in urbe*, a garden city, in the most literal sense (Figures 2 and 3). Thomas Fuller waxed lyrical on this theme, reflecting in his *Worthies of England* (1662) upon the civilising effect such a green and pleasant landscape must have upon the men and women fortunate enough to enjoy it:

> Norwich is (as you please) either a city in an orchard, or an orchard in a city, so equally are the houses and trees blended in it, so that the pleasure of the country and the populousness of the city meet here together. Yet, in this mixture, the inhabitants participate nothing of the rusticalness of the one, but altogether of the urbanity and civility of the other.[16]

Thomas Baskerville (1618), another of the many seventeenth-century travellers to leave a vivid pen-portrait of the city, was frankly disappointed by the River Wensum, which, in his opinion, lacked the necessary breadth and grandeur to present a suitably imposing urban vista.[17] It was, moreover (as so many local people had bitterly complained for the previous four hundred years, if not longer), badly polluted with the noxious waste created by the leather and cloth industries upon which trade depended.[18] Yet he, too, could not but be impressed by Norwich's 'ancient flint wall, with towers at convenient distance for defence, and gates for entrance'. He praised the unique pattern of 'gardens, orchards and enclosures', the 'large and well-built' parish churches, the 'very stately castle' with its massive dyke, and the generous provision made for 'people wearied with the toils and care of their fore-past life' in the Great Hospital, which had been founded for the city's poor in 1249. Most of all, though, the central market place, another salient feature of the city's medieval topography, seized his imagination (Figure 8). Its size was matched by the gargantuan piles of food on sale there. One superlative follows another: 'the greatest shambles for butchers' meat I had ever yet seen', abutted on a similar emporium for poultry and dairy produce, the quarters of veal vying with mounds of eggs and cheese. Cheek by jowl with heaps of grain and a 'great store of gingerbread' were stalls selling fish commandeered from the Yarmouth quays in such quantity as to leave the port itself virtually empty.[19]

Long after Norwich had slipped down the league table of England's largest and most prosperous cities, the market remained – and still remains – a major tourist attraction. The poet and essayist, George Granville

FIGURE 2. Bishop's bridge with its gate, the River Wensum and the surrounding meadows. Detail from Samuel and Nathaniel Buck's south-east prospect of Norwich of 1741, which provides a panorama facing west. (*Norfolk Heritage Centre, photograph by Terry Burchell*)

Barker, who visited Norwich in the late 1930s, was as struck by its size and diversity as Baskerville had been over three centuries before:

> The market place itself, with its apparatus of stalls and boxes and tarpaulins, its variety of smells from fruit and meat and flowers and fish, its cobbles and lavatories, its vendors with hoarse voices and its continual bustle, looks and smells and tastes like limbo: there is a real thrill in spending a morning wandering around it.[20]

By far the best-known accounts of Norwich in the late seventeenth and eighteenth centuries come from the pens of two travellers with a keen eye for the economic and social developments then affecting town and country alike. Celia Fiennes (1689) and Daniel Defoe (1724) have both left perceptive and frequently quoted descriptions of England's second city in its prime. Struck, like Baskerville, by the scale and profusion of the markets, Fiennes commented approvingly on the broad, clean and well-paved streets, the sophisticated water supply and the distinctive medieval

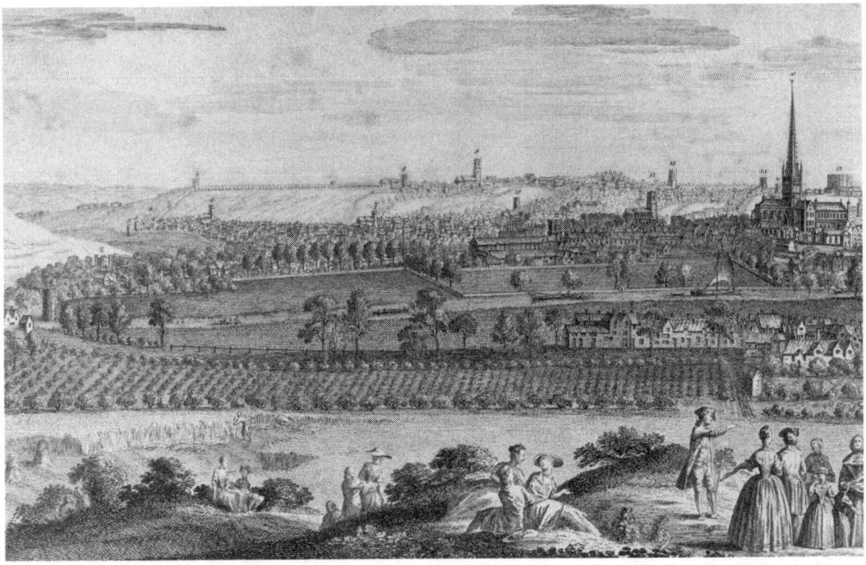

FIGURE 3. Norwich, 'the city of gardens', viewed from the suburb of Pockthorpe, from Samuel and Nathaniel Buck's north-east prospect of Norwich of 1741. (*Norfolk Heritage Centre, photograph by Terry Burchell*)

architecture, with its glassy knapped flint. From her vantage point on the castle mound she observed that 'the whole Citty lookes like what it is, a rich, thriveing industrious place', its wealth based upon the 'great perfection of the textiles, 'which is the whole business of the place'.[21] Defoe likewise pronounced Norwich 'an antient, large, rich and populous city'. Its deserted streets, which on weekdays gave the appearance of a ghost town, were, he reflected, a sign of prosperity, since the inhabitants were 'all busie at their manufactures ... in their garrets at their looms, and in their combing-shops ... twisting-mills and other work-houses'.[22] The industrious Dutch had taught a valuable lesson.

Norwich emerges from these accounts as a buoyant regional capital, feeding – and feeding off – the most fertile and productive hinterland in medieval and early modern England.[23] Arriving from France for a year's study, in 1784, the young François de la Rochefoucauld immediately identified the reasons for its long-term commercial success. He made copious notes on its manufactures, 'which for centuries have been steadily increasing, but which have never known so much activity as there is today', and was (uncharacteristically) amazed by the brilliance of local society, conceding that it far outshone anything in provincial France. Influenced, no doubt, by his friendship with the agricultural reformer, Arthur Young, he attributed this longstanding prosperity to the blessings of nature and topography:

> The town has the advantage of being almost in the middle of the county, and having very good soil all round it, cultivated by a large number of labourers and providing fully for the town's great consumption. It stands in an area where grain of all kinds is abundant, where all breeds of livestock are raised, where malt especially makes a good price ... It is by water that Norwich receives all its provisions in grain, and all its coal, of which the consumption is considerable; for its dyes and the preparation of cloths ... its wools arriving spun from different parts of England and Ireland; in a word, all its consumption requirements and all the raw materials for its manufactures. All the manufactures themselves are taken the twenty miles to Yarmouth, and through that port ... exported to all parts of Europe.[24]

This happy state of affairs was not destined to last. Other visitors, and some inhabitants, too, felt the city had been trapped, like a fly in amber, in its medieval past. The narrow streets, which earlier generations of tourists had found quaint and interesting, began to seem cramped and dirty, the flint buildings simply old-fashioned. In a world obsessed by Enlightenment concepts of progress, there was no place for such relics of a bygone age as the fourteenth-century walls and gates, which, it was now claimed, prevented the healthy circulation of the air and impeded the view. A campaign, begun in 1783, led to the demolition of the gates a decade later, while the walls ('a nuisance that smells rank in the nose of modern improvement') were left to collapse.[25] This bid for modernity was not, however, a portent of real and lasting prosperity. Once famed for its path-breaking approach to public health, Norwich now lagged behind other cities with their wide streets, grand municipal buildings and temples to commerce. The graphic account of overcrowded dwellings, of 'very bad and very defective' water supply, inadequate drainage, congested burial grounds and frequent epidemics presented in William Lee's *Report on the Sanitary Condition of the City and County of Norwich* (1850) confirmed the impression that decline had, indeed, set in.[26] Significantly, his findings appeared within a few months of Borrow's *Lavengro*, with its nostalgic evocation of vanished greatness. The causes of this decline and the city's eventual recovery will be considered in the second volume of *The History of Norwich*. It is appropriate at this point to examine the various attempts made by local scholars to document the history of England's second city in its prime.

Norwich boasts a long and impressive antiquarian tradition, notable for the interest shown by its historians, from William Worcester onwards, in the study of space and topography as well as the more predictable subjects of genealogy, heraldry and civic politics.[27] Worcester, who retired to Norwich after the death of his demanding employer, Sir John Fastolf of Caister, compiled his *Itineraries*, an early type of historical guidebook, in the 1470s. He was especially well placed to note, in careful detail, the measurements of its great medieval buildings, but relied more upon his imagination when it came to writing about its origins. In keeping with contemporary tradition, the region's first city needed a suitably distinguished founder, whom Worcester identified as Gwytelinus, king of the Britons. Sad to say, this mythical figure was not the builder of the exquisite 'blanch flour' castle, nor did Julius Caesar himself extend the fortifications, although to a scholar seeped in the legends of Rome such a tale must have seemed eminently plausible.[28] In other respects, though, Worcester proved a model topographer, recognising the importance of buildings in the urban landscape and the need to describe them in as much detail as possible. Norwich occupies only a few pages in his work, however, and the best part of three centuries elapsed before the city received the attention it deserved. There were, meanwhile, occasional straws in the wind, but nothing came of them. John Caius (d. 1573), the eminent Norwich-born physician, remained close to the friends of his boyhood and disclosed in the preface of a book on the sweating sickness (which he wrote in 1552, apparently for their benefit) that he had started to compose a 'chronicle of the citie of Norwiche, of the beginninge and thinges done ther from time to time'. It was, unfortunately, a retirement project, 'the matere wherof yet rude and undigested lyeth by me, which at laisure I intende to polishe, and to make an end of that I have begunne'.[29] Like so many undertakings of this kind, it never saw the light of day.

Later generations of scholars, including John Camden (d. 1623), Sir Henry Spelman (d. 1641) and Sir William Dugdale (d. 1686), drew upon the Norwich records, but, despite the remarkable flowering of antiquarian studies during the seventeenth century, a history of Norfolk on the scale of Dugdale's *Antiquities of Warwickshire* never materialised. This was not for lack of interest or enthusiasm. One local gentleman, overwhelmed by Dugdale's achievement, begged him, in 1659, to take up the challenge. He was assured of rich rewards, or, should he expire in the attempt, 'a statue of gilded brasse in the market place at Norwich to your memorie and for the encouragement of ingenious posteritie'.[30] This mark of honour was eventually accorded to Dugdale's friend, the physician Sir Thomas Browne, whose antiquarian publications contain surprisingly little on his native city. His work on Norwich was confined to an account of the tombs and monuments in the cathedral, published posthumously as the *Rerpertorium*, a lament on the destructive power of iconoclasm recently experienced in 'the late civill warres'.[31]

It was not until the eighteenth century that the first sustained attempts were made to write the city's history from its vast store of muniments. Despite the energy and commitment of a 'little society of Icenian antiquarians', which numbered Bishop Thomas Tanner (d. 1735) and Peter le Neve (d. 1729) in its ranks, few of these projects came near fruition.[32] Although he produced a history of King's Lynn, Benjamin Mackerell (d. 1738), did not live to publish his companion volume for Norwich, which remains in manuscript to this day.[33] His contemporary, John Kirkpatrick, sometime treasurer of the Great Hospital, made even slower progress. The great mass of transcripts and jottings from the archives accumulated before his early death, in 1728, collected dust for over a century.[34] Through the efforts of the collector, Dawson Turner, some of these notes finally appeared in 1845 as *A History of the Religious Orders and Communities of the Hospitals and Castle of Norwich, Written about the Year 1725*. William Hudson, who combined his duties as vicar of the parish church of St Peter Parmentergate with a passion for local history, subsequently brought out *The Streets and Lanes of the City of Norwich* (1889), which incorporated a good deal of his own research along with Kirkpatrick's.

Hudson is now chiefly remembered as editor of a clutch of the city's most important medieval legal documents,[35] and for his energetic collaboration with its honorary archivist, J. C. Tingey. Together they reclassified the civic records on their removal from the guildhall to the newly created Castle Museum in 1894, produced a much needed catalogue five years later, and then compiled the two-volume *Records of the City of Norwich* (1906–10), which still constitutes a major source of reference for historians of English towns. Hudson's work is notable for his lively – and in some respects pioneering – sense of the urban landscape and of the importance of environmental issues, subjects which figure prominently in this present volume. It is worth noting, for example, that in 1896 he wrote a short and extremely influential book for the popular market to explain *How the City of Norwich Grew into Shape*.[36]

Interest in local history had, meanwhile, been greatly stimulated by the foundation of the Norfolk and Norwich Archaeological Society. An enthusiastic public meeting, chaired by Bishop Stanley in January 1846, was followed a year later by the first number of *Norfolk Archaeology*, one of the earliest journals devoted to county and regional history which were to become such a feature of nineteenth-century British scholarship, both amateur and professional. 'Antiquity properly called forth', pronounced the editor of this gloriously eclectic volume, 'lends her torch to history; nor does Religion herself disdain to allow its gleam to penetrate her sanctuary'.[37] The blaze was indeed a bright one. Thanks to the apparently insatiable demand for articles on aspects of Norwich's past, the antiquaries of Hudson's generation maintained a level of productivity which would today gladden the heart of any university appointments committee.[38]

Their efforts were, none the less, overshadowed, and perhaps not a little inhibited, by the existence of Francis Blomefield's magisterial survey of the city's history and buildings, first published serially in instalments between 1741 and 1745. It formed the second part of his projected *Essay towards the Topographical History of Norfolk*, left incomplete on his death in 1752, when he was 'snatched away in the midst of his labours' at the age of just forty-seven.[39] Like so many historians of the region before and since, Blomefield found it impossible to meet an over-optimistic deadline. Having easy access to the massive archives of Peter le Neve and Thomas Martin (d. 1771), two more scholars who found it easier to collect than to write, he launched an ambitious fund-raising proposal. The entire work was to be published in regular monthly 'numbers' between 1734 and 1736: an impossible target which reflects the enthusiasm of a young and inexperienced beginner. As the enormity of his task became all too clear, schedules slipped and it was not until 1739 that the first part (including the borough of Thetford) was finished.[40] 'I am well apprized what number of carpers and enemies this work will meet with', a chastened and more cynical Blomefield observed in his introduction, adding, with some feeling, that 'they must be such as know not with what difficulty, length of time and expense the *materials* for this *Essay* have been got together'.[41] Illness and the manifold problems of running his own press held up work on Norwich, to which he turned next, although he at least lived to enjoy considerable acclaim for his meticulous study of its topography and institutions. For the last two centuries, indeed, Blomefield's county history has remained the only work to cover the sweep of Norwich's medieval and early modern past in significant detail and depth.

A number of authors have since produced short, single-volume histories of Norwich,[42] but none have attempted a full-scale academic study, which seeks to integrate the growing body of archival, architectural, topographical and archaeological material now at our disposal. This apparent diffidence on the part of scholars is understandable, given the sheer profusion of sources, which, in terms of chronological breadth, must rank among some of the best in Europe. From an early date the city fathers took great care to organise and preserve their records. The compilation of the only known surviving English medieval urban cartulary, the Norwich

Domesday (1394–97), along with the Book of Customs (1306–11), the Old Free Book (1384), the *Liber Albus* (1426), the Book of Pleas (*c.* 1454), the Mayor's Book (1526) and the *Liber Ruber* (1562), demonstrates their keen sense of the importance of the civic archive.[43] Perhaps like John Carpenter, who produced a book of laws and customs of London (where he was common clerk) in 1419, they were galvanised into action by the loss of so many experienced and knowledgeable aldermen during outbreaks of plague. This left untried office holders in desperate need of written guidance.[44] At all events, a plethora of measures for the greater security and better management of a rapidly expanding body of records followed in the late sixteenth and seventeenth centuries. Yet, despite their abundance and the wealth of historical evidence they contain, the Norwich records are still under used, most notably for the medieval period. The recent *Cambridge Urban History of Great Britain*, i, *600–1540*,[45] has, for example, comparatively little to say about the city, a reticence which appears all the more striking given the attention which its contributors have paid to London, York and Bristol.

A mere glance at Hudson and Tingey's *Revised Catalogue of the Records of the City of Norwich* (1898) serves to explain why so many projects remain, like Kirkpatrick's, largely unfinished. 'Better by far he had contented himself with amassing less and turning what he had got to account', Dawson Turner shrewdly remarked,[46] although it is easy to see how this indefatigable scholar became buried under a pile of evidence as overwhelming as the mountains of food on display in Norwich market. To the city's own archives must, of course, be added the legal and administrative records of central government, stored in the Public Record Office, Kew, and the copious records of the Dean and Chapter of Norwich, which date from the eleventh century.[47] The scale of the historian's task is further compounded by the steadily increasing volume of secondary printed works, on topics ranging from the medieval Jewish community to the insurance industry, which now illuminate discrete aspects of the city's history and culture. Specific institutions, such as the cathedral, the castle, several hospitals and schools, the Town Close charity, the public library and the university have also been studied in depth, adding yet more pieces to this constantly expanding jigsaw.[48]

Full as it is, the written record illuminates only one part of the picture. As in Borrow's day, Norwich's medieval heritage still dominates the landscape, for, as well as its celebrated castle and cathedral, the city still possesses over thirty parish churches, some outstanding examples of domestic architecture, a guildhall, two bridges,[49] the finest surviving friary complex in England and two hospitals, all of which were built before the

FIGURE 4. The cow tower, cathedral and pastures of the Great Hospital (formerly St Giles's hospital) in the nineteenth century. (*Trustees of the Great Hospital, with permission from Ms Brigid Land*)

Reformation. Despite the effects of sustained periods of iconoclasm in the sixteenth and seventeenth centuries and sweeping changes in both ecclesiastical and secular fashions, a good deal of its rich material culture still survives from this period, most notably in the remarkable stained glass of St Peter Mancroft, the city's richest church.[50] Incomplete but substantial stretches of the walls, and the great Cow Tower which dominates the arc of the Wensum as it curves southwards, constitute a permanent reminder of the late medieval defences which cost so much to build and maintain (Figures 4 and 5). The published reports of the Norwich Survey and Norfolk Archaeological Unit, frequently cited in the pre-Reformation chapters of this volume, have, moreover, brought to light swathes of the city's buried past. The vital importance of archaeology in understanding its origins and growth is apparent from Brian Ayers' *Norwich* (1994, revised 2003), which explains how the built environment developed from the mid-Anglo Saxon period onwards.

Despite its title and ambitious agenda, *Norfolk Archaeology* published comparatively little of note on excavations in Norwich until after the Second World War, when urban archaeology emerged in Britain as a specialist field in its own right.[51] Early work by E. M. Jope (1948) and

FIGURE 5. Bishop's bridge and the Wensum from the south, in the 1840s, showing Mousehold Heath. (*Trustees of the Great Hospital*)

J. G. Hurst (1954–55), along with an exhibition at Norwich castle on the growth of the city in 1963, paved the way for the creation of the Norwich Survey.[52] As Jope recognised, archaeology offered the 'chief hope of understanding the early history of most English towns', although the Survey's aim from the outset was to approach this and other questions from an interdisciplinary angle, using documentary evidence as well as material culture in its quest to explore the changing urban environment.[53] Drawing its inspiration from existing projects at Winchester and King's Lynn, this pioneering venture marked a decade of collaboration between the University of East Anglia, the Department of the Environment and the City Council. The Survey began its programme 'of recording and publishing the evidence for the origins and development of Norwich' in 1971.[54] When the last excavation ended, seven years later, thirty-eight sites of varying size and importance had been examined, generally in response to the exigencies of urban development.

Inevitably, in a city as rich in archaeological and architectural resources as Norwich, the initial preoccupation with its Anglo-Saxon origins soon widened to embrace aspects of later settlement and growth, extending well into the early modern period. In addition to a series of brief interim reports which appeared annually in *Norfolk Archaeology*, three full-length monographs were envisaged: the first two appeared in 1982 and 1985 respectively, but the third was delayed by the tragically early death, in 1988, of the project's charismatic leader, Alan Carter.[55] A number of articles by individual members of the team, separate volumes dealing, respectively, with the pottery and other important finds, and an analysis of the documentary evidence for the zoning of medieval crafts, were, however, published in the interim.[56] The appearance, in 1975, of James Campbell's survey of Norwich's development and topography in the *Historic Towns* series constituted another major contribution to our knowledge of the city, providing solid foundations upon which others have since built.[57]

Founded in 1973, initially under the aegis of the Scole Committee, as the first shire-based archaeological unit in the country, the Norfolk Archaeological Unit had, meanwhile, been concentrating its efforts upon the rest of the county. As the Norwich Survey wound down, and ceased excavating, it assumed responsibility for the city, too, and began digging there in 1979. Early reports on a Saxo-Norman waterfront site near Fye bridge and on the north-east bailey of Norwich castle were followed by monographs about other major excavations, such as St Martin-at-Palace Plain and the early riverside settlement at Fishergate.[58] The Unit also produced a series of pamphlets for the general reader, notable for their accessibility and use of documentary evidence along with the archaeological record.[59] It is a tribute to the achievements of both the Survey and the Unit that so many contributors to this volume have drawn upon their work, and that the study of medieval Norwich is now well on its way to becoming the interdisciplinary enterprise envisaged three decades ago.

No single author can hope to tackle such an embarrassment of riches over a sustained chronological period. This, the first volume of *The History of Norwich*, spans the Anglo-Saxon era to the mid sixteenth century, and brings together the work of fourteen historians and archaeologists, with the aim of doing justice to at least some of the many topics which make Norwich's story so fascinating during this lengthy period. Every city has its own tale to tell. Norwich's is clearly very different from those of great industrial centres and flourishing ports, such as Cardiff, Glasgow, Nottingham and Sheffield, all of which have been the subject of lengthy histories concerned with more recent events.[60] Its story is, in comparison to theirs, loaded towards a great medieval and early modern past, during which the church dominated the urban landscape and the lives of the men, women and children who lived and worked in it. It is ironic that Norwich, which, according to the 2001 Census, now has less time for organised religion than any town in England, may once have been the most religious city in Europe, or so Norman Tanner suggests.[61] Its cathedral and nunnery, its hospitals, friaries, parish churches, schools and chantry chapels, its hermitages, anchorholds and beguinages (unique to England) reflect the vibrant spiritual life of its residents, whose wealth was channelled into schemes for the construction and embellishment of these powerhouses of prayer. During the sixteenth and seventeenth centuries, no doubt under Dutch influence, devotional practices took a more austere turn, pushing forward changes in worship initiated during the Reformation. Protestant or Catholic, religion played a prominent part in shaping the political, social and cultural life of the city, as many chapters in this volume demonstrate.

From the late Anglo-Saxon period onwards, Norwich's economy followed a cycle of expansion and stagnation, sometimes in direct opposition to wider national trends. The Norman Conquest, which transformed the city's physical appearance almost beyond recognition, and proved by far the most cataclysmic event in its long history, triggered a period of boom and population growth. By the time of the Domesday survey in 1086 it may have been home to as many as 8000 souls or more.[62] Norwich's development into a regional capital was further accelerated by the foundation of the cathedral in 1096 and the construction of one of Europe's most remarkable – and flamboyant – Norman castles. Two centuries later, Norwich presented a confident, successful exterior as a major centre of international commerce with a flourishing mixed economy, but signs of retrenchment and decline were already apparent. The influx into the city of poor labourers from the surrounding countryside, desperate for work, pushed the population up as high, perhaps, as 25,000 by the early 1330s. Expansion was not, however, accompanied by rising prosperity. The number of residents may have fallen somewhat over the next fifteen years, but many continued to live in the crowded and dirty conditions where pestilence breeds. It is now hard to determine the full extent of the devastation caused by the Black Death of 1349–50, largely because it marked the beginning of a long cycle of epidemics. Further outbreaks of plague in the 1360s and 1370s (and thereafter at regular intervals over the next two centuries) curbed any incipient recovery, not least because the young were especially vulnerable. At a generous estimate, the population cannot have exceeded 8,000 in 1377, and hovered around 11,000 (less than half of the early fourteenth-century figure) by the 1520s.[63]

Yet there were lights amid the gloom. Unlike some English cities, such as Coventry and York, late medieval Norwich was not blighted by protracted economic stagnation. On the contrary, the expansion of the worsted trade brought a striking upturn in the fortunes of the ruling elite, which still leaves its mark today. It was during this period that the parish churches and friaries were rebuilt and refurbished, and handsome residences (such as Dragon Hall) were constructed near the busy staithes along the Wensum. A royal charter of 1404 bestowed county status upon the city, which was henceforward governed by a mayor and sheriffs. Commercial and cultural links across the North Sea flourished. When annotating a copy of Virgil's *Aeneid*, one Norwich friar compared the channel between the island of Tenedos and Troy to the sea separating England from Flanders, an obvious analogy to anyone who rubbed shoulders with the *nouveaux riches* at this time.[64] The concentration of wealth and power in a few hands was, inevitably, a cause of friction, which, as noted above, gave rise to occasional outbursts of disorder. On balance, though, Norwich appears to have been firmly governed by magistrates who took seriously their obligations to the deserving poor, and who increasingly assumed wider responsibilities for morality, health and safety. Their task was far from easy, especially during the recessionary years of the mid sixteenth century. Although by the 1520s Norwich had assumed a proud position as England's second city, it had to fight hard to retain this accolade.

Just as the Norman Conquest led to a dramatic restructuring of urban space, so too the Dissolution of the Monasteries had an immediate physical impact upon 'the city of churches'. Buildings disappeared or changed their use; the trappings of 'popery' vanished almost overnight. A sense of the devastation occasioned by the ongoing process of reformation emerges from a letter written in 1560 by John Bale (d. 1563) to Archbishop Matthew Parker (d. 1570). The former, who had spent his younger days as a Carmelite friar in Norwich before embracing the Protestant faith, and the latter, a local boy made good, both regretted the wanton vandalism that had accompanied the dismemberment of the Catholic Church. Having itemised what little remained of the great store of books known to him in his youth, Bale pronounced it 'a very pytiefull case that our contray men are so uncircumspecte and, as it were, unnaturall to the olde monuments of their nacyon'. In his opinion, a far better example had been set by 'the learned Germanes', whose respect for their cultural heritage put the English to shame.[65] Although, by and large, Norwich's rulers managed to steer a careful course between religious extremes, avoiding the worst excesses of iconoclasm and repression, the mid sixteenth-century city presented a far from united front. The problems of rampant inflation, food shortages, civil unrest and a slump in the cloth trade proved harder to control than religious enthusiasm. An explosive combination of social, economic and doctrinal grievances resulted in the 'commosyon' of 1549, when the city briefly became a focus of violent insurrection. Kett's Rebellion, which drew on a long tradition of popular protest, may be considered the last medieval uprising in England, and reflects the inherent instability generated by decades of uncertainty and change.

This volume ends on a more positive note with a study of public health and provision for the sick in the medieval and early Tudor city. Both topics, also addressed thematically over time in volume two, assume an importance in *The History of Norwich* rarely accorded to such matters in histories of other English cities.[66] This in part reflects the interests of scholars currently working on Norwich, which is exceptionally rich in documentary and archaeological sources for medical history.[67] As we have seen, the city's early preoccupation with cleanliness, space and charitable provision meant that seventeenth- and eighteenth-century visitors invariably commented upon these things, no doubt with every encouragement from their hosts. The diarist, John Evelyn, conducted personally around Norwich in 1671 by none other than Sir Thomas Browne, had every inducement to praise the healthy environment, although since he himself was a celebrated campaigner against atmospheric pollution in the capital he was better placed than most to appreciate the 'prospect sweete' before him.[68] François de la Rochefoucauld, in turn, admired the corporation's generosity towards the poor, the high standards of care in its 'houses of industry' (where, contrary to established practice, children were allowed to remain with their parents) and the fine new Norfolk and Norwich Hospital. 'I never in my life saw an infirmary so clean', he told his father, 'the buildings are so well adapted to the needs without the least excess'.[69] Far earlier visitors, less anxious to record their impressions for posterity, evidently voiced similar opinions – or so the minutes of the Tudor assembly would have us believe. Norwich was, after all, the first city in England to raise a compulsory public rate, in the 1540s, for the acquisition and support of its largest hospital, and was already by then modelling its schemes of poor relief on the best continental practice.

It is, none the less, impossible to cover in equal depth all the events and institutions which feature in well over a thousand years of the city's development, or to explore the lives of the individuals who have made their mark upon it. Many important aspects of Norwich's past, such as its castle and cathedral, have already been examined in detail elsewhere and readers are referred to the bibliography at the end of this volume for the most important titles. Others, such as civic ritual in the late medieval and early modern period, are currently under investigation, and will add to the growing stack of publications which draw upon the city's exuberant material culture as well as its archives.[70] A number of major topics still remain unexplored or under-researched, and it is hoped that scholars will now take up the challenge. Norwich's North Sea connection, which emerges so vividly in this volume, had a formative influence upon its life and culture long before the arrival of the Strangers during the mid sixteenth century, yet a comprehensive analysis of these complex networks has yet to be undertaken. The city's relations with its medieval hinterland, most notably regarding the supply of foodstuffs and the raw materials for the worsted and leather industries, also demand further attention.[71]

The aim of this volume is to advertise the great wealth of Norwich's archival and material resources, and convey a sense of the riches of its medieval past. The impact of this past still strikes today's visitors as it struck those of the seventeenth and eighteenth centuries, creating a pleasing sense of harmony and organic development. It awaits further study. 'Norwich', as Nikolaus Pevsner remarked, 'has everything',[72] an opinion eloquently shared by Granville Barker, to whom we may leave the last word:

> For, so some places are places where things are lost or found, and others have a feeling of the familiar or the foreign, Norwich is a place where variety meets. Rivers, periods, architectural styles, religious opinion ... the antique and the contemporary, the historical and the ecclesiastical, the spiritual, the temporal and the intemperate, the sophisticated and the unsophisticated ... Norwich has got itself sorted out according to use and not according to architectural theory. It works, and it has always worked and it will always work. It is the triumph of maudlin acumen, the success of common sense ... not only house proud, but town proud, and after all with some reason.[73]

1

The Urban Landscape

Brian Ayers

> Norwich has everything – a cathedral, a major castle on a mound right in the middle, walls and towers, a … medieval centre with winding streets and alleys, thirty-five medieval parish churches, and a river … It even has hills.
>
> Nikolaus Pevsner, *The Buildings of England*, 1962[1]

'It even has hills' – not high but occasionally steep – and an assessment of the urban landscape superimposed upon these could indeed take up an entire book.[2] This more modest appraisal of the development of Saxon and medieval Norwich must, nevertheless, start with an appreciation of the hills and of the valleys between them. The truism that 'history is what people make of their geography'[3] is particularly apposite in the case of Norwich where, for over a millennium, citizens have infilled valleys and scarped slopes, modifying an environment which belies Noel Coward's now weary aphorism 'very flat, Norfolk'. The city is located in the valley of the River Wensum where the margins of the river are narrowed by gravel terraces lying between the slopes of Mousehold to the north and east and the Ber Street escarpment to the south and west. Neither hill is a great eminence – barely 130 feet above sea level – but the effect of the enforced narrowing of the valley was to provide a situation where the river could be forded or bridged, its water used domestically and industrially, and its banks colonised for wharves and warehouses, all at the centre of a rich agricultural hinterland accessible to the sea (Figure 6).

The land on either bank of the river was also cut by subsidiary valleys, each containing streams or 'cockeys', which flowed into the Wensum.[4] Although all have now disappeared from above ground, the existence of these streams not only helped to determine urban layout but for centuries continued to act as topographical reference points.[5] The largest such stream, the Great Cockey, occupied a marshy valley which archaeological excavation has shown almost certainly determined the western boundary

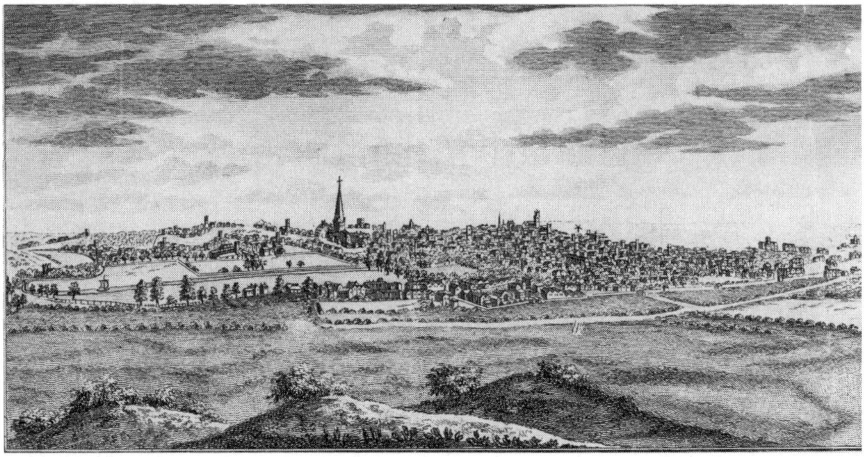

FIGURE 6. North-east prospect of Norwich from Marcus Armstrong's map of 1781, showing the hills and the valley of the Wensum. (*Norwich Castle Museum and Art Gallery*)

of the pre-conquest borough south of the River Wensum.[6] Its course still marks the parish boundary between St Peter Mancroft and St Andrew.

Geography is thus a primary determinant of the form of the city. Examination of the topographic skeleton which was laid upon the geography, however, is no simple matter. Indeed, in the late nineteenth century, the Reverend William Hudson could state that 'it would be a fruitless task to attempt to trace out in detail the topographical development of Norwich [before the thirteenth century] because we have no evidence to teach us'.[7] Historical evidence is indeed lacking but other, principally archaeological, evidence does exist. To be fair to Hudson, the operative phrase in his statement is 'in detail'; earlier he had sought to understand urban development in Norwich in broad terms. He was hampered, though, by an imprecise chronology, coupled with then prevalent misconceptions concerning the date of the construction of the castle.[8]

Chronology is important because only by a chronological analysis of the skeleton of the medieval city is it possible to explain the great size of medieval Norwich. The walled city, seen as 'vast' by Celia Fiennes in 1698,[9] was a late medieval result of a combination of urban developments over a period of half a millennium. The walls, only completed in the 1340s, encompassed a settlement which had it origins as early as the eighth century but admitted of Danish and Norman influence as well as that of the Anglo-Saxons. Although large, the walled area was still insufficiently broad to enclose all existing settled areas: Heigham to the west was omitted, becoming a suburb by default rather than by design. It is necessary to dissect the known extent of the late medieval landscape in order to reconstruct its development from a pre-urban environment to an urban one.

The density of prehistoric activity, notably from the Bronze Age and later, in the vicinity of Norwich, particularly to the south in and around the Yare and Tas valleys,[10] suggests that the medieval city also overlies many features of prehistoric date. Few of these have been located in the centre of the city, although a possible Bronze Age post-hole building on Palace Street and a partial ring-ditch and Iron Age pits at the Millennium Site are exceptions, both from excavations conducted as recently as 1999.[11] As yet, however, any impact upon subsequent topography cannot be ascertained. Roman influence is much clearer. While the principal centre of Roman urban life in east-central Norfolk was the town of *Venta Icenorum* (Caistor St Edmund), some three miles south of Norwich in the valley of the River Tas, Roman roads ran through the site of the medieval city. One such road was a northern extension from Caistor of Pye Street, the road north from Colchester. It is probable that it entered Norwich by crossing the River Yare at Lakenham, running up Long John Hill and thence northward *via* Ber Street.[12] It crossed the river north of Charing Cross and then proceeded northward along Oak Street. This north-to-south road was intersected by an east-to-west route (sometimes referred to as 'Holmstrete Way') at Charing Cross. 'Holmestrete Way' entered the city from the east, cut across the low-lying land of Cowholme (now largely playing fields east of the cathedral) – almost certainly on a gravel causeway – before leaving the city along what is now the Dereham Road.[13]

Both routes took advantage of the geography of the site. The north-to-south road crossed the Wensum in an area where the river braided around a number of small islands, facilitating the construction either of bridges or of a ford.[14] The east-to-west road may have forded the river at the site of the surviving medieval Bishop's bridge, a site known to be the lowest possible fording point on the Wensum and Yare river system.[15] While neither road seems to have supported any significant Roman settlement,[16] the location of each may have been a determinant in the positioning of post-Roman fifth- or sixth- century cremation cemeteries.[17] One of these seems to have lain on the site of the church and churchyard of St Michael-at-Plea. The location is a low eminence, but nevertheless a commanding site, overlooking both the Wensum valley to the north and east and that of the Great Cockey to the west, the Roman road passing immediately to the north.

The road would have crossed the Great Cockey, rising up the far slope of the Cockey valley to intersect the north-to-south route. Again the site is a dominant one, now occupied by the church of St Gregory, Pottergate. It can be argued that both St Michael and St Gregory are early foundations. The former was known as St Michael *Motstow* or 'meeting place near the market', a name perhaps deriving from a more ancient moot or meeting place associated with the preceding cremation cemetery. It was subsequently also the site of the archdeacon of Norwich's court,[18] emphasising its importance within early administrative organisation of the borough. The parish of St Gregory seems to have played a formative role in the development of the western part of the city. It has been suggested that the parishes of four other churches (Saints Laurence, Margaret, Swithin and Benedict) were created out of that of St Gregory;[19] and, as St Laurence is known to have been in existence between 1038 and 1066,[20] such subdivision implies that St Gregory is an early foundation.

Without exploratory excavation and the recovery of dateable material, it is not possible to verify a likely foundation date for either of these churches. A Middle Saxon date (mid eighth to ninth century) cannot, however, be ruled out for two reasons. First, the limited evidence for Middle Saxon activity in Norwich – largely finds of Ipswich ware pottery – indicates that such settlement as there was occurred predominantly in riverside areas, precisely those occupied by the parishes of St Michael and St Gregory.[21] Secondly, another important riparian parish church on the south bank, St Martin-at-Palace, has been excavated. The extant building contains the oldest standing fabric in the city (long-and-short work of mid eleventh century date in the east end), but the archaeological investigation also uncovered two earlier timber buildings. One of them cut a pre-existing burial, the radiocarbon date for which cannot be later than the Middle Saxon period.[22]

The accumulated evidence is admittedly tenuous, but it is sufficient to offer comparison with the early place-name evidence for two specific localities, namely Westwick ('the western settlement' or 'western port') and probably Conesford ('the king's ford').[23] It has been suggested that, taken together, the place-names, archaeological material and perhaps the above-mentioned churches may indicate areas of 'proto-urban' settlement. Currently this seems to be stretching matters too far, especially with regard to a developing urban topography. The three churches all lie close to the east-to-west Roman road, but there is as yet little evidence for early urban activity in their immediate hinterlands: not a single Middle Saxon building has been positively identified by archaeological excavation, nor can any streets be postulated as dating from the eighth or early ninth centuries.

At first sight, data from the north bank of the Wensum might offer greater likelihood of Middle Saxon urban activity. Here, excavation on Fishergate in 1985 uncovered relatively large quantities of Middle Saxon material but, as on the south bank, no evidence for actual settlement.[24] It is tempting to locate the port of Norwich, the Middle Saxon 'north *wic*', on this bank of the river but, to date, it is only possible to suggest limited activity prior to the third quarter of the ninth century.

Thus, despite the availability of a geographically-preferred site and some evidence for settlement, it is not currently feasible to propose urban occupation in Norwich for the Middle Saxon period. By the second quarter of the tenth century, however, coins were being minted in the city;[25] and, by the 980s, Norwich is documented in the *Liber Eliensis*, when, together with Cambridge, Ipswich and Thetford, it was 'of such liberty and dignity that if anyone bought land there he did not need witnesses'.[26] The impetus for the development necessary for the establishment of a mint and the acquisition of both legal and social status was almost certainly provided by the Danes from the late ninth century onward.

While there is little material of this date which is unequivocally Danish in origin from the city, there *is* considerable evidence from the tenth century and later to imply a strong and sustained Anglo-Scandinavian presence (Map 1). Artefacts representing all the major Scandinavian styles have been located: these include tenth-century Borre style brooches,[27] a later tenth-century Mammen style cross-shaft,[28] an early-eleventh century Ringerike mount,[29] and an early twelfth-century Urnes style capital.[30] In addition, Scandinavian place-name elements are common, from the almost ubiquitous suffix *gata* (gate, meaning 'street') to personal names such as Toki. *Tombland* derives from *täm* meaning 'empty', the 'empty or open land' being used as the market place by the eleventh century.[31] Comparison of the Anglo-Scandinavian names with the few solely Old English names is informative; the Danish or hybrid Danish names relate to the topography, naming streets. The Old English names generally either refer to natural features (such as the River Wensum or *wændsum*, which means 'winding') or broadly geographic locations (such as *Mereholt*, a 'boundary wood').[32] It might be suggested that pre-Danish settlement was almost indistinguishable from the surrounding environment, but that Danish activity fostered urbanisation.

Church dedications with Scandinavian associations imply as much. While there were two churches in the medieval city dedicated to the Norwegian king, St Olaf (which cannot predate the 1030s as he was not canonised until after his martyrdom in 1030), there were also two churches dedicated to St Clement, a saint popular in Denmark and other Scandinavian countries.[33] One of the churches, which survives as St Clement Fyebridge or Colegate, is located in a position common to churches with such a dedication in many Anglo-Scandinavian boroughs, to wit, on the main road (Magdalen Street) through the borough where that road either cuts through defences or, as here, crosses the river (similar examples can be drawn from Lincoln, Cambridge and London). St Clement's in Norwich is not recorded before 1252 but it is almost certainly pre-conquest in origin. The parish was initially large, extending well beyond the bounds of the late medieval city wall, with tithe payments being made accordingly.[34] Later churches within the walls paid two-thirds of their tithes to St Clement's,[35] suggesting that, as the city grew, so the parish became fragmented. The church could possibly have been founded in about 900, a date consonant with its Scandinavian-preferred dedication, in a location which topographical analysis and archaeological excavation indicate was central to activity on the north bank.[36]

Excavation has now confirmed a supposition based upon analysis of the surviving topography that a defensive bank and ditch existed north of the river. This seems to have run from the Wensum at St George's Street (west of Magdalen Street) in a D-shaped arc northwards and then south to reach the river once more to the east of Magdalen Street, probably close to the church of St Edmund off Fishergate.[37] The ditch was nearly thirteen feet in depth and, with its rampart, is morphologically similar to defensive earthworks around other Anglo-Scandinavian boroughs, notably Ipswich, where excavation at Foundation Street in 1985 indicated an early tenth-century construction date, similar to that suggested for the structure in Norwich.[38] The Norwich defensive earthwork has the river to the south and marshy ground or streams to the west and east (the Muspole and the Dalymond respectively), a further topographic feature paralleled elsewhere, as, for example, south of the Witham in Lincoln. The enclosure is bisected by Magdalen Street, with the church of St Clement located centrally on the main axis where that axis crosses the river.

The river crossing at this point is now undertaken *via* Fye bridge. The earliest bridge over the Wensum was a causeway of timber extending from Colegate on the north to Elm Hill on the south.[39] Unfortunately, the dating of this causeway is problematical. Material excavated in 1896, and again in 1974, included Thetford-type ware (tenth- to twelfth-century in date); and, although further excavation in 1999[40] succeeded in recovering part of a pile from the causeway complete with its bark, a dendrochronological date proved elusive.[41] An early crossing must nevertheless be suspected, linking the north bank to known tenth-century activity to the south.

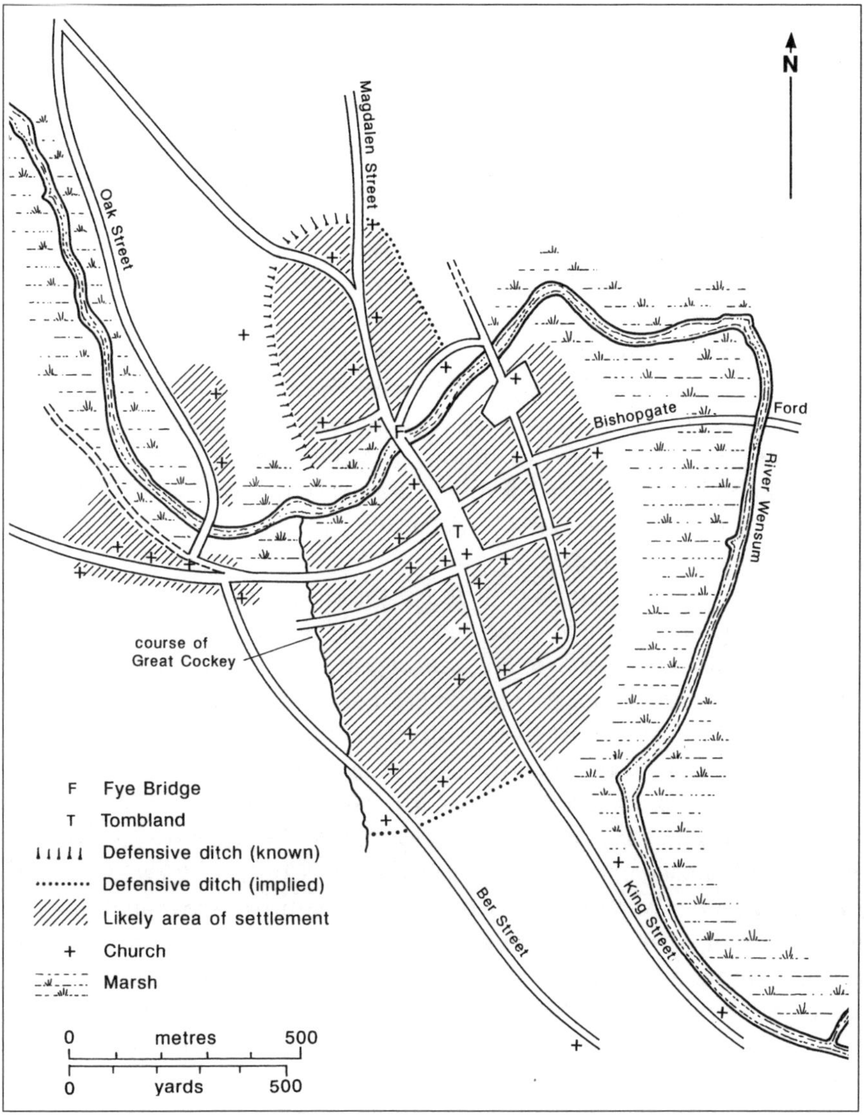

MAP 1. Anglo-Scandinavian Norwich. (*Phillip Judge*)

In summary, therefore, there is now (just) sufficient evidence to suggest a defended Anglo-Scandinavian enclosure on the north bank of the Wensum, probably constructed soon after 900 in response to resurgent Anglo-Saxon pressure led by Edward the Elder of Wessex. This enclosure may also have acted as a centre of urban activity following the Wessex conquest of the East Anglian Danelaw in 917; the Athelstan coins mentioned above had to be minted in a location that was not only urban but defended, according to Athelstan's own decrees issued at Grateley in Oxfordshire in 935.[42] The occupation and utilisation of this enclosure certainly entailed development of an urban landscape, probably prior to the reconquest. The primary route was that of Magdalen Street, which ran north to Stump Cross,[43] where the road forked. The north-westerly fork ran past the church of St Botolph, probably a pre-conquest foundation and one dedicated to an East Anglian saint. Churches bearing this dedication are frequently located close to gateways in defences (such as those at Aldgate, Aldersgate and Bishopgate in London), as would have been the case here, where Botolph Street passed through the defensive bank and ditch. The northern fork also traversed the defensive earthworks, close to another church, that of All Saints.[44]

Subsidiary routes must have included the riverside streets of Fishergate and Colegate. Both would have run from Magdalen Street towards the defences, although gates here are unlikely; indeed, the surviving topography at the junction of Colegate and St George's Street militates against such a possibility. A further east-to-west street can be suggested at St Saviour's Lane and possibly also at Golden Dog Lane. Calvert Street seems to be a surviving intramural road of which a lost element can be seen in property boundaries on the 1883 Ordnance Survey map of the area between Botolph Street and Magdalen Street. The western part of Cowgate at least may have fulfilled a similar intramural function. This bare urban skeleton, however, is the limit of current understanding; excavation has yet to recover a single pre-conquest building north of the river,[45] although it does seem to indicate that pre-1066 settlement was largely confined within the enclosure, extramural development in areas such as Oak Street being suburban at best.[46]

Anglo-Scandinavian activity also extended across the area south of the Wensum. It should be noted that all the stylistic finds mentioned earlier are from south bank sites, although relatively few of them are dateable to the tenth century and hardly any to the late ninth century.[47] All these sites lie east of the Great Cockey, but recent excavation at the Millennium Site west of the stream has uncovered evidence for Anglo-Scandinavian goldworking in the form of an ingot, a crucible with traces of gold, and fragments of litharge which indicate the smelting of precious metals.[48] These discoveries were located within the context of a pattern of land divisions at variance with the rectilinear post-conquest plots associated with the Norman development of the area. Danish influence can thus be demonstrated to be extensive within Norwich, although evidence would at present suggest that urban development on the south bank, while originating in the tenth century, is unlikely to date before 917, in contrast to probable development north of the Wensum.

Urban topographic growth south of the river was, however, soon to become much more extensive than that to the north. It too was constrained by geographic determinants, being bounded by the river to the north and east and the Great Cockey to the west. To the south, the land rises sharply up the Ber Street escarpment with only a narrow shelf extending along the river. This shelf, now known as King Street but originally as Conesford and subsequently Conesfordgate,[49] was clearly an early primary route. Not only were two churches with Anglo-Scandinavian dedications located here (St Clement and St Olaf or Olave), but a third, that of St Etheldreda, is probably also a pre-conquest foundation. Furthermore, excavation has recently uncovered evidence for pre-conquest buildings on four sites, extending from St Olave's parish in the south to that of St Peter Parmentergate in the north.[50]

King Street, has, none the less, always been an extension of the urban core. This lay to the north, centred on Tombland, which lies between King Street and the river crossing northward to the defended Anglo-Scandinavian borough. The post-conquest development of the castle, cathedral precinct and, in the thirteenth century, the Franciscan friary, all obscure the pre-conquest situation. Yet it is clear from archaeological and topographical evidence that settlement was extensive by 1066. In part also, an understanding of the urban landscape can, for the first time, be gleaned from documentation.

Pre-conquest documentary references to Norwich are both rare and relatively late.[51] In contrast, the Domesday Book entry is detailed if occasionally exasperating in its omissions. The account mentions seven churches by name, the geographical locations of which extend from St John de Sepulchre at the southern end of Ber Street to Saints Simon and Jude close to Fye bridge in the north, and from St Martin-at-Palace in the east to St Laurence in the west.[52] In other words, mention of these four churches alone implies that Norwich south of the river in 1066 was already approaching the size of its late medieval walled successor. Domesday also contains numerous references to dwellings, houses, pasture and meadow, as well as mills and at least twenty-five churches or chapels.

Norwich was large, with 1320 burgesses, perhaps reflecting a population of between 5000 and 10,000 people. Some of these individuals would have lived north of the river, the limited evidence for which has been outlined above. What did the provision of housing and other facilities mean in terms of the emerging urban environment to the south?

Notwithstanding the deleterious impact of major post-conquest institutions on the existing fabric and topography, the survival of topographic evidence is such that, when combined with information from archaeological excavation and a judicious use of later documentary sources, much can be gleaned with regard to the earlier urban landscape. Within the cathedral precinct, for instance, it is possible to postulate a hypothetical pre-conquest rectilinear street pattern which extended northward to the river, south to present-day Mountergate and westward into the surviving streets of Elm Hill, Waggon and Horses Lane, Queen Street and Bank Street.[53] Recent archaeological work has expanded the understanding of this pattern. Excavations beneath the site of the Franciscan friary in 1993 have been supplemented by discoveries on Mountergate and north of Palace Street. At Mountergate, an early, probably pre-conquest, alignment of the street was uncovered, having been abandoned when this particular thoroughfare was closed and moved northward by the Austin friars in the fourteenth century.[54] Off Palace Street, a fragment of a probable lane lies fossilised within post-medieval buildings as an enclosed yard; it was recorded when evaluation excavation of the neighbouring plot uncovered evidence for eleventh-century foreshore consolidation against the river.[55]

It has been postulated that the apparent regularity of the street pattern could be the result of a degree of planning by the forebears of the influential magnates mentioned in the Domesday survey.[56] Excavation suggests that the pattern extended over the area north of Mountergate and as far west as the line of the Great Cockey. Such a settlement would have enjoyed a relatively secure position, being bounded by the river to the east and north (and the defended enclosure north of that) with the marshy Cockey valley to the west. Only to the south would an artificial boundary have been required. A logical position for such a boundary would have been to continue the western end of Mountergate over the hill (parallel to Stepping Lane) to the Cockey valley. Excavation in 2000 immediately south of Stepping Lane revealed a ditch some six and a half feet deep and thirteen feet wide, which was probably a modest defensive feature, perhaps with the lane forming an intramural road.[57] It is possible that a continuation of the ditch was uncovered in 1989 during the Castle Mall excavation, having subsequently been recut as part of the ditches around the Norman castle.[58]

The location of this ditch supports the consideration of Norwich in the eleventh century as a 'double *burh*', examples of which are known from elsewhere in the reconquest areas of lowland England. Five sites mentioned in the *Anglo-Saxon Chronicle* can be cited, namely Bedford, Buckingham, Hertford, Nottingham and Stamford, with London and possibly Cambridge in addition.[59] At a more regional level there is also the example of Thetford, where a probable tenth-century bank and ditch south of the river were supported by a similar defensive earthwork to the north.[60] Such double *burhs* linked by bridges seem to have been established to control rivers: Edward the Elder in particular constructed new fortifications opposite pre-existing Scandinavian examples, as was the case at Nottingham.[61]

The northern defensive work in Thetford probably acted in this manner, supplementing existing fortifications to the south. A similar situation may have prevailed in Norwich, where a defended area south of the Wensum supplemented the enclosure to the north, to which it was linked by Fye bridge. It follows that the dating of the Stepping Lane ditch is critical, as it provides a context for urban fortification south of the river. A tenth-century date ought to place the construction of the fortification – and indeed the street layout of the town south of the river – within the proactive post-917 reconquest period. A later tenth- or early eleventh-century date, however, would suggest a defensive work undertaken in response to threats posed by the Anglo-Danish wars of the reign of Æthelred. It should be remembered that, in 1004, Norwich was famously visited by Swein of Denmark and his host, who 'completely ravaged and burnt the borough'.[62]

The discovery that the borough south of the Wensum was defended is confirmation of an hypothesis first promoted by the late Alan Carter, although the defensive ditch is located further south than his suggested line.[63] Carter further proposed that such a defended borough would have had a tenth-century nucleus; and recent results from excavation, notably at Castle Mall and the Greyfriars site, do indicate that urban activity was underway by this period.[64] The work at Castle Mall has now identified over twenty tenth- and eleventh-century buildings from deposits predating the castle, including sunken-featured or cellared examples. At the Greyfriars site three structures associated with some form of industrial activity were located, one of which may have been used for metal-working.[65] Such evidence for the economic base of the town is now readily apparent from a number of sites, especially those connected with the pottery industry. Excavations on Bedford Street and Lobster Lane – on either side of the Great Cockey – have revealed kilns and waster heaps associated with the manufacture of 'Thetford-type ware' pottery, an almost ubiquitous earthenware surviving from the later tenth to the early twelfth centuries.[66] Interestingly, the pre-conquest production sites lie east of the Great Cockey; those on Lobster Lane date from the twelfth century and are the latest in the sequence, perhaps offering further confirmation that the Cockey formed the boundary of the early borough, with suburban activity taking place to the west.[67]

The industrial activity of the borough was complemented by a developing commercial framework. As we have already seen, a market seems to have been established on Tombland by the eleventh century – and probably earlier. Excavation is revealing evidence for localised specialist activity,[68] including crafts, such as woodturning and leatherworking,[69] and the development of commercial waterfront facilities.[70] These discoveries not only demonstrate changes in the urban topography as a result of the intensification of occupation and utilisation of the available land,[71] but organic finds (for example, timber) also indicate management of the wider environment through processes such as pollarding and coppicing.[72] Such activity must have been necessary given the density of population in Norfolk in general, as well as that of Norwich in particular, and the ensuing high levels of consumption of wood.[73]

An adequate and regular timber supply was critical, as within pre-conquest Norwich, in common with other English towns of the period, buildings were generally constructed of wood. Most churches, too, were of timber although the stone building at St Martin-at-Palace may have been completed by 1066, and other stone churches could also have existed. Excavation has recovered the plan of one pre-conquest timber church, a previously unknown building complete with soakaway for a font and a graveyard.[74] This building was constructed in the first half of the eleventh century and has been identified as an early form of stave church, the common timber church type of northern Europe.[75] Its location helps us to reconstruct the urban plan that was destroyed, in this instance, by the early Norman castle. In common with many of the probable pre-conquest churches in Norwich, it seems to have been located on a street corner: surviving examples of this situation (with later fabric) include St Mary the Less, St Michael-at-Plea, St Peter Hungate and Saints Simon and Jude.

Norwich was sufficiently urban by the eleventh century to begin acquiring suburbs. The most significant of these seems to have been a development westward along St Benedict's Street, marked by the creation of the four parishes of St Benedict, St Laurence, St Margaret and St Swithin. Excavations south of the defensive ditch on King Street have also uncovered eleventh-century post-built structures. Development in places such as Oak Street was perhaps less suburban than a continuation and intensification of pre-urban activity. In contrast, recent excavations on Heigham Street have failed to locate anticipated pre-conquest material;[76] suburban growth here would therefore seem to be a post-Conquest activity.

It is thus possible to characterise, in broad terms, the urban landscape of Norwich on the eve of the Norman invasion. It is also possible, although outside the scope of this chapter, to characterise the types of support systems – economic, social and administrative – necessary to sustain the town. There are as yet, however, insufficient data to undertake spatial analysis of the pre-conquest town in order to assess both its relative wealth and status and the uses to which space itself was put within the borough. Assessments of population density remain vague and, accordingly, it is not possible to correlate population density with economic indicators of urban sustainability. All these desiderata remain to be addressed as they do in large part for the post-conquest period, although here also recent work has clarified much concerning the development of the urban landscape.[77]

The Norman Conquest initiated one of the two greatest periods of change in Norwich prior to the second half of the twentieth century (the other being the dissolution of religious houses and ensuing closure of parish churches in the sixteenth century) (Map 2). Within a quarter of a century, Norwich had increased in size by some 30 per cent; its centre had been redeveloped ruthlessly, with new institutions deliberately obliterating old topographies; and the physical appearance of the built environment itself was altered radically by the introduction of prolific usage of stone, both local and imported. Domesday Book graphically illustrates how economic and political power had shifted to the Norman elite by 1086, although it is clear that, in the short term at least, the effects of the flight of Anglo-Saxon burgesses and economic disruption were acute: 'those fleeing and others remaining have been utterly devastated partly by Earl R(alph)'s forfeitures, partly because of fires, partly because of the King's tax, [and] partly by Waleran'.[78] Forfeiture must have started soon after the Conquest; the abbot of Ely was one who lost a house this way, although it was restored to him between 1071 and 1075.[79]

The shift of power was also manifest in the development and use of the urban topography, the most obviously enduring symbol being the castle. Construction of this complex perhaps began as early as 1068, and must have been well advanced by 1075 when it was besieged by a royal army under Archbishop Lanfranc during the revolt of the earls of Hereford and East Anglia.[80] Recent excavation has suggested that work in the eleventh century may have been undertaken in two principal phases: a relatively small mound or motte, a possible defended entrance to the north east and two baileys, being followed by massive enlargement of the mound and defensive ditches.[81] The completed earthworks dominated the pre-existing town, most of which lay to the north and east but some of which was destroyed beneath the castle ramparts. It blocked east-to-west routes and severely inhibited north-to-south communications. As a result, a curving route was established around the western perimeter of the precinct (London Street, Castle Street and Back of the Inns), concentric with the defences. This new street marked the edge of the royal liberty of the castle (the 'Castle Fee') until 1345 when the precinct, save for the mound and the south gate, passed to the city.[82]

The earthworks may have been vast but construction of the keep from about 1095 onward was and remains an extraordinary statement in secular architecture (Plate 1). Norwich castle was then the only royal castle in Norfolk and Suffolk, two of the most populous counties of England in the eleventh century,[83] and thus the centre of royal administration. The keep has been acclaimed as 'architecturally the most ambitious secular building in western Europe', and described as a 'colonial architecture – designed to overwhelm'.[84] Its construction not only provided an unambiguous declaration of Norman power but was also a physical expression of the role of Norwich within the Anglo-Norman kingdom. The tenth century saw Norwich develop as a shire town; the Norman Conquest made it a regional capital (Figure 7).

The translation of the seat of the bishopric to Norwich in 1094 emphasised this growing regional importance. Again, the impact of such an institution, with its attendant Benedictine priory, was profound upon the pre-existing urban landscape. Although it is difficult to assess the exact nature of urban occupation in the area of the cathedral precinct,[85] it seems that at least two churches were demolished (St Michael Tombland and Holy Trinity) and three others enclosed within the cathedral precinct (St Ethelbert, St Mary-in-the Marsh and St Helen). The principal access to the borough from the east (Bishopgate) was diverted, removing a direct link eastward south of the river until the construction of Prince of Wales Road after 1860. Tombland became one of several matters of dispute between the cathedral priory and the citizens, a dispute sometimes violent,[86] and one which lasted until a celebrated *concordat* achieved centuries later in 1524.[87] The precinct was fortified, but the ecclesiastical liberty extended beyond the walls, encompassing land in Norwich both north of the river and between Tombland and St Martin-at-Palace Plain.

The physical impact of the castle and the cathedral was great, and so was the cultural expression embodied in both. Not only were stone buildings of such magnitude and complexity hitherto unknown in Norfolk, but the

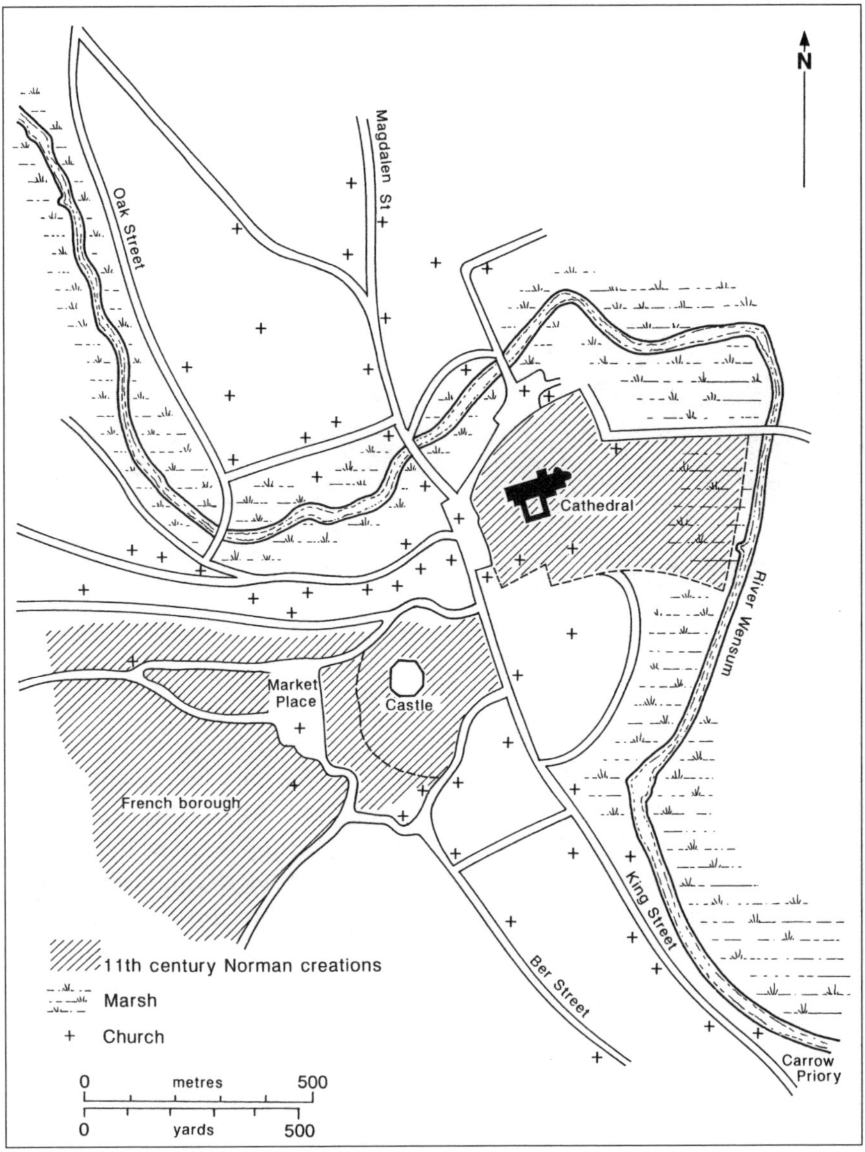

MAP 2. Norman Norwich. (*Phillip Judge*)

FIGURE 7. Norwich castle keep before refacing, after Henry Ninham. (*Norwich Castle Museum and Art Gallery*)

structures emphatically linked Norwich to mainstream developments in Europe. Progenitors for the keep and its decoration have been identified in the northern Loire region in France,[88] while Norman French examples, such as the church of St-Etienne in Caen, have been posited as models for work at the cathedral.[89] Norwich had been an Anglo-Scandinavian borough with houses, workshops and churches similar to those in the towns of northern Europe.[90] Influences from across the North Sea survived and even prospered, but the developing city was also becoming Norman-French.

Other than the castle and the cathedral, the urban landscape demonstrates this most ostentatiously in the establishment between 1071 and 1075 of an apparently new urban development west of the Great Cockey, the borough for the '*Franci de Norvic* [French of Norwich]'.[91] This borough, often thought of as green field development,[92] may have been constructed in part above a small suburban area of the pre-existing town. It centred on a new market place (Figure 8), which superseded but did not completely replace that on Tombland. It was also associated with 'a certain church', most probably that of St Peter Mancroft, which, unlike most of the

FIGURE 8. Norwich market place in 1809, by Henry Ninham after John Sell Cotman. (*Norwich Castle Museum and Art Gallery*)

churches in the Anglo-Scandinavian borough, was evidently built of stone from the outset. Recent analysis of the fabric of the late medieval church indicates that the fifteenth-century rebuilding was initiated by a new east end springing from an existing central tower.[93] It is thus possible to visualise a great Romanesque cruciform church dominating the market.

Long narrow tenements still survive in parts of the French Borough, notably off Gentleman's Walk and, prior to the late 1930s, north of St Peter's Street.[94] Many probably date from the initial laying out of the streets in the third quarter of the eleventh century, but such is not necessarily always the case; excavation at the Millennium Site uncovered evidence that similar tenements on the Bethel Street frontage were only established in the mid twelfth century, replacing earlier, wider tenements which seemed to focus on St Peter's Street.[95] Norman acquisition of earlier properties could also lead to change in the pattern of holdings; land east of St Martin's bridge was laid out afresh in the twelfth century with tenements sixty feet wide.[96]

The Millennium Site also revealed a further innovation of the Norman period – stone-built houses. Evidence for two such structures was located, of which one could probably be dated to the 1160s.[97] Other archaeological discoveries include the remains of two mid thirteenth-century buildings excavated off King Street behind the later medieval Dragon Hall,[98] a possible third belonging to Ranulph Wankel in 1297, also on King Street,[99] and the discovery in 1981 of a stone house still standing in excess of six and a half feet in height at St Martin-at-Palace Plain.[100] It is indicative of the particularity of these buildings – and the impact that they had upon contemporaries – that all of the above structures appear in early documentation, sometimes as topographical indicators, the only exception (paradoxically, since it is the best-preserved) being the last.[101]

A further stone house survives above ground on King Street, that now known as the Music House. Its complex history involves two twelfth-century phases,[102] the second of which was probably the work of the family of Isaac, the celebrated late twelfth- and early thirteenth-century financier. Isaac was only the most prominent figure amongst an important group of newcomers to Anglo-Norman Norwich, the Jews. This community, with exceptions such as Isaac, lived close to the castle as befitted a persecuted minority, the members of which were technically the vassals of the king and thus entitled to royal protection. The Jews of Norwich are some of the best documented in England, as a third of the country's surviving medieval Hebrew deeds relate to their community, as do half of the Latin ones involving Jewish parties.[103] This relative wealth of documentation enabled a partial mapped reconstruction of the Jewry to be plotted,[104] although, to date, the Music House remains the only building known unequivocally to have been occupied by Jews.

Norwich was thus changed topographically, culturally and socially by the Norman Conquest. While it also grew spatially with the French Borough, it was in addition extended both north and south of the river. Expansion to the north was in part inspired by the early bishops, who established two hospitals, one of which was north of the growing city (the Magdalen hospital, elements of which still survive within the Lazar House Library). The other lay immediately east of the fortified Anglo-Scandinavian borough and was supported by the church of St Paul.[105] Ribbon development along the northern part of Magdalen Street can also be detected, the church of St Margaret *in combusto* being established in about 1100.[106] South of the Wensum, expansion along the river is apparent from the above-mentioned twelfth-century stone buildings; and archaeological excavation is now also uncovering evidence of further foreshore consolidation, presumably for commercial use, with revetments, or retaining walls, of willow and oak.[107] The creation of St Paul's hospital on the north bank of the Wensum probably took place contemporaneously with removal of the early tenth-century Anglo-Scandinavian defensive earthwork. Excavation evidence suggests that these defences had gone by the mid twelfth century,[108] topography once again reflecting changing social imperatives. Residents of the Anglo-Scandinavian town had sought collective security; Norman colonisation protected an elite – be it secular in the castle or ecclesiastical within the close.

The Norman Conquest was clearly disastrous for most of those living in Norwich in 1066 but it was essentially a short-term disaster. The centralisation of authority in the castle and cathedral, with strong support for the development of the borough itself (the French Borough seems to have been created by the king and the earl of East Anglia as 'the king had two parts and the earl the third'),[109] must have led to investment with concomitant economic expansion. This is difficult to quantify in the twelfth century, due to a lack of relevant documentation; the archaeological record, however, clearly shows evidence of extensive trade contacts from northern Europe to southern France;[110] and data are accumulating for diverse urban industrial and craft activities.[111] Investment in infrastructure, such as wharves and warehousing, indicates a thriving economy, and it is likely that surplus wealth was also being directed towards churches. As we shall see, the four round-towered churches of the city which survived until the Second World War – one still stands with another having been rebuilt – are late eleventh- and twelfth-century examples of Norman investment.[112] Leper hospitals were established outside the urban area;[113] and the foundation in the 1140s of Carrow priory, a splendid cruciform church with a central tower and a building second in size only to Norwich cathedral,[114] is further indication of solid economic growth – despite the political upheavals of King Stephen's reign.

Norwich at the end of the twelfth century was thus greatly changed from its Anglo-Scandinavian predecessor. It contained prestigious buildings of international quality; it had expanded in size to overtake London in spatial area; it had probably reached its full medieval complement of over sixty parish churches, most of which were no less probably built in stone;[115] and its economic base appears to have been diverse, with craft and service industries as well as a developing mercantile elite catering to local, regional and national markets.

The large spatial area of the city at the beginning of the thirteenth century was therefore a result of two interacting factors: the diverse origins of settlement, fuelled largely by economic considerations, and the exploitation of opportunities offered by geography (Map 3). The low hills and watercourses were clearly critical in determining settlement layout, although, since the nature of the regional economy arguably dictated that Norwich was going to be a large city in any case, it was perhaps extremely fortunate that the geography offered room for expansion. Norwich, after all, had to cope with a very large population. Absolute numbers are notoriously difficult to calculate, but the presence of sixty parish churches, with merely 250 souls to a parish, implies a minimum of 15,000 people. The numbers could have been considerably greater; and indeed, by the first decades of the fourteenth century, it has been postulated that the city's population may have been as high as 25,000 people.[116]

The paucity of early thirteenth-century documentary evidence means that archaeological data have to be utilised in order to deduce the probable economic base and attendant urban development necessary to support this potentially very large population. Fortunately, information is again forthcoming in the late thirteenth century (notably in the enrolled deeds), when men and women engaged in over 120 different crafts and trades can be enumerated, ranging from textile, leather and metal workers to builders, agricultural workers and those in service trades. The impact of all this activity upon the urban landscape was profound. In the first instance, despite the size of Norwich, space for living and working was constrained. The city contained large areas of open land (such as substantial low-lying parts of the cathedral close) which could not be developed, or were being utilised for other activities. Quarrying was the most obvious, an operation which simultaneously occupied land and removed it; the scars remain today along Rouen Road.[117] Secondly, the nature of urban activity put pressure upon the environment and forced change. Thus infilling of the river margins, while often an economic necessity in order to reach deeper water, was also a practical one, providing more space for buildings and ancillary facilities. Such infilling has been discovered on a number of excavations, with only rare instances of a permanent arrest in activity (as at Quayside, where the present riverside wall represents a line probably established as early as 1146).[118]

The occupation of marginal land increased from the thirteenth century, presumably serving as an indicator of population pressure. The stone buildings behind Dragon Hall on King Street were constructed above deposits dumped east of the gravel shelf towards the river. Upstream, infilling off Westwick Street started in the twelfth century, leading to the creation of long tenements running north from the street to the river.[119] The Cockey valley was infilled, deposits of thirteen feet in depth being recovered below the Royal Arcade in 1988.[120] There was even pressure on streets which were little used. In 1250, Roger de Burg was fined for an encroachment upon 'the King's way upon the Key [Quayside] from the Bridge of St Martin to Fybrigge, where carts were used to pass with Merchandises'.[121] He was ordered to remove it; but the same offence was

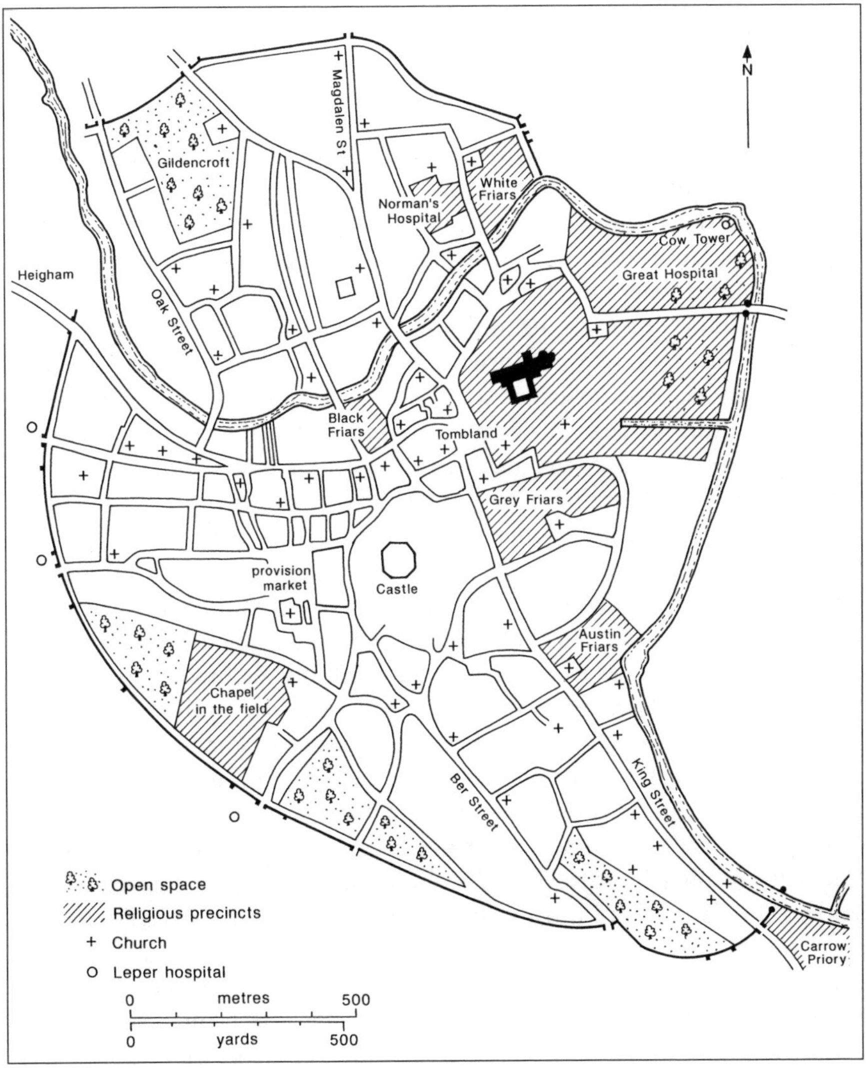

MAP 3. Late medieval Norwich. (*Phillip Judge*)

committed by Maud de Catton and three of her neighbours in 1285–86. Maud had built a fish-house upon the quay and, although all four defendants were fined, it seems that the obstacles remained.[122]

Development on marginal land was not confined to secular activity. The hospital of St Giles was founded in 1249 in Cowholme, on low-lying pasture to the north east of the cathedral. It was an episcopal endowment and the land had the advantage of being held by the bishop. The site was also one which symbolically helped to fulfil the purpose behind the foundation, marginal land reflecting the position of hospitals throughout Europe 'as brokers between heaven and earth'.[123] Such considerations, whilst applicable in a context where the bishop held ample quantities of land, were not, however, the driving force behind settlement by the various orders of friars who began to arrive in Norwich from 1226 onwards. Their desire to create urban friaries was just as spiritual, but the almost invariable placing of their institutions next to rivers or at some distance from the city centre (or both) was a result of practical necessity.

The friars were latecomers to the medieval urban scene with a mission to preach directly to the resident community. Their convents were therefore designed to facilitate access by lay people and were built as near to the centres of urban life as possible. This necessitated the use of marginal land, none more marginal than that eventually occupied by the Dominican friary (Blackfriars) after 1307. This institution, the buildings of which largely survive,[124] was erected on a site which was only fully created through the amalgamation of earlier properties after some twenty years of effort.[125] Even then, the steeply-sloping riverside location required massive infill to the north in order to provide a level platform for the spacious cloisters.[126] Similar infilling took place at the riverside site of the Augustinian friary on King Street.[127] The buildings erected by the friars were some of the largest and most impressive in the medieval city. The surviving Dominican church is about 265 feet in length and occupies the full extent of the available east-to-west space between Elm Hill and St George's Street (Figure 16). Much of the capital for this spectacular undertaking came from the citizens, who were also investing in their own houses, parish churches and public works. These last also impacted upon the landscape, not always to universal approval. The construction of new city water mills was mooted in 1401–2, when a site was surveyed, although the structures themselves were not completed until 1430. The abbot of St Benet Holme then complained that the mills 'stopped the water, so that it overflowed the banks, and damaged his land on both sides'.[128] The river banks themselves needed regular maintenance; in 1400, for example, William Blakehommore, his wife Margery and Jeffry de Bixton gave a messuage, lime kilns, a garden, a house and shops to the city 'towards the repairs of the banks of the River Wensum'.[129]

The greatest single corporate act, however, was the construction of the stone city walls, largely completed between the 1280s and 1345. Although intended to be funded by murage grants from the crown, their completion was only made possible through the largesse of a single individual, Robert Spink, as the city acknowledged with gratitude.[130] Bishop's bridge, the only surviving medieval river bridge, was built and fortified at his expense: excavation in 1999 revealed part of the south face of the gate tower (the only element of the twelve city gates now extant);[131] and it is possible that the carved male and female heads beneath the outer arch represent Spink and his wife. The walls which, in addition to the gates, included some forty towers, extended for two and a half miles and required prodigious quantities of materials (a figure of some 40,000 cubic metres has been suggested).[132] Late in the fourteenth century, building accounts survive for the construction of a single, admittedly large, tower in the angle of the river north east of St Giles's hospital (the cow tower). These record expenditure on 170 carts of stone, as well as carts of sand, lime and bricks,[133] with materials being brought not only from Norwich but also from further afield: William Knape, *botman*, for example, was paid 20d. for the carriage of 200 *sparres* (fir poles) from Great Yarmouth (Figure 4).[134] The lime-kilns for such constructional work would alone impact upon the landscape, as is known from documentary evidence for similar activities off King Street, together with a sixteenth-century reference to the attendant pollution problem.[135] A lime-kiln of twelfth- to fourteenth-century date was excavated on the Millennium Site in 1999, perhaps having been associated with one of the stone houses also identified there.[136]

Construction therefore was a service industry with a substantial presence in the urban environment, in terms of both the extraction and preparation of raw materials, as well as the visibility of finished products. On the other hand, manufacturing also impacted upon the landscape, either physically or culturally. Documentary evidence implies that much industrial activity may have been zoned,[137] a sensible and logical situation given the often noxious and indeed dangerous activities undertaken. Thus, while they worked everywhere, skinners were frequently to be found in riverside locations, such as Mountergate, where infilling of the river marshes gave access to water supplies;[138] some leatherworkers concentrated on the sub-leet of Ber Street;[139] and bell-founders worked in marginal areas such as World's End Lane (although the bell-founding family of Robert Brasyer operated in St Stephen's parish).[140] Potters, who were a notorious fire hazard, seem to have ceased to work in the city altogether after the mid twelfth century,[141] presumably because of their incompatibility with urban living, but perhaps also for economic reasons, such as the difficulties of obtaining raw materials.

The most striking industrial grouping is that of cloth-finishers in the western part of the city. Here place-name evidence alone is instructive: *Letestere rowe* (Westwick Street) for dyers; *Blekestereshole* (lost) for bleachers; *Le Fulleres holes* (lost) for fullers; *le Scherereshil* (Charing Cross) for shearmen; and *Madelmarkette* (Maddermarket) for the sale of dyestuffs.[142] Excavation has recovered a dyehouse off Westwick Street, complete with furnaces for heating dye vats and a drain to allow the effluent to run to the river,[143] upstream of the rest of the city: another indication of the impact of industry upon the urban environment. Textile workers clearly made use of urban facilities – an order of 1344 concerning the upkeep of the city defences decreed that 'no man hang cloths to dry on the walls of the city nor in the ditches'.[144] There were tenter grounds for drying cloth in Chapelfield.

The textile trade in general was crucial to the Norwich economy, leading to both public and private investment. In 1384, the city purchased land north of the market place for a cloth *seld*, or bazaar,[145] hoping thereby to control trade both through the imposition of tolls and to ensure quality. A fragment of a sixteenth-century rebuild of this complex survives at the corner of Lower Goat Lane. City merchants enriched themselves through cloth, none perhaps more handsomely than Robert Toppes, who built a magnificent hall on King Street in 1427, achieving access to the river by an astute use of the existing topography.[146] Similar buildings sprang up elsewhere; excavation in 1999, for instance, uncovered evidence for a substantial, possibly fourteenth-century, stone-built hall house further north on King Street.[147]

Many of the greater merchants' houses were constructed above stone-built, brick-vaulted undercrofts, over sixty of which survive. These frequently had a dual purpose: provision of secure, fireproof storage space and the creation of a building platform for the house above. Buildings on the north side of Bedford Street, for example, took advantage of one of the steeply-sloping hills of Norwich by being erected above such undercrofts, thus again demonstrating a creative use of marginal land. The greatest surviving suite of undercrofts is that beneath the Bridewell, itself a fine example of a stone-built late medieval merchant's house owned by the influential Appleyard family.[148]

Buildings such as the Bridewell now constitute part of Norwich's historic environment and can be studied by architectural historians, but archaeological excavation is the only methodology available for achieving a better understanding of the types of housing occupied by the majority of the city's medieval residents. Extant standing structures are all from the upper end of the social scale, even Pykerell's House in Coslany, the smallest surviving domestic dwelling, being a hall house with service rooms.[149] Slightly more modest structures with cellars beneath timber ceilings were uncovered on Pottergate in 1973;[150] and work at Alms Lane in 1976 recorded probably the best sequence of house buildings discovered in the city to date.[151] These included earth-walled constructions, evidence for which has now been located at a number of sites in the clearly less affluent parts of the city.[152]

The building stock throughout the medieval period would have been numerically dominated by such relatively poor dwellings, often thatched or covered with shingles (wooden tiles),[153] with numerous outbuildings, cess- and rubbish-pits and wells. Street coverings were of gravel until the thirteenth century; a road surface of this date uncovered beneath the Franciscan friary was metalled in cobbles.[154] The surface was cambered with side channels for rainwater. Within ecclesiastical precincts, drainage was more sophisticated; very recent excavation (2001) at 65 The Cathedral Close has uncovered two drains vaulted in Caen stone which served the Benedictine priory.[155] At the Franciscan friary, an extensive system of drains has been recorded, with subsidiary channels running into a main east-to-west flint-covered drain.[156]

The number and extent of ecclesiastical precincts formed a major visible element of the urban landscape. They were augmented by the profusion of churches which, despite occasional losses or closures,[157] still totalled over fifty at the end of the middle ages. These were nearly all parish churches with rights of burial, although not all the graveyards could cope with the increasing pressure of the urban population – by 1316, the parish of Saints Simon and Jude needed to utilise a separate graveyard which was laid out across the road in the parish of St George.[158] The church of St George itself came under pressure. It had probably been established about 1100 as an encroachment upon Tombland, and by the late medieval period commercial resurgence had led to the creation of market stalls in the eastern part of the churchyard, stalls which subsequently fossilised into shops. These still exist, crowded tight against the east window of the church without any rear yards. Similar encroachment can be seen east of St Peter Mancroft.

Such competition for space in the late medieval city is perhaps especially manifest in the manner in which investment in church buildings led to excessively large structures extending beyond their original boundaries. Common lanes were occasionally closed (as happened to those running through the precinct of the Blackfriars in 1345),[159] and churches also extended across them, as was the case at the churches St John Maddermarket and St Gregory. In addition, the construction of late medieval chantry chapels meant that churches grew substantially: the grandiose extant chapel built at the east end of the south aisle of St Michael Coslany in the very early sixteenth century by Robert Thorp constitutes a good example of this kind of development.[160]

Thorp's chapel (Figure 9) is faced on the exterior with remarkable flushwork; and such ostentation was a general feature of the late medieval churches of the city, most notably St Peter Mancroft, which has an extraordinary hammerbeam roof, covered with a timber ceiling. The use of glass, metalwork, fabric and paint is evident from the few survivals, including such avowedly austere institutions as the now demolished Francisan friary. Here, fragments of Purbeck marble and painted glass, as well as an oyster-shell palette, have been found by excavation. This last retained traces of paint, including azurite, a bright blue which was more costly to produce than gold leaf.[161] Ostentation spread to secular buildings as well. Chequerwork was used on the east gable of the guildhall; it has been suggested that this was a visual pun, reminding citizens of the building's function as an exchequer, through analogy with the chequer table of the medieval accountant.[162]

Despite the construction of its stone churches and a substantial guildhall, Norwich reached the end of the medieval period as a city as vulnerable to fire as any of its contemporaries. Two such devastating conflagrations broke out in 1507, perhaps destroying as much as 40 per cent of the urban area. Dramatic evidence of the destruction was uncovered on Pottergate in 1973, when the remains of a series of houses were excavated and buildings were seen to have collapsed into underlying cellars.[163] The events presaged similar, if more deliberate destruction some thirty years later during the Dissolution. The rapidity of loss in the 1540s still astonishes – the Franciscan friary was obtained by the duke of Norfolk, who proceeded systematically to demolish the buildings and sell the materials, leaving a practically empty site by 1560,[164] while at least eight churches had been closed or demolished by 1564.[165] The large walled area of Norwich, however, ensured that rebuilding from the fires and redevelopment of the vacated ecclesiastical sites rendered extramural development unnecessary until the nineteenth century.

The study of a developing urban landscape such as that of Norwich is one which draws upon a range of disciplines. It is, however, essentially forensic, seeking a better awareness of the general in the particular. There is thus great potential to enhance our understanding of the growth of the city

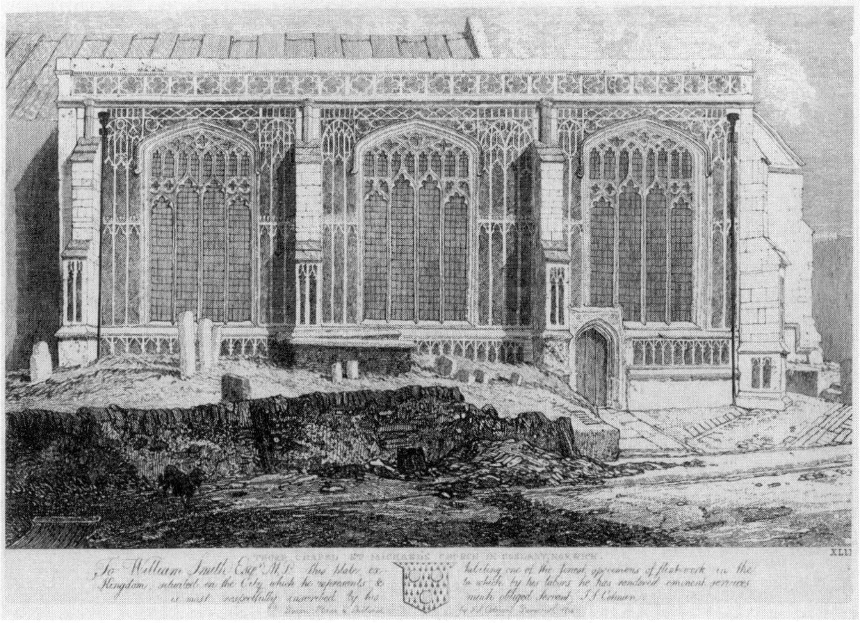

FIGURE 9. South elevation of the Thorp chapel at the church of St Michael Coslany, 1814, by John Sell Cotman. (*Norwich Castle Museum and Art Gallery*)

as a community, as well as a physical entity. Discoveries such as those on Pottergate, for example, can inform historical approaches to specific debates, not least concerning the vexed issues of urban decay and decline in later medieval England. These remain controversial topics.[166] It has recently been argued with some force that the study of long-term social change in towns needs to utilise and integrate archaeological data – that is, evidence from material culture – with documentary information in a more sophisticated manner. The Pottergate site was taken as an example:

> The increased durability of the housing stock means that the economic cycle becomes divorced from the building cycle, and often the main potential occasion for rebuilding occurred after a fire. The extent of reconstruction after an extensive fire could be an important yardstick with which to measure decline, but the congruence of archaeological and documentary evidence is rarely as illuminating as Pottergate ... it is necessary to look for both a chronological and a geographical change because a comparison between core areas and suburban areas would pay dividends ... One of the lessons to come from the work at Norwich is to realize the discrepancy, for example, between the

> documentary evidence for the congested area of Pottergate in the later fourteenth century and the archaeological assessment of it as an area just on the verge of development ...[167]

In other words, the evidence of the urban fabric across a great and diverse city such as Norwich has the potential to illustrate long-term changes in society which are not necessarily evident from the type of data hitherto used by economic and social historians. This underlying structural change can be interpreted 'in more social ways, and in ways more appropriate to the archaeological data, so that we can learn about the condition of late medieval urban society'.[168] For instance, the study of the use of urban space can inform our understanding of hierarchies just as constructional, artefactual and palaeo-environmental data can illuminate living standards.[169]

The urban landscape, therefore, is not merely the empty parchment or paper upon which the history of the city is written; Norwich is a document itself. The interaction of the geography and topography can help to provide a chronology, and it should always be remembered that the detailed fabric – both above and below ground – is not fossilised but dynamic, being subject to constant change and renewal; it both provides a context for the life of the city through time and a means to understanding the engines of social and economic change which produced its distinctive character. It also has great potential for contributing new data and therefore stimulating new concepts. It is 'a fine old city, truly ... view it from whatever side you will ...'[170]

2

Norwich before 1300

James Campbell

> 1272, on the day following the Feast of St Laurence [11 August], the citizens of Norwich laid siege around the precincts of the monastery. When their insults failed to gain them admittance, they set fire to the main gate into the monastery ... they burned the dormitory, the refectory, the guest hall, the infirmary with its chapel, and indeed almost all the buildings within the precincts of the monastery. They killed many members of the monastery's household, some subdeacons and clerics, and some lay people, in the cloister and in the monastery. Others they dragged off and put to death in the city, others they imprisoned. After they had gained entry into the buildings, they looted all the sacred vessels, books, gold and silver, and everything else that the fire had spared ... Afterwards the justices of the lord king had certain of the delinquents dragged to the gallows by horses, then to be hanged, and their bodies thereafter to be burned.
>
> Bartholomew Cotton, *Historia Anglicana*[1]

By the late thirteenth century the population of Norwich may well have exceeded 15,000.[2] If so, it could have been the most populous of English provincial towns, and beyond doubt it was somewhere near the head of the list. Such earlier figures as we have (all fiscal) tell the same story: Domesday Book, the exchequer records for royal levies from the twelfth century to the late thirteenth, the subsidy assessments for 1334.[3] William of Malmesbury, writing in about 1125, emphasised the populousness and commercial wealth of Norwich.[4] The same could have been said a century before, and for centuries to come. Perhaps the most striking thing about Norwich was its wide extent: the medieval enceinte enclosed about a habitable square mile.[5] This was a place of wide open spaces and of gardens.[6] This extraordinary city was the metropolis of an extraordinary area, the Holland of England, one might say. Domesday Book records a population in south-east Norfolk of a density matched in only one other area of England, and that a smaller one.[7] In at least one part of Norfolk the 1086 population of some villages matched that recorded in the census of 1801.[8] There are similar indications in later centuries.[9]

London was, of course, much more populous than Norwich; but the picture might be considerably different were one to compare not the cities, but the cities together with the areas within easy reach. The east Norfolk environment was not only densely settled but also economically developed; it has been powerfully argued that in some places agriculture had developed by around 1300 to the point at which grain yields sometimes corresponded to those of the eighteenth century.[10] The area included not only such productive arable, but also a great tract of grazing marshes, created by the draining of the 'Great Estuary' (which accompanied the withdrawal of the sea between the Roman collapse and the Norman Conquest).[11] Defoe, much later, described it thus: 'a long tract of the richest meadows and the largest, take them altogether, that are anywhere in England'.[12] Crucial to the economy of this part of East Anglia was water transport: a major set of rivers converged on Breydon Water: Wensum, via the Yare, Waveney, Bure, Ant, Thurne. Norwich certainly owed much, maybe almost everything, to its position on the waterway web. Specially important was the city's river link to Yarmouth, whose urban development was under way by 1086. By 1334 only four provincial towns (or, by another calculation, five) were assessed more heavily for the subsidy. Norwich was assessed at a little less than Yarmouth.[13] Nowhere else in England were two such major places so close together. Norwich and Yarmouth were often at odds; but their economic roles must have been complementary.

Particularly significant in the economy of our area were two commodities: herring and peat. The Yarmouth autumn herring fishing was a great source of food: quite likely the most important single source of food in England. The herring was almost the potato of the middle ages. Most herring for England came from Yarmouth.[14] At least from the eleventh century Norwich had a herring interest and may have been a base for herring fishing. The riverside properties in Norwich owned by midland monasteries from the thirteenth century were more probably associated with the acquisition of herring than (as has been suggested) the disposal of wool.[15]

A major feat of research demonstrated in 1960 that the Norfolk broads are peat-mines, flooded in consequence of a rise in sea levels beginning in the late thirteenth century.[16] The quantities involved were enormous. One example: in a peak year (1326) Norwich cathedral priory alone consumed 410,000 peats.[17] Fuel was no minor item in the medieval economy. Thus the herring industry depended upon salt and the production of salt required great quantities of fuel. So too did the pottery industry, very important at Norwich until about the middle of the twelfth century.[18]

The intimacy and grip of the links between Norwich and its rural environment are everywhere observable. The estates of the cathedral priory were largely concentrated in Norfolk, especially eastern Norfolk.[19] So too were those of St Giles's hospital (much lesser, but not inconsiderable).[20] The names of the property-involved inhabitants of late thirteenth- and early fourteenth-century Norwich demonstrate to what an extent they (or their progenitors) had come to the city from rural Norfolk (and, in lesser numbers, Suffolk). William Hudson suggested that Norwich, towards the close of the thirteenth century, had attracted within its sheltering privileges natives of perhaps three hundred Norfolk and perhaps sixty Suffolk, towns, villages and manors.[21]

By the late thirteenth century the sources for at least some of the life and nature of Norwich are fairly good. Domesday tells us much about the city some two hundred years before. With that exception, the further back one goes the thinner and more ambiguous the sources become. Yet the weakness of the early sources is by no means a necessary indication of Norwich's real importance. Much of what was there by 1300 may have existed well before. Our knowledge of Edward I's Norwich therefore sets an agenda for inquiry into earlier development. For this reason it is appropriate to begin at the end of our period and proceed from the relatively well known to the increasingly obscure.

How did the people of Norwich live? An important fact here, indicating the status of the city as a major economic centre, is the large number of trades carried on there. Hudson found references to 131 different trades in documents of the later thirteenth century.[22] A recent analysis of the avocations of the people mentioned in enrolled deeds between 1285 and 1311 shows that the most frequently occurring 'industrial' category is that of leather-workers, especially shoemakers.[23] Next most strongly represented were those who produced or traded in textiles, accounting for 15 per cent of the 'known trade population'.[24] Weavers (*factores pannorum*) appear second in a list of the trades of Norwich, *c.* 1273.[25] The long importance of textiles in Norwich makes it interesting to know when the textile trades first became prominent there. The earliest indication comes in 1201–2 where Norwich appears ninth among towns making payments to the crown to be allowed to buy and sell dyed cloth as they used to.[26] From the fourteenth century Norwich was celebrated for the trade in worsted, the unfulled cloth no doubt connected with Worstead (about twelve miles north east of the city). As early as 1295 worsted was sold in Dublin.[27] A clear indication of the production, or finishing, of cloth is an agreement of 1286 between the citizens of Norwich and woad merchants from Amiens and

Corbie.[28] All told, there is enough to show that cloth production and trading were important in Norwich by 1300; one cannot quantify beyond that. If the leather and textile trades were conspicuous in Norwich, the many others presumably included agriculture and horticulture. The Cuningham panorama of 1558 gives an impression of what the city had been like for many centuries: it shows wide meadows and gardens, and cattle grazing within the walls (Figure 1).[29] In the mid twelfth century we learn of a poor woman of Norwich who made her living by fattening pigs.[30] She would not have been the only one who lived in such a way.

It is fairly easy to sketch, but not at all easy to analyse, the society of early medieval Norwich. By the later thirteenth century (and probably earlier), and as in all towns, there was a small elite of men, usually described as merchants or mercers, pretty wealthy and likely to serve as bailiffs of the city.[31] We get glimpses of a proletariat, such as the men working for a penny a day, for whom the city's custumal (probably late thirteenth-century) expresses extensive distrust.[32] The gap between rich and poor is illustrated when our sources allow occasional glimpses of houses. An account of a felonious entry into a house in Fyebridgegate in 1263 describes how first the miscreants battered down iron-bound oak doors; then, having entered the courtyard, broke into the hall; and, then, into the 'chamber of the hall'.[33] They were out to rob an important dwelling arranged round a courtyard. Contrast Bartholomew Cotton (monk of the cathedral priory) on a great flood in 1290: he says that it dragged whole houses into the river; these can hardly have been substantial.[34] Most of our documents relate to the relatively better off; and our knowledge of these has been usefully advanced by the scholars who have analysed closely the deeds enrolled between 1285 and 1311. Thus they show that the number of people recorded as participating in property transactions (or mentioned in ways suggesting that they were property-owners) in these years was 3851; that the total number of habitable properties in Norwich around 1340 was of the order of 1870; and that in *c.* 1311 the proportion of tithing men in Mancroft leet who are known to have been real property-owners was 13 per cent.[35] Such figures conceal as much as they reveal. But they introduce some helpful reality. For example, if all, or nearly all, of those who appear in the enrolled charters were probably citizens (*concives* or *pares*, as the custumal has it), admitted to the liberty and liberties of the city, then the figures indicate that, although such men were doubtless a minority, it was not so very small a minority.[36]

An almost astonishing feature to emerge from the enrolled deeds is this. Of the 966 people to whom a 'trade' is assigned, about a quarter (247) can be described as 'ecclesiastical': 119 are described as *capellani*, sixty-nine as *clerici*.[37] This was a society in which the boundaries between lay and clerical were somewhat vague. Some of those in priests' orders would have been married and leading lay lives; many *clerici* would have been literate men in minor orders, not real ecclesiastics, and some may not have been ordained at all. It is likely that a proportion of the clerics in question were investors: Norwich property could have been a popular home for savings.[38] A good few of the *clerici* were, probably, professionals engaged in the written and legal business of a busy city. Simply to consider the practised hands of the enrolled deeds is to apprehend that the clerks concerned did a lot of other writing too.[39] The business of Norwich must have involved correspondence and account keeping. From 1295 the accounts for the cathedral priory estates reflect remarkable sophistication, notably in the attempt to indicate true profits and losses.[40] It is known that the obedientiaries of the cathedral priory employed *clerici* from outside the monastery.[41] Maybe the advanced accounting reflects the expertise of such men?

One might argue that the leading economic activity of Norwich did not lie in the leather trades, nor in the textile trades, nor in the great urban standby of taking in one another's washing. Rather did it lie in religion: in the following sense. From an economic point of view such an institution as Norwich cathedral priory was an apparatus which extracted money from the countryside and spent it in the town. The net income of the priory in about 1300 is estimated at £2500. If some 30 per cent was expended in the scattered cells of the priory, £1750 annually would have been left for the cathedral priory at Norwich.[42] How was it spent? Fifty or sixty monks had to be maintained. Their servants and employees were more numerous; at an estimate there were some 150 of them.[43] Add the families and dependants of these servants and functionaries, and the economic significance of the priory, as by far the biggest employer in town, is plain enough. This is so even without taking building work into account, which for several centuries must have been a serious source of expenditure and employment. [43] One other great landowner resided, if intermittently, in the city: the bishop. Herbert de Losinga, the first occupant of the see of Norwich, built a fortified residence to the north of the cathedral in about 1100; some hundred years later, Bishop Salmon planned the expansion of his *palacium*.[44] A bishop's household would be a spending presence numbered, at the very least, by the score. There were other ecclesiastical dignitaries with economic weight. A crucial episode in the grim story of St William (1144) turns on his having an offer (or feigned offer) of a job in the archdeacon's kitchen: clearly a plum.[45]

The relationship between the cathedral priory and the city was complicated to the point of explosion. When Herbert de Losinga established the *sedes* (seat) of the East Anglian see of Norwich he did it on the grandest scale, seeking to establish something like a *cité episcopale* of a continental kind. His acquisitions included not only that part of the Anglo-Saxon town which became the cathedral precinct, but important areas on the precinct's western fringe which remained part of the commercial town, and rural properties such that the city was largely enclosed by priory lands.[46] Unsurprisingly, as soon as we have documents capable of showing city-priory tension and hostility (that is by the thirteenth century) they show it.[47]

Hostility boiled to a terrible crisis in 1272.[48] In June a fair was being held on Tombland, the open space that lay just outside the precinct of the cathedral priory but which was largely under its jurisdiction (Map 3). The 'citizens' drove 'the men of the priory' into the close. A priory man with a crossbow shot a 'citizen' and killed him. Tense weeks followed. The culmination came in the second week of August. An attack was launched on the cathedral; and the close was invaded. A great fire broke out: probably semi-accidental in origin. Most of the monastic buildings and much of the cathedral were burned.[49] The intruders killed a number of the priory men, though all the monks escaped. The furore was intense. On 14 September King Henry III came to Norwich. Alleged participants in the riot were put on trial: some thirty were hanged. The bodies of some (perhaps all) were burnt; this was the penalty for arson. The affair did not end there. Wider inquiries indicated that the prior was not innocent of provocation. He was deposed and the priory lands taken into the king's hand. The matter was not (more or less) closed until Edward I presided over a settlement by which the city paid the priory £2000 in indemnity.

The great riot is, understandably, better documented than any other episode in the early history of Norwich. Chronicle accounts express fiercely opposed points of view. Beyond doubt these Norwich events of 1272 belong to a long context of town and cowl conflicts in several towns.[50] Such struggles were nationally traumatic. It was not for nothing that the king himself came to Norwich; came in the last weeks of his life, for Henry died on 12 November. In assessing blame, we can accept many of the accusations made on either side: the prior probably did behave aggressively; the townsmen retaliated with a vengeance. The scale of the August encounters tended towards warfare rather than mere riot. The prior strengthened his forces with three shiploads of bad lots from Yarmouth.[51] The townsmen's attack was not just that of a mob: at least at one juncture the Norwich authorities (or some among them) seem to have sought to assemble and deploy the city's forces as they were organised for national defence.[52] That priory men were dragged into the city and put to some kind of trial rather suggests that municipal institutions were involved, low though their royally accepted jurisdiction was. Among the approximately 175 townspeople known to have been involved or accused were men of considerable status and worth; some had held leading office as bailiffs.[53]

For Norwich, as for London and other English cities, the thirteenth century was an age of iron. For example, when the 'Disinherited' rebels against Henry III sacked Norwich in 1266, their plunder was commonly said to have been worth 20,000 marks (£13,333) or more, and to have filled 140 carts.[54] At about the same time the city was subject to a royal fine (rather unfairly one might think) because it had been occupied by de Montfort's supporters.[55] Norwich must have taken other hard knocks in earlier generations, for example when it was captured by the earl of Leicester in the rebellion of 1173–74,[56] or when it was occupied by the forces of Prince Louis of France after the death of King John.[57] Or again Norwich may well have suffered during the last years of Stephen's reign and the first of Henry II's, when the city was presumably the capital of the great fief which Stephen gave to his younger son, William.[58]

Three themes stand out in the history of Norwich in the epoch of the great riot: a disturbed society; an ordered society; and possibly something of a new deal. Our London source has something interesting to say about the forces from Yarmouth which the prior brought to resist, or oppress, the townsmen; namely that they were bad men who *tempore turbationis regni* (in the time when the kingdom was disturbed) had become thieves, ravagers and evil-doers.[59] This was a society stricken by a civil war whose impact may have been as disturbing as that of the great civil war of the seventeenth century, a society partly arming against itself. For instance, it is unsurprising that the outraged monks of Norwich rebuilt their precinct wall in 1286, but interesting that other such communities followed their example.[60]

By a kind of contrast with such apprehension of violence, when one considers the records of the legal pursuit of those involved in the great riot, the elements of order revealed are striking. Thus one of the records of the procedures against people implicated in the events of 1272, as it lists thirty-five of them, specifies for each his tithing man: 'he was in the tithing (*decennia*) of Adam Cawal in Coslany', and so forth.[61] This relates to the frankpledge organisation of Norwich of which, thanks to the preservation of several leet court rolls from 1288 onwards, quite a lot is known.[62] The organisation revealed is notably interesting, not least because of its partly (or even wholly) Anglo-Saxon roots. Pre-conquest Norwich was administratively and legally an organisation or unit known as a hundred. Like many, or most, East Anglian hundreds it was divided into subdivisions: leets. In the late thirteenth century there were four of these, each with a court, approximating to a hundred court (Map 11). Such jurisdiction may not seem to amount to much: it embraced petty offences, nuisances, market regulation. Much of what they dealt with was the smallest change of local government: coping with people who built muck-heaps on the king's highway or deposited dead cats in a pit at Lothmere.[63] These courts do not seem to have had the ability (or drive) actually to collect most of the fines they levied.[64] For all that, the system mattered, above all in representing and enforcing the system of frankpledge. This required that every male of twelve or over had to be a member of a defined group, notionally of ten, with mutual responsibility for producing one another before the law. Each tithing had a leader, the 'tithing man' or 'chief pledge'. Plainly, this system was working in Norwich.

One of the surprising things about early medieval England is the extent of its almost ant hill-like organisation. The point has been admirably illustrated by Professor Jenks, who shows how the assessment of an Edwardian tax on movables could involve at least 10,000 separate teams.[65] Such a society as that of Norwich was thus not only considerably stressed, but also considerably organised. Harsh conflicts certainly there were: witness not only what happened in 1266 and 1272 but also the tortuous case involving accusations about the Jews, which dragged on throughout the 1230s. This seems to have brought about an earlier visit to Norwich by Henry III and gave him probably his first acquaintance with the anfractuosities of the city.[66] But such clashes were much rarer in the fourteenth century (though not so clearly in the fifteenth). Urban society contained forces for order and peace; as indeed did the English polity as a whole. Thus it is reasonable to entertain the possibility that the development of urban representation in parliament did something to reconcile hitherto colliding forces and to modify and mollify attitudes which had been such that towns were seen, and saw themselves, as partly and almost necessarily opposed to kings and nobles. So, it may have mattered, seriously, that Norwich is one of the twenty-two towns known to have sent representatives to each of the seven parliaments of Edward I for which there is reasonably complete information on membership.[67]

The nature and development of the internal government of Norwich between the eleventh century and the fourteenth are not easy to determine.[68] That the city was a hundred by itself before the Conquest would have given its court a degree of judicial competence. The Norman borough seems to have been recognised as a separate entity in the reign of Stephen, but there is no clear evidence for this later.[69] The first royal charter to Norwich comes from early in the reign of Henry II. It confirms to the citizens all the customs and liberties they had enjoyed under Henry I and says that anyone who has withdrawn from their customs and payments is to return.[70] This is one of a number of short grants to towns aimed at restoring the pre-Stephen position. No other grant is known until that by Richard I, made on 5 May 1194.[71] Norwich was one of many towns to profit by (and pay for) such charters from Richard and John. The 1194 charter (Plate 2) granted the citizens the right to commute their payments to the crown for a fixed annual charge (*firma burgi*); freedom from toll throughout England; the same liberties and customs as London; the right to elect their own reeves; and other privileges.

It is a question how far the charter of 1194 did any more than confirm what was already *de facto* the case. A convincing instance is that of the fee farm, fixed at £108; there is pipe roll evidence which takes this odd sum back to the early years of Henry II.[72] How old were the 'customs' mentioned in the charter of Henry II? It is likely that in long-established towns many of their customs derived from before the Conquest.[73] Particularly important may have been rules relating to the tenure of property. Consider these rules of Norwich as they emerge in the custumal and thirteenth-century deeds. There was more freedom in the transfer of property than was normal in the countryside. Thus in Norwich land which had been acquired by purchase could be devised by will. Although inherited land could not be devised, this rule could be evaded by deploying the entitlement to sell.[74] It is important that leasing had a more complete sanction of law in boroughs than it did in the country at large.[75] By, or before, the late thirteenth century, leasing and renting were normal in Norwich. Many of the inhabitants lived in properties which were leased. Bundles of rents or leases were bought and sold.[76] There is much for the legal historian to explore here. In any case it is plain that the leasing and renting of urban property was a significant factor in the economic life and development of Norwich. It is plausible to suppose that urban property was an important field for investment. It is a question how far the 'customs' confirmed in the twelfth century relate to a position comparable to that of the later thirteenth century. An important element in the life of the city by the thirteenth century, if not earlier, was the provision made for the efficient handling of property transactions and litigation. Deeds relating to property could be made public before the bailiffs at least from about the middle of the century. From 1285 or before such deeds could be officially enrolled; this was not mandatory, but considerable use was made of the facility.[77] An advantage of the bailiffs' court was that it was frequently in session:

at least once a week. A most important function of that court may well have been to hear cases relating to property in the town and to provide quick justice.

The administration of the city changed between the twelfth century and the thirteenth. Round about 1223 the authority of two reeves was replaced by that of four bailiffs.[78] It is a little curious that, unlike most important thirteenth-century towns, Norwich did not get a mayor.[79] Why was this notable lack not made good till 1406? A likely answer is that the four bailiffs each represented one of the four leets and that the history, and not least the sprawling topography, of the city helped to make the quaternary arrangement more acceptable than that of a unitary mayor.[80] The bailiffs to some extent increased their powers in the thirteenth century, for example by gaining the franchise of return of royal writs in 1256.[81]

What the municipality did not gain in 1194, or at any time in the thirteenth century, was major criminal jurisdiction. The city's rights did not extend beyond *infangthief*: the right to try (and, if appropriate, hang) a thief in possession of the stolen goods. There was a terrible furore in 1285 when the bailiffs and community tried and punished a man called Walter Eghe, who, although he may have been a thief, had not stolen in such a way as to empower the city court to hang him. Erring Norwich was, for a time, taken into the king's hand.[82] The most important liberties and rights enjoyed by the city were those with an economic bearing: not only the relatively free and flexible customs relating to the tenure and transfer of urban property, but also the control of marketing arrangements via the leet courts, and, not least, control over guilds.[83] Because the city was an organised entity, it could do such things as (in 1285) appoint an alderman of its 'hanse' to guard its interests in fairs at other places.[84]

Very likely the charter of 1194 partly legitimised some of what already went on. But it was granted in circumstances of tension, not to say crisis, and so may also have had a radical aspect. The charter was issued at Portsmouth on 5 May. King Richard was there because, having returned from his German captivity in March, he was about to set sail to seek to restore his power in Normandy. He had already tried to cross on 5 May but did not make it until a week later.[85] The immediate context of the charter was therefore that of a king selling liberties as he raised all the money he was able. Could there have also been an element of necessary conciliation there? When Richard returned from Germany he had to fight to regain full control in England, for example by a brutal siege of Nottingham castle.[86] At some time in 1193 or 1194 there was a large royal garrison in Norwich castle.[87] Why? Fear of a French invasion seems unlikely at this juncture. What was, probably, at stake was royal control of Norwich. The need to control towns may have been related to the military potential of burgesses. Henry II had intended such people to be armed.[88] John's government saw Norwich as having military capacity when he ordered that it was to provide twenty armed men to serve on the Continent in 1212.[89] The 'views of arms', which were a feature of the later medieval organisation of Norwich, may have had long antecedents.[90] It is not easy to judge the moods and attitudes of men such as the Norwich burgesses in about 1200, not least to guess how much they may have known of other towns and other countries. There could have been a more experienced radicalism in Norwich than readily appears from our sources. The grant of the charter of 1194 may have owed something to the pressure of an increasingly demanding citizenry with an armed capacity.

Norwich was more changed by the Norman Conquest than it had ever changed before (in so short a time); or than it was ever to change again. In this revolution four elements were linked: the castle, the new town, the cathedral and the Jews. The keep of Norwich castle still dominates much of the inner city. It is a statement in 'the architectural language of power'. A 'fortified palace' whose keep, though now refaced and gutted, still reveals its brilliant origins.[91] The earliest reference to the castle comes in a letter from Archbishop Lanfranc in 1075 saying that, after it had been regained from rebels led by Ralph, earl of East Anglia, it was held by 300 armoured men, accompanied by slingers and engineers.[92] A major fortification is implied; and, indeed, Domesday Book suggests it replaced some ninety-eight messuages; and archaeology indicates a sequence of post-Conquest earthworks on an increasing scale.[93] The castle, as now we see it (in part), was probably an expression of the organising power and 'expensive taste' of King William II (Figure 7).[94] The keep was, arguably, commenced after *c.* 1090 and completed by *c.* 1120. Its richly decorated exterior would have been all the more impressive if, like most major Norman buildings, it was painted.[95] Henry I's Christmas sojourn at Norwich in 1121 may indicate the completion of the keep. Maybe he was the first king of England to have come to Norwich. The castle may have been intended as a provincial palace. It was also the centre of control, defence and administration for the most populous part of England. For a period the garrison was provided by the important (but obscure) system of castle guard; the abbey of Bury supplied ten knights for each quarter of the year; and other tenants in chief made similar provision. This presence of fairly numerous East Anglian knights in Anglo-Norman Norwich must have had social and political importance, possibly reflected in the nature of the castle, and, indeed, of the Norman borough.[96] The system of castle-guard was modified in the twelfth century and in the thirteenth appears to have been abandoned or commuted, though the constable had serjeants at his disposal.[97]

Domesday refers to a 'new borough' at Norwich, established when Earl Ralph granted land for the founding of a new borough 'between himself and the king'. Domesday indicates that in 1086 it held forty-one burgesses living under the direct authority of king and earl, that Roger Bigod then claimed fifty more and that other Normans had between one and fourteen. This new borough lay on the west of the city and resembles a similar development at Nottingham (Map 2). Both were in a contemporary tradition of urban foundation in Normandy.[98] The list of landowners there shows (as does a list of those in the main borough 'from whom the king does not have his custom') that urban property was already being acquired as an investment; for surely someone who has two or three or five *manses* is more plausibly seen as an investor than as a lord. The number of holdings in the new borough had grown from thirty-six (or forty-two) at some earlier date, probably that of its foundation.[99] This growth contrasts with the sad state of the main town as described in Domesday Book. A striking total of 480 burgesses or former burgesses could no longer pay their dues; another thirty-two had left Norwich altogether. The survey sketches the sources of the troubles of a population being entirely devastated ('*omnino ... vastati*' – strong words, of a kind not often heard in Domesday): the forfeiture of Earl Ralph after his 1075 rebellion, fires, royal taxation.

An element in the comparative prosperity of the new Norman borough must have been its market place. This was on the same site as the present Norwich market place, though then with an additional strip to the south.[100] East Anglian market places deserve more attention than they have received. In most of England (for example in London) the market place was a wide street, or streets, sometimes a space at a cross-roads. There is something rather special about such vast rectangles as those of Norwich and Yarmouth – that at Yarmouth is believed to be the most extensive in the land. What was the purpose of these unusually wide spaces? By the late thirteenth century Norwich market place was the home of very many stalls and shops: you could buy all sorts of things there. Not *everything*, however: livestock, and bulky goods such as timber, were sold elsewhere.[101] Suppose (one cannot prove it, but it is a fair guess) that similar circumstances prevailed in the eleventh century. The big market place stands for an extremely commercial society, such that there was much buying and selling of a wide variety of goods. The prosperity of the new borough would have depended partly on its providing a better forum for trade than the old one had done. The old market place had probably been Tombland. Although the impact of the Conquest on Norwich was hard indeed, the success of the French borough intimates underlying movements towards prosperity.

Norwich cathedral tells the same tale. The definitive move of the *sedes* of the East Anglian see to Norwich took place in 1096, having been in the air for some time. Bishop Herbert de Losinga, a man of high ability, acquired a vast site, including what had been part of the town. He made the new cathedral a monastic one; and inaugurated monastic building to the south of the cathedral. Fortified accommodation for the bishop followed to the north. De Losinga gained a substantial endowment for the new cathedral and its monastery. An important element in this was the manor of Thorpe, bordering the city on the east with dependent settlements to the west and south. The cathedral rose by stages: the eastern end, including bays of the nave, was completed by 1119, the rest of the main building was up by 1148.[102] It is not surprising that the church took long to build; for it is titanic. Of the twelve biggest churches of approximately this period, those on the same scale as St Peter's, Rome, nine are English, and one of them is Norwich. Comparison of seventeen relevant churches in England and abroad shows that Norwich cathedral was exceeded in length by only four: Old St Peter's (Rome), Speyer, Winchester and (by a hair's breadth) Bury.[103]

How was so vast a project funded? Lacking financial accounts, we must guess. Losinga secured good gifts. The newly increased estates of the see were rich, though maybe not so rich as the bishop had hoped. A significant, if unquantifiable, source may have been taxation. Losinga seems to have gained the right to levy a land tax, a carucage, on all estates in the diocese and to have instituted a levy on churches (perhaps all churches). Both taxes seem to have continued till John of Oxford (the fourth bishop of Norwich) gave them up at some point between 1197 and 1200.[104] These levies may have been exceedingly important. East Anglia's great cathedral church must have been a product of East Anglia's great wealth. These may well have been boom times. The Domesday *valets* (evaluations), for lands other than *terra regis* (that of the king), of Norfolk rose vastly between 1066 and 1086: by 38 per cent, a higher figure than that for any other shire.[105] The Suffolk rise was the fifth highest, 20.5 per cent. Some of these increases may have derived from the iron greed or efficiency of Norman landlords; but that need not be the whole story. In building up the estates and power of his church, Herbert de Losinga displayed wide ambitions and economic acumen. There were two rising ports on the Norfolk coast. He secured control of one, Lynn, and established a firm base in the other, Yarmouth. Not for nothing had he been prior of the monastery of Fécamp, an important Norman port. One is reminded of the Flemish Baldwin, abbot of Bury St

Edmunds from 1065, who had by 1086 developed a newly planned quarter of his town, straight in front of the main gate of the monastery.[106]

Not the least important introduction to Norwich by the Normans was that of the Jews. The Jews of Norwich first come to notice in 1144 in connection with the 'martyrdom' of William of Norwich.[107] The story is a horrible one; for it marks the emergence of the lie about Jewish ritual murder. A boy of about seven or eight, William, was murdered at about Eastertime 1144. The story was invented that he had been sacrificed by the Norwich Jews. This was believed by a faction among the cathedral monks. For a time they did not prevail, but in the end they did; and William's body, moved by successive stages to an honoured place, became the centre of a cult, for a time a burgeoning cult. (For all its many advantages, Norwich cathedral had hitherto lacked a saint of its own.) There were further outbursts of violence against the Jews in 1190 and in the 1230s.[108] The Jewish community, of never much more than two hundred, was probably some sixty strong when expulsion came on the orders of the crown in 1290.[109] The Norwich Jews were more important than numerous. Their leading members in the late twelfth and earlier thirteenth centuries were rich indeed: in particular Jurnet and his son Isaac, who was 'obviously the outstanding plutocrat of his generation, not only in Norwich but possibly in the whole of England'.[110] The financial activities of the Norwich Jews are specially well documented (Plate 3). For example, the 'day book' rolls of 1225–27 provide information on over three hundred loans: one to a monastery, a few to noblemen, most to gentry, a handful to peasants, artisans and citizens.[111] Their business transactions extended over much of East Anglia. There is no doubt that their community was dependent on royal power, almost as an arm of government. Not for nothing did most Norwich Jews live near the castle.[112]

Late Anglo-Saxon Norwich is, in a way, up to a point, well recorded. Domesday gives a fuller account of it than any we have for most continental towns of the day. As we have already seen, assiduous and sophisticated archaeological work has advanced knowledge remarkably indeed. Yet, the reality of Norwich before 1066 remains a matter for speculation and, not least, for the delineation of ignorance. How populous was the city? Domesday indicates, depending on how you interpret it, a 'recorded population' of between 1437 and 1518 for 1066, though it also says that there were 1320 burgesses in the time of Edward the Confessor.[113] A repeated suggestion that the real population was, say, between 5000 and 10,000 depends on the deployment of a 'multiplier' related to hypothetical household size and on turning a blind eye to the possibility that an essentially fiscal record may exclude an urban proletariat at least as numerous as the burgage holders with their households. How extensive was the city? Our best single piece of evidence is Domesday's indication that there were between forty-nine and fifty-four churches and chapels in 1066. Probably there were never more than about sixty-five churches in medieval Norwich.[114] The implication of the Domesday account of churches (reinforced by archaeology) is that the city was already very extensive, though we do not know how thickly settled.

What were the functions and occupations of the city? Four principal elements fall under consideration: government, residence, manufacture and the sea. England was a much-governed country. Indications of this in regard to Norwich are as follows. As we have just noted, Domesday says at one point that in 1066 Norwich had 1320 burgesses. This number is rather contradicted by other Domesday statements; its duodecimal nature is, however, suggestive of the city's involvement in a tight fiscal organisation. So too are indications that before the Conquest the geld assessments imposed upon one hundred adjacent to Norwich, and of part of another, had been raised, it may well be in response to the increasing prosperity of the city.[115] From the earlier tenth century to nearly the time of the Conquest, East Anglia was under the authority of earls, the last of whom was the future King Harold II. Where was that authority based? A fair guess is at Norwich. A late thirteenth-century source suggests that the earls had a palace by Tombland, the central open space of late Anglo-Saxon Norwich.[116] If so, this was a major fact about the city; but it is unverified. An indication of the administrative weight of Norwich is that, according to the twelfth-century *Liber Eliensis*, it was one of four places in Norfolk, Suffolk and Cambridgeshire at which those buying land needed no witnesses.[117] A major centre of government might be expected to have attracted residents and property owners of status, and this would have been a significant economic factor.[118] We know only a little about landowners in pre-conquest Norwich. A very important one was Archbishop Stigand. His sister also had property there. So too did his brother Æthelmaer, bishop of East Anglia, who, Domesday tells us, owned a Norwich church 'not by reason of the bishopric but by inheritance'. These circumstances, and Stigand's Norse name, suggest that he may have been a Norwich man 'of Norse trading stock'.[119] If so, he was the most successful Norwich man ever, so far. The Toki who gave his name to suburban Tokethorpe may have been the Toki who appears in Domesday as a significant Norfolk landowner.[120] The abbeys of Bury, probably Ely, and maybe already Ramsey, had establishments of some kind in Norwich.[121] This is as far as our knowledge of the properties and residences of the powerful in Norwich goes; there could have been more such; and this could have been important.

Late Anglo-Saxon Norwich was a major manufacturing place. This is most demonstrably so in the case of pottery. Until, from the 1950s, modern archaeology began to illuminate early Norwich, there was only one piece of evidence for pottery manufacture there: a long street, called Pottergate. It has now been shown that much pottery was made there and thereabouts; from the tenth century (or maybe a little earlier) until approximately the mid twelfth cooking pots and storage jars were produced in Norwich, as elsewhere in Eastern England, in quantities unmatched since Roman times.[122] The semi–indestructible quantities of pottery give it (and its distribution in the countryside) an assured role in the archaeological record. Other manufactures would have mattered even more. In noting the prominence of the leather trades in Norwich around 1300, we remember that, six generations earlier, the unfortunate 'Saint' William started off in just such a Norwich trade as the first known English apprentice.[123] His biographer, Thomas of Monmouth, is explicit: 'he was entrusted to the skinners to learn the skinners' craft'. Archaeology shows that leather-working was already in hand in late Anglo-Saxon Norwich. So too was metal-working, the manufacture of combs and such from bone and horn, wood-working (all tableware was made of wood) and probably (though not quite demonstrably at this date) cloth and clothing.[124] The environment of Norwich came to be densely populated. One of Adam Smith's major arguments was that the possibility of specialisation of function, the key to economic progress, related to density of population. It has been argued on archaeological grounds that the tenth century saw, at least in some places, a markedly increased availability of rather ordinary manufactured goods.[125] Maybe Norfolk's population growth, in affecting the demand and market for manufactured everyday goods contributed to the rise of Norwich, where consumer goods were made for peasants who could now afford them.

Another part must have been played by the sea. Here the former 'Great Estuary' must have figured prominently. It seems broadly certain that between the fifth century and the eleventh the sea retreated and the lands it left were drained.[126] The when and how of this are still vague. Norwich was, of course, always accessible by water. The most important quays until the eleventh century were those immediately downstream of Fye bridge; the construction of the cathedral and castle partly blocked this area off; later, the main quays were further downstream in Conesford. It is, however, uncertain how large the ships which could reach the city were. The most powerful instance of this problem is as follows. Tens of thousands of tons of stone were brought to Norwich, from Caen and from the midlands, for the building of cathedral and castle. Did the vessels carrying it come direct upriver, or did their cargo have to be transhipped at Yarmouth?

An indication of Norwich's maritime connection is the considerable prominence there of herring. There are two references to herring renders from Norwich in Domesday, including one from Thorpe.[127] The abbey of Bury drew a last of herring (probably 12,000) from its Norwich property. Further evidence of the significance of herrings at Norwich is that from the thirteenth century until 1816 Norwich owed to the crown an annual render of twenty-five herring pies. It is possible that this obligation was as old as the eleventh century; for the service of carrying the pies fell on a holding in a nearby village, and what might be the same service is recorded in Domesday.[128] A third Domesday render to the crown illuminates (ambiguously) another aspect of the maritime trade of Norwich. The city had to provide a bear, with dogs to bait it. The poor beast must have come from outside England. Was this an indicator of extensive trade, say, with Scandinavia? Or simply of an exotic import line? Most of what we know of the overseas contacts of Norwich comes from occasional post-conquest references, and it is always a question as to how far they stand for something which had been going on for a long time. Thus the life of St William, writing of the mid twelfth century, mentions 'a merchant of Cologne who had brought wine in a ship from that part of the world'.[129] This reference adds weight to the implications of another of 1200 or 1201 which mentions wine 'by the measure of Norwich'.[130] And one wonders how far finds of Rhineland pottery in late Anglo-Saxon Norwich take the wine trade.[131] A comparable example is that of timber. We know that by the late thirteenth century timber was imported to Norwich from Germany; for the cathedral priory sent its carpenter to Hamburg to select timber for the rebuilding after 1272.[132]

Whatever the doubts and difficulties – and they are many – no one can question the economic importance of Norwich in the generations before the Conquest. The indicators of its high rank among English towns are conclusive. Archaeological work of the greatest value has done much to establish the extent and nature of the development of the city, not least to the south of the river. The evidence of parish and hundredal boundaries is strongly indicative of expansion.[133] While there is too much that we do not know about, say, later tenth- and eleventh-century Norwich, much is reasonably clear and becoming clearer. The same is not true of earlier centuries.

The greatest mysteries relate to the period between the fifth century and the tenth. Inquiry is greatly hindered by lack of written evidence; almost completely absent in East Anglia. For the years between the seventh century and the ninth two questions highlight the problems and the possibilities. Is it likely that there was no emporium site between Ipswich and York? Did one at, or near, Norwich fill part of the gap? Emporium is a term used to denote such sites as those detected and partly explored, for example, at Southampton, London west of the former Roman city, and Ipswich: dating from between the seventh century and the ninth, covering some tens of hectares, providing considerable evidence for trade and manufacture, and demonstrating a suggestive relationship to centres of royal authority.[134] They are also found on the opposite shores of the North Sea and the Channel. All these settlements would be called towns, did not the term seem too presumptuous. Generalisations about them may be ventured. Their wide extent must exclude an explanation for their existence, such as is sometimes offered, that it depended on the supply of luxury goods. Their locations, with easy access to the sea, must be significant. Their economic function has to be considered in the light of fairly recent discoveries which owe much to extensive use of metal detectors. This has brought to light two important phenomena. First, that in parts of the period concerned very large amounts of coin were in circulation: it seems that in the earlier eighth century there was as much or more coin about, in large parts of England, than there was for centuries to come.[135] Secondly, a considerable number of 'productive sites' have been discovered. This comfortably indeterminate expression indicates countryside sites which can quite plausibly be suggested to have been those of markets; on the basis of finds of coins and small metal items.[136] It is beginning to seem possible that the emporia formed the upper level of an economy in which the extensive use of coin was associated with the widespread distribution of relatively low value goods. In short, we may begin, with necessary hesitation, to see the emporia rather as one may see *late* Anglo-Saxon Norwich: as centres of manufacture of consumer goods also enjoying involvement in maritime trade.

There is a reasonable case for searching for an emporium in East Anglia in addition to Ipswich. 'Search' might indeed have to be the word; one has only to bear in mind for how very many years the relevant sites at London and York were undiscovered. How suggestive is the very name Nor*wich*? It appears that places of the kind under discussion were called '*wics*' and that in English toponymy the relevant place name element is that in the palatalised form 'wich'.[137] This element need not, but can, indicate a place of economic significance.[138] The 'wich' in Norwich (the name first appears on coins of the early tenth century or possibly of the late ninth) could indicate an emporium site there or thereabouts.[139] Finds from the appropriate period have been made at Norwich, in particular of Ipswich ware, and especially north of the river. As one scholar has put it 'the amount of eighth century material found there implies a settlement involved in more than just farming and fishing'.[140] That alone is not adequately convincing evidence for an emporium. But it has to be borne in mind that for all the good archaeological work that has been done in Norwich in the last forty years the area under consideration is enormous, and the parts of it where there has been little or no archaeological inquiry are numerous.[141] English emporia were generally set up in close association with centres of royal authority. If there was such a centre near Norwich it was probably Thorpe, because Thorpe appears in Domesday Book and later as the centre of a really big estate, at some stage a royal estate.[142] It could, as such, have been very old: there is no telling for certain. An extension of emporium problems, another version of them, comes in the ninth and very early tenth centuries. From *c.* 870 until *c.* 920 East Anglia was under Danish rule. This regime is almost entirely undocumented. There are important possibilities on which we have little to help us beyond place-names, archaeology (good but insufficient) and guesswork. For example, it *could* be that the island of Flegg was at some stage a major Danish base.[143] Perhaps Norwich was the centre of Danish power in East Anglia. It may also be that the city's origins as a major centre of commerce and manufacture belong to the Danish period and that we should see Norwich as a kind of Dublin. Some of the place-names of Norwich are Scandinavian. Scandinavian artefacts have been found. Such evidence does no more than provide some modest fuel for speculation.[144]

In short, for all the solid fact of the city, and notwithstanding long study, much about the story of Norwich is almost completely veiled, as yet unknown. So much is plain to anyone who considers the possibilities of its past before about 1000. Two illustrations of why agnosticism is imperative are these. One, the caverns in the chalk under and near the city; there is extensive evidence that these are vast.[145] That a double-decker 'bus collapsed into one of them in 1988 is a minor indication of their scale.[146] They may be exceedingly old and of long-lasting importance. The Caen or Barnack stone facing of the walls of the cathedral and castle enclosed fillings largely of flint. How far could the flints have come from the mines beneath the city? Another mystery is that of the great timber causeway, a hundred yards long, crossing the Wensum at Fye bridge. It was found in 1896 and has been further investigated since, but not conclusively dated.[147] It is well possible that for a long period this causeway was the lowest crossing of the Wensum Yare; and, if so, a key point for a wide area.

New and arresting areas of doubt have been opened by increasingly sophisticated analyses of the medieval English economy. Thus the 'commercialisation' of that economy has been notably explored by Richard Britnell, who concluded that there were really major changes between the time of Domesday and that of the Black Death.[148] In putting his complex account beside what may be known, or guessed, about Norwich, from the eighth century onwards, questions about the relationships between the qualitative and the quantitative present themselves very forcibly, for one cannot but suspect whether large parts of East Anglia were adequately 'commercialised' by the eleventh century or, conceivably, earlier. Recent work has made us look at East Anglia in new lights.[149] We end with questions. What was the relationship between Norwich, Norfolk and London?[150] For example, why are Norfolk names and people so prominent in late thirteenth- and early fourteenth-century London? Can one take the (possibly too limited) evidence of early fourteenth-century acknowledgements of debt as indicative of the extent to which partly 'industrialised' Norfolk was financed from the countryside and its little towns, not by sources in the local metropolis of Norwich?[151] The more you know, the more you realise how little you know. The study of the social, political and economic history of early Norwich is, very distinctly, in its infancy. That history cannot be fully understood until some boreal Braudel enables us to place it in a full North Sea context.

3

The Churches

Jonathan Finch

> The prayers were read especially well for so old a man as the incumbent, who is on the shady side of three score years and ten – when the duties of preaching came he seemed exhausted and his voice faltered. There is an old system of Clerk and Sexton here with their usual roles. Also one could not but admire the old system of worshipping God in contrast to the flummery now introduced into many churches.
>
> Thomas Lord, wool merchant, on the service at St George Tombland, 29 June 1884[1]

There are many aspects of Norwich that might be proffered in its long claim to be one of England's foremost cities, but none stand more surely than the number and splendour of its medieval churches.[2] Norwich has long been famous as the 'city of churches' and it has been the ecclesiastical buildings – particularly the parish churches – that have given form and character to its development since it began to expand in the tenth and eleventh centuries. The church still loomed large in the eighteenth century; and John Kirkpatrick's view of the city shows a prospect of domestic buildings mustered behind the fourteenth-century walls, their gables and dormer windows regularly punctuated with sturdy flint towers marshalled around Everard's elegant cathedral spire (Figure 6). When the master mason, Robert Everard, completed the spire in 1498, however, the city must have seemed a hive of building activity. In what might arguably have been the greatest transformation of its landscape since the Norman foundation of the cathedral and the castle, nearly every parish church in the city was subject to some form of alteration. Some were radically rebuilt and laid out in a new open plan form, whilst others, notably in the poorer areas, could only stretch to a new porch or windows. Such was the extent of rebuilding during this period that it is impossible not to see it as a regeneration of civic identity, since within the process were embedded the fortunes and aspirations of the city and its inhabitants. Here was the material expression of two key aspects of life in Norwich: faith and fortune.

Despite their obvious role in the history of Norwich from its very beginnings to the present day, the city churches still await extensive and systematic study. The work that has been done so far has tended to take one of two approaches. The first and most necessary consists of individual parish histories which have concentrated upon the church as the focal point of these specific communities. More recently, architectural historians have meticulously pieced together the evidence from moulding profiles and tracery forms to identify particular masons or workshops operating in the city and across the region during the medieval period. Their research aims to understand the growth and spread of ideas across both time and space, but its impact on our knowledge of ecclesiastical architecture in Norwich is not always immediately apparent. Not all churches, for example, display the tell-tale mouldings or pier forms associated with these architectural innovators. This chapter seeks to draw together a range of published and unpublished work to provide a more general overview of architectural development. It will suggest a chronology of building and investment to complement that already established from the documentary record, in order to provide the context within which each parochial story sits. It will then attempt to identify what are perhaps the most intriguing issues arising from such a survey. These fall into three roughly chronological sections with three distinct objectives in mind: first, to assess the evidence for, and the reasons behind, the proliferation of churches in Norwich; secondly, to explain the lack of evidence for ecclesiastical building in the thirteenth and fourteenth centuries; and finally to understand the motives behind the transformation of the parish churches in the fifteenth century.

An essential starting point is to account for the sheer number of churches in the city – which takes us back to its very foundation. It is clear from Domesday Book that Norwich was well provided with places of worship around the Conquest, as between forty-nine and fifty-four churches and chapels are recorded in 1086.[3] Only eight, however, are mentioned by name as having existed before 1066: All Saints,[4] Holy Trinity (Christchurch),[5] St Laurence, St Martin,[6] St Mary,[7] St Michael Tombland,[8] Saints Simon and Jude, and St Sepulchre.[9] St Gregory's and St Clement's can be added to the list, as it has been argued that characteristics of their parishes and locations are suggestive of early foundations.[10] St Vedast's (later corrupted to St Faith's) has also been identified as a pre-conquest foundation because of the section of a tenth-century interlaced cross shaft found in a building near the site in the nineteenth century.[11] The churches of St Edmund and St Helen may also be candidates for pre-Conquest foundation, along with St Cuthbert's, St Mary the Less, St Michael-at-Plea and St Peter Hungate.[12]

Richard Morris has attempted to address the issue of why there were so many churches in certain medieval towns and cities, which he sees as a reflection of early traits of urbanism, dating from before 950.[13] He also hints at the significance of Danish involvement during those early periods, since most cities with a multitude of churches are found in the east: Norwich, Lincoln and York being the most obvious.[14] Despite the striking numbers involved, Morris argues that such places were far from overchurched. The top five cities in the eleventh century – London, Winchester, Norwich, Lincoln and York – were substantially larger than any other towns in England, having attained states of development which placed them in a class of their own. This was the urban premier league, and the proliferation of churches within these cities was as much a reason for their membership as it was a manifestation of that status.[15]

Although documentary sources suggest that around twenty-five churches might be a fair indication of the number of pre-conquest foundations in Norwich, the chronology of investment in them around the Conquest is still unclear. We are, however, fortunate that evidence is emerging about the form they took. A church discovered beneath the north-east bailey area of the Norman castle supplies the best information.[16] The building was probably constructed in the first half of the eleventh century, but only survived for around seventy-five years before it was buried beneath the castle earthworks. It was a two-cell structure with a rectangular nave roughly twice as long as the slightly narrower chancel, and was of post-in-slot construction, with possible evidence for a soakaway for a font.[17] A wall of similar construction was found within the nave of St Martin-at-Palace during excavations, but it was not possible to be certain that it belonged to an early church, despite its east-west alignment.[18] A second timber building survived as seven post-holes, delineating the south wall and the south-western corner, to the north of the first. Significantly, a fragment of grave cover had been used to pack one of the post-holes. The fragment indicates that the building dated from the mid eleventh century, and also lends weight to the view that it was a church, since material from earlier burials was available for re-use.[19] In contrast to the partial excavation of St Martin's, the complete excavation of St Benedict's revealed no structure earlier than the eleventh century, although three burials predating the fabric again raised the possibility that an earlier church was situated elsewhere on the site, beyond the scope of the excavation.[20]

Tantalisingly little remains of this Anglo-Saxon achievement in terms of

FIGURE 10. The church of St Mary Coslany, 1828, by James Sillet. The round tower, with its distinctive triangular-headed sound holes, is thought to date from after the Conquest. The two-storey south porch, faced in ashlar, is typical of the additions made to Norwich churches in the fifteenth century. (*Norwich Castle Museum and Art Gallery*)

standing fabric or architectural detail. Most of the fabric that was once thought to be Saxon has, in fact, now been reclassified as 'Saxo-Norman' and cannot be assigned with certainty to the earlier phase. The long-and-short work evident on the east end of St Martin-at-Palace, for example, which marks out the width of an earlier chancel, was once thought to be Saxon.[21] The excavations at St Martin's were unable, however, to demonstrate that it represented a pre-conquest phase, and more recent scholarship has sought to redefine the technique involved as 'Saxo-Norman'.[22] The fragment of long-and-short work on the north-east corner of the chancel at St John Timberhill is also now thought to be post-conquest because it uses Caen stone – a material introduced into the city by the Norman builders of the cathedral – rather than the Barnack limestone deployed at St Martin's.

The presence of Caen stone also serves to undermine the common belief that the round-towered churches in Norwich are pre-conquest. The tower of St Mary Coslany (Figure 10), for instance, has a distinctive belfry with two triangular-headed openings supported by a central baluster, which have been confidently defined as a pre-conquest or Saxon trait, yet close inspection revealed the central baluster to be of Caen stone.[23] Further proof that round towers were not indicative of pre-conquest structures was provided by the excavation of St Benedict's, which could not be dated any earlier than the eleventh century.[24]

The city has two other surviving round-towered churches: St Julian's and St Etheldreda's.[25] St Julian's gained fame as the home of the anchorite, Julian of Norwich, and, although it is now a pastiche of post-war restoration, the three windows on the north wall exposed during restoration are of a Saxo-Norman style.[26] The Romanesque doorway now within St Julian's was salvaged from another bombed church, St Michael-at-Thorn. The round tower at St Julian's is unusual in that it is thickened at the junction with the west gable, rather than displaying the customary form of support offered by quadrant pilasters to either side.[27] St Etheldreda's tower has been reduced to little more than a stump, crowned by a late medieval polygonal belfry. The use of chevron decoration marks out the early surviving fabric of the church as post-conquest, whilst the changing level and decoration of the string course suggests that the eleventh-century chancel began slightly to the west of the present chancel arch.[28]

Cartographic evidence may allow us to add another round-towered church to those already known in Norwich. St Mary-in-the Marsh was one of the pre-conquest churches enclosed within the cathedral precinct when it was created in the late eleventh century.[29] The church is thought to have been destroyed in the late sixteenth century, although its position has long been associated with a flint wall preserved within a row of eighteenth-century buildings in what is now the Lower Close.[30] Even so, an eighteenth-century plan of the tenement, made just before it was redeveloped, seems to include the church. It shows what appears to be a round western tower, nave with a south porch and a transept chapel on the south side, complete with buttresses, and chancel (Map 4).[31] Its survival into the eighteenth century would account for the use of its chancel fabric as a spinal wall in the new buildings.

The debate concerning round-towered churches has hitherto turned largely around a single issue: whether they were pre- or post-conquest. The answer that they may be both, but that most are probably post-conquest, should not be taken as the last word about them. The question we should now ask is *why* these expensive and fascinating structures were built: not least because the people who paid for them either belonged to, or were firmly under the heel of, a new elite with its own highly distinctive architectural style. The current explanation is that older techniques lingered on among the indigenous craftsmen. Thus, for example, the round-splayed windows of the cathedral's refectory range were built in a 'Saxon' style during the 1090s. Such an explanation may serve for minor aspects of a large construction programme, but seems less valid for prestigious public statements, such as church towers. It also makes the unwarranted assumption that there was no choice or 'agency' in church design at a crucial moment of foundation and rebuilding. We are asked to assume that, despite the complexity of marrying a round tower to a gable wall, and despite the extraordinary cost of building a church (of which engineering the tower was a considerable part) the patrons exercised little or no preference – they simply got what the master mason provided. Alternatively, one might argue that round towers were actively *chosen* by patrons to reflect the antiquity of the site, or even the cultural identity of those involved: either of an individual patron or of the parish as a whole. Such a supposition may seem fanciful. Yet it is important to explore the significance of these churches in terms other than the inability of Saxon masons to produce anything else. It has been argued that towers might be the articulation of a Baltic community, drawing links with similar churches in parts of northern Germany.[32] Perhaps during the Saxo-Norman rebuilding of these churches an older established identity was deliberately enshrined in the most prominent feature. We should remember that the topography of Norwich was radically transformed by the Norman plantation of castle and cathedral. Elements of the Saxon town were completely obliterated and its foci reoriented. In the context of symbolic, even defiant, display through architectural endeavour, the conservative design of a number of city churches cannot be regarded simply as a reflection of the masons' inability to replicate Norman architecture. It ought at least to be considered in the wider context of statements about indigenous identity.

The deployment or use of 'antiquated' styles of architecture leads us to another element of the late Saxon townscape: the nature of the pre-conquest ecclesiastical hierarchy. In order to uncover which, if any, of the churches once served as Saxon minsters, a number of sources must be drawn together. There seem to be four main candidates: St Clement's, St Gregory's, Holy Trinity (Christchurch) and St Michael Tombland. Both St Clement's and St Gregory's can claim to be early foundations and their parishes may once have been much larger. St Clement's dominated the *wic* settlement on the north bank of the River Wensum, and also claimed two-thirds of tithes from land in other parishes, which has prompted speculation that it may have been a minster.[33] St Gregory's was notable for providing sanctuary – a right perhaps linked to the survival of its fourteenth-century door ring of a lion's head devouring a man (Figure 11).[34] In addition, the church can boast four round brick openings encased by a later refacing of the tower, which have most recently been described as Saxon.[35] If this *is*, indeed, the

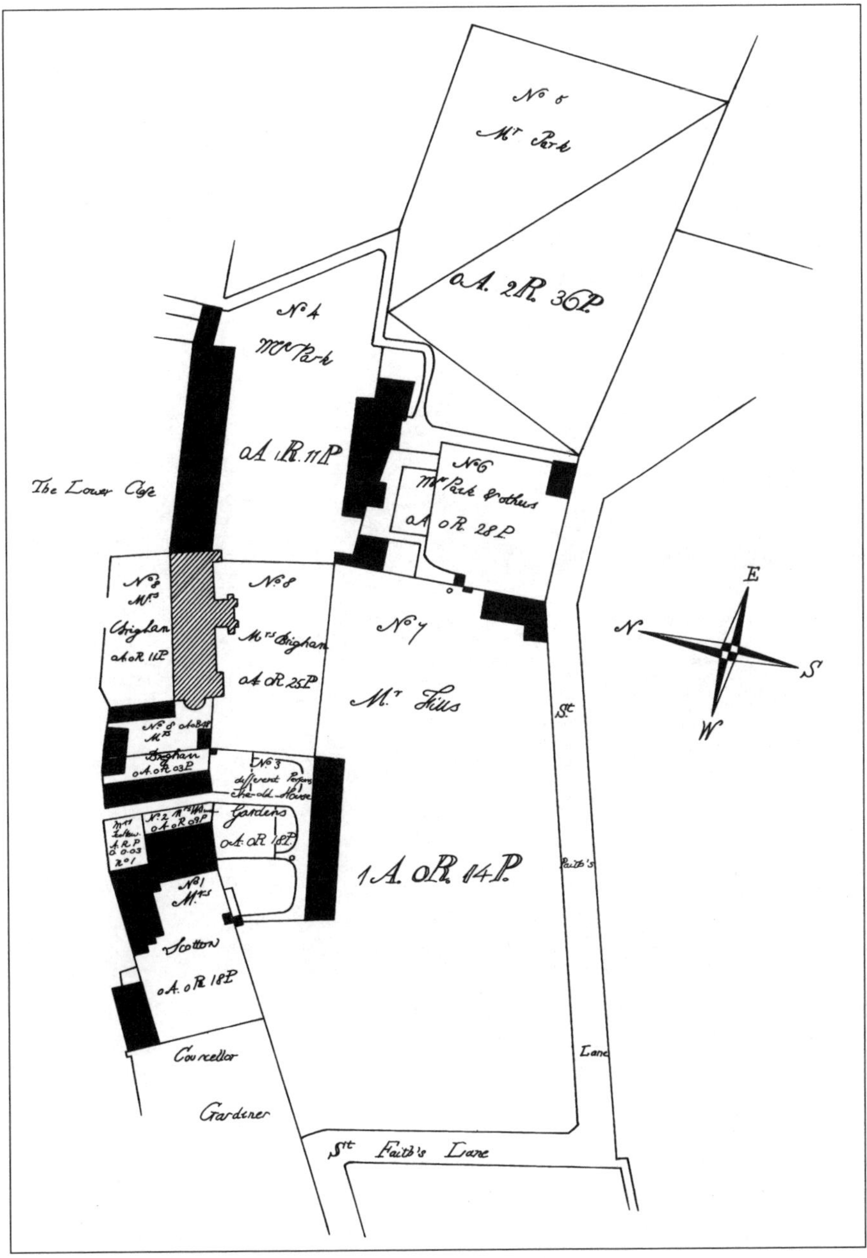

MAP 4. Plan of the Gascoin and Lines estate in the cathedral close, *c.* 1760. This plan of the south side of the lower close before redevelopment appears to show the outline of the church of St Mary-in-the Marsh (shaded) with a round west tower, south porch and transept, NRO, DCN 127/11. (*Norfolk Record Office, redrawn by Sven Schroeder*)

FIGURE 11. Medieval door ring from St Gregory's church. Although dating from the fourteenth century, the ring adopts an earlier design and may demonstrate the right of sanctuary offered here. (*Norwich Castle Museum and Art Gallery*)

case, then firm evidence of a pre-conquest tower would strongly suggest a minster church of some size and consequence.

Nothing is known about the structure of St Michael Tombland or Holy Trinity (Christchurch), although the location of each has been deduced from associated finds. St Michael's situation in Tombland was suggested by the discovery of a walrus ivory pectoral cross in 1878, during the excavations for the public toilets. The delicately carved cross (Plate 4), now in the Victoria and Albert Museum, has been regarded as confirmation of the church's early status and wealth, although not all art historians agree with the early date originally ascribed to it, preferring one around 1100.[36] Domesday certainly describes St Michael's as the richest pre-conquest church in the borough, as it then held one carucate of land worth 20s.[37] It has been argued from a detailed reading of the Domesday Book, and from the complex exchanges of land necessary to create the cathedral precinct, that St Michael's was a minster church, and possibly a royal foundation.[38] Its position, in an open market place, flanked by an episcopal residence to the northern end and, reputedly, by a palace of the earls of East Anglia to the south, was certainly one of the most prestigious in the Saxon town.[39]

The location of Holy Trinity (Christchurch) has been pinpointed by the reconstruction of the Saxon topography and the discovery of burials that were cut by the cathedral's foundations and eventually exposed during excavations on the north side of the cathedral's north transept.[40] It would appear that the early church lay at the cross roads of two important routes, but was swept away by the cathedral that shared its dedication. Significantly, perhaps, the architectural decoration of the cathedral's north transept is remarkable for its overtly 'antiquated' Saxon iconography and rich sculptural decoration.[41] This material has been read either as an 'anomaly' within the Romanesque building or as a symbolic space designed to link Herbert de Losinga (d. 1119), the first bishop of Norwich, with Felix, the first bishop of East Anglia (d. 647), whose effigy was displayed on the external face of the transept.[42] This is a persuasive argument, which connects the episcopal palace with the cathedral by means of the north transept.[43] It carries even greater force if we assume that the north transept did not simply replicate the architectural vocabulary, but actually incorporated fragments of the important Saxon church it replaced. There are a number of suggestive parallels for early minsters being subsumed by later cathedral foundations. In Hereford, for example, the parishioners of St John's, which had a claim to be the primary church of the town, worshipped in a chapel in the north transept of the cathedral church following the destruction of their church *c.* 1100 when the episcopal complex was enlarged.[44] If this speculation is correct, then the reused architectural elements, such as the three large beasts' heads, are a unique insight into the scale and decoration of the larger churches in Saxon Norwich. They are also indicative of a prosperous and powerful borough.[45]

Although St Michael's was probably the most prestigious pre-conquest church in the city, the fact that others can stake interesting claims to rival it suggests that the ecclesiastical hierarchy was well established and richly endowed before the Norman campaign of rebuilding which has left its legacy of round-towered churches. Indeed, the evidence for eleventh- and twelfth-century investment in churches is far more readily apparent than that produced during the subsequent two centuries. It is clear that by 1300 the parochial framework within the city, as elsewhere throughout the country, had been tightened up to prevent further private foundations, as the papacy exerted its power and opposed the secular ownership of churches. By the mid thirteenth century, therefore, the number of churches and chapels had reached a peak at around sixty (Map 5).[46] This was followed by fifty years or so of stability in the number of churches servicing the city. A gradual process of parish amalgamation then occurred over the later fourteenth century. Forty-six churches existed by 1520, a number which was further reduced after the Reformation, with another five lost to bombing and fire in the 1940s. This leaves thirty-one medieval churches in the city today.

The architectural contribution of the thirteenth and early fourteenth centuries is not now immediately apparent in the churches of Norwich, perhaps due to changing priorities for investment, but more probably because of the overwhelming impact of subsequent building campaigns in the fifteenth century. The Decorated style, pioneered by the Ramseys in the cathedral cloisters (especially the prior's door into the church), must undoubtedly have had an impact elsewhere.[47] Today, however, the style survives most visibly in the window tracery of various city churches, much of which is actually Victorian replacement of earlier stonework. None the less, most – if not all – of this was restoration work, replicas replacing the eroded or damaged original. The finest pieces are to be found in the east windows at All Saints, St Clement's, St Giles's and St John Maddermarket. Only that at St John Maddermarket has escaped complete replacement by the Victorians, and even here there has been heavy restoration. This striking five-light east window is far more extravagant than most Decorated tracery in the region and is the earliest element of the church, possibly dating from *c.* 1340–50.[48] Of the five ogee lights, the tracery of the outer and middle is taken higher to create two large ogee mouchettes (a curved dagger shape), each filled with six further mouchettes which fold around a central pair of ogee quatrefoils (Plate 5). The apex is filled with four more mouchettes, topped by an ogee lozenge. The combination of verticality within and between two highly decorated and curvilinear frames creates a remarkable window.[49]

Elsewhere across the city Decorated forms can be seen in the aisle windows at St Augustine's, in the clerestory tracery at St Gregory's, and in the tower tracery at St Margaret Westwick. These all retain simple curvilinear features. Much of this work can, in fact, be dated to the end of the first

1. The south bailey area of Norwich castle in the 1860s, with the Norman keep, refaced in the 1830s, in the background. By an unknown photographer, the picture probably advertises the new cattle market of 1862. (*Brian Ayers*)

2. The charter of Richard I to the city of Norwich, 1194, NRO, NCR, 26A/2A. (*Norfolk Record Office*)

3. Caricatures of Norwich Jews and devils from an exchequer roll of 1232–33, PRO, E401/1565. (*Public Record Office*)

4. Twelfth-century walrus ivory pectoral cross, excavated outside the cathedral precinct in Tombland. (*Trustees of the Victoria and Albert Museum*)

5. The east window of the church of St John Maddermarket. Dated *c.* 1340–50, this window is one of the finest elements of Decorated architecture to survive in any of the city's churches. (*Jonathan Finch*)

6. The interior of the church of St Peter Mancroft, looking north east towards the chancel chapel (with its stained-glass east window). The chapel provided the architectural inspiration for the whole interior. (*Jonathan Finch*)

7. The interior of St Andrew's church, looking north east. The shafts of each pier are separated by a casement moulding, thereby creating an impression of slenderness rather than mass. The vertical emphasis is further enhanced by the blind panels which connect the arcade to the clerestory, drawing the eye upwards. (*Jonathan Finch*)

8. The chancel roof of the church of St George Colegate. In 1496 William Wright was paid 8s. 4d. for the three crown braces which structure the roof. The continuous curve from the wall posts to the apex provided an elegant line without involving a heavy outlay on timber. (*Jonathan Finch*)

9. The east wall of Thorp's chapel on the south side of the church of St Michael Coslany, *c.* 1500. The delicate white ashlar filled with dark flint frames the large east window, offering a remarkable display of wealth and craftsmanship. (*Jonathan Finch*)

10. Mural monument to Mary Gardener (d. 1748) in the church of St George Tombland, executed by Peter Scheemakers. A winged putto holds a shrouded portrait of the deceased, conveying the growing emphasis on personal loss to be found in monuments to women from the urban bourgeoisie. (*Jonathan Finch*)

Parish Churches and Chapels

1. All Saints Fyebridge
2. All Saints Timberhill
3. Christ Church/Holy Trinity
4. St [John de] Sepulchre
5. St Andrew's
6. St Anne's
7. St Augustine's
8. St Bartholomew's
9. St Benedict's
10. St Botolph's
11. St Catherine's/St Winaloy's
12. St Christopher's
13. St Clement's
14. St Clement Conesford
15. St Crowche's
16. St Cuthbert's
17. St Edmund's
18. St Edward's
19. St Ethelbert's
20. St Etheldreda's
21. St George Colegate
22. St George Tombland
23. St Giles's
24. St Gregory's
25. St Helen's
26. St James's
27. St John Maddermarket
28. St John the Baptist Colegate
29. St John the Evangelist Conesford
30. St John Timberhill
31. St Julian's
32. St Laurence's
33. St Margaret at Newbridge
34. St Margaret Fyebridge
35. St Margaret Westwick
36. St Martin at Oak
37. St Martin at Palace
38. St Martin in the Bailey
39. St Mary Coslany
40. St Mary in the Marsh
41. St Mary the Less
42. St Mary Unbrent
43. St Matthew's
44. St Michael at Plea
45. St Michael at Thorn
46. St Michael Conesford
47. St Michael Coslany
48. St Michael Tombland
49. St Olave's
50. St Olave Conesford
51. St Paul's
52. St Peter Hungate
53. St Peter Mancroft
54. St Peter Parmentergate
55. St Peter Southgate
56. St Saviour's
57. St Simon and St Jude
58. St Stephen's
59. St Swithin's
60. St Vedast's

Religious Institutions

A Cathedral Priory (Benedictine)
B Site of Carrow Priory (Benedictine)
C Site of College of St Mary in the Fields
D The Great Hospital

E Dominican Friary (Blackfriars)
F Site of Franciscan Friary (Greyfriars)
G Site of Carmelite Friary (Whitefriars)
H Site of Austin Friary

MAP 5. Sites of the churches and religious houses of medieval Norwich. (*Sven Schroeder*)

quarter of the fifteenth century, in a period when Perpendicular styles had already taken hold. It is important to realise that, rather than being simple relics of an earlier age, Decorated and Perpendicular styles were evidently used together quite deliberately by master masons to articulate the rhythm of the building.

The paucity of thirteenth- and early fourteenth-century architecture in Norwich churches seems to be the result of the extent to which almost every church was rebuilt or refenestrated in the fifteenth century. The documentary records, in particular the accounts kept by the obedientiaries of the cathedral priory (which held the advowsons of around a score of city churches), cast a valuable light on this period of investment.[50] It is hard to tell if the levels of expenditure maintained by the priory were similar to those at churches which were not owned by a religious institution with a sharply declining budget.[51] An analysis of the 1368 inventory of church goods in the archdeaconry of Norwich suggests that provision of liturgical vestments, books and other paraphernalia in those churches appropriated to the priory was not noticeably worse than elsewhere in the city.[52] Even so, the work implemented by the priory seems to have been piecemeal, rarely costing more than the income it received annually from each of these churches. Since the amounts raised could be as little as one-fifth of revenues from rural parishes, the likelihood that upkeep and maintenance were under-funded remains very real.[53]

The most important running repairs were intended to keep chancels glazed and watertight, with thatchers and plumbers regularly employed for this purpose. There was rarely enough money to do more than replace a single complete window or door each year. The limited documentary evidence suggests that expenditure on chancels was kept under close control, and this may explain why east windows in particular have survived into the post-medieval period. Money was spent on maintaining the chancel and its expensive liturgical fittings and furnishings, rather than on bold statements of patronage. The naves of churches, on the other hand, were subject to waves of investment during the fifteenth century by increasingly wealthy parishioners, who were financially responsible for this part of the building. Despite this rather negative picture, the income received by the cathedral obedientiaries from their churches seems to have reached a peak towards the end of the fourteenth century. This was generally maintained into the fifteenth century, suggesting that parish life and commitment were far from faltering.

It would likewise be wrong to think of the fourteenth century as a period which saw no major ecclesiastical building campaigns in Norwich. Many of the surviving fifteenth-century arcades and windows are actually set within fabric dating from the previous century, when many churches realised the full extent of their plan form. But there was also another focus for ecclesiastical building in the thirteenth and fourteenth centuries which is far from evident today – the religious orders. One of the early foundations was the Benedictine nunnery, known today as Carrow abbey, in 1146. The church, which was nearly two hundred feet long, was the largest Norman building in the city after the cathedral, and must have been one of the most important construction programmes of the late twelfth century, although little now survives of the ornamental work. Carrow abbey sits at the southern edge of the city, outside the walls, but the churches of the friars were a dominant presence right in the heart of Norwich that has, consequently, all but vanished today (Map 6). The Franciscans (Greyfriars) arrived in 1226 and occupied a large site east of the castle, straddling the modern Prince of Wales Road; the Carmelites (Whitefriars) followed in 1256 and established themselves near the river, north of Whitefriars' bridge; and the Austin friars settled next to the Wensum by King Street in 1290. Little is left of the architecture of these important institutions: only the fourteenth-century arch known as the Arminghall Arch survives from the Whitefriars, and is an impressive sculptured portal with royal figures in the niches (Figure 17).[54] The site of the Greyfriars was recently excavated, but negligible evidence of its architecture came to light. The site of the Austin friars was all but destroyed by development in the 1970s.[55]

Norwich does, however, boast one real gem from the lost heritage of the religious orders – the church of the Blackfriars, which is the best-preserved friary church in the country. The Dominicans originally established themselves in St Clement's parish on their arrival in Norwich in 1226, then acquired the site of the suppressed Friars Penitential, just south of the Wensum, in 1307. Between 1325 and 1345 they built a church and precinct there. A fire in 1413 destroyed much of the fabric, but the rebuilding programme (*c.* 1440–70) preserved the plan and layout, with its majestic 265 foot long church. The surviving architectural features include parts of the cloister, and even some remnants of the original fabric from the Friars Penitential. The remains of Beckett's chapel and the adjoining early brick undercroft with its central stone pier are of that original build, whilst the five south-aisle windows and the east window, all with reticulated tracery, are elements from the fourteenth-century Dominican friary.

The mid fifteenth-century building known officially today as St Andrew's Hall (but also by its medieval name of Blackfriars) is an important landmark in the development of the Perpendicular style (Figure 16). Its window tracery is associated with the Coltishall-born Reginald Ely, who, as the first master mason of King's College, Cambridge, was probably responsible for designing the famous chapel in the early 1440s.[56] The rebuilding of the friars' church in Norwich was financed by donations which came predominantly from established county families. Sir Thomas Erpingham (d. 1428), whose arms appear along the clerestory of the nave, was one of the most generous patrons of the religious orders, financing the rebuilding of Blackfriars, installing a lavish stained glass window at the Austin friars, and also constructing the Erpingham Gate at the cathedral (Figure 23).[57] Erpingham may have been the most prominent local patron of his day, but the transformation of Norwich's parish churches was to be the result of investment by the new mercantile and civic elite who dispensed their considerable bounty closer to home.

The rebuilding of Blackfriars during the mid fifteenth century came at a pivotal point in the transformation of Norwich's ecclesiastical landscape. Aristocratic patronage spread across a wide range of religious institutions was gradually being displaced by mercantile investment. This focused increasingly on the parish churches, which, during the fifteenth century, were radically recast. Their exterior appearance and internal arrangement were both transformed – they were unified by the singular architectural vocabulary of the Perpendicular style. The process was achieved through the increasing confidence, wealth and generosity of the mercantile elite, who focused on the parish churches as an expression of pride in their city. It is hard to conceive the sheer scale of this outlay, but the disruption it would have caused to the patterns of everyday life must have been obvious to all. Given the sense of purpose and commitment involved, there can have been little doubt that a very deliberate strategy was being pursued.

The history and archaeology of this building campaign is only gradually being revealed; establishing its exact chronology is difficult. The architectural style – for all its poise and refined beauty – is hard to date precisely. Master masons borrowed earlier forms and motifs, thereby hampering the efforts of today's architectural historians. Documentary sources have shown, however, that the undoubted thrust of investment came in the mid fifteenth century, between around 1425 and the 1480s. During this period, and certainly until the dawn of the sixteenth century, nearly every church in Norwich underwent some form of extension, addition or rebuilding.[58] Some of the most prestigious, notably St Peter Mancroft, St Andrew's and St Gregory's, were subject to comprehensive restructuring, while smaller churches had porches or chapels added, or were systematically refenestrated, to achieve a sense of modernisation. The emphasis was on creating lofty, spacious interiors in which the architecture seemed to defy the engineering. Slender piers supported clerestories that flooded the naves with light, and expanses of glass in the aisles added to the effect. The ideal plan form was box-like with a wide nave accentuated by the addition of aisles, and an increasing disregard for the architectural division between chancel and nave.

One of the first parish churches to display the new style was St Giles's, which seems to have been planned in the early fifteenth century as an extraordinary statement in Perpendicular. The lofty west tower is the highest in Norwich (120 ft), even before one takes into account its topographical position on the ridge above the river valley. The emphasis on the buttresses, two to each face, suggests that the height of the tower was part of the original plan, although the final section with its unusually large traceried openings appears to have been the work of a different mason or workshop. Inside, the sense of height and space within the nave is accentuated by the slender piers, which lead the eye to the remarkable roof with projecting angels. The piers, which are composed of four asymmetrically arranged shafts, are of particular note. Towards the aisles, the shafts are equidistantly separated by plain hollow-chamfer mouldings, but on the nave side the piers are elongated, with the fourth shaft pushed forward into the nave on a pair of double-ogee mouldings, creating a greater sense of scale and depth. Dating the building campaign is difficult. The first documentary reference to all this activity is a bequest for the 'emendation of the church' in 1386. More specific evidence suggests that the tower was almost finished by 1424, whilst stylistic parallels for the stepped pier-bases point to an early fifteenth-century date.[59] The unusual pier form is also found at Blickling and at Carbrooke, which was in progress in the 1440s, but requests by senior civic officials for burial in the nave of St Giles's during the 1430s suggest it was then sufficiently near completion for such august ceremonies.[60] St Giles's was a radical new architectural statement in the city, and it is significant that, at this early stage in the development of the Perpendicular plan form, the chancel was left in its fourteenth-century state. Later building programmes in other parishes would remodel and greatly reduce the chancel. Ironically, at St Giles's the chancel fell into disrepair and was demolished in the sixteenth century, only to be rebuilt by the Victorians.

Today the most visible form of the Perpendicular transformation of the city's churches is exemplified by St Peter Mancroft, the most prestigious parish church in later medieval Norwich and one of the finest in England. Founded within the new French borough in the eleventh century and towering over the Norman market place, St Peter's was a statement of power and a focus for the new topography of the town. Little is known of the earlier church that stood on the site, but it has been suggested that by the late fourteenth century it had aisles, a Lady chapel, transepts and a central tower.[61] Despite the apparent architectural uniformity of the Perpendicular church, it appears to have been completed in a series of short campaigns. More significantly, the vision of a grand open church seems only to have crystallised once work was under way. The impetus for rebuilding came when the advowson passed from the abbey of St Peter in Gloucester to the neighbouring college of St Mary in the Fields in 1388.[62] A new tower was begun in the early 1390s to the west of the church, straddling the western boundary of the churchyard (as was the case at St John Maddermarket). The awkward relationship between the tower and the west end suggests that it may originally have been conceived as a free-standing structure. Other work in progress in the late fourteenth century seems to have been the demolition of the central tower, which would have left a section between the chancel and nave to be made good. A bequest to the new clerestory in 1431 indicates that restructuring was then well underway. The chancel also attracted attention in 1393, perhaps as a result of the eastern extension of the churchyard in the 1370s.

The transformation of St Peter's took its lead from the north chancel chapel, which was added to the old church *c.* 1440–45 (Plate 6). The mismatch between the eastern arcade base of the north chapel and the floor levels in the chancel suggests that the exact form of the church, particularly its raised east end, had not yet been planned. Soon after work on the chapel began, however, the college of St Mary's donated a full year's profits from the church to rebuild the chancel. This intensive campaign embraced the eastern end of the church, a new south chapel, the south transept and possibly that to the north as well. The programme is especially significant because of the effort made to match the detailing and fenestration of the two chapels and the transepts in order to create a unified architectural whole. The transformation of the chancel, which was probably complete by 1455, was either allied to or followed by a similar effort on the nave and aisles of the church, although this is much harder to date. A series of shorter building campaigns from the east towards the western tower was substantially finished by 1479, when 40s. was left for the new leading of the church. Work on the tower continued into the first decade of the sixteenth century, including presumably its adaptation from a free-standing structure to one engaged with the nave and aisles.

A near-contemporary scheme was also underway at St Gregory Pottergate. There are, indeed, a number of interesting parallels between the chancels of these two important churches. Most obviously, both have raised eastern ends and passageways running beneath them. Both also make use of brick, particularly in the vaulting. Dating the programme at

St Gregory's is more difficult, although the earliest reference to work on the chancel is from 1394, when the cathedral priory paid £4 'to the making' of it.[63] Unfortunately, such a date bears little relation to the present structure and, as the example of St Peter Mancroft has already demonstrated, it is not inconceivable that the chancel fabric could have been reworked again in the first half of the fifteenth century. There are a number of stylistic indications that the nave was extensively remodelled during that period. The clerestory windows are dateable to *c.* 1425 by comparison with those in the tower of St Saviour's; and the use of tracery in the aisles copied from the north walk of the cathedral cloister also points to the first half of the fifteenth century.[64] The internal aisle walls also have wall arcades to articulate the rhythm of the bays: a popular feature of the city's churches during the mid fifteenth century (as can be seen at St George Colegate). The date of the chancel fabric is therefore open to conjecture; but, although it might be difficult to suggest a fourteenth-century date, it is equally hard to argue for one later than St Peter Mancroft, where the stepped eastern end does not seem to have been part of the rebuilding scheme until the mid 1440s.

It is at the west end of St Gregory's, however, that the architecture is most puzzling. The porches were clearly built up against the pre-existing tower, which, as we have seen, may contain earlier Saxo-Norman fabric. The relationship between the aisles and the porches is more complex: it has been proposed that the aisles were built up to the new porches with the intention that they should eventually extend further west, embracing the tower and replacing the porches altogether. But there is no way of being sure what the original scheme was, only that, once the aisles abutted the porches, they were refaced to give the appearance of a single unified entity. The layout of the tower and porches was obviously important, since plans changed at some point during the rebuilding process. The tower arch had been built to a single full height, yet a chapel platform was then inserted, cutting across the lower western window. Access to the new chapel level and the space above is from a staircase in the north porch, which was originally entered from the north aisle. Since the porches were later additions it is difficult to determine how this upper level was previously reached – or indeed if it was always accessible.[65] The addition of porches at some point in the fifteenth century was clearly associated with the insertion of the chapel in the tower, and was therefore part of a considerable reorganisation of space and liturgical foci at the west end of the church.

Confirmation that the building campaign had reached its full extent, and that the porches were not, after all, to be rebuilt as the final bay of the aisles, comes with the magnificent fifteenth-century wall-painting of St George on the west wall of the north aisle (Plate 22). It is now considered to be one of the finest murals of its period in the country. Recent discoveries of more surviving paintwork in the south aisle (an Annunciation and images of Saints Ambrose, Augustine, Gregory and Jerome) suggest that the whole church displayed the same unrivalled quality of work, transforming a bold interior design into something quite breathtaking.[66]

If rebuilding plans at St Peter Mancroft were altered in the light of work on the chancel of St Gregory's, then St Andrew's, the last great church to be comprehensively rebuilt, drew on St Peter Mancroft for inspiration (Plate 7). Perhaps learning from the periodic nature of rebuilding at St Peter's and the architectural hitches it produced, St Andrew's seems to have been a comprehensive restructuring with one outcome in mind – to create the largest uniform interior space of any city church. Although the old tower was retained, the rest of the church was completely demolished to allow John Antell a free hand. This included finally abandoning the architectural division between nave and chancel, presumably with the consent of its patron, the same College of St Mary in the Fields that had generously underwritten so many schemes at St Peter's. The result was a soaring interior. The five-bay nave is flanked by identical aisles and flooded with light from the huge windows, which borrow their tracery from St Peter Mancroft, and from the clerestory where two windows were placed above each arcade arch. The tracery of each clerestory window continues down as blind panels to meet the arcade arches, signalling the hand of the master mason who also created Shelton church in South Norfolk and St George Colegate in Norwich. Although there is no distinct chancel as such, the single aisleless bay at the eastern end is demarcated by three steps up from the nave. At the west end, the earlier tower originally had openings to the north and south to light the vault which was entered from the west. When the north and south porches were added during the sixteenth-century rebuilding of the nave, their outer openings were not hung with doors, thus preserving the light to the inner tower vault. Unusually, however, the entrance into the church from these porches is to the nave aisles rather than into the tower and the centre of the nave, as at St Gregory's. Above the vault within the tower, again as at St Gregory's, was a chapel of 'Our Lady in the Steeple'. The architectural spaces at the west end of these new city churches were clearly being defined through changing patterns of use.

The campaigns to rebuild these three prestigious churches reveal some fascinating insights into the process of transformation. At St Peter Mancroft the overall plan appears to have changed in the course of work which took the form of a series of shorter campaigns. The ongoing programme at St Gregory's may have been affected by these decisions, as the two buildings vied for pre-eminence (and financial support) in the centre of the thriving city centre. Finally, the work at St Andrew's was planned from the outset with a clear and radical design in mind to create a particular form of church.[67] Architectural and documentary evidence from other churches in the city reveals that the piecemeal approach to rebuilding was by far the most common, as might be expected.

St George Colegate, perhaps 'the finest example of late medieval parish church architecture in Norfolk and one of England's best', evolved in this manner, despite the apparent uniformity of the finished building.[68] As at St Peter Mancroft, the final rebuilding began with the north chancel chapel (*c.* 1463–72) and possibly included the north aisle, as this contains windows with the earliest tracery evident in the church. As was the case at St Gregory's, the cathedral priory was responsible for the chancel, where work was undertaken in the late 1490s. The chancel was roofed in 1496, when William Wright received 8s. 4d. for three 'crown braces', presumably pairs of braces, in addition to the 20s. paid to him and his servants for work on the chancel stalls. The simple 'crown brace' roof has wall-posts which curve up to the principals without a break in the profile of their curve (Plate 8). The advantage of this form, which is found across Norwich, was that it could be built with relatively slight timbers, having no tie beam, queen or crown post.

Activity in the chancel was stimulated by plans to rebuild the nave, which began with the tower and included a south porch giving access to the upper stage of the tower. In common with other city churches, including St Margaret Westwick, which is stylistically linked to St George's, this porch may originally have been free-standing on three sides, but was soon abutted by an enlarged south aisle. The nave interior is by John Antell, who worked on St Michael Coslany and St Andrew's, yet here the style is refined to a simplicity that underplays the technical risks taken in building such a wide nave with a heavy flat roof.[69] Showing kinship with St Andrew's, the nave roof (*c.* 1500) rests its great weight on the reinforced clerestory, although the size of the windows belies its important structural role. Furthermore, in contrast to the lightly structured pitched roof in the chancel, the nave roof utilises massive timbers, proclaiming its quality and expense.

The final work was on the south aisle, which was built in the sixteenth century with characteristic wall arcades and straight interior jambs to the windows: another stylistic form deployed across the city during the early years of the century. One final aspect of this stage of rebuilding at St George's is the stripped-down tracery in the windows. This may have been a deliberately austere feature intended to highlight the fine roof and fittings. On the other hand, space had to be found for an elaborate glazing cycle which had been commissioned at the same time; at least five bequests were made for glazing windows there during this period.

Windows and window tracery were an important statement for any church, and stylistic similarities link a number of them across the city, including the Blackfriars' church mentioned above. It has been identified as a form of tracery known as 'Yorkshire Ogee' because of its early manifestation in the east window of York Minster (*c.* 1400), although its distribution is concentrated in East Anglia and Lincolnshire.[70] Despite their rarity elsewhere, varieties of Yorkshire Ogee tracery were frequently used in Norwich during the later fifteenth century. They can be found in some of the major building projects, notably the east windows of the aisles at St Peter Mancroft and in the chancel of the Blackfriars' church, both dated to some time after *c.* 1440. Although the original innovator of the form remains elusive, it was revived in the city at the end of the fifteenth century, having possibly been reintroduced by John Antell. He arrived in Norwich from Cambridge, where – like Reginald Ely – he had been master mason working on the design of King's College chapel.[71]

Antell has been identified as the master mason responsible for rebuilding an important group of city churches, pre-eminent amongst which is St Michael Coslany, described as 'the finest late gothic achievement in any of the churches of Norwich'.[72] The piers have a lozenge section, enriched with vertical mouldings that carry up into the arch, and can be linked to similar piers at St Andrew's, St George Colegate and Shelton. The tracery on the north and south aisles may likewise be associated with contemporary work at St Martin at Oak and St Andrew's. The most extraordinary architectural feature at St Michael's is undoubtedly the flushwork at the east end of the south aisle (Plate 9). Built at the turn of the fifteenth century, the Thorp chapel was established as a chantry by Alderman Robert Thorp. The east and south faces constitute a 'quite unparalleled *tour de force*'.[73] The flushwork frames each of the windows with blind tracery. On the east end the four-light tracery forms extended ogees, and on the south aisle it produces more complex lights with stepped transoms (Figure 9). Above the four-centred windows, circled quatrefoils are placed within spandrels created in bands of flushwork, being topped on the east by *fleur-de-lys*. The pale limestone is picked out against the glass-black flint to create a dazzling filigree effect which speaks for the wealth and ambition of the age. Thorp's chantry chapel was the first element of what we have seen to be a typical campaign of rebuilding by rapid stages. Construction got underway in earnest *c.* 1498, with the nave following, and the north aisle nearing completion by *c.* 1516.[74] The remodelling, however, was never completed and the south side of the church, begun at the east end with such spectacular promise by Thorp, is caught in time, half finished. The two bays of the south nave aisle represent half its intended length, since the western arcade pier is still embedded within the junction of the temporary west wall of the aisle and the fourteenth-century south wall, through which the arcade was being punched.[75] The pier itself was temporarily packed in with bricks to fill the void where the original fabric had been hacked away. So the west end of the south wall still retains its mid fourteenth century window and door, a last glimpse of the earlier church.

All these examples serve to illustrate the processes employed to effect the transformation of the city's churches in the fifteenth century. Similar piecemeal development that was subsequently manipulated to appear unified is apparent at St Laurence's and St George Tombland, where the ashlar facing of the clerestory masks the different campaigns of nave and chancel rebuilding. The architectural uniformity of many city churches may have been the result of similar sleight of hand, but the fact that stylistic and spatial uniformity was held at a premium should not be overlooked. This kind of plan is often explained as a conscious emulation of the friary churches dedicated to preaching, or rather to listening, yet this argument makes sweeping assumptions about the use of such spaces. The dominant concern of fifteenth-century popular religion was purgatory, not preaching. The fittings and furnishings of parish churches were covered with pleas for intercession on behalf of the departed. Paradoxically, as church interiors were unified into a single space, with far less emphasis on the chancel, that space was being divided to accommodate chantries. Most bequests for intercessory prayers and masses financed a limited cycle or time span, and few required the dedicated architectural space created for perpetual chantries such as Robert Thorp's.[76] Instead, they merely required an altar for the stipendiary priest. Altars proliferated in response to this growing demand, and St Michael Coslany was not atypical in having at least eleven by the end of the fifteenth century.[77] The interiors were designed not so much with the purpose of providing accommodation for the living as for the commemoration of the dead. The grand space was a frame within which the miniaturised spaces of the chantry altars could be arranged, served and periodically replaced.

The architectural elements that remained, such as the tower space and porches, were therefore of increasing significance as permanently defined spaces. Porches proved to be a particularly attractive investment for many patrons in the fifteenth and sixteenth centuries, providing a discrete architectural element for the display of secular or religious iconography (Figure 10). They were also extremely visible, serving as key elements in processions as well as being the theatre for numerous rituals, transactions and oath-taking. Moreover, they also provided valuable extra space, particularly as they were almost all two-storey structures. The role of the porch and parvis has been neglected by architectural historians, who remain focused on either ornamental detailing or the more liturgically prestigious east end. Yet the humble upper rooms within these churches were clearly important to the parish, either as accommodation for the clergy or as vestries, libraries, schoolrooms and meeting rooms for the numerous guilds that attached themselves to the churches.

The increasing significance of structural elements, such as porches towards the western end of churches, was matched by a declining emphasis on the chancel in the same buildings. An appropriate degree of prominence was achieved in the great churches discussed above by raising the level of the chancel rather than extending its area or augmenting its liturgical furniture, which had been the hallmark of fourteenth-century church improvements. Some architectural historians have seen this shifting focus within parish churches as a reflection of the growing power of the laity at the expense of the clergy. Yet we will be unable to appreciate the full complexity of the issues involved until we understand the multiple roles played by each separate element of the fabric.[78]

What cannot be doubted is that the fifteenth-century rebuilding was an initiative driven forwards by the parishioners themselves. The nave was traditionally the responsibility of the parish, which relied on donations and bequests from those who used the church to maintain the fabric. Consequently, improvements to the body of the church have been seen as a measure of lay wealth. There is, however, considerable evidence from Norwich to suggest that the laity were also taking responsibility for redeveloping the chancels of several important churches. St Peter Parmentergate underwent a complete rebuild between around 1486, when a bequest refers to 'the making of the new church', and the first decade of the sixteenth century, when burials were requested in the porch (1504) and the vestry was described as 'new' (1512).[79] There are several interesting elements within the church, the two most immediate being the window tracery, which is devoid of all cusping, and the nave roof, which is one of only two in the city to employ tie beams.[80] The old chancel roof was sold in 1497, raising £1 3s. 4d. for the infirmarer, who owned the advowson. This suggests that work on the chancel and nave was progressing in tandem. Fifteen years later, the infirmarer paid off loans of over £10 for the project, including 53s. 4d. to the masons Richard Haus and William Hermer, who had, significantly, been apprenticed to John Antell. Further sums for work on the chancel were, however, paid to the churchwardens, who represented the parish but were evidently overseeing the entire project.[81] A similar arrangement appears to have been in place in the mid fifteenth century at St Peter Mancroft, since Robert Pert's bequests for rebuilding the east wall of the chancel were entrusted to a group of parishioners rather than the clergy.[82] Indeed, it has been argued that the parish initiative at St Peter's can be traced back to the decision to transfer the living in the late fourteenth century.[83]

An analysis of the payments received by the cathedral priory from its appropriated churches in the city makes it clear that the revenue from tithes and oblations was mysteriously declining in the second half of the fifteenth century.[84] Since this cannot be related to any significant downturn in the urban economy, it is possible that parish money was being diverted as gifts to these building programmes. The extent to which the priory condoned, or even encouraged, this behaviour is less easy to judge, as it must have felt a real fiscal impact at a time when its own revenues were dwindling fast. Since the Norwich Benedictines were involved in many of these building campaigns, it is hard to believe that they would not have been aware of parishioners' expenditure.

Determined parishioners are evident at St Martin-at-Oak, St Sepulchre and St George Colegate, where the cathedral priory made subventions to the building costs, and the parish itself drove forward and paid for the reconstruction of the chancels. The nave at St Sepulchre was complete by *c.* 1475. The chancel followed, with the infirmarer releasing the profits (just over £5) from the church in 1480 as a contribution to the costs.[85] A bequest was made in 1492 for leading the roof, but work also started on two matching transept chapels. They were evidently built over a long period, as that to the south was described as 'new' in 1500, whilst orders for the construction of one to the north in a similar manner were not issued until 1536.[86] The process of extension thus continued at St Sepulchre's right up to the eve of the Dissolution. Even so, it is worth noting that the chosen design was not the vast, open space of St Andrew's or St Peter Mancroft, but a more traditional, even antiquated, plan of an aisleless nave with two transept chapels.

St Michael-at-Plea, St Mary Coslany and St Peter Hungate also belong to this group of churches which eschewed the grandiose developments manifest in what might be termed the 'civic' churches. Although lesser works continued across the city well into the sixteenth century, St Stephen's was the last major project. The earlier church, of which only the tower porch survives, was rebuilt from about 1530, as it was being glazed by 1533 although the construction work was not yet finished.[87] Payments by the chamberlain of Norwich cathedral priory for repairs to the chancel are recorded in 1522 and 1523, suggesting that the rector, Thomas Boyer, may have been initially responsible for the rebuilding initiative. References of 1534 to a letter of fraternity awarded to the notary, Robert Coraunt, by the grateful chapter provide evidence that parishioners became even more heavily involved, for Coraunt had apparently paid for an entire phase of the enterprise.[88] Work on the nave appears to have progressed first along the south then the north, and from east to west, during the 1540s. Evidence of the parishioners' response to the doctrinal changes of the Reformation can be seen in the rood turret, which begins as an integral part of the fabric but is abandoned higher up in favour of a window. It therefore looks very much as if the – now potentially heretical – plans for a rood loft were abandoned during the strict Edwardian reforms of the 1540s. The conviction of the parishioners that they should pursue their building project in the face of such radical religious change is testimony to their own vision of what the church stood for. It also, perhaps, reveals their involvement in that very process of Reformation.

St Stephen's demonstrates that church building could be carried on through the Reformation. In fact the real boom had actually begun to lose impetus much earlier, in the 1490s, long before the first signs of trouble. The fifteenth-century legacy served the parishioners well over the next five centuries, despite the loss of some churches in parish amalgamations after the Dissolution. The many survivors continued to function as the complex social arenas they had always been. Levels of monumental commemoration actually peaked during the early eighteenth century. The chancel at St George Tombland and the nave of St Andrew's, for example, then acted as a gallery for the prestigious school of local sculptors, as well as a pantheon for the urban elite (Plate 10).[89] There are close parallels with the situation in medieval Norwich, when the local brass workshops all but excluded products from London.[90] Although the traditional picture is one of post-medieval decline in the fabric of these churches, they were still celebrated on eighteenth-century maps and views of the city, and they still formed the focus for political rivalries.[91] Just as in the medieval period, so in the modern, if one is to appreciate the true wealth of this architectural legacy one must attempt to understand how the churches were used, just as much as how they were built. It was through *use* that the parish churches of Norwich helped to structure the everyday life of visitors and citizens alike. From the very outset, these same churches served to define the city both in terms of its topography and of its identity. They still perform this role with distinction. It is by using churches sympathetically that this great medieval legacy can be sustained and taken forward as part of our shared history.

4

The Religious Houses

Christopher Harper-Bill and Carole Rawcliffe

> But above all are their riches displayed in the church treasures; for there is not a parish church in the kingdom so mean as not to possess crucifixes, candlesticks, censers, patens, and cups of silver; nor is there a convent of mendicant friars so poor, as not to have all these same articles in silver, besides many other ornaments worthy of a cathedral church in the same metal. Your Magnificence may imagine what the decorations of these enormously rich Benedictine, Cistercian and Carthusian monasteries must be. These are, indeed, more like baronial palaces than religious houses …
>
> *A Relation of the Island of England … about the Year 1500*[1]

In the diversity of its religious experience medieval Norwich presented a microcosm of western Christendom. Although not yet a cathedral city before the Norman Conquest, it was divided into numerous parishes, each of which boasted a church endowed by groups of wealthy inhabitants, often with its own hereditary incumbent. The foundation by a French bishop of a monastic cathedral in 1096 introduced into this emergent regional capital a rule of life regarded throughout the Latin West as the yardstick of Christian observance. Respect for these practices was, in later centuries, sporadically shaken rather than destroyed by conflicts over legal rights, most notably the violent confrontation of 1272, when the citizens took to arms in defence of their privileges.[2] By then, however, the cathedral priory ranked as only one among several monastic houses in Norwich and its environs, the rest of which had forged close, generally more cordial, links with the lay population.

In 1146 a female Benedictine community was established at Carrow, in imitation of many such pre-conquest institutions in the old kingdom of Wessex. During the twelfth century several hospitals, which were barely distinguishable from monasteries, sprang up in and around the city.[3] Houses of Augustinian canons, whose brethren publicly embraced the new ideal of clerical celibacy and the service of the poor, proliferated in the hinterland at this time. Most of them owned some property in Norwich, where their members must have been familiar figures as they went about their ecclesiastical and secular business.[4] It was this order which proved the inspiration for Bishop Walter Suffield's 'Great Hospital' of St Giles, endowed by him in 1249 as both a refuge for the sick and a house of prayer. Even more dramatic, however, was the impact in the thirteenth century of the friars, those shock troops of the papal campaign for the reformation of sinful souls. They played a crucial role in promoting among a wider lay public the devotional ideals of the twelfth-century cloisters and schoolrooms. By 1300, Norwich had thus experienced every major European development in the practice of institutional religion; and, despite shifts in fashion, each was to remain integral to its spiritual and social life until the Dissolution (Map 6).

A generation after the Norman Conquest, the landscape of Norwich was transformed by the reconstruction of the castle as one of the most impressive secular buildings in north-western Europe, and by the building of a new cathedral church.[5] Both were statements of colonial domination over a town whose economic fortunes were in the ascendant. The erection of an urban cathedral followed the general policy of moving the site of sees from the countryside to major centres of population. The sheer physical presence of the cathedral complex, staffed by monks (according to one of the few practices of the Old English church of which the conquerors approved) was meant to inspire awe (Plate 11 and Figure 12). The area designated for the precinct was, indeed, impressive. Work began almost immediately, in 1096, at its western extremity, on a building which took fifty years to complete and was, from the outset, envisaged as a church on a grand scale in the continental style. It ranks as the most formidable manifestation of the 'episcopal imperialism' which characterised the activities of the founder and first bishop of Norwich, Herbert de Losinga.[6]

In essence, the plan of the new cathedral was that of a great Roman basilica. It was built in stone shipped from Barnack, from Quarr in the Isle of Wight and, for the most important work, from Caen in Normandy.[7] The east end comprised four bays; the choir originally extended beyond the crossing to the second of the fourteen bays of the nave. The construction of an altar for the congregation in the third and fourth bays of the nave suggests that the laity enjoyed easy and frequent access. Monastic orders are said to have taken greater care of the spiritual welfare of the lay community in the twelfth century than was later to prove the case,[8] although, in the early days, it looks as if the most frequent visitors were merchants and artisans from the French borough rather than natives. Certainly, the

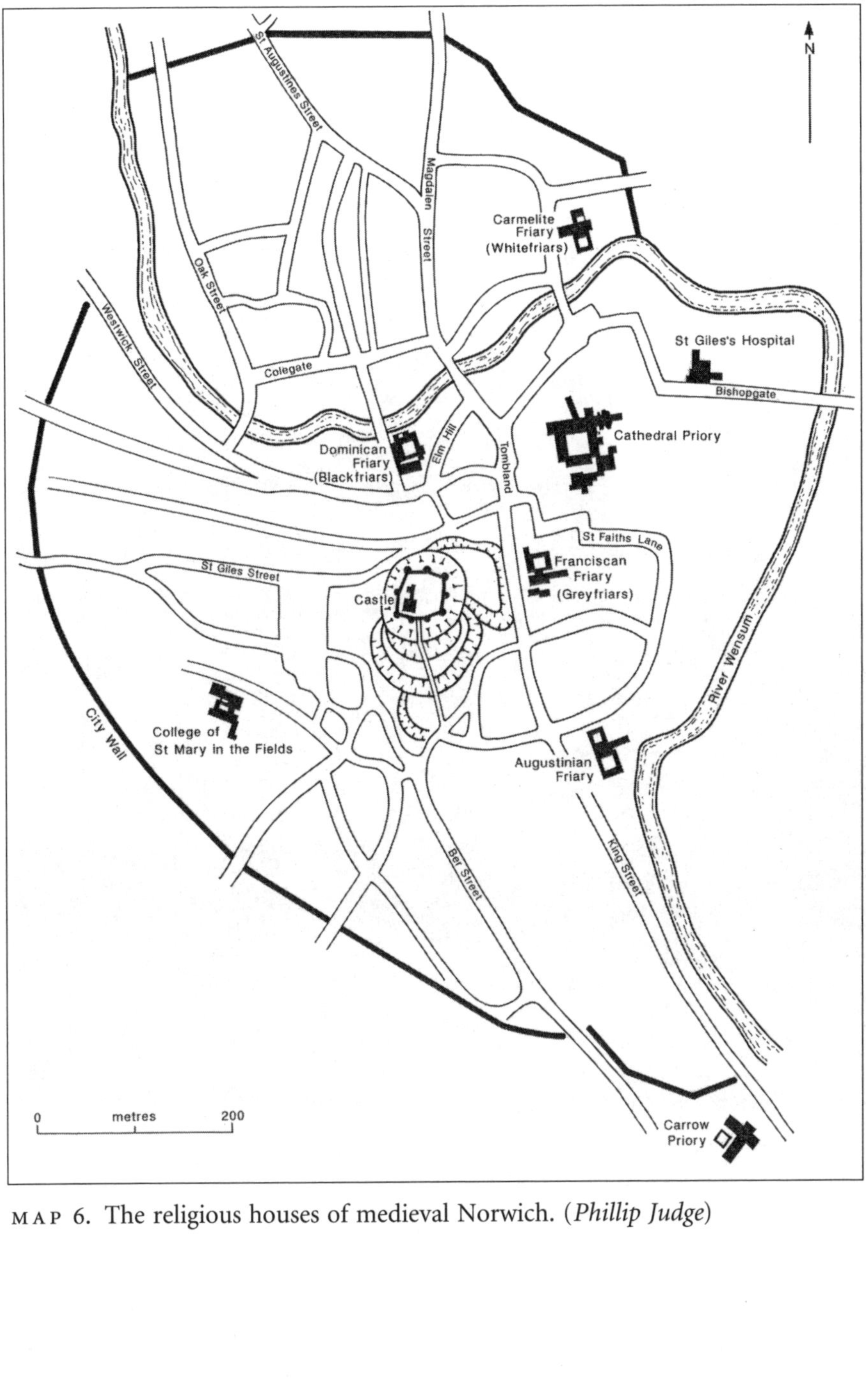

MAP 6. The religious houses of medieval Norwich. (*Phillip Judge*)

FIGURE 12. The west front of Norwich cathedral, after John Britton. (*School of World Art Studies, UEA*)

liturgy performed at Norwich was that of the Norman monastery at Fécamp, where Herbert had been abbot. Because this was a new foundation, the French usage did not have to be forced upon a reluctant congregation, as had been the case at Glastonbury.[9] Above the church rose the great central tower, visible from the city and lavishly decorated, as if to emulate, or even rival, the castle keep. The core of Herbert's episcopal palace, to the north of the church, was hardly less imposing, being itself a small *donjon* (Figure 13).

Architectural symbolism was not confined to the initial construction. After the cathedral monks had emerged, vindicated by royal judgement and retribution, from the riot of 1272, their community reasserted its privileged status in obvious ways. In the final decade of the thirteenth century the great Norman tower was heightened by the addition of a spire pointing heavenwards, and the new Ethelbert gate (*c.* 1317) was lavishly decorated by a façade rich in imagery (Figure 14). The battle between St George and the dragon and the figure of Christ displaying His wounds were surely intended as pointed allegory of the triumph of good over evil.[10] It has been suggested that, over a century later, the neighbouring Erpingham gate was decorated with images of religious orthodoxy – the crucifixion, the Trinity and the eucharist – as a challenge to those Lollard heretics who were currently under vigorous investigation by Bishop Alnwick (1426–36) in his palace.[11]

Within the walls, too, imagery and visibility were paramount considerations. The enclosure of the precinct was always theoretical rather than real.[12] In his visitation of 1309, one of Bishop Salmon's main concerns was that the priory hall court, 'which is common and seen by many', should be kept clean of all dung and rubbish, lest the monks' negligence become a matter of common gossip.[13] The Carnary chapel, built by Salmon as a proud reassertion of episcopal status, was faced across the approach to the west door of the cathedral by a row of leased shops and stalls (Figure 15). The citizens of Norwich must have had frequent recourse to the precinct for commercial as well as religious reasons, while a constant stream of visitors came from further afield. There were bailiffs or tenants of outlying estates, county gentry, fellow Benedictines and, at the highest level, members of the royal family with their swarms of retainers. In 1343, for example, an enormous strain was placed on the priory's resources by an exceptionally heavy round of four visits from the king and three from the queen.[14] The great and the good would doubtless have been taken around the new cloister to admire the striking sequence of Apocalypse bosses, and allowed to walk in the numerous gardens, redolent with spiritual allegories.[15] A wider public had also to be impressed. The waterfront of the precinct was enhanced by a swannery, which clearly advertised the status of the cathedral priory to

FIGURE 13. The gateway to the bishop's palace, 1814, after John Sell Cotman. (*School of World Art Studies, UEA*)

FIGURE 14. The Ethelbert gate, 1817, after John Sell Cotman. (*School of World Art Studies, UEA*)

FIGURE 15. The Carnary chapel, occupied from the 1540s onwards by Norwich School, from Higham's *Excursion through Norfolk* of *c.* 1819. (*World Art Studies, UEA*)

passing boatmen. The cellarer's dovecote, just inside the southern gate, presented further evidence of temporal power. The sacrist's doves, as they flew out from their refuge in the northern wall of the church, symbolised more dramatically the spiritual role of the community. Everything possible was done to create a landscape of ecclesiastical lordship which would transmit an appropriate message to guests as well as neighbours.

Norwich cathedral was a bipartite institution: the seat of the bishopric as well as the home of a monastic community.[16] In 1126 Pope Honorius II confirmed the founder's intention, which had grown even more determined after his failure to annex the great exempt abbey of Bury St Edmunds, that Norwich should be the mother church of the counties of Norfolk and Suffolk. Like all his English colleagues, the bishop fulfilled both a spiritual and temporal role. He was the father and judge of his flock, but also a tenant in chief of the crown with burdensome responsibilities to the king and the realm. The episcopal estates were assessed in the *Valor Ecclesiasticus* of 1535 at £1050 gross and £979 net, which made the bishop probably the wealthiest magnate in Norfolk.[17] Between the late eleventh and the sixteenth centuries, the occupants of the see were mostly royal nominees with experience of secular government at the highest level. William Raleigh (1239–43) and Simon Walton (1257–66), for example, had been senior royal judges, John Wakering (1415–25) keeper of the rolls of chancery, and James Goldwell (1472–99) king's secretary. Many were cosmopolitan figures who brought the wider world of western Christendom to Norwich. John of Oxford (1175–1200) had been Henry II's roving ambassador during the Becket conflict; William Bateman (1343–55) served as a papal judge at Avignon as well as being a king's clerk; and the colourful Henry Despenser had, in his youth, fought in Italy as a mercenary commander. Only five of the twenty-eight bishops between foundation and dissolution were themselves monks. Two, Walter Suffield (1244–57) and John Salmon (1299–1325), were popularly regarded in Norwich as saints, although neither was officially canonised. Because of the secular demands made upon them, the bishops were only sporadically resident in their cathedral city; when not engaged in government business, they moved between their various houses, such as Gaywood (near King's Lynn), the two Elmhams and Terling in Essex. Unlike some English prelates, though, they were not excluded from their own cathedral by a chapter jealous of its autonomy. Although there were some acrimonious disputes between the bishop and the monks under John of Oxford and the choleric Henry Despenser, these were disruptions of a normally harmonious relationship. When they were confronted by violent hostility from a significant element of the citizenry, as in 1272 and 1443, they instinctively presented a common front.

From the thirteenth century onwards the machinery of episcopal administration functioned whether or not the bishop was personally present. His sacramental functions were frequently delegated to a suffragan, often the head of a local monastery, or to a senior friar, while his jurisdictional role was exercised by his Official, the most senior of a growing staff of university trained lawyers. By the 1350s, and probably much earlier, all priests in charge of parishes were bound to come to Norwich at Whitsuntide with lay delegates from their flocks, and to process and make compulsory offerings at the cathedral.[18] Two weeks later, according to a settlement of 1390, the city clergy had to stage their own procession.[19] Twice a year, at Easter and Michaelmas (29 September), from the early twelfth century onwards, the heads of other religious houses, the rural deans and representative clergy from each deanery met in synod at the cathedral to pay their dues, resolve disputes and, if necessary, submit to corrective discipline.[20] By the late thirteenth century judicial procedure had become more complex and specialised. The bishop heard important cases in his court of audience, sitting in the chapel of his palace, as happened between 1428 and 1431, when Bishop Alnwick passed sentence on several Lollards, some to be burnt at the stake.[21] Routine deliberations took place in the consistory court in the cathedral, which was presided over by its own official. Penances, too, were undertaken here: this might result in a flogging, but more often by the late fifteenth century was likely to involve a humiliating appearance at the head of the Sunday procession. Lesser jurisdiction was delegated to the dean of Norwich, the urban equivalent of those rural deans whose rapacious activities were exposed by an inquisition of 1286, or by the dean of the priory's own liberties.[22] Although the ecclesiastical courts were inevitably resented by prosperous citizens when they themselves were brought to book, or had to pay for probate, they were systematically utilised by the better sort as a means of enforcing good behaviour upon the lower orders.[23]

The cathedral priory housed a relatively large community, originally intended for sixty monks, both Norman and Anglo-Saxon. The complement had risen to sixty-seven on the eve of the Black Death, which cut a swathe through the cloister. Recovery proved slow but steady, with numbers reaching fifty in 1381 and fifty-six in 1441. There was then a gradual decline from forty-seven in 1499 to thirty-two in 1534.[24] Probably a dozen or so should be deducted from these totals to account for monks absent at the dependent cells and at university. Even so, recruitment held up well, falling only slightly below that at the great Benedictine abbey of St Albans, which had initially been far larger. In the later Middle Ages, when it is possible to deduce the origins of monks from the place names they adopted on entering the monastery, the majority appear to have come from Norfolk villages, predominantly on the priory estates.[25] There were, however, always a few from city families, often those living in close proximity to the monastery in the parishes of St Martin-at-Palace and St Mary-in-the Marsh. Most were associated with the brewing, victualling or building trades, upon which the monks relied, while a handful boasted connections with the ruling elite. Unlike the nuns of Carrow, though, the monks did not regularly recruit from the aldermanic class.[26]

The population of the precinct was far larger than these numbers might suggest. At a conservative estimate, from the late thirteenth century onwards about 150 people were permanently employed as officers and servants, in addition to a group of corrodians (that is pensioners who had either purchased sheltered accommodation or had been imposed upon the monastery by the crown).[27] Their ranks were swollen at regular intervals by a small army of craftsmen and their employees working on major building projects, such as the construction of the cloister. The various departmental heads, known as obedientiaries, had always spent heavily on commodities such as wine and spices, and, as the direct exploitation of monastic estates declined during the later Middle Ages, the volume of local trade increased. The priory also offered a great deal of occasional and casual employment to individuals such as molecatchers and laundresses, to whom payments were regularly made. Nor was the exchange in one direction only: surplus supplies of honey and saffron were sold on the open market, as were seeds and young plants from the precinct gardens, which seem to have served as a local nursery.[28]

Twice in the fourteenth century and five times between 1494 and 1532 the proceedings of visitations conducted by the bishop or his commissaries afford a glimpse of the internal life of the monastery. The evidence poses many problems. On the one hand, the visitor was obliged to seek out abuses and eradicate faults rather than praise excellence, while, on the other, a clean bill of health might conceal a conspiracy of silence. The injunctions of Bishop Salmon (1309), who was himself a monk, expressed anxiety about the time consumed by administration. The daily grind of bureaucracy kept many monks away from the choir, where the full round of the Benedictine liturgy was performed. Since this, the *raison d'être* of any monastery, offered an intercessionary ritual for patrons and benefactors, as well as the community itself, the bishop ruled that two-thirds of the monks should always attend, and that everyone should be present on feast days. Mass books were standardised and a new clock provided to regulate the monastic day. Such measures were crucial, since the cathedral offered a model of liturgical practice for the entire diocese.[29] Not surprisingly, in view of the difficult economic circumstances then facing major landowners, Bishop Bateman (1343–55) took a more pragmatic approach, being principally concerned to balance the books. In order to set the house on a sounder financial footing, he insisted upon the presentation of regular departmental accounts and created a reserve fund for emergencies. Yet he, too, kept an eye upon the spiritual health of the brethren, criticising their tendency to eat meat and dine out with friends in the city. Along with this worrying departure from the monastic ideal went a penchant for colourful clothes and an even more alarming laxity in the matter of female visitors, who had apparently been frequenting the precinct at night.[30]

Slackness of discipline could hardly be prevented in an age when English monasticism had lost much of its eremitical zeal. Familiarity with women was alleged against some monks in all five of the visitations held between 1494 and 1532.[31] The prior himself set a poor example, being charged with adultery in 1514, at which time the sub-prior was said to be conducting a very public liaison with a tradesman's wife. As was so often the case, vanity went hand in hand with lust. Clothing had grown even more ostentatious, a tendency which nocturnal dances in the guest hall may well have exacerbated, since beribboned pumps were then *de rigueur*. The young monks came in for particular criticism, preferring to gossip and play cards or dice rather than study. Indeed, the most serious revelation to emerge from these reports concerns the bitter friction which had apparently developed between the generations, a phenomenon which some might regard as evidence of declining standards and others as an inevitable feature of life in a large residential institution. In either case, the citizens of Norwich must have come to regard the monks, with all their imperfections, as only too human. Respect for these fallen knights of Christ may well have declined among the laity, who turned increasingly to others for spiritual guidance.

The cathedral priory had originally been endowed with a substantial income, both from land and spiritualities (that is revenues from churches and tithes).[32] Nearly four and a half centuries later it was said to be worth £874 net, roughly the same as the abbeys of Battle in Sussex and Hyde in Winchester, both of which were royal foundations.[33] Thanks to the generosity of successive bishops, by the end of the twelfth century the monks held property in over a hundred Norfolk manors, with significant outliers in Suffolk and even Chalk in Kent.[34] More significant, however, was the grant by Henry I of the manor of Thorpe on the eastern outskirts of Norwich, along with its appurtenances at Catton, Lakenham and Arminghall. These suburban properties and the various rights and franchises that accompanied them were to cause protracted disputes between the citizenry and the monks. Equally controversial was the king's concession of a ten-day Whitsuntide fair to the cathedral priory, along with jurisdiction just outside the precinct in Tombland, Ratton Row and Holme Steet, as well as in St Paul's parish and around the hospital of St Mary Magdalen in Sprowston (one mile north of Norwich).[35]

It seems likely that, before the late twelfth century, the Norwich Benedictines followed the practice evident in other monastic houses and leased out most of their estates. From then onwards, however, a combination of high inflation and rapidly expanding markets encouraged the direct cultivation of demesnes, especially for grain production on a commercial scale. Adopting a system of centralised control and intensive farming practices, the priory had, by 1300, become one of the foremost pioneers of profit and loss accountancy in England.[36] According to a papal tax assessment of 1291, gross income had almost reached £1000, half of which came from land.

This was, in fact, a considerable underestimate, as the internal accounts of 1295–96 record profits of no less than £1571 from the temporalities alone, which suggests that the monks could then rely on annual receipts of around £2500 gross. Although the costs of demesne farming, in terms of wages, buildings and equipment, were far from negligible, the monks appear to have been the richest landowners in Norfolk, save for the bishop himself. This happy state of affairs was not destined to last. The cumulative impact of endemic plague from 1349 onwards spelt little short of disaster for England's great religious houses, as prices plummeted and wages shot upwards. From a maximum of 3000 acres in 1300, by 1430 the area of priory demesne under direct cultivation had slumped to a mere twenty-seven acres. Henceforward almost all the community's income derived from rents, supplemented during the four decades before the Dissolution by useful sums raised from the sheep kept for wool and hides.

Despite an initial recovery after the first ravages of plague, revenues declined throughout the later Middle Ages. Indeed, the superficially impressive receipts of £2200 recorded in 1363–64 appear less encouraging in light of the fact that all the obedientiaries were then overspending and the house was already £600 in debt. By the 1470s income had fallen to £1500 a year, although by dint of stringent economies each department had at least struggled out of the red. This is the last point at which we can achieve an overall picture of monastic finances, which appear to have remained in credit despite a further decline in gross receipts. The figure of £1061 gross presented by Henry VIII's commissioners in the *Valor Ecclesiasticus* was probably quite accurate, and reveals that, until the very end, a shrinking budget was relatively well managed, in the face of testing circumstances.

Although they exercised none of the wide ranging jurisdictional authority possessed by the Benedictines at Bury St Edmunds, the Norwich monks exploited their franchises in and around the city to the full. This inevitably soured their relations with the ruling elite.[37] A series of incidents from the 1240s onwards so inflamed feelings that, in 1272, a scuffle outside the monastery gates between the prior's servants and a group of residents escalated into one of the most violent attacks on a religious house to occur in medieval England. At least thirteen people (but no monks) were killed in the ensuing assault, which inflicted serious damage on the precinct. The perpetrators, who included some of the bailiffs and other leading citizens, were excommunicated, thirty of the ringleaders being sentenced to death. The city was placed under interdict and its liberties, which were suspended by Henry III, restored only after the payment of a massive fine. A period of calm ensued, the restoration of amicable relations being helped, perhaps, by the priory's notable contribution to poor relief during the 1280s.[38] But the underlying problem, which arose from the general vagueness of, and inconsistency between, royal charters awarded to the monks and those granted to the city, did not go away. There was hardly a decade between the 1370s and the Dissolution when some contentious issue did not arise. In 1380, for example, and again in 1441, the city government threatened to disenfranchise any citizen who initiated litigation in the prior's court; and in 1486 the uprooting of posts, which the mayor had planted within the monastic liberty to mark his authority, caused another fracas. These relatively minor incidents were punctuated in January 1443 by a second major confrontation, known as Gladman's Rising, after the merchant of that name who led a march through the streets, thereby unleashing further disturbances. Once again the mayor (who forced the monks to surrender their charters) and citizens were fined and their liberties temporarily suspended.[39] After a temporary lull, sporadic sniping resumed until 1524, when Cardinal Wolsey finally brokered a settlement between the two parties. The struggle had lasted for three centuries, sometimes, as in the case of John Gladman's protest, being exacerbated by the factionalism of civic politics. It is worth stressing, however, that in the Peasants' Revolt of 1381, when there was widespread violence against local ecclesiastical landowners, including the monks of Bury St Edmunds and the nuns of Carrow, the priory escaped attack. Nor, in a city where seventeen churches within the walls and a further eleven in the immediate vicinity were owned by the cathedral priory, does there appear to have been any serious conflict over the payment of tithes and other spiritual dues. This contrasts sharply with London, where disputes of this kind were common from the fourteenth century onwards.[40]

The parochial system was already well developed in Norwich at the time of the priory's foundation, and it was to their parish churches that most of the citizens pledged their main religious loyalty. The cathedral did, however, provide a variety of additional benefits, which were readily available to visitors. It was dedicated to the greatest of spiritual patrons, the Holy Trinity, but its monks were keenly aware of the need to develop local cults, with a more immediate appeal to the populace. The search for relics and the crowds of pilgrims they attracted (and perhaps diverted from other lucrative shrines at Bury St Edmunds and Ely) provides the background to the extraordinary posthumous career of William of Norwich, whose earthly remains proved a magnet to visitors during the third quarter of the twelfth century.[41] The cathedral also owned a phial of the Holy Blood of Christ, brought from Fécamp at this time, and by the fourteenth century boasted at least three shrines to the Virgin Mary and one to St Sitha of

Lucca, the patron saint of domestic servants. All attracted veneration, as for a short while did the tombs of Bishops Suffield and Salmon.[42] But the greatest incentive to pilgrimage, especially by those who lived nearby and could repeat the experience, was the prospect of acquiring a series of papal indulgences.[43] These promised remission of the penalties to be incurred in the next life for sins committed on earth, and thus facilitated a speedier passage through the torments of purgatory. Popes Gregory IX (1249) and Nicholas IV (1291) each granted relief of one year and a quarantine (forty days) to those who visited at specific times with a contrite heart. In 1317 visitors to the new Carnary chapel secured one hundred days. An indulgence of seven years and seven quarantines, offered in 1363, raised money to repair storm damage; and in 1473 at the behest of Bishop James Goldwell, who had been the king's orator at the papal curia, Sixtus IV awarded a remarkable twelve years and twelve quarantines to pilgrims. Most spectacular of all in this period of rampant spiritual as well as economic inflation was the indulgence of the Portinacula (1398), which bestowed full remission of sins. It was revoked in 1402, having contributed not a little to the rise in offerings at the high altar. Reassurance of a less tangible kind came from the sermons that were regularly to be heard at the cathedral, sometimes by large outdoor congregations gathered in the precinct. In the mid-thirteenth century the bishop and prior preached regularly during Lent and Holy Week; and for a while the city's friars also performed this office until their religious opinions gave cause for concern. In about 1360 the prior wrote to Gloucester College, Oxford, alleging that certain mendicants had expressed views 'against the norm of sound doctrine and the liberty of the church'.[44] At about this time two Austin friars addressed parliament on the vexed question of excessive ecclesiastical possessions: views which may have struck a chord with the citizens and commonality of Norwich, given their struggle over rights and franchises.[45]

Considerable attention has been recently been paid by historians to religious guilds and confraternities as a manifestation of lay piety.[46] Five of the nineteen craft and religious guilds of Norwich pursued some form of religious activity in the cathedral. The pelterers claimed St William, the boy martyr, as their patron, an appropriate choice given the fact that he had been apprenticed as a skinner. Most notably, the prestigious guild of St George, which, from 1452 onwards, was effectively synonymous with the city government, maintained a chantry in the nave, where mass was celebrated every year with great solemnity on 23 April, and held its ceremonial dinner at the bishop's palace.[47]

An imperfect but telling index of devotion to the cathedral may be found in the testamentary bequests made to it by residents of Norwich between 1370 and 1532. During this period 35 per cent of those whose wills survive remembered either the cathedral or (less often) the priory, their numbers rising significantly over the years from 14 per cent before 1439 to no fewer than 61 per cent after 1518.[48] Although the value of individual legacies was generally declining from shillings to pence, the rising number of gifts more than compensated for this reduction. Some were purely conventional marks of respect to the mother church of the diocese, but others suggest that, however far it may have departed from the monastic ideal, the city's oldest and most traditional religious house had recovered at least some of its initial popularity, as that of the friars suffered a slight, but significant, decline. Such evidence accords with national trends following the revival of the English church begun in the reign of Henry V.[49] Moreover, on a day to day basis, shared bonds and reciprocal interests often outweighed the impact of disputes between the mayor and the prior. Indeed, the latter sometimes hosted dinners for members of the ruling elite.[50] As one of their number, Alderman John Cambridge (d. 1442) had, for example, been party to some tense exchanges over rights and franchises, yet he did regular business with the priory, where his nephew, William, was a monk. The young man and six other brethren were remembered in his will, made just one year before John Gladman took to the streets. However difficult relations may sometimes have been at a civic level, the monks and their immediate neighbours generally enjoyed a happier *modus vivendi*, marked by compromise as well as conflict.

Although it towered over the city, in both a physical and spiritual sense, the cathedral priory did not stand alone. During the later middle ages, the eastern margins of Norwich, facing symbolically as well as geographically towards the Holy City of Jerusalem, were dominated by an arc of imposing religious houses. From the Benedictine hospital of St Paul and the Carmelite friary to the north of the Wensum, past St Giles's hospital and the cathedral, which faced each other across Holme Street, and the Greyfriars further south, the city's spiritual defences extended to Carrow priory, just beyond the walls. Visitors approaching from the south east could not but be impressed by the massive cruciform Norman church and walled precinct of the city's only nunnery, which played a notable part in its history from the mid twelfth century until the arrival of Henry VIII's commissioners.[51] The priory's extramural situation, outside the Conesford gate on one of the main routes into Norwich, reflects its original function as a hospital, run by a small community of religious women. In 1146 two of these professed sisters, Seyna and Lescelina, obtained support from King Stephen and Bishop Everard for the foundation of a Benedictine priory, dedicated, like the hospital, to the Virgin Mary, the house (or more specifically its church) having already attracted a donation of land worth 25s. 'in the fields of Norwich' from Stephen some nine years earlier.[52]

Carrow's distinguished patronage marked it out as the only royal foundation among East Anglia's eleven medieval nunneries. For many years it had also ranked as the largest, a distinction not entirely welcomed by the nuns, who complained to the pope in 1229 'that the English nobility, whom they cannot refuse, had obliged them to receive more sisters than they could support'.[53] The more socially prestigious house of Campsey Ash in Suffolk eventually overtook Carrow in size, as the latter's numbers declined from a healthy average of about twenty-seven professed sisters during the second half of the fourteenth century to no more than ten in 1532.[54] This common phenomenon, apparent in male as well as female monasteries, was not, however, accompanied by either indifference or hostility on the part of the civic elite. On the contrary, despite occasional disagreements of the kind which frequently clouded relations between urban and religious corporations at an institutional level, their regard for the nuns themselves lost none of its original warmth.

The loss of the cartulary recording grants of land and franchises to Carrow priory makes it impossible to reconstruct the house's early history in any detail, but there can be little doubt that the residents of twelfth- and thirteenth-century Norwich eagerly followed King Stephen's lead in assisting the new nunnery. As was later to prove the case when Bishop Suffield founded his hospital in Holme Street, endowments from this quarter were numerous but generally modest, for the most part comprising fixed (assize) rents of a few pence, leviable in perpetuity upon property which remained in the hands of the donors and their heirs.[55] An undated parchment roll of about 1285 lists no fewer than 180 such rents, scattered across thirty city parishes. The care taken to record the names of past and current tenants, terms of payment and location suggests that, as so often happened, it had become increasingly difficult to keep track of, let alone raise, all the money.[56] In addition, the nuns either bought or were given a number of urban properties which could be leased competitively to tenants. The bulk of their income, however, came from extensive estates in the Norfolk countryside and a handful of appropriated rural livings, whose patronage lay in the gift of the prioress and whose revenues were paid into her coffers.[57] Of especial interest in the present context, though, is her acquisition of the advowson of the neighbouring parish church of St James, Carrow, as well as those of All Saints Timberhill, St Julian and St Edward (united by 1305) Conesford, and St Catherine Newgate, within the city walls.[58] St Julian's and St Edward's each possessed anchorholds, as did the nunnery itself. As we shall see, their occupants figured prominently in the religious life of the urban community, greatly enhancing the convent's reputation and moral authority. Its nuns and their dependants thus maintained a strong spiritual and economic presence in both Norwich and its south-eastern suburbs, reinforced by their right to hold court over their tenants in that part of Conesford known as Little Newport (Map 7).

The ownership of property and franchises was always a potential source of friction in medieval England, especially on the outskirts of a large city. The land around the convent in Trowse and Bracondale constituted an exempt jurisdiction, where the prioress was theoretically free to exercise full legal authority, extending to rights of probate and the use of her own gallows. The grant by King John, in 1205, of an annual fair lasting four days in early September further consolidated her position, since it also entitled her to levy tolls on all sales of corn within the city during that period.[59] This was, however, easier said than done. Always sensitive to any threat to their own hard-won commercial freedom, the civic authorities eventually negotiated an agreement, in 1290, whereby the prioress would relinquish these tolls, along with her view of frankpledge in Little Newport, in return for a fixed quantity of wheat payable each year at the start of the fair. It is apparent from this document that ill-feeling had also arisen over damage caused to the priory's crops by carts coming and going through the Needham gate. The ensuing compromise, whereby the gate was to be closed to heavy traffic for four months before the harvest, suggests that both parties recognised the need for friendly coexistence, despite occasional disagreements over wandering animals and rights of way.[60]

Whatever passing irritation the nuns of Carrow may have caused the citizens paled into insignificance when compared with the latter's protracted struggle to wrest control of the cathedral monks' exempt liberties in and around Norwich. In this respect, at least, the city and the convent shared a common adversary, for the sisters had also become embroiled in a series of disputes with their fellow Benedictines. During the first half of the fourteenth century conflict focused upon the payment of tithes in Bracondale, immediately to the west of Carrow, where the cathedral chapter claimed superior jurisdiction.[61] The award of county status to the city, by a royal charter of 1404, marked an escalation of hostilities. Its imprecise definition of 'suburbs and hamlets' meant that the rulers of Norwich were emboldened to exploit every possible chink in the monastic armour, not least by making common cause with the sisters at Carrow. A signal opportunity arose twelve years later, when the then prioress, Edith Wilton, and one of her nuns were appealed by a local woman for inciting, abetting and

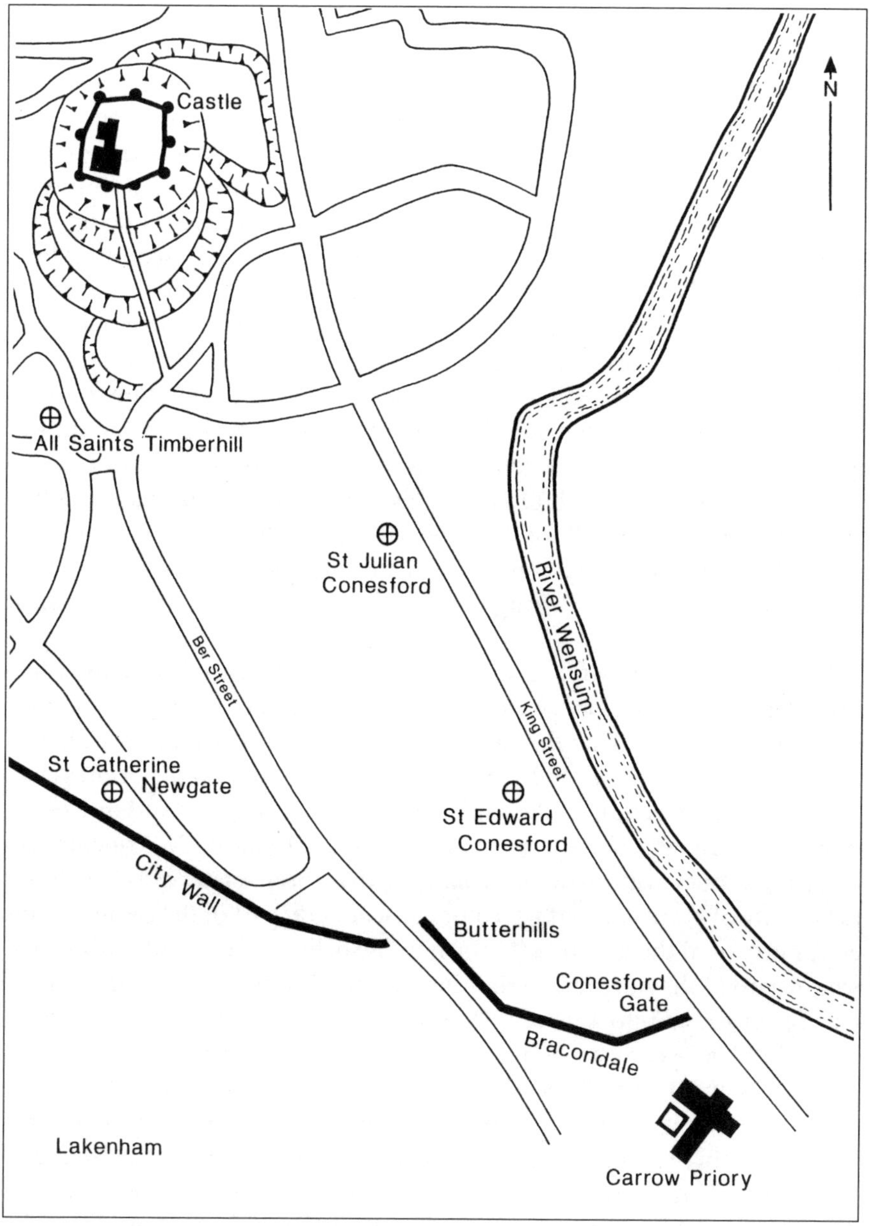

MAP 7. Carrow priory and its environs. (*Phillip Judge*)

harbouring the seven malefactors who had battered her husband to death *cum quandam vauga vocata 'molspade'* and other agricultural implements at Lakenham (another cathedral liberty). The case went to trial in the autumn of 1416 before the court of king's bench at Westminster, where the two women, who had been imprisoned in the Marshalsea, appeared in person to answer the charge of accessory to murder. Significantly, their defence hinged upon the fact that Carrow was part of the new county of *Norwich* rather than that of Norfolk as specified in the legal documentation; and it was on this technicality that they were finally acquitted by a local jury in July 1418. The principal assailant, William Coteham, secured a royal pardon not long afterwards. This case was clearly of major importance for the city in establishing its suburban boundaries, and at least two transcripts of the proceedings were preserved in the corporation records, along with copies of the royal charters previously awarded to the nuns.[62] Nor can it be coincidental that bail was offered for the accused during the summer of 1417 by a clutch of Norwich's most eminent citizens, including the town clerk, Thomas Rous, and the MPs, John Bixley and Robert Dunston. Rous was subsequently paid £4 by the city for his work on its behalf in the king's bench and 'taking counsel for defending all matters against the prior'.[63]

We shall never know for certain if members of the cathedral chapter had prevailed upon the victim's widow to instigate these proceedings with offers of practical support. That the case was part of a longer and more sustained offensive is, however, beyond doubt. In the summer of 1416 the prioress had herself begun an action in the same court against the prior and one of his monks for driving off cattle, *vi et armis*, from her land in Bracondale and extorting money with menaces. Claiming that these estates also lay within the county of Norwich, and were not consequently part of the cathedral liberty, she carried the day in 1417, much to the delight of the civic authorities, who regarded the outcome as another landmark victory. She also sued the pair for breaking into a close of hers at Norwich and destroying her trees and fish.[64] Half-yearly accounts compiled by the chamberlain of the cathedral priory in April 1418 record heavy legal costs of £50 *in expensis versus Carhowe*, well over half this sum being spent on litigation involving a collusive but otherwise unspecified lawsuit between the perfidious citizens and the nunnery.[65] As early as 1415–16, advice was being sought by the mayor on 'the right of our community and our liberty at Carrow', so the evidence for long-term complicity seems overwhelming.[66] The prohibitive cost of such high-profile law suits, as well, perhaps, as an awareness of the need for unity in their ranks, led the two Benedictine houses to reach a settlement in October 1419. The prioress then recognised the exempt liberties claimed by her adversaries, while securing confirmation of her grazing rights, as well as the convent's own independent areas of jurisdiction.[67]

That the Carrow nuns should sympathise with the aspirations of the ruling elite is hardly surprising, since – in contrast to the cathedral monks – many of them came from prominent mercantile families, such as the Cooks, Earlhams, Elyses, Pygots, Segrymes and Wetherbys. Had she wished, the cellaress, Margaret Folcard, who was daughter of a Norwich alderman and sister of a councillor for Mancroft ward, could have called upon the expertise of her rich and successful kinsmen while drawing up her accounts in the 1460s.[68] Such connections might prove lucrative as well as politically advantageous. Thomas Virly's handsome bequest of £10 in silver, made to the priory in 1380, was probably intended to commemorate various female relatives who had taken the veil there.[69] Yet there were drawbacks, too. Because of their close links with the corporation, the nuns could hardly escape involvement in the internecine struggles which polarised the city in the third and fourth decades of the fifteenth century. As leader of the disruptive minority faction, the alderman of Conesford ward, Thomas Wetherby, incurred considerable obloquy at this time, not least because of his association with the cathedral priory and William de la Pole, the hated duke of Suffolk.[70] Since his daughter, Alice, had joined the community, and he himself was a parishioner of St Julian's, Wetherby's decision to beat a retreat to the precinct of the nunnery, where he and his wife had been granted a large house for life, may be explained in purely personal terms. It is, none the less, tempting to speculate that the convent, like St Giles's hospital and the cathedral priory, sympathised with the duke's supporters, and was temporarily marching out of step with the majority of the ruling party. The city records certainly hint at tensions. In October 1436, while the divisions among the elite were at their height, two aldermen and commoners were appointed by the assembly to negotiate with the prioress's counsel 'regarding all matters, quarrels and debates' then at issue between them.[71]

Quite possibly the nuns had come to regret their earlier stand against the cathedral monks, or at least had been persuaded by Wetherby that their best interests lay in forging a united front with their fellow religious. The sweeping settlement imposed on the city in the aftermath of Gladman's Rising of 1443 not only upheld the rights of the cathedral priory, but also ruled that the nunnery at Carrow was not, and never had been, a part of Norwich.[72] These were turbulent times for the sisters, who may themselves have faced internal disciplinary problems. The antiquary, Anthony Norris, claimed without supporting evidence that Wetherby was placed in control of the house's temporalities by Bishop Brown in 1442–43, following the removal of the prioress, Alice Waryn, for maladministration. The beleaguered alderman had only two years to live, though, and seems already to have been in poor health, which suggests that he is unlikely to have been recruited from outside. His widow, Margaret, ended her days there, while another daughter, who married the influential lawyer, John Jenney, boarded at Carrow for long periods as a paying guest.[73]

The harsh realities of economic life in late medieval England meant that all but the most sequestered of religious houses had to open their doors to high-status tenants and boarders. Such a potentially disruptive lay presence brought mixed blessings. On the one hand, it introduced the world and its temptations to the cloister, and thus appeared especially subversive in female houses, yet, on the other, it offered an irresistible combination of financial and political benefits. During the fifteenth and early sixteenth centuries, the Carrow nuns earned a few extra pounds each year by leasing tenements, houses and chambers in the precinct to influential county gentry and lawyers, such as William Aslak, Robert Damme and the courtier, Andrew Sulyard, who needed accommodation near Norwich.[74] The widows of prominent local landowners and citizens, including Agnes and Anne Appleyard (1456 and 1520 respectively), Amy Aslak (1456) and Lady Eleanor Wymondham (1503), also rented lodgings there, perhaps intending to devote their sunset years to contemplative seclusion. The house supported vowesses as well as anchoresses, and, as we shall see, attracted a formidable circle of pious female patrons. In addition, weekly boarders made a substantial contribution to its coffers. In 1455–56, for example, they and their servants accounted for almost £17 (about a seventh) of net receipts, some, such as the four young sons of John Ilberd and the two daughters of Thomas Elys, being almost certainly entrusted to the nuns for their early schooling.[75]

For this reason, as well as the ties of kinship which existed between the nuns and the more affluent citizens of Norwich, potential disagreements of the kind described above rarely got out of hand. One final dispute, concerning pasture land at Butterhills, just inside the Ber Street gates, flared up in 1488. For several years the corporation occupied the meadows, paying the nuns a token rent of 10s., until in 1523 the arrangement was formally ratified. On this occasion, Carrow priory was described as lying 'in the county of the city of Norwich', a concession which the mayor and aldermen must have been anxious to secure. It is worth noting that these 'dissensions and discords' yet again – and not coincidentally – came to a head during another period of friction between the city and the cathedral priory, then under arbitration by none other than Thomas, Cardinal Wolsey.[76]

Caught in the crossfire between two implacable opponents, the Carrow nuns were to a significant extent the casualties of an unusually protracted boundary dispute. On a daily basis, their relations with the people of Norwich were far from acrimonious. In common with the city's other religious communities, they made a significant impact upon the local economy. Expenditure on labour and building materials in 1456 came to £12, while almost three times as much was spent on provisions. The priory also a recruited a steady stream of laundresses, cooks, maids, millwrights, gardeners, coopers, smiths, masons, carpenters and agricultural workers, being one of Norwich's major employers. Although the ratio of servants to sisters fell, along with the number of paying guests, there were always more of the former than the latter, their ranks probably augmented by the inevitable 'hangers on' who received clothing and food in lieu of payment. Like many other Norwich residents, the nuns confined their eleemosynary activity to their own dependants, and were not, despite their charitable antecedents, given to the wholesale distribution of largesse.[77]

Because of their smaller size and the almost complete loss of records sustained at the Dissolution, medieval English nunneries are generally far less well documented than the leading male houses, such as Norwich cathedral priory. The fortunate survival of a handful of account rolls from Carrow is thus especially welcome, since it not only permits a unique insight into the management of the house, but also into the state of its finances. Compiled by the cellaress, who controlled virtually all the budget, they reveal that, despite strenuous efforts, it was becoming difficult to balance the books. Although they hovered around £90 in the early sixteenth century, and had slumped to a mere £64 by the Dissolution, revenues had been almost twice as high during the 1450s. The nunnery was then slightly more affluent than St Giles's hospital, while enjoying about a twelfth of the income of the cathedral priory.[78]

TABLE 1

Accounts of the cellaress of Carrow priory in pounds

Year	*Arrears due*	*Current receipts*	*Overspent last year*	*Current expenses*	*Balance on paper*
1455–56	4	130	6	122	+6
1484–85	–	88	–	96	–8
1503–04	13	91	31	64	–9
1520–21	–	91	10	102	–21
1529–30	4	94	–	81	+17

Source: NRO, NRS 26882–84 42 E8; Hare MSS 5954–55 277x1. See also Redstone, 'Three Carrow Account Rolls', pp. 41–88.

Despite their apparent simplicity, medieval accounts can be hard to interpret, since once theoretical receipts and current outgoings had been itemised in such a way as to prevent deceit or evasion on the part of the official in question, long-term debts and uncollected revenues had to be factored into the final calculations. That the figures meticulously set down on parchment by the cellaress and tabulated above might bear scant relationship to the actual state of her coffers is, for example, apparent from the first and last of these rolls. A parchment schedule attached to the account for 1455–56 lists overdue rents and other outstanding sums totalling almost £99, as well as *additional* debts of £42 owed by the obedientary herself. Litigation alone had plunged the priory £17 into the red, while the chaplain had evidently gone unpaid for several years. Some rent collectors and tenants were evidently no more than a year behind in their payments, but the situation still appears considerably less promising than the comfortable balance of £6 in hand recorded at the end of the main account suggests.[79] Although the level of long-term debts and arrears had evidently subsided by the sixteenth century, similar entries at the foot of the accounts for 1529–30 reveal that, contrary to appearances, the cellaress was in reality almost £9 over budget.

Problems of this nature were, however, ubiquitous in a period of population stagnation, when low rents, rising wages and falling agricultural prices spelt trouble for monastic landowners. By and large, the nuns seem to have done their best to adapt to testing circumstances, first by abandoning demesne farming on almost all their estates and, secondly, through a process of economic diversification, notably through investment in wool production for the burgeoning local cloth trade. Like the cathedral monks and brothers of St Giles's hospital, they turned to sheep farming as a supplementary and less labour-intensive source of income, building up their flocks from a mere 152 animals in 1485 to an impressive 807 in 1520.[80] The persistent belief that late medieval English nuns were poorly educated spendthrifts, incapable of rendering proper accounts or managing their own affairs, has been comprehensively challenged by recent studies of female religious.[81] Setting aside the uncertain circumstances surrounding Thomas Wetherby's arrival at Carrow in 1442–43, the only clear instance of financial and administrative abuses coincides with the dramatic fall in revenues in the late fifteenth century. A critical visitation report of 1492, when the prioress failed to render any accounts, found that the house was not only riven with factionalism but that her dishonest servants (*mali servientes*) had caused 'great damage to the goods of the priory'.[82] From the limited evidence at our disposal, standards of book-keeping otherwise appear to have been high. The attack upon the priory during the Peasants'

Revolt of 1381, and the ritual burning in central Norwich of deeds and court rolls seized by the rebels, confirms that, in the aftermath of the Black Death, at least, the nuns were no less ruthless than other unpopular ecclesiastical landlords in exploiting every available source of income.[83]

The cost of maintaining the great priory church of St Mary placed an additional strain upon this diminishing budget. Help was, however, forthcoming from the citizens and local gentry whose personal links with the sisters, their priests and servants proved a potent stimulus to charity. Some wished to be buried at Carrow, and paid handsomely for commemoration, often leaving further sums to be shared among the sisters.[84] Robert Blickling, esquire of Norwich, who was interred there beside his late wife in 1452, promised the sisters over £13 to roof their new dormitory, while also bequeathing 20s. to the anchoress who lived in the precinct.[85] Less than a decade before the Dissolution, Elizabeth Yaxley, widow of a Norwich lawyer, left 66s. 8d. to pay for her burial before the image of the Virgin 'at the hieghe aulters ende' and the celebration of a hundred masses. She also gave the nuns 'a clothe of tappestery werke stored with the nativite, resurreccon and epiphany to hange in theyr churche at solempne feestes to remember myn husbandes soule and myn'.[86]

That the convent was able to capitalise upon the trepidation felt by affluent East Anglians as they contemplated the Last Judgement is further revealed in the sale of indulgences. Although they could not match the generous terms on offer at the cathedral, these slips of parchment were still well worth the price. In 1391, for example, the pope offered a hefty remission of four years and 160 days' enjoined penance to anyone who contributed to the upkeep of the fabric of St Mary's church.[87] Since none of the sacristan's accounts have survived we can only guess at the sums given to her as alms. Other donations came from the guilds and fraternities which worshipped at the convent. Chief among them was the Norwich guild of spurriers and saddlers, whose members congregated from 1385 onwards 'a-forn the ymage of oure lady at the heye auter in the chirche of nunnes in the nunrye of Carrowe ... in worchepe of cryst and of his moder and alle halwen [saints] and amendement of here soules'. Every year the brothers and sisters processed solemnly in their liveries from the cathedral to the nunnery, where they heard mass, made offerings and presented heavy candles to illuminate the high altar. When any of their number died, they undertook to 'seyn for his soule in the chirche of the nunrye of Carrowe *dirige* and masse'.[88]

Unlike secular clergy and religious in higher orders, nuns were themselves unable to administer the sacraments, including mass and confession.

For these potentially lucrative services the men and women of medieval Norwich generally turned to parish priests and friars. But other avenues were open to the sisters of Carrow. In common with many other English nunneries, the priory exercised considerable influence upon the inner religious life of the neighbouring community, not least in fostering new, often intense, forms of private devotion. This was done in part through preaching by resident and visiting clergy, since the spacious nunnery church offered as fine a setting for the propagation of the Word of God as did the city's friaries and larger parish churches, none of which could equal it in size.[89] With its many images, side altars and chapels, St Mary's had served as an appropriate setting for the consecration of Bishops Suffield of Norwich and Burgh of Llandaff in 1245.[90] Local congregations regularly gathered there as well. The text of one fifteenth-century sermon, delivered at Carrow on the feast of the Assumption, still survives, and confirms that the priory was a centre of the Brigittine spirituality which so profoundly affected figures as diverse as King Henry V and the East Anglian mystic, Margery Kempe.[91] The house's anchoresses, of whom Dame Julian of Norwich is now by far the most celebrated, played an important role in transmitting and explaining these ideas to the laity, who turned to them for guidance in times of emotional crisis. Although unusual in terms of its length and fervour ('mych was the holy dalyawns that the ankres and this creatur haddyn be comownyng in the lofe of owyr Lord Jhesu Crist many days that thei were to-gedyr'), Margery's visit to Julian's cell in Conesford well illustrates the wider pastoral activities undertaken by such holy women.[92]

The latter's namesake, Dame Julian Lampet, subsequently occupied the anchorhold in the precinct, inspiring numerous bequests from those who valued her counsel. In 1447 Joan, Lady Bardolf, left her over £6, on the understanding that she would continue to support one of the apparently sick or elderly women who was currently living with her until she died, and then assist another. This interesting requirement suggests that, far from embracing a solitary life, the anchoresses (who are known to have kept servants) gathered about them small groups of like-minded acolytes, maintained where necessary with financial help from pious matrons. Many of the Norwich testators who left money to the nuns certainly remembered the recluses at Carrow and Conesford with affection. The merchant, Robert Baxter (d. 1432), for example, set aside about £4 to be shared among them all, while Alderman Wetherby and his wife disposed of considerably more. Margaret Wetherby's gift of her warm cloak to the anchoress at Carrow betokens a close personal relationship established over many long East Anglian winters. So too does the will of Katherine

Kerre (d. 1498), a prosperous and devout Norwich widow, who left money and clothing to three individual nuns, as well as a cash sum and 'my gown furred with ffoxe and the boke that she hath of me' to the anchoress at St Julian's. A female friend was promised the amber rosary with gilt paternosters 'that wer the ankeres of Carrowe', and which clearly constituted a treasured possession, charged with spiritual power.[93] Katherine's sister and executor, Christine Veyl, had evidently retired to live in the precinct as either a lodger or a vowess by the 1480s, having previously cared for the local hermit, Richard Ferneys (d. 1464), around whom an impressive circle of learned women revolved. Prominent among them was Margaret (d. 1481), the relict of Alderman Richard Purdans, whose many legacies to the community at Carrow included *unum librum anglicanum*.[94] Although tantalisingly few references remain to the ownership of books by the nuns and recluses themselves, silence cannot be equated with either illiteracy or indifference. Three illuminated psalters survive from what may well have been a substantial collection produced for the sisters by Norwich scribes at the behest of wealthy patrons.[95]

Joanna Scrope, who spent time as a young boarder at Carrow with her mother, Lady Eleanor Wymondham (d. 1505), in the early sixteenth century, has been immortalised by the court poet and rector of Diss in Norfolk, John Skelton. His mock elegy on the death of her 'litle prety sparow', slain among the black-robed sisters by 'Gyb our cat savage', furnished Eileen Power with proof positive that English nuns were as flighty as their tame birds.[96] More interesting, though, than the evidence these verses provide of the understandable delight medieval religious took in their pets, is the impressive list of books that Joan is said to have read. Skelton does not, unfortunately, tell us exactly where she acquired her polished education, but it looks very much as if some of the titles (which include chivalric romances, history books and poetry by Chaucer, Lydgate and Gower) were available in the nunnery.[97] All were in the vernacular, probably in early printed editions by William Caxton. It is worth noting in this context that Katherine Mann, an anchoress attached to the Norwich Blackfriars, was supplied by the heretic Thomas Bilney (d. 1531) with illicit copies of William Tyndale's translation of the New Testament and his *Obedience of a Christian Man*.[98] The Carrow nuns and their recluses appear to have remained staunchly orthodox, but there is no reason to suppose that they were any less anxious to improve their minds – and souls – through study.

What of the sisters themselves? As we have already seen, a significant proportion of the Carrow nuns belonged to influential Norwich families, while the county gentry and yeomanry supplied the rest. Notwithstanding attempts by the papacy to stamp out the ubiquitous practice of demanding 'dowries' from female postulants, it was expensive for a girl to assume the habit. Entry fees were, however, occasionally subsidised at Carrow, and it looks as if some of the legacies bequeathed to individual nuns constituted a type of bursary or exhibition for those of limited means with a true vocation. The above-mentioned Elizabeth Yaxley left one of the sisters an annual rent of 3s. 4d. for life, a 'litle goblette with the cover of sylver' and the sort of basic possessions ('a payre of browde shetes, ij platteris, ij dyshes, ij sausers, a litle chafer, a litle ketyll, a litle potte, a lowe pewtre candylstycke, a playne table clothe, a playne towell and xs. [ten shillings] of lawfull money'), which suggest that she needed a generous patron.[99] In an age when monastic poverty and the renunciation of the world had gone the way of all flesh, most nuns relied upon their families to keep them in a degree of comfort appropriate to their station. From her father, a successful Norwich barber-surgeon who died in 1459, Isabel Welan received a legacy of 66s. 8d., followed shortly afterwards on the death of her mother by two pairs of best linen sheets, a feather bed with hangings to match, a red embroidered counterpane and tester, a mazer and two drinking bowls.[100] Significantly, she was named as executrix by both her parents, a task which made her responsible for the welfare of their immortal souls as well as the settlement of their earthly estate. Such marks of trust were not simply bestowed upon dutiful daughters. Being women of considerable authority as well as proven administrative experience, the prioresses themselves were popular in this respect. During the early sixteenth century, Isabel Wygon, the penultimate holder of this office, invested heavily in the rebuilding of the west range of the priory. She refurbished her own lodgings and the guest house there with, *inter alia*, a decorated fireplace bearing her rebus, which was prominently displayed in the carved doors and roof spandrels, too. Here, indeed, was a fitting place to entertain patrons and potential benefactors.[101]

Perhaps because it so demonstrably catered for the cloistered daughters of Norwich's wealthier citizens and the spiritual demands of an educated elite, Carrow priory did not attract the sheer volume of testamentary bequests which, as we shall see, were showered upon the city's four friaries. Even so, 16 per cent of a sample of 615 wills drawn up by citizens between 1370 and 1532 contain legacies to the priory and its female community. The local clergy were rather more generous, eighty-one out of a potential 289 testators being disposed to favour them, often because of a close personal connection. These priests held the nuns and anchoresses in high esteem, some, such as William Baxstere (1438), John Dowes (1439), William Walsingham (1475) and William Hallys (1478), actually electing to be buried in

St Mary's church.[102] Thomas Waterman (d. 1547), parson of All Saints Timberhill, remembered his former patrons fondly long after the Dissolution had severed all formal ties between them. His bequest to the last prioress of 'a ring of golde with the five wowndes [of Christ]' seems especially poignant.[103]

Although they enjoyed the right to elect their own prioress, free of outside interference, the nuns were, like the Benedictine monks, subject to regular visitations by the bishop of Norwich. That of 1492 has already been mentioned. Three less damning reports, for 1514, 1526 and 1532, also survive and provide an engaging vignette of life in a small community of ageing sisters, whose principal earthly concerns focused upon the weakness of the beer and insufficiency of their diet (common grounds for dissatisfaction among the late medieval religious). With their silk waistbands, addiction to tittle-tattle and fondness for Christmas festivities, the few young nuns invited censure from their disapproving elders, although their complaints reveal none of the bitter factionalism apparent at the cathedral priory. Nor were there any serious breaches of discipline of the sort perpetrated by the monks. Some services were allegedly rushed at an unseemly pace; the observance of certain festivals was patchy; and, perhaps inevitably, relations with the laity had become a shade too easy-going. There was also, if Skelton is to be believed, a fondness for domestic pets deemed inappropriate in women dedicated to God. This catalogue of minor grievances and peccadilloes suggests that, on the eve of the Dissolution, the convent was essentially well managed, if, perhaps, lacking the spiritual fervour of an earlier age.[104] The royal commissioners who inspected it in 1535 certainly found no cause for complaint, observing that the eight remaining nuns were 'of very good name by repute of the county' and that the house, although shabby, had been properly maintained.[105] Carrow had clearly seen better days, but still inspired respect, even in the most hostile quarters.

The friars were a revolutionary force in the thirteenth-century church, the front line of a 'counter-reformation' directed against heresy, rampant in various regions of continental Europe, but also against religious ignorance and indifference, wherever they might be found.[106] The four main orders were diverse in origin. St Dominic (*c.* 1170–1221) had been convinced and determined that sound academic training was essential for those charged with combating dissent within the church. St Francis's (1181–1236) vision was more charismatic, based on his conviction of the need to follow unreservedly, as a matter of personal commitment, the example of Christ's own life and sacrifice. Dominic recognised that voluntary poverty was an invaluable manifestation of intent for those committed to a life of evangelisation, and so he adopted the Franciscan example of mendicancy, albeit in a less extreme form. The papacy gently obliged Francis to adopt the organisation and educational structures pioneered by Dominic, which would prove essential if his order of Friars Minor was to serve as a missionary force beyond the hills of Umbria. A generation later the same necessary discipline was imposed on 'the various fringes of almost lunatic (if beautifully lunatic) extremists'[107] of central Italy who were moulded into the Order of Augustinian Hermits, and on the refugee hermits from the Holy Land who were banded together as the Carmelites. When they came to England these four new groups, whose great strength was to combine the religious enthusiasm of the Mediterranean world with strict adherence to an organisational structure and missionary programme determined by the papacy, were welcomed by reforming bishops, by young university students and by the poor. They were, on the other hand, fiercely resented by many elements within the institutional church which felt their own vested interests to be threatened.

The friars were essentially an urban movement: only in towns could they effectively beg, and in the same towns there was a multitude of souls to be saved. So it was no accident that, soon after their initial landfall in England, all four of the main mendicant orders rapidly established themselves in Norwich.[108] They came as poverty-stricken radicals, settled on the margins of the city. Yet, within a century, their convents were dominated by magnificent churches, frequented and patronised by the most prominent figures of city and county society. Until the catastrophe of the English Reformation, which made inevitable the abolition of orders directly answerable to Rome, they appear in Norwich, as elsewhere, however loud the satirical criticisms of their enemies,[109] to have satisfied the religious aspirations of all social classes within the city and its region.

The Dominicans (also known as the Black Friars or Order of Preachers), who arrived in England in 1221, and the Franciscans (the Grey Friars or Friars Minor), who landed three years later, both came to Norwich in 1224. The difference in time scale arose because the Dominicans were determined to found new houses only when they could provide a minimum complement of thirteen friars, while the Minorites adopted a characteristically reckless policy of expansion. Both groups settled at the limits of the medieval city: the Dominicans across the river in the northern suburbs on a square of land extending north/south from the present Golden Dog Lane to the river, and east/west from the church of St George Colegate to that of St Clement at Fye bridge;[110] the Franciscans on land given to them by John de Hastingford to the south of the marketplace at Tombland between the churches of St Vedast and St Cuthbert in Conisford, in an area well within the limits of the late Saxon town but by then depopulated.[111] The great difference between the two endowments was that the Dominicans were initially granted the parish church of St John the Baptist, while the Franciscans presumably had to construct for themselves a small oratory, probably not unlike the tiny original chapel of their order at Cambridge.[112] From all that we know of the vocation of the early friars, it is certain that they would have made a rapid impact on the city by their preaching and, in the case of the Franciscans especially, by the almost ostentatious austerity of their lifestyle.

Nearly thirty years elapsed before other orders of mendicants arrived in Norwich. The Pied Friars were established in the 1250s in Conesford and the Friars of the Sack by 1258 in the parish of St Peter Hungate.[113] Any influence exerted by these two groups proved short lived, as their death knell was effectively sounded in 1274, when the Second Council of Lyons forbade such lesser orders of friars to admit any new postulants, as a sop to those powerful elements in the church which opposed mendicancy *in toto*.[114] The Carmelites (Whitefriars) who arrived in Norwich in 1256 were a colonising party sent from the house at Burnham Norton, Norfolk, established in 1242, whose co-founder was Sir William de Calthorpe, nephew of Bishop Walter Suffield. They settled in the parish of St James, just north of the river, on land given by Philip, son of Warin of Cowgate, merchant.[115] It was not until 1288–89 that the fourth of the larger mendicant orders, the Augustinian (or Austin) friars, reached the city. The site given by their founder, Roger Minyot, supplemented by a tenement donated by John Chese, lay to the south of the Franciscans, on King Street in Conesford, with a river frontage near St Anne's staithe.[116] Norwich now, like almost all the major cities of thirteenth-century western Europe, had its full complement of friaries.

By the time that the Austin friars appeared, the longer established orders had embarked upon the piecemeal extension of their original sites. In contrast to the older monastic and canonical orders, the mendicants were committed to corporate as well as individual poverty, but the preaching and teaching roles which they had been allocated by the papacy made the strict application of such a policy simply impractical. In the mid thirteenth century English Franciscan university teachers were instrumental in diluting St Francis's gospel of absolute poverty in favour of the security of property now deemed essential for the efficient conduct of their mission.[117] The reality of the situation was recognised almost incidentally by Pope Clement IV in 1265 in his bull for the Augustinians, *Ad consequendam gloria*, which decreed that the friars, as orders grounded in poverty, should by their rules and constitutions have no possessions *beyond the bounds of their churches, monasteries and cloisters.* This did not, of course, prohibit the enlargement of their precincts, and proved a notable stimulus to expansion.[118]

By 1276 the Norwich Dominicans had acquired no fewer than six messuages, and in 1280 they enclosed their site with a wall. There were further grants and purchases up to the turn of the century. A major development occurred in 1307 with their petition to the crown for permission to occupy the site of the Friars of the Sack, of whom there was by now only one aged survivor, in the parish of St Peter Hungate. One of the reasons for the request was the alleged difficulty of access to their present church. Armed with the necessary royal licence to enlarge and build upon their new site, the Dominicans embarked upon an urgent campaign of acquisition of various plots, some of them substantial, so that by 1322 they held a solid block of land. In the 1330s the citizens, alarmed by such determined territorial expansion, themselves petitioned Edward III against Dominican encroachments, perhaps because the central location of the new Blackfriars seemed likely to pose a similar threat to civic liberties as that already presented by the cathedral priory. The royal response was that the acquisition of plots adjacent to the old Friars of the Sack was not detrimental to the city, but that any lying farther afield on the south side of the river would have to be surrendered – a response in complete accordance with the papal ruling of 1265. In 1345 the new Dominican precinct was rounded off when the Blackfriars obtained a royal licence to enclose the lane running through it.

The Franciscans too had gradually augmented their original site from 1226 to 1285, when they also acquired a royal licence to close a lane to the south of their plot to enlarge the precinct. By this stage the long conflict within the order between advocates of strict poverty, as preached and practised by St Francis, and those who considered that a secure convent was essential to house 'luxuries' such as books, had been won by the latter party.[119] In 1292 the Greyfriars obtained Edward I's consent to acquire no fewer than eighteen separate blocs of land; in 1297 and 1299 two further lanes were enclosed; and in the latter year permission was granted to incorporate three more plots. The Friars Minor now owned an extensive site on which an imposing new complex of church and claustral buildings was begun, probably near the King Street frontage.

The other orders rapidly followed suit. Although the Carmelites had received some modest grants at the time of their original settlement, the main period of their territorial expansion began in 1322, when they acquired a messuage for the enlargement of their dwelling place (Whitefriars). Further properties were added between 1332 and 1345. Meanwhile, on 25 August 1343, they occupied the choir of their new church, which was finally dedicated thirty-nine years later. By 1344 the new cemetery had been consecrated; in 1359 a lane to the east of the house was enclosed; and one further messuage was secured in 1380. The Augustinians did just as well. A mere five years after their arrival in Norwich, they had obtained six additional messuages by gift or purchase, and in 1325 yet another, from the abbot of Langley, specifically for the enlargement of their house. Their last major acquisition, in 1368, was the church of St Michael of Conesford. This marks the end of any large-scale expansion by the mendicant convents within the city. It was now merely a matter of rounding off the four sites and building upon them, although, as we shall see, the churches and cloisters themselves represented a major capital investment. Despite the one instance of resentment against the Dominicans in the early 1330s, it is notable that no complaint apparently came from the people of Norwich in 1352 in response to the royal inquisition into mendicant property throughout England.[120]

The early to mid fourteenth century witnessed a great phase of rebuilding of the mendicant churches, which transformed the landscape of late medieval Norwich. This was a local manifestation of a western European phenomenon, and reflects the confidence of the surviving orders of friars in their pastoral mission following the groundbreaking papal constitution *Ad fructus uberes* (1281). Martin IV had thereby authorised them to assume pastoral and sacramental functions in any diocese or parish without the consent of the officiating bishop or parson. The confidence – and wealth – generated by this high-water mark of their privileged status was hardly dented by Pope Boniface VIII's ruling in *Super cathedram* (1300) that bishops should license individual friars to act as confessors (there is a steady stream of such licences in later medieval bishops' registers) and that, to allay the resentment of the secular clergy, the mendicants should give a quarter of burial fees and offerings to the parish church of the deceased.[121]

Large churches were needed for preaching, and also for the burial of those whose income or status entitled them to a tomb or grave in the interior, rather than outside in the cemetery. After 1310 the Dominicans built a spacious new church on their new site south of the river, with conventual buildings to accommodate sixty friars. This was destroyed by a disastrous fire on 4 May 1413, after which they moved back to the original site north of the river, which in turn was burnt to the ground in 1449. That the return *ultra aquam* had not been intended to be permanent is indicated by the commencement of further work on the southern site from about 1440. Wills reveal that the infirmary and hospice were being rebuilt in 1458, the library in 1459 and the steeple of the church around 1462. The surviving chancel (Blackfriars Hall) and nave (St Andrew's Hall) are the most complete remains of any substantial mendicant church in England, and represent rare physical evidence of the impact of these orders on English towns and cities (Figure 16).[122]

The earliest Franciscan buildings had also been destroyed by fire in 1238, and King Henry III himself gave £20 towards rebuilding. After the expansion of the site, however, work began on a new church, which was to remain in use until the Dissolution. It was presumably built in the transitional Early English or Decorated style, with the normal Franciscan straight east end. The dimensions, given by the fifteenth-century antiquary, William of Worcester, are impressive, the overall length being about 250 feet (choir 105 feet, tower space 42 feet, nave 101.5 feet).[123] This is similar to Norwich Blackfriars (overall length 254 feet), and among English Franciscan churches was equalled only by Coventry and surpassed solely by London. The probable width was 56 feet (compared with 77 feet for Blackfriars), while the main cloister measured 106.75 feet square. There was probably a second cloister and a second cemetery, and the whole complex was by 1324 walled, with at least four gates. The Carmelite church was only slightly less striking in its dimensions (225 feet in length, with a choir of 105 feet, an ambulatory space of 40.25 feet, and a nave 80.5 feet long and 63 feet wide). In addition, the spectacular portal, known as the Arminghall Arch, with its sculptures of royal figures, advertised powerful temporal connexions just as good as – if not better than – those of the cathedral priory (Figure 17).[124] Determined not to be outdone, in 1360 the Augustinians demolished the church of St Michael of Conesford (only formally granted to them by Sir Edmund de Thorp eight years later) to build a splendid new conventual church.[125]

As for numbers of brethren, it is possible to gauge the population of all four friaries in the early fourteenth century. The Dominican convent housed fifty-three friars in 1326 and 1328, the Franciscans numbered approximately fifty, as did the Carmelites in 1326, while the Augustinian accounted for forty in 1325 and thirty-seven in 1328. There were therefore some 190 friars operating within and out of Norwich, moving around the small towns and villages of their respective limitations, or preaching circuits, especially during Advent and Lent, in search of alms and of souls. This compares to probably fewer than sixty monks in the cathedral priory. At the Dissolution, dispensations to serve as secular priests were granted to just sixty-two Norwich friars, but the decline in numbers had probably been rapid as the storm clouds gathered in the 1530s. It has been estimated that the number of friars in England in 1500 stood at about two-thirds of the level before the Black Death, which would give a figure of approximately 124 for Norwich, compared to forty-six cathedral monks (some of

FIGURE 16. The late fifteenth-century church of the Norwich Blackfriars from the south. (*Norfolk Heritage Centre, photograph by Terry Burchell*)

whom were absent in distant dependent houses).[126] Bearing in mind that there were also communities of all four orders at Cambridge, Lynn and Gorleston (outside Yarmouth), of Dominicans and Augustinians at Thetford, of Franciscans at Walsingham and of Carmelites at Blakeney and Burnham Norton, as well as nine friaries in Suffolk, it is obvious that almost to the end the mendicants had the capacity to make a great impact on the religious life of East Anglia.

That four such magnificent churches could be built in a city already so well provided with parish churches, and such numbers of friars be supported alongside the numerous secular clergy, is itself testimony to the popularity of the mendicants, at the very least until the end of their building programmes. For they had only the generosity of their benefactors on which to rely, since they lacked the extensive landed endowment of the Benedictine monks, or even of the nuns at Carrow and the city's larger hospitals. Apart from complaints about Dominican expansion in the heart of Norwich, there appears to have been remarkably little conflict between the citizen body and the mendicant convents. The city apparently subsidised the extension of the Franciscan precinct in 1292 and its elite attended services at Greyfriars in the fifteenth century.[127] In 1488 the Carmelites, desiring the security of a patron and in absence of any living heir of their initial benefactor, Philip Cowgate, successfully petitioned that the mayor, sheriffs, aldermen, merchants and citizens of Norwich should be considered the founders of their house, thus binding themselves tightly to the civic government.[128]

Neither, indeed, is there any significant evidence from Norwich of hostility to the friars from the monks of the cathedral priory – in marked contrast to the resistance to Franciscan settlement shown by the Benedictines of Bury and the Augustinian canons of Walsingham. Nor did the secular clergy offer any opposition. Such few disagreements as did occur were, with one exception,[129] over territory and franchises rather than wider theological issues. There were disputes between the cathedral priory, as proprietor of many city parish churches, and the Carmelites in the late thirteenth century, and in the 1270s the latter agreed to return any offerings made to them by parishioners of these churches. This was, however, at a time when the mendicants were coming under intense pressure throughout western Europe. The final agreement, made a century later in 1376, that a quarter of any funeral offerings to the Carmelites should be remitted to the parish church of the deceased, was merely in accordance with the above-mentioned ruling of Boniface VIII in *Super cathedram*.[130] In 1433 the rector of St Peter Hungate sued for the recovery of tithes and offerings he had lost because of the wholesale acquisition by the Dominicans of properties within his parish. The dispute was finally settled some twenty years later, when he was promised a quarter of all legacies left to the Blackfriars.[131] This represents remarkably scant evidence of conflict over a period of three centuries, during which the 'mendicant problem' continued to be a matter of lively, sometimes acrimonious, debate across western Christendom.[132]

What benefit did the people of Norwich derive from the presence of the friars? First, surely, preaching of a high quality, for which the mendicants won a formidable reputation, the Dominicans through their rigorous academic training, the early Franciscans through their sheer joy in God's creation. The friars' ability to attract large audiences by their use of parable and anecdote, designed to render lay congregations receptive to profoundly serious points or moral theology, was demonstrated long ago.[133] The nave of Blackfriars is obviously an auditorium, and outside it to the south lay the preaching yard, with an outdoor pulpit designed to attract even bigger crowds. The Norwich Dominican John Somerton, who attended Cambridge in 1468–69, produced a volume of *Sermones per annum*, as did the near contemporary Augustinian John Sloley.[134] The cathedral monks may have been irritated by certain friars when they preached in the cathedral, but they were happy to enlist them as mediators in their ongoing dispute with the city over exempt liberties. During one

FIGURE 17. The Arminghall Arch, originally at the Norwich Carmelites, after John Sell Cotman. Even in its somewhat dilapidated state, the arch conveys a sense of the decorative quality of the medieval precinct. (*School of World Art Studies, UEA*)

outbreak of hostilities, in 1493, for example, the Franciscans performed their traditional role as arbitrators at a meeting held in their own house.[135] The Paston Letters reveal that they had assumed the same peace keeping function in 1423 during a private quarrel between William Paston and Walter Aslak.[136] More common, if not mundane, was the reconciliation through confession and penance of the individual sinner with God and with particular individuals whom he or she had offended. The ministration of this sacrament was one of the great complaints of the parochial clergy against the friars, who were alleged to exploit – even abuse – their position by soliciting money (and other favours) from penitent sinners. Yet they nevertheless persisted. John Brackley, superior of the Norwich Franciscans, was a supportive confessor of the great military commander, Sir John Fastolf of Caister;[137] and it is highly likely that the many Norwich testators who made special bequests to individual friars were paying tribute to their spiritual directors.

To be effective, preaching, confession and even arbitration required education, most especially in moral and pastoral theology, to which the indispensable medieval preliminary was instruction in Latin grammar. If, in the early years, Francis and his companions had sanctified poverty, Dominic and his immediate successors had insisted on the carefully structured education of the brethren as the prerequisite for missionary activity, and the Dominicans' highly successful strategy was soon imitated by the other mendicant orders.[138] By the mid thirteenth century the Dominicans and Franciscans had established themselves as leading lights of the theological faculties of the major European universities, and this scholarship at the highest level was deliberately filtered downwards through the convents of each order. Every Dominican friary soon had its own classroom, where all brethren destined for the priesthood attended lectures and engaged in practice disputations. As well as biblical studies, the curriculum included Raymond of Penaforte's *Summa de casibus*, a treatise by the great Dominican canonist on confession and penance.

The other orders adopted this scheme, too. Each of the Norwich friaries ranked as a *studium* of its order, to which brethren from all over England and beyond might be sent for further training. Most is known of the Franciscan school.[139] Adam de Wodeham lectured here on the *Sentences* of Peter Lombard between 1329 and 1332, before moving to Oxford; his widespread influence on the development of late medieval theology has only recently been rediscovered. Nicholas of Assisi, an Italian Franciscan, studied in the city during the late 1330s and kept a notebook of the lectures he attended. Peter de Candia, later to be another distinguished theologian and the future Pope Alexander V, also spent some time here before going to

Oxford in the 1360s. A near contemporary, by no means as distinguished, was the English Franciscan Walter Wiburn, who produced many very long Latin poems, especially of Marian devotion, now considered 'extremely tedious to the modern reader'.[140] John Bale, the Protestant evangelical and bibliographer, who had himself been a Norwich Carmelite, included in his compilation of distinguished pre-Reformation writers some twenty Norwich friars, most of them from his own order.[141] There was certainly an impressive intellectual 'infrastructure' to support the friars' preaching and literary activities. In the 1450s Prior John Keninghale built a new library at Whitefriars, which Bale later described as the most beautiful in the order. Part of it still remained under lock and key in 1658, when the antiquary, William Dugdale, asked Sir Thomas Browne to help him obtain 'sight of a manuscript of Landaffe which may be usefull to me'.[142] The most munificent benefaction by any Norwich citizen to the friars was the 100 marks [£66 13s. 4d.] left to the Augustinians in 1457 by the above-mentioned Margaret Wetherby for a new library, conditional upon visual commemoration of herself and her late husband there, as well as prayers for their souls.[143] A bequest of 1459 reveals that the Dominicans had then also built a new library.[144] That the learning of the mendicants mattered to some citizens of Norwich is suggested by wills which differentiate between the friars according to status; for example, a bequest of 1484 to the Franciscans left 12d. to each master of arts, 4d. to each priest and 2d. to every other friar.[145] Respect for education as well as religious aspirations may have impelled Isabelle Moode, a Norwich widow, when in 1505 she left money to a named Franciscan to make her stepson a friar and support him until he might be ordained a priest.[146]

Each of the city friaries provided a venue for at least three guilds or confraternities, thereby accounting for twelve to the cathedral's five. In fostering such popular institutions in their own churches the friars were imitating their Mediterranean brethren, as well as established practice in Norwich, where many guilds were attached to parishes.[147] The evidence for the existence of these guilds comes primarily from returns made to a government enquiry of 1388–89 and from bequests in last testaments. Both the Franciscans and Dominicans housed a confraternity of Our Lady (Dominicans 1360, 1398; Franciscans 1498) and the Carmelites had a confraternity of Her Annunciation. The Dominicans and Austins each accommodated a guild of the Holy Cross or Holy Rood (Austins 1492–1506; Dominicans 1527). There was a Franciscan guild of St John the Evangelist; St Christopher and St Margaret were patronal saints of confraternities at the Austin friars; and both Carmelites and Franciscans were home to guilds of St Barbara, the patron saint of prisoners and those in danger of sudden death.

The craft guilds of the candlemakers and shoemakers met respectively at the Carmelites and the Austins, their respective dedications to St Mary and St Augustine emphasising that, whatever their other corporate concerns, they assembled with profoundly religious intent.[148]

The friaries also contained sites or objects of particular religious devotion, to which bequests of money, plate, vestments and jewels were made.[149] The altars and chapels of the Blessed Virgin at the Greyfriars, Blackfriars and Whitefriars were the religious centres of the guilds dedicated to her. There was a chapel of St Anne, the mother of Mary, in the Franciscan church, and an image of her at the Carmelites. Bequests were made to Our Lady of Pity (the *Pietà*) at the Austin friars and Greyfriars. All this reflects the ever-growing emphasis on the life and death of Christ and on the Holy Family in fifteenth-century popular religion. There were stained glass windows of the early saints: Lawrence at the Carmelites and Catherine at the Austin friars. Nearer to late medieval times, there was a chapel of St Thomas Becket at the Carmelites and a statue of him at the Franciscans, while a link with the heroic days of the order was provided by an image of St Peter Martyr at the Dominican church. The choice was eclectic, perhaps reflecting a bias towards dedications and images which would appeal to female religiosity.[150]

The existence of most of these statues, images and lights is known only because late medieval testators requested burial in proximity to them. Initially, in the early thirteenth century, the friars had provided burial in their cemeteries for those humble yet pious folk who could not aspire to interment by the monks or canons, but who sought the spiritual advantages of the barrage of prayer, and specifically masses, offered by a religious community. Long before the end of the century the friars had become the intimates of the great and good, from the level of the royal court to that of urban oligarchies, and as a result persons from a remarkably wide range of classes and occupations desired a final resting-place in the Norwich mendicant convents. Almost one in ten lay testators from the 1370s to the second decade of the sixteenth century requested burial there, although there was a sharp drop to 4 per cent in the period between 1518 and 1532, perhaps as a result of new ideas filtering in from the Continent.[151]

In the mausolea of the friars' churches the minor aristocracy and county gentry of Norfolk lay alongside the worthies of the city. The first recorded knightly burial is that of Sir Oliver Ingham in 1292 in the Carmelites; the roll call down to 1420 includes only knights, gentlemen and their ladies; but in 1423 John of Earlham, citizen and merchant, was buried there. In 1383 William, Lord Morley, was interred in the Austin friary, bequeathing to it amongst other things his best black horse and a complete set of vestments, both probably accoutrements of a splendid funeral. In 1452 Edmund Sedgeford, citizen and mercer, requested that a marble slab be placed on his grave in Blackfriars, before the altar in the north part near the window glazed with the history of the *Magnificat*; and fifty years later Dame Joan Blakeney too wanted marble set over her grave in the Lady chapel.[152] The mendicant churches were full of funeral monuments and memorials. In the aftermath of the Black Death there was a strong desire for ostentatious commemoration of the dead, which achieved its finest expression not in any single tomb but in the great new east window given by Sir Thomas Erpingham in 1419 to the Austin friars, displaying the arms of all those noble and knightly families who had died out because of lack of male issue since 1327 – eighty-seven families in all.[153] There was also a great armorial window at Blackfriars, towards which Erpingham was no less generous. The friars had not, however, abandoned their original spirit of inclusivity to the extent that these examples of worldly pomposity might suggest – among those who sought burial with the mendicants in the fifteenth and early sixteenth centuries were a coverlet weaver, a hardware man and a limeburner, prosperous by their endeavours, perhaps, but hardly of elevated social status. A true cross-section of classes, trades and professions found solace in burial with, and commemoration by, the friars.

What was urgently required, by those interred in or outside the mendicant churches and by benefactors who sought burial elsewhere, was the spiritual suffrage of the friars. The well-to-do might aspire to a chantry, such as that established before 1459 at Blackfriars by Ralph Skeet. From outside the city Sir Ralph Kerdeston of Claxton in 1445 left to the Austins 300 marks (£200) for three friars to celebrate masses for himself and his wife for all time, and in 1516 Sir James Hobart, formerly attorney general to Henry VII, also requested a chantry there (although it is not certain that either was ever established).[154] Most testators, of course, could not afford their own perpetual chantry, but they might become confraters of a mendicant house (which was different to membership of the smaller guilds described above). Pope Sixtus IV in 1479 issued an indulgence to the whole Franciscan order that members of its confraternity might have total forgiveness for all their sins once in their lifetime, along with the promise of a letter ensuring plenary remission, even for the most serious sins reserved to the pope, at the hour of their death.[155] Several Norwich lay testators describe themselves as members of the Franciscan confraternity, and Margaret Est in 1484 mentions her 'letter of pardon' from the Norwich Greyfriars, of which house she was a sister. There are letters of confraternity extant from the Franciscans (1433) and the Carmelites (1504, 1517), and an example of an 'open' Carmelite letter of 1512, which left a blank for the insertion of the recipient's name – an obvious indication of mass production for a popular market.[156] Pope Leo X granted the whole Augustinian order the administration of another plenary indulgence (full remission of all sins), and this is probably the origin of the *Scala Coeli* at the Norwich Austins.[157] There were some, however, who preferred the security of prayer at Rome itself: in 1497 John Aylmer, esquire, left thirteen marks (£8 13s. 4d.) to a named friar to go on pilgrimage to Rome after his death on his behalf.[158]

Between 1370 and 1532 each of the four mendicant houses received bequests from between 42 and 47 per cent of Norwich testators, although, as with requests for burial, there appears to have been a falling-off after 1517. Most testators left an equal sum, ranging from a few pence to one mark (13s. 4d.), to each friary, but perhaps more to a particular house if they sought burial there.[159] Deathbed bequests were not confined to the city itself – a group of wills proved in the early months of 1499 before the archbishop's commissaries contains gifts from as far away as Holt to the north and Eye to the south, including a donation of £2 to each house from an esquire of Gunton. In this small sample alone, a total of seventeen testators left between them over £5 to each house, a grand total of £22 1s. 4d. over a five-month period – the equivalent of four years' wages for a labouring man.[160] Other bequests were made in kind: vestments, ornaments, books and wine for the celebration of mass, the gift of a Norwich vintner. Some legacies suggest that the pristine poverty and asceticism of the early friars was by the fifteenth century as much a thing of the past as the strict monastic rule at Carrow and the cathedral. Bequests were now made to provide pittances, or mealtime luxuries, for the convent; many directed legacies to individual named friars, sometimes the kinsman of the testator. Such 'laxity', however, did not discourage the inhabitants of late medieval Norwich from trusting in the efficacy of the friars' prayers, any more than it prompted a loss of respect for the sisters at Carrow, the brothers of St Giles's hospital, or the Benedictine monks.

A common request was for a trental of thirty masses, but more affluent testators established what were, in effect, short-term chantries. Bequests to the Franciscans, for example, included five marks (66s. 8d.) to sing masses for a year (1467), fourteen marks (£9 16s. 8d.) for two years (1477), and a promise of four marks a year (53s. 4d.) for three years of commemoration (1488). Deathbed bequests were, in fact, only the tip of the iceberg. As has been demonstrated for parish churches and hospitals, so too for the mendicants: the living were eager to build up spiritual capital during their lifetimes. Norwich convents had their own 'limitations', large groups of vills where the brethren of one house of each order had the right to collect alms. The importance of such financial considerations is emphasised by the agreement in 1259 between the competing Dominican convents of Norwich and Dunwich about the extent of their respective territories.[161]

One point deserves particular emphasis. Almost from their inception the mendicant orders had faced fierce hostility from many of the bishops of western Europe, resentful of their exemption from episcopal control; and from the parish clergy, fearful of the loss of offerings to the friars. As we have seen, the papal bull *Super cathedram* had been intended as a compromise, but the controversy between secular clergy and friars rumbled on into the early sixteenth century. The anti-fraternal satires of Chaucer and Langland were, in part at least, a reflection of this hostility. At Norwich, however, there is little evidence of such endemic tension, and a significant percentage of the secular clergy of city and region chose burial in one of the friaries, while many more made bequests to them. In 1418, for example, the rector of Bixley promised a set of vestments in return for burial in the Franciscan precinct and the prayers of the brothers, and in 1499 the rectors of East Raynham and Shimpling, a chaplain of Wymondham and a Norwich priest each made legacies to the friars, three of them to all four orders.[162] Such bequests argue against any deep-felt resentment of their ministrations.

In a great city such as Norwich the friars were in their ideal milieu. There was for them here no spectacular mission, such as they had faced in the thirteenth century in the heresy-ridden towns of northern Italy, southern France and Flanders. There was, however, a great deal of pastoral work to be accomplished in an environment where the citizen body was alienated, occasionally spectacularly so, from the monastic chapter of the cathedral church, which represented overt ecclesiastical wealth and jurisdictional privilege, and where the parish churches, however thick on the ground, were poorly endowed in terms of property and thus unlikely to attract learned incumbents. The thirteenth century is usually seen as the heroic age of the mendicant orders, after which they lost their primitive idealism and, like their monastic predecessors, became mired in prosperity and privilege. The Norwich evidence suggests that, here at least, they remained a vigorous and popular element within a united church until the very eve of the Dissolution.

The chapel of St Mary, in the fields to the south-west of the city, was founded shortly before 1248 by John le Brun, priest, who settled upon it the advowson of the church of St George in Tombland, of which he was, presumably according to the custom of the city, hereditary incumbent. He also donated the church of St Andrew, where his brother, Geoffrey, was rector.

Another brother, Matthew le Brun, gave the church of St Mary Unbrent.[163] The chapel, established as an act of family piety, was initially intended to serve as the adjunct to a hospital, but Bishop Suffield's popular foundation of 1249 attracted so much patronage that John may well have been prompted to change his mind.[164] It was as a liturgical centre that St Mary's later attracted other endowments and was transformed into an important secular college in which both the bishop of Norwich and the city corporation had a keen interest. It thus came to act as a bridge between the ecclesiastical and civic authorities in a way in which the cathedral never did.

The great period of expansion was the later fourteenth century. The *Taxatio Ecclesiastica* of 1291 credits St Mary's with revenues of only £4 10s. 3d. a year, and, although this is surely an underestimate, it remained at this date a minuscule institution in financial terms. The *Valor Ecclesiasticus* of 1535, however, records an annual income of £111, of which over £63 came from spiritualities, although, because of numerous pensions and fees chargeable to the college, the net value was only £82 12s. 8d.[165] In 1350 the above-mentioned churches of St Andrew and St George were appropriated to the college, which henceforth received the rectorial income. Royal approval was given for the appropriation of Moulton church and a moiety of Fressingfield, Suffolk, in 1361, and of Easton in 1374. Field Dalling church was similarly acquired in 1384, and forty marks (£26 13s. 4d.) was then paid to the crown for licence to appropriate St Peter Mancroft, recently acquired from the monks of Gloucester. The rectorial income from the other moiety of Fressingfield was added in 1420. This steady expansion of revenues and the acquisition of what was to become the city's most spectacular parish church was attended by the extension and elaboration of the college buildings, most of the evidence for which comes from testamentary bequests. In 1374 the precinct wall and a common kitchen were being constructed, and between 1377 and 1379 work proceeded on the cloister. The choir of the church was being roofed with lead in 1428 and 1433, and the rebuilding of the church (perhaps by then the nave) was progressing in 1458. It is not known whether William Fake's exhortation was heeded when, in his will of 1483, he asked that his grave before the Rood should be surrounded by twenty-four marble paving stones as an example to others to floor the whole church in this fashion.

The full complement of the foundation comprised the dean and ten prebendaries. Five of the prebends were assigned to dignitaries holding offices, and the others were named after the main masses to be celebrated in the church. From an early date the collation of all these prebends pertained to the bishop – a welcome increase in patronage for a diocesan burdened by a monastic cathedral chapter which provided no lucrative benefices for his own ambitious clerks. In the last half century of the college's existence, at least, the normal roster appears to have shrunk to the dean and seven prebendaries. On the other hand, the proportion of graduates amongst them rose over the years, from seventeen out of forty-two institutions in the period 1370–1449, to thirty-eight out of forty-seven between 1450 and 1532.[166] There were certainly some cases of non-residence, most particularly among those appointed by the crown during vacancies of the see. In 1492, for example, the dean, Master John Neele, was fully occupied in a key role in the household of Arthur, prince of Wales;[167] and at least four of the seven prebendaries, including the bishop's brother, were currently – or had been – engaged in diocesan administration. Some of them might always be found in residence at any one time, however, being aided in their liturgical duties by six *conducti* (hired chaplains) attached to the various chantries established by the college, and also by other clerks not in holy orders and by boys, whose presence suggests a trained choir. Testamentary evidence from 1415 and 1455 reveals that one of Norwich's many anchorites was attached to the community.[168]

St Mary's provided a focal point for the city's clergy. Of those whose wills survive, 21 per cent made bequests to the college, as compared with 6 per cent of lay testators. It was here that the Corpus Christi guild of priests, on the octave of that feast, held an annual procession, mass and dinner, with a requiem mass next morning.[169] This guild was founded, allegedly, in 1278, only fourteen years after the official recognition of the feast by Pope Urban IV, and was in continuous existence until 1546, with a brief revival in Queen Mary's reign.[170] St Mary's also, however, attracted civic, and indeed popular, loyalty. Since the college was established on open ground, just within the walls, there was not the potential for jurisdictional conflict which marred the city's difficult relationship with its cathedral. Before the guildhall was built the city government often met at the college, and from 1456 a solemn annual obit (or memorial) service for civic benefactors was held there, involving the massed ranks of the corporation, the masters of all the guilds and thirteen paupers.[171] Among the six chantries founded at St Mary's were prayers in perpetuity for the souls of William Appleyard, later mayor (1388), John Alderford, a prominent citizen (1406), and William Setman, mercer and later mayor (1412).[172] The college seems to have been particularly diligent in maintaining its chantries, perhaps because the city government acted as guarantor and could apply coercion to forestall lapses in devotion. The tailors' guild, dedicated to the Ascension of Christ and to the Blessed Virgin, met there, and possibly also the more affluent and influential mercers, whose parish church of St Peter

Mancroft had such close links with the college.[173] The confraternity of the Annunciation of the Blessed Virgin, both socially and politically the most important guild in the late fourteenth-century city, had its home at St Mary's until 1402, when it disappears, probably merged with the Bachelry guild. This, in turn, was eventually absorbed into the company of St George, which became, effectively, synonymous with the corporation of Norwich.[174] The greatest public display of the integration of the college into the life of the city occurred on Corpus Christi Day, when the mayor, sheriffs and aldermen processed to St Mary's with thirty-two guilds carrying their banners.[175] Until its dissolution in January 1544, the college expressed the religious spirit of the city far more than did the cathedral.

It has become the new orthodoxy that the English Reformation was a very gradual process, the effects of which were not fully absorbed until well into the reign of Elizabeth I.[176] In Norwich, however, the consequences, in terms both of the topography of the city and its ecclesiastical personnel, were more dramatic. The cathedral, of course, survived, albeit with a smaller complement of clergy whose membership lacked the corporate solidarity of their Benedictine predecessors.[177] The hospital of St Giles, too, unusually for such an institution, was preserved under new municipal management, stripped however of its liturgical magnificence and the intercessory role which had hitherto been its *raison d'être*.[178] The nunnery of Carrow was dissolved in 1536, the college of St Mary in the Fields in 1544, and both churches were demolished. The sumptuous house built by the last prioress of Carrow was preserved, a monument to the withdrawal of the superior from the convent which has been seen as one of the significant weaknesses of late medieval monasticism; it would make a fine residence for successive generations of prosperous city businessmen. The collegiate buildings of St Mary's could also easily be converted into a mansion, and two centuries later, in 1754, the Assembly Rooms were built on this site.[179]

Even so, the most visible change must have come with the dissolution in 1538 of the four friaries. Their occupants had, by their vocation, been active in the very heart of the community, both in the city and its region, preaching, teaching and collecting alms. For nearly three hundred years the mendicants had offered up prayers and masses for the souls of their benefactors, many of whom sought burial within their precincts. Their schools had made a notable contribution to the city's reputation as a centre of education, even of learning. Yet, within a few years three of the four great mendicant churches had been razed. The Carmelite plot changed hands many times in the next century. The Franciscan site was for twenty years rented by the duke of Norfolk to a brewer, but was purchased by the city in 1559 and used as a common staithe; it was subsequently broken up into many small holdings, and the 'great house', probably that occupied by the suffragan bishop, was demolished in 1565–66.[180] The fate of the other friaries is symbolic. The bulk of the Augustinian site soon passed to the Paston family, and was known as Conesford Place, while a garden there remained in the hands of the dukes of Norfolk.[181] Blackfriars escaped demolition because it was snapped up by the corporation with an eye to accommodation for the grammar school. After the scholars decamped into the cathedral precinct, the nave was converted into an assembly hall and the chancel retained as the municipal chapel.[182] Once it had become obvious that suppression was inevitable, there seems to have been a determination that the king should not be the sole beneficiary.

By 1658 only a hazy recollection of Blackfriars' history remained in staunchly Protestant Norwich. It was then that Sir Thomas Browne, who was helping his friend, William Dugdale, with the local section of his *Monasticon Anglicanum*, observed:

> Here is in this citty a convent of Black Friers, which is more entire than any in these parts of England ... I conceive it were not fitt in so generall a tract to omit it, though little can be sayd of it, only conjectur'd that it was founded by Sir John of Orpingham or Erpingham whose coat [of arms] is all about the church and six-cornered steeple.[183]

In Norwich, as in the rest of England, after the crown had taken its profit, it was the aristocracy, gentry and urban oligarchies who gained materially from the dissolution of the religious houses. Whether the benefit was also spiritual and educational is a more debatable question.

5

Medieval Glass-Painting

David King

> Stevenson, a tradesman, an alderman of Norwich and laterly a great dealer in painted glass, the plunderer of all the painted glass particularly in the Norfolk churches he could legally lay his hands on no matter has fitted up the windows of this chapel [Costessey Hall] ... I myself laid out some money with him and possess about six very fine subjects amongst which a crucifixion, on which he told me after I had bought it came from the Grey Friars Norwich. I call'd on him at his house when I was in Norwich with Mr and Mrs Hudson Gurney.
>
> Reverend D. J. Powell, 1815[1]

'English stained glass is the least appreciated of the medieval pictorial arts.'[2] Thus begins a recent study of medieval glass-painting in this country. The author cites the destruction of the vast majority of the windows made, the fragmentary condition of what survives, and problems of restoration, rearrangement, access and lack of publication as some of the reasons for this neglect. To his depressing list could be added, particularly in the case of Norfolk, the many instances where glass has been moved from its original location. Yet the medium has much to offer as a reflection of many aspects of medieval life for the student of art, religion and society, not least in Norwich, where insights into regional styles, workshop practice, the religious and political concerns of patrons and popular piety, amongst other topics, can all be gained from a study of its painted glass.

The glass in the county is spread over about 275 buildings and some of the main collections are to be found within the city walls. Norwich was one of the most important cities for the medium, rivalling the better-known centre of York in the number of glaziers whose names have survived. It produced glass not only for the city itself but also for a considerable hinterland in Norfolk, Suffolk and further afield.[3] This chapter confines itself to the painted glass made in and for the city from the twelfth to the sixteenth century. In order to fill in the huge gaps in the material record it uses the evidence not only of the glass extant in Norwich buildings, but also that which is now in museums and collections elsewhere. It also draws upon documentation relating to Norwich glaziers, antiquarian descriptions of material now lost and, of especial interest, the large amount of painted glass recovered from excavations in the city in recent years.[4]

There have been glaziers in Norwich from at least the thirteenth and probably the twelfth century. The earliest document recording the name of a glazier in the city dates from 1241, when Bartholomew le Verer (meaning glazier), son of Simon le Sauvage, is mentioned as owing 10s. to the Jew, Abraham.[5] He was, however, almost certainly not the first to work there. The evidence is exiguous, but the probability is high that the art was introduced into the city at some time in the twelfth century. There is no information about any glazing activity in Norwich during the Saxon and early Norman periods, such as there is for other parts of England, but tenth-century blue window glass has been excavated at Thetford, and painted window glass has been found, or is documented, for the period *c.* 1100–1160 at a small number of sites in England, including Ely cathedral, where a head of about 1150 and other fragments of drapery and decoration have been uncovered.[6] Documentary references to Osbernus *vitrearius* in three deeds of Ramsey abbey of between 1114 and 1160, and to Daniel *vitrearius*, another Ramsey monk of the early twelfth century, who later became abbot there and then at St Benet Holme in Norfolk, bring the use of glass nearer to Norwich in the twelfth century, but could refer to glass-makers rather than glaziers.[7] The most persuasive evidence is a single fragment of twelfth-century painted glass decorated with a foliage pattern found in Norwich during the excavation prior to the construction of the Castle Mall.[8] The most likely provenance for this piece would have been the chapel in the castle keep, probably finished by 1121 when Henry I stayed there over Christmas.[9]

The same masons who built the castle also worked on Bishop Herbert de Losinga's cathedral, which was begun in 1096 and completed by 1145.[10] There is no documentation for any glazing of the cathedral windows before the thirteenth century, but glazed they must have been: and in such an important building with painted glass of the highest quality. So, for example, were the windows of Prior Conrad's choir at Canterbury, which was consecrated in 1130, but possibly not glazed until the middle of the century.[11] Moreover, the large dimensions of the Norman north transept windows at Norwich look as though they were specifically designed to allow for the maximum area of glass.[12]

Bartholomew le Verer could have been engaged a little after 1241 on the new axial Lady chapel at the cathedral built by Bishop Walter Suffield

(1244–57), but by the mid thirteenth century there is evidence that the use of painted glass had become more widespread and extended to ordinary parish churches.[13] Most of the church architecture of this period in Norfolk has been destroyed by later rebuilding, but there is *in situ* stiff-leaf grisaille glazing in Drayton church of *c.* 1250, done by the same glazier who appears to have glazed the refectory at the nearby Horsham St Faith's priory, where a fine fragment of grisaille was found. Both buildings are on the outskirts of Norwich. Stiff-leaf grisaille was made for many buildings in thirteenth-century England and remains have been unearthed in the city on a variety of archaeological sites; it is clear that this type of work, sometimes combined with coloured glazing, must have been very common.[14]

The first recorded glazier employed by the Benedictines was Nicholas Fayerchild, who received one shilling in 1279–80 for taking down glass shields in the cathedral. In 1283–84 he and his sons were given a robe worth the considerable sum of 20s. by the master of the cellar. Between 1283 and 1304 another glazier called William le Verer also appears on the cathedral payroll.[15] It is worth noting that in 1303 his daughter sold a property to Robert Painter in St George's, Tombland, which lies just outside the precinct.[16] In the same parish in 1285 Peter Pictor (Painter) was living almost next to a tenement that had recently belonged to Augustin le Verer.[17] Between 1286 and 1310 a group of glaziers, painters and illuminators were involved in property transactions in the parishes around the west end of the cathedral precinct, so it is probable that they were living and working there and deriving some of their commissions from the monks, notably from the building of the cloister.[18] The construction of three imposing friaries in the city in the thirteenth century must also have provided a lucrative source of employment.[19]

The earliest extant panel of glass, as opposed to excavated fragments, that can with some certainty be assigned to a Norwich provenance has hitherto been thought to have come from Oxford, but can now be attributed to the Norwich Greyfriars, whose church just to the south of the cathedral was being built in the 1290s. It is a charming donor figure, now in the Burrell Collection in Glasgow, depicting Beatrix of Valkenburg.[20] She was the third wife of Richard of Cornwall, king of the Romans and an ancestor of Thomas Howard, duke of Norfolk, who acquired the friary buildings at the Dissolution. Such an important association with the ducal family may explain why the glass survived. Beatrix was buried in the Oxford Franciscan church, to which the panel has previously been ascribed, but a clear line of provenance from the Norwich Greyfriars can be established. The Franciscan connections of the donor figure are confirmed by the heraldic pattern of *barry gules and sable* used to patch her mantle, which is as close as the glazier could get for technical reasons to *barry gules and argent*, the arms of the Franciscan saint, Elizabeth of Hungary, before whom Beatrix perhaps originally knelt (Plate 12). Elizabeth herself played a significant part in the devotional life of the city, her cult having spread rapidly across Europe within a few years of her death in 1231. It is interesting to note that the late thirteenth-century stylistic affinities of this rare survival are with France and Germany, countries with which the Franciscans had close links. The style of the panel and the building history of the friary date the panel to the last decade of the thirteenth century.[21]

There is a gap in the documentation of Norwich glaziers and in the extant glass from about 1311 until the 1340s, apart from a few fragments of naturalistic leaf grisaille, such as those still to be seen in the chapel over the Ethelbert gate to the cathedral. Possibly the political upheavals and economic dislocation of the period contributed to this decline, but the vagaries of survival of both documents and glass make firm conclusions difficult. Evidence for activity from around 1340 onwards is more plentiful. Excavated glass found on the site of the Norwich Greyfriars points to a second mid fourteenth-century glazing campaign after the initial work in the 1290s.[22] Panels of the Virgin Mary and St John that would have flanked a Crucifixion and are now respectively in the Victoria and Albert Museum and the Burrell Collection can also be more tentatively assigned to the Franciscan church.[23] At this time, a number of glaziers were living in King Street opposite the entrance to the friary, such a concentration suggesting that there was ample work to keep them in gainful employment.[24]

Glass dateable to between 1370 and 1390 has been found at a site further down King Street opposite the church of St Peter Parmentergate.[25] Whether it was discarded when that church was rebuilt in the late fifteenth century, was debris from a glazier's workshop or came from the nearby Augustinian friary is unclear, but it demonstrates that the glaziers then documented in the city were working in a style close to that seen elsewhere in glass and manuscript painting. A few canopy fragments of this date have also been leaded into a window in St Gregory's church, and it appears that the east window of St Edmund's Fishergate was being glazed in 1374, at least if the provisions of the will of Henry Wynke, chaplain, were carried out.[26] This is one of several legacies for the provision of a painted window to be made in medieval Norwich. The main motivation for bequests for church building, decoration and furnishing was to keep the donor's name and those of his or her friends and family clearly in public view, so that others would be moved to say prayers for their souls, thus leading to a shorter stay in Purgatory. A window was a very visible gift, especially an east-facing one above an altar, and a priest in particular might also have in mind the provision of a spiritually edifying image for the faithful whom he had taught and served before his death. As well as beautifying a church (which many of Norwich's wealthy residents would have regarded as a commendable activity in its own right), stained glass thus seemed to advertise and educate. It offered powerful spiritual propaganda and a sure route to paradise. In a literal as well as a figurative sense, it brought enlightenment to the congregation.

No city glass of the International Gothic period (*c.* 1390–1430) has survived, although panels made at this time for county churches may have come from Norwich workshops.[27] A remarkable window executed in 1419 for the now lost church of the Augustinian friary in King Street still existed in the eighteenth century. It was given by the influential courtier and hero of Agincourt, Sir Thomas Erpingham, and was an extraordinary heraldic *tour de force* of more than eighty shields with an inscription in French explaining that it commemorated all the lords, barons, bannerets and knights who had died without male issue in Norfolk and Suffolk since the coronation of Edward III in 1327.[28] Display of rank and lineage was another important element in medieval stained glass, and heraldry played a major part in this from the thirteenth century, as we have seen already. This apogee of armorial artistry has been described as symbolising 'the unity of the warrior-landowning class of East Anglia' of which Sir Thomas had been a notable leader. He and his two wives were later to be seen in a window in the cathedral made at, or before, his death in 1428. An eighteenth-century engraving of this fine memorial survives (Figure 18).[29]

If the picture of Norwich glass painting up to 1400 has seemed patchy with much reliance on documents, excavated fragments and conjecture rather than actual windows, the situation in the fifteenth and sixteenth centuries is very different, since the vast bulk of medieval glass surviving in Norwich is from this period. By far the most important collection is that in the church of St Peter Mancroft, where the remains of at least ten windows may still be found.[30] This glass is of national and international significance for the quality of its painting, for what it tells us about medieval stained glass workshop practices, for the interest of its subject matter and as a prime example of glazing in a high-status civic context. It is now mainly in the east window with lesser remains in others, one panel in the treasury and three others in collections elsewhere. The glass is described here as if it were still in the windows whence it originally came. That which survives the best is the Toppes window, made between about 1450 and 1455 for the east window of the north chancel chapel. The chapel was dedicated to St John the Baptist, and it was here that the mass of the Name of Jesus was

FIGURE 18. Engraving of 1793 of a lost window depicting Sir Thomas Erpingham and his wives, *c.* 1428, originally in the north choir aisle of Norwich cathedral. (*Norwich Castle Museum and Art Gallery*)

celebrated, to which the glass subtly alludes. The cult of the Holy Name was a comparatively recent development, and its popularity among the mercantile elite of Norwich, who made up the congregation of St Peter's, is worth noting.[31] An eighteenth-century description of the window by the Norwich antiquary John Kirkpatrick allows a reconstruction. Above a picture of the donor, Robert Toppes, the richest merchant in the city who was three times mayor, his wives, and a display of family heraldry (Figure 19), was placed a Marian cycle depicting the Infancy of Christ and the Death, Funeral and Assumption of the Virgin Mary. In the tracery stood three tiers of figures, English sainted kings, bishops and archbishops, with the Coronation of the Virgin completing the Marian cycle beneath.

This window was made by the leading glazing workshop in the city at the time. It belonged to John Wighton, who also glazed the council chamber of the Guildhall, where some of his work can still be seen, and became an alderman in 1453 when Toppes was mayor.[32] The same workshop, employing at least three painters with very different styles, executed several other commissions in the church. In the south chancel chapel were three windows of between about 1450 and 1455 relating to the assumed dedication of this part of the church as the Lady chapel. A genealogy of Christ in the

FIGURE 19. Stained glass depiction of Robert Toppes and his family, *c.* 1450, originally in the east window of the north chancel chapel, and now in the east chancel window, of the church of St Peter Mancroft. (*National Monuments Record*)

tracery of the east window was flanked in the south-east window by a representation of the Holy Kindred in the tracery. The depiction of Jesus' extended maternal family appealed to late medieval lay piety, especially to the prosperous merchants and their wives who would have gazed upon and appreciated the imagery, with its focus on the importance of fertilty and lineage.[33] We can only guess at what was in the main lights of these two windows, perhaps a Tree of Jesse and a Life of St Anne, as the Guild of St Anne later met in this chapel. The original disposition for the next south window is fortunately clearer: tracery lights held an Annunciation and Visitation (Plate 25) in a different style from the other windows. Main lights panels in this same style, and therefore probably from the same window, portray a Franciscan donor, suffragan bishop Robert Ringman, who died in 1453, with the seraphic St Francis, the Franciscan St Elizabeth of Hungary distributing alms (Plate 27) and two scenes from the life of St Margaret of Antioch. All this glass is now to be seen in the chancel east window. As well as relating to the dedication of the Lady chapel, its iconography also links in with widespread female devotion to the cults of St Margaret and St Anne, both of whom had strong associations with childbirth and were venerated throughout the region. It may have also have alluded to the forthcoming birth in 1453 of Prince Edward to the pregnant Queen Margaret of Anjou, who had visited Norwich in that year. The last mentioned window may have been painted by Helen Moundford, the only recorded female glazier in Norwich and a member of the Wighton company.

Her husband, William, also worked for John Wighton and was a Dutchman.[34] His hand may be discernible in some other glass at St Peter Mancroft and elsewhere, including two scenes from a Passion window, which was probably that for which Thomas Bumpsted left the remarkably generous sum of £10, payable over four years, to glaze the east window of the north transept in 1445. He possibly also executed a magnificent series of main-light seated female saints of which two panels survive and for which Flemish art may have been an inspiration. Two later commissions from Norwich glaziers were originally in the side windows of the chapel of St John the Evangelist, the more westerly depicting a life of St John of *c.* 1480–1500 given by another mayor, William London, and the other donor figures, inscriptions and heraldry commemorating the Elys and Garneys families, probably of *c.* 1526. Although they constitute only a small part of the original, these survivals give some idea of the sheer opulence of Norwich's richest and most spectacular parish church, and of the investment made in it by its affluent parishioners. Naturally, others followed suit. This was, indeed, a 'boom' period for the city's glaziers, when the great rebuilding programme spread into virtually every parish, and new glazing schemes replaced those deemed outdated or insufficiently attuned to the demands of lay patrons.

A similar combination of fifteenth- and sixteenth-century glass may, for example, still be seen in the church of St Peter Hungate, which was refurbished by the Paston family in the mid fifteenth century and where an additional sixteenth-century glazing campaign was undertaken in the chancel (Figure 20).[35] Much of the glass has now been collected into the east chancel window, but all the other windows of the church except two retain lesser remains. Once again, John Kirkpatrick, and his fellow antiquarian, Francis Blomefield, help to make sense of what is left.[36] The sixteenth-century glass belongs to the chancel, where the second window on the south displayed the figures of the Four Evangelists now seen in fragmentary form in the east window. Opposite in the second north window was a matching series of the Four Doctors of the church, of whom Saint Gregory is seen in the east window.[37] In the first south window Blomefield records the kneeling figure of a tonsured priest dated 1522, now in the east window, which probably gives the date of the reglazing of the chancel. He also refers to some lost glass, which was probably a representation of the Seven Sacraments. This subject, together with others such as the Seven Works of Mercy, was included in the influential decree *Ignorantia sacerdotum* made by Archbishop Pecham in 1281 listing the basic tenets of the faith that priests should teach to their congregations. Seven Sacrament windows are, however, much more common in the west of England; in East Anglia the subject appears more frequently on late medieval fonts, possibly to reinforce orthodox belief in the sacraments against the incursions of Lollardy.[38]

The fifteenth-century glass was made for the transepts and nave of this small but well-appointed parish church. The presence of several kinds of tracery-light figure suggests that originally there was a Coronation of the Virgin and series of kings and patriarchs, apostles, female saints and angels, all typical of Norwich glazing of this period. Demi-figures of angels holding texts, now in the east window, and a north transept window came from the heads of main lights, but of the glazing below that level there are no survivals except for a few fragments now set in the borders of the windows and elsewhere. These hint at the subjects of some of the fifteenth-century main-light glazing: an Annunciation, the Three Magi, the Four Doctors (again), St Christopher and some patterned quarry glazing. As late as the eighteenth century the church still possessed a figure of Thomas Andrew, the rector, who died in 1468, in the east window of the north transept.[39] The priestly and valedictory content of the *Nunc dimittis* texts held by some of the angels would have been a suitable accompaniment and possibly

FIGURE 20. Stained glass depiction of St James the Greater and St Simon as children, *c.* 1460, reset in the chancel window in the church of St Peter Hungate. (*David J. King*)

came from that window. The series may have been completed in the matching east window of the south transept.

Lesser remains of fifteenth-century glass can be seen today in the churches of All Saints, Fye bridge, where there are fragments of another Holy Kindred window, St John Maddermarket, where there are also a few fourteenth-century pieces, St Michael-at-Plea and St Swithun. Blomefield found evidence of a payment of 1s. 8d. made at St Laurence's church in 1643 to 'Goodman Perfett for the putting out of the superstitious inscriptions in the church windows', and also described a mass of heraldic glass of about 1500, which was probably originally accompanied by religious imagery. All that now remains of what must once have been a striking display is a mosaic of fragments in one light of the east window of the north aisle. In the east window of the north chapel of St Michael Coslany, which was attended by some of the city's leading merchants, is another jumble of fragments and heraldry, some of which may relate to the building date of *c.* 1511 given for the chapel.[40]

Certainly there was no lack of successful glass-painters in the city during the late fifteenth and early sixteenth centuries.[41] For example, just four years after the death in 1481 of John Moundford, who seems to have taken over and continued the workshop of Alderman Thomas Wighton, and to whom can be attributed the important glass of the late 1470s at East Harling, it is recorded that William Heyward entered the freedom of the city as a glazier. Living in Conesford, he soon began to occupy various civic offices, as was normal for a freeman, becoming constable, councillor and chamberlain and finally alderman in 1505, the only glazier apart from John Wighton to rise so high in the ranks of the elite. He was also a member of the prestigious guild of St George. He was very active in the field of property transactions, too, not just for places in which to live and work but also, it would appear, as investments. One acquisition relating to his craft activities may have been the purchase in 1493–94, together with a tailor and a baker, of four shops and a tenement on the east side of Conesford (now King Street) which abutted onto a property formerly owned by another glazier, Thomas Durham. Several other glaziers are known to have worked in this street, probably in direct continuity from their fourteenth-century predecessors described above. Two years later, however, Heyward sold a tenement north of the river in the parish of All Saints, Fye bridge, along with John Wattok, glazier, Wattok's wife, Margery, Robert Gylmyn, glazier, and John Bettys, citizen, an indication that he was also working in partnership with craftsmen established elsewhere. Wattok, who had been apprenticed to William Gylmyn, held civic offices across the water in the first two decades of the sixteenth century and was left a gown worth 10s. in Heyward's will. The will was proved in 1506 and also contained a bequest of money to glaze the east window and one of the side windows of the chancel of the church of St Peter Parmentergate, if it was built within the next four years. Other beneficiaries included the guilds of St George and St Luke, which met in the cathedral, and those of the Holy Cross and of St John the Evangelist, which worshipped, respectively, in the Augustinian and Franciscan friaries. Both these latter institutions and the church of St Peter lay close together on Conesford Street. Heyward had two apprentices, Robert Baly and John Tenche; and another glazier, Nicholas Grene, probably worked for him as well. Perhaps the most interesting feature of his career was that he also produced monumental brasses.[42] Glaziers with two occupations were not unknown in medieval Norwich and are also to be found in London, but Heyward may possibly have developed into an entrepreneur with various business interests rather than a versatile craftsman who himself demonstrated such a range of skills. He would, on the other hand, have found it comparatively easy to execute designs for both windows and monumental brasses.[43] Certainly, artistic resemblances between depictions on glass and brass have been noted, although these are more convincing in the years following Heyward's death.[44]

William Heyward was an important figure in the community in the later fifteenth and early sixteenth centuries. Unfortunately, it is has not been possible as yet to attribute any of the extant glass-painting in the city or county to his atelier. We know that in 1503 he was paid by Thomas Sharington of Cranworth to glaze a window in Thuxton church at just over one shilling a foot. The commission required him to depict the Transfiguration, a relatively unusual subject, with figures of Sharington and his wife Katherine, kneeling below and wearing coats of arms.[45] Almost inevitably, this glass has been lost.

The influential college of St Mary in the Fields was not only patron of St Peter Mancroft, but also of the second most important parish church in the city, St Andrew's, which still retains important glass of the sixteenth century, having been rebuilt from about 1478 onwards.[46] St Andrew's stood on a hill above the great preaching church of the Blackfriars, and looked down upon one of the public spaces used for civic pageants, so the need for display was clearly paramount. There survive in the easternmost south aisle window parts of the original glazing of the east chancel window. We should remember that the east window, the most important in any church, stood behind the high altar and framed the celebration of mass. Comparison with the similar but rather later remains still in the east window of St Stephen's shows that both churches had a Crucifixion flanked by related Old Testament scenes in this central position, each being of five lights, with the Crucifixion occupying the central three lights, and the Old Testament parallels, namely the sacrifice of Isaac and the raising of the Brazen Serpent, in the first and fifth respectively (Figure 21). It is these Old Testament scenes that have partially survived at St Andrew's. The glass, which can be dated by the building history to about 1509, shows a marked shift in style since the late fifteenth-century life of St John window at St Peter Mancroft, being much more realistic and heavily influenced by Flemish or French glass-painting. In another south aisle window is a fascinating panel that was originally part of a series in the south clerestory depicting the Dance of Death, the only surviving example of this theme in England in the medium of glass.

FIGURE 21. Stained glass depiction of the sacrifice of Isaac and the raising of the Brazen Serpent, *c.* 1509, originally in the chancel window, now reset in a south aisle window, of the church of St Andrew. (*National Monuments Record*)

This reflects the late medieval preoccupation with the possibility of sudden death, especially in the time of plague.[47] It dates from the last decade of the sixteenth century, and depicts a skeleton leading away a bishop. Although broader and cruder in style than the glass from the east chancel window, it would have been very effective in its original lofty position (Plate 29).[48]

St Stephen's parish church was the last to be extensively rebuilt in medieval Norwich. The glass mentioned above in the bottom half of the east window (the top having been glazed in the early nineteenth century with imported German glass) may be dated by an inscription to 1533, just two years before the Dissolution. It depicts the same Old Testament scenes in the outer lights, but lights two and four have retained subsidiary parts of the original large Crucifixion, although the central figure of Christ has gone. The style is different from the earlier but iconographically related St Andrew's east window glass, being characterised by unusually hard-edged and precise brushwork.[49]

The glass in both St Andrew's and St Stephen's church raises the important question of continental influence on Norwich glass-painting. This probably began in the twelfth century with the Normans, but is of particular interest in the sixteenth century since many glaziers from the Netherlands and Germany worked in England at this time, and we know of at least one instance of the importation of glass made in France. No record of foreign glaziers active in Norwich has, however, been found in this century, and, although the style of the glass in each of these churches strongly reflects continental work, it is impossible to say whether this indicates the secondary influence or the actual presence of glaziers from abroad. Design links between the two churches and with contemporary glass at Shelton suggest that at least some of the glass in question was made locally.[50]

The guildhall beside the market was built between 1407 and 1453, but in 1511 disaster struck when the roof of the mayoral council chamber collapsed. When the building was restored in 1534–37, some of the original 1453 glazing appears to have been reused, but additional new material was installed, a few pieces of which survive in the three eastern windows mixed in with both older and post-medieval glass (Plate 13).[51] Members of the ruling elite thus had a fine opportunity to advertise their sense of civic pride, as well as their own wealth and status. They seized it with vigour. The large east window was glazed by the executors of John Fuller (d. *c.* 1526), mercer and city councillor. It contained heraldry and a figure of St George with the inscription *Domine fac Salvum Regem* (God save the King).[52] The two small flanking windows were the gift of Alderman Thomas Necton (d. 1556): one depicted his merchant's mark and the other his rebus.[53] The glazing of the first window on the north was likewise commissioned by Robert Ferrour, draper and mayor in 1526 and 1536. His coat of arms, *gules a cross flory argent*, which once appeared there, can still be seen in glass from the deanery, now in St Andrew's chapel in the cathedral, on a shield held by an angel; others hold the arms of Henry VIII, Cardinal Wolsey and Bishop Nykke of Norwich. This glass presumably marks the final settlement in 1524–25 of the long and bitter dispute between the city and the cathedral priory, which was achieved through Wolsey's intervention, an interesting but by no means unique example of glass moving into the political sphere. Ferrour's guildhall window presented a salutary message in 'the story of the Corrupt Judge who was flayed alive for false judgement', with a descriptive text in English. It included the lines

> Lette all Men se, stedfast you be,
> Justyce do ye, or els loke, you fle.

This was both an admonition and a warning to those who sat in judgement in the mayoral council chamber that they avoid the fate of Sisamnes, the venal judge condemned by the Persian king, Cambyses, to be flayed alive. This well-known cautionary tale was, for example, the subject of two panel paintings executed in 1498 by Gerard David for the town hall in Bruges. Such 'justice pictures' adorned many town halls in the Netherlands and in Germany in the fifteenth and sixteenth centuries, and their appearance in the guildhall in Norwich attests to a strong and abiding Flemish influence in the city. This may be corroborated by the presence in the surviving glass of a small Flemish panel depicting a man pleading before a seated king, which seems to be a scene from this same story; the glass is dateable on style to the 1530s.[54] The adjacent north window was given by Robert Jannys, grocer and mayor in 1517 and 1524, and contained, in addition to his merchant's mark and the heraldry of his trade, a scene and text reminding the onlooker how death comes to all.[55] The two opposite windows came from two other leading dignitaries, Nicholas Sotherton (mayor in 1539) and Augustine Steward (mayor in 1534, 1546 and 1556). The first south window included a depiction of the Judgement of Solomon, another theme of especial significance to the civic officers who held their courts here.[56]

Steward had a series of six roundels (which may have been Flemish) illustrating the parable of the Good Samaritan in his house, which is a reminder of the importance of domestic glazing in the city in the fifteenth and sixteenth centuries.[57] The topic's theme of charity to the stranger was one not all of Norwich's rulers took to their hearts, but its didactic importance is unambiguous. Now in a south aisle window in the parish church of St George's Colegate, but probably of secular origin, is a fifteenth-century roundel depicting a man sheltering from the rain, one of a series on the popular medieval theme, often illustrated in books of hours, of the labours of the months (Plate 14). Similar series are known to have been made for domestic contexts and are now in museums or private ownership. One set made shortly before 1500 came from the old parsonage of St Michael Coslany, and another of early sixteenth-century date may have belonged to a house in this parish owned by Thomas Pykerell, mayor in 1525, 1533 and 1538. A series of the Nine Worthies, of which King David and Judas Maccabaeus are now in Marsham church, is also said to have been displayed there.[58] The inspiration for this latter series could have come from the residence of that famous warrior, Sir John Fastolf, in Pockthorpe, just outside Norwich, where the Nine Worthies were also to be seen, presumably made some time before his death in 1459. These fragmentary remains give a tantalising glimpse of the sumptuous decoration originally to be seen in late medieval houses in Norwich. Fastolf's elaborate glazing schemes at Caister Castle, near Yarmouth, must have been the talk of the county.[59]

The Reformation brought an end to the painting of religious imagery on glass in the city, but the craft has continued almost without a break to the present day. Heraldic glazing provided much work up to the eighteenth century, followed in the nineteenth by a resurgence stimulated firstly by the wholesale importation of medieval and renaissance glass from the Continent and later by the Gothic Revival.[60] Modern glaziers have concentrated mainly on the conservation of what is left of this rich heritage of glass-painting. As has been seen, it helps us in so many ways to understand the lives and aspirations of the men and women who commissioned and looked upon it.

6

Religious Practice

Norman Tanner

> All shall be well and all manner of things shall be well.
> God all-wisdom is our kindly mother.
> Thus was I learned that love is our Lord's meaning ... and in this love he hath made all things profitable to us.
>
> Julian of Norwich, *Revelations of Divine Love*[1]

Norwich's prominent place in medieval England is apparent throughout the first part of this book. This chapter seeks to bring together the various facets of Christianity in the city and to relate them more generally to the broader canvas of religious life in medieval Europe. Norwich was a remarkably religious city by the standards of western Christendom as a whole. It might, indeed, be possible to argue that it was Europe's *most* religious city. A few disclaimers are, however, required at the outset. In terms of quantity – the number of Christians, the number of churches and so forth – there is no suggestion that Norwich can be compared with, say, Paris or Venice or even London. Norwich was never one of the largest urban centres of medieval Europe in terms of population. On the other hand, Norwich was more than a provincial capital. It was a city of European standing and has a right to be compared with other such cities. It has been argued that the population reached a peak of around 25,000 or even more in the 1330s, rather than the previously proposed figures of about half that number.[2] Moreover, Norwich's close links with the Continent, especially the Low Countries, both geographically and through trade, meant that it was more 'European' than the other provincial capitals of medieval England: York, Coventry and Bristol. Indeed, one might say that late medieval England had two European cities: London and Norwich.

The argument, therefore, about Norwich being the most religious city in medieval Europe is not just qualitative: premised only on the intensity of religion in the city, irrespective of its size. It is based, rather, on a mixture of quality and quantity, so that Norwich's standing as a European city is an integral part of the argument. A parallel claim might be made for, say,

Siena in northern Italy: a city of similar importance and of exceptional religiosity.[3] The suggestion would not be regarded as outrageous if made for Siena and it bears examination for Norwich, too. The words 'most religious' also need some justification. Can we say that one community or country is *more* religious than another, varying in time and according to circumstances? It may seem foolish to ask such intimate questions at all, since they are surely answerable by God alone. The issue is, moreover, an inner one that is not susceptible to outer historical verification. My sympathies are somewhat with this view but not completely so. If it were wholly true, church history would lose much of its interest. Moreover, while our inner state is beyond, it is not wholly beyond: there seems some link between outer manifestations and inner reality. At least the following chapter proceeds upon this assumption.

At the pinnacle of religious fame, Norwich compared favourably with any other European city of the time, thanks to the star attraction of Julian of Norwich, the anchoress and mystic. Her single book, *Revelations or Showings of Divine Love*, surviving in a long and a short version, places her among the greatest mystical writers of all times and all religions. The love of God, the motherhood and feminine nature of God, her optimistic tone, epitomised in the words revealed to her, 'All shall be well and all manner of things shall be well',[4] sound well to modern ears and offer the hope of salvation for all people. Currently Julian may be the most popular of all medieval Christian mystics alongside Hildegard of Bingen. Every aspect of her theology and spirituality seems to have been explored.[5] Three critical editions of her *Revelations* have appeared in the last twenty-five years;[6] an anthology of excerpts from the *Revelations* has sold over 100,000 copies worldwide, and has seen translations into Japanese and Korean.[7] Other attractive features of Julian's spirituality have been identified: heaven is becoming our true selves; how our deficiencies are transformed into good rather than annihilated; God as a 'playful lover'; Julian's pastoral concern for people living in the world.[8]

Was Julian an isolated peak or part of a much larger mountain range? She did not appear unusual in her lifetime, rather being part of a large and flourishing tradition of hermits and anchorites in Norwich. Margery Kempe came from Lynn to seek her counsel and there is further evidence of her respected position within the religious life of the city; on the other hand, there is no evidence of interest in her writings or a special cult to her during her lifetime or immediately after death.[9] Her book of *Revelations* has come down to us through the almost chance survival of a handful of manuscripts, a single fifteenth-century one for the shorter version and a few from the seventeenth century for the longer.[10] It was only in the second half of the twentieth century that Julian suddenly achieved international fame. It might be argued that late medieval Norwich was unable to see a genius in its midst, or perhaps that Julian regarded her thoughts as so unusual that she sought to keep them secret. My preference is to think the quiet respect she enjoyed in her lifetime, combined with the exceptional veneration in which she is held today, indicate a remarkable woman who was representative of the city's deep Christianity.

Some fifty other hermits and anchorites are known to have lived in medieval Norwich: half a dozen of them in the late thirteenth and early fourteenth centuries, then a long gap until the appearance of Julian at the end of the fourteenth century, and the others in the fifteenth and early sixteenth centuries. The number, so far as is known, was substantially more than for any other city in medieval England, with the possible exception of much larger London, and seems remarkable by the standards of any European city. None of them has acquired a reputation in any way comparable to Julian's but the characters of several of them emerge from the records. They divided roughly equally between men and women; and while a number of them were priests or members of religious orders, both male and female, the majority were lay men and women. All the women were anchoresses, that is to say living in a cell, or 'anchorage', which was usually attached to a religious house or a parish church. While some of the men were similarly tied to an anchorage, hence called 'anchors', more of them were described as hermits, who, as well as providing various material services to the community, such as looking after a gate or bridge of the city, were free to wander.[11]

The most colourful of them was Thomas Scrope. Born shortly before 1400, possibly the grandson, legitimate or otherwise, of Richard le Scrope, first Baron Scrope of Bolton,[12] he became a friar at the Carmelite house in Norwich, but, according to John Bale, writing in the mid sixteenth century and himself once a friar there, he left the friary and was to be seen around 1425, 'clad in a hair shirt and a sack and girded with an iron chain, preaching the gospel of the kingdom of God and proclaiming that the new Jerusalem, the bride of the Lamb, was about to come down from heaven'. Bale believed that Scrope's eccentric behaviour upset his religious superior, Thomas Netter, the prior provincial of the English Carmelites, and that a frightened Scrope returned to his friary in Norwich, this time as an anchor. He remained there for some twenty years, during which time he appears to have written several books. He then reverted to an active life. He went to Rhodes as a papal legate, was consecrated bishop of Dromore in Ireland, and acted as a suffragan bishop in the diocese of Norwich for some twenty-eight years. Finally, according to Bale, he spent each Friday of the last years of his life as a barefoot itinerant preacher in the diocese, dying in 1492 aged almost a hundred.[13]

Another character was Richard Ferneys. He lived as a hermit in the city for many years in the mid fifteenth century, probably moving his residence to different places there and ending as 'hermit of Newbridge', one of the bridges over the Wensum, though whether he was responsible for its upkeep is unclear. At least in his early years as a recluse he may have journeyed outside Norwich. Thus, in 1429, in the earliest known reference to him as a hermit, he was bequeathed the large sum of £40 – the approximate equivalent of eight years' annual income for a building worker – by Robert Baxter, a former mayor of the city, 'to make a pilgrimage for me to Rome, going round there fifteen times in a great circle, and also to Jerusalem, doing in both places as a true pilgrim does'.[14] We are not told whether he accepted the challenge, but Baxter presumably had some knowledge of the kind of things he might be prepared to undertake. Towards the end of his life, Ferneys himself made a will that provides a glimpse of his comfortable living conditions and of the society of other hermits and anchorites with whom he maintained contact. His bequests totalled several pounds in money and a variety of household items, and his beneficiaries included two attendants – one being described as 'my boy' (*puer meus*) and the other, a woman, as 'my guardian or nurse' (*custos mea*), as well as several other hermits and anchorites in the city.[15] These hermits and anchorites were appreciated and encouraged by the citizenry: a tribute to Norwich's support for unusual forms of religious life. One in five surviving wills made by local people in the fifteenth and early sixteenth centuries contained bequests to them, substantially more than in London and other cities.[16]

Notable, too, is the presence in Norwich of two or three communities closely resembling continental beguinages, which are the only such communities identifiable in medieval England. An unknown number of women, variously described as 'sisters living together' and 'sisters dedicated to chastity' are recorded as residents of a tenement in St Swithin's parish from 1427 to 1444; a second group of three women, similarly designated as 'sisters' or 'poor women', 'under a vow of chastity' and 'dedicated to God', occupied another tenement nearby in St Laurence's parish from about 1442 to 1472; there may have been a third group in the parish of St Peter Hungate at about the same time. Although the words 'beguines' or 'beguinages' do not appear in the records, there are striking resemblances, strengthened by the frequent references to the tenement in which the second group lived as 'recently belonging to John Asger': he was probably the merchant from

Bruges of that name who became mayor of Norwich in 1426. The tenement may have been a gift from him to the women, thus linking Norwich with the Low Countries, a centre of the beguine movement.[17]

The hermits, anchorites and communities resembling beguinages are worthy of attention for several reasons. They form one of the most notable features of religion in the city and constitute an important reason why it may be considered an exceptionally religious place; in this respect Norwich surpassed all other English cities.[18] The support given to them by the citizens as well as the fact that they represented a 'lay' movement ties them into popular religion at a grass-roots level. They situate religion in Norwich within a European and wider world, which encompasses Thomas Scrope's departure for the island of Rhodes, the bequest to Richard Ferneys for him to go on pilgrimage to Rome and Jerusalem, possible links between beguines in Norwich and Bruges and the international fame of Julian of Norwich today.

Another remarkable feature of the religion of medieval Norwich – the one that probably strikes visitors most today – is the parish churches (Map 5). The first decisive development seems to have occurred sometime in the eleventh century. The Domesday Survey of 1086 recorded between forty-nine and fifty-four chapels (*capellae*) and churches (*ecclesiae*) in the city, the majority of which were the forty-three chapels that, it says, 'the burgesses hold' (*tenent burgenses*).[19] Subsequently, in ways and at times that are obscure, these churches and chapels developed into the approximately sixty parish churches that the city contained in the mid thirteenth century. Thereafter there was a gradual decline in numbers – two churches were absorbed into the Dominican and Augustinian friaries, some were pulled down, others were reduced to the status of chapels-of-ease – but we can say with some confidence that in 1520 the number stood at forty-six. To a certain extent the four friaries (Franciscan, Dominican, Carmelite and Augustinian), with their large churches, preachers and religious services, challenged the role of the parish churches. Nevertheless, the small drop in numbers from about 1250 represents a development rather than a decline in importance. Between the fourteenth and early sixteenth century almost every parish church in the city that was not demolished was extensively rebuilt on a grander scale. Larger buildings meant that fewer were needed, especially following the dramatic slump in population occasioned by plague. Certainly these new churches, as any visitor to Norwich can still see, must have been large enough to accommodate the citizens; except perhaps for a short time in the early fourteenth century, if the higher estimate of a population of around 25,000 in the 1330s is correct.[20]

How remarkable were Norwich's parishes and parish churches? For England the number was high but not wholly exceptional. London had over twice as many for a much larger population, while York and Lincoln had only slightly fewer than Norwich for somewhat fewer residents. Yet the number of parish churches in English towns – principally those that were already major towns in the eleventh and twelfth centuries, when parish churches were being built in great numbers throughout the country – was notably high, proportional to population, by the standards of Europe as a whole. Venice, for example, one of the largest cities in western Christendom, had about seventy parishes; and Bruges, at one time the largest city in the Low Countries, with about 41,000 inhabitants in the 1340s, had only twelve during the late middle ages, though some of these boasted more than one imposing parish church. While it would be foolish to push the argument to the point of claiming that the number of parish churches in Norwich was wholly exceptional, it was nevertheless, by any standards, in terms of the city's population, very high.[21]

In terms of quality, too, the record is impressive; the churches were not empty shells devoid of purpose. The evidence to this effect comes mostly from the late middle ages. When the bishop of Norwich made an official visitation of the city's parish churches in 1492, he found at least one priest serving almost every church and a total of no fewer than eighty-nine serving the forty-six churches altogether.[22] And when the archdeacon of Norwich undertook a similar inspection in 1368, he noted in almost all of them a striking quantity of items for the celebration of the liturgy and virtually all the service-books that archbishops Winchelsey and Reynolds of Canterbury had regarded as obligatory for parish churches in the southern province to possess. St Peter Mancroft, the largest and grandest of the parish churches, had the following collection, mostly for the celebration of the eucharist: ten complete sets of vestments for a priest, deacon and subdeacon, each set usually comprising a cope, chasuble, two tunicles and three albs; fourteen other sets of vestments for single priests, five other copes and four capes for boys; nine frontespieces for altars and large quantities of altar linen as well as carpets and pillows; eight chalices, two cups for hosts and a pyx; dishes, cruets, candlesticks, (hand) bells, crosses, four banners, four thuribles, an aspersorium, a vessel for chrism oil, a mitre and a pastoral staff; and various service-books, including seven missals, six breviaries and three psalters. The collections of many other churches parallelled on a smaller scale that of St Peter's, where in the early sixteenth century an even more lavish collection of service-books, vestments, plate and other ornaments was recorded.[23]

Evidence of lay piety also comes from the wills of the citizens, which survive in significant numbers from 1370 onwards. More testators made bequests to parish churches than to any other religious institution: 95 per cent of the laity left something to at least one parish church. Some bequests were of large sums of money or costly items, indicating special interest in the welfare of a particular church. For example, John Coppyng, a mercer, left to St Andrew's in 1430 the money needed to buy a missal costing up to twenty marks (£13 6s. 8d.) and a vestment costing up to £20; John Terry, a former mayor, left forty marks (£26 13s. 4d.) to St John's Maddermarket in 1524 to buy a silver and gilt cross; John Gilbert, another former mayor, left the munificent sum of one hundred marks to St Andrew's to buy a vestment or an ornament. Alice Carre left to St Stephen's parish church her best coral beads to beautify the images of various saints on their feast-days and her small coral beads to be 'daily about the image of St Anne'; John Basse wanted his best tippet to be decorated at his own expense with buttons and tassels and given to St Martin of Coslany 'to cover the sacrament on dead days and interment days'. Testamentary evidence also helps to explain and document the extensive rebuilding of the city's parish churches in the late middle ages. Bartholomew Appleyard, for example, left £20 in 1386 to lead the roof of his parish church, St Andrew's; Richard Browne, a former mayor, left forty marks in 1461 to build the steeple of Holy Cross, so that he might be 'remembered together with my brother Sygrim [alderman Ralph Segryme] and all my good friends'. Robert Pert left £20 to the *economi* of St Peter Mancroft in 1445 to pay for a new gable at the east end of the church; this was in the middle of the period during which the church was completely rebuilt. It is interesting that he entrusted the money to parishioners, not to the clergy. John Reynolds, a grocer, offered the parishioners of St Andrew's £6 13s. 4d. in 1499 for a window, if they built a new church. He too expected the initiative for constructing the church to come from the parishioners and entrusted his money to them rather than to the clergy. But it would be wrong to see much of a divide between the laity and the priesthood in this matter; the parish clergy made plenty of similar bequests to the churches for which they had been responsible.[24]

These bequests touch on the wider issues of the art and architecture of Norwich's parish churches, which were of pressing concern to the elite of the medieval city. Suffice it to say here that St Peter Mancroft surely rivals in beauty and elegance any parish church anywhere, while the surviving panels of the two late medieval retables depicting scenes from the life of Christ which are now preserved in the cathedral – the so-called Despenser retable (Plate 15), kept in St Luke's chapel, and the panels formerly in the parish church of St Michael-at-Plea, now preserved in St Saviour's chapel

– provide a glimpse of the high level of artistic achievement in the city.[25] This was placed unreservedly at the disposal of its religious institutions.

Any city that claims – or whose claims are put forward – to be the most religious city in medieval Europe requires a tradition of intellectual eminence. Norwich's claims are stronger than might first appear. There was no medieval university in the city, but recent research suggests that too much importance should not be accorded to Oxford and Cambridge during this period, and that intellectual life in late medieval England had many foci.[26] London, for example, with its Inns of Court, the royal court, houses of religious orders and other intellectual attractions, provided some such centres outside the two universities; Norwich and York, each with four friaries and a cathedral, a large secular clergy, an educated laity and many schools, offered others.[27] The Franciscan friary in Norwich attracted students from abroad including the future pope Alexander V; conversely the cathedral priory exported its learned monk Adam Easton to Rome where he became a cardinal.[28]

The number of beneficed parish clergy – rectors and vicars – who are recorded as university graduates when they were appointed rose markedly towards the end of the middle ages: from 8 per cent (twelve out of 158) between 1370 and 1449 to 32 per cent (twenty-three out of seventy-one) between 1450 and 1499 and 42 per cent (twenty-five out of sixty) between 1500 and 1532. The evidence for the unbeneficed clergy – parish chaplains and stipendiary and chantry priests, who together made up the large majority of the secular clergy of the city – is much scarcer but it is clear that, while university graduates among them were much fewer than among the beneficed clergy, they were not unknown.[29]

Of the books of the secular clergy, the most intimate and revealing picture comes from the inventory of the goods of John Baker. He was probably the rector of two churches in the city, St John Maddermarket and All Saints Ber Street; he appears not to have been a university graduate and died, probably in middle age and still rector of both churches, in 1518. The inventory, drawn up after his death, mentions twenty-six books by name and 'twenty other small books'. The biggest group of the identified books consisted of legal works, mostly of canon law: the *Decrees*, the *Decretals* and *Sext*, which comprised the three main parts of the basic text of medieval canon law, the *Corpus iuris canonici*; a book by William Lyndwood (d. 1446), probably his work on English canon law called *Provinciale*; commentaries on canon law by three foreigners, Bernard of Compostella (d. 1267) from Spain, William Durandus (d. 1296) from France and Italy, and Panormitanus (d. 1445) from Italy; and dictionaries of legal terms and abbreviations. Baker clearly took his parochial responsibilities very seriously, especially when it came to preaching. There were five collections of sermons by, probably, the English Carmelite friar, Richard Maidstone (d. 1396), John Fisher (d. 1535), bishop of Rochester, two Dominican friars, Vincent Ferrer (d. 1419) from France and Johannes Herolt (d. 1468) from Germany, and an anonymous collection as well. The remaining books were *Legenda aurea*, the famous collection of saints' lives by James de Voragine (d. 1298), archbishop of Genoa; two other works by German Dominicans, Albert the Great (d. 1280) and John Nider (d. 1438); a Latin-English dictionary; a breviary in two volumes; and a Bible, though it is unclear whether this was the Latin vulgate or an English translation. The books indicate conservative tastes and a keen interest in the law of the church. At the same time, the collections of sermons, in particular, suggest a pastorally minded priest; and the number of works by foreigners reflects an outlook that was far from insular.[30]

Baker's is the only surviving inventory listing the goods of a secular priest of pre-Reformation Norwich. Since no books *at all* were mentioned in his will we may reasonably conclude that ownership was presumably much wider among other members of the clergy than the surviving testamentary evidence suggests. Books mentioned in these wills are, even so, quite numerous and we can say, in brief, that they reflect conservative tastes, like Baker's. On the other hand, many works were comparatively recent classics in their field; and the number by authors from other European countries is again impressive.[31] Maybe, the secular clergy were also able to make use of the libraries of the cathedral priory, the friaries and other religious houses.

Wills also provide some evidence of the books owned by the laity, though here, too, ownership was probably more extensive than the wills suggest. One wonders, again, whether some testators drew upon the resources of religious houses or of the secular clergy, such as the learned masters of St Giles's hospital, many of whom were graduates and who maintained close relations with members of the city's ruling elite. Most of the books were standard liturgical works, chiefly missals, breviaries, primers and psalters. The only Bible mentioned before the end of Henry VIII's reign was that left in 1542 by William Cannered, a butcher: it is unclear whether it was a Latin or English version. Three women, all widows, making their wills towards the end of the fifteenth century, owned interesting collections that included works by or about saints and mystics from abroad (Plate 16). Katherine Kerre left a 'book of St Katherine' (of Alexandria, or Siena, or Genoa?); Isabel Liston bequeathed to her daughter a 'book of Saint Margaret's life' (Margaret of Antioch or of Scotland?)

and an 'English book called *Partonope*', presumably a version of the twelfth-century French romance, *Partonopeus de Blois*. Margaret Purdans left an 'English psalter' to a priest and her 'small psalter' to her son. Her taste in reading matter is further reflected in her gift of two books to convents of nuns: 'Le doctrine of the herte', which was probably a translation of *De doctrina cordis*, the treatise addressed to a woman on how to lead a devout life usually ascribed to bishop Grosseteste of Lincoln, and an 'English book of Saint Bridget' (probably containing the prayers and mystical writings of the popular Swedish saint). To a certain Alice Barley Margaret bequeathed 'a book called Hylton', almost certainly by the fourteenth-century English mystic, Walter Hilton.[32]

Books were, of course, only one way through which the citizens could grow in knowledge of Christianity. Other ways came through hermits and anchorites living in the city; and by attendance at parish churches with their regular liturgical round and other communal activities. Hopefully, too, the laity benefited from the learning of the clergy and vice versa. There was also instruction through preaching. We should not, however, forget that religious music also helped to inspire belief, for singing was at the centre of the liturgy, including the divine office sung in the cathedral and various religious houses, not least St Giles's hospital, which possessed a sizeable choir trained in polyphony and no fewer than three organs (Figure 22). Chantries, which were numerous in Norwich, could offer plainsong and other, more elaborate, forms of music: St Peter Mancroft, with its many chantries, both perpetual and temporary, may have provided an almost daily concert of religious music.[33] Taken together, and avoiding an undue concentration upon either book-learning or the importance of Oxford and Cambridge, the evidence of Norwich suggests a deep and creative knowledge of Christianity, one that points to an exceptionally religious city in the best sense.

Pilgrimages were both a form of devotion – through penance or thanksgiving or petition – and a way of encountering the wider Christian world. Robert Baxter's legacy to the hermit Richard Ferneys to make a pilgrimage for him to Rome and Jerusalem is noted above. Several other citizens left bequests in their wills for vicarious pilgrimages. Many of the shrines were in East Anglia. Thomas Oudolff, for example, a priest who was a widower, instructed his executors to hire one man to go 'naked in his shirt' to the Holy Rood of Beccles and another to go barefoot to Our Lady of Walsingham, which, along with St Thomas of Canterbury, was the most popular shrine in England. Abroad the most favoured destination was Rome, where the priest-pilgrim was often instructed to say masses for the testator and

FIGURE 22. Late fourteenth-century processional from the Great Hospital, now unique in providing coloured diagrams of liturgical ceremonies (the priests are seen from above as tonsured heads). The name Holdiche records a post-Dissolution owner after the hospital library was destroyed, BL, Add. MS 5734, fo. 90r. (*British Library*)

his family and friends. The English hospice in Rome was host to a number of pilgrims from Norwich: an average of some two a year in those years between 1479 and 1514 for which records survive. Edmund Brown, a merchant who made his will in 1446, followed Robert Baxter in his interest in long pilgrimages. He instructed his executors to hire one man for seven shillings to go on foot to St Thomas of Canterbury, another for five marks to journey to St James of Compostella, and a third, for a sum to be negotiated, to go to the shrine of the Holy Blood at Wilsnack in Germany.[34]

Norwich, principally its cathedral, was also a centre for pilgrimages. Margery Kempe came to the cathedral to 'offer' there both before and after her long journey to the Holy Land.[35] The account rolls of the cathedral priory record donations to various shrines there from the late thirteenth to the early sixteenth centuries. A steady stream of offerings 'to the high altar' peaked at about £120 for each of several years around the Jubilee of 1400, when the priory obtained a special papal indulgence. Smaller sums were collected at the shrines of St Mary and St William and of two bishops of Norwich, Walter Suffield (d. 1257) and John Salmon (d. 1325). Richard Caistor, vicar of St Stephen's parish in Norwich from 1402 until his death in 1420, enjoyed a reputation for holiness that drew pilgrims to his grave from as far afield as Kent.[36] Since the monks owned the living, they presumably shared in its success, although by far the most important and lucrative of their late medieval shrines was at St Leonard's priory, a cell of the mother house just outside the city walls to the east of Bishop's bridge. Martin Heal has recently analysed the dramatic rise in revenues (reaching a remarkable total of £43 in 1454–55) apparent during the fifteenth century, as floods of pilgrims came to venerate a lavishly decorated statue of the patron saint. Nor did visitors simply offer a token penny: from Sir John Fastolf came a piece of crystal containing silver relics; while the Yorkist knight, Sir Andrew Ogard, presented a silver image of a boy, perhaps an *ex voto* for his own sick son. An image of the earl of Suffolk also hung there in 1425, along with an impressive array of jewellery.[37]

Craft guilds and pious confraternities formed another notable feature of the city's religion. Between the mid thirteenth and early sixteenth centuries – the golden age of these associations in Norwich as elsewhere – approaching a hundred crafts and trades in the city are mentioned as having their own guilds (or taking part in guild-like activities). In addition, records indicate about half that number of pious confraternities, which were usually attached to parish churches and religious houses rather than to crafts or trades.[38] The primary role of the guilds was the economic, social and political regulation of their respective crafts or trades, but they also had important religious functions. A central feature was the annual 'day' of the guild, usually the feast day of the saint to which it was dedicated, comprising a mixture of social and spiritual activities: a mass for living and dead members, other devotions and finally a fraternal banquet. Many guilds made provision for members in need, not least so far as funerals and obits were concerned. They were most visible, however, when taking part in various civic and religious processions. Ordinances issued by the city government in 1449 ruled that: 'All tho persones that shall be clad in the clothing of craftis ... shall at all tymes be charged to all walkings [and] ridings to the worship of the advow [patron] of the craft on the principall day.' There is additional evidence of communal processions undertaken by all the guilds, together with the mayor, sheriffs and aldermen, on major feast days, notably All Saints, Christmas, Epiphany and Corpus Christi.[39]

By the eve of the Reformation the guilds of the city were performing a cycle of twelve mystery plays on Whit (Pentecost) Monday. As at York, each play was probably acted several times in different parts of the city, being drawn round on a movable float or cart. The twelve plays in the cycle were: *The Creation of the World*; *Hell*; *Paradise* (the only play whose text survives); *Abel and Cain*; *Noah's Ship* (Plate 17); *Abraham and Isaac*; *Moses and Aaron with the Children of Israel and Pharaoh with his Knights*; *The Conflict of David and Goliath*; *The Birth of Christ with Shepherds and the Three Kings of Cologne*; *The Baptism of Christ*; *The Resurrection*; and *The Holy Ghost*.[40] It has been suggested that these plays provided the inspiration for the masons who carved the stone bosses in the nave of the cathedral. They certainly did much to transmit knowledge of the Bible to ordinary men and women.[41]

Many of the activities of the pious confraternities appear similar to those of the guilds, though information about most of them is fragmentary and extends little beyond knowledge of their existence. The most famous was St George's, which was given a royal charter in 1417 and was effectively united to the city government in 1452, so that the outgoing mayor of the city automatically became the head, or alderman, of the confraternity. Its account rolls, which survive from 1420 to 1547, give details of its large membership, numbering some two hundred in the early sixteenth century, the material and spiritual help it afforded to members, living and dead, and its celebrations on the feast of St George. The latter comprised mass in the cathedral, an elaborate procession and pageant depicting the exploits of their saint and a lavish banquet.[42] Norwich was not exceptional in its guilds and confraternities. They did not compare in importance with the livery companies, craft guilds and confraternities of London, still less with the Scuole of Venice.[43] They show, nevertheless, that Norwich participated in this important aspect of medieval urban religion in a way that was appropriate to its standing as a major provincial capital.

'The second commandment is this: You shall love your neighbour as yourself' (Mark 12: 31). Charity towards one's neighbour is an integral part of most religions, including Christianity. Norwich boasted many charitable institutions, which were supplemented by private philanthropic initiatives on a grand scale.[44] The evidence of wills reinforces the strong sense of personal piety and social obligation already described. Almost two in every five testators from the city, in the late middle ages, left one or more bequests to the sick-houses (originally leper houses) just outside the gates – usually a bequest to each house or to each individual living in them – while more than one in three gave to St Paul's hospital. These figures appear substantially higher than those for late medieval London, where fewer than a fifth of testators remembered a hospital. Sixteen per cent of testators from Norwich left a bequest to prisoners in the guildhall or in the castle. Many set aside the residue of their estate, or part of it, to be disposed for their soul 'in alms to the poor or in works of mercy and charity'; some left money for the poor to pray for them or to attend their funeral services. The bequests of two testators stand out for their scale and imagination. Robert Jannys, a wealthy grocer and former mayor who made his will in 1530, wanted a penny to be given to each of eighty poor persons every Friday for twenty years – a bequest that, if fulfilled, would have amounted to almost £350 (Plate 21). He also bequeathed £20 for the marriages of 'maidens', presumably dowries for poor brides, to be distributed at the rate of 20s. each. The most radical approach came from Richard Caistor, the vicar whose reputation for holiness is discussed above. Apart from a bequest of £10 for buying two antiphonaries for his parish church, he wanted all his wealth to be given to the poor on the grounds that 'the goods of the Church, according to canon law, belong to the poor'.[45]

It is now time to return to the suggestion that Norwich was the most religious city in medieval Europe – by focusing on two points: the apparent absence of heresy in the city and, secondly, the harmony of old and new. Heresy, at least when understood as organised dissent within the Christian community, appears to have been almost non-existent in England before the appearance of John Wyclif and Lollardy in the late fourteenth century. Thereafter England, along with Hussite Bohemia, was home to the most serious dissenting movement anywhere in western Christendom. The apparent failure of Lollardy, a vibrant reform movement within Christianity, to make much impression in Norwich is remarkable. The city was never a centre of its adherents as were London, Coventry, Bristol, Leicester and some other towns of southern and middle England.

The most crucial evidence for this relative absence comes from the records of the prosecution of Lollards conducted by Bishop Alnwick of Norwich throughout his diocese between 1428 and 1431. They form the fullest records of heresy trials anywhere in late medieval England and, of the fifty or so individuals who were convicted at them and whose places of residence were mentioned (only a handful were not), only two came from Norwich: Thomas Wade, a tailor, and the wife of a certain John Weston. A few other comments made at the trials suggest that some citizens had been influenced by Lollardy.[46]

Either side of this prosecution there are only a few isolated hints of heresy in the city before the start of the English Reformation. A somewhat vaguely worded complaint from the cathedral priory in about 1360, that the friars of Norwich were preaching 'against the norm of sound doctrine and the liberty of the Church', probably refers to their criticisms of the Benedictine monks rather than to more serious heresy.[47] John Bale, the early Protestant reformer and erstwhile Carmelite, maintained that Richard Caistor, the vicar of St Stephen's, was a Wycliffite, but there is no evidence to substantiate this claim, beyond his evident austerity and love for the poor. The martyrologist John Foxe said that a priest from Norwich called Thomas was degraded from the priesthood and burnt in the village of Eckeles (almost certainly Eccles in south Norfolk) in 1510, presumably for heresy. Francis Blomefield claimed (without citing any sources) that Thomas Bilney, who was also sent to the stake for his evangelical activities, was a native of Norfolk, probably of Norwich or East Bilney, and Foxe recounts that he had preached in Norfolk before his arrest by Bishop Tunstall of London in 1527. Bilney was, indeed, arrested for the last time at Norwich in 1531, when Thomas More asserted that he had 'infected various people of the city before'. His only identifiable disciple there was an anchoress attached to the Dominican friary, probably Katherine Mann: he gave her two controversial works by Tyndale – *Obedience of a Christian Man* and his translation of the New Testament – but said, to calm her conscience, that he had never taught her anything heretical.[48]

There is no reason to think that the apparent absence of heresy results only from a scarcity of evidence. Certainly the diocese of Norwich had a succession of bishops noted for their concern about Lollardy: Henry Despenser (1370–1406), John Wakeryng (1415–25), William Alnwick (1426–36), Thomas Brown (1436–45) and Richard Nykke (1501–35), in particular.[49] They might be expected to have been especially vigilant towards their capital city. The fact, however, that Lollardy was comparatively strong in other parts of East Anglia, shown notably by the trials of 1428–31, makes its relative absence from Norwich all the more remarkable.[50] One line of argument might be that Lollardy was suppressed rather than rejected, that fear kept it out of the city. It is true that many of those found guilty in the 1428–31 trials, though from outside, suffered within it: three were burnt to death as relapsed heretics; others were ordered to be beaten or to undergo 'solemn penance' there.[51] In the early sixteenth century, moreover, several people from other parts of the diocese who were convicted of heresy were executed in Norwich.[52] Did fear of punishment restrain potential Lollards or simply force the movement underground? There may be some truth in the argument but it does not seem an adequate explanation.

The more likely eventuality is that, because religion in Norwich was so rich and diverse that it catered for the tastes of almost everyone, the inhabitants did not feel the need for, or the attraction of, Lollardy as they might have in a more spiritually barren landscape. How then is the success of the Reformation in the city and Norwich's subsequent nonconformist tradition to be explained? This is a big question that is difficult to answer. It is true that there were outside factors, notably the arrival of the Strangers, some five thousand Protestants from the Low Countries, in the late sixteenth century.[53] But there may be unease with the argument that the Reformation was largely imposed on Norwich from above or from outside, overwhelmingly against the wishes of the citizens, as some scholars have argued for the country as a whole.[54] Late medieval Norwich was an unusually religious city and there was a great change in the forms of worship as the Reformation progressed. It rapidly made the transition from a kind of almost Baroque, high-church Christianity to becoming a puritan stronghold. If Christianity, or religion more generally, is regarded as something static, then this change is very difficult to explain. If, on the other hand, religion is envisaged as more ongoing and developing, changes of outward form will cause much less surprise; a very religious community will, and should, grow and change in this way while remaining deeply religious. Indeed, to remain static would indicate a lack of depth to the faith.[55]

The second point is the remarkable harmony or blending of old and new in the religion of medieval Norwich. Or, to extend the point further, the way in which the people of the city were able to maintain both creativity and continuity in their religion, much to suit all tastes, preserving depth and variety, while also achieving relative harmony and unity. This genius constitutes an important reason for Norwich to be considered medieval Europe's most religious city.

We should not, however, ignore the other side of the coin. What about the assault of 1272, when the citizens attacked the cathedral priory, looted and burned it and killed some thirteen of the priory's servants and tenants? Tension between city and priory persisted, acute at times, and erupted again in 'Gladman's Insurrection' in 1453, though on this occasion nobody was killed.[56] There was, too, the great blot on the city's reputation regarding its Jewish population. In 1144 the death of a young apprentice skinner of the city, William, led to accusations, almost certainly false, that some Jews had ritually crucified him. It was the first time this kind of story, later known as the blood libel, received widespread notice in England and thereby Norwich became instrumental in the development of anti-Semitism both at home and abroad. Attacks on Jews occurred in Norwich, as in many English towns, in 1190, and they were finally expelled from the city, as from the rest of England, exactly a century later.[57] At a different level, the fullest recorded visitation of the city's parishes in the middle ages, that by the bishop of Norwich in 1492, provides evidence of considerable lay absenteeism from the mass. Nine men and women were accused of not attending their parish churches on Sundays and feast-days. Three publicans were charged with keeping their taverns open during divine service. Of one woman it was alleged that 'she observes an evil custom with various people from neighbouring households, who sit with her and drink during the time of service'. At another visitation in 1430, more wilful obstinacy had been alleged against two men from Catton in the suburbs of the city: 'They deride divine service and are unwilling to hear mass on feast-days, chattering continuously and obstructing the service.' These and other visitations, along with court records, document various cases of sexual immorality and bad behaviour on the part of both laity and clergy.[58]

This shadow side certainly existed, though it has a context. The citizens' disputes with the cathedral priory involved economic, legal and political issues more than religious ones, and there were good day-to-day relations between the two sides as well as sporadic conflicts. An illuminating snapshot of cordiality is provided by an account roll of the priory's cellarer for the year 1431–32, which records payments for 'minstrels of the city and other players performing before the lord prior, the mayor of the city and others on the day of the banquet at Christmas'. A Christmas dinner was held then and in other years, bringing together both the priory and the city government. In the case of the visitations, it is noticeable that most complaints came from the laity: rather than giving vent to anticlericalism, they wanted better standards to be observed both by themselves and by individual members of the clergy. Nothing suggests, moreover, notably low standards in Norwich compared with other towns and cities. The attacks on Jews and their expulsion must be seen in the sad context of anti-Semitism throughout western Christendom; they were not peculiar to

Norwich. Intolerance is a great danger of religious fervour, yet the latter's more positive aspects should be appreciated, notwithstanding this inherent weakness. It may be counted to the city's credit, moreover, that the cult of St William, with its encouragement of anti-Semitism, appears to have been quickly cold-shouldered by the citizens.[59]

The main argument in favour of the harmony of old and new must surely be the impressive amount of positive proof. The two most remarkable features are the parishes and the hermits and anchorites. The number of parishes and the ways they developed, remaining at the centre of the city's religious life, provide good evidence of the strength of popular religion. The remarkable community of hermits and anchorites shows the imagination of the city in its religion. In these and many other respects Norwich was a leader in Europe, not just in England. Indeed, it is the coming together of so many notable features that makes Christianity in medieval Norwich so very striking and of such absorbing interest.

One other feature demands attention: that is, the number of priests and members of religious orders in the city. It may seem a strange topic with which to conclude, since the clergy, both secular and regular, are sometimes seen as forming a discrete clerical establishment at odds with lay piety, almost oppressive of true religion. But this is largely a misconception: the clergy are better seen as an extension of lay piety than as being opposed to it. After all, priests and religious spent the first twenty or so years of their existence as lay people, before they entered upon their new ways of life. Criticisms of the laity against the clergy – including those made in Norwich – were nearly always that the latter were not priestly and religious enough, that they remained too attached to their former ways of lay life, not that they were too clerical and distant.

The most complete statistics for priests and men in religious orders in Norwich come from the bishop's visitation of the city in 1492. Eighty-nine priests were recorded as being attached to the forty-six parish churches; about twenty-seven more belonged to the colleges of secular priests or held various ecclesiastical offices; forty-six monks lived in the cathedral priory; and an average of perhaps thirty friars might be found in each of the four friaries, which were not included in the visitation. The total thus stands at almost 300 priests and male religious.[60] This means that, if a figure of about 10,000 for the total late fifteenth-century population of the city is accepted, then over 5 per cent of the male population of the city, and a much greater proportion of the adult men, were priests or members of religious orders. For other periods of time the evidence is much less complete, but it looks as though the proportion of priests and male religious to the total population of the city remained much the same, the population peaking in the

11. The east end of Norwich cathedral, *c.* 1876. (*N. Batcock and the School of World Art Studies, UEA*)

12. Stained glass depiction of Beatrix of Valkenburg, *c.* 1290–1300, attributed to the church of the Norwich Greyfriars. (*Burrell Collection, Glasgow*)

13. Stained glass of *c.* 1453, re-set in the central east window of the guildhall council chamber. (*National Monuments Record*)

14. Stained-glass roundel depicting one of the labours of the months, 1460–80, in a south aisle window of the church of St George Tombland. (*Dennis King*)

15. The Despenser retable, 1370–1406, was probably made for the refurbished sanctuary of Norwich cathedral, and was almost certainly the work of local craftsmen. The heraldry around the frame commemorates those who contributed to the building fund as well as the picture. (*Dean and Chapter of Norwich Cathedral*)

16. Late medieval alabaster of female saints, including Margaret, the patron saint of women in childbirth (with dragon), in the church of St Peter Mancroft. (*Carole Rawcliffe*)

17. Fifteenth-century stone roof boss of Noah's ark in Norwich cathedral nave. Depicting a sequence of biblical events from the creation to the last judgement, these lively carvings were influenced by the mystery plays performed by the trade and craft guilds of Norwich. The tale of Noah naturally appealed to the fishmongers. (*Dean and Chapter of Norwich Cathedral*)

18. Fifteenth-century roof boss of Adam and Eve in Norwich cathedral nave. Congregations throughout the city were constantly reminded of the consequences of the Fall, as were the crowds who watched the annual cycle of mystery plays. (*Dean and Chapter of Norwich Cathedral*)

19. Spandrel in the fifteenth-century roof beams of Dragon Hall, *c.* 1430. Built by the wealthy alderman, Robert Toppes, the hall not only served to advertise his personal wealth and status, but also the authority of the guild of St George. (*Len Riches*)

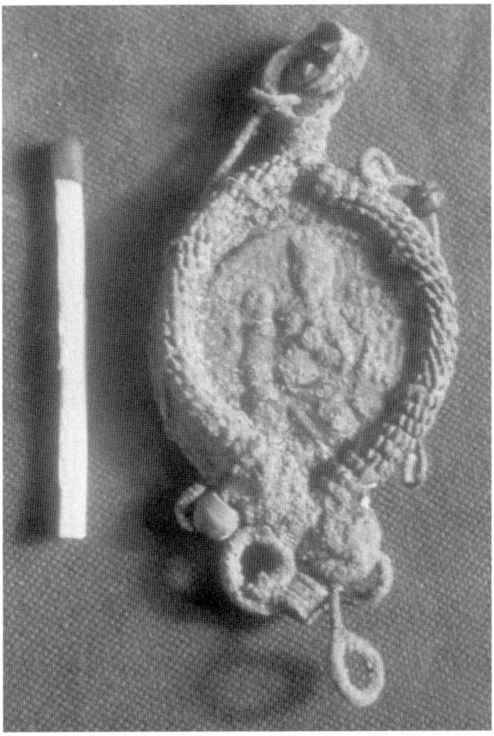

20. Late medieval pilgrim badge from the shrine of the *sancta roba* in Cologne, unearthed during an excavation in Pottergate, Norwich. (*Norwich Castle Museum and Art Gallery*)

21. Alderman Robert Jannys (d. 1530), the richest Norwich merchant of his day, with Death as a tipstaff, from a series of civic portraits in the Norwich Blackfriars. The verse, eliciting thanks for his good works, originally appeared below his shrouded image in a stained glass window, now lost, in the guildhall council chamber. (*Norwich Castle Museum and Art Gallery*)

early fourteenth century, falling sharply after the Black Death and recurrences of the plague, and slowly recovering from the middle of the fifteenth century.[61]

Nor was Norwich the home of an alien clerical population, in the way that Chaucer and Langland described London as a magnet attracting ambitious priests from outside the city.[62] The evidence of the birthplace of ordinands recorded in the episcopal registers indicates that Norwich was producing roughly as many secular priests as were living in the city. Added to this is the large number of young men who were mentioned in their parents' wills as being priests or members of religious orders. Between 10 and 11 per cent of all the sons mentioned were so described, and even these figures understate the true situation, since they do not include children who became priests or entered religious orders after their parents made their wills. These testators came predominantly from the upper ranks of Norwich society. That such a high proportion of their sons (and daughters) entered the church shows that the older and more institutional forms of religion still had considerable appeal for a class of young men that one might expect to have produced its fair share of radicals. Here too was a blending of old and new, a certain harmony between the institutional and charismatic. The proportion of sons opting for an ecclesiastical career showed no decline on the eve of the Reformation, indeed it was slightly higher between 1490 and 1532 than between 1370 and 1489. Some of these home-grown clergy, it seems, stayed in Norwich while the majority lived and ministered elsewhere.[63]

It is perhaps fitting to end on a topic – the value of the priesthood and of life in a religious order – that was as much debated in the middle ages as it is today. Then, as now, men and women argued over the nature of true religion. Ending with men may cause regret. On the other hand, the chapter began with the anchoress Julian of Norwich, who today is by far the best known figure, religious or otherwise, to have lived within the medieval walls. She, pre-eminently, illustrates that the religious phenomenon of medieval Norwich was as feminine as it was masculine: a fact supported by much other evidence. It obviously cannot be *proved* that Norwich was the most religious city in medieval Europe, but hopefully it has been shown, at least, that the city was one of exceptional piety in medieval Christendom.

7

Economic Life

Elizabeth Rutledge

Hec est Norvycus panis ordeus et halpeny pykys
Clausus porticus domus Habrahae dyrt quoque vicus
Flynt valles rede thek cunctantibus optima sunt hec.
(Here is Norwich. The best things on offer to the loiterer are these: barley bread and halfpenny pies, the closed porch of a Jew's house and foul street, flint walls, reed thatch.)

Walter Rye, *Tourist's Guide to Norfolk*, 1892[1]

When the Black Death hit Norwich early in 1349 the city included a built-up area as large as in 1789 and probably housed a level of population that was not to be equalled until the late seventeenth century.[2] That mid fourteenth-century Norwich should have been a substantial city is not surprising. Its hinterland was both populous and wealthy (Map 8). In the lay subsidy assessment (taxing personal goods) for 1334 Norfolk enjoyed the second highest average assessment per square mile of any English county after Middlesex, and the population of eastern Norfolk was such that a density approaching 500 persons per square mile has been suggested for some districts.[3] Not all the surrounding countryside, of course, was prosperous and the immigration of land-starved peasants looking for work no doubt helped to fuel what appears to be a considerable rise in the population of Norwich throughout the late thirteenth and early fourteenth centuries.

Different areas of the city are likely to have grown at different rates. Recent immigration into the leet of Conesford (one of the four major administrative divisions of the city), for instance, probably explains the presentment of forty-one men in 1299–1300 for not being in a tithing. This was the compulsory registration of all adult males who had lived in the city for over a year and a day.[4] Tithing records also show that the adult male population of the market parish of St Peter Mancroft rose by 59 per cent between 1311 and 1333, while the male population of the outer parish of St Stephen more than doubled over the same period. Extrapolation from the figures for these two parishes to the rest of the city suggests a total population of possibly 15,000 to 17,000 in 1311, rising to nearly 25,000 by 1333. Norwich may have continued to expand into the 1340s, though Hollingsworth's estimate of a population of 41,000 at the Black Death is based on dubious premises.[5] Lack of equivalent data makes it impossible to compare the early fourteenth-century population of Norwich with that of other leading English towns. In size the city may have come second only to London, then credited with around 80,000 inhabitants, though this is by no means certain. Internationally its population was somewhat, but not dramatically, below that of cities on the other side of the North Sea, such as Bruges (with 41,000 souls in 1348) and Ypres.[6] Norwich was also relatively wealthy. In a ranking based on taxation by the English crown between 1154 and 1312 it appears along with Bristol, Lincoln and York in the leading group of provincial towns.[7]

In common with many pre-industrial centres, Norwich at the start of the fourteenth century had a broad-based economy.[8] Occupations are known for a total of over 2500 secular men and women engaged between 1275 and 1348 in around 130 different trades (Table 2).[9] The latter figure in itself confirms the status of Norwich, as there is a broad relationship between the number of recorded occupations and urban size. Winchester, for example, with a population of about 10,000, had seventy known occupations, while London boasted 175.[10] Almost twenty additional trades, including those of axesmith, appleseller, feltmaker, lacebraider, leadbeater, quernstone dresser (*quernehacker*) and digger of wells (*wellemakere*), as well as makers of balances, baskets, mattresses and ropes, occur at Norwich only as bynames. Apart from two women, no one has been included simply on the strength of an occupational byname, such as Roger le Bakestere or Isabel le Taliour;[11] the trades mentioned in such bynames might have been those of a father, grandfather or husband and may not have been carried out in Norwich at all. Sometimes the trade given in the byname can be confirmed; Anselm le Armurer supplied Norwich cathedral priory with light helmets, cuirasses and other armour in 1338–39.[12] Elsewhere it is clearly not applicable; Thomas le Clerk was known as an *acuarius* or maker of needles, while John le Combestare appears in the Norwich enrolled deeds as a fishmonger (*piscenarius*). This problem was appreciated by contemporaries, and where necessary the situation was made clear by such unambiguous descriptions as Richard Clericus *clericus* and Henry le Peynter *peynter*.

The first two columns in Table 2 give an insight into the nature of this economy. Of the total trade population known for the period, almost half (44.5 per cent) was engaged in manufacture of some kind, whether it was

MAP 8. The hinterland of late medieval Norwich. (*Phillip Judge*)

heavy, such as tanning, or light manufacture, such as tailoring or candle-making. Another quarter (25 per cent) provided food and drink, and 15 per cent (from merchants to chapmen) were occupied in trade. This is a conservative figure for victualling, as it would have been considerably higher had it included the 837 additional men and women fined between 1288 and 1313 for offences connected with brewing.[13] Nine per cent of the remainder provided a range of services, from what would now be considered as the professions, offering medical and legal aid, down through the ranks of barbers and a fencing master to carriers and boatmen. Another 4 per cent were employed in the building trade, while the artistic community, consisting of makers of stained glass (glaziers), sculptors (gravours), illuminators of manuscripts, minstrels, artists (painters) and a possible storyteller (spellere), accounted for one per cent. Despite the availability of large areas of open land enclosed within the city walls, agricultural occupations are hardly mentioned, making up less than half a percentage of the total. It seems likely, however, that grazing sheep were a common sight in the less developed parts of the city (Figure 4), and many citizens bought or rented land in the countryside. Three of the six known shepherds owned property in the outer parishes of St Katherine, St Clement and St Augustine, and in 1288 Beatrice la Qwyte and her friend were accused of pulling wool from the fleeces of John Moll's sheep in the Ber Street area.[14]

No single industry dominated the manufacturing sector. Here, as in many other towns of this period, leather was important, with similar numbers employed in the production of leather (tawying, tanning or currying) as were engaged in the production of cloth (dyeing, bleaching, fulling and weaving): between 7 and 7.5 per cent of all occupations each. The same proportion undertook metal work as armourers, bellfounders, cutlers, furbishers, goldsmiths, latoners (workers in base metal), locksmiths, needlers, smiths, spurriers and tinkers. Most of the remainder (17 per cent, comprising cordwainers who made fine footware, glovers, shoemakers, girdlers, hatters, hosiers, skinners and tailors) were engaged in turning cloth or leather (and sometimes metal) into articles of clothing.[15] In addition comparatively small numbers of artisans produced other leather goods (mainly saddles and bridles) or a range of items made from wood, bone or horn (knife handles, bird snares, gaming boards, bows, arrows, barrels, hurdles and spoons). Much of this industrial activity took place not simply within the walls but in the very heart of the city: near the market place and along the stretch of river separating the northern from the southern half of Norwich. The discordant sounds of metal working and the noisome smells associated with tanning, fulling and dyeing must have been part of the mental landscape of any child brought up in the city during this period (Map 9).[16]

Two industries missing from the surviving sources are the making of clay pottery and boat-building. In both York and London the term 'potter' was used as an alternative to 'brasier' and the potters made metal pots.[17] There is no reason to believe that the situation was different at Norwich. Clay pottery used in the city was imported from elsewhere in Norfolk and overseas. On the other hand, boat repair must have been carried on at Norwich and the building of small boats may have been a speciality among certain wrights or carpenters. Norwich cathedral priory regularly used carpenters for work on its boats in the 1330s.[18] Sea-going vessels, however, were another matter and the lack of a major boat-building industry in Norwich was probably recognised by the crown when Norwich, unlike other Norfolk ports, was not ordered to send ships to Berwick-on-Tweed in 1301.[19]

While this analysis gives a broad picture of the economy of Norwich before the Black Death, it has its limitations. Unlike the freeman rolls of later periods, there is no single source for this date that consistently lists individuals by their occupation. Most of the evidence only mentions trades occasionally, as an additional means of identification, and some is biased towards particular trade groups. This means, for example, that occupations are not recorded for a number of leading citizens, who needed no further description. The problem of bias, on the other hand, leads to the probable over-representation of the provisioning trades listed in the Table because fishmongers, butchers, poulterers, chandlers, cheesemongers and cooks were regularly fined by name in the surviving leet rolls between 1288 and 1313. The same is true of the tanners, presented for using ash rather than oak bark to create an inferior product. By and large, however, the determining factor was wealth. The major source for the evidence of most trade groups is the series of Norwich enrolled deeds and these only provide information on the sector of the population affluent enough to own property. This was always a minority: in the parishes of St Stephen and St Peter Mancroft the proportion of men who were property owners fell from 13 per cent to 6 per cent during the course of the early fourteenth century, further limiting the scope of the deeds as an historical source and the section of society represented (Map 10).[20]

Few economies, moreover, are static and the rest of the Table aims both to provide greater detail and give some idea of the changes taking place at this date.[21] Because of the vagaries of the different sources used for the periods 1286–1305 and 1320–39, the best approach is an analysis of the changes apparent from the evidence of the Norwich enrolled deeds, which provides more an indication of how well the different trades were doing economically than an exact comparison of overall figures.[22] The total number of references to occupations in the deeds fell by 12 per cent between 1286–1305 and

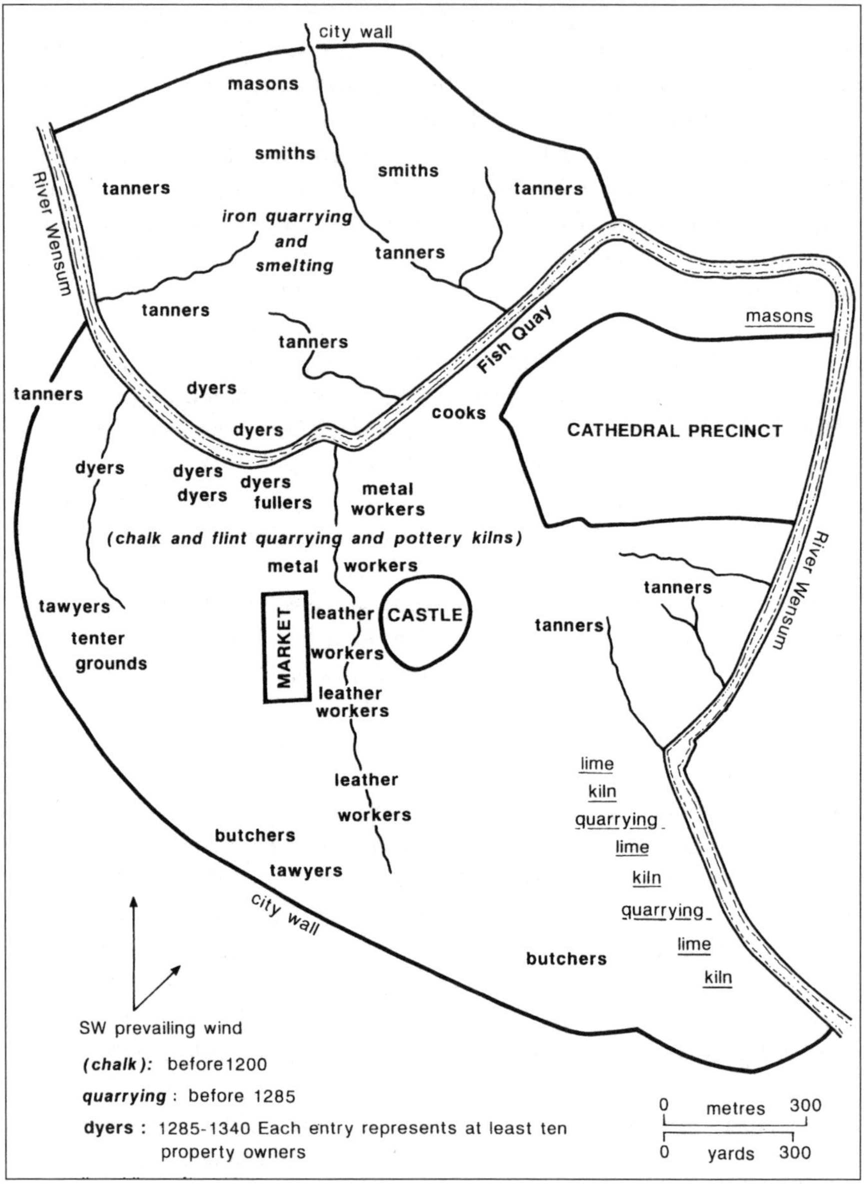

MAP 9. Industrial activity and pollution in late medieval Norwich. (*Phillip Judge*)

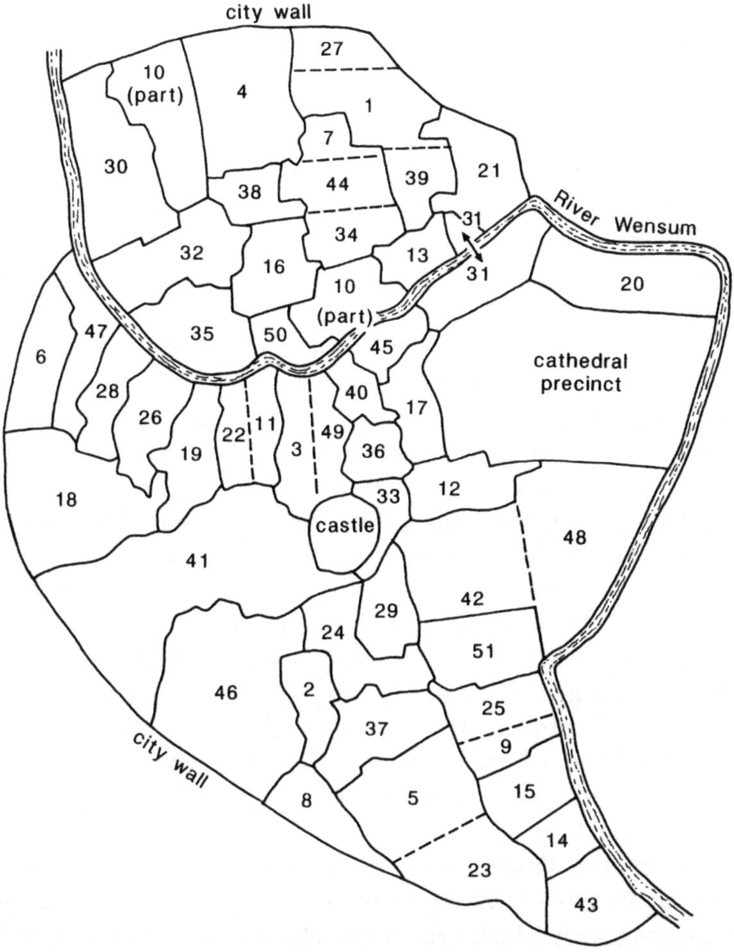

1 All Saints Fyebridge
2 All Saints Timberhill
3 St Andrew
4 St Augustine
5 St Bartholomew
6 St Benedict
7 St Botulph
8 St Catherine
9 St Clement Conesford
10 St Clement Fyebridge
11 St Crowche
12 St Cuthbert
13 St Edmund
14 St Edward
15 St Etheldreda
16 St George Colegate
17 St George Tombland
18 St Giles
19 St Gregory
20 St Helen
21 St James
22 St John Maddermarket
23 St John Sepulchre
24 St John Timberhill
25 St Julian
26 St Lawrence
27 St Margaret Fyebridge
28 St Margaret Westwick
29 St Martin at Bale
30 St Martin at Oak
31 St Martin at Palace
32 St Mary Coslany
33 St Mary the Less
34 St Mary Unbrent
35 St Michael Coslany
36 St Michael at Plea
37 St Michael at Thorn
38 St Olave
39 St Paul
40 St Peter Hungate
41 St Peter Mancroft
42 St Peter Parmentergate
43 St Peter Southgate
44 St Saviour
45 SS Simon and Jude
46 St Stephen
47 St Swithin
48 St Vedast
49 St Christopher
50 St Margaret Newbridge
51 St Michael Conesford

MAP 10. The parishes of late medieval Norwich. (*Phillip Judge*)

1320–39, with the result that any trade that managed to maintain, or actually increase, its numbers between these two periods was doing very well.[23]

Fortunes differed both between and within the various trade groups. The overall numbers of provisioners fall dramatically between 1286–1305 and 1320–39, in large part because no leet rolls survive for the latter period. Over half of the group were never wealthy enough to own property and some of the lesser occupations initially represented in the deeds, such as the cheesemongers and the poulterers, appear to have been squeezed out of the property market. The same may also be true of the poorer fishmongers, though, as will be seen, the numerical decline among the wealthier members of this group probably has an alternative explanation. Conversely, other major provisioners (butchers, bakers, chandlers and taverners) not only retained their position in the property market but were also taxed on a relatively high level of personal wealth in the lay subsidy of 1332. In numbers assessed for the subsidy the provisioning trades as a whole come second only to the mercantile sector and are far ahead of any other occupational group (Table 2).[24] As in York and London, victualling so large a city was clearly a profitable business. It is interesting that the number of known bakers consistently outnumbers the cooks, although the latter were named when fined for breaches of civic regulations, while the bakers were not. Ironically, the only list of named bakers is of seven men who had *not* broken the assize of bread in 1288. This suggests that before the Black Death the urban poor of Norwich ate bread rather than hot fast food supplied by the cooks: for a casual labourer earning 1d. a day a halfpenny pie would constitute a rare extravagance.[25]

Another successful, though modest, group consisted of the building trades, with an increase in numbers of over 50 per cent. Norwich was unusual in having such a high proportion of masons in relation to other building workers.[26] Their number clearly reflected important projects taking place within the city, such as the immense circuit of the flint city walls and the building of the friaries,[27] and Norwich men were probably employed on parish churches and at religious houses throughout the region. The figures also indicate, however, that masons were more likely than carpenters or other building workers to be wealthy enough to enter the property market, though they do not appear to have been rich in personal goods. None was assessed for the subsidy in 1332.

Less buoyant as a whole were the clothing trades. Whereas the shoemakers and cordwainers held their own, some of the smaller groups, such as the girdlers, glovers and hatters, seem to have moved out of the property market altogether. The greatest casualty was the hosiers. These were initially a wealthy group in Norwich, investing in property such as bakeries, market stalls and fixed rents; two of their number were still prosperous enough to be assessed for taxation in 1332. Variously known as *caligarii*, chaucers or hosiers, they occupied a quarter on the east side of the market associated with the leather workers. Nevertheless, six of the hosiers active in 1286–1305 are known to have owned frames for stretching cloth (tenters). The assumption is that they were involved in making woollen as well as leather hose. In particular they may have produced the woollen hose with leather soles that could be worn in the place of shoes or boots.[28] By 1320–39, however, only one hosier owned a tenter, and a possible reason for the hosiers' decline is that the making of (often multi-coloured) woollen hose had passed to the tailors, leaving them to supply the much smaller market for leather hose. The tailors' rise was certainly rapid, with the numbers owning property almost doubling between 1286–1305 and 1320–39. Even so they were not a particularly wealthy group: many tailors did not evidently possess any property, and only three of all those documented between 1320 and 1339 were assessed for the subsidy of 1332.[29] This suggests that they played little part in the lucrative cloth trade; the growth in numbers probably reflects an increased demand for their garment-making services from an expanding population.

The most noticeable contrast, however, is the difference in fortunes between the leather producers and the cloth workers. By 1320–39 there is a 45 per cent reduction in the number of property-owning tanners operating within the city. The poorer tawyers seem to have moved out of the Norwich property market altogether. The tanners cured cattle hides with bark while the tawyers treated the lighter sheep or goat skins with alum or oil. This fall in the number of leather producers, apparent in other English towns, was not the result of a decline in the demand for leather in Norwich. The numbers of shoemakers and cordwainers in the city remained constant and the saddlers and bridlemakers show a slight increase. It has been suggested that tanners left the towns to avoid urban regulations, but at Norwich, as at Winchester, they may also have reacted against the pressure of increasing urban development and the rival demands of the cloth industry on the vital water supply.[30] Throughout this period the Norwich tanners show a tendency to move upstream, considerably reducing the earlier concentration exploiting the cockeys (or small streams) joining the river south of the cathedral. If continued, this movement would have taken them outside the city walls. Those staying in the city remained a wealthy group, with over a quarter of individuals known between 1320 and 1339 being assessed for the 1332 subsidy. The tawyers, by contrast, were always poor. They operated on the fringes and were also associated with the village of Trowse to the south. The lower number of tawyers may not accurately reflect the level of demand for the lighter skins. There is some evidence that the Norwich cordwainers (known, as at York, as *alutarii*) may have carried out their own tawying.[31]

In contrast to the decline in leather production, this period saw a considerable increase in the number of known cloth workers, despite the fact that there is little evidence for a developed weaving industry in the city. It has been accepted for some time that early fourteenth-century Norwich was a centre for cloth finishing rather than production and this is borne out by the figures presented in Table 2.[32] The small group of shearmen (who shaved the nap from the cloth to create a smooth finish) more than doubled its numbers between 1286–1305 and 1320–39, and the larger population of dyers increased by almost 50 per cent. Dyeing was among the more profitable occupations in the city, with ten dyers being assessed for the subsidy in 1332. In comparison, the number of known weavers is small and remained steady throughout the period. Poor weavers would not own property, but a large working population might be expected, like the tailors, to be more evident in other sources. On the other hand, an ulnager (a royal official responsible for assaying cloth) was appointed for worsted (unfulled) cloth of *Northwys* in 1315,[33] and the regular, if undramatic, appearance of weavers from 1327 to 1348 in the incomplete freedom rolls of this period suggests that weaving in Norwich may have been on the increase. The 1330s and 1340s may also have been a time of technical innovation in the weaving industry two centuries before the arrival of the Strangers effected such a transformation in 'Norwich stuff'. John Kempe, who came to England from Flanders before 1331 to teach his system of weaving, may be the John Kempe de Gaunt (Ghent) who had settled in the parish of St Peter Mancroft by 1333.[34]

A source of income not mentioned at all in the Table, though it was also on the increase, was profit from lettings.[35] As the population of Norwich grew, so did the need for rented accommodation, whether under a formal lease, a monthly or weekly tenancy or simply on an *ad hoc* basis as a lodger. As early as 1311 at least three-quarters of the households in the leet of Mancroft may have been living in property they did not own (Map 11). Most of this demand was met by landlords who were both secular and private. In contrast to the situation at Oxford,[36] no more than 3 to 3.5 per cent of the city's housing stock was in the hands of ecclesiastical institutions and most of this consisted of single holdings owned by religious houses situated within the diocese. Rents were a useful source of income at many levels of Norwich society, from the wealthy man, whose principal holdings consisted in part of tenements leased out (*redditus*), to poorer residents, such as John Bete (himself the tenant of Stephen Besaunt) who took in lodgers.[37]

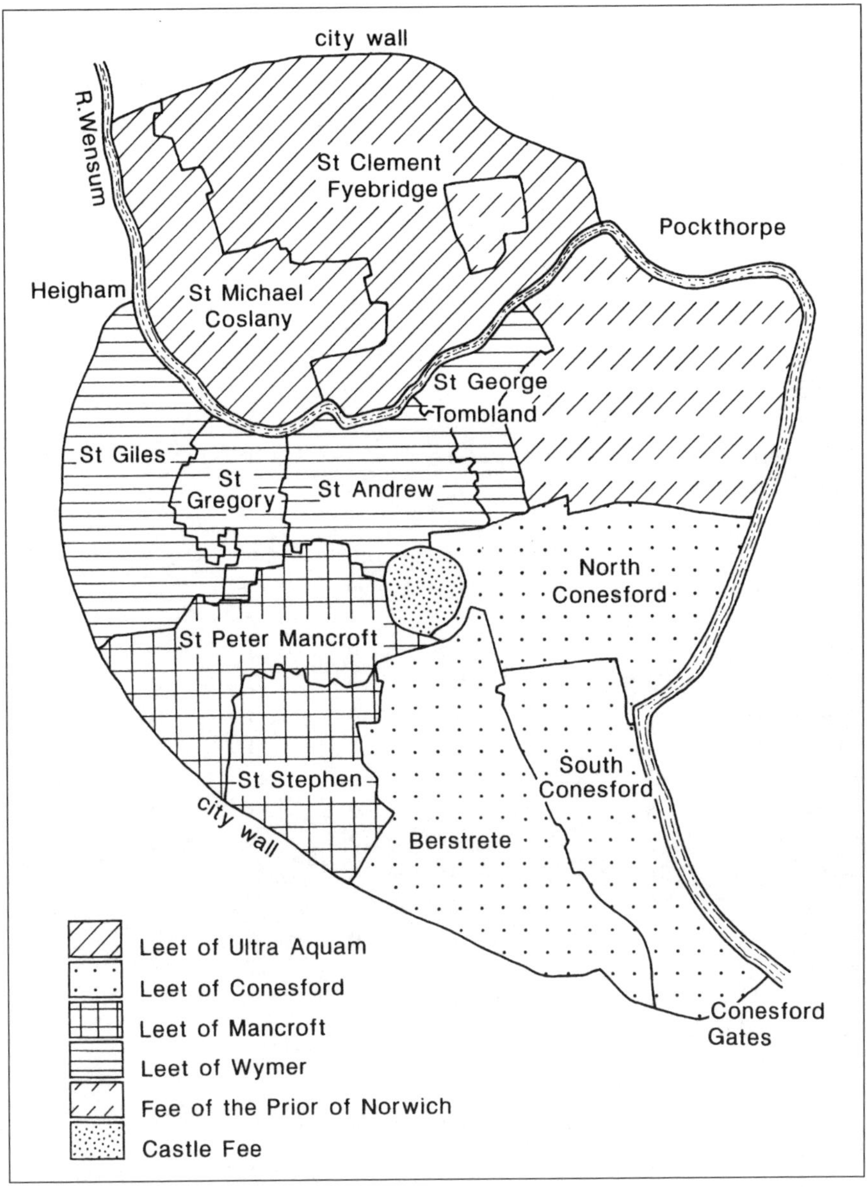

MAP 11. The leets of late medieval Norwich. (*Phillip Judge*)

TABLE 2

Inhabitants of Norwich with Known Occupations, 1275–1348

Occupations	*Active, 1275–1348 known:*		*Active, 1286–1305 known:*		*Active, 1320–1339 known*		*1332 lay subsidy*
	From all sources	*From deeds*	*From all sources*	*From deeds*	*From all sources*	*From deeds*	*Nos assessed*
Agriculture							
Gardener	1	1	1	1	0	0	0
Parker	1	1	0	0	1	1	0
Shepherd	6	3	1	1	4	2	1
Warrener	2	0	1	0	1	0	0
Total	*10*	*5*	*3*	*2*	*6*	*3*	*1*
Artists							
Glazier	3	3	0	0	0	0	0
Gravour	2	0	0	0	1	0	0
Illuminator	3	3	1	1	1	1	0
Musician/actor	9	5	2	2	4	2	0
Painter	14	9	9	5	4	2	0
Storyteller	1	0	1	0	0	0	0
Total	*32*	*20*	*13*	*8*	*10*	*5*	*0*
Building							
Builder	1	0	0	0	1	0	0
Carpenter	39	24	12	8	22	11	1
Lath maker	1	1	0	0	1	1	0
Limeburner	1	1	0	0	1	1	0
Mason	33	29	9	9	17	15	0
Plasterer	5	0	2	0	1	0	0
Plumber	5	3	2	2	3	1	1
Reeder	14	4	1	1	7	3	0
Roofer	6	3	3	1	2	1	0
Sawyer	1	0	0	0	0	0	0
Tiler	4	2	0	0	3	2	0
Total	*110*	*67*	*29*	*21*	*58*	*35*	*2*
Clerical and legal							
Attorney in court	7	0	2	0	6	0	1
Clerk	147	111	83	70	31	22	2
Public notary	1	1	0	0	1	1	0
Scrivener	3	2	1	1	0	0	0
Summoner	1	0	0	0	0	0	0
Total	*159*	*114*	*86*	*71*	*38*	*23*	*3*

Occupations	*Active, 1275–1348 known:*		*Active, 1286–1305 known:*		*Active, 1320–1339 known*		*1332 lay subsidy*
	From all sources	*From deeds*	*From all sources*	*From deeds*	*From all sources*	*From deeds*	*Nos assessed*
Cloth production							
Bleacher	1	1	0	0	1	1	0
Chaloner	2	1	0	0	2	1	0
Comber	5	2	2	0	2	1	0
Dyer	81	63	23	23	35	32	10
Fuller	34	19	10	6	10	7	1
Quilter	1	1	1	1	0	0	0
Shearman	32	22	5	5	16	12	1
Weaver	40	28	12	10	14	11	2
Total	*196*	*137*	*53*	*45*	*80*	*65*	*14*
Clothing and accessories							
Cordwainer	87	53	26	21	41	24	5
Girdler	7	6	4	4	0	0	0
Glover	25	19	14	11	2	2	0
Hatter	25	14	12	10	11	5	2
Hosier	37	35	25	25	9	8	2
Purse maker	4	1	2	1	2	0	0
Shoemaker	86	63	33	30	41	27	2
Skinner or fripperer[1]	90	4	35	21	28	17	5
Tailor	86	52	18	17	51	32	3
Upholder	4	3	0	0	2	2	0
Total	*451*	*293*	*169*	*140*	*187*	*117*	*19*
Distribution							
Chapman	8	6	4	4	4	1	0
Coalman	2	2	2	2	0	0	0
Coper	1	1	0	0	1	1	0
Draper	66	59	34	33	31	30	11
Exporter of cloth and worsted	2	0	0	0	2	0	0
Exporter of wool	30	0	11	0	15	0	5
Exporter of wool, importer of cloth	2	0	1	0	2	0	0
Featherman	1	0	1	0	0	0	0
Flaxman	1	1	1	1	0	0	0

Occupations	*Active, 1275–1348 known:*		*Active, 1286–1305 known:*		*Active, 1320–1339 known*		*1332 lay subsidy*
	From all sources	*From deeds*	*From all sources*	*From deeds*	*From all sources*	*From deeds*	*Nos assessed*
Horse coper	1	0	0	0	0	0	0
Importer of cloth	1	0	0	0	1	0	0
Importer of woad	2	0	0	0	2	0	0
Ironmonger	1	1	1	1	0	0	0
Linen draper	35	32	31	29	7	7	3
Mercer	23	17	10	10	12	9	3
Merchant	164	143	71	66	84	74	36
Saltman	2	1	1	1	1	0	0
Woad dealer	7	6	6	5	2	2	0
Woolmonger	40	31	17	14	19	16	2
Worsted seller	2	0	0	0	2	0	0
Total	*391*	*300*	*191*	*166*	*185*	*140*	*60*
Leather production							
Currier	6	5	4	4	2	1	0
Leatherkerver	2	2	0	0	2	2	1
Parchment maker/seller	11	7	2	2	3	1	0
Tanner	147	79	95	45	29	25	7
Tawyer	17	6	13	4	0	0	0
Total	*183*	*99*	*114*	*55*	*36*	*29*	*8*
Leather work							
Bottle maker	1	0	1	0	0	0	0
Bridle maker	20	12	6	6	10	6	1
Collar maker	1	0	0	0	1	0	0
Saddler	29	19	6	6	15	10	2
Total	*51*	*31*	*13*	*12*	*26*	*16*	*3*
Metal work							
Armourer	5	2	1	1	3	2	1
Bellfounder	5	5	3	3	1	1	0
Cutler	28	23	9	8	16	14	2
Farrier	4	3	0	0	3	2	0
Furbisher	4	3	2	2	2	1	0
Goldsmith	36	27	19	17	16	9	3
Latoner	26	14	1	1	19	10	1
Locksmith	4	2	1	0	3	2	1
Needler	8	3	5	3	2	0	0

Occupations	*Active, 1275–1348 known:*		*Active, 1286–1305 known:*		*Active, 1320–1339 known*		*1332 lay subsidy*
	From all sources	*From deeds*	*From all sources*	*From deeds*	*From all sources*	*From deeds*	*Nos assessed*
Potter	4	2	1	1	2	1	0
Smith	59	38	21	15	20	15	1
Spurrier	1	0	0	0	0	0	0
Tinker	3	0	1	0	1	0	0
Total	*187*	*122*	*64*	*51*	*88*	*57*	*9*
Miscellaneous services							
Barber	23	16	7	7	9	4	2
Fencing master	1	1	1	1	0	0	0
Janitor	1	0	1	0	0	0	0
Laundress	2	0	0	0	1	0	0
Money lender	2	0	2	0	0	0	0
Physician	5	3	2	1	4	3	0
Porter	3	1	0	0	1	1	0
Servant	11	1	6	0	3	1	0
Squire	2	1	0	0	1	1	0
Surgeon	2	1	1	1	0	0	0
Trone operator	1	1	1	1	0	0	0
Total	*53*	*25*	*21*	*11*	*19*	*10*	*2*
Provisions							
Baker	108	80	51	39	51	41	12
Butcher	85	40	49	19	26	21	6
Chandler	41	16	15	6	18	8	3
Cheesemonger	28	2	14	1	1	0	0
Cook	73	21	42	10	17	7	1
Corn seller	2	0	2	0	0	0	0
Cumin seller	1	1	1	1	0	0	0
Fisherman	6	3	3	1	3	2	0
Fishmonger	194	79	138	44	40	35	12
Fishmomger (freshwater)	9	2	3	1	0	0	0
Flour seller	1	1	0	0	0	0	0
Leek seller	3	2	0	0	1	0	0
Maltster	15	0	10	0	0	0	0
Miller	4	1	2	1	0	0	0
Mustard seller	1	1	0	0	0	0	0
Oatseller	11	0	2	0	0	0	0
Oil seller	1	0	1	0	0	0	0
Pepperer	2	2	0	0	2	2	0

Occupations	*Active, 1275–1348 known:*		*Active, 1286–1305 known:*		*Active, 1320–1339 known*		*1332 lay subsidy*
	From all sources	*From deeds*	*From all sources*	*From deeds*	*From all sources*	*From deeds*	*Nos assessed*
Poulterer	23	7	20	6	3	2	0
Provisioner	1	1	0	0	0	0	0
Pudding seller	1	0	1	0	0	0	0
Spicer/ apothecary	32	25	11	10	19	15	2
Taverner	36	29	17	13	14	12	4
Unguent seller	3	3	3	3	0	0	0
Total	*681*	*316*	*385*	*155*	*195*	*145*	*40*
Transport							
Boatman	14	6	1	1	5	3	0
Carter	17	6	6	4	4	0	0
Total	*31*	*12*	*7*	*5*	*9*	*3*	*0*
Wood, horn and bone							
Birdsnare maker	1	0	1	0	1	0	0
Board maker	1	0	0	0	0	0	0
Bowmaker	3	1	0	0	2	1	0
Card maker	1	1	0	0	1	1	0
Cooper	21	12	3	3	12	6	0
Fletcher	1	1	1	1	0	0	0
Handle maker	1	0	1	0	0	0	0
Hirdle maker	2	2	1	1	1	1	0
Horner	1	1	1	1	0	0	0
Spooner	2	1	2	1	1	1	0
Turner	5	1	1	1	3	0	0
Wheelwright	1	1	1	1	0	0	0
Wright	5	1	0	0	3	1	0
Total	*45*	*22*	*12*	*9*	*24*	*11*	*0*
Grand Total	*2580*	*1563*	*1160*	*751*	*961*	*659*	*161*

Source: The evidence produced in this table derives from an ongoing database, whose sources are discussed at length in note 8 above.

Note: [1] It is not always possible to distinguish the skinners (*peliparii*), who were furriers, from the smaller group of fripperers (*phelipparii*), who dealt in second-hand clothes.

In a city of this size, where over 40 per cent of the known trade population engaged in the provision of food, drink and clothing, much of the economy of early fourteenth-century Norwich was both internal and circular.[38] William Bele the butcher might sell the hide of his slaughtered ox to Thomas Elys the tanner.[39] Thomas could pass his poorly tanned hides (because of using ash rather than oak bark) on to Richard de Wotton the shoemaker and Henry Papunjay the saddler. Henry could buy bread from John de Thwaite the baker and cheese from Alice, the wife of Hugh Cristemesse the poulterer. Alice and Hugh might be too busy to do their own brewing and so have to get their ale from Botilda la Braceresse. Botilda in turn could go to Peter de Pulham the fripperer (*feliper*) for second-hand clothing, or buy cloth from Thomas de Cokefeld the draper to be made up by William Ardaint, the one-eyed tailor. William Ardaint would be shaved by Richard de Erilyens the barber, who, when buying his house in the parish of St Michael-at-Plea, would need to use the services of Robert de Buxston, a minor clerk. Robert was not a freeman but tried to increase his income by trading. Waiting to acknowledge the deed at the bailiffs' court, he risked food poisoning by eating one of the pies that John Jaune had reheated more than two or three times. Jaune in his turn bought the meat for the pies from William Bele. And so on. Nevertheless, no city could be entirely self-sufficient. Goods needed to be bought in: food (at the least grain, fish and animals to be slaughtered), fuel, timber for building, reed for thatch and raw materials (iron and wood) for manufacture, as well as large quantities of pottery (found in innumerable excavations), wool or cloth and more luxurious items such as wine from Gascony, gold and silver for the goldsmiths, dye, lead, freestone and window glass. A boat coming up the river from Great Yarmouth that sank off Cantley in 1343 was laden with sea-coal, salt, iron from Sweden, wooden boards from Riga, onions and herring.[40]

Little is known for certain about the inland and import trade of Norwich, though there are hints at specialisation. The two men described as 'coleman' may have imported charcoal or sea-coal for the use of the smiths and limeburners. The 'yrenmonger' probably brought in iron from the Baltic, and there was also a dealer in flax and no fewer than nine possible importers of woad for dyeing. Two men are known to have specialised in the supply of salt, a very important commodity, especially in a city so involved with the fish trade, and right at the end of the period a horse dealer or *mercator equorum* became a freeman. Though there was a cattle market, the wealthier butchers themselves are likely to have reared or fattened their own cattle on the pastures of Trowse or Lakenham. Masons may have organised their own building materials and some taverners negotiated the import of wine. John de Beston, taverner, imported fifteen tuns and four pipes of wine through Great Yarmouth in 1340–41. This was not necessarily just for consumption at his tavern. In 1339–40 he sold three tuns of wine to Norwich cathedral priory for the substantial sum of £10 15s. 3d.[41] Much of the wide range of imports, however, especially goods from abroad, came into Norwich by the hands of undifferentiated merchants (*mercatores*).

To finance this economy, goods imported had to be offset, in part, by those exported from the city. Three commodities were of especial importance to late thirteenth- and early fourteenth-century Norwich: fish, wool and cloth. Fish, of course, was a vital part of the medieval diet (not least because of the great number of fast days) and this is reflected in the strikingly high number of men and women known to have been engaged in its supply (Table 2).[42] Most of those mentioned were not themselves fishermen. Fish were caught in the Wensum and the Yare and two men from the leet of Conesford, some fishermen belonging to Norwich cathedral priory and men from Surlingham were all fined between 1288 and 1293 for using the wrong size of net in city waters.[43] (Norwich claimed jurisdiction over the Yare as far as Hardley Cross, about fifteen miles down river).[44] Most of the known suppliers, however, were fishmongers who forestalled, or attempted to corner, the market by buying fish *en route* to the city. In specific presentments between 1288 and 1313 individuals were charged with riding to Brundall to buy oysters from a boat there, buying fish from a boat on the river below Carrow and purchasing freshwater fish at Trowse.[45] A wide choice, both salt and freshwater, was available. Barbel, cockles, codling, crabs, crayfish, eels, fry, ling, oysters, pikerel, plaice, razor shells (*rasours*), roach, ruff (a type of perch), salmon, *skreyth* (?crawfish), smelts, sole, sprats, stockfish (dried cod) and whelks were all for sale in Norwich in the spring of 1337.[46]

The major trade, however, was in herring. Great Yarmouth, the wealthy outport of Norwich, was renowned for its herring fishery and large numbers of herring must have been consumed within Norwich alone. Herring, however, could also be cured and sent further inland. In 1273 and 1274 the abbey of Waltham, Essex, was granted safe conduct for bringing herring from Norwich to Waltham, and this was by no means exceptional.[47] Leicester abbey bought fish from Norwich in 1286;[48] in the late thirteenth century no fewer than four Cistercian abbeys (Warden and Woburn in Bedfordshire, Garendon in Leicestershire and Combe in Warkwickshire) owned property in the Conesford area of Norwich, near the river, almost certainly as a base for the purchase of herring. It is highly probable that Norwich fishmongers also dispatched supplies of fish into the midlands, though the only evidence is that one of their number, John le Prestesone, was involved in an assault at Cambridge in 1316.[49] By the time of the Black Death, however, the part played by Norwich in the distribution of herring may have declined. All four Cistercian abbeys moved out of Norwich, probably abandoning the direct purchase of fish in favour of reliance on local dealers. When Lady Katherine de Norwich, who spent part of the year in the city, stocked up with a last of red herring in 1336–37, the purchase was sent direct from Yarmouth to her manor of Mettingham in Suffolk.[50] Similarly, between 1339 and 1349 herring for the Clare household were transferred from Yarmouth to Bardfield, Essex, and Bury St Edmunds, Suffolk, without passing through Norwich.[51] Norwich would have continued to supply its immediate hinterland beyond the Yarmouth river system, but this decline in the provision of more distant markets probably accounts for the reduction in the number of Norwich fishmongers wealthy enough to own property between 1286–1305 and 1320–39. Even if its scope had been reduced, however, the supply of fish still remained a profitable business and twelve of the later fishmongers were assessed for subsidy in 1332.

The second important commodity was wool. Contrary to widespread popular belief, Norfolk was not a leading wool-producing county at this date. Its wool was of comparatively poor quality and worth only about £4 for a sack of twenty-six stone.[52] Nor was Great Yarmouth a major centre for its export. The port handled only about 2 per cent of national wool exports between 1297 and 1336.[53] Nevertheless, both the home and export trade in wool were attractive to Norwich men. No fewer than forty late thirteenth- and early fourteenth-century citizens were described as woolmongers (*lanatores*, *leyners*, wolmen or wollemongeres). Only three of these, however, also appear as exporters. Together with two others fined at Norwich for selling wool and wool fells outside the market, they may well have been primarily engaged in bringing wool into the city to sell. By and large, one needed far greater reserves of capital to trade at this level. The export of English wool was dominated by alien (foreign) merchants in the late thirteenth century, but by Edward II's reign more than half of the wool passing through Yarmouth was being handled by Norwich-based entrepreneurs. Altogether over a fifth (thirty-six) of the Norwich men described as merchants are known to have taken part in the trade, along with another thirty-two property-owners, not specifically described as merchants. Most of them were only small scale exporters, few shipping the average thirty sacks a year regarded as the minimum for a serious trader. Even so, wool seems to have been a regular part of their business. John le Gloz, for instance, was a constant exporter of wool between 1309 and 1321. In the year beginning 29 September 1309 he paid custom for one sack and twenty-three stone shipped on 20 October, four sacks and one and a half stone on 28 October, one sack and twenty-two stone on 25 February, one sack and two and a half stone on 2 March, twenty-five-and-a-half stone on 11 April, two sacks and nineteen and a half stone on 2 July and finally, one of his few more substantial exports, seven sacks and half a stone on 17 July. Though the individual amounts exported by John de Gloz are probably below average, the pattern of frequent small-scale shipments is universal.[54] Yarmouth was not the only port available and some of these men also exported small amounts out of King's Lynn.[55] There was also some Norwich involvement in the limited export from Yarmouth of the other customable goods: woolfells and hides.

The active participation of Norwich merchants in the wool trade continued during the débâcle caused by Edward III's foreign policy in the late 1330s and early 1340s.[56] Despite the generally low quantities handled by individuals, wool was clearly an important export for the Norwich mercantile class. Cumulatively the trade could be highly profitable and large amounts of money were involved. In 1311 seven men, including four Norwich merchants, claimed that they had sold wool at Bruges and elsewhere to the value of over £1000.[57] Some idea of the government's dependence on the trade can be gauged from the fact that by 1340 the amount of duty payable per sack, which for most of this period stood at 6*s.* 8*d.*, had risen to £4 for native merchants and over £5 for foreigners.[58]

Not all the wool exported from Great Yarmouth, even by Norwich men, necessarily passed through the market in Norwich. Two Norwich exporters, Robert de Aula (or de la Sale) and Roger Hardegrey, bought wool direct from Lakenheath in Suffolk in 1320 and 1345 respectively.[59] Yet the Norwich wool market was clearly of some importance. Until 1326 the wool staple, in so far as it boasted a formal existence, was based in Flanders or Artois. In that year it was moved to England and shared between eight towns, of which Norwich was one. This development heralded an attempt to impose firmer control over continental trade. Alien merchants could now only buy wool in a staple town and even native merchants had to keep their wool in one for forty days before exporting it. By the following year, however, there was already some relaxation of the regulations and though home staples were reimposed in 1333, they were short lived. It seems likely that the brief presence of the staple, though underlining the importance of wool in its commercial life, made little practical difference to the economy of Norwich. There is virtually no change in the number of known woolmongers between 1286–1305 and 1320–39, suggesting that Norwich was already an entrepôt for the sale of wool by 1300; it was probably because of this active market that the city was chosen as a staple town in

1326. Nor would a staple have greatly increased the number of alien merchants in the city. The part played by foreigners in the Yarmouth wool trade at this date was limited, declining further from 4.6 per cent of the total exported in 1323–29 to a mere 3.5 per cent in 1329–36.[60]

While almost 28 per cent of the entire distributive trade group is known to have been involved in marketing wool, an even higher proportion, at least 34 per cent, was engaged in the marketing of cloth. Cloth came in three main forms: linen, broadcloth and worsted. By the end of the thirteenth century linen products (made from flax or hemp), as well as worsted (an unfulled woollen cloth from north-east Norfolk), were established as luxury items.[61] Both were among presents sent by the city to the royal justices in 1300–1.[62] Of the total of thirty-five Norwich linen drapers known for the whole of this period all but four were active between 1286 and 1305. As owners of stalls in the *lindraperia* or Linendrapers' Row in the market, these men are likely to have purchased their linen cloth from the producers in the parishes around Aylsham (some linens were known as 'aylshams'). They could then arrange for the cloth to be dyed before selling it on, either for home use or to general merchants for wider distribution; as early as 1301, both worsted and 'aylshams' were a regular import into Oxford.[63] With the turn of the century, however, the Norwich linen drapers suffered a dramatic decline. No new linen draper appears in the Norwich enrolled deeds after 1308, and the description altogether vanishes from this source after 1318. Only seven men were still active between 1320 and 1339 and four of these had diversified, being known alternatively as draper or merchant.[64] This is despite the fact that the Norfolk linen industry continued to flourish well into the mid 1340s, when an ulnager was appointed specifically to control the production of linen cloths from Aylsham, Beetley and Salle.[65] There is no indication that the trade was taken over by the Norwich mercers, whose numbers remained relatively stable. Two factors are likely to have led to this decline. The first is the loss of an earlier export market (implied by a request from foreign as well as native merchants in 1314 for improved standardisation of 'aylshams') to the growing linen industry in Flanders and the Low Countries, which now set the benchmark. The second is the apparent migration of a number of Norfolk-based mercers, who specialised in both linen and worsted wares, to London, bypassing Norwich for more than the local distribution of linen cloth.[66] It is not surprising that a part of Norwich market place was described as the *former* Lyndraper Rowe in 1357.[67]

Drapers performed the same role in relation to broadcloth (fulled woollen cloth) as linendrapers did to cloth made from flax or hemp. They would have bought local cloth from the producers, organised its finishing with the fullers and dyers, and sold the final product on the market. A third of all the drapers are known to have owned their own stalls in the drapery or in Omanseterow. (The latter took its name from *omansete*: cloth worked by one man or wide enough to cover one person.)[68] The drapers are also likely to have dealt in cloth from the Continent, though they were not necessarily engaged in its import. Few drapers were also described as merchants. When the ulnage accounts of the 1330s recorded the seizure at Great Yarmouth of striped cloth from Flanders belonging to ten Norwich men, eight of the ten were known merchants but none was a draper. The haul included cloth from the Dutch and Belgian towns of Aardenburg, Dendermonde, Ghent and Louvain (Map 12).[69] Foreign merchants were also involved in this import: five men of Brabant had sixty-five pieces of cloth worth £210 confiscated in Norwich in 1317.[70] On the whole, the drapers were a wealthy group and they probably sold as well as purchased their cloth well beyond the confines of Norwich. One draper, Thomas de Cokefeld, was given safe conduct to travel to trade in Boston, Lincolnshire, in 1318 along with three other citizens.[71] Another, Robert de Long, was owed £20 by a man from Hampshire in 1320,[72] while a third, Robert de Holveston, was engaged in actions in the court of common pleas at Westminster for the recovery of the remarkable sum of £752 owed by a number of different defendants in 1305 alone.[73] It is unlikely, however, that much of the local cloth handled by the drapers went abroad. Though Norwich men were exporting some broadcloth in the 1330s, even then the amounts were small compared with the shipments of worsted.[74] By the time the detailed accounts for cloth exported from Yarmouth begin in 1348–49 the quantity of broadcloth mentioned is negligible.[75]

In London trade in worsted cloth was the preserve of the mercers.[76] Assuming the same was the case in Norwich, worsted appears to have played a much smaller part in the economy of the city during this period than did broadcloth. In both 1286–1305 and 1320–39 there were about three times as many known drapers as mercers. This is surprising, considering that the mercers might have been expected to take over some of the trade in linen fabrics relinquished by the linen drapers. There is also no evidence that they participated in the growing export market. When custom duties were first charged on cloth exported by nationals in 1347, Great Yarmouth, together with Bristol and Ipswich, was one of the chief ports involved in a trade that, in Yarmouth's case, consisted almost entirely of worsteds. Yet, in spite of the activities of some Norwich entrepreneurs, the most prominent being William de Dunston who exported 226 worsted cloths in 1348–49 and 410 in 1349–50, Norwich involvement overall was limited. Less than a quarter of the worsteds exported through Yarmouth in these two years may have been handled by Norwich-based men and none of those involved were described as mercers.[77] The relative wealth of the three cloth distributive groups can be seen from the 1332 subsidy assessment. Eleven drapers were taxed, but by this time all three of the linen drapers assessed, and two of the three mercers, were known as merchants rather than specialists, suggesting that the latter occupations were only really profitable when coupled with diversification or overseas trade.

Both the occupational descriptions and the concentration upon fish, cloth and wool in the surviving sources can suggest a far less varied pattern of trade than actually existed. Versatility was the hallmark of the Norwich mercantile class, both at home and abroad. In this they resembled the Norfolk corn-dealer, William Bauchun of Blofield, who between 1301 and 1331 sold a range of commodities to Norwich cathedral priory, including axes, jars for wine, coloured paints and iron. He was also instrumental in the purchase of cloth for the monastic servants' robes.[78] At home John de Gnatishale, otherwise known as a Norwich draper, supplied the cathedral priory in 1333–34 with 67s. 2d. worth of spices.[79] Conversely, Peter de Scothowe, a Norwich spicer, exported wool. Abroad, Roger de Blakeneye, citizen of Norwich, complained about the loss of his goods when the ship *Nicholas*, bound for Hamburg, was driven off course to Bremen in 1333. His share of the cargo consisted not only of two scarlet cloths, fourteen woollen cloths, seventy-one cloths of worsted and eight 'coverletz', but also silk garments (*cendals*), girdles and silk bags, knives, rings, silver spoons, armour, beds, robes and chests.[80] Clearly wool as an export could be supplemented not only by broadcloth and worsted, but also by a wide range of other articles manufactured in Norwich or bought at fairs further afield.

An important aspect of the economy of Norwich lay not in its better-known exports but in its invisible earnings and services. Norwich was both an ecclesiastical and a secular centre. The cathedral priory, four major friaries and other important religious institutions brought in many visitors. The cathedral was a recognised, though lesser, place of pilgrimage.[81] The city served as an administrative base for both the archdeaconry of Norwich and Norwich diocese, though diocesan business was also transacted at the bishop's other East Anglian palaces and elsewhere in the region. The royal administration, for both Norfolk and Suffolk, was exercised by the sheriff from Norwich castle. This would have required a permanent clerical staff and a sizeable archive; in 1311 three men were pardoned for placing two forged writs on the files among the sheriff's writs at Norwich.[82] Certainly the rulers of Great Yarmouth recognised the importance of Norwich as a legal centre. The borough accounts for 1331–32 record payments to Godfrey

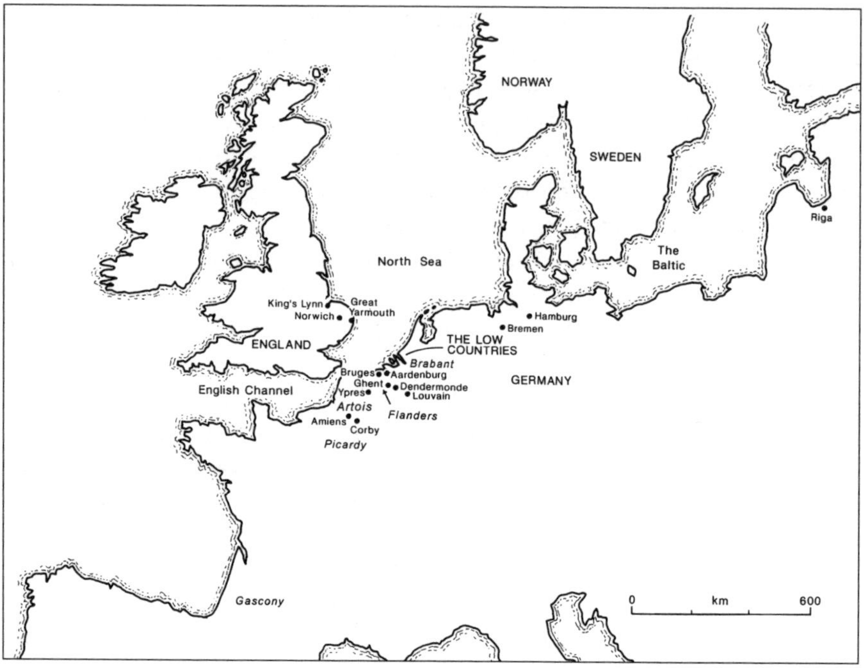

MAP 12. Trading links between Norwich and the Continent, *c.* 1300–1350. (*Phillip Judge*)

de Colneye for three journeys to Norwich to return royal writs and deal with business arising from gaol delivery and an inquest on the death of Henry atte Key of Langley, who had been killed at Yarmouth.[83] Norwich castle was the main gaol for county prisoners awaiting trial and four-fifths (616) of major criminal trials in Norfolk between 1307 and 1316 took place in the city, necessitating the presence of juries from every corner of the county and sometimes beyond.[84] Finally, both creditors and debtors from further afield would have come to Norwich to acknowledge and register debts under the provisions of the parliamentary Statutes of Merchants of 1283 and 1285.

As well as being the region's most important administrative centre, Norwich was a major provider of services and luxury goods. Legal, medical and canonical expertise was available, along with the services of a fencing-master (skyrmeschur) and other specialists.[85] As the Table shows, in the matter of consumer products early fourteenth-century Norwich had far more to offer than barley bread and halfpenny pies. In addition, the presence of large numbers of chaplains and literate administrators must have created an educated society, encouraging like-minded individuals to take up residence in the city. Though property in Norwich may undoubtedly have been seen as a good investment, it was social factors which seem to have motivated both rural clergy and knightly and baronial families to purchase a foothold here. More than three-quarters of the eighty benefices whose parsons appear as parties to conveyances in the enrolled deeds lay within a twenty-mile radius of the city (including the nearer parts of Suffolk), and almost half of these lay within ten miles of Norwich. In other words, most of these properties were held by clergy whose benefices were close enough to allow them to live in Norwich, with all its cultural and social advantages (and opportunities for additional employment), while still serving their cures. Similar considerations seem to have influenced the local knightly and baronial families. Of twenty-nine members of such families owning property in Norwich at this period two thirds also owned a manor within ten miles of the city and all but three owned one within twenty miles.[86] It was therefore quite unnecessary from a practical point of view for them to acquire a Norwich residence, as access to luxury goods and services would have been easy enough from their country estates. That the lure of Norwich was largely social can be exemplified in the case of Katherine de Norwich. Katherine was the widow of Sir Walter de Norwich (d. 1329), a former treasurer of the exchequer. She had rights of dower in a number of Norfolk and Suffolk manors, the closest to Norwich being Blackworth, about five miles from the city in the parishes of Stoke Holy Cross and Howe. Her household accounts survive from late September 1336. After periods of residence at Mettingham, Suffolk, and Blackworth, she moved to Norwich in January 1337 and remained there until at least the end of April, when the detailed accounts cease. Her stay included the anniversary of Sir Walter's death on 20 January when she held a great dinner costing almost a sixth of the expenditure recorded in the whole seven months' account.[87]

The purchasing power of Katherine de Norwich is just one aspect of the contribution made by women to the economic life of the city. This is difficult to quantify as women were rarely accorded occupations except as bynames, which could derive from their fathers or husbands.[88] They were, however, regularly fined for breaches of regulations governing the sale of food and drink, and so it is apparent that at Norwich, as in other medieval towns, many women both married and unmarried were involved in this activity. Cheese, oats, fish, flour, malt and ale could all be bought from women, with some specialities, such as the retailing of oats and cheese and the brewing of ale, being almost exclusively in their hands. St Giles's hospital used older women to care for the sick poor and paid a succession of laundresses at the rate of 2s. a year.[89] Other traditionally female occupations were domestic service and prostitution. Female as well as male servants are sometimes mentioned in the sources, though few are named. Matilda Staunford, described as a former servant in 1329, acts as a reminder that service could merely be one stage in a woman's life. Prostitution (another occasional source of income) seems to have centred around a lane east of St Andrew's Hill in the leet of Wymer. This was known as Gropecuntelane or *Turpis Vicus* (possibly the foul street mentioned in the verse at the beginning of this chapter); the removal of certain common prostitutes from the area caused an affray in 1313.[90]

References to service, prostitution and brewing might give the impression that all these women were poor. Such was by no means the case. Women who brewed, for instance, came from a wide cross-section of Norwich society, from Katherine atte Hill, a single woman who was fined regularly between 1289 and 1300 for breaches of the assize of ale and probably considered brewing to be her main source of income, to Mazelina the wife of Odo de la Bothe, four times bailiff of Norwich between 1291 and 1297.[91] All brewers, however, had to be above the poverty-line to afford the necessary equipment and have access to a hearth;[92] and even single women traders could be quite as well off as male artisans. Gundreda le Puddingwyf and Margery le Melewoman, sellers of puddings and flour respectively, were both wealthy enough to have a stake in the property market. Similarly, the former servant Matilda Staunford owned a property in the parish of St Peter Mancroft. Altogether single women in Norwich were an economic power to be reckoned with. Between 1285 and 1311 unmarried or widowed women made up 13 per cent of all known property owners and twenty-eight women were assessed for the subsidy in 1332. Two wealthy women, Letitia Payn and Katherine de Kyrkeby, possessed the resources to set up perpetual chantries in 1316 and 1332 respectively. These were an expensive, and therefore relatively unusual, form of commemoration. Katherine's endowment consisted of Abraham's Hall in the parish of St Peter Mancroft; the property took its name from Abraham fitz Deulecresse, a wealthy Jew who was executed for coin-clipping and blasphemy in 1279.[93]

How far women's work extended into the manufacturing sector is more difficult to determine. They made candles; and in 1300 Beatrice de Dilham was fined for her failure to follow the regulations governing the fulling of cloth, one of the few forms of manufacture that was controlled almost as strictly as the provision of foodstuffs. If Beatrice could run a fuller's business there is no logical reason why women should not have been involved in other manufacturing trades. A potential obstacle, whether they were dealing in manufactured articles or provisions, was the restriction of trade to freemen of Norwich. Only one woman, Anselna the daughter of Philip de Bauburgh, appears on the few surviving freedom rolls of this period.[94] It is therefore not surprising that a number of women, like men, were fined for trading as citizens without being free. On the other hand, part of the general charge against brewers in the leets of Conesford and Mancroft in 1300 was the offence of passing off strangers' goods as their own, which required the women concerned to be treated as citizens.[95] They may, like Anselna, have paid for entry to the freedom, but it is also possible that the wives, widows or single daughters of freemen were permitted to trade.

Norwich could never have grown into such a major city without its populous and relatively wealthy hinterland. It was on this immediate area that the city principally depended for food, timber, immigrants and cloth, and as a market for the sale of its goods, both imported and manufactured. Lying at the head of the navigable river system, where goods had to be transferred from boat to cart, and cut off by the Fens from easy routes to the midlands, Norwich could appear isolated both from the rest of England and within the county. In 1342 the collectors of Norfolk wool were permitted to transport it to Lynn as well as Norwich, as previously ordered, because the city was too far away for many.[96] This dependence worked both ways. By 1300 Norwich was of a sufficient size to affect the agriculture of its region markedly. A population of about 25,000 three decades later would have required 41,250 quarters of grain annually to provide the staples of bread and ale.[97] The intensive cropping of poor soils in the region has been seen as driven by the requirements of Norwich; demand from the city also encouraged the commercial production of butter and cheese in central and south-east Norfolk. On the other hand, there is no sign in Norfolk of the large-scale cultivation of oats as a cheap food that can be found in the environs of London, and possibly Oxford and Canterbury.[98] Both oats and the far more expensive wheat were on sale in Norwich, but by and large, in the major barley-producing county of Norfolk, barley bread must have been the comparatively nutritious food of the urban poor.

In other respects the impact of Norwich upon its hinterland varied with distance. Villages within a few miles of the city walls, though outside the city's jurisdiction, probably maintained a close connection. As there were no other official markets within a radius of some ten miles of the city,[99] they would have used Norwich as their market town, though not necessarily as their only source of food. Corn, cheese and poultry were, like fish, regularly bought *en route* to Norwich market, possibly at informal markets in the suburbs where tolls were not levied. This was also a prime area for investment by many Norwich citizens, whose rural property was mainly concentrated within an arc of five miles, south and west of the city.[100] For most other purposes, however, twenty miles seems to have been the effective limit of Norwich's real commercial influence.[101] Most of the areas to which residents extended credit under the provisions of Statute Merchant lay within this radius, as did the wider holdings of inhabitants transferred by final concord (a secure form of legal title registered in the court of common pleas) and the rural benefices of clergy apparently resident within the city. Here, however, the resemblance between these three groups ends. Norwich men offered credit with greatest frequency to debtors in the neighbouring hundreds to the north and south, where they presumably had contacts for the supply of raw materials, cloth and foodstuffs. They entered fewer such contracts east towards Great Yarmouth or within the more distant southern hundreds along the Suffolk border.[102] The rural holdings of the citizenry were also localised, but seem to have been concentrated along easily accessible routes out of the county irrespective of distance from Norwich.[103] Very little interest, for instance, was shown in the parishes north and north west of the city, or in most of the southern parishes outside a ten mile limit, including north Suffolk. Instead holdings were clustered between the Bure and the Yare towards Great Yarmouth, along the Ipswich road towards London, and, most noticeably, along the road towards Watton and a southern crossing of the Fens from Downham Market (Map 8). It is also noticeable that, although several Norwich men held property in or near King's Lynn (no doubt reflecting its use for the export of wool), none did so in the north coast ports.

These two patterns as a whole probably indicate the limits imposed on the influence of Norwich by the neighbouring commercial centres of Great Yarmouth and Lynn. The latter, with access through its river systems not only to west Norfolk and Suffolk but also to Bedfordshire, Cambridgeshire, Huntingdonshire and Northamptonshire, was virtually independent of Norwich. Great Yarmouth, while acting as the outport of Norwich *via* the Yare, also stood at the mouths of the Bure and the Waveney, giving direct access to the rich agricultural and cloth-producing region of north-east Norfolk and to north Suffolk. Nor was the wealth of Yarmouth solely dependent upon trade. Its medieval importance derived largely from its herring fishery, involving direct links with London fishmongers and foreign merchants; in 1332 both the total and *per capita* personal wealth of its inhabitants was greater than that of its larger neighbour.[104] It is hardly surprising that the rich Yarmouth merchant Oliver Wyth, who died in 1291, appears to have had comparatively few links with Norwich.[105] In contrast, the benefices of rural clergy with city property were evenly spread within the entire twenty-mile radius, including the relevant area of north Suffolk, while the proximity of their nearest manor to Norwich appears to have been the factor drawing knightly and baronial families into its orbit. Economically Great Yarmouth may have inhibited the influence of Norwich, but it posed no threat as a social and cultural centre.

The full extent of Norwich's trading area is more difficult to gauge. Norwich men were involved in assaults in Cambridge in 1316 and 1333, were accused of killing a falcon, worth the remarkable sum of £20, in Hertfordshire in 1317, and needed safe conduct before travelling to trade at Boston in 1318.[106] Commerce could be an eventful, as well as a profitable, business in this period. There was obviously some, though to judge by the debt certificates only a limited, connection with London.[107] These few references, however, must grossly underestimate Norwich's national market. The drapers of Norwich could not have remained so wealthy, nor the dyers have increased their numbers by half, without a substantial inland trade in broadcloth as well as worsted. The importance of the overland routes to the economy of Norwich may be reflected in the strategically positioned rural holdings of the urban elite. On the whole, the city's foreign trade is more visible. Great Yarmouth was the natural port, but not the only outlet used. The export of wool from King's Lynn has already been mentioned; and imported woad belonging to two Norfolk men was seized at Ipswich in 1345.[108] In 1297 John But of Norwich even had wool arrested at Sandwich in Kent, but this was exceptional.[109] The wool staple permitting, Norwich's trading links overseas lay mainly on the other side of the North Sea, rather than the English Channel, and occasional references between 1308 and 1333 to the goods of Norwich merchants place them *en route* to or from Flanders and Picardy, in Norway or in Germany.[110]

Throughout this period the government of Norwich lay in the hands of four bailiffs, elected by the community. The office of bailiff was dominated by members of the mercantile class. Though they made up less than 15 per cent of the known trade population, merchants, linen drapers, drapers, mercers, woad dealers and exporters of wool and cloth together account for no fewer than three quarters of the forty-eight bailiffs whose occupations are known with any certainty.[111] Apart from a small group of clerks, there were two dyers, two hosiers (reflecting their earlier importance) and two spicemen/apothecaries, one fishman and one taverner. The dominance of this commercial elite is not surprising. The position was no sinecure (the early fourteenth-century custumal imposed a heavy penalty of £2 on anyone refusing to serve if elected), and merchants of any type would best be able to spare the time and expense involved.[112] The preoccupations of the city government were raising the fee farm due annually to the king (for most of this period between £110 and £120) and the maintenance of law and order. Failure in either of these respects, as the city knew to its cost, could lead to the forfeiture of its liberties. In 1272, after the attack on Norwich cathedral priory, and again in 1285, after the execution of a thief without due process of law, the liberties were seized and the city ruled for a time directly under the crown.[113] This understandable concern with civic obedience is apparent from the early fourteenth-century custumal, whose first ten chapters deal with criminal matters.[114]

The bailiffs were also intent to uphold, and if possible increase, the liberties of the city. Thus in 1305 they purchased leet (minor criminal) jurisdiction over Great Newgate in the parish of St Stephen; in 1330 they successfully maintained their right to waste ground within the city; and in 1345 they acquired jurisdiction over much of the castle fee from the crown, as well as the clerkship of the market.[115] Individuals were expected to be as vigilant as the authorities: in 1289 John de Disce was fined after he had failed to assert his rights as a freeman of Norwich not to pay toll at markets and fairs.[116] The bailiffs were also concerned to uphold a citizen's right to be impleaded in the city court, rather than in the central courts at Westminster, particularly where land in Norwich was involved.[117] In 1305, for instance, they claimed the superiority of their court in a number of cases where widows were seeking dower in their former husbands' Norwich property.[118] Defending the city's liberties in this respect was not just a matter of prestige. Paying the fee farm every year can have been no easy task, quite apart from meeting the day-to-day running expenses of civic government. At the beginning of the fourteenth century the entire rental income available to the rulers of Norwich, including the old landgable rent, raised barely £10.[119] In these circumstances, as the citizens reminded the king in 1326, judicial profits made an important contribution to their overall finances.[120]

Several factors added to the problems faced by the bailiffs in the realm of law and order. One possible source of tension was the presence in Norwich of foreign nationals. The remnant of the Norwich community of Jews, the source of earlier unrest, was expelled by the crown in 1290. Merchants from the other side of the North Sea and English Channel were, however, active in Norwich throughout this period. In 1285 an agreement was reached with merchants from Amiens and Corby bringing woad into the city; and in 1317 cloth worth £210 was seized from five merchants of Brabant to satisfy the loss of English goods taken at sea by Brabanters.[121] Interestingly, the cloth was confiscated in Norwich because the sheriff of Norfolk and Suffolk could not find goods of sufficient value elsewhere within the county, a fact which underlines Norwich's role as a centre for foreign merchants. One of the woad merchants, Peter le Mauner, together with Thomas le Fruyter, another alien, became so assimilated that they were described as citizens and merchants of Norwich in 1308 and have been included in Table 2.[122] Nevertheless, despite the selection of Norwich as a staple town in 1326 and 1333, the number of foreign merchants present in the city may have declined over this period. By 1329–36 aliens accounted for only 3.5 per cent of the wool exported from Yarmouth and for none of the worsted exported from the port in 1348–49.[123] The import of woad was also partially taken over by local men. In 1345, for instance, seventeen tuns and one pipe of woad were seized at Ipswich from Richard Spink and John Mouner, citizens of Norwich.[124] While John Mouner may have come from Picardy, Richard Spink's origins apparently lay far closer to home in Cambridgeshire.[125] This reduction in the number of alien merchants operating within Norwich, did not, however, preclude the presence of other foreign nationals. The friaries drew in students from as far afield as Italy,[126] and more generally the presence of such names as John le Long de Amyens (a poulterer) , Henry Trunch de Braban (a goldsmith) and the John Kempe de Gaunt already mentioned testifies to the continuing links between Norwich and the Low Countries.

Another potential cause of discontent was the wide disparity in income between rich and poor within the city. Even a small operator such as John le Gloz could export wool worth a total of £78 in one year, when a whole year's wages for a labourer was unlikely to rise much above one pound. Men like Robert de Holveston, with his bad debts of £752, were operating in a different league altogether. Because of immigration from an over populated countryside, this gap between the rich and the poor was, if anything, increasing. Within the leet of Mancroft the proportion of the population owning their own homes more than halved during the course of the early fourteenth century and real property became increasingly concentrated in the hands of a declining number of well-established residents. The same may have happened to personal wealth, and it is unlikely that more than 8 per cent of all Norwich householders were assessed for the subsidy of 1332.[127] If, as is quite probable, a number of them were visiting merchants, the real percentage was even lower.[128]

The fundamental problem faced by the bailiffs during this period was that of governing a city whose rapid physical expansion was not being matched by economic growth. Despite its recent difficulties over law and order, Norwich at the very start of the fourteenth century had an air of prosperity. In 1311 as many as 13 per cent of all men over the age of fourteen in the parishes of St Peter Mancroft and St Stephen were owner-occupiers. Property owners here and elsewhere in the city included glovemakers, when gloves were still a luxury item, girdlers, making ornamental girdles of silk, wool and linen as well as leather belts, decorative painters and workers in precious metals. The city served as a centre for the distribution of herring from Great Yarmouth and of the fine napkins, towels and kerchiefs produced by the linen industry of north-east Norfolk. By the eve of the Black Death the situation looked very different. Immigration from an over-populated countryside had resulted in an increase in the number of urban poor, leading to deteriorating living conditions and a polarisation of incomes. The city had declined as an entrepôt for fish and linen goods and as a leather producer. Wool exports had been disrupted and Norwich men as a whole had demonstrably failed, both at home and abroad, to exploit the growing trade in worsteds. From the late 1330s exports and imports through Great Yarmouth must, moreover, have been affected by problems over the silting of the harbour.[129] Though traffic continued it probably required transhipment into smaller boats, thereby increasing costs. Inland the series of disastrous harvests from 1315, followed by cattle and sheep disease, would not only have increased the number of poor immigrants but also affected the purchasing power of the hinterland on which Norwich partly relied for the sale of its manufactured items.[130] Certainly Norwich's luxury trades seem to have become less profitable. Between 1286–1305 and 1320–39 the numbers of known painters, glovers, girdlers and bellfounders all fell, while the goldsmiths were overtaken by the latoners, who worked not in precious metals but with tin and bronze. It is perhaps not surprising that by 1334 Norwich had slipped to seventh place among provincial towns in terms of taxable wealth.[131] In contrast to other centres, however, the one bright spot in the economy of Norwich was its cloth industry. The numbers of known dyers and shearmen rose noticeably between 1286–1305 and 1320–39, thus stimulating a demand for cloth to finish. At first they may have relied primarily on cloth brought in from the countryside. There was always, however, a small home weaving industry and the limited evidence available suggests this was on the increase. In short, during the course of the early fourteenth century Norwich seems to have moved from being a prosperous city with a wide industrial and commercial base to a city with a far greater proportion of urban poor heavily dependent upon a single industry.

8

Order and Disorder

Philippa Maddern

> the offys of teching and chastysyng longyth ... to euery gouernour aftir his ... degre, to the pore man gouernynge his pore houshould, to the riche man gouernynge his mene, to the housebond gouernynge his wif, to the fadir & the moodir gouernynge her childryn, to the iustice gouernynge his contre, to the kyng gouernynge his peple.
>
> *Dives and Pauper*[1]

In 1465 William Fielding and John Brydde of Ely entrusted John Deynes to take two hundred head of cattle to Norwich for sale. Unfortunately for them, within a week Deynes had been imprisoned by the sheriffs, 'for the preservacon of the good rewle of the same Citie'. The case came before the court of chancery at Westminster, Fielding and Brydde claiming that Deynes had pledged their cattle for his release from wrongful imprisonment. In their vigorous defence, the sheriffs of Norwich, Walter Fornfield and Richard Anyel, left an intriguing example of what they considered credible rhetoric about late medieval civic order. Like other cities, they asserted, Norwich was accustomed 'for the conseruacion of the good rewle, peez and prosperite' of the town to imprison and try such 'mysgouerned and mysrewled persons' as 'diseres, hasarders, auowtrez, fornicatours, burgaleres, baudre and breker of housez'.[2] Deynes, they said, during his five-day stay in Norwich had 'vsed the dice [and] the hasard provoking and causyng men, prentice and servaunts of the seid Citie to the same in unlefull tymes'. He had also:

> brake mens howsez be nyght ... and at last brak oop by nyght tyme the house of on Robert Smyth ... he that tyme being at Hull ... and ther made afrey vpon his wif and ther wold haue lyen by hir.

He then spent the night with a servant of the household, and 'in that abhomynabil doyng was taken by the officers of the seid Sheriff'. Brought to the Guildhall, he confessed his 'abhomynabill offencez' before the mayor and sheriffs, and 'putte hym in ther rewle'. They fined him one hundred shillings (equivalent to a working man's annual wage), and he produced twenty bullocks as surety for his release. In reply, Fielding and Brydde blamed the sheriffs themselves for any misrule. Deynes, they claimed, had lodged at Smith's house 'by lycence of suche persones as the seid Robt gave auctorite to, that ys to sey Margery wyfe of [Robert]'. It was Fornfield and Anyel who, 'for their unlawful and extorcious getyng', allowed 'divers mysgoverned wymmen occupyng comyn Bawdery' to stay in the house, 'and yf ther were eny mysgovernaunce with eny woman in the said hous yt was don by the fauour and wylfull assent of the said Margery and the agrement of the said servaunt'. The sheriffs indignantly defended the honour and good order of Smith's household. The couple were, they wrote, 'of right good and honest conversacon and rewle as wele in ther household as in al other wise'; they themselves had arrested Deynes on good grounds, 'accordyng to their office'.[3]

This case encompasses many intriguing features of public order and disorder in late medieval Norwich. In their stiff defence of civic bureaucracy, the sheriffs' language is all of rule and misrule in the public sphere. Yet throughout the account private and public order intertwine as if the two were an indistinguishable whole; moral, social and political order are equated in a manner foreign to twenty-first century readers. This kind of discourse is quite typical of concerns about civic life expressed in and about Norwich from the 1250s to the seventeenth century. Certainly the sheriffs' assertions that 'good rule' was under threat simply re-echo claims from the late fourteenth century onwards that the city was on the brink of rebellion, unresolvable conflict, misrule and dissolution. Civic and royal authorities continually agreed on this point, if on no other. Thus, a petition of 1377–78 described the commons as '*moelt grauntement contrarious*'; and a Norwich friar, annotating his copy of the *Aeneid* in the aftermath of the Peasants' Revolt, wrote scathingly of the local mob and its propensity for insurrection. The 1415 composition between various factions of the city government cited 'discordes' by which 'the Cite hath be diuided, dissoyled and in poynt to ben distroyed'. The preamble to a 1424 indenture drawn up between the mayor, sheriffs and aldermen alleged that dissension among the city's governing body had caused it to be 'hevyly voysed for lak of good and vertuous governaunce'.[4] In March 1437, the earl of Suffolk, attending a general assembly in Norwich, proffered a letter from the king rebuking 'certeyn divysyon and debate fallen among the Cytezeyns', which, he asserted, was likely to cause 'the diselacyon and distruccyon of our seyd Cyte'. A petition made in the 1450s refers to 'grete riotts, debats and trespasses doon withynne the said citee' in 1437. In a letter (*c.* 1446–47) to the sheriffs, aldermen and commoners, Sir John Clifton, governor of the city during a seizure of its liberties, resorted to beseeching the Holy Spirit to 'graunte you grace to be as wele rewlyd as I wold that ye were'.[5]

As in Deynes's case, dangerous disorder was taken to comprise a vast range of behaviour and attitudes. Private quarrels, tax grievances, breaches of economic regulations, failures to undertake civic responsibility, disagreement among the governing classes, arson, domestic violence and infidelity, street riots, armed attack on the city from outside, and what was vaguely termed 'lak of good governaunce', all, as we shall see, apparently equally signified civic disorder. In Norwich's early fourteenth-century custumal, the assault of one city-dweller by another was therefore no mere personal offence; the convicted assailant was to pay not only due amends to the victim but a heavy fine to the bailiffs 'for breaking the peace (*pro pace violata*)'.[6] In 1373 those refusing 'to pay a tax assessed upon them for causing the barge to be made to the aid of the Lord King' were roundly termed rebels.[7] When called upon to impose order on their apparently uneasy city, fifteenth-century city assemblies were in the habit of organising time, people and places with almost obsessive minuteness. On just one day, for instance (14 December 1453), the range of regulations included orders for the lights which were to be displayed over the Christmas period from five till nine every evening, the times of opening and closing of the city gates, the curfew that was to apply to servants after eight at night on pain of imprisonment for defaulters, the responsibility of innkeepers to answer for the good behaviour of their guests, and the carriage of muck out of the city by water.[8]

To take our sources seriously, therefore, we cannot confine an analysis of public order in medieval Norwich to events that modern sensibilities might denounce as disorderly. No doubt an understanding of the extent and nature of major outbreaks of crime and violence is important. To comprehend the actions of late medieval law-makers and law-enforcers in Norwich, however, we need to reconstruct also the civic and mental world which transformed what we would consider private, and (or) comparatively minor, offences – such as dicing, whoring, or possessing an offensive muckheap – into metonyms of serious public disorder.

If late medieval Norwich was a disorderly city, it was certainly not for want of institutions or authorities to reform it. From at least 1223 until 1404 the city's four great leets each had its own leet court, over which a bailiff presided (Map 11). The bailiffs also sat together to hear cases from the whole city. Each leet was subdivided into smaller areas, from which legal presentments could be made, accusing specific individuals of particular offences. At least in theory, the entire free, adult, male population of each leet was organised into tithings, whose strict duty it was to present any crimes or misdemeanours in their sub-leet, through their capital pledges, or spokesmen. Every leet had its own constable, sub-constables and collectors of amercements (the latter perhaps being the permanent serjeants of the bailiffs) to help enforce the rulings of the courts.[9] Their remit, as Walter Hudson remarked, was astonishingly wide: among a myriad cases heard between 1287 and 1391, women and men were presented for avoiding tolls, failing to register in a tithing, selling substandard goods, overpricing ale, practising excessive usury, feeding pigs on crown land, infanticide, obstructing the roads, drunkenness and leprosy.[10] Nor were leet courts the only avenues of legal control. Wronged individuals could and did pursue their opponents in local ecclesiastical courts, a practice brought to light by surviving charges in the leet courts of impleading a citizen in the court Christian in matters which did not concern marriages or wills.[11]

Even more elaborate governing structures emerged during the fourteenth and fifteenth centuries. By the 1340s it was traditional for the citizens *seu maioris partis eorum* (or a majority of them) to elect twenty-four men to represent them in communal business.[12] By the 1360s, at the latest, the twenty-four were assisted by a common assembly, which approved urban taxes and framed the commercial and civic regulations governing Norwich's internal affairs. Two groups were entitled to some share in this city governance: the 'commons' and the more elite *bon gents* or *probi homines*, who had either served as bailiffs, or commanded the status to do so. Even members of the commons regularly attended city assemblies and approved the legislative decisions made there.[13]

After the city's incorporation in 1404, at least 155 officials every year staffed an impressive political and legal bureaucracy. Peaceful governance of late medieval Norwich apparently required, according to contemporary belief, the united efforts of a mayor and his recorder, two sheriffs, twenty-three aldermen, sixty common councillors, a common speaker, a common clerk, two coroners, four claverers (or key-bearers), a chamberlain, a treasurer, two supervisors, at least three justices of the peace besides the mayor, sixteen constables, two sergeants, one sword-bearer, thirty masters of craft guilds, an overseer of the dykes, and four overseers of the walls and towers; quite apart from the customary leet officials. If, as has been estimated,[14] the fifteenth-century population of Norwich varied roughly between 5000 and 10,000 people, then, not counting participants in the leet system, between 1.6 per cent and 3.1 per cent of the city's *total* population were governing officials at any one time. Granted that only adult men could hold office, and that neither secular nor regular clergy were appointed, a very rough estimate would suggest that, in the fifteenth century, between one in twelve and one in twenty-three of all adult lay freemen were at some stage in their lives directly involved in keeping the good order of the city.

Even this formidable array of officers and institutions did not comprise the whole of Norwich's regulatory mechanisms. Throughout the period the king or his itinerant justices might sit at Norwich, enacting the awsome spectacle of royal justice in sheriffs' tourns, gaol deliveries and sessions of the peace at the castle and gaol, which, even after the city's grant of liberties in 1404, formed a separate administrative island in the heart of Norwich.[15] After 1404, Norwich city, as the equivalent of a shire, had its own justices of gaol delivery, including the mayor and other aldermen, who were empowered to try felonies.[16] Since both city and county justices of gaol delivery could impose capital punishment, the power of the state to root out urban disorder was rendered vividly present to late medieval citizens. In 1438–39, for instance, John Slynge, John James and Stephen Dykere, all Norwich men, were sentenced to hang following their trials in Norwich before the Norfolk justices of gaol delivery for arson and attempted murder, breaking and entering and stealing.[17] At the same time, the personal and moral regulation of the old leet courts survived in the activities of fifteenth-century mayors and aldermen. In July 1434, for instance, Katherine Florens was required to appear before the mayor in the guildhall to swear to the fact that during the whole of her marriage to John Florens, despite repeated attempts by Thomas Grys to seduce her, he had never actually 'violated' (*violavit*) her.[18] Similarly, in 1439 Joan and Henry Mayster's marriage broke up in *discenciones et discordis*; Henry had allegedly beaten his wife so severely that the blood flowed 'to her ankles' (*sanguinem ... usque ad eius talos decurrentem*), and he finally turned her out of the house. The mayor, one of the sheriffs and the coroner took it upon themselves to arrange for Joan to live in another household until they could 'provide for a mature settlement' (*maturionem concordiam ... providerent*) between the couple.[19]

At the other end of the spectrum from household disturbances, external order occupied the minds of city rulers. From the mid thirteenth century till at least the end of the fourteenth century, the city's military defences were gradually, but steadily, strengthened. In 1253 the citizens gained royal licence to enclose the town 'with dykes (*cum fossis*)'; in 1294 the city walls began to rise. In 1342 a wealthy citizen, Richard Spink, donated thirty springalds (catapults) to be mounted on the walls, which were intended, so the city said, to resist any attack by *enemys notre siegnor le Roi.*[20] By 1355 a view of arms in Norwich mentions gunners and gunpower, and by 1385 the city's artillery included some fifty expensive guns distributed around its gates and towers (Figure 1).[21] These defences hardly rendered the city impregnable. More recent historians have suggested that the purpose of late medieval city walls was less to provide military security than to construct an emphatic sign both of the unity of the city, and of the distinction between urban space and surrounding rural jurisdictions.[22] Yet the willingness of Norwich's richer citizens to pay not merely for walls but for armament may suggest that among the distinctly urban characteristics they wished to display was a capacity to maintain their city's integrity by repelling besiegers and repressing internal disorder.

Preoccupations with maintaining peace and securing the due obedience of the populace to their leaders were also embodied in the regulations of religious institutions, which could act as microcosms of civic order. Initiation rites of devotional guilds established the subordination of new members to the rule of the guild officers.[23] The structure of the pre-eminent guild of St George, as described in a manuscript of the early 1430s,[24] closely replicated city government, with an alderman being analogous to the mayor, two masters mirroring the role of the two city sheriffs, two beadles, and a body of twenty-four members chosen, like a common council, to represent the whole. All guild members were to be 'gouerned and reuled by the Aldirman' in all guild business; any disputes between them were to be laid before the alderman and masters, who would 'here and examine bothe parties and … sette hem in pes and reste if they mown be'. The slightest duties of guild members were minutely specified; they were instructed on how, when and where to buy, wear, and dispose of their guild livery; what to offer at the annual St George's Day mass; what part to take in the procession when one of their number, armed as St George, battled a mock dragon through their city streets; and under what conditions they might be permitted to be absent from the subsequent feast. The language of the ordinances mimicked pronouncements on urban, and indeed national, public order. Members 'founde rebelle and contrarious' against the governors of their voluntary association could be fined 40s. Admittedly the rules of the St George guild were exceptionally lengthy and precise; but since all religious fraternities must have had some governing precepts, and since Norwich hosted at least forty-six pious confraternities in the period between 1370 and 1532, it seems that many Norwich citizens submitted willingly to intense communal organisation of some part of their devotional lives.[25]

Whether the subjects of these all-embracing systems of government gave either heartfelt respect or habitual obedience to their superiors' edicts is impossible now to say. The urban elite, however, attached great importance to its institutions, determinedly upholding both their authority and their magnificence. The bailiffs' accounts for 1295–96, for instance, record the purchase of a banner for the use of the constables, apparently to raise the visibility and prestige of their office.[26] Thirteenth- and fourteenth-century bailiffs rated their dignity so highly that they formally classified the actions of underlings who refused to take their oaths of office as '*maximo contemptu*' against the bailiffs.[27] Attempts to sidestep their jurisdiction were immediately and heavily punished. In 1290–91, the tanners were fined the large sum of one mark (13s. 4d.) because 'they correct transgressions which ought to be pleaded before the bailiffs'.[28] Diligent efforts were made to force lesser inhabitants of the city at least to demonstrate outwardly their personal accountability for the city's peace and welfare. In the thirteenth to fourteenth centuries, tithing rolls were conscientiously updated and reluctant freemen routinely presented and fined for such irresponsibility as failing to register in a tithing, not attending the leet courts, or harbouring unregistered city-dwellers.[29] By about 1308, the makers of the custumal were gravely worried that the large number of day labourers in the city might be effectively immune to legal sanctions, because they had no property by which they could be attached to appear in court.[30] Jurors and capital pledges were presented for concealing offences or failing to discharge their official reponsibilities.[31] Fifteenth-century members of the St George's guild who were unaccountably absent from assemblies or masses were likewise regularly noted, and occasionally fined, as were members of the aldermanic bench, or even commoners, who missed city assemblies.[32]

It is worth looking in more detail at one of our most informative sources on thirteenth- and fourteenth-century Norwich perceptions of public order. From the surviving presentments and amercements of the leet courts, unequally distributed over the period 1288–1391, we should be able to tell which issues were thought by the tithingmen and juries to warrant the scrutiny of the courts. Tabulation of the published cases supports the contention that the courts dealt with an astonishing variety of misdeeds, excluding only such major crimes as homicide. Table 1 (below) also shows, however, that few of the complaints would nowadays be seen as particularly threatening. By far the commonest allegations concerned economic regulation, or enforcement of civic responsibility. Offences against the assize of ale or bread, at over one-fifth of all cases, formed the largest single body of misdeeds. Together with forestalling or regrating goods (attempting to corner the market or offering merchandise for resale), and perpetrating bad or fraudulent workmanship, this category of economic offences amounts to over one half of all cases (53.3 per cent). Civic offences, such as avoiding the leet courts, not registering in a tithing, harbouring the unregistered, buying and selling without being a member of the freedom, knowingly concealing offences and wrongfully raising the hue, make up nearly another quarter of all allegations (24.2 per cent). Assault, menaces, blood-drawing and hamsoken (mayhem) come a bad sixth in the list of popular offences (4.8 per cent). Causing a nuisance or obstruction (blocking watercourses, digging up highways, or owning a noisome dunghill) and theft (including receiving stolen goods, or harbouring thieves) were the only other single categories to register more than 3 per cent of total allegations. The more sizeable 'Other' group is highly miscellaneous, combining various economic offences (such as taking wheat out of customers' bushels, selling tallow and candles secretly, making a fixed-price agreement), moral and social regulation (two foreigners presented as 'tipplers [sellers, not drinkers] of beer', one charge of dicing, one of excessive usury, and nine accusations of nightwalking), a variety of administrative peccadilloes (not delivering up treasure trove, concealing or selling found goods, avowing corn to be fee of the prior of Norwich) and other offences, including misuse of common or royal resources (catching fish against the assize, digging turves out of the city ditch and feeding pigs on the king's wall).[33]

TABLE 3

Cases in Norwich leet courts, 1288–1391

Type of offence, in order of frequency	Percentage (of 1659 cases)
Offences against assize of ale/bread	21.8
Avoiding leet/not registered in tithing/harbouring those not in tithing/buying and selling though not of the freedom	20.6
Forestalling/regrating goods	19.8
Practising fraudulent craft/selling bad meat/cooked food	11.7
Other	7.4
Assault/hamsoken/menaces	4.8
Making nuisance/obstruction	3.8
Asporting goods/receiving stolen goods/harbouring thieves	3.1
Raising the hue wrongfully	2.4
Making rescue/wrongful distraint/wrongful attachment	1.4
Concealment of misdemeanor/refusing oath of office	1.2
Impleading in court Christian on secular matters	0.8
Purpresture	0.7
Avowing foreigners' goods as one's own	0.6
Total	100.0

In all these statistics, the only cases which could possibly be classed as violent or serious crime are one presentment of harbouring felons, one of illegal imprisonment, one in which 'John the Redepriest' was to be arrested on suspicion of having killed his illegitimate baby, and a presentment of menacing in 1374.[34]

While both the admonitions of rulers and the range and elaboration of peace-keeping mechanisms might suggest that late medieval Norwich residents experienced constant social and political division and the continual risk of terrifying lawlessness and violence, the records of the city's main legal forum suggest that serious and violent crimes were not the chief preoccupation of law-keepers. Of course, few historians nowadays would be prepared to take the simple pronouncements of civic elites at face value. At the very least, all commentators had their own reasons for stressing civic discord, which might derive less from the actual state of the city than from other exigencies. The urban leaders castigating the contariety of the commons in 1377–78, for instance, were trying to persuade Richard II to grant powers to the bailiffs and the twenty-four to pass ordinances without the consent of their supposedly recalcitrant councillors. They apparently found no reason to use their newly-granted authority for some years after it had been gained.[35] Heavy-handed government regulation may signify either a genuine need to suppress crime and disorder, or that there was a perceived value to urban governments in promoting the meticulous supervision of almost all aspects of civic life, independent of the actual crime rate. Indeed, the one thing we can certainly tell from the elaboration of governing structures in late medieval Norwich, and the range of their concerns, is that to these urban rulers 'good governance' implied not merely the creation of a largely law-abiding and non-violent environment, but also the maintenance of whole sets of highly-regulated and often strictly stratified cultural worlds within the city. Good governors, according to the actions of the Norwich elite, regulated the economic order of the city, making sure that distinctions between the commercial opportunities of citizens, non-citizens and outsiders were rigidly observed. They maintained specific devotional and ceremonial observances; protected the physical health of both the city and its inhabitants; ordered the times of day at which specific activities could take place; and, as in Deynes's case, saw an indissoluble connection between an individual's moral behaviour and the 'good rule' of the entire city.

This reading of the assumptions of Norwich governors does not prove that serious and violent crime was rare in Norwich in the period between 1250 and 1500; but it does suggest that the case for a violently disturbed city remains to be proven. What evidence do we have of either serious social tension, common and long-lasting divisions among the governing classes, or consistently high levels of violent crime in late medieval Norwich?

In terms of social division so grave as to lead to serious disturbance, it is true that well-attested outbreaks of major public disorder occurred. In 1235 it was alleged that a *maxima civitatis multitudo* assaulted the officers of the sheriff of Norfolk, who had attempted to protect Norwich Jews from the attacks of their neighbours.[36] No one denies that in August 1272 around 170 citizens attacked the priory by the Ethelbert gate and succeeded in burning down some of its buildings.[37] In 1381, during the Peasants' Revolt, Geoffrey Litster and his army entered the city, looted and extorted money from some richer citizens, and executed Reginald de Eccles, a Norfolk justice of the peace.[38] In January 1443, it was alleged, a crowd of about one hundred people assembled *ad insurreccionem*, and threatened to besiege and burn the priory if an indenture of 1429 recording an agreement between the city and the priory were not returned to them.[39] Even four mass public outbreaks (1235, 1272, 1381 and 1443) hardly constitute continuous social disorder over the space of 265 years from 1235 to 1500. At the apparent average rate of one major outbreak every sixty-six years, Norwich might seem considerably more peaceful and united than many twentieth-century cities. Besides, whether these events were generated by urban class enmities is very doubtful. The two attacks on the priory appear to have been supported by city-dwellers from a range of social ranks, up to and including prominent members of the urban government. Fifteen office-holders have, for instance, been identified among the named rioters of 1272.[40] In both 1272 and 1443, the supposed insurgents seemed primarily concerned with maintaining, and if possible extending, the city's control over its own jurisdiction and urban space. In 1272, the citizens alleged (admittedly after the event) that incursions into the city by the prior's men constituted the setting up of a 'false castle' (*castrum adulterinum*) in the king's city, against the king's peace, and hence that it was lawful for them to attempt to 'subdue and assault' (*gravare et expugnare*) the king's enemies, if necessary with fire, though they admitted that Christians should not in general burn down sacred buildings.[41] The geographical and jurisdictional limits of the prior's powers within and around Norwich were in dispute at least as early as 1233, when a plea between the burgesses of Norwich and the prior over the liberty appears in the curia regis rolls.[42]

Frequent legal bickering characterised late medieval city-priory relationships in general; and the claim that the citizens were actually protecting the king's rights was to have a long history. By 1290 a fine (or formally binding agreement) had been made between the prior and the citizens 'concerning Common of Pasture in Eaton and Lakenham'.[43] Leet courts presented the prior and his servants for such offences as allegedly feeding pigs on the king's wall, or fishing against the assize (1290–93).[44] At least twice (1380 and 1441) city assemblies tried to enforce on citizens a boycott of the prior's courts.[45] The years 1416 and 1417 saw the priory and the city engaged in a kind of legal and ritual competition for authorisation. Each accused the other of hearing cases in areas in which they had no jurisdiction; and the mayor, sheriffs and aldermen, in order to assert their rights to fish in the river at Trowse, sponsored an official fishing expedition, including a triumphal procession back to Norwich and a ceremonial fish-distribution to all citizens, carried out to the chant of 'We are in possession by right and by our liberties of this City of Norwich we have caught them'.[46] The events of 1272 and 1443, therefore, seem to have been occasional, but not typical, products of the long-running and intensely felt (but generally legally expressed) tension between two prestigious and authoritative bodies uneasily juxtaposed in a small administrative space.

Certainly, too, the events of 1381, though doubtless terrifying to some citizens, did not display the deep-riven social conflict which briefly devastated towns such as London, York or Beverley. In Norwich, the one casualty was not a member of the urban government, and few Norwich citizens seem to have been involved; the city was the place of origin of only eight of all Norfolk rebels later presented at the hundred courts.[47] That late medieval Norwich was heavily socially stratified is, of course true, and those who were ruled sometimes expressed their dissatisfactions trenchantly. In the early fourteenth century, for instance, the 'middle people' petitioned vigorously against what they considered to be oppressive and unjust taxation levied on them by the city government.[48] Yet social discontents, just as they did not markedly provoke urban conflicts with the priory, also apparently rarely caused violence among citizens, let alone anything approaching social revolution.

Divisions among the governing elite are obvious at some points in the city's history. In the years following incorporation, such serious disputes arose between the common assembly of the city and the twenty-four 'prudhommes' that the influential Norfolk knight and courtier, Sir Thomas Erpingham, had to be called in to produce an acceptable arbitration.[49] After a mayoral election in 1433, so hotly contested that both sides appealed to governmental intervention to support their candidate, the 1437 elections were marred by what the losing side later asserted to be a riot.[50] The agitation against the priory in 1443 was itself initiated by a bitter dispute in the city assembly on 25 January 1443 over whether the city should use its seal to ratify formally an indenture of arbitration in the ongoing dispute.[51] Again, however, such events were perhaps untypical of late medieval life within the walls. It has been argued that potential destabilisation caused by conflict between the governing elite and the wider group of 'commons' in the late fourteenth and fifteenth centuries was generally forestalled not by stricter legal controls but by well-agreed protocols of negotiation and arbitration.[52] One apparent result of the dissension of the early fifteenth century was an indenture of 1424 in which the Norwich elite registered their consent to a set of procedures to protect group solidarity under almost any circumstances. By this agreement, aldermen undertook not to campaign for political office, nor to sue any quarrel against their peers, or even to be party to any such dispute. Instead, they would submit to peer arbitration.[53] The indenture did not, or course, prevent the development of deep political rifts among the elite in the 1430s. But a counterweight to this observation is the fact that the mayor's court books from 1424 to 1449 record dozens of securities of the peace offered by members of the ruling classes to each other, many of them specifically guaranteeing the participants' consent to abide by arbitrament. Evidently at least some of the upper class were doing their best to stick to their self-imposed rules of solidarity.[54]

Finally, it is important to establish what is known about daily levels of major crime and violence in late medieval Norwich. Were they high enough to warrant intense levels of anxiety, and justify strict supervision in the medieval city? Possibly, but such an argument must be speculative at best, granted the extremely sporadic survival of records from Norwich peace sessions, coroners' sessions, gaol deliveries, bailiffs' courts and mayor's courts. Individual records rarely suggest high rates of serious crime. For instance, the only major case preoccupying John Cottesmore, John Fray, John Caumbrigge, Robert Baxter and Thomas Wetherby, justices of gaol delivery for the city sitting on 1 August 1430, was one of alleged counterfeiting by Geoffrey Grenewode, a Norwich saddler, who had, according to an indictment made before their predecessors on 11 April, forged coins called 'pens of to pens'. The August session remanded him to prison until the justices could scrutinise the original indictments. Aside from his case, the justices cleared three people arrested on suspicion, because no indictments had been preferred against them.[55] Reports of Norwich gaol deliveries for a scatter of years between 1482 and 1501 show no evidence that the justices curbed violent crimes. There were no recorded allegations more serious than 'suspicion of felony', and almost all the suspects were apparently either acquitted or released without indictment.[56] Instead, like other Norwich lawgivers, the justices of gaol delivery spent much of their time examining moral or spiritual matters, which they were not, in fact, competent to determine. In the Epiphany sessions of 1500, for example, the names of three 'women baudes' were noted. Hugh Pye, the heretic burned at Norwich in 1428, had been sent to the bishop for examination from a gaol delivery held in the city on 20 July 1424.[57] That of 21 February 1429 heard a detailed indictment of how three Norfolk men, together with two others from Suffolk and one from London, had held a heretical school at Earsham, maintaining such dangerous opinions as the inability of any priest to make bread into Christ's body, the legitimacy of eating meat on any day of the year, the inefficacy of confession, and that saints' images *nullo modo sunt adorandi.* Two of the adherents, apparently carried away by their own rhetoric, broke into a local church and destroyed an image of St Andrew. Having made a lengthy examination, however, the justices in the case correctly decided that their only option was to deliver the prisoners to the bishop for judgement.[58]

As for Norwich peace sessions, a single record of presentments made to the justices on 30 December 1440 lists intriguing, but not particularly violent or riotous, cases. Some allegations reflected the long-running disputes between city and priory over the limits of each other's jurisdiction. The prior and his servants were twice presented for attacking the city's sergeant and rescuing from him a man he had arrested for debt; and the prior's servants were also accused of breaking into a free tenement belonging to Robert Chapeleyn, mayor of Norwich in 1436, and cutting down timber. Four strange presentments allege that the houses of John and Margaret Fedymend and Richard and Beatrice Hervy were both twice broken into in November-December 1440, and that in both cases the malefactors assaulted the husband and 'carnally knew' (*carnaliter cognovit*) their wives. These may reflect attempts to manipulate categories of legal presentment in order to punish the clients of known prostitutes.[59] The remaining allegations – theft of cloths, unlicensed obstruction of a roadway – recall vividly the minute concerns of the earlier leet courts.[60]

Coroners' records are in fact the only ones which document a significant proportion of cases of violent crime in the medieval city. But the only surviving run is from 1263 to 1268, when thirty-six cases were heard. Of these, fourteen clearly reported accidental death or theft; and in five of the remaining twenty-two cases, either the coroner's jury swore that the death investigated was accidental, or the crime was imputed to slayers outside Norwich, or the suspect was cleared by compurgation.[61] Seventeen possible instances of murder over five years in a city whose population may, at a guess, have totalled 10,000 would give an average murder rate of thirty-four per 100,000 of population.[62] This figure is admittedly far higher than modern homicide statistics. The fourteen homicides reported from the whole of Norfolk in 2000–2001 constituted only 1.74 per 100,000 of the estimated mid 2000 Norfolk population of 803,900.[63] On the other hand, Norwich's late thirteenth-century figures are less than a third of those reported for mid fourteenth-century Oxford (110 per 100,000).[64] Perhaps, then, all that can be safely concluded is that small samples give such wildly variant readings as to defy generalisations about crime rates. We should also note that modern medicine is infinitely better equipped to deal successfully with injuries to the person which in the past invariably proved fatal.

Granted the haphazard survival of Norwich legal records, it could be argued either that major crime outbreaks are lost in the *lacunae*, or that serious indictments were taken to the central courts. But central court records are also equivocal at best on the scale of disorder at Norwich. Among the 7546 cases listed in the published curia regis rolls between 1224 and 1242, only eight concerned either Norwich land or Norwich people. Of these, three were argued out over rights to dower, another dealt with landownership, the fifth was a suit of trespass and the sixth a legal dispute between the burgesses and the prior over the liberties of the city. Only two possibly comprise allegations of serious crime.[65] In one, a party of Norwich Jews was accused of kidnapping and circumcising a five-year-old boy. Though at least three of the alleged perpetrators were eventually executed, it seems most likely that the case represented not a major outbreak of crime but a custody dispute over the unfortunate child between the Norwich Jewish community and one of its male Christian converts.[66] The other case alone, recording the incident in 1235 when the bailiffs of the city pleaded that the sheriff of Norfolk had arrested city officers without cause, while the sheriff himself counter-accused the bailiffs of failing to halt anti-Semitic arson in the city and allowing the citizens to beat his officers, could plausibly represent open public disorder. It is, however, clear that social anxieties in thirteenth-century Norwich were on occasion channelled into active anti-Semitic aggression (Plate 3); but also that even at this early stage the question of public order was entangled with problematic distinctions between royal and communal authority.

Any comparison between Norwich and other parts of England in terms of its crime statistics is almost impossible to establish, though by limiting the analysis to one series of records over a comparatively short period some tentative observations emerge. Table 4 gives the percentages of the various kinds of charges appearing from Norwich in the king's bench records between 1422 and 1442 as compared to the same statistics from the rest of the East Anglian circuit for that period. These figures are the more significant in that, if Norwich could be described as a disorderly city in any twenty-year period in the late middle ages, surely it should be during the years when both the city-priory tension, and divisions within the city's governing bodies came to a head.[67] Table 4 should therefore show whether or not these events reflected or produced a general breakdown of law and order in the city.

TABLE 4

Allegations in Norwich king's bench cases compared with the rest of East Anglia, 1422–1442[68]

Alleged offence	*Other East Anglian cases: (Percentage of 2937)*	*Norwich cases: (Percentage of 201)*
Asporting goods	22.5	16.4
Trespass (close-breaking)	36.6	14.4
Assault	15.9	21.4
Rape/Abduction	4.3	9.0
Menaces	4.5	8.0
Homicide	2.0	0.5
Riot	0.6	1.5
Mayhem	0.4	0.0
Maintenance/or embracery	4.1	19.9
Other	8.9	9.0
Total	100.0	100.0

At first sight, the figures might suggest a troubled community, since allegations of non-violent crime (alleged trespass, or asporting goods) comprised a much lower percentage of cases from Norwich than from the rest of the East Anglian circuit. On the other hand, Norwich percentages of apparently more violent offences were consistently, though not spectacularly, higher.[69] Closer investigation, however, reveals some prosaic reasons for these disparities. Among the fifty-nine Norwich cases of assault and menaces, nine separate bills appear, each lodged on the same day by a different well-heeled Norwich businessman (including one alderman), each monotonously reiterating that, on 26 May 1440, John Wymondham had assaulted and menaced the plaintiff so that he could not continue his accustomed trade.[70] Since Wymondham himself had already secured the indictment of all nine complainants at a sheriff's tourn on 21 October 1439 for breaking into his park at Gressenhall and stealing sheep and cattle, there is more than an equal chance that the bills reflected no actual crime, but a well coordinated attempt by a group of prosperous citizens to put some legal pressure on their adversary in the course of a property dispute.[71] Even if we suspend disbelief and assume both the park-breaking and the charges of menacing to be true, it seems certain that collaboration among the 'victims' procured the proliferation of allegations of assault and menaces. Reducing these nine charges to one would therefore more accurately reflect the figures of alleged crime at this period. It would also lower the percentage of alleged assaults and menaces in Norwich to 18.1 per cent and 4.2 per cent respectively: that is, either not significantly higher than, or slightly lower than, the percentages in the rest of East Anglia.

Similarly, any alarm at the apparent fact that Norwich had more than double the rate of rape and abduction evident in the rest of East Anglia should be allayed by the observation that, of the eighteen cases, ten alleged the abduction of a servant, two more of a serf, and one of a monk of Langley. Certainly in these three last cases, and probably in the last thirteen, we must suspect that the alleged abductees had simply left their original employment for greener pastures. If that were so, then the alleged incidence of rape and abduction in Norwich would fall to the low figure of 2.7 per cent of all crimes. The higher proportion of these cases coming from Norwich may thus represent not disorder in the city, but the comparative plethora of employment opportunities it offered to discontented servants, labourers and even monks.

Only the anomalous proportion of cases of maintenance and embracery remains to sustain any argument that Norwich was more violent, lawless and disordered than other places in East Anglia between 1422 and 1442. But of all possible crimes, maintenance is the least likely to have involved violent disorder, or to have attracted a significant proportion of guilty verdicts. In all East Anglian records where a detailed indictment is available, the charge in fact involved bribing jurors with money or food rather than threatening them with force.[72] Thus John Wymondham, evidently following up his allegations of park-breaking against Gregory Draper and other Norwich notables, alleged in the Hilary term of 1441 that jurors in the case had taken money, food and drink from Draper to give a favourable verdict at sessions held in Norwich in June 1440.[73] If these cases undermined law and order, at least they did so by non-violent means. Furthermore, guilty verdicts on the charge of maintenance and embracery are so rare as to preclude any certainty that the offence took place. None of the defendants in the forty Norwich cases was convicted, while eleven were acquitted, or obtained a *sine die*. It is therefore possible that this array of charges testifies not to the disorderly state of late medieval Norwich, but to the sophistication of Norwich litigants, who knew that one way to harass opponents at law into settlement was to allege maintenance and embracery against them.

Hence crime statistics do not unequivocally support the argument that Norwich was a place of violence and disorder. Surveying practically all surviving court cases seems also to present puzzling incongruities in the definition of late medieval public order there. Why did urban rulers so commonly bemoan the dangerously disordered state of their city, yet concentrate their judicial efforts on relatively minor and civil offences? It would be interesting to know what exactly the citizens who rioted against the priory in 1272 and 1443 thought they were doing. We might also ask why Jewish men who had tried to reclaim one of their boys from a Christian household had to die for it. It is also curious that justices of gaol delivery, who lacked the authority to determine cases of heresy, nevertheless spent significant time examining them; and even more so that members of the guild of St George were compelled to turn out every year to support a parade in which a dressed-up knight battled a fictive, though fire-breathing, dragon through the streets of their city. How can we make sense of a boundary between public and private disorder so ill-defined that the mayor, aldermen, sheriffs, justices of the peace and justices of gaol delivery all felt impelled to investigate and regulate the sexual and marital goings-on of individual urban households, and the visitors in them?

Perhaps both the range and the nature of events classed as disorderly in late medieval Norwich make sense only in the context of a much wider and more organic ideal of order underlying the rhetoric and actions of governors and city-dwellers alike. It has rightly been observed that the idea that the urban community could be characterised as a human body – literally an incorporation – was widespread in late medieval English towns. But the implications of the metaphor extend beyond the often-quoted quest for urban purity and the consequent banishment of antisocial elements to the outskirts of medieval cities.[74] Once identified as a body politic, the late medieval city could very easily be described as one step in a hierarchy of politicised entities. The universe could be represented as a body; so, in descending order, could a nation, a city and a household.[75] Most of these organisms also consisted of a voluntary congregation of individuals (the household of the man, his wife, and their dependents, the city of the free citizens, and so forth); but at all levels of this hierarchy of polities, right governance could best be envisaged as a metaphor of bodily construction. Even the individual body could be seen as a collective of parts ruled by the soul. Thus Sir John Fortescue (d. *c.* 1475), drawing heavily on Thomas Aquinas's *On Princely Government*, taught that rule of one leader over many in all organisations where many members were 'coordinated into one' was quintessentially organic and hence natural:

> In the corporeal universe, the earthly bodies are regulated by the first body, which is celestial, and the same are governed by the rational creature, and man's body by his soul, and the parts of the soul, that is passion and desire, by reason, and all the members of man's body by the head and the heart.[76]

Each level of political association, from the human body upwards, necessarily had a 'head'. 'A people does not deserve to be called a body whilst it is acephalous', Fortescue succinctly commented.[77]

Bodily order thus became a powerful symbol of all forms of governance, an idea which gained force from Augustinian notions of the origins of all political regulation. Though, as Fortescue remarked, St Augustine of Hippo (d. 430) subscribed to the classical theory that polities derived from people grouping together to ensure justice and to further their common interests,[78] he also assumed that such groupings became strictly necessary only after the Fall. In the Augustinian view of the prelapsarian state, institutions of governance were not needed, because the common good was willed by God, and the created universe was as yet completely obedient to God's will. Hence the universe formed an ideal political organism, in which all members – angels, humans, animals, plants – freely and without coercion carried out their allotted roles for the good of all the others. This state of consensual obedience to divine order functioned even within the marriage, and the physical bodies, of Adam and Eve. Augustine hypothesised that, as the universe was infinitely beneficial to them, so their own bodies suffered neither disease nor accident; and as they accepted gratefully the just rule of God, so their partnership was one of loving consensus, without domination on Adam's side or disobedience on Eve's. Similarly, as each effortlessly obeyed God, so all their bodily organs freely obeyed their soul's will, producing (among other salutary effects) sexual intercourse without lust and hence without shame.

Since this potentially anarchic, but perfectly ruled, system was sustained only by the complete obedience of all parts of the cosmos to their creator, it could not survive Adam and Eve's disobedience. At the taking of the forbidden fruit, disruption and insubordination invaded the whole universe. Subjects (including wives) became inherently rebellious and intractable; rulers (including husbands) easily succumbed to selfish 'lust for dominion'. In such a new and dangerous world, individuals might well group together for common protection; yet they also needed firm government to check pride and disobedience.[79] The rebellious physical body thus became the instigator of sin, a site of shame, the theatre of the 'carnal rebellion (*contentionem*) ... that we sustain in our limbs and blighted being', and a metonym of all social and political disorder.[80] Only by consciously and painstakingly rebuilding their obedience to God could humans recapture any semblance of the ideal order of the prelapsarian universe.

Such political theology may seem distant from the world of late medieval English city-dwellers; yet its messages were firmly embedded in popular urban media. In the late fifteenth-century East Anglian N-town play cycle (probably performed in Norwich), *The Creation and Fall of Man* explicitly contrasts the state of Adam and Eve before and after the Fall in Augustinian terms of obedience and rebellion (Plate 18). In Eden, God promises that the whole world 'xal be buxum at thi byddyng', providing unstintingly 'flesch and fysch and frute of prys'. Correspondingly, Adam and Eve are 'blythe and glad our lordys comaundement to fulfyll'. Their disobedience produces the inevitable revolution in natural power-relationships.[81] 'Alas, alas ffor this fals dede, my flesly frend my fo I fynde' exclaims Adam, neatly encompassing both Eve and his own mutinous body parts in the transition from obedience to rebellion; while for Eve the expulsion from paradise represents loss of nature's bounty, loss of her own ruling 'wit' and the beginning of harsh rule by her husband:

> Now stumble we on stalk and ston
> My wyt a wey is fro me gon
> Wrythe on to my necke bon
> Wt hardnesse of thi honde.[82]

The postlapsarian world is forthwith represented in the plays as a polity in which good and evil types of governance – Augustine's two notional cities – struggle for supremacy. Significantly, the play of *The Entry into Jerusalem* is prefaced by a speech in which Lucifer, announcing himself 'Prince of this werd', complains that Christ's disciples, as his 'bedellys', are bringing back 'eche town and cety' to godly obedience. In defence, the devil must encourage both disobedience to legitimate rule, and disturbance of the established social order. His entertaining harangue encourages his urban audience to ape extravagant fashions, to 'sett at nowth' the laws of church and state, and to delight in destabilising social ranks by dressing above their means and their estate: 'A beggerys dowter' should 'cownterfete a jentyl woman dysgeysyd as she can'.[83]

What, then were the corollaries of this reading of the origin and nature of political entities such as cities? The combination of viewing the human body as both microcosm and true representation of political structures, and of positing that all systems of order, from the individual body upward, were struggling against the disastrous consequences of the Fall, had several important effects. First, the prime duty of the head of every polity, at whatever level, was the same: to extirpate disorder and encourage obedience among subordinate members of the metaphorical body. As the quotation from the fifteenth-century tract, *Dives and Pauper*, which opens this chapter, makes plain, discipline had to be maintained at every level of society. After the incorporation of 1404, therefore, a Norwich justice of the peace, as a 'iustice gouernynge his contre' could regard himself as having exactly the same kinds of power and responsibility that any other ruler – from a husband to a king – might exercise. A second supposition follows. Under this conceptual scheme, issues of public order could hardly be confined either to a narrow range of crimes, or to what we would now call the public sphere. It was the duty of the urban ruler to ensure that all parts of the body politic, in all their functions, were duly obedient to godly order. Failure even in one of the smaller political units of the city – for instance, the household – would inevitably produce disruption elsewhere. The author of *Dives and Pauper* expressed hearty approval of the Deuteronomic law that the parents of incorrigibly disobedient children should deliver them for punishment to 'the rewlours of the cite', because:

> God bad that al the people of the cite ... schuyldyn slen [slay] that vnbuxum [disobedient] child with stonys in example of al othre. For whan yong folc waxyn rebel to fadir and moodir but they ben chastysyd and withstondyn in the begynnynge, their schul schendyn [destroy] the comounte of the people be roberye and morde [murder] and manslaute, be colligaciouns and wyckyd companyys and makyn rebellion and rysynge ayens her souereyns and so ben cause of distruccion of the lond, of the cite and of the comounte.[84]

No wonder, then, that the rulers of Norwich showed themselves simultaneously perpetually overanxious about the good order of the city, and indefatigably interested in even the minutest detail of urban institutions and activities. At the highest level, theirs was the responsibility of seeing that city space, and the city's inhabitants, were regularly, ritually and visibly ordered in that service to God which alone could restore the perfect rule of paradise. At Christmas, Epiphany and All Saints members of all craft guilds and fraternities were bound to attend the mayor, sheriffs and aldermen, in order of rank, as they solemnly processed to the cathedral; and by the 1450s the order of the annual Corpus Christi procession, from the least prestigious craft (reeders) to the wealthiest merchants, was laid down in a city ordinance. From the 1420s onwards, St George's day marked the special procession of the guild of St George, in which a man dressed as the saint and attended (as his assumed status demanded) by both a sword-bearer and a banner bearer, battled a fire-breathing dragon through the streets of Norwich (Plates 19 and 22). The pageant was accompanied by the mayor, aldermen and guild members, on horseback and in livery, with twenty-four priests preceding them, the cantors of the cathedral chanting, and the bells of the cathedral ringing.[85] The dragon, the symbol of Lucifer, the archetypal rebel against God, was thus slain by a martyred saint, the icon of Christian obedience, amid the ritual affirmation of the church and the applause of a nicely-graded populace. This annual restoration of heavenly order thus seemed to produce, and to be produced by, correct social order and harmonious relations between the church and the lay world.

Ultimately it was this understanding of public order which made such good sense of Justice William Yelverton's proposal of 1452 to produce a partial merger between the guild of St George and the city government. While the devotional functions of the guild remained distinct from those of the mayoralty, the overlap in personnel between the two groups was institutionalised; every member of the common council of the city was to be admitted to the guild, the ruling alderman of the guild was invariably to be the outgoing mayor of the city, and dismissal from either group entailed removal from the other.[86] It is, no doubt, right to suggest that one aim of this settlement was to enhance the solidarity of the ruling classes, which had been severely strained in the disturbances of the 1430s and 1440s.[87] But it also institutionalised the regular performance, by the governing body, of rituals of godly obedience, and hence drew on the deeper perception that public order ultimately depended on the right relationship between urban rulers and their God.

The perceived importance of this relationship may also have encouraged both the apparent anti-Semitism in Norwich in the thirteenth century, and the later anxiety of justices of gaol delivery to unearth cases of heresy and send them for judgement. It is worth noting that fire – possibly partly as a symbolic purification – was used against both heretics and Jews. In 1235 it appears that city authorities were unwilling to prevent arson against Jewish families; while in 1428 official conflagrations publicly despatched the heretics Hugh Pye, William White and John (or William) Waddon to their final judgement.[88] No doubt short-term causes, too, influenced the timing of these events; there was a general upsurge in anti-Lollard persecution between 1428 and 1431, linked, as has been suggested, to the need to impress the forthcoming Council of Basle with England's orthodoxy.[89] But since both heretics and Jews were held to have chosen knowingly to reject God's will, they formed groups clearly vulnerable to any inclination by the urban government to bring their city back to godly order by purifying it of perceived anti-Christian elements.

The metaphor of the body politic also demanded that the physical, institutional and political integrity of the city should command a high priority with its citizens. The walls of the city obviously emphasised its organic unity, its notional impermeability, as well as its capacity to resist any who opposed the king's authority. Hence the government of Norwich was, at least intermittently, careful to maintain its defences in good order. Less obviously, however, economic regulation of the freedom of the city provided a clear administrative distinction between members of the body politic and those outside it – a distinction which was monotonously enforced by the prosecution of commercial offences in the leet courts. Those who sought to blur the boundaries of the urban body by buying and selling although they were not included in the freedom, or by acting as agents of those outside the freedom, had to be punished. Furthermore the persistent antagonism between city and priory may have derived some of its heat from the deep-seated conviction that a body politic with two heads would resemble a dangerous freak of nature. Especially after incorporation, the mayor needed to show himself to be sole ruler of his independent county. Any hint that the prior might justifiably act as a competing secular authority within the city space would jeopardise the whole metaphor of right rule which legitimated the city government.

At a lower social level, the typological connection between all levels of government within the city meant that households, too, must be closely regulated. If urban households were disordered – if wives, children and servants swerved from their allegiance to male household heads – then, as the author of *Dives and Pauper* implied, public order would inevitably be at risk from adulterous women and delinquent children. The anxieties of the mayor, sheriffs and coroners to repair the violent discord in Henry Mayster's marriage, the examination of possible cases of adultery in the mayor's court, and the determination of the sheriffs in the Deynes case to assert that Robert and Margery Smyth were of 'good and honest conversacon and rewle as wele in ther household as in al other wise', and to categorise John Deynes as an adulterous interloper, made excellent sense in terms of late medieval understandings of public order. In this conceptual system, to make any distinction between public and private would be to jeopardise the safety of the whole city. As head of the corporation, the mayor had to be not only the city's ruler, but also, ultimately, its marriage counsellor, if he was to fulfil his role properly.

Finally, the bodily health of each individual presumably also both witnessed to, and reproduced, the good order subsisting in the city as a whole; an assumption which may have added point to the attempts of governors to ensure the cleanliness of the city and the health of its inhabitants.[90] This notional entity also required moral regulation. On the simplest analogical level, since intemperance, gluttony, drunkenness, lechery and even the company of 'dees [dice] pleiers and hasardours' would disorder an individual's health,[91] it is no wonder that leet courts, sheriffs and justices alike punished tipplers, bawds and gamesters as part of their task of procuring civic welfare and order. But late medieval discursive links between swearing and dicing, due worship of Christ, bodily integrity and social disorder were even more profound and complex than the simple body and city metaphor would imply. Thomas Gascoigne (d. 1458), for instance, noted in his *Loci e libro veritatem* that the sinful were inclined to swear '*horribiliter*' by the parts of Christ's body – His eyes, His blood, His heart, the nails in His hands and feet – whereupon, in punishment, God made them die, bleeding from the same parts of their own bodies.[92] Swearing here appears as a re-enactment of the dismembering of Christ's crucified body, hastening the mortal dissolution of the individual's own anatomy. An early fifteenth-century *pietà* wall-painting from Broughton, Buckinghamshire, portrays the links between dissolute behaviour, attack on the physical body of Christ and the consequent disordering effects on the social body of humanity with shocking vividness. The dead Christ lies in Mary's lap, surrounded by flashily-dressed sinners whose words and deeds literally tear him apart. The bones of one arm and one leg protrude from Christ's torn flesh; one misdoer triumphantly holds a dismembered hand, another a foot, a third Christ's heart. Directly beneath the Christ figure two men sit with a gaming board between them. One holds a cross; despite this, the other is in the act of murdering him with a vicious sword blow to the head.[93] To those attuned to medieval body politics, the message is clear. Dissolute behaviour constituted a direct and rebellious attack on Christ's physical body; which, in true Augustinian fashion, was instantly refracted in a violent breakdown of public and social order.

It is easy for us to see, in major outbreaks such as the attack on Norwich priory in 1272 or the murder of Reginald de Eccles in 1381, signs of a public order crisis in late medieval Norwich. But the high visibility of these cases to our eyes may be misleading. To late medieval citizens of Norwich, imbued with Augustinian notions of bodily order and political theory, major riots and crimes may have borne a very different meaning. The citizens viewed their actions in 1272 and 1443 at least partly as a legitimate defence of their urban administrative space. These events, to them, may not even have seemed as destabilising as the shoals of what we would call minor, or private offences which engaged their attention in the local courts. Theology and political theory may seem remote from the practical problems of governing a late medieval city, and were hardly explicitly cited by the rulers of late medieval Norwich. But the scope and nature of their activities – their determined oversight of civic responsibilities, city walls, godly devotion, marital fidelity, street cleaning and moral behaviour – cannot be fully understood unless we are willing to enter that rich world of godly politics and ideas about the body in its widest possible sense which informed, sustained and legitimised late medieval Norwich governments in their pursuit of the ideal of the well-ruled city.

9

Trade

Penelope Dunn

> Then a lamentable plague travelled by sea to Southampton and on to Bristol, where almost the whole population of the town perished, snatched away, as it were, by sudden death, for there were too few who kept their beds for more than two or three days, or even half a day. And hence cruel death spread everywhere with the passage of the sun ... After the plague many buildings, both large and small, in all the cities, boroughs and townships, decayed and were utterly razed to the ground for want of occupants ... For there was no memory of so unsparing and savage a plague since the days of Vortigen, king of the Britons, in whose time, as Bede records in his history of the English, there were not enough left alive to bury the dead.
>
> *The Chronicle of Henry Knighton* for 1349[1]

A survey which begins with a city devastated by the loss of about two thirds of its population might be expected to dwell on the tragic short-term aftermath and gloomy long-term desolation following the Black Death of 1349–50. Indeed, descriptions of several towns and cities in the later middle ages are coloured by a sense of decline, and many historians have taken a largely negative view of the urban experience in the 150 years after the calamitous fourteenth-century plagues.[2] Yet, in contrast to the response of some English provincial centres, the economic and commercial history of Norwich in the later fourteenth and fifteenth centuries is characterised by the pragmatism with which the city adjusted to massive losses from the pestilence. An initial influx of immigrants contributed to the partial replacement of the diminished population. The largest number of entrants for any year in the history of the *Liber Introitus Civicum*, or Old Free Book, is recorded in 1349–50, when 120 men paid to join the Norwich franchise.[3] In the previous year only twenty-one individuals had taken up the privilege and it seems that immigrants from outside Norwich were mostly responsible for the gradual provision of new citizens in the months following the loss of so many leading residents.[4] A similar phenomenon can be noted in 1369, after another outbreak of plague, which indicates that relatively prosperous newcomers were always willing to fill the ranks of the elite citizen body. With hardly a hint of the catastrophic events which had taken place within living memory, the later fourteenth-century records underscore the city's resilience in attempting a fresh start in the wake of the disaster.

In the short term, successive epidemics had eased the pressure on space and resources, which had previously characterised the overpopulated city. The 8,000 or so residents of the 1370s probably achieved a level of prosperity similar to that apparent elsewhere in the country.[5] What is striking about Norwich's experience is that this prosperity was effectively sustained throughout the fifteenth century as well.[6] While other important commercial centres, such as York, declined, by 1525 Norwich was the largest and wealthiest provincial city in the country, second only to London.[7] How far this success should be attributed to the astute financial policy of the ruling elite will be examined here. It will also be argued that the city's industry, and the trade it generated, contributed most to Norwich's economic buoyancy during a period when other towns claimed to be experiencing acute financial difficulties.

Commerce, roughly defined as 'financial transactions or the buying and selling of merchandise', was crucial to Norwich's survival and prosperity during the middle ages.[8] Commercial interaction was, of course, the lifeblood of all medieval towns, whose markets, offering year-round facilities for wholesaling and retailing, were central to their very existence. The town's function as a place of exchange, where members of urban and rural communities made purchases and sold their goods, was vitally important and generated the funds essential for effective government. Not surprisingly, members of the mercantile elite comprised the most affluent group within Norwich society and filled the ranks of its aldermen.[9] The wealthiest citizens were usually those merchants who made sufficient money through their commercial endeavours to finance the church, to underwrite municipal projects and ecclesiastical and lay building work, to obtain royal charters and present petitions in parliament. They were also expected to contribute generously toward charitable works, not to mention the costs of the day-to-day running of the city and the annual payment of its fee farm, which stood at £128 2s. 4d. a year in the late fourteenth century.[10] Money, the key to high political office and the surest route to power in late medieval Norwich, was made in abundance through overseas and national trade. But commerce, in the widest sense of the word, went on at every level of the social hierarchy, from the womenfolk who bought and sold their daily bread to visiting Florentine merchants, such as Balthasar Lumbard, with lucrative business contacts in the city.[11] Trade was just as important to someone like Peter of Stody, a common 'fripperer' who recycled and sold old clothes,[12] as it was to men such as Hugh Holland, who made at least nine shipments of goods, together worth over £400, from Great Yarmouth in the year 1388–89 alone.[13] Buying and selling was the way in which the majority of townsmen and women earned their livings and thereby secured the basic necessities of life. This chapter will examine the commercial dealings undertaken by Norwich people in the late middle ages, at an international, national and local level, and the ways in which commerce shaped the fortunes of all classes of civic society during this period.

It is impossible to explore the trade of any city without providing some account of its chief industry. Textile production, encompassing both the finishing and the manufacture of cloth, was the principal industry of late medieval Norwich and its hinterland. Indeed, textiles became increasingly important for the city's economy in the century and a half following the Black Death of 1349–50. Worsted, a cloth peculiar to Norwich and the villages north of the city (whence its name was derived), was highly versatile both as a luxury fabric, for prestigious items, such as altar cloths and bed hangings, and as an inexpensive clothing material that required little or no fulling.[14] Fulling was the process by which woollen cloth was 'felted', by pounding it in soap or fullers' earth, before it was stretched on a 'tenter-frame' to dry.[15] Instead of being fulled, worsted was woven from yarn made from long-stapled wool that had been teased out into slivers with hot combs. The combed wool was then spun into yarn with a stone or pottery spindle rather than a conventional wheel.[16] After being woven into cloth, worsted was often sold 'white', ready for finishing elsewhere. It might then be dyed and sheared, with the nap of the fabric trimmed away to leave a smooth surface. Finally came 'calendering' or hot-pressing, which gave the cloth its characteristic fine gloss.[17] Because the stages in its manufacture were not so labour-intensive or time-consuming, worsted was less expensive to produce than broadcloth.[18] Developments in the city's textile industry before the Black Death saw a shift from the long-established business of finishing broadcloth produced in rural Norfolk. Because of economic diversification, Norwich now emerged as a significant centre for the actual manufacture of both broadcloth and worsted and, crucially, as the region's principal outlet for the distribution of worsted cloth.

The role of the city within Norfolk's textile industry changed radically, in terms of the production as well as the distribution of cloth, over the course of the fourteenth and early fifteenth centuries. In the second half of the fourteenth century worsteds began to be produced commercially inside the city walls, and textile manufacture came to equal if not surpass the cloth finishing trades in importance for the Norwich economy. During the reign of Richard II (1377–99) the number of weavers identifiable in the city records increased dramatically.[19] No more than fourteen weavers have been found for the period 1320–39, and only eleven of them come to light as property owners, trustees or witnesses in the enrolled deeds of the period.[20] Between 1377 and 1399, however, ninety-five are named in the surviving leet court rolls, the Old Free Book and the enrolled deeds and wills, almost half appearing in the deed rolls alone.[21] In contrast to the total of twenty-four weavers of substance listed in the Old Free Book during the fifty-year reign of Edward III (1327–77), the much shorter reign of his grandson saw fifty-nine of them enter the freedom.[22]

The number of individuals employed in the cloth-finishing industries also increased in the late fourteenth century: admissions to the freedom of dyers and fullers rose from twenty-three registered under Edward III to forty-three under Richard II. By the 1390s the proportion of weavers to fullers and dyers was roughly two to one, which reflects the demands, in terms of intensity of labour and rates of productivity, made by their respective crafts. It is unclear how much broadcloth was actually manufactured in the city, nor do we know when the weaving of worsted actually surpassed that of broadcloth. This had probably occurred, however, by the mid fifteenth century when the numbers of fullers entering the franchise began to decrease.[23] By 1490 seven times as many weavers as fullers were registered as freemen. The Norwich textile industry had initially developed to provide the expertise for finishing the broadcloth made in the city's hinterland, but there was a subsequent trend towards widespread worsted and broadcloth production in the city itself after the Black Death.

At the same time as levels of cloth production dramatically increased, Norwich gained a valuable monopoly over cloth distribution in the county. The city had probably always exercised a degree of unofficial supervision over standards of manufacture across Norfolk, but its powers were formalised in the later fourteenth century when the ruling elite established the 'worstedseld'.[24] This was part of a wider initiative to increase the revenue of the community of Norwich while enforcing stricter control over trade and industry in the city. Situated in the same block of buildings as the common inn, near the tollhouse on the edge of the market place, the 'worstedseld' enabled the authorities to achieve both of these aims. Henceforward, *all* worsted cloths were to be checked and sealed there by approved officials before being sold by enfranchised citizens. In 1388 a civic ordinance prohibited the sale of any Norfolk or Norwich cloths other than at the seld.[25] This effort to restrict the lucrative trade in worsted was initially a great success: the seld raised £15 1s. 8d. in the financial year 1394–95 and an annual average of at least £18 during the 1390s.[26] The seld's effective monopoly proved short-lived, however. There were complaints as early as 1414 that it had been abandoned and that sales were taking place illegally elsewhere in the city.[27] Although the 'worstedseld' evidently ceased to play any significant part in the worsted industry, the city itself retained a prominent role in the organisation and distribution of worsted throughout the region.[28] Indeed, the demise of the 'worstedseld' confirms that the strength of the civic industry and its factors was considerably greater than the ability of the civic authorities to control it.

Textile production, and worsted in particular, remained the city's major industry throughout the later middle ages and accounted for a higher percentage of entries into the franchise than any other section of the economy. Between 1400 and 1549 textiles continued to increase their share of new citizens recorded in the Old Free Book. This rose from about 30 per cent between 1400 and 1474 to 34.6 per cent between 1475 and 1499; then, during the first half of the sixteenth century, it remained fairly steady at just under 38 per cent.[29] In short, weaving was always the leading occupation of recruits to the freedom, and thus of participants in the process of government, although cloth finishing still figured prominently in the commercial life of the city.[30] The impact of the expanding textile industry on the topography of Norwich is apparent from the transfer of industry, labour and wealth to the ward of Ultra Aquam (Map 11). By 1500 textile workers, and weavers in particular, were moving across the Wensum from Westwick to settle around Colegate. Evidence of the construction of good quality housing and of expensive building work carried out on the churches of St George Colegate and St Michael Coslany during this period reveals the cloth-workers' obvious prosperity (Plates 8 and 9). Despite fluctuations, the textile industry endured and, in the long term, was to prove indispensable for Norwich's continued prosperity. Whereas the wealth of a city such as York diminished in the face of growing competition from the booming rural cloth industry of the West Riding, Norwich remained a flourishing centre of manufacture. It thereby postponed for at least four centuries the process of decline.[31] The production of cloth and the trade in finished cloths fundamentally shaped the late medieval economy of Norwich and the composition of its ruling elite. It is now time to take a closer look at the people involved in, and affected by, the changing commercial fortunes of the city's leading industry.

In July 1393 Alice, the widow of Ralph Skeet of Norwich, paid the substantial sum of £10 for a royal pardon for:

> the sale contrary to parliamentary statute of thirty-five sarplars of wool to certain merchants of Bruges, her said husband having in his lifetime given them to one William Denis, his apprentice, to take to the staple of Calais, which was at the point of removal to England, and her husband dying, the wool was in danger of being lost because it lay there so long, to avoid which the apprentice caused it to be sold outside the staple without the knowledge of the said Alice or the executors.[32]

Alice's brush with the eagle-eyed authorities who enforced the protectionist policies of the crown provides a useful introduction to the international trade of Norwich in the late middle ages. Surviving national customs accounts, together with references of this kind in the printed calendars and, to a lesser extent, the local customs accounts preserved in the Yarmouth borough court rolls, supply enough evidence for us to sketch in broad brushstrokes the activities of Norwich merchants overseas.[33] The loss of many national customs accounts and the fact that Norwich merchants are not always named in the Yarmouth local customs records, because they enjoyed freedom from toll there, make a more comprehensive overview of Norwich trade impossible. But the late fourteenth-century sources are surprisingly detailed and a comparatively large number are still extant for the reign of Richard II. These accounts record the date a ship entered or left port, the ship's name, its port of origin and master, the name of each merchant, and the type, quantity and value of goods on board. They also tell us the amount of custom due.

The case of Alice Skeet concerns wool, one of the principal English exports of the fourteenth century. The peak in the wool trade from Yarmouth in 1353–54, when 3336 sacks left the port, was largely because the wool staple was temporarily located in Norwich at that time.[34] The wool staple was a fixed point or points, at home or abroad, which changed periodically during the middle ages, through which all wool had to be exported by law.[35] Norwich was one of the home staples and, when it was situated there, the concentrated trade naturally boosted the export of wool through the nearest and most convenient port, Yarmouth.[36] Yarmouth wool exports declined after 1370, as cloth became the major export from the port, and for most of the fifteenth century no raw wool passed through it at all.[37] But while it lasted Norwich men certainly played a significant part in the Yarmouth wool trade: particulars of account from 1385–86 disclose, for example, that six prominent city merchants exported 164 sacks and 10.5 cloves of wool in that year alone.[38] A total of 277 sacks of wool was shipped from Yarmouth that year, which suggests that Norwich traders then handled about 59 per cent of its business. The extant records indicate that

Norwich men exported at least 296 sacks and 18.5 cloves of wool through the port during the reign of Richard II, on which they paid a hefty £740 16s. 2d. in customs or subsidy.[39] Despite the decline in local wool exports, ten named late fourteenth-century merchants were still investing substantial sums of money in overseas shipments. Evidently not all of the county's wool was being consumed by the burgeoning local worsted industry.

The quotation above furthermore highlights the government's strict enforcement of the regulations concerning the wool staple, as the only place where wool could be legally traded, and the perils of operating outside it. For most of the later fourteenth century the staple was based in Calais. As a result, Norwich's wool merchants may have been disadvantaged in comparison with traders in other commodities, who encountered no such constraints.[40] They were restricted to plying the Calais route, although the chief market for their wares at this time lay directly across the North Sea in the Low Countries.[41] Not surprisingly, in such an unpredictable economic climate, families diversified in order to safeguard their interests: Henry Lomynour, for example, specialised in the export of wool, while his brother William and nephew Nicholas concentrated solely on worsted. The decline in wool exports from Yarmouth was linked to national developments, whereby cloth began to replace wool as England's major commodity for sale overseas, a trend clearly apparent in the Norwich mercantile community.

Yarmouth was the major outlet for the export of worsted cloth and, as we have seen, the trade probably peaked in the mid to late fourteenth century. Worsted exports from the port accounted for 3275 cloths in 1350 compared to 12,000 in 1400–1.[42] By this time Norwich entrepreneurs had vanquished all local competition, in large part because of their successful 'worstedseld' policy. A comparison with the Yarmouth cloth merchants certainly demonstrates this supremacy. From the evidence of the tunnage and poundage accounts, only nine Yarmouth burgesses were engaged in the cloth trade between 1388 and 1399. Of these only five exported cloth valued at more than £20 in any single year, and none of those active in 1388 were still trading a decade later.[43] In contrast, eighteen Norwich merchants shipped cloth through Yarmouth during the same period. No fewer than fourteen exported cloth worth more than £20 in a single year and three, Thomas Hert, William Lomynour and John Worlyk, are mentioned in both 1388 and 1396.[44] The evidence from this source alone is testimony to the wealth of the city's mercantile elite. Thomas Hert's shipments were worth at least £469 12s. 10d.; William Lomynour's bore a valuation of £432 19s. 2d.; and in 1388 alone Alice Skeet's husband, Ralph, exported cloth worth £376, which no doubt explains why the crown was so interested in his affairs. It is worth noting that, at this time, the average prosperous Norfolk manor yielded a net rental income of around £40 a year.[45] Not only worsted cloth was exported but a multitude of broadcloths, *mantelanum*, kerseys, *pannus strictus* (narrow woollen cloth), 'matessales' (cloth from Mattishall) and the popular worsted mixtures known as fulled worsted, linen worsted and 'damdokes', to name but a few.[46]

The fortunes of the worsted trade through Yarmouth fluctuated during the course of the fifteenth century and historians may have been premature in charting its rapid decline.[47] The evidence is too thin to support such a gloomy diagnosis, although worsted exports from England did fall considerably during the first half of the fifteenth century. The available Yarmouth data suggest that the total number of worsteds exported each year was about 1000 doubles and 200 singles between 1446 and 1464, there being a significant increase to about 1800 doubles and 200 singles in the period 1468 to 1482.[48] This tallies well with the conspicuous rise in the number of worsted weavers joining the franchise of Norwich in the later fifteenth century, although we should also remember that the mid fifteenth century was a period of profound recession. Cloth exports in general from Yarmouth appear to have grown at a striking rate once the economy began to recover. Between 1515 and 1520 the average number of cloths exported stood at roughly six times that recorded during the early 1450s, despite ongoing problems caused by the silting up of the harbour entrance.[49] Notwithstanding periodic slumps and the occasional lamentations of the craft, which like others was prone to hark back to an earlier golden age, worsted undoubtedly remained Norwich's greatest export throughout the later medieval period.[50] Substantial quantities may possibly have been sent by road to London by the turn of the sixteenth century but, whatever the mode of transport adopted, continental records still frequently refer to 'Norwich White'.[51]

Norwich men did not export wool and cloth alone but traded in any commodities likely to turn a profit. Predictably, in an age when fur was not only of great practical value but also a notable mark of status, many of them invested in it, either as a business staple or occasional sideline.[52] William Sporle, for example, was a pelter who exported thousands of rabbit, lamb and cat skins in the 1380s and 1390s.[53] During his early career Richard Purdans, who served as mayor in 1420 and 1433, exported rabbit skins and 500 otter skins worth sums, which, for an individual of his wealth, represented little more than pin money.[54] In the early part of our period Yarmouth merchants dominated the fish trade: only five Norwich citizens, William Gerard, John Palmer, John Pope, William Stalon and Reginald de Norwich, apparently challenged this monopoly.[55] By the end of the fifteenth century, however, their astute successors had moved into the herring industry, presumably capitalising on the long-term decline of the port and collapse of its mercantile community by the 1470s.[56] Walter Niche specialised in grain, shipping quantities of barley and wheat, while other city merchants also dealt in malt.[57] Skins, fish and grain were often shipped along the coast, for redistribution from other English ports, because water transport offered a cheaper and quicker alternative to road haulage for national trade. The export of agricultural produce appears to have increased dramatically after 1470, possibly because Norwich men diversified their activities in response to the mounting competition from Londoners in the textile markets of the Low Countries. That decade also saw a glut in the barley market, which forced producers to ship their grain elsewhere in search for profit.[58] Even so, exports accounted for only half of the city's overseas commerce in the late middle ages; goods imported for sale there reveal yet more about the urban economy.

The wide diversity of continental merchandise brought into the city is immediately striking, as is the scale of investment involved. In 1388 at least seventeen Norwich merchants were trading abroad, and five of them had imported goods worth over £150.[59] Thirteen of their Yarmouth rivals were then active in foreign markets, but only two apparently returned with cargoes valued at more than £40.[60] This provides further evidence that Norwicians had taken a clear lead, being significantly wealthier and more heavily engaged in overseas trade by this date. The materials required for the all-important textile industry dominated imports, and it was usually cloth merchants who dealt in the supplies essential for broadcloth and worsted manufacture. In 1393, long before he achieved notoriety for his involvement in city politics, Thomas Wetherby exported worsted and imported quantities of merchandise, including woad, eight bales of 'menemadder' (madder of middling quality) and a quantity of black soap.[61]

The chief dyes imported were woad, often described specifically as 'Riplandwadde', and madder, which, respectively, produced the vibrant blues and reds so popular in medieval England. The records differentiate between 'cropmadder', made from the roots of the madder plant, 'mollemadder', which was somewhat inferior, and the most commonly imported 'menemadder', for general use. The scale of these shipments seems quite small, especially when compared to the cargoes of woad worth £640 entering Bristol in one month alone.[62] In contrast to Bristol, the bulk of dyes used in Norwich may have reached the city by road or sea from London by the fifteenth century, rather than being imported directly from the Continent.[63]

Woad thrives in sunny, south European climates, but usually came to

Yarmouth in ships of Zeeland, while madder was grown on the North Sea islands of Zeeland itself.[64] At least six Norwich merchants dealt in madder during the late fourteenth century, confirming the existence of a significant dyeing and finishing industry for cloth in the late medieval city (which boasted its own madder market). Other dyes mentioned in the customs accounts are weld, known as dyer's rocket, from which came yellow, and different types of alum, such as 'alum de Roche' and 'alum folie', which additionally served for fixing less stable dyes. Large quantities of imported soap were used in the textile industry for scouring new wool; and wood ashes were also shipped in for the manufacture of further supplies.[65] Equipment for deployment in textile production was imported from the late fourteenth century: in 1475–76 no fewer than sixty-six fullers' kettles, which were the large lead pans used for fulling and dyeing, came through the port of Yarmouth.[66] Cards, combs, pins and needles also appear regularly in the customs accounts.[67] The demand for certain types of fabric had, meanwhile, to be met from overseas, and the import of linen and canvas cloth continued throughout the period. A type of coarse cloth called bustyan was brought in occasionally, while Iperlyngs, which were linen cloths from Ypres, and canvas called 'westsale' and 'spynale' were frequently unloaded on the staithes of Norwich during the late fourteenth and early fifteenth centuries.[68] The once thriving domestic linen industry of the earlier fourteenth century had been taken over by competitors from Prussia, Flanders, Brabant and Zeeland.[69]

Besides the raw materials and manufactured goods destined for the textile industry, Norwich's import trade featured minerals, timber and other building materials. There was a steady flow of iron, much of it probably from Sweden and some from Spain, and less frequently copper. Large cargoes of timber arrived from overseas: most commonly 'rigold', from the Baltic, but also wainscot, a fine quality oak; 'barelborde', for making casks and barrels; 'clapholt', or boards cut to make barrel staves; and 'deles', which were fir or pine timber boards.[70] Similar items included bowstaves, tables, wooden trays, chests and occasionally ships' masts. Pitch and tar were popular imports; and manufactured items for use in the building trade included axes, nails, scythes, paving stones, tiles and bricks. The continuing demand for such goods further confirms the existence of a flourishing construction industry and comes as no surprise in view of the ambitious ecclesiastical and secular building programmes currently taking place in the city at this time.[71]

As might be expected, imports of food and drink brought luxuries as well as staple foods to Norwich. Olive oil, often from Seville, rice, almonds, dried fruit and dates came from southern Europe to the tables of the wealthy citizens and clergy, while less exotic cargoes of rye, garlic, vinegar, stockfish, dragonfish and lampreys also reached the city by sea. Spices, such as cumin, aniseed and liquorice, were frequently included in shipments, but the principal medieval condiments, ginger and pepper, are never mentioned in the records. These were almost certainly purchased from London wholesalers, who sent them, either by road or coastal vessel. They therefore leave no trace in the customs records.[72] Salt was another staple from continental markets, although Norwich merchants did not generally import it directly. They either purchased their salt from coastal traders after the custom had been paid elsewhere, or bought it at Yarmouth for shipment up river to Norwich.[73] Nine merchants are known to have supplied the city with salt during the reign of Richard II. The trade was evidently considerable, because five of them imported just over 514 weys of salt in 1379–80 alone.[74] The demand remained heavy throughout the fifteenth century.[75] Evidence from the national customs records of the shipment of wine to Norwich is also limited. Of the eighteen men with cargoes of wine on the *Christopher* of Great Yarmouth in June 1388, for example, only two were Norwich merchants, and they accounted for only three tuns between them.[76] Likewise, city traders paid customs on only ten of the 311 tuns brought into Yarmouth in 1449.[77] Although a mere handful of local merchants supplied the Norwich market directly during the late fourteenth century, this certainly does not reflect a low demand for wine. On the contrary, as with salt, it was probably obtained from other English ports, in this case with closer links to France, or else via middlemen on the Yarmouth quays.[78]

It is impossible here to describe all the many and varied items which crossed the seas to late medieval Norwich. The catalogue is almost endless, and testifies to the prosperity and economic diversity of England's second city.[79] Large quantities of wax were needed to supply the households, churches and religious institutions of the city. Paper was available in many different varieties: paper 'scrivable' for writing and paper 'spendable' for wrapping, along with 'roraline' and the ominous sounding 'coffyn' paper, whose special uses are now unknown. Norwich's expanding book trade was clearly well supplied, as were the city's counting houses. Domestic goods included basins, dishes, pans, kettles and coal.[80] Aloe oil and 'calmyne' (calamine) were used for medical purposes. The many looking glasses imported suggest that the more affluent citizens were as concerned about their appearance as the stern moralists and preachers of the period feared. For Norwich had clearly become a city of dandies. 'Doblettes' from the more fashionable Continent were eagerly purchased alongside 'brusches', 'strawenhattes' and 'blakhattes'.[81] In the 1470s 'cofinhatts' and 'splithatts' were imported in great quantities. Much of the wealth generated by the export of cloth was promptly reinvested in the necessities for textile manufacture, but the growing range of less essential items on offer confirms that standards of living were generally improving lower down the social ladder, while luxuries were available for purchase by the affluent elite of Norwich and its hinterland.[82]

The origins of the ships which docked at Yarmouth can tell us regrettably little about the sources of the goods they carried, but they do reveal a pattern of commercial contacts with the Continent. By 1400 the international trade connections of Yarmouth, as reflected in the ports of origin of the vessels which sailed there, were far more concentrated than they had been before the Black Death. The case of Ralph Skeet and his wool exports confirms that the ports of northern France, and most notably the staple of Calais, still exerted a powerful attraction in the late fourteenth century. Vessels from the Hanseatic ports of Lübeck and Danzig were regular visitors to Yarmouth in the reign of Richard II, but the vast majority of ships came from Holland and Zeeland.[83] By the mid fifteenth century the ships of the Hanseatic League of Baltic ports had disappeared from the Yarmouth records, leaving those from the Low Countries an effective monopoly over the carrying trade across the North Sea.[84] Relations between Norwich merchants and the Hanse declined during the late medieval period. In 1385 a dispute between England and Prussia led to the confiscation of the goods of eighty-eight English merchants in Prussia. A list of the individuals concerned included fifteen Norwich citizens, whose losses allegedly came to £937 13s. 4d.[85] This figure accounts for a sixth of the entire claim for compensation. Yet after a similar incident in 1442 there was no mention of any merchants either from Norwich or Yarmouth.[86] The almost complete reliance on trade routes to and from the Low Countries became an increasingly bitter source of conflict between East Anglian merchants and their London rivals. In 1421 Norwich men were among those who protested against the appointment of a Londoner, John Wareyn, who had been chosen as constable of the community of English merchants in the Low Countries without the consent of any provincial merchants.[87] Objections to the domination of London over trade to Holland and Zeeland recurred throughout the fifteenth century.

Norwich merchants usually joined together to ship their goods, sometimes hiring a whole vessel between them, as they did in December 1388 when Ollard Johannson's *Seintemarieschipp of Arnemuth* left Yarmouth with a cargo of worsted, cheese and rabbit skins owned solely by a consortium of Norwich exporters.[88] Sea-going vessels in the middle ages were comparatively small, but it is unlikely that any ventured up the shallow river as far as Norwich.[89] Consequently, the transhipping of goods into smaller river vessels to navigate the twenty-mile stretch of the Yare and then the Wensum must have added considerably to the overheads incurred in international and coastal trade. This perhaps explains why Norwich-owned goods arrived at and departed from the port in large joint shipments, thereby spreading transportation costs. Norwich merchants also tended to use the same vessels and shipmasters repeatedly, establishing long-term contracts with certain mariners. The *Katherine of Canmfer* of Brixis Outresson, for example, appears in three different customs accounts, five times importing and on eight occasions exporting the goods of Norwich merchants between December 1396 and October 1400.[90] The speedy turn-around of ships entering and leaving Yarmouth adds credence to the concept of the North Sea as a busy lake. With remarkable dispatch, the *Seintemarieschipp* of Ollard Johansson arrived on 6 December 1388 with a mixed cargo belonging predominantly to Norwich entrepreneurs.[91] She set sail only two days later, on 8 December, laden with Norwich-owned worsted, cheese and skins, and on 26 December was back again with a shipment including madder, canvas, soap, oil and wax.[92] Johansson's ship had crossed to a continental port, disposed of its cargo, had reloaded and returned in the space of just eighteen days during the potentially stormy month of December. The apparent ease and speed of travel across the North Sea emphasises the closeness of East Anglia's continental neighbours.

Norwich merchants evidently preferred to employ foreign rather than local vessels to carry their goods. Of the 118 ships used by them during the reign of Richard II only nine were Yarmouth-owned. Norwich itself was clearly not a community of mariners and shipbuilders. So far as we can tell, only one ship, the *Christopher* of William Heynsson, was described as a Norwich vessel in the fourteenth century.[93] Another, the *Peter*, was conveyed in a deed enrolled in the mayor's court, but this was probably a river vessel.[94] When the king requested a new barge from the city in 1372 the prolonged negotiations and difficulties which ensued occupied a disproportionate amount of the assembly's time.[95] By the later fifteenth century, however, Norwich merchants were becoming more personally involved in shipping. Walter Aldrich of Norwich owned a vessel which transported cloth from Yarmouth for his fellow citizens in 1454–55, and during the 1470s at least six Norwich-owned ships can be identified. This was possibly a result of the general decline of Yarmouth, which, as we have seen, offered Norwich merchants an opportunity for expansion into an area previously dominated by the port's mercantile community.

Some of the risks of overseas trade have already been described. Confiscation of goods because of political conflict, as occurred during the 1380s when Prussia employed commercial sanctions against the English, was not uncommon. The Hundred Years' War with France made the threat of piracy and enemy action all the more likely.[96] On the other hand, Norwich traders themselves were not above making a profit from the intermittent free-for-all which affected shipping in this period. No less a person than the mayor, Thomas Elys, was accused in 1454 of receiving stolen figs and raisins seized from a French ship, the *Mary* of Rouen, in spite of a promise of safe conduct.[97] He was perhaps following the dubious example of his father, Bartholomew, who had himself been accused of smuggling in 1408.[98] The case of Alice Skeet highlights the problems likely to arise when apprentices and factors were left to manage the affairs of a busy merchant. The delegation of routine arrangements for international trade to representatives in Yarmouth and abroad must have been unavoidable for merchants who were often leading members of the city government and MPs. Yet some agents were remarkably experienced. Hamon Claxton seems to have pursued a long career as a factor overseas: he was working in Middelburg in 1454 and again appears in the Low Countries sixteen years later, being then paid £5 per annum and half his expenses to act for Richard Hoste there.[99] Claxton undoubtedly had alternative sources of income and was a man of considerable means, so we may assume that he represented other merchants on the Continent, in addition to running his own business.[100] During the course of his sojourn overseas Claxton encountered some of the hazards mentioned above at first hand when a French fleet captured him and held him prisoner until Thomas Elys paid his ransom. The ruthless opportunism which no doubt explains his success is apparent from Claxton's refusal to refund the money, a breach of faith which resulted in litigation.[101] The use of subordinates was unavoidable but risky, since unreliable or dishonest agents could be a liability. Elys's own apprentice, Robert Hoste, for example, was responsible for the loss of an entire consignment of his master's goods, which led the hapless Elys to begin another case in chancery.[102]

Despite their many commitments at home, prominent Norwich men sometimes spent long periods abroad, and the connections between them and their continental counterparts were not just commercial. John Asger, who became mayor in 1426, came from 'Seland' and was described as a merchant of Bruges.[103] His son John seems also to have been born in the Low Countries and acquired a letter of denization from the king in 1431.[104] Just as Norwich merchants were often to be seen in the towns and cities of Flanders, Brabant, Zeeland and Holland, there was a reciprocal 'foreign' presence in late medieval Norwich well before the arrival of the Strangers in the sixteenth century. There are references to at least forty-five such 'aliens', Dutchmen in particular, in the two surviving late fourteenth-century leet court rolls of 1374–75 and 1390–91; and about 137 aliens were living in Norwich in *c.* 1440.[105] They most often got into trouble for trading outside the franchise, but were also not infrequently the victims of violence. For example, the cordwainer John de Northwick threatened to beat and kill two Dutchmen and then robbed them of just 7½d. outside Needham gates as they tried to flee the city.[106] Yet notwithstanding the occasional fracas, the link between Norwich and the Low Countries, based on commercial dealings and personal and dynastic ties, was deeply entrenched by the late fourteenth century. Whatever the potential dangers involved, hundreds of city merchants chose to chance their money and even their lives in overseas trade during the late middle ages. As with most high-risk ventures, the rewards were often great.

The wealthiest late fourteenth-century merchants were, without exception, prominent members of the ruling elite.[107] This trend continued throughout the fifteenth century, when many Norwich mayors were leading overseas traders.[108] Individuals of more modest means were also engaged in continental and national commerce. William Blackmore never achieved the status of bailiff, though he helped to elect office-holders in the reign of Richard II. Even so, he appears twice in the Yarmouth local customs records for 1377 as an importer of hides and sea-coal from Tyneside.[109] Many other citizens are likewise occasionally mentioned undertaking small-scale transactions, which suggests that overseas and coastal trade was not limited to the upper echelons of society. Nor were women excluded from international markets. We have already seen how Alice Skeet took over her husband's business after his death. Margaret Aylward likewise managed her late husband's affairs in the 1470s.[110] Interestingly, some women even set up in business while their husbands were still alive. Alice Pouchmaker of Norwich paid duty at Yarmouth on one last of barley destined for the city in April 1380.[111] This transaction was definitely made during the lifetime of her then husband, Peter, because the couple together sold a property in the parish of St Andrew two years later.[112] Another striking outcome of this survey is that the governors of Norwich and the sizeable group of citizens involved in overseas activities were not synonymous. Indeed, whereas successful merchants almost invariably held high office in the city, many other politically active families do not feature in the customs accounts at all. Neither Bartholomew Appleyard nor his son William, the first mayor of Norwich, appear to have had much direct interest in overseas trade; nor did Thomas Spink, who belonged to a well-established dynasty in the late medieval city. International commerce, though of profound importance for the economy of Norwich in this period, was not the only route to wealth and status. Trade within the region provided an alternative path to riches and sufficient profits could evidently be made from local and national commerce to provide the means to secure an *entrée* into the elite.

In contrast to the detailed records available for the study of international commerce, the evidence for Norwich's national trade network is very limited. Because they were exempt from paying toll at Yarmouth, little trace of the activities of late medieval citizens can be found in the local customs accounts. This is a great loss given the importance of coastal trade, which accounted for about 70 per cent of all shipping activity through the port of Exeter in the late fourteenth and early fifteenth centuries.[113] From the glimpses to be seen in the records of central government and the courts at Westminster, we may assume that Norwicians were similarly involved. We have just seen, for instance, that William Blackmore was shipping hides from Newcastle to London or Norwich in 1377, while John de Winterton, in partnership with William de Bury of London, acquired a licence to transport a substantial cargo of 1000 quarters of malt from Yarmouth to London at this time.[114] The coastal trade in hides, coal, food and wine was considerable throughout the late medieval period, and the shipment of herring and grain from Yarmouth and King's Lynn to the Tyne in return for coal was particularly important.[115]

Crucial for both international and coastal commerce was the river which provided access to and from Norwich. The city was dependent on this one route to the open sea because, unlike Lynn, with its extensive waterways reaching as far as the midlands, it was relatively land-locked and otherwise lacked navigable communications.[116] It is important to note that, during the middle ages, travel by road was beset by problems, including crime, the cost of draught animals, carriages and labour, and the poor quality of the roads themselves. Expensive, perishable products, such as wine, or heavy items, including millstones, had to be transported by sea, and this, as we have seen, strengthened existing links between the city, other English ports and the Continent. The vital function of the river was an ongoing concern of the authorities, who issued regular commissions to keep it clear and operational.[117] Furthermore, the rulers of Norwich realised that trade could be better controlled and tolls more comprehensively levied on goods entering the city if the staithes on the river were in their own hands. As part of the reform programme during the 1370s, they not only set up the 'worstedseld', but also purchased the Old and New Staithes in Conesford (Map 15).

It was decreed that all ships were henceforward to be unloaded and loaded there under penalty of arrest and a heavy fine. A revised list of tolls on goods entering Norwich was then set in place.[118] The city also demanded a compulsory payment called 'windage' for the use of the communal crane and storage fees for the obligatory use of its warehouses. This monopoly provided a steady revenue of between £10 and £30 a year throughout the later middle ages and demonstrates the continued importance of Norwich as an inland port.[119]

The distribution of goods shipped into Norwich must have generated substantial profits from across the region and beyond, but we have no firm statistics to guide us. The regional trade network of the wealthy Norwich merchant Robert Toppes (d. 1468) is revealed in a list of the debts due to his executors in 1492.[120] In addition to 116 sums in Norwich, his estate was still owed money in no fewer than fifty-one towns and villages across Norfolk and also named debtors in Hadleigh, Bury St Edmunds, Bungay and Beccles in Suffolk. His various financial dealings, meticulously recorded in a 'great book', had clearly extended to individuals throughout and beyond his home county. The list embraces a wide range of trades and occupations, ranging from labourers to landowners. Somewhat more impressionistic evidence comes from the market in worsteds. By the late fourteenth century worsted was being sold to religious houses outside Norfolk: in 1386, for example, Bicester priory bought three pieces for 5s.; and Boxley abbey in Kent made similar purchases at this time.[121] References in the Paston Letters describe Norwich worsted being sold at Winchester in 1471; and an inventory of the goods of John Mayho, a clothier of Chew in Somerset, made in 1495, records 'iii coverlytes of Norwich Makyng'. It was popular with senior clerics: Geoffrey le Scrope, canon of Lincoln (d. 1382), left his chamberlain a 'Norfolk bed with birds ...'; and Dr John Selot, master of St Giles's hospital, Norwich, deemed it an appropriate gift to make altar frontals for his old college.[122] Norwich worsted was obviously renowned throughout England, and it is significant that textiles from Norfolk were to be found in other major textile producing areas, such as Somerset and Lincolnshire. Cloth from Norwich was distributed across the country by sea and by road and these busy routes in turn brought merchandise to the city, connecting it to a wider national and international network.

The transport of worsted cloth by road to London for export overseas probably increased during the late middle ages.[123] Contacts of this kind certainly encouraged the development of strong working relationships between Norwich merchants and those in the capital.[124] In addition to noting the partnership of John de Winterton and William de Bury, other references in the records of central government confirm that Norwich merchants had regular dealings with their counterparts in London.[125] As well as business partnerships, reciprocal patterns of migration between Norwich and the capital were quickly established. John Chittok, who served as mayor of Norwich in 1457 and 1466, is described in the city records as '*civis et mercator de London*' and, because of what we today might call his dual citizenship, possessed the rare privilege of being able to trade through the port of London.[126] Walter de Berney (d. 1382), who described himself as a citizen of London in a will registered in Norwich, clearly had a strong affiliation with his new home and left considerable bequests to Norwich cathedral, the hospital of St Giles and the chapel of St Mary in the Fields, as well as other religious institutions in both cities.[127] Some of Norwich's leading mercantile families kept a representative in the metropolis, being well aware of the commercial advantages at stake.[128] Sometimes such connections between the two cities were maintained for several generations. A Norwich deed of 1430, for example, records a sale of property in the parish of St Peter Mancroft by Nicholas Wought, *alias* Nicholas Norwich, citizen and grocer of London, son and heir of John Wought, late citizen of London, son and heir of John Wought, late citizen of Norwich.[129] During the political conflicts of the mid fifteenth century, the crown made John Welles, a London alderman and MP with strong East Anglian connections, and Thomas Catteworth, a citizen of Norwich and sometime mayor of London, wardens of Norwich.[130] Commercial, political and dynastic connections between the city and the capital were deep-rooted, if occasionally contentious, in this period.

Buying and selling took place daily within the city walls. Transactions were not confined to residents, for Norwich was an important regional centre where people from its wide hinterland would come to sell or exchange their agricultural produce. By the fifteenth century Norwich had eclipsed its two main regional rivals, Yarmouth and Lynn, as the commercial and social capital of the locality, and men from towns throughout the region sought advancement there.[131] The reasons for its predominance are various: the decline of Yarmouth has already been noted; Lynn also suffered from the contraction of the wool trade, and the growing power of the Hanse, and, unlike Norwich, was geographically too far distant to profit from the worsted industry.[132] Local sources add further to the long list of commodities available for sale in Norwich. An inventory of stock belonging to the grocer Richard Ballys, dated 1499, demonstrates that urban, rural and continental products might all be purchased in a single marketing operation. Worsted cloth and Norfolk honey were to be found in Richard's shop alongside raw materials, such as soap, alum, resin and brimstone, and foreign luxury wares, including spices and oils.[133] The eclectic choice of goods on offer in Norwich provided something to tempt all but the poorest members of city and county society.

Commercial activity might involve formal transactions in shops, such as the one belonging to Richard Ballys, stalls and selds, or be little more than a quick sale from portable baskets and trays. The main area for buying and selling in the city, as today, was the market place in the central parish of St Peter Mancroft.[134] Then, as now, it comprised permanent stalls in rows, where particular traders, such as butchers, apothecaries and cooks, congregated (Map 13). Arranged around its perimeter there were a few substantial buildings, such as the murage loft, which was used for the collection of tolls. The space below the rows was where country retailers sold their produce from baskets, booths, tents and carts on market days.[135] The city government recognised the economic potential of the market, and, as yet another part of its late fourteenth-century reform programme, bought up all the stalls, placing them in communal ownership. As with the staithes in Conesford, protective legislation was then put in place. Meat and fish were only to be bought and sold from these stalls and nowhere else; leases were to extend no longer than three years; and subletting was strictly prohibited.[136] This proved to be a more workable and enduring scheme than the 'worstedseld', as revenue from renting out the market stalls never fell below £74 per annum between 1397 and 1436. Perhaps with the continued success of the central market in mind, attempts were made to establish two annual fairs in Tombland in 1482.[137] Given the fraught relations between city and cathedral over the exercise of jurisdiction in this part of Norwich, it is hardly surprising that so controversial a gesture ended in failure. But it at least provides an example of the city leaders' willingness to risk new ventures. The market continued to provide the city with a dependable income throughout the late middle ages. It undoubtedly contributed to Norwich's economic buoyancy and ability to pay the royal fee farm of around £125 per annum when other urban centres were falling by the wayside.[138] The fifteenth century also saw the construction of visible symbols of the city's self-confidence and pride with the building of the guildhall, completed in 1412, and the New Mills in 1429.[139]

Anyone with money to spend or surplus goods to exchange could buy or sell in late medieval cities, but officially only freemen were permitted to engage in wholesale transactions. The commercial privileges of citizenship in Norwich included the right to trade retail in the city, to set up a shop, to take apprentices and to be exempt from paying tolls on goods going in and out of the city and through the port of Yarmouth.[140] Despite attempts

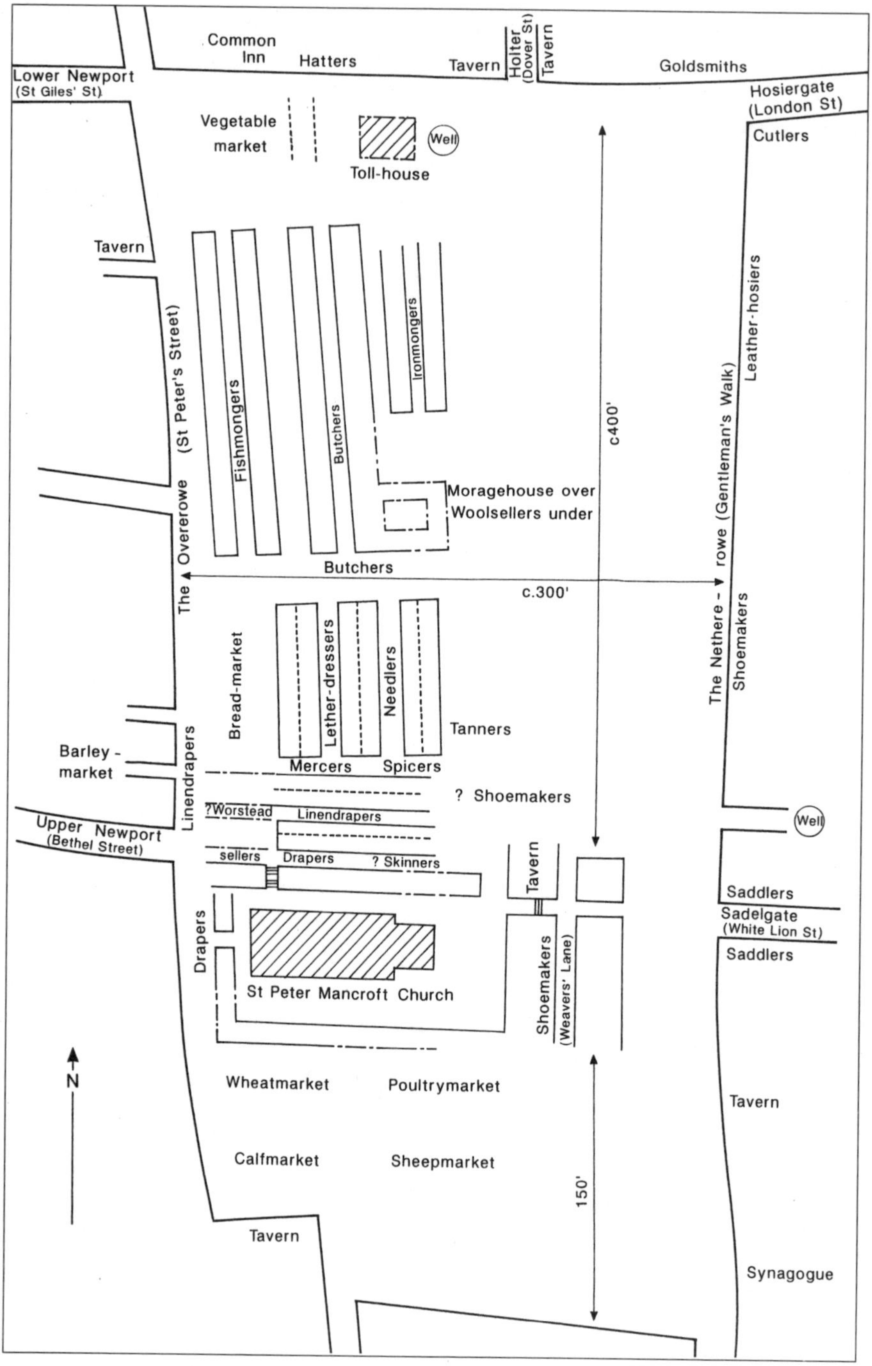

MAP 13. Norwich market place in the later middle ages. (*Phillip Judge*)

in the 1370s and 1380s to enforce penalties for operating outside the franchise more strictly, some affluent, property-owning artisans chose not to join the freedom and paid small regular fines in the leet court instead. The freedom of Norwich was less rigidly enforced than that of York, for example, where breaches of the regulations restricting retail trade to freemen incurred a heavy penalty.[141] So long as the Norwich authorities were able to secure either the routine payments made by newcomers to the freedom or fines in the leet courts for exemptions they were happy with the system. In fact, the controls and regulations enforced through the courts seem to have been well organised and effective.

Besides trading outside the franchise, the most frequent commercial offence was forestalling, in other words cornering the market in a specific commodity and attempting to sell it in unauthorised places at an unreasonable price. Such conduct was clearly a matter of concern to the authorities, since in periods of dearth it threatened to provoke popular unrest, even food riots. The rich were often the worst culprits. In 1374, for example, the wealthy city taverner and merchant John de Gaywood 'forestalled so many eggs in the market that he filled twenty-eight barrels at diverse times and sent them out of the kingdom to foreign parts'.[142] The following year Roger Calf was similarly fined for buying 'oysters by forestalment in divers boats, so that when one boat is at the Staith for the sale of oysters another boat or two shall be at Thorpe until the first boat is emptied and sold, and then the rest of the boats come up for sale; and whereas the common people were wont to have 100 oysters for 1½d., Roger sells them for 2d.'[143] The hustle and bustle of incessant commercial activity was therefore regulated to some degree by admissions to the freedom, assizes of quality control and the prevention of outright profiteering. All individuals involved in trade and commerce, from wealthy overseas merchants to city hawkers and hucksters, were, at least in theory, subject to an established system of legislation and tolls, ranging from national customs dues at one end of the scale to local impositions and assizes at the other.

Many dramatic changes affected the people of Norwich during the late medieval period. The horrors of plague reduced the city's population by as much as two thirds. The Hundred Years' War, bullion shortages, upheavals in continental markets and tense diplomatic relations combined with the transition from wool to cloth export further to disrupt the overseas trade of Norwich merchants. Yet the city's resilience in adapting to changing circumstances, the establishment of a sound financial policy in the late fourteenth century and, most important, the growth of industry and trade in the city itself ensured Norwich's prosperity at a time when several other urban centres appear to have stagnated or been in decline. There were naturally low points in the history of the city's economy, notably between 1440 and 1460, when depressed markets and political conflict led to a slump in rental income,[144] but Norwich none the less emerged as England's second city by the early sixteenth century. The enthusiasm, perseverance, willingness to take risks and sheer sense of adventure of the mercantile elite, along with the diversity and entrepreneurial activity of its small-scale traders, enabled Norwich to thrive as an important regional capital and as a principal national and international trading centre in the late middle ages.

10

The Urban Elite

Ruth H. Frost

> Well and lawefully to your cunnyng and powere ye shall susteyn executen and mayntene ye lawes libertes fraunchises gode customes and ordenaunces of ye Cite of Norwich and ye pes and tranquillite in ye same Cite.
>
> *Oath of the mayor of Norwich*[1]

The Norwich Chamberlains' Roll of 1453 records a bill submitted by John and Walter Ingham for expenses incurred by their father, Thomas Ingham, and by Robert Toppes when Ingham and Toppes were MPs for Norwich in 1445–46. The bill ends by noting: 'Item, in the somme of all the dayes of the parliament with iij dayes allowed outeward and iij dayes hoomwerd is x^{xx} xv (215) dayes. And the seid Robert and Thomas Ingham abyden v (5) dayes for to speke with the Lord of Suffolk and other lords for to sue to their grace and to knowe their will.'[2] Although Toppes and Ingham spent more time on parliamentary business than most of the Norwich MPs who served between 1400 and 1520, the two men were typical in many other respects: both were aldermen, and both combined offical business with lobbying for city interests and other local concerns. During this period, the task of representing Norwich in parliament and presenting its case to people of influence fell predominantly to aldermen and other members of the ruling class. While being an MP probably had heightened importance during times of internal or national tension, the city always relied on its representatives, aldermen and other leaders to advance and defend its interests. Periods when this relationship broke down – as was the case during the 1430s and 1440s – served to highlight the importance of a stable, conscientious elite.

Not surprisingly, the city of Norwich in 1520 had changed considerably since the early 1400s. For instance, despite periodic setbacks, its population increased steadily over the course of the fifteenth century. By 1520 it was the second-most populous city in England, with at least 11,000 inhabitants.[3] Yet it experienced economic problems and pressures, the worst of which occurred between 1440 and 1460, a period of national as well as local conflict.[4] The worsted trade, however, seems to have revived considerably from this point onwards;[5] and, despite economic fluctuations, late medieval Norwich approached the sixteenth century in a stable state. Unfortunately, the first decade of that century brought disaster to the city: fires in 1505 and 1507 consumed at least 20 per cent, and perhaps over 40 per cent, of its housing.[6]

Throughout these vicissitudes, the business of civic government continued. Indeed, the basic structure of government remained largely unchanged for much of that time. In 1404, a crucial date in its history, the city received a royal charter that authorised the annual election of a mayor, thus abolishing the offices of the four bailiffs.[7] It is likely that the charter resulted in part as a reward for Norwich's generosity to Henry IV in 1402, when the king faced a costly revolt in Wales.[8] Yet, although the hierarchy of command changed because of Henry IV's charter, the type of men holding the highest civic offices did not. In the first ten years after the disappearance of the bailiffs, for example, five men served as mayor who had previously acted as bailiffs of Norwich. Similarly, of the twenty individuals who held the position of sheriff between 1403 and 1412, eleven had been bailiffs before 1403.[9]

In addition to establishing the grander and more prestigious office of mayor, the charter of 1404 granted county status to the city and recognised it as a legal and administrative entity separate from the county of Norfolk.[10] As a result of this important concession, citizens of Norwich (or their representatives) were thereafter allowed to elect two sheriffs each year.[11] Yet this was not a wide franchise, as citizens comprised only a small fraction of the male inhabitants of Norwich. A citizen had to possess the freedom of the city, which gave a vote in municipal elections and exemption from 'toll and lastage through England and all the ports of the sea'.[12] In return, citizens were expected to pay taxes, serve if elected to office and obey the ordinances of the city.[13]

The 1404 charter also paved the way for further changes in the government's structure, notably the creation of a ruling elite of twenty-four men, together with an outer circle of eighty councillors. By 1417 the twenty-four were being termed 'aldermen'.[14] Their participation in the leadership of the city had a precedent: a petition addressed to Richard II in 1378 referred to the four bailiffs and twenty-four citizens 'elected each year for the commune of the said town'.[15] References to the 'twenty-four' also appear in assembly rolls of the fourteenth century. The original purpose and jurisdiction of this body are unknown, but it seems likely that its members were at first bound to attend assemblies and form a quorum, and that subsequently they sought to consolidate and regularise their administrative power.[16] It would also appear that, as relations with the crown grew in complexity and civic concerns called for a well-organised mouthpiece, Norwich relied on 'a manageable, limited and intelligent body to deal with the outside world and represent it to the city'.[17]

The implementation of such major structural changes inevitably encountered resistance, and over the course of the next twenty years the citizens were involved in various disputes among themselves. These were often exacerbated by conflicts involving local landowners and other interested parties, and on occasion generated such animosity as to necessitate the use of outside negotiators. For example, in 1414 the 'commons' of Norwich asserted that the twenty-four had governed autocratically without the consent of the wider commonalty.[18] Consequently, a ruling now known by historians as the Composition of 1415 was promulgated; this proved crucial in refining and defining the duties of the aldermen and of the common council.[19] Negotiated by the influential courtier and Norfolk knight Sir Thomas Erpingham, the Composition instituted several changes in constitutional structure and established new electoral procedures. For instance, the twenty-four 'concitizens' (or aldermen) were to hold office in perpetuity as in London and might be removed only for reasonable cause.[20] The common council was reduced from eighty to sixty, and subject to annual elections. Whereas the four wards of Norwich were each to be represented by six aldermen irrespective of size, common councillors were assigned on a proportional basis: twelve for Conesford, sixteen for Mancroft, twenty for Wymer and twelve for Ultra Aquam (Map 11). The aldermen were powerless to enact anything binding on the city unless the commonalty, represented by the sixty councillors, approved.[21] If the latter believed an issue needed to be debated at length, they could ask for further deliberation. In addition, the 1415 Composition set the dates and formal machinery for the election of the mayor, sheriffs and other officers.[22] By granting councillors the right to vote for certain offices and insisting upon a formal process of consultation, the Composition imposed several checks upon the powers of the mayor and aldermen.[23]

The structures laid down in the 1415 agreement remained in place, with only a few changes, throughout the fifteenth century. Henry V tacitly approved them in 1417 when he issued a charter almost identical to the Composition.[24] One final document, the Tripartite Indenture of 1424 between the mayor, sheriffs and aldermen, further defined the duties of the aldermen and influenced the development and direction of the aldermanic body. According to the indenture, they were individually and collectively obliged under oath to give good counsel to the mayor, keep the matters discussed among themselves secret, support their fellows and avoid speaking slanderous words about other aldermen.[25]

The documents that fashioned Norwich's late medieval government also generated much of the pomp that accompanied office holding. The mayor, for example, could have a sword carried before him in the presence of everyone save the king.[26] The Composition of 1415 called for the mayor and aldermen to be arrayed in clothes worthy of their estate, which meant that the mayor was permitted to wear a furred and lined cloak appropriate to the season of the year.[27] In an age keenly aware of the close connection between dress and status, such matters went far beyond mere ceremonial: they constituted a clear statement of political authority. Residents of Norwich were expected to show proper respect to the mayor and aldermen; failure to do so could result in fines or other punishments. Sometimes office-holders were the victims of assaults or verbal abuse. In 1512 Thomas Musterder (who later became an alderman himself) was brought before the mayor's court and fined £10 for calling the alderman John Marsham 'Gresij face and Bocherfface'.[28] The scale of the fine, which was equivalent to the annual income of a parish priest or gentleman of modest means, reflects the severity of the offence.

The most important and ostentatious member of the ruling class was the city's mayor. Chosen from those aldermen who had already served as sheriff, the mayor was elected for a year. Indeed, the demands of the office made it financially prohibitive for most candidates to serve longer than that. Some men even paid to be exempted from this burdensome obligation, although the vast majority of eligible candidates did not. Mayoral elections were held on 1 May (the feast of the apostles Philip and James). The Composition of 1415 stipulated that on election day citizens who lived in Norwich were to gather in the guildhall with the sixty common councillors and nominate two candidates. Their names were then submitted to the current mayor and other aldermen for secret ballot, and this inner circle cast the deciding vote.[29] The assembly did not seek to increase participation by demanding that all aldermen who had been sheriffs take a turn as mayor, nor did it discourage re-election. The lister Richard Ferrour, for example, served as mayor five times between 1473 and 1499. The Composition did, however, prevent too great a monopoly of power by insisting that no candidate had been mayor within the previous three years.[30] Perhaps because it consumed so much time as well as hard cash, there was not a demand for wider involvement in office-holding at this level, and most of the men who served more than once presumably did so through a sense of civic obligation. Although some individuals were eager to avoid office, the absence of regulations requiring aldermen to serve and the low rate of fines upon aldermen and councillors who failed to attend mayoral elections suggests that in most years suitable and willing candidates were ready to stand.

The type of man who held civic office in Norwich remained consistent throughout the fifteenth century and into the first two decades of the sixteenth, as did the profile of wealth and achievement. Indeed, an alderman of 1508 would almost certainly have recognised an alderman of 1428 as a like-minded equal. The first rung up the ladder was enrolment as a freeman of the city. Records of civic freedoms go back at least to 1317.[31] Although the early evidence is incomplete, there can be little doubt that relatively few men and almost no women took this step. On average, fewer than forty people entered the freedom each year during the second half of the fifteenth century. Like other cities, such as York, medieval Norwich offered three different routes into the freedom: patrimony, apprenticeship or redemption.[32] Those admitted by patrimony (because their fathers were already freemen) paid no entrance fee; those who entered by apprenticeship paid 13s. 4d. for much of the fifteenth century; and those newcomers or other citizens who enrolled by redemption paid a range of fines, from 20s. to at least five marks (66s. 8d.). In addition, new freemen were charged for enrolments and clerks' fees.[33] After acceptance by the wardens of their craft if they had been apprentices, the new freemen swore their oaths of allegiance before the mayor and assembly.

After entering the freedom, most men who aspired to the highest civic office began their slow climb to the top from the bottom rung, holding various lesser elected posts and waiting a number of years before joining the aldermanic circle.[34] Among the eighty-three individuals first elected aldermen between 1461 and 1509, for example, only two entered civic government at that exalted level. Most followed a traditional *cursus honorum*: they acted first as constable, then as councillor, with service later perhaps as chamberlain or auditor. For many a term as sheriff preceded aldermanic election.[35] In some ways, this *cursus honorum* was akin to an apprenticeship, as it bestowed valuable political and administrative experience.

During the fifteenth and early sixteenth centuries mercers, grocers and drapers dominated the aldermanic circle, and the majority of mayors followed these occupations. This monopoly lessened towards the end of the fifteenth century, however, and more craft representation emerged. Weavers, bakers, listers and scriveners managed to gain office with some regularity, as, more occasionally, did goldsmiths, glaziers and other prosperous artisans. Nevertheless, many of the less salubrious crafts were entirely excluded from power – tanners, for example, never gained entrance – and the growth in craft representation took place within a limited context and with mixed approval. The mayoralty also continued to be occupied by members of the same mercantile elite.

It was possible for an able, worthy man to change his affiliation from a lowly to a more prestigious craft and thus succeed to office. Following his aldermanic election in 1508, the butcher Robert Brown agreed to enrol as a mercer and forswear butchery.[36] In addition, a newcomer to Norwich might also aspire to advancement if he possessed the right qualifications or had sufficient means. In 1489, for example, John Crome paid 26s. 8d. to enter the civic freedom. Originally from Salle in Norfolk, Crome became an alderman in 1503. While exclusive, therefore, the aldermanic circle was not entirely closed. Certainly, once a man reached aldermanic office, he usually retained it for life. Yet, as protests in 1500 against two aldermen illustrate, the citizens had means of redress if they perceived that an individual was not upholding his duties or behaving in an appropriate manner.[37] This, however, was a rare occurrence, and restraints on the aldermen seem rarely to have been exercised from below. It was more common for the aldermen and councillors to discipline one another for misdemeanours or dereliction, accomplishing this through fines or public reprimands.[38]

Members of the ruling class of late medieval Norwich were bound together not only by their oaths of office, but also by a complex amalgam of social and economic relationships, akin to the sinews of the body politic. Many were linked by blood or marriage, or by the affective ties of apprentice and master. For instance, about half of the aldermen first elected between 1461 and 1509 appear to have been connected by close familial ties with others who either served with them, belonged to a previous aldermanic generation, or were to serve in a future one. If the maiden names of all their wives were known, the figure would almost certainly be considerably higher. At least nine aldermen were themselves the sons of aldermen, while one was a nephew. In addition, it appears that there may have been as many as six pairs of brothers in this group. Many examples exist of intermarriage amongst aldermanic families, most notably that of Thomas Wilkyns, who was an alderman between 1489 and his death in 1492. His sons, Ralph and Thomas, each married daughters of aldermen, with Thomas the younger marrying Agnes, daughter of Thomas Caus, and Ralph marrying Anne, daughter of Thomas Aldrich.[39] Thomas the elder was himself also the brother-in-law of alderman Robert Rose.[40] Not surprisingly, the widows of senior officials sometimes remarried within this elite. The limited evidence at our disposal reveals that a minimum of five

FIGURE 23. The Erpingham gate of Norwich cathedral, *c.* 1819, after John Sell Cotman. Contructed in *c.* 1428, when the bishop was leading an attack on heresy, the gateway is replete with symbols of Catholic orthodoxy. (*Norfolk Heritage Centre, photograph by Terry Burchell*)

aldermen in the late fifteenth and early sixteenth centuries married their colleagues' widows, although the number was probably greater.[41] Like tended to marry like so as to preserve their hard-won reserves of capital and property, while also ensuring that marriages took place between equals. The Norwich aldermen were not unique in this practice. Intermarriage was common among late medieval merchant families of York, Beverley and Hull.[42]

The mayor and aldermen dominated the ruling class of late medieval Norwich, joined by those common councillors who rose up the *cursus honorum*. Not all members of the elite were office-holders, however. Some prominent men gained exemptions, or died before scaling the peaks of civic fame. (Women, however rich and influential they might be in their own right, never held elective office.) Other leading residents included members of the county gentry, many of whom were never formally involved in the mechanics of government. Indeed, the majority of residents, rich or poor, did not possess the freedom of the city, and the aldermen and other officials comprised a tiny percentage of the population. The aldermen, councillors and those affluent enough to avoid civic obligations never exceeded one per cent of Norwich's householders. Indeed, after 1500, they numbered no more than half of one percentage of the city's heads of houses.[43]

Between 1400 and 1520 the aldermen ranked amongst the wealthiest residents of Norwich, but they were not alone in this respect. A taxation list of 1451 records the names of 163 people with annual incomes ranging from £2 to £200. It reveals that many of the richest were not actually citizens of Norwich. Some may even have been visitors rather than residents, but others did own houses there. On the other hand, no fewer than twenty of the twenty-four aldermen of 1453 appear on this select list.[44] A different type of fiscal document, the 1489 subsidy return, reveals that the aldermanic class held a sizeable share, but not all, of the most lucrative (or highest assessed) real estate within the city. Several common councillors had acquired valuable holdings as well. By then, however, few members of the gentry rated as leading property-owners, despite the fact that some had invested in the local market.[45]

The affluence of the Norwich aldermen is not surprising given what we know of civic elites elsewhere in England. The aldermen of fifteenth-century London, for example, were invariably recruited from among the most prosperous citizens,[46] and wealth and suitable occupations were likewise factors determining the choice of men elected to high office in York.[47] Close behind the Norwich aldermen in this respect came the common councillors. When assembled for meetings in the guildhall, the two groups would have represented most of the cream of Norwich in terms of secular wealth. One of the richest aldermen of the early sixteenth century was the draper Thomas Aldrich. In his will of 1528 he left a total of £1400 in cash to his three sons, £100 to his daughter (the prize secured by Ralph Wilkyns), and other gifts of cash and kind as well as property in Norwich and the outlying areas.[48] His position compares more than favourably to that of the county gentry. It has been argued that fifteenth-century London merchants with reserves of capital worth £1000 and above were the financial equals of knights and barons whose annual landed incomes were £200 or more.[49] If this is the case, Aldrich's estate would have rivalled, if not surpassed, the resources of some of the leading Norfolk gentry.

Unlike most citizens, the aldermen probably had the leisure to hold office, due in part to their comfortable status. These prosperous figures tended to fulfil their duties for a variety of reasons, including civic pride and a sense of public responsibility. Other motives were more calculated.[50] Wealth itself may have prompted some merchants and leading craftsmen to seek office so as to preserve order and foster an atmosphere that would uphold their commercial privileges and profits.[51] Some probably became aldermen or councillors in the hope that such a move would bring them trade and foster other useful connections. The electors, who had vested interests of their own to protect, seem to have endorsed the role of prominent citizens, or so the relatively small number of election disputes between 1400 and 1520 would suggest. Wealth offered proof of competence, acumen and ability, traits desirable in leaders. Since the aldermen also served as representatives of the city, their obvious success undoubtedly made a more favourable impression upon visiting dignitaries. This was, after all, a world in which appearances mattered.

By any yardstick, medieval Norwich was governed by only a few men, an oligarchy in the strictest sense of the word, which formed an exclusive and exclusionary group. 'Oligarchy' has become a loaded word among historians. In theory, it means government by the few, but in practice it tends to be associated with government by the few, rich and self-interested.[52] Perhaps 'aristocracy' is a more appropriate description of the Norwich aldermen; not surprisingly, they viewed themselves as an elite with the authority to act on the community's behalf and for that community's moral good. As the aldermen were human, however, they were not themselves immune from sin, both venial and mortal. Some were absent from meetings or half-hearted about their commitment. For example, between 1461 and 1509 at least eight assembly meetings were cancelled because of insufficient attendance.[53] Some officers succumbed to corruption, favouritism, profiteering or indifference. John Peterson, a Norwich brewer, brought a suit against Richard Ferrour and Thomas Veyl, sheriffs of Norwich, alleging that they conducted inquests 'for ther owne coveityce (covetousness) and for their singuler lucre'.[54] John Richeman, a 'bedman' of Norwich, lodged a complaint regarding an action of debt of £17 'ontrewly commensid' against him by Thomas Bewfeld. Bewfeld allegedly owed the money to the alderman, William Ramsey, and Richeman believed they had conspired together to cheat him. The plaintiff justified his appeal to the court of chancery 'yn so moche as the seid William Ramsey ys one of the Aldermen within the seid Cite entendynge by hys great myght and poer to condempne your seid Oratour yn the seid summe which were to the utter impoversshyng of hym ...'[55] Although Richeman's plea may have been one frequently adopted by less influential suitors when confronting those in authority, the bedman made a clear connection between Ramsey's status as an alderman and his personal influence.[56]

Despite occasional litigation arising from alleged abuses of power, the majority of office-holders seem to have proved worthy of their electors' trust. Many, if not most, of the leaders were apparently motivated by a sense of civic and Christian duty. They shared a belief that, as the richest, most successful citizens of Norwich, they had a moral responsibility to govern.[57] They also felt a responsibility to make charitable donations, subsidising civic projects and giving goods or money to the imprisoned, sick and destitute. In doing so, of course, they expected to be remembered for their bounty and to have prayers said in their memory. The alderman and grocer Thomas Aleyn provides a typical example of this. His will of 1453 contains bequests of 2d. to each bedridden pauper in Norwich or in St Giles's hospital and of one halfpenny to every other ambulant pauper living thereabouts.[58] A more spectacular legacy was that of the alderman and bed-weaver John Jowell, whose will of 1499 stipulated that a total of £30 should be spent on the poor and bedridden within the city.[59] The civic projects patronised by the aldermen usually included the repair of walls, gates and the banks of the river, along with the paving of streets. In 1465, for instance, the mercer, Richard Hoste, bequeathed four marks (53s. 4d.) to pave the 'Holter', which was a lane near the Maddermarket, and in 1498 the scrivener and notary Stephen Brian left £10 to repair the walls in St Stephen's ward, where he had served as alderman.[60] Aldermen's wives also made charitable bequests of this kind. In her will of 1504, Katherine, widow of Thomas Bewfeld, set aside £5 for the upkeep of the city walls and £2 for the 'emendyng' of the river.[61] A number of aldermen bequeathed money for the 'common lyvelod' and for the common weal, giving broad discretionary powers to their executors and to the city.

Phrases such as 'common lyvelod' richly illustrate the belief in a shared civic identity and purpose.[62]

Some assaults or threats were made against civic officers, and when these happened they were usually dealt with swiftly and sternly. On the whole the residents of Norwich appear to have accepted the aldermen and the exercise of their authority with relative equanimity.[63] This suggests that few flagrant abuses of power occurred, especially towards the close of the middle ages. Norwich in the late fifteenth and early sixteenth centuries rarely saw disagreements over elections, those which did occur being sorted out quite easily, in marked contrast to some of the earlier disputes. This was probably because, from 1452 onwards, no serious attempts were made to alter the system of government, which inevitably provoked controversy among those who felt excluded. It would be naive to assume that this tried and tested system had no critics, but from the mid fifteenth century until the 1540s the city was largely spared 'usurpationary' unrest. The economy and government of Norwich appear to have been stable enough to satisfy most residents.

The late medieval burghers of Norwich have been praised for the 'sound political instinct by which they steadily directed their way into the broad track whose ultimate goal is civil freedom, rather than the narrow road of privilege'.[64] This view, expressed in 1894, now strikes the reader as predictably whiggish, for the aldermen of 1400–1520 certainly did not seek to broaden participation in elective office, nor did the citizens actively attempt to overturn or even question the privileges associated with wealth and success. In many ways, civic government existed to preserve the status quo, and the aldermen stood to benefit far more from such an agenda than most residents. In their own eyes and by the standards of the time, however, they appeared generous, morally upright and conscientious. The system rested on the concept of duty and on a sense of hierarchy and order in society; most aldermen recognised their place and the obligations that accompanied it.

Members of the ruling class of Norwich between 1400 and 1520 tended to be conventional and conservative, intent on maintaining the system they knew because they believed it to be good, effective and proper. They did not differ greatly in type or outlook from their peers in the governments of late medieval York or London or Bristol. Their ties were uniquely East Anglian, even so, and their wills reflect their loyalty to Norwich and its environs. Clashes of personality and of interest occasionally ensued within the aldermanic group and sorely tried the system at times. The machinations of Thomas Wetherby and others in the 1430s and 1440s are the best known of these aldermanic disruptions.[65] For most of the 120-year period in question, however, the oaths that bound the aldermen to one another and to their city largely held firm, resulting, with some exceptions, in a stable government for late medieval Norwich.

A stable, loyal civic government was, of course, in the interests of the English crown. The tumult experienced by Norwich in the 1430s and 1440s graphically illustrates the practical consequences of political instability. Henry VI (or more accurately those ruling in his name) took away the city's liberties twice in those two decades; the second period of forfeiture alone lasted from 1443 to 1447. On both occasions the crown appointed wardens to govern Norwich while it was in disgrace and imposed heavy fines on the city.[66] In 1452 the royal justice (and former city recorder) William Yelverton mediated an agreement between the guild of St George and the citizens. The guild was restructured in large part to help preserve civic order and ensure that factionalism would not disrupt the government again. Henceforward, the mayor and aldermen automatically became guild members, bound together not only by civic oaths but also by guild oaths and rituals.[67] The city turned to the throne in subsequent years for help with arbitration in various disputes. In 1482, for example, a longstanding quarrel with the Benedictine monastery of St Benet Holme was finally resolved with help from the king's brother-in-law, Earl Rivers.[68] After 1447, however, a chastened and more circumspect city did not give the government at Westminster further cause to remove its liberties, internal troubles being generally settled in court or through other peaceful means.

Whereas the king sometimes had to respond to problems in, or petitions from, the city of Norwich, more often than not it was the aldermen and councillors who were obliged to answer a variety of summonses from central government. On occasion the crown appealed to duty, loyalty and patriotism and requested loans from Norwich. Such appeals were not uncommon: Norwich lent an average of £90 per year to Henry IV and of £100 each year to Henry V.[69] Occasionally the city loaned money in the clear hope of receiving something tangible for its support. The advance of 1000 marks to Henry IV in 1402 was, as we have seen, made on the assumption that a favourable charter would follow.[70] Although some loans were probably written off from the start, many were made in the expectation that they would be repaid promptly. In 1435–36, for instance, Norwich loaned £100 to the king, money that had in turn been advanced by Alderman Gregory Draper and others. Five years later the loan was still outstanding. Hoping to use some of the £100 for a gift to win over the king's uncle, Humphrey, duke of Gloucester, the assembly allowed Draper and the other creditors to sue in the exchequer at Westminster for its repayment.[71]

According to the eighteenth-century antiquary Francis Blomefield their presumption 'gave great offence'.[72]

Civic officials realised the advantages to be gained by advancing loans or responding promptly to royal letters patent when it was in their power to do so. At times the city employed more direct approaches to gain favour or money from the king, sending members of its ruling elite to London to petition him and his ministers directly. After the Norwich fires of 1507, for instance, Thomas Aldrich, Robert Brown and Henry atte Mere were sent to the privy council to relay the city's misfortunes to the king and to try to enlist his aid in assisting the afflicted and helping rebuild the city. As was so often the case with the miserly Henry VII, no immediate largesse was forthcoming, and in August 1508 the city dispatched Aldrich, atte Mere, John Clerk, William Hert and John Marsham to appeal again to the king and solicit an answer regarding its pleas.[73]

Besides lending money to the king, the ruling class was asked to demonstrate the city's loyalty to the crown in other ways. Occasional visits by monarchs or royal consorts provided what was, quite literally, a spectacular opportunity to show support, as these events required that Norwich prepare for its distinguished guests and provide lavish entertainment and hospitality for their entourages.[74] Not surprisingly, when a member of the royal family entered the gates, the mayor, aldermen and common councillors led the city in greeting him or her. When Henry VII arrived on a formal progress during the first year of his reign, the mayor, sheriffs, aldermen and craft masters welcomed him, all dressed in scarlet.[75] Spectacles and pageants were usually organised in honour of the visitor, and this involved much planning and expense. The Westwick gates served as the site of a stage bearing an elaborate pageant of angels, banners, giants, patriarchs, apostles and virgins, designed to greet Edward IV's queen, Elizabeth Woodville, and her entourage in 1469.[76] In addition to the cost of such displays, the city had to find money for appropriate gifts, not only for the royal guest but also for his or her principal attendants, who were powerful figures in their own right. Aldermen were always involved in raising such funds and, as was often the case when assessments were made, this task could be onerous.[77] On the other hand, it paid to cultivate friends in high places (Plate 23). Sometimes this investment brought immediate results: in 1482 Edward IV ended his visit to Norwich by granting it the right to hold two more fairs. As it happened, they were not commercially successful, and by 1486 brought few participants and garnered no profits.[78] The city had, however, exploited the benefits of patronage to the full.

Members of the royal family were not the only ones to be entertained by civic officials or to receive costly gifts. The chamberlains' accounts show that presents were also given to nobles and others of influence, in the hope that they would remember Norwich kindly and press for advantages on its behalf at court. Sir Thomas Erpingham, Henry IV's 'right-hand man',[79] received many such gifts. Erpingham provided advice on judicial matters and was also 'willing to bring Norwich's needs to the king's attention'.[80] Striking while the political iron was white hot, as early as the autumn of 1399 the city was lavishing food, drink and money on the powerful Lancastrian knight. These ultimately bore fruit. Erpingham was instrumental in obtaining the 1404 charter for Norwich that established the mayoralty, gave the city county status and brought about the other key changes described above.[81] While such gift-giving today would give rise to suspicions of bribery, in the fifteenth and sixteenth centuries it was an accepted and expected practice. In turn, Erpingham funded some substantial building works in Norwich. He commissioned the Erpingham gate outside the cathedral in thanks for the English success at the battle of Agincourt (Figure 23); he helped to rebuild the Dominican church in Norwich; and he sponsored the now-destroyed east window of St Michael's Conesford.[82] He funded many charitable enterprises after his death, as well. In his will of 1428 he bequeathed a total of £22 to the sisters and poor inmates of two Norwich hospitals, to prisoners in the castle and guildhall, and to male and female recluses within the city.[83]

Whereas royal visits were potentially diverting and perhaps even profitable to the city and its tradesmen, royal musters offered fewer tangible benefits. Evidence of musters survives throughout the documented proceedings of the late medieval city assembly, reflecting the state of the realm and its defences.[84] In January 1461, for instance, the city responded to a commission of array from the beleaguered Henry VI, then fighting to retain his throne against the house of York. After considering the commission's request, the assembly agreed to raise and support 120 armed men for six weeks at 6d. *per diem*. The commonalty had to pay for eighty men, while the aldermen and former sheriffs undertook to fund the rest.[85] At the very start of the century, in 1401, Henry IV asked Norwich to build and outfit a royal barge.[86] A similar request was received in 1462 from Edward IV. Norwich eventually hired *The Katherine* of Bishop's Lynn and paid for half of its crew.[87] Later, Norwich and other towns responded to royal summons with less alacrity, often sending a minimum of troops or supplies. Fortunately, such lukewarm responses did not stir the king's displeasure.

In addition to documenting requests for troops or resources to assist in the defence of the realm, the medieval records of Norwich contain information about royal tax assessments imposed on the city. One of the most common forms of taxation in the fifteenth century was the tenth and fifteenth. This tax was levied on the moveable goods of the laity, at a rate of one fifteenth of their value in the countryside and of one tenth in boroughs and on the royal demesnes.[88] Norwich was expected to meet a fixed sum or quota, but could raise the money however it saw fit. The assembly elected men to assess and to levy the tax. Once again, aldermen and common councillors took the lead in collecting and paying towards it. For instance, a tax assessment of 1468 required twenty-four assessors, eight of whom were aldermen. At least ten of the others were councillors and three were constables.[89] Another form of taxation that made heavy demands upon the ruling class was the benevolence, or so-called 'free gift' presented to the king by his grateful subjects.[90] Aldermen and councillors were expected both to implement the benevolence and to contribute generously to it. Failure to do so could result in punishment: in 1481 a former mayor Robert Portland was fined 6s. 8d. for abrogating his responsibilities regarding the collection of a benevolence from people 'worth more than twenty marks'.[91]

Because the mayor and sheriffs were direct representatives of the crown, specific obligations accompanied their offices. The mayor acted as royal escheator for Norwich during his term in office, receiving 'dues or forfeits' that belonged to the crown and generally watching after the king's financial interests.[92] The sheriffs were responsible for raising the yearly fee farm and accounting for it at the exchequer.[93] In addition to their fiduciary duties, the mayor and sheriffs also performed a judicial role. The mayor was charged with maintaining law and order within the city and ensuring that the common law of England, as well as the rulings of local courts, was upheld. The sheriffs, in turn, served the king's writs.[94]

Preserving the king's peace and administering justice were crucial responsibilities for the mayor, sheriffs and aldermen, and between them they oversaw several courts.[95] The royal charter of 1404 authorised the mayor to appoint four '*probi homines*' (worthy men) to act as justices of the peace in all matters except felonies.[96] These justices held sessions of the peace four times a year, as well as arranging special ad hoc sessions when necessary.[97] In 1452 a new royal charter changed the procedure that had hitherto determined how the justices were to be chosen. The charter begins by pardoning the citizens for the offences that had caused their liberties to be suspended by the crown in the 1440s. It refers to confusion surrounding the role and selection of justices of the peace and notes that petitions asking for clarification of relevant terms had been submitted to Henry VI. The petitions, dated to the 1440s, evidently constituted a response to the disruptions caused by Thomas Wetherby and others. Each called for Norwich to be subdivided into smaller administrative districts and pleaded for limits to be imposed on aldermanic powers. The 1452 charter ignored these specific requests.[98] Indeed, it reinforced the existing hierarchy by stipulating that all aldermen who had already served or might in future serve as mayors of the city were henceforward automatically to become justices of the peace and remain so as long as they stayed in office. In addition, the current mayor and recorder would also sit on the bench. The same charter also authorised the justices (or four of them at least) to investigate all felonies, trespasses and the like that occurred in the city and its liberties.[99]

Members of the ruling class were also called upon to sit on the numerous royal commissions which enabled the government to conduct its business and maintain order in the regions. For example, in 1423 Richard Purdans, an MP and former mayor, served as a commissioner of gaol delivery in Norwich.[100] The alderman and MP Ralph Segryme likewise acted as an agent of the crown: in 1449 he was commissioned to distribute a tax allowance in the city; he served on an important commission of oyer and terminer during the aftermath of Cade's rebellion; and, in 1452, he was dispatched to inquire into the wreck of a Prussian ship off the Norfolk coast.[101] The crown expected these commissions to run with efficiency. Although members might meet and cultivate useful contacts, especially when they travelled outside Norwich on royal business, it seems likely that many such appointments merely added to a heavy workload while bringing little or no tangible personal gain.

The members of parliament for Norwich provide additional examples of men who incurred temporal and financial burdens because of office-holding. They were supposed to be reimbursed for parliamentary service. The customary rate for a member representing a prosperous urban community in the late fifteenth century was usually 2s. *per diem*, the equivalent of a skilled craftsman's weekly wage. Because it set such store by appearances, Norwich had initially paid a more generous 3s. 4d., although financial difficulties meant that by 1460 the city had been obliged to follow this trend. Indeed, from about 1440 onwards members often had to plead for payment, and long delays could ensue before full settlement was made.[102] In several cases, a special tax was levied upon residents in order to raise money for the MPs' wages and expenses.[103] In 1474, for example, the assembly debated how to find the wages owed to John Awbry, who had been an MP two years earlier. In response, Richard Ferrour, a former mayor, offered to forgo the twenty marks (£12 13s. 4d.) due to him if two conditions were met: Awbry and Thomas Bokenham, his fellow MP, would each remit their own wages, and any alderman then owed money by the city would likewise pardon the municipality its debts.[104] Awbry appears to have

22. Wall painting of St George and the dragon, *c.* 1500, in St Gregory's church. Occupying the entire west wall of the north aisle, the painting was part of a lavish decorative scheme, including the Annunciation and the Four Latin Doctors. (*David King*)

23. The ceiling of the new chancel of St Giles's hospital was completed after a royal visit in 1383. It contains 250 panels bearing the arms of Anne of Bohemia, queen to Richard II, who probably paid for it. (*National Monuments Record*)

24. John Parkhurst, the first Elizabethan bishop of Norwich (1560–75), at the age of sixty-four. (*National Portrait Gallery*)

25. Stained-glass panel of the Visitation, *c.* 1450, in the church of St Peter Mancroft. St Elizabeth, on the right, wears a laced maternity smock of a kind popular in the period. The scene depicted had particular resonance for pregnant women, who feared a stillbirth or miscarriage. (*National Monuments Record*)

26. Early sixteenth-century carved wooden bench end of St Margaret and her dragon in the nave of the Great Hospital church. Presented by the master, John Hecker, in the early sixteenth-century, this image would have reassured female members of the congregation. (*Carole Rawcliffe*)

27. Stained-glass panel of St Elizabeth of Hungary feeding the poor, *c.* 1450, in the church of St Peter Mancroft. This reminder of the obligations of the rich to the poor served to stir the consciences of the city's ruling elite, who worshipped here. (*National Monuments Record*)

28. One of a long sequence of fourteenth-century stone roof bosses in the cloister of Norwich cathedral depicting the Apocalypse. Here a tonsured monk lies prostrate beneath the plague-bearing angel described in the Book of Revelation: a stark reminder of the Black Death. (*Ken Harvey*)

29. Death claims a bishop in the last surviving stained-glass panel of a late fifteenth-century dance of death in the clerestory of St Andrew's church. (*National Monuments Record*)

been unmoved by Ferrour's public-spirited offer: local levies were raised to pay him the considerable sum of £32 he claimed for his cumulative parliamentary service.[105] Ferrour's proposition exemplifies another hidden cost of office: the moral pressure to accept a reduction or remission of substantial fees, or to make voluntary donations to causes. The honour of representing England's second city was offset by the lavish sums spent on display and entertainment while parliament was in session.

These considerations made some citizens reluctant to attend parliament more than once: in 1461 Robert Toppes and Edward Cutler prudently asked to have their wages guaranteed before they returned to Westminster after a prorogation. Despite the woes associated with stalled payments, parliamentary service none the less retained its prestige. Throughout the fifteenth and early sixteenth centuries members were consistently chosen from the very pinnacle of Norwich's urban elite. For instance, a majority of the twenty-three men who sat for Norwich between 1422 and 1461 held all three offices of sheriff, alderman and mayor during their careers. Only three of the MPs occupied none of these important posts, although two out of three were busy lawyers who served at least briefly as recorder of Norwich and had their fingers firmly upon the civic pulse. Several other MPs also practised as lawyers, but the majority were merchants and mercers.[106]

Of the forty men who served as MPs between 1400 and 1461, just over half sat more than once, which suggests a powerful strain of civic responsibility.[107] Some were returned often: the alderman John Bixley attended four parliaments between 1413 and 1419, for example, and the wealthy Robert Toppes served five times between 1437 and 1461.[108] As a result, most parliamentary teams that represented Norwich boasted at least one experienced MP who knew his way around the corridors of power. There were occasional exceptions between 1400 and 1461, notably towards the end of the period.[109] It may be that men were less eager to stand for parliament towards the close of Henry VI's reign because they were aware of the potential delays in the payment of wages and the dangers of close involvement in an increasingly volatile political situation as the country moved towards civil war. Nevertheless, for much of the fifteenth century Norwich was able to send at least one seasoned representative to parliament. The resulting continuity must have helped considerably when it came to learning the complex customs of the lower House and to furthering Norwich's interests there.

Many of the statutes passed between 1400 and 1520 that directly concerned Norwich reflect the city's interest and investment in the worsted industry. In 1410, for example, the House of Commons adopted a petition securing 'a grant to Norwich of the ulnage (assay and measurement) of worsted cloth in Norfolk over a period of seven years'. Sir Thomas Erpingham played a key role in acquiring this important concession, thereby justifying the careful cultivation of his 'good lordship'. The city rewarded its two MPs, merchant Robert Dunston and lawyer William Ampulford, with healthy purses in gratitude for their hard work.[110] A statute of 1442, designed to regulate the weaving of worsted cloth in Norwich and Norfolk, was likewise the result of intensive lobbying.[111] In 1512 John Clerke MP introduced a Bill further to protect the Norwich worsted industry by restricting one of the processes used in making worsteds to persons approved by the mayor of Norwich and two representatives of the craft.[112] Not all of the hard-won legislation regarding the worsted industry was, however, destined to endure: a 1495 statute concerning worsted shearers in Norwich was partly repealed less than ten years later on the ground that the provisions had been 'craftily obtained, to make the worsted-shearers a different craft or trade from the shearman's craft'.[113]

In addition to attending the Commons and perhaps conducting some business of their own, MPs often undertook errands or negotiations on behalf of the city while at Westminster. Indeed, from the local perspective, these additional responsibilities were often of far greater importance.[114] It was therefore to the city's advantage to choose tried and tested insiders, familiar with its particular concerns and interests. Sometimes these men worked to secure favourable trade agreements or preferential tariffs. At other times MPs were involved in legal business, especially concerning contested franchises and commercial matters. In 1427, for instance, MPs Thomas Ingham and John Alderford met two lawyers while they were in London, probably to take advice about the bitter dispute between the city and the cathedral priory. Elected again in 1429, Ingham continued to pursue this case, now assisted by his fellow MP, Thomas Wetherby.[115] One remaining duty expected of MPs was to report on parliamentary proceedings to the assembly.[116] On 30 May 1421, for example, Robert Baxter and Robert Dunston rendered their public account of the parliament they had just attended.[117] Such occasions gave the urban elite an invaluable opportunity to hear current news and gather impressions from trusted sources.

From its MPs to its recorders, mayors, aldermen, councillors and sheriffs, and thence downwards through the ranks of its lesser officials, the city of Norwich relied on men in a variety of positions to defend its interests, maintain the peace, meet its obligations to the crown, and oversee day-to-day activities within the walls. A certain *quid pro quo* characterised dealings between the city and the king, as well as between individual members of the ruling elite and the civic government. High-ranking officers expected a degree of respect from the people they governed. The citizens in turn looked for dedication and attention to duty from their elected and appointed officials. The government of Norwich, as represented by this august hierarchy, worked to uphold the king's interests but looked for occasional concessions and favours in return.[118] In their turn, successive monarchs expected the city to be loyal and properly responsive to royal needs.

Throughout the period 1400 to 1520 civic leaders were frequently tested by internal, external and natural events. The success or failure of their responses often depended on a delicate balancing act, weighing the interests of the city on one hand against the crown's demands on the other. When all went well, the urban elite benefited personally from a protectionist environment that encouraged trade and restricted competition. When troubles ensued, however, it was the mayor, aldermen, sheriffs and other members of the ruling class who were first called to account, often being obliged to reach into their private coffers and pay more in taxes or loans. Despite the demands upon their time and resources, the majority of eligible candidates between 1400 and 1520 none the less agreed to stand for office and did not seek exemption. Even during the financially straitened 1440s and 1450s Norwich had a sufficient pool of dependable, committed individuals on whom to rely. Some expressed occasional frustrations with their burdens, especially when they were owed wages or waited for loans to be repaid. Yet the appeal of office and a strong sense of duty appear to have predominated. With comparatively few exceptions, late medieval Norwich was the beneficiary of this culture of civic responsibility.

11

The Reformation

Ralph Houlbrooke and Muriel C. McClendon

> Amongst many Cities in this *famous Kingdome*, beholding vnto God for the Ministry of the Word, you in your Citie are not the least beholding. Euery *Sabbath* day, in many of your *Churches* is the Word *preached*, and almost *euery day* in the weeke, the preaching of the same is painfully *continued.*
>
> *A Learned and Fruitfvll Sermon, Preached in Christs Church in Norwich by Mr Newhouse, late Preacher of Gods Word there* (London, 1612)[1]

It has been suggested that Norwich remained during the Reformation a deeply religious city even though the outward expressions of its religious feeling changed. The argument that the Reformation was imposed on Norwich against the wishes of its citizens likewise occasions unease.[2] Religious activity in Norwich soon began to run through the new channels cut by the Reformation, and there was indeed some early support for Protestantism in the city. Equally clearly, however, the major changes were imposed by the government in London. They involved the destruction of most of the lively and familiar religious institutions which had dominated the late medieval landscape, and deeply divided the city. The avoidance of serious conflict was largely due to the efforts of the magistrates, who, though themselves of various religious opinions, were anxious to minimise internal disharmony and external interference. The traumatic events of the mid fifteenth century, still fresh in the collective memory, must have constituted a painful reminder of the consequences of dissension.

Henry VIII's break with Rome and achievement of supremacy over the English Church, completed in 1533–34, did not lead inevitably to further religious change. Financial need, however, combined with moderate reforming aspirations on the part of Henry or his advisers soon led to far-reaching measures, especially the dissolution of religious houses (1536–40). Royal injunctions of 1536 and 1538 discouraged 'superstitious' aspects of saints' cults and required the placement of a vernacular Bible in every parish church, among other things. In 1539, anxious about divisions caused by new religious ideas, Henry reasserted some fundamental Catholic doctrines in the Act of Six Articles. But though the brakes had been applied, the engine had not been put into reverse. Henry's evangelical archbishop of Canterbury, Thomas Cranmer, survived his master. In Edward VI's reign (1547–53) he played a key role in further reforming measures. Intercessory institutions, especially chantries and parish confraternities, were dissolved by virtue of a statute of 1547. Images were banned by royal authority along with a number of traditional religious ceremonies. Parliament passed further Acts permitting the marriage of priests and two Acts of Uniformity (1549 and 1552) imposing English orders of service in two Books of Common Prayer, the second of which was clearly underpinned by Protestant doctrine. The confiscation of church bells and ornaments not required for Protestant worship was ordered in 1553.[3]

Norwich cathedral priory, uniquely, escaped dissolution altogether. It was the only English monastery to be directly transformed into a community of secular priests headed by a dean and chapter (May 1538). The four Norwich friaries were dissolved in the same year. In 1540 the city was granted the Dominican house, which it later turned into an assembly hall (St Andrew's Hall), chapel and granaries. The city's craft guilds met there for their feasts and elections from 1543 onwards. The other three friaries, however, all came into private possession: the Franciscans' premises were granted to the third duke of Norfolk in 1540. The secular college of St Mary in the Fields, which contained eight chantries, was granted in 1545 to Miles Spencer, the last dean of the college, a conservative but conformist churchman. The corporation gained control of three of the city's many hospitals, St Giles's and Hildebrond's by royal grant, and St Paul's on a long lease from the dean and chapter in 1565. Hildebrond's was dissolved and St Paul's eventually turned into a bridewell. In Edward VI's reign the corporation also bought the chapel of the Carnary college within the cathedral close; this ultimately became the premises of the city's school. The guild of St George survived, albeit under a new name, its ordinances purged of 'superstitious' observances. The city acquired the endowments of several other confraternities, which were in July 1548 ordered to be applied to the cleansing and maintenance of the River Wensum. A certificate drawn up early in Edward's reign showed that thirty city churches had already disposed of church goods amounting to the huge total of over £1218. Altogether Norwich in the broadest sense managed to keep for itself much of the proceeds from the destruction of Catholic institutions.[4]

During Edward's reign, when the pace of religious change was at its fastest and most unsettling, unrest in the city reached its peak. The evangelical preacher Thomas Bilney, a fierce critic of saints' cults, had been burnt in Norwich as early as 1531.[5] A few years later the mayor's court began to deal with indiscreet or disorderly expressions of religious opinion, both conservative and radical. These cases became markedly more numerous in 1547–49. Kett's Rebellion drew much of its support from the poorer elements in the Norwich population. Kett's rebels have traditionally been perceived as supporters of the Reformation. Some people nevertheless resented the plunder of church goods. The bid for the throne made by the Catholic Mary I (1553–58) from her Kenninghall residence after Edward VI's death in July 1553 was strongly supported in Norfolk.[6]

The first phase of the Reformation in Norwich owed little to its local magnates. The third duke of Norfolk was a staunch opponent of Protestantism, though his imprisonment for treason (1546–53) removed him from the region altogether. Bishops Richard Nykke (1501–35) and William Rugge (1536–49) were notorious conservatives. Thomas Thirlby (1550–54), an able conformist administrator, seldom visited Norwich. John Hopton (1554–58) was a whole-hearted enforcer of the policies of Mary I. She had the mass restored by her first parliament (1553), and ordered the married clergy to be deprived of their livings. Her paramount goal of reunion with Rome was achieved in her third parliament (1554), but she could not risk alienating powerful political opinion by confiscating monastic or chantry endowments from their new owners. It fell to Hopton to proceed against religious dissidents under medieval anti-heresy legislation restored in 1555. Several of those who refused to abjure their beliefs were burnt in Norwich, though only two were Norwich people.[7]

The religious settlement made by Elizabeth I (1558–1603) was Protestant, but conservative in various respects. Committed Protestants hoped that church services would be purged of all 'popish' survivals. But personal preference or a desire to appease religious conservatives caused Elizabeth to prevent a more thorough reformation of worship. She even made some small conservative amendments to the 1552 Book of Common Prayer and insisted that surviving ceremonies be observed. Those who persisted in pushing for further reforms or conscientiously objected to the ceremonial requirements of the settlement became known as 'puritans'.[8]

Bishop John Parkhurst (1560–75), the first Elizabethan bishop of Norwich (Plate 24), shared some of the puritans' aspirations. A more powerful local magnate, however, was Thomas Howard, fourth duke of Norfolk from 1554 to 1572. His magnificent palace in the heart of Norwich and his good relations with the city's oligarchs gave him immense influence. His wide network of friends and clients included several men of conservative, even Catholic, religious outlook. Parkhurst's freedom to promote local reformation was also limited by the inherited personnel of diocesan administration. This very reactionary group included William Mingay, the diocesan registrar, who, as mayor in 1561, entertained the duke at a magnificent feast.[9]

Parkhurst welcomed the arrival of the Flemish and Walloon 'Strangers' from 1565 onwards. This community of Protestant exiles, ultimately well over 4000 strong, had its own church orders and services, much more in line with puritan ideas than the hierarchy and liturgy of the Church of England. Yet the possible influence of the Strangers over religion in Norwich has proved impossible to pin down. There is no certain evidence, for example, that four East Anglian heretics who were burnt between 1579 and 1589 got their ideas from the Strangers. Some of the incomers may have supported the separatist Robert Browne, active in Norwich around 1580, but there is nothing to show that the example of their churches inspired him or his collaborator, Robert Harrison.[10]

The duke of Norfolk's downfall and his execution in 1572 ended this period of dominance of the county's politics by one man. Religion was an important element in the local conflicts of the ensuing period. Bishop Parkhurst found vigorously Protestant allies among the Norfolk gentry. He encouraged 'exercises of prophesying', that is discussions of scriptural texts by groups of clergy, but Elizabeth, fearing controversy, turned decisively against them. Parkhurst's successor, Edmund Freake (1575–84), was keen to implement the queen's policy, and allied himself with conformists and religious conservatives among the gentry. One of Freake's allies, the Catholic Sir Thomas Cornwallis, a Howard protégé and ex-privy councillor to Mary I, bought and rebuilt the former college of St Mary in the Fields in Norwich as one of his residences.[11]

Elizabeth's last archbishop of Canterbury, John Whitgift (1583–1604), was a willing and active upholder of uniformity in the church. He demanded that all clergy subscribe their complete acceptance of the Book of Common Prayer, but had, however, to accept a modified subscription from many puritans. Several members of the privy council disliked his methods of enforcement. His policy provoked during the 1580s a national puritan campaign, including attempts to bring the issues of worship and church order before parliament, and the production of county surveys designed to show the parlous state of the clergy. Locally, Freake's two successors, Bishops Edmund Scambler (1584–94) and William Redman (1594–1602), were more temperate, discreet, and in tune with the feelings of puritan-inclined gentry and clergy.[12]

In Norwich, as in England as a whole, the Reformation opened religious divisions. Roman Catholic recusants were very few in Norwich.[13] The main fault line in the ruling class and the clergy probably lay between conformists (some of them religious conservatives who had only gradually settled down within the Elizabethan Church) and moderate puritans who prized the powerful preaching of God's Word and sought so far as possible (without splitting the church) to minimise the elements of ceremony in worship. Among the middling and lower ranks of society, however, there was an unquantifiable but possibly substantial minority deeply dissatisfied with Elizabeth's inadequate Reformation. This chapter will explore these divisions and the crucial relationship between clergy and laity. Who played the greater part in shaping the character of Protestantism in Norwich? Evangelical clergy, many of whom came to Norwich from outside, or the city's lay rulers and populace?

The course and outcome of Norwich's Reformation were shaped in important ways by the city's magistrates, the mayor and aldermen who were responsible for maintaining local peace and prosperity. The vast majority of recorded conflicts among city residents that stemmed from religious change during the crucial years 1535–58 were resolved in the mayor's court, rather than in church courts. Such controversies in Norwich were fewer in number and less intense than historians have found elsewhere, and the ruling elite adopted a rather unusual strategy in handling them. The magistrates almost never sought out religious dissidents, whether they were traditionalists or advocates of greater religious reform. Consequently, nearly all the cases they heard resulted from complaints brought to them by local residents. Whatever the charges, the magistrates customarily dismissed such allegations or took no action against those involved, with a few notable exceptions.

While Norwich's leaders endorsed each of the official Tudor religious settlements in a formal sense, they did not enforce religious conformity with the rigour required by each directive. They therefore never sought to adopt and enforce Catholicism or Protestantism exclusively. The magistrates repeatedly failed to alert outside authorities about the activities of religious dissidents in their jurisdiction or to punish religious offenders as required by parliamentary statute. The men who ruled sixteenth-century Norwich, it seems, were willing to tolerate a measure of spiritual diversity among the residents of the city, as well as among themselves.

The evidence for this variety of religious belief among civic leaders comes from wills, the only personal documents left in any significant number by Norwich's sixteenth-century aldermen. Although the use of wills to determine a testator's religious inclination is fraught with difficulty, a careful reading of the Norwich sources reveals that the city's ruling group was divided in matters of observance and doctrine throughout nearly the entire Reformation era.[14] The seventeen wills drawn up by aldermen during the last two decades of Henry VIII's reign, for example, show a predominantly conservative group, with only two testaments that did not fit the traditional medieval pattern of calling on saints or bequeathing money for commemorative masses.[15] Nine aldermen made wills during Edward VI's reign. While this group of testaments poses particular interpretative problems, as a traditional bequest might easily have attracted unwelcome official attention, it also reveals religious heterogeneity among the magistrates. Two wills disclose the testators' commitments to known Protestant clergy, while two others demonstrate an attachment to traditional Catholic practices and objects.[16] Wills from the Marian period raise similar difficulties for a modern reader, as Protestant testators might have been reluctant to declare themselves openly. Catholic ones, on the other hand, possibly feared the reversal of the Marian settlement and were therefore reluctant to make traditional bequests in such uncertain and volatile circumstances. Eight of the thirteen aldermanic wills written at this time offer evidence of Catholicism, three contain suggestive clues that the testators harboured Catholic sympathies and two defy any classification whatsoever.[17]

It would not be until the Elizabethan era that the city's ruling group became more unified, now along Protestant lines. There was, indeed, sufficient support among them to hire some of the hot Protestant clergymen who had begun to congregate in Norwich as early as the 1560s to preach before the corporation.[18] An examination of the testaments left by the men who served as aldermen during Elizabeth's reign reveals that, while all of them fell within acceptable Protestant parameters, some indicate a stronger commitment to the new faith than others. Thus, when Nicholas Norgate, who served South Conesford ward from 1559 until his death in 1568, penned his will, he left money to support sermons to be given by four preachers selected by Bishop Parkhurst.[19] Thomas Parker, Ber Street ward's alderman between 1559 and 1570, left bequests to George Gardiner, dean of the cathedral, and prebendary John Walker, both of whom were among the more forward of the Protestant clergy at this time.[20] Similarly, the 'apostle of Norwich', John More, received legacies from Ellis Bate in 1574 and from John Aldrich in 1582.[21]

Sometimes aldermen openly acted upon their religious convictions. According to John Bale, the East Anglian Protestant reformer and ex-Carmelite friar, Robert Rugge, brother of Bishop William Rugge and then mayor of Norwich, along with the steward, John Corbet, a gentleman from Sprowston, apprehended Bale's wife Dorothy while she was visiting the city in 1545. The two interrogated her about her husband and threatened her with indictment on charges of felony and treason. Some evidence suggests that both Rugge and Corbet (members of the duke of Norfolk's circle) held traditional religious views, making them likely candidates to be upset by Bale's presence in Norwich. But there is no record of an appearance by, or charges against, Dorothy Bale in the mayor's court book, suggesting that the two harassed her alone, in an essentially private capacity.[22] The future alderman, Andrew Quasshe, demonstrated his Protestant sensibilities in 1548 when he publicly objected to the reorganisation of the great civic guild of St George, even after its annual celebrations had been adapted to conform to the directives of Edward VI's Protestant settlement.[23] In the autumn of 1553, just months into Queen Mary's reign, the mayor, Henry Crook, was heard publicly to rejoice at the return of the mass.[24] During the Marian persecution of Protestants, Alexander Mather actively participated in the diocesan interrogation of the lay preacher Robert Watson. In the account of his travails composed after he fled to the continent, Watson additionally singled out Aldermen Thomas Codd (brother of the last Catholic master of St Giles's hospital) and Thomas Marsham as 'enemies of Christ' for the role that they played in his ordeal.[25]

Yet these kinds of declarations appear to have been rare, and, as a group, the magistrates tended to avoid such intervention in religious conflicts. Their doctrinal differences did not prevent them from cooperating as a corporation. In addition to the way in which they managed to diffuse religious conflicts, they worked together to take advantage of the official assault on the church when they thought that the city could benefit from it, despite the disagreements among them. In the later 1530s, for instance, city magistrates acted to exploit the dissolution of the friaries. In 1538, they wrote directly to Thomas Cromwell to request his assistance in securing the house of the Norwich Blackfriars at its surrender. On 1 June 1540 the Blackfriars' house and lands were granted to the citizens of Norwich for £81. Having gained valuable experience through these dealings with the government, the authorities moved quickly and effectively to gain control of St Giles's hospital seven years later. In marked contrast to the majority of English urban corporations, the rulers of Norwich lost no time in seizing this valuable opportunity to reform their system of institutional relief for the poor.[26]

The magistrates also worked together in reshaping the city's public culture as they reacted to the Reformation's assault on traditional ritual. In response to directives to reduce the cycle of pageants, plays and processions that had punctuated the civic calendar in the pre-Reformation era, city leaders revived some ceremonies, reinvented others and added new observances that highlighted temporal events rather than traditional religious ones. These new rituals allowed Norwich residents to come together to celebrate the civic body and the triumphs of Tudor government with few, if any, references to religious doctrines and practices. This reinvented public spectacle was very much in keeping, therefore, with the magistrates' practice of not imposing religious homogeneity.[27] When the feast of St Mary Magdalen (22 July) became one of the numerous holy days abrogated by Henry VIII in 1536, the magistrates reinvented rather than abandoned it. They established a similar festival – the 'watch' in Pentecost week – to be celebrated at a different time of year from the traditional one. The new ceremony continued to feature the mayor and aldermen, dressed in armour and parading on horseback. But it omitted all of the customary homage paid to Mary Magdalen. From a ritual that had honoured a female saint and also served political and economic purposes, the magistrates' armed procession became a wholly secular but no less splendid civic occasion.[28]

In the ensuing years, the magistrates invented completely new ceremonies to be observed in Norwich that were not narrowly religious in focus. In 1537, for example, they mounted an elaborate spectacle to mark the birth of Prince Edward, Henry VIII's long-awaited male heir. Similar celebrations commemorated Tudor military successes, including Edward Seymour's sack of Edinburgh in 1544 and the 1546 treaty of Ardres that ended the war with France.[29] In Edward VI's reign, the magistrates sought to redesign the annual celebration of the guild of St George, purging its overtly Catholic elements. Perhaps because it so conspicuously struck at the roots of Norwich's medieval past, this particular reform produced the first open strife about a major ritual event. In other respects, however, the elite moved as one: in 1549, after the defeat of Robert Kett and his rebels, an annual service of thanksgiving was held at St Peter Mancroft in Norwich for more than a century.[30] The magistrates continued to devise new ceremonies in the later sixteenth century, although at a slower pace. In Mary's reign, the corporation staged a three-part show to mark Alderman Augustine Steward's third term in mayoral office. There was also a celebration of England's military victory at St-Quentin, France, in 1557.[31] Finally, and in keeping with this upsurge of patriotism, Norwich was one of the few communities in England to institute an annual thanksgiving service after the defeat of the Spanish Armada in 1588.[32]

By the end of the sixteenth century, Norwich magistrates had proved remarkably successful at containing religious divisions and quarrels so they did not escalate out of control. Because of their judicious practice of *de facto* toleration and the reshaping of public culture, neither the crown nor the church was given much reason to intervene in the city's business, as it had done so dramatically in the previous century. Fortunately for this policy, the gentry and nobility of Norfolk, most of whom were religious conservatives before the accession of Elizabeth, played little direct role in Norwich's religious affairs. Only John Corbet and Sir Roger Townsend, a Norfolk JP during Henry VIII's reign, sought to exercise any such influence, and then only infrequently.[33] The course of the Reformation in Norwich, therefore, demonstrates that sixteenth-century magistrates learned to compartmentalise their religious beliefs, effectively creating a distinction between private religious faith on the one hand, and public action and civic loyalty on the other.

The primary instrument through which Norwich's magistrates handled the conflicts that resulted from changing religious doctrines and practices was the mayor's court, one of the three main instruments of justice in the city. They also staffed the other two most important courts. The mayor and a select group of aldermen who had previously served as mayor acted as justices of the peace in the court of quarter sessions. In addition, all of the aldermen then in office constituted the court of aldermen, which dealt with a wide range of civil and commercial disputes, as well as civic business. Boundaries between these bodies were fluid: cases presented to the mayor's court and the quarter sessions were heard by the same people; the distinction between meetings of the mayor's court and the full court of aldermen was not always clear and their records were not kept separately.[34]

Recent research has revealed that Norwich's voluminous civic records, particularly the mayor's court books, are critical sources for the study of the Reformation in the city. Members of the ruling elite appear to have exercised nearly complete control over the management of incipient doctrinal conflict during the most important phase of the Reformation era. Cases of religious conflict first appear in the city court records in the 1530s. From that time until nearly the end of the century, the magistrates confronted a wide variety of beliefs among Norwich residents. They ranged from views espoused by the medieval church to those that strayed well beyond the boundaries imposed by any Tudor settlement. Very quickly, though, the magistrates established a pattern of disciplining religious offenders lightly or not at all, no matter whether the cause for their appearance in court stemmed from over-enthusiastic support of traditional or reformed doctrines and practices. For example, the mayor and aldermen appear to have taken no action against the capper Thomas Myles, when in July 1535 six witnesses reported inflammatory remarks which, if they were indeed his, would clearly have placed him outside the religious mainstream. Myles had asserted that 'the sacrament of the [Aulter] is or was asmoche in his capp presse as it is ... in the chirche' and that 'the sacrament of the [Aulter] was aswell on the [Norwich] Castill ditch as in the chirche'. He had also attacked the Creed, the rite of confirmation, images, saints and pilgrimages, as well as the reactionary old Bishop Nykke.[35]

Similarly, when William Thakker appeared before city magistrates later that same year for criticising the sermons of John Barret, he seems not to have been disciplined. Barret, divinity lecturer at the cathedral, was a close friend of John Bale, and has been credited with playing an important role in Bale's conversion.[36] Even when the magistrates did punish religious dissidents, they usually imposed a light penalty. One Henry Niker was gaoled, probably for only a very short time, for having broken an Ember Day fast in 1537.[37]

The strategy of defusing local religious conflicts in order to deflect outside attention from civic affairs became more difficult during Edward VI's reign, when such conflicts increased markedly. Some Norwich residents engaged in iconoclasm, attacked the priesthood, broke down altars and expressed radical views, while others criticised the doctrine of royal supremacy, disregarded Edwardian religious innovations and disparaged reformed preachers. The mayors and aldermen nevertheless refused to punish religious offenders harshly, despite the heightened challenge to civic authority posed during these years. Ralph Gylmyn was bound to good behaviour in 1547 for having denied the Real Presence, but he was never called before the court again.[38] Thomas Bedys was committed to ward in 1548 for declaring that the preacher Thomas Rose was 'a ffalse knave and here lyke a false p[rea]cher'. On the following day, however, the magistrates released him 'upon the truste of amendment'.[39] A man named Thurston was simply warned to hold his tongue in 1549 when he appeared in court for having claimed 'all priests' wives were whores'.[40] The mayor and aldermen sentenced John Dyxe to gaol until he could find sureties, in June 1553, after he had disturbed a service at the parish church of St Martin-at-Oak when the priest had commanded fasting to observe the feast of St John the Baptist. It is not clear, however, that Dyxe ever actually served his sentence or found the sureties required.[41] The magistrates remained committed to tolerating religious differences in order to preserve unified civic authority, although that policy had been shown to rest on somewhat fragile foundations.

This pattern of refraining from vigorous prosecution of religious offenders evident from the mayor's court records becomes quite striking during periods when particularly severe penalties were imposed by the government for religious nonconformity. During the last years of Henry VIII's reign, when the death penalty hung over anyone who denied the key points of belief and practice ordained for the English Church in the Six Articles,

Norwich city magistrates did not make a single arrest for violations of the Act. This stood in stark contrast to the situation in London, where an eager corporation led the investigations that resulted in the imprisonment of hundreds of suspected heretics.[42]

Similarly, when Queen Mary's government passed the heresy laws of 1555 that set the stage for the subsequent trial and execution of close to three hundred Protestants, religious conflict virtually vanished from the pages of the mayor's court books.[43] In fact, only two residents of Norwich died in the flames, and both of them were arrested because of self-incrimination, and not because the magistrates took the initiative in rooting out heretics. The first, Elizabeth Cooper, a pewterer's wife, died at Lollard's Pit in Norwich in July 1557, along with Simon Miller of King's Lynn.[44] Cooper had interrupted a service at St Andrew's to retract publicly an earlier recantation of her Protestant beliefs. It appears that she was arrested only because one of the congregants demanded that the sheriff, Thomas Sotherton, also a parishioner there, take her into custody. As Cooper went to the stake, along with Simon Miller, Cicely Ormes, the wife of a worsted weaver from St Lawrence's parish, declared her support for the pair. She called out that 'she would pledge on the same cup that they drank on'. Also in the crowd was John Corbet, the former city steward, who turned her over to diocesan authorities. Ormes was examined and imprisoned for nearly a year before she was executed in September 1558.[45]

The *de facto* toleration practised by Norwich's magistrates was neither theorised nor codified in law. It was inherently unstable and could not be enforced at all times. The deaths of Elizabeth Cooper and Cicely Ormes as Protestant heretics during Mary's reign demonstrate that point clearly. Nevertheless, for most of the Reformation period, city leaders were effective in fending off the inquiries of outside officials by countenancing spiritual diversity among local residents and remaining politically unified despite their own confessional differences.

Those differences began to disappear at the time of Elizabeth's accession. The influenza epidemic that swept through England in 1558–59 took the lives of ten of Norwich's aldermen, at least six of whom were Catholic. While it is difficult to identify the doctrinal affiliations of their replacements, it seems likely that the religious composition of the aldermanic bench changed dramatically during Elizabeth's first two years on the throne to become strongly Protestant.[46] The most interesting evidence of the Norwich magistracy's religious reorientation after 1558 comes not from their past proclamations or their wills but from their practice of governance. The magistrates continued their policy of tolerating differences between Protestants and Catholics as well as the developing diversity among Protestants. Although they presided over the execution of a number of Protestant heretics in the 1570s and 1580s, none were from Norwich, and the magistrates had not been involved in their apprehension or conviction. In addition, there is no evidence that they took any action against, or were even officially aware of, the activities of the separatist Robert Browne and his followers.[47] Given their history of religious toleration, this does not necessarily reflect an emergent Protestant solidarity in their ranks. In other areas of governance, however, the magistrates demonstrated a new and strong Protestant ethic. Without imposing religious uniformity, they embarked on a campaign of moral and social discipline closely related to their own religious reorientation.

Just after Elizabeth became queen, the pages of the Norwich mayor's court book began to fill with references to petty criminal and moral offenders in far greater numbers then ever before. The magistrates meted out harsh disciplinary punishments for theft, vagrancy, illicit sexual behaviour and a number of other social transgressions. After 1561, the hitherto rare crimes of 'evil rule' and 'ill rule' were commonly recorded, often without any additional description of the illicit act committed. Although various antisocial misdemeanours had been noted in the court books intermittently before this time, the correction of such faults became a much more regular and frequent feature of court sessions after 1558. The mayor and aldermen punished these offences by routine whipping, expulsion from Norfolk, setting in the stocks and imprisonment. The timing of the sudden upsurge in punishment points to the beginning of a deliberate effort to impose moral discipline on the city's inhabitants through the office of the mayor's court, in striking contrast to the magistrates' continued toleration of religious diversity.[48]

The prime focus for the pious devotion of the citizens of late medieval Norwich was the parish church. About fifteen of them were closed or demolished between 1530 and 1564, mostly between 1540 and 1553, especially in the northern and Conesford wards. Some of these churches were already very vulnerable because of late medieval parochial unions following depopulation in the fourteenth century. Several, however, were being repaired and receiving generous bequests until within a few years of their final demolition. The crown, the grantees of monastic advowsons, the corporation, and the dean and chapter all profited from the process of dissolution, but often at the expense of parishioners who had little say in the matter. In March 1551 the cathedral chapter leased the church of All Saints Fyebridgegate to the mayor and citizens of Norwich for five hundred years. In May, the dean deceitfully assured the anxious parishioners that their church had been neither given nor sold; the very next month, the parish was united to St Paul's and the church pulled down. The closure, union or adaptation of churches was not a new phenomenon. Never, however, had so many disappeared in so short a space of time.[49]

Not all Norwich churchgoers were so impotent in the face of change. Another important development was the acquisition of a larger share of ecclesiastical patronage by some parishioners or their representatives, especially in the wealthy Wymer ward. Twenty of the city's post-Reformation parishes comprised appropriated benefices without vicarages, over half of which belonged to the dean and chapter, while the rest had been owned by other religious houses. Many of these appropriated benefices were miserably poor. Yet among them were also two of the wealthiest in Norwich: St Andrew and St Peter Mancroft. Formerly belonging to the nearby college of St Mary in the Fields, both were sold by the crown and eventually bought by feoffees acting for the parishioners: St Andrew's in 1559 and St Peter's in 1581. Representatives of the congregations of the two most important city parishes thus assumed responsibility for choosing their own ministers. The advowson of St Benedict's, formerly appropriated to Buckenham priory, was also bought by the parishioners after the Dissolution. The mayor and corporation gained control of appointments to St Helen's Holme Street (1547) and St Etheldreda's (1550). Parishioners leased the right of appointment to at least two of the cathedral chapter's donative cures for part of the period. In 1603, four of the city's rectories were said to have been vacant for twenty years, and the churchwardens of three of them (St John Maddermarket, St Lawrence and St Margaret) had taken over the responsibility of paying a curate.[50]

Many Norwich parishes were served by stipendiary clergy who enjoyed little security and received poor remuneration. A high turnover of personnel and the serving of two or more cures by the same minister in order to make ends meet were commonplace throughout this period. The proscription of prayers for the dead and the dissolution of chantries removed the clergy's most valuable source of supplementary income. The endowment of special sermons by Protestant benefactors offset these losses to some extent, but these were plums for ministers held in high esteem. Robert Hill, one such minister, wrote in 1611 of the 'uncertaine allowance' provided even for the city's preachers, and 'the meane estate they must ever needs live in'. In 1606 the clergy of Norwich went so far as to petition parliament for a tenth of current rents in the city, but the city's MPs opposed the resulting Bill, and the ministers were persuaded to desist by means of a promise of a fresh assessment on the parishes to increase their wages. Voluntary contributions were not enough to provide a sufficient maintenance, privy councillors told the city's mayor and justices, in view of the unwillingness of the 'inferior sort' to pay their share.[51]

Thomas Bilney's 1531 journey to Norwich and subsequent martyrdom heralded the Reformation in the most dramatic fashion. He was, however, in Norwich for a very short time, and it is not clear how much lasting influence his preaching had. By the late 1540s there had gathered in the city an outstandingly strong cluster of evangelical clergy. Dr John Barret was appointed its divinity lecturer by the cathedral priory before its dissolution, confirmed in this position by the dean and chapter in 1542, and presented by the king to the rectory of St Michael-at-Plea in 1550. The preacher Thomas Rose's adventurous career had already included incitement to iconoclasm in Essex in 1532 and spells of imprisonment, hiding and exile before he arrived in Norwich around the beginning of Edward VI's reign, when he was described as preaching at St Andrew's. Henry King was a prebendary of Norwich cathedral between 1548 and 1554. All three, but especially Rose, provoked strongly hostile reactions from some of the laity. It seems that one of King's sermons was also criticised in 1547 by Matthew Parker, possibly a more moderate evangelical. When Parker tried to dissuade Kett's followers from further rebellious actions in 1549, his words were so angrily received that he had to flee their camp.[52] In some ways the most remarkable figure among the Norwich preachers of Edward's reign was Robert Watson, who had in 1539 created a major stir when he challenged Bishop Rugge's teaching concerning free will. Unlike Barret and Rose, he had then been resident in Norwich for over a decade. In May 1549, even though a layman and twice married, he was presented by the king to a prebendal stall in the cathedral. A 'preacher in those days of good Estimacion', he was chosen by Kett's rebels to be one of their 'captains'. Thomas Coniers, priest of St Martin-at-Palace, next to the cathedral, conducted services in English at the rebels' request. Two other clerical activists were William Stampe and Andrew Colby. Stampe, with a band of sympathisers, broke down the altar in his church of St Augustine in May 1549 against the will of the parishioners. In June 1551 he had to do penance for conducting services with his cope deliberately turned inside out. Colby, too, may have been involved in altar smashing, and in 1552 told his parishioners that he was going to break a fast: an act of overt defiance against established Catholic doctrine.[53]

The Marian regime faced remarkably little effective resistance from this large band of evangelical ministers. John Barret conformed almost immediately, and received royal authorisation to preach. Early in 1554 the corporation assured the duke of Norfolk that he had celebrated mass according to the queen's proceedings. In 1555, Barret debated the doctrine of transubstantiation with his old friend Robert Watson, imprisoned for his refusal to attend mass, before Watson subscribed his own qualified acceptance of it. In June that year, Thomas Rose confessed before an impressive audience of county and city notables and clergy that Christ was really present in the sacrament of the altar after the words of consecration. Both Watson and Rose fled abroad soon afterwards. They tried to explain their words away, but the bloodless capitulation of these two leaders of the early Reformation in the city was a propaganda coup of immense value for Bishop Hopton. It goes some way towards explaining the paucity of lay martyrs in Norwich. At least eleven Norwich clergy were deprived of their benefices or dismissed from their cures for marriage. But none of these men was executed. Some, like John Salisbury, erstwhile dean of Norwich cathedral, and his colleague, Henry King, submitted and served in the Marian church. Others fled or lay low.[54]

Only some years after Elizabeth I's accession did a new Protestant clerical leadership emerge. A shared commitment to vigorous preaching and organised discussion of the scriptures, along with conscientious objections to vestments and other aspects of formal worship, were to mark out some of these men as 'puritans'. Among the first such preachers known to have been active in Elizabethan Norwich were George Gardiner, minister at St Andrew's church from 1562, George Leedes, curate at St Stephen's from about the same time, and John Machett, rector of St Clement's. They were joined in 1564 by John Walker, who came to St Peter Mancroft as its senior minister. These men may have led the exercise of prophesying (the exposition of scriptural texts by a group of ministers) which began around that time, probably with the encouragement of Bishop Parkhurst.[55] At this stage, Elizabeth's opposition to all such exercises had not yet crystallised.

John More emerged as the leading Norwich reformer during the 1570s (Figure 24). Like George Gardiner, More was a northerner who had been a scholar at Christ's College, Cambridge, and he too became minister of St Andrew's (in about 1573). He soon made his mark. In December 1573 Bishop Parkhurst reported that More was the only Norwich minister who refused to wear the surplice for fear of causing offence to his congregation. He also described him as godly and learned, and said that he had done much good in the city.[56]

Both Bishop Parkhurst and Archbishop Parker died in 1575. Some Norwich ministers took advantage of this unusual hiatus in ecclesiastical authority to establish a 'Prophesie' in Norwich cathedral on Monday mornings. Nineteen or twenty 'godlie Exercises of preching and Catechizing' allegedly existed in Norwich during this halcyon period. Bishop Freake ended them and suspended the puritan clergy. In September 1576 six Norwich ministers, including Richard Crick, George Leedes, John More and Thomas Roberts wrote to Lord Burghley protesting their loyalty and detestation of heresy, along with 'all puritanisme and suche like'. They dared not accept the ceremonies which had divided the church, and begged him to use his influence both with the queen and their new bishop. Thomas Roberts, the young rector of St Clement's, had emerged as More's principal lieutenant. Crick had been a minor canon and chaplain to Bishop Parkhurst. At last, in August 1578, after lobbying on the ministers' behalf by sympathetic local gentry, and pressure on Bishop Freake from privy councillors, all except one of these men were licensed to preach. They were, however, first required to acknowledge that the ceremonies, order and government of the Church of England were 'so farre tollerable' that nobody should on their account refuse to participate in its services.[57]

More and his colleagues had lay support. In November 1576 two laymen and a minister were ringleaders of the opposition in St Andrew's parish to the clergyman whom Freake appointed in More's place. They rebuked him openly as a turncoat and false preacher. Freake found the mayor and aldermen unwilling to deal with these men. Only after the intervention of Francis Wyndham, a local gentleman, did they commit the protesters to prison, where sympathisers brought them food and wine. The increasing radicalism of a section of lay opinion in Norwich is shown by a petition to the queen of about 1580 subscribed by 175 men which called for the removal of the 'dumbe ministrie' and the establishment of a Presbyterian church order. Among the signatories were Robert Browne and Robert Harrison.[58]

The zeal of local people for further reformation attracted Robert Browne to Norwich and provided the basis of support for the independent congregation which he established together with Harrison. Norwich separatism may have survived their departure from the city in 1581. About three years later, twenty Norfolk ministers wrote to ask for the privy council's help in the face of Archbishop Whitgift's demand for subscription to his three articles. They had kept their people from Browne's schism only with difficulty, even when there was plenty of preaching available in the parish churches. If they were to be deprived and replaced by incompetent ministers, they feared that a serious division in the church would result. A much longer list of sixty-four Norfolk ministers 'not resolved to subscribe' to the articles, headed by John More of St Andrew's, included a number of other Norwich activists, such as Thomas Roberts and George Leedes. Most puritan clergy later accepted a modified form of subscription. Moderate puritans had to tread a narrow path between offending their own consciences and possibly alienating many of their more radical parishioners

FIGURE 24. John More, 'The Apostle of Norwich', from an engraving of 1620. (*National Portrait Gallery*)

through the use of vestments and ceremonies, on the one hand, and being deprived of their benefices or dismissed from their cures, on the other. One Norwich minister to be deprived was the later famous John Burgess, briefly rector of St Peter Hungate, who allegedly sacrificed this living in 1590 rather than cause such offence to his parishioners. John More, veteran of at least two puritan campaigns, himself managed to survive at St Andrew's till his death in 1592. Various examples of nonconformity were presented in the bishop's visitation of 1597. At St Peter Hungate Master John Holden, Burgess's successor, did not read the whole service every Sunday. Master William Welles of St George Colegate baptised in a basin set into the font, rather than the font itself, and did not go on Rogationtide perambulation. Both Holden and Welles, however, survived in Norwich long after 1597. Only one man, the otherwise unknown Master Awldham, curate of St John Sepulchre, was reported for failing to use the surplice, and he at once agreed to do so in future.[59]

Two famous puritans, William Burton, who was in the city in the 1580s, and Robert Hill, who was minister at St Andrew's at the turn of the century, described the abundance of preaching in late Elizabethan and Jacobean Norwich. The Word was preached every Sunday in many churches, and well-attended sermons were also delivered on most or all weekdays. Both men mentioned the hospitable welcome which the preachers received in aldermen's houses. Hill particularly singled out Francis Rugge, three times mayor, in this connection. 'But howsoever the Arke of God's Covenant be beautifully set up in your severall Temples', Hill wrote, 'yet to you of S[t] Andrewes hath God appeared in exceeding beauty'. He doubted whether any one parish in the kingdom had been 'so successively blessed with learned and laborious Ministers', as St Andrew's had been for almost sixty years. John More had for twenty years preached amongst his flock almost every day, besides holding his 'private conferences' among their families. Hill had for over five years worked alongside Thomas Newhouse (d. 1611), another powerful preacher and pastor at St Andrew's, who (Hill thought) had something of the spirit of William Perkins, foremost puritan exponent of practical divinity. The parishioners of St Andrew's were proudly conscious of their position in the vanguard of the Norwich Reformation: inscriptions over the aisle doors recorded the translation of the church from 'extreme idolatry' in 1547, the first year of Edward VI, and Elizabeth I's re-establishment of the gospel.[60]

The majority of the Norwich clergy were, however, far less well qualified than the ministers of the quite exceptional parish of St Andrew's. In 1563, thirty-three parishes were listed in the record of the archdeacon's visitation. Only five incumbents were named for the city's fifteen rectories and vicarages. Only four men were distinguished by the title 'magister' (which should have indicated the possession of a master's degree, but was sometimes respectfully accorded to clergy with lesser academic qualifications), including George Gardiner, George Leedes and John Machett. By 1593 a considerable improvement had taken place. Nine of the city's parishes then had incumbents. At least twelve of the Norwich clergy had degrees: two a BA, nine an MA and one, Ralph Furness of St Andrew's, a BD. Twelve men were described as preachers or able to preach, including two non-graduates. Three of the twelve were public preachers.[61]

This was indeed a handsome endowment. But nine clergymen were presented in the bishop's visitation in 1597 for failing to provide monthly sermons, let alone give them in person. This tends to corroborate the damning evidence presented in the puritan survey of the Norfolk clergy (*c.* 1586), which had found eight non-preachers in Norwich, serving between them thirteen of the city's cures. Two men, both of whom served two cures each, were described as 'a drunkard' and 'negligent, given to drinking' respectively, and a third was claimed to be 'no minister'. In about 1603 John Lowe, who allegedly served three parishes, faced many serious accusations brought by his parishioners at St Benedict's, among them that he had been a drunkard, a persistent sex-pest and a 'sturrer upe of contention amongest his neighbores' for almost twenty years in his several parishes. He did indeed preach, but maliciously and bitterly. Lowe for his part claimed that the ringleader of the complainants was 'a greate precisian, or puritan as they call them'.[62]

The obstacles to the realisation of the puritan vision of reform included not only the inadequacy of poorly paid clergy but also religious conservatism and positive attachment to ceremonies and ornaments. The cathedral, with its corporate life going back to monastic times and its tradition of liturgical music and formal worship, loomed over Norwich and controlled the appointments to many city livings (Figure 25). During two brief interludes, around 1550 and 1570, it looked as though the cathedral might be captured for forward Protestantism. In the early 1570s the chapter was indeed dominated for a time by moderate puritans, but after the advent of Bishop Freake the chapter members most involved in cathedral affairs were mainly dependable conformists. Three of the senior ministers of the foremost parish church in Norwich, St Peter Mancroft, gained cathedral prebends. John Walker was one of a group of prebendaries who in 1570 allegedly attempted innovations, including the destruction of the organs in the choir. (For puritans, organs had no place in the pure worship of God.) The one who served longest in the cathedral was, however, Hugh

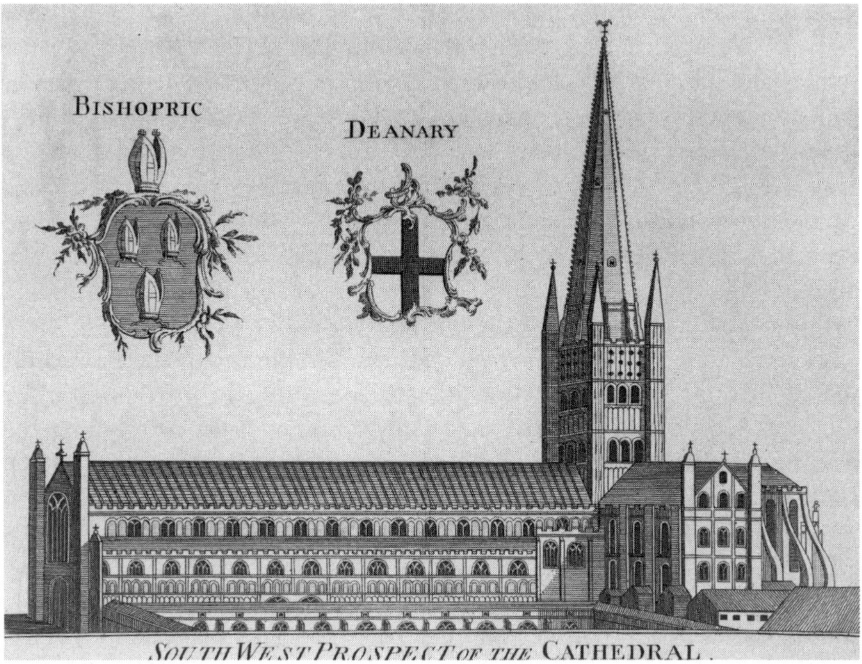

FIGURE 25. South-west prospect of Norwich cathedral, proudly displaying the arms of the bishopric and the deanery. (*Norfolk Heritage Centre, photograph by Terry Burchell*)

Castleton (1577–1616). He was first among Norwich ministers in obedience in 1573, according to Bishop Parkhurst, and was later one of Bishop Freake's principal supporters.[63]

A number of cathedral minor canons also served as ministers in the city. Some of these men were poorly qualified for pastoral work. Bishop Freake collated two in succession, Germain Gardiner and Thomas Thwaites, to the church of St Simon and St Jude. This was a parish which needed strong leadership. The godly sort there had been scandalised in 1573 by the antics of a disruptive group which rang the bell during sermons and caused the *Magnificat* to be sung by 'lewde boyes' when the minister read it. (One of these boys was almost certainly a cathedral chorister.) Thwaites, who probably occupied the living from 1582 to 1604, was no graduate, did not preach and was presented for neglecting various duties in 1597.[64]

Some of the most fertile ground for the development of a non-puritan style of churchmanship was to be found in parishes under the cathedral chapter's wing. The parishioners of St Gregory's, according to Bishop Parkhurst, still resisted the destruction of their roodloft in 1573; the parish contained several 'adversaries', like one Debney, who called the Geneva psalms 'Gehenna psalms'. The parishioners showed a notable pride in the fabric of their church, for whose 'beautifying' the considerable sum of about £110 was to be raised in 1626. St Stephen's was the best of the cathedral's Norwich livings. Its church, whose rebuilding was splendidly completed as late as 1550, housed several memorials to registrars, scribes and proctors of the Norwich consistory court and their families: Godsalve, Mingay, Rant, Styles and Atkins. These men were conservative in outlook; a Mingay and a Rant would be prominent among Norwich's seventeenth-century royalists. Miles Spencer (d. 1570), long serving-chancellor of the diocese and devoted servant of Bishop Nykke, lived in this parish and frequently held his court in the church.[65]

The Reformation's effects on Norwich were complex as well as far-reaching. Those who benefited materially from the Dissolution or transformation of medieval religious institutions and the confiscation of their endowments included the city's corporation and the inhabitants of some of its more favoured parishes. A number of poorly endowed parishes ceased to exist. Opinion in the city was deeply divided by religious innovation. Although there was very little outright resistance to change, and most Norwich people conformed outwardly to the requirements of successive governments, the city certainly contained till the 1560s several leading citizens who were strongly conservative in their religious sympathies. Vociferous disagreement and verbal invective recorded in the mayor's court book began in the 1530s and reached their peak in Edward VI's reign. The city's lay rulers sought throughout to contain internal disagreement, prevent external interference and turn change to Norwich's advantage as far as possible. With some exceptions (especially during Mary's reign) they showed very little desire to punish religious dissidents.

Norwich attracted notable evangelical preachers from the 1530s onwards. The collapse of civic Protestantism in the face of the Marian reaction is therefore striking. The very fact that John More could be dubbed 'the Apostle of Norwich' conveys the sense of a sharp change in tempo, if not a new beginning, in the early 1570s. The 'grave senators' of Elizabethan Norwich enforced social discipline through the mayor's court and supported godly preachers largely chosen by inhabitants of a cluster of city parishes. But the puritan vision of a 'holy city' was still some way short of realisation by the 1590s. Several parishes still lacked resident preaching ministers; and some clergy, in the cathedral and elsewhere, were ceremonial conformists of a more conservative persuasion. By 1580, it is clear, there was a widespread demand for further reformation on the part of a militant minority of layfolk whose aspirations could only be satisfied by more radical puritanism or separation. The transformation of the powerful religiosity of late medieval Norwich into new forms and institutions had been far from smooth or complete.

12

Kett's Rebellion

Andy Wood

> The rable of Norffolke rebelles, ye pretend a common-wealth. How amend ye it? By killing of gentlemen, by spoiling of gentlemen, by imprisoning of gentlemen? A marvellous tanned common-wealth. Why should you thus hate them? For their riches or for their rule? ... Is this your true duetie ... to disobeie your betters, and to obeie your tanners, to change your obedience from the king to a Ket? ... In countries some must rule, some must obeie, everie man maie not beare like stroke: for everie man is not like wise.
>
> Sir John Cheke, *The Hurt of Sedition*, 1549[1]

Patrons of the gentlemen's lavatories at the Castle Mall shopping centre in Norwich are confronted, as they exit, with a perplexing image of popular disorder.[2] When the Mall was completed in the early 1990s, the walls of its cafeteria were decorated with a mural depicting the history of the city. On Saturday lunchtimes, harassed parents now struggle with their hungry toddlers before a tableau of Norwich's turbulent past. It so happened that the section of the murals depicting the major popular insurrection in the city – Kett's Rebellion of 1549 – was located opposite the entrance to the toilets (Figure 26). This shows a portly Robert Kett seated beneath his fabled Oak of Reformation. Sitting below Robert is the clerk of the court of popular justice that met under the Oak; around him stand his grave, elderly advisers; in front of Kett stands a representative of Protector Somerset's council, a royal herald entitled the king of arms; and behind the herald is a posturing boy, lifting his tunic to reveal his bared buttocks. Between Kett and the king of arms the artist depicted two adult rebels. One raises a hammer above his head, while the other lifts a sickle, the two implements forming a cross. Unfortunately (perhaps as an ironic comment upon the eclipse of organised socialism after 1989?), this element of the mural has been obscured by the control panel for the Mall's sprinkler system. None the less, its symbolism should be obvious: the crossed tools, alluding to the unity of town and country labourers, originated with the

FIGURE 26. Mural by Piers Wallace in the Castle Mall shopping centre, Norwich, depicting the interview between Robert Kett and the royal herald on Mousehold Heath in 1549. (*Norfolk Archaeological Unit*)

Bolshevik Revolution of 1917, and remain a potent symbol of the International Socialist Movement. Whereas the significance of the mooning boy is less than immediately obvious, the crossed hammer-and-sickle, despite its occlusion, highlights both the historical role played by the labouring people of Norwich in what is often described as an 'agrarian revolt', and the modern appropriation of Robert Kett's Rebellion by Norfolk radicals and socialists.

For the first three hundred years following the defeat of his insurrection, Robert Kett's name stood as an official byword for the chaos that flowed from popular politics. Like the medieval rebels Wat Tyler and Jack Cade, Kett was invoked by conservative writers in order to damn mob politics. It was not until the early nineteenth century that he was rehabilitated. Norfolk Chartists, radicals and (later) trade unionists and socialists, confronting many of the same issues that they felt had led to rebellion in 1549 – rural poverty, low wages, legal prohibitions on popular organisation – saw in Kett's Rebellion a precursor of their own struggles. Robert Kett's current good name originates from this ideological reorientation of mid Tudor history. Labour-voting, twentieth-century Norwich embraced the yeoman rebel from Wymondham as one of its own: the ridge upon which

Kett's command post stood is now known as Kett's Hill; the remains of that building (originally Surrey Place, the palace of the earl of Surrey) have become Kett's Castle; below Kett's Hill stand a pub and a garage named after the local hero; the great brass doors of Norwich's interwar city hall depict Robert Kett's horrible death in December 1549, hanging in chains from the walls of Norwich castle. Glowering across the marketplace from city hall stands the castle itself, in 1549 the symbol of royal authority within the city. But here too the modern rehabilitation of Robert has left its mark. A plaque unveiled in 1949 commemorates (and in part apologises for) Robert Kett's execution in the following terms:

> In 1549 AD, Robert Kett, yeoman farmer of Wymondham, was executed by hanging in this Castle, after the defeat of the Norfolk Rebellion, of which he was the leader. In 1949 AD – four hundred years later – this Memorial was placed here by the citizens of Norwich in reparation and honour to the memory of a notable leader in the long struggle of the common people of England to escape from a servile life into the freedom of just conditions.

Academic historians often condescend to such public representations of the past.[3] But the contrasting styles of the plaque on the castle and the shopping centre mural hint at a historical contradiction within the ideology of Kett's Rebellion. Somewhere between the jokiness of the Castle Mall mural, with its mysteriously mooning boy, and the sombre plaque on Norwich castle, lies a genuine conflict at the heart of sixteenth-century popular politics. Whereas the plaque of 1949 identifies only one source of rebel politics in 1549 – that of the disciplined struggle of 'the common people' – the humorous late twentieth-century mural illuminates a fundamental contradiction within rebel ideology: that between order, represented by Kett under his Oak of Reformation, and the festive disorder personified by the rude boy.

In order to appreciate the significance of this dichotomy, we must return to the events of 1549 themselves. This chapter will therefore begin with a brief account of the 1549 rebellions within Norfolk. It will then use the incident depicted in the Castle Mall mural as a starting point for an assessment of rebel ideology, looking in particular at the insurgents' religious attitudes; at the significance of rebel divisions; and at the theme of social conflict. Thereafter, it will briefly describe the pattern of disorder elsewhere in the country in 1549, before illuminating the peculiar intensity and violence that characterised Kett's Rebellion in Norfolk. Finally, comes an examination of the role played by the inhabitants of Norwich in the rebellion, focusing on the ambiguous behaviour of the city's elite towards the rebels; the underlying social tensions within the mid Tudor walls;

and the strong support shown by many labouring people in Norwich towards the rebel cause.

The Castle Mall mural depicts an event that took place on 24 August 1549. For the preceding six weeks, Norwich had been surrounded, and periodically occupied, by a large rebel force led by Robert Kett.[4] Yet the insurrection began without Kett; and although history has given his name to it, the Norfolk rising was best known until the 1580s as the 'commotion time'. According to Holinshed's *Chronicles*, trouble started in Norfolk in early June 1549, when the inhabitants of Attleborough broke enclosing fences on their common land. On 6 July, the Attleborough rioters led a general attack on enclosures, including those recently erected by Robert Kett, a wealthy yeoman tanner from Wymondham. The assault on Kett's enclosures took place on 9 July, and ended in Kett offering to lead the rebels himself in an attempt 'to subdue the power of Great men'.[5]

The rebels moved swiftly, gathering support as they marched. On the evening of 10 July, they met with Norwich sympathisers at Eaton Wood, and were subsequently joined by the mayor, Thomas Codd, and a delegation of aldermen, who came to hear their complaints. Kett asked Codd's permission to move his host through Norwich on his way to Mousehold Heath, a large area of common land bordering the eastern side of the city, where they intended to establish a camp (Figure 5). Denied such permission, Kett's host skirted Norwich, arriving at the heath on 12 July. According to later exaggerated estimates, some 20,000 people converged upon Mousehold Heath. Captured gentlemen were imprisoned in Surrey Place, in the city's gaol and in Norwich castle. With its commanding views over Norwich, Surrey Place became Kett's military headquarters; he administered justice in Thorpe Wood, adjoining the southern edge of the heath, under his Oak of Reformation (Figure 27). Here Kett and his councillors maintained order over the 'commotioners'. Lists of rebel complaints were drawn up for the attention of Protector Somerset's council, and handed to royal representatives on their periodic visits to the camp.[6] Since the death of Henry VIII, England had been governed by a council of leading noblemen, headed by the Lord Protector, the duke of Somerset, whose attempts at social reform earned him some popular approval. Like other rebel groups, Kett's 'commotioners' hoped to win his support for change within their locality.

Over the succeeding weeks, the rebels' negotiations with Somerset became increasingly fraught, especially after they seized the city on 22 July. Receiving news of the fall of Norwich, the council sent an army of 1500 men, under the command of the marquis of Northampton, to confront Kett's rebels. This force arrived on 31 July. One day later, during running

FIGURE 27. An eighteenth-century depiction of Robert Kett beneath his 'oak of reformation' on Mousehold Heath. (*Norfolk Heritage Centre, photograph by Terry Burchell*)

street battles within the city, the rebels defeated Northampton's small army. Following the rebel victory, Norwich entered a period of dual control: the city authorities continued to function, but real power lay with the rebels. By late August, the situation was transformed by the arrival of a new royal army. This large force was led by the earl of Warwick and numbered somewhere between 8000 and 12,000 men. The hard core of Warwick's host comprised a body of foreign mercenaries and mounted gentry, including many Norfolk gentlemen keen to punish their tenants for their impudence. The king of arms' presence at the Oak of Reformation on 24 August 1549 therefore had a dual purpose: preceding Warwick's arrival, the herald came to offer pardon and instruct the rebels to depart; but he also came to negotiate, acting as a kind of go-between. For all its jokey qualities, the incident depicted on the shopping centre mural therefore represents a moment of profound tension in the history of Norwich. We shall now look more closely at the encounter between the king of arms and the rebels, before proceeding to an examination of its significance.

According to Alexander Neville's 1575 history of the rebellion, the earl of Warwick dispatched the king of arms on the assumption that he would be able to persuade the rebels to disarm 'by the hope of pardon and impunity', and so save the lives of the hostage gentry in Surrey Place.[7] He was doomed to disappointment. Although the captives remained safe, Neville claims that unruly elements within the Mousehold camp demanded their death. Significantly, unlike rebels in many other parts of the country, the Norfolk 'commotioners' consistently refused pardons, and their negotiations with royal representatives were conducted in a spirit of truculent defiance.

The king of arms was met by forty mounted rebels, who led him out of the city and up to Mousehold Heath. Here he encountered 'rankes of the Rebels ... every one uncovering their heads, as it were with one mouth and consent all at once (for the most part) cried, God save King Edward, God save King Edward'. While he awaited the arrival of Robert Kett, the herald spent his time denouncing the rebels as 'the scumme of the people', and warning them that, although he brought another pardon, this would be their last opportunity to save themselves, because 'Warwick hath most solemnely sworne, [that they] shall never hereafter be offered [pardon] againe: but ... he would pursue [them] with fire and sword'. The assembled rebels remained unconvinced by the herald's peroration:

> When he had made an end, although many ... trembled ... for the guilt of Conscience ... yet neverthelesse all of them ... being grievously offended with his speech ... reviled the Herald ... with shouts and cursings: some calling him Traytor, not sent from the King: but had received his lesson from the Gentlemen ... to bring them a sleepe with flattering words and faire promises to deceive them in the end ... Others said, that pardon in appearance seemed good and liberall, but in truth would prove in the ende lamentable and deadly, as that which would be nothing else; but Barrels filled with Ropes and Halters. And that painted coate distinct, and beautified with gold; not to be ensignes of an Herald: but some peeces of Popish Coapes sewed together.

Indifferent to this display of plebeian fury, the herald moved up the hill, and began to repeat his speech. This time, his oration was interrupted by an obscene display of rebel contempt:

> It happened before he had made an end of his speech, that an ungracious boy, putting down his breeches, shewed his bare buttockes, and did a filthy act: adding therunto more filthy words.

It is this incident that provides the basis for the humorous scene depicted in the Castle Mall mural.

From a late twentieth-century perspective, influenced by the burlesque humour of *Monty Python* and *Blackadder*, the excremental incident may seem amusing; but, at the time, both its immediate context and effects were gravely serious. The 'ungracious boy' was (in an ugly, but deliberately political display) demonstrating his ostentatious contempt both for the negotiations and for the king of arms' office. The response of the royal forces to this insult was correspondingly brutal:

> At the indignity whereof, a certaine man being moved (for some of our men were on the river, which came to behold) with a bullet from a pistoll, gave the boy such a blow upon the loines, that sodainely strooke him dead.

The soldier's reaction was taken by the rebels as confirmation of the now deceased 'ungracious' boy's point: that the negotiations were false, and that the gentry could not be trusted. Rebel horsemen came flying from the scene, crying

> O my companions, we are betrayed. Doe you not see our fellow Souldiers cruelly slaine before our eyes, and shot thorow? ... For surely this Herald intendeth nothing else, but we ... may most cruelly be slaine of the Gentlemen.

At this point, Robert Kett arrived, and 'joyned himselfe with the Herald and minded to have spoken with Warwicke', but was pursued by 'a mighty rout of Rebels' who cried after him 'whither he went', promising that they should remain 'his companions and partners, both in life and death'. Observing the apparent collapse of Kett's authority, the king of arms 'willed Kett to goe backe againe, and stay his concourse and tumult'.[8]

This incident sealed Kett's fate. Upon the return of the humiliated king of arms, the earl of Warwick ordered a bombardment of the city. This opened three days and nights of claustrophobic street-fighting. For a while, the outcome hung in the balance: on 25 August, after the rebels had burned part of the southern parishes, Warwick received a delegation of city oligarchs, who pleaded with him to withdraw. After refusing, Warwick considered breaking the bridges that linked the poorer northern parts of the city to its prosperous centre, leaving the northern wards in rebel hands. Relief for the royal forces came on 26 August, with the arrival of a thousand fresh mercenaries. With his expanded forces, Warwick cut the rebels' supply lines into the countryside. Moved by a prophecy which told of success at Dussindale (a low, flat valley between the southern edge of Mousehold and the River Yare), on 27 August the exhausted rebels moved to Dussindale, where they pitched stakes and awaited Warwick's onslaught. Battered by successive artillery bombardments and cavalry attacks, they finally collapsed. Kett fled the field, only to be captured the following day. Many rebels had already been hanged during the fighting within Norwich; after this crushing defeat further mass executions followed in the city.

Meanwhile, Robert Kett was being interrogated at Norwich castle. In November, he and his brother William were convicted of high treason in London, and returned to Norfolk. William was hanged from the tower of Wymondham Abbey, while Robert was suspended in chains from the walls of Norwich castle on 7 December 1549.

Let us return briefly to the confrontation between the king of arms and the rebel crowd on Mousehold Heath on 24 August 1549. We can see now how that confrontation enables us to make sense of the mooning boy in the shopping centre mural, while also suggesting how this apparently humorous gesture was really full of latent violence. Furthermore, the encounter between the rebel crowd and the king of arms reveals some important contradictions within rebel ideology. According to the account, we see the herald arriving at the Mousehold camp, anticipating negotiations with the leadership. But such negotiations were frustrated by the mocking behaviour of the rebel rank and file. The conclusion of the incident, in which the herald told Kett to return to his tumultuous followers, raises the question of who was leading whom on Mousehold Heath. The collective speech attributed to the rebels suggests something of their attitudes to religious politics – and so hints again at internal conflicts within their camp.

Historians of Tudor rebellions conventionally distinguish between the Norfolk uprising, which they present as resulting from 'economic' grievances, and the Western Rebellion underway at the same time in Devon and Cornwall, which is traditionally presented as 'religious' in its concerns.[9] In contrast to the devout Catholicism of the Western rebels, historians typically present the Norfolk rebels as uniformly Protestant. Such assessments tend to be based upon a single document, the list of complaints submitted by the leadership of the Mousehold camp to Protector Somerset in July 1549.[10] These articles include denunciations of dealings by local clergy in the land market, and demand the provision of educated preachers capable of teaching 'pore mens chyldren' to read the catechism and primer. Historians interpret these demands as an endorsement of Somerset's radical programme of evangelical religious reform. On the other hand, the rebel speech reported by Neville – in particular, the sarcastic assessment of the king of arms' gorgeous surcoat, bearing the royal insignia, as 'some peeces of Popish Coapes sewed together' – suggests a rather different assessment of the Edwardian Reformation.

The reported speech contains a hint of how the recent sequestration of church goods may have been regarded by many Norfolk rebels. Although historians of the Reformation often present the population of East Anglia as more receptive to Protestant ideas than many other parts of the realm, both the suppression of the monasteries and the steady removal of the traditional furnishings of the parish churches during the Henrician and the Edwardian reformations stirred significant hostility within Norfolk. Would-be rebels in Walsingham in early 1537, for instance, recognised a connection between the dissolution of 'all the abbeys in the cuntrey' and the oppressions committed by the gentry: 'for the gentle men buye upp all the grayn, kepe all the catal in their handes and hold all the fermes that poor men cann have no living'. Throughout the later 1530s, and again during the reign of Edward VI, grumbling against the removal of church goods was reported from both Norfolk and Norwich. Notably, one such plebeian complainant, Robert Burnam, had been an ardent rebel during Kett's rising.[11] Such evidence jars with the implicit statements of support for Somerset's religious reforms presented in the Mousehold articles.

Neville's account of the confrontation between the king of arms and the rebel crowd illuminates the outstanding aspect of Kett's Rebellion: the peculiarly violent conflict between the Norfolk gentry and the 'pore commons' assembled on Mousehold Heath. This is made apparent in the rebels' suspicion that the gentry would not honour any pardon offered by Somerset. The Norfolk insurgents' rejection of the pardon contrasts with the willingness of 'commotioners' in many other counties to negotiate with, and to submit to, the authorities. It will be argued here that the violent ferocity that characterised the closing stages of the 'commotion time' in Norfolk resulted from the rebels' rejection of successive offers of pardon; the next part of this chapter will explore the deep, structural conflicts within urban and rural society alike that underlay the Mousehold rebels' suspicion of the offers of pardon made to them. But in order to appreciate the significance of local patterns of social conflict to the violent resolution of the Norfolk rebellion, we must first locate Kett's Rebellion within the wider history of the 'commotion time' of 1549.

Ironically, although it remains the best-known rebellion of that year, the Norfolk insurrection came late in the 'commotion time'. By the outbreak of the Attleborough rising in early July, the commons of many other counties south of Trent had already risen in armed rebellion; and some had been subdued, either through negotiation or repression.[12] Although the rebellions expressed deep conflicts within Tudor society, the immediate cause of the 'commotion time' lay in Somerset's social and religious policies. His decrees enforcing the Edwardian Reformation were often bitterly resented, and in April 1548 led to a Cornish rising. In contrast, his opposition to the enclosure of common land met with widespread popular support. For generations before 1549, wealthier farmers and powerful lords had fenced off pieces of common land, privatising their use. This development was felt by many in mid Tudor England to be reaching a dangerous level. Following anti-enclosure proclamations of June 1548 and April 1549, royal commissioners were instructed to collect information concerning the illicit enclosure of land. This policy inspired the large-scale popular destruction of enclosures and demonstrations concerning other agrarian and urban grievances. Although in some areas, such as Wiltshire, Sir William Herbert immediately repressed these gatherings without waiting for royal authority, elsewhere, as in Kent and Sussex, the local gentry and nobility acted with greater moderation as intermediaries between the council and the 'commotioners': as Edward VI noted, the spring rebellions were appeased 'by fair perswasions, partly of honestmen among them selfes and partly by gentlemen'.[13] The 'commotion time' therefore had its origins, in the spring of 1549, in armed demonstrations in support of Somerset's enclosure policies, albeit sometimes tinged with hostility to the ongoing Reformation. May Day saw the spread of insurrection across many southern counties. In June 1549, the commons of Cornwall and Devon rose in rebellion against Somerset's religious policies. By midsummer, the relative quiet of the commons of East Anglia seemed peculiar.

Somerset's announcement of a new Enclosure Commission on 9 July, coupled with the absence of many leading gentlemen at Windsor, where they were answering a summons from the council to organise military action, drew the commons of East Anglia into the 'commotion time'. A pioneering essay of 1979 has shown how large-scale rebellion revealed itself in Norfolk, Suffolk and Cambridgeshire at almost exactly the same time: that is between 9 and 11 July.[14] Kett's Rebellion therefore seems to have been but a late example of a more widespread phenomenon, as across southern England prosperous men such as Robert Kett placed themselves at the head of rebel camps. By July, the leaders of these camps encountered Somerset's representatives, who encouraged them to submit written complaints to the council, and to disarm. Like other aspects of rebel behaviour, violence was controlled and ritualised. Notoriously oppressive gentry who fell into rebel hands were roughed up and humiliated, but (with one notable exception, in Yorkshire) were not killed.

In one significant respect, though, the Norfolk rebels deviated from the general pattern of the 'commotion time'. The 'commotioners' of Norfolk not only refused to disarm, but actively frustrated the royal representatives' attempts at negotiation. This was not the only area where the demonstrations of the 'commotioners' led to armed violence. In Wiltshire and Cambridge the local authorities immediately repressed insurrection, with some loss of life. In Devon and Cornwall, where conservative religion defined rebel grievances, and in Oxfordshire and Buckinghamshire, where hostility to the Reformation coloured complaints, the 'commotion time' also ended in substantial violence. But in Norfolk, as we have seen, the leadership of the Mousehold camp was careful to downplay rebel hostility to the Edwardian Reformation. We return, therefore, to our defining question: why did Kett's Rebellion lead to such massive bloodshed?

Blame for the violent end of Kett's Rebellion has more recently been placed upon Sir William Parr, the marquis of Northampton (Figure 28). It was he who led the small royal army to Norwich on 31 July, only to be forced into ignominious retreat on the following day. He has been charged with incompetence, his defeat leaving the duke of Somerset with no alternative but to crush the Norfolk rebellion:

> The Protector might indeed have got away with the whole great gamble [that is, his appeasement of the rebels] if the Marquis of Northampton had not blundered when he led his expeditionary force from London into Norfolk, combining lack of local knowledge with political ineptitude: his mishandling transformed the Norwich encounter from negotiation to bloody battle. Once Norfolk exploded into really murderous violence, Somerset's strategy came crashing down, and the Privy Councillors could vent their feelings on him and on the commons of England.[15]

According to this analysis, Northampton's blunders had far-reaching consequences, forcing Somerset to abandon his appeasement of the rebels and resort to repression. The failure of Somerset's policy towards the 'commotioners' undermined his political position, as it justified the gathering critique within ruling circles of the 'Good Duke's' leniency towards the rebellious commons.[16] This critique acquired armed force in the military coup of October 1549, in which Somerset was displaced by the earl of Warwick, fresh from his victory over the rebels in Norwich. Such an emphasis upon the centrality of the events of 31 July and 1 August is of fundamental importance in understanding the outcome of Kett's Rebellion. Playing with counterfactuals, we might imagine (as this interpretation invites us to) a different outcome to Northampton's arrival on 31 July, in which the Mousehold rebels followed their counterparts in Suffolk, Sussex and Kent and accepted Somerset's pardon in return for the consideration of their complaints. In the context of elite politics, Somerset's position would thus have been secured and his social reforms would have continued. In Norwich, as elsewhere, the memory of the Mousehold rebels would most likely have faded away; there would have been no 'Kett's Rebellion', distinct from the 'commotion time', to remember.

Although Northampton stands accused of having 'blundered', it is

FIGURE 28. William Parr, marquis of Northampton, by Thomas Athow. (*National Portrait Gallery*)

unclear how he might have redeemed the impossible situation that faced him on 1 August. His small army was intended to intimidate the rebels into negotiations, rather than to confront and defeat them. His conduct during the battles of 31 July and 1 August might be compared with that of Lord

Grey who, possessed of an army of similar size, had put the rebels of Oxfordshire and Buckinghamshire to flight after battle in mid July.[17] But unlike Lord Grey's opponents, Kett's rebels remained concentrated as a single body, dominating Mousehold Heath and Norwich. Although Northampton was apparently unfamiliar with the city, he was accompanied by a number of leading Norfolk gentlemen who knew it very well. Northampton's conduct therefore did not stem from any 'lack of local knowledge'. It seems equally unreasonable to blame the failure of negotiations upon Northampton's 'political ineptitude': in part, because the rebels had opened hostilities a week before his arrival, when they had seized Norwich; and also because they did not present him with any real opportunity to negotiate. Such negotiations often formed the closing drama in the rituals of early Tudor rebellion, from which would flow public submission and the private settlement of grievances. Northampton's clear expectation of such submission derived not so much from his peculiar naivety as from the logic and structure of early Tudor rebellion itself.[18] Only in retrospect is it possible to criticise him for his failure to recognise the concealed military threat posed by the rebels.

As events transpired, the rebels' pretence at negotiations proved no more than a strategem to seize the military initiative. On the morning of 1 August, Northampton received 'information that att Pockthorp gates was a iiii or v c [four or five hundred] persons to submit themselves and receive the king's pardon'. Accompanied by some of his forces, he therefore proceeded to Pockthorpe gates where he found only twenty rebels, led by John Flotman of Beccles, who engaged him in argument (Map 15). Northampton and his herald stood upon the corner tower of the gates, from where the rebels were offered the king's pardon. In answer, Flotman said that 'hee defyde [Northampton] and seid hee was a traytour nor wulde of his pardon, nor had deservid pardon but that they were the king's true subjects'. At this point, word was brought to Northampton 'that the rebellis had entrid the cittye neere the hospitall'.[19] The negotiations were revealed as a clever device, designed to distract Northampton from the main rebel onslaught near the Great Hospital at Bishopgate (Figure 29). Northampton's small, divided force was therefore left under the authority of his second-in-command, Lord Sheffield, to face the rebel attack. During a series of running engagements, Sheffield was knocked from his horse and hacked to death. Confused and leaderless, the royal troops fled Norwich.

If Northampton made a mistake, it lay in underestimating the military threat posed by the Mousehold rebels. The Norfolk rebels' consistent willingness to fight their opponents represented a breach of the rituals of Tudor rebellion: in earlier uprisings of 1525 and 1536, as in many places in

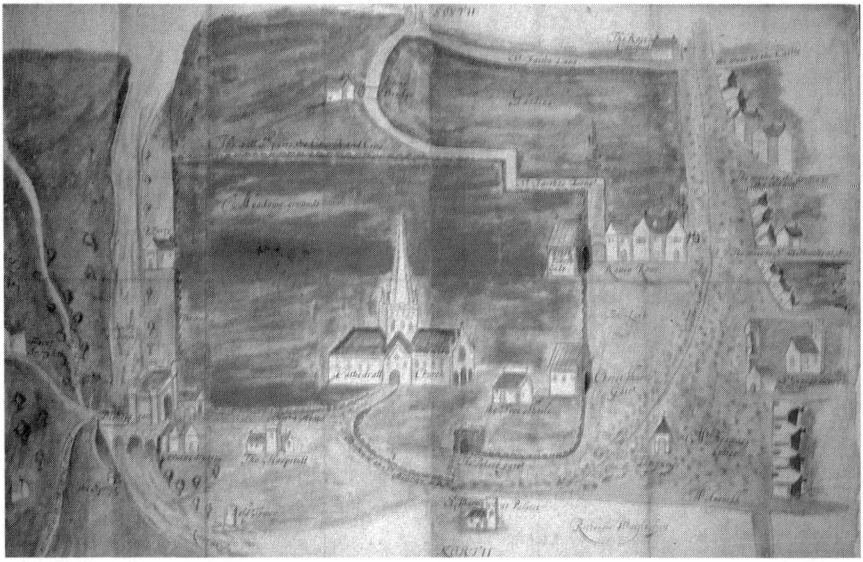

FIGURE 29. A map of the cathedral and its environs of *c.* 1630 shows bishop's bridge, the hospital meadows and the route taken by Kett's rebels as they stormed the city on 1 August 1549. Lord Sheffield was killed on the bend in the road by the hospital, NRO, ACC 1997/215. (*Norfolk Record Office, by permission of Mr Peter Hornor*)

1549, rebels had assembled in arms, but subsequently disbanded upon the offer of a pardon and a promise that the local elite would represent their grievances to the crown. In defiance of these conventions, Kett's rebels deliberately rejected the intercession of urban oligarchs, country gentry and royal heralds on numerous occasions: on 10 July, the mayor of Norwich attempted to persuade the rebels to return home, but was rejected. The following day, Sir Roger Woodhouse brought carts of food and beer to the 'commotioners'. In contrast to events in Sussex, where the earl of Arundel's conspicuous display of such traditional hospitality had smoothed his successful negotiations with the rebels, Woodhouse was beaten up and taken prisoner.[20] On 21 July, York Herald confronted the rebel leadership on Mousehold Heath. Upon the rejection of his offer of pardon, he had denounced the Norfolk rebels as traitors. The following day, they seized Norwich. On 1 August, Northampton offered pardon to the rebels assembled at Pockthorpe gates, but was mocked. On 24 August, as we have seen, the king of arms was verbally abused while attempting to deliver yet another olive branch. Finally, surrounded by Warwick's victorious mercenary troops at the sanguinary conclusion of the battle of

Dussindale, some insurgents still continued to refuse the royal pardon, exclaiming that

> they suppose[d] this mention of pardon, deceitfully offered by the nobles; to be nothing else, but [as a means] whereby ... they should all then, the last bee led to torture and death. And in truth, whatsoever they pretend, they know well ... this pardon to bee nothing else, but vessels of ropes and halters, and therefore have decreed to die.[21]

The extreme violence of the closing stages of the Norfolk 'commotion time' resulted not from the individual failings of the marquis of Northampton, but rather from the rebels' fundamental distrust of the pardons that were offered repeatedly to them. This distrust was the product of bitter conflict within both urban and rural society in Norfolk.

The intensity of social conflict in early sixteenth-century rural Norfolk has become notorious. Landlords' attempts to enclose common fields, increase rents, extend deer parks and expand their sheep flocks created lasting antagonisms throughout the countryside. Richer and poorer villagers, often at one another's throats over other issues, joined forces against a common enemy: the gentry. The Reformation heightened such conflicts. The Dissolution of the Monasteries and the radical changes to church ornaments and services were often understood as attempts by the 'gentlemen' to destroy the cultural and spiritual basis of plebeian community, at the same time as their aggressive seigneurialism undercut its material basis. Social and economic historians have long understood these conflicts as providing the deep causal basis for Kett's Rebellion.[22] Moreover, they also help to explain the refusal of the Norfolk commons to accept the validity of the pardons offered to them: by 1549, the commons had grown used to confronting what they saw as the gentry's 'treachery'.

Historians have tended to present Kett's Rebellion as a rural uprising, in which urban conflicts played only a minor role.[23] In standard accounts of the rebellion, the city of Norwich provides merely the passive backdrop to the closing dramas of the insurrection; the inhabitants are portrayed as the helpless victims of the rebels. Yet the antagonistic relations within mid Tudor Norwich strongly influenced the events of July and August 1549. Moreover, it will be argued here that anxieties on the part of the city's rulers about the depth of these fissures undermined their confidence in dealing with the rebels, thereby generating a weak and contradictory policy towards the 'commotioners'. The rest of this chapter will be concerned with the urban context of Kett's Rebellion. First, it will briefly elucidate some of the fundamental conflicts which divided mid sixteenth-century

Norwich. Secondly, it will look at the response of the city's governors to the rebels. Lastly, it will examine the nature of rebel support within Norwich.

Social conflict in Tudor Norwich shared many similarities with that affecting the countryside. Just as rural commoners criticised the administration of government and justice by the gentry, so, as in other early modern towns, vicious disputes occasionally exploded in Norwich over issues such as popular participation in civic government, entitlements to common resources, local taxation and the crown's harsh fiscal demands. There seems to have been a particularly anxious quality to the assertion of urban authority in early modern England. The elaborate displays of this authority all too often contrasted with the deliberately confrontational language used by the poorer classes to describe their social superiors: the Norwich capper who in 1513 called an aldermen a 'shytebreke' might stand for many.[24] In flagrant contrast to its structural and economic diversity, the social order tended to seem harshly bipolar to contemporary eyes. Whereas richer inhabitants were sometimes inclined to see their poorer neighbours as a threatening, disease-ridden burden, so the labouring classes used the same social terminology as their rural counterparts when describing the oppressions of the 'rich men', whom they condemned as 'traitors' and 'churles', and denounced for their corrupt monopolisation of local government.[25] Indeed, the artificial distinctions made by historians between 'urban' and 'rural' experiences dissolve at this point, for popular perceptions of economic change tended to present grasping merchants and sheep farming gentlemen as locked in a joint conspiracy to destroy the poor.[26]

Plebeian senses of economics were articulated most clearly in the seditious speech recorded immediately before and after the 1549 rebellion, in which urban workers and rural labourers alike stood accused of having denounced the 'gents and richemen'. These were said to 'have all [the] catell and wolles ... in ther hands nowe a dayes and the pore peple are now famysshed'.[27] Social conflicts within the city arose principally over access to resources and space: in lanes and courtyards, on common lands and in the market place. Attempts by affluent inhabitants to extend or improve their properties were sometimes understood by their poorer neighbours as part of a plan to squeeze the 'pore comons' out of the city altogether.[28] We should not lightly dismiss such anxieties. Tudor Norwich was delineated into richer and poorer parishes, with the poorer classes largely concentrated north of the river, and in the southern parishes (Figure 30). Sharp, face-to-face conflict was also manifest upon the city's common lands outside the walls, which came under pressure from poor urban dwellers and commercial sheep-farmers. The same is also true of the extensive resources

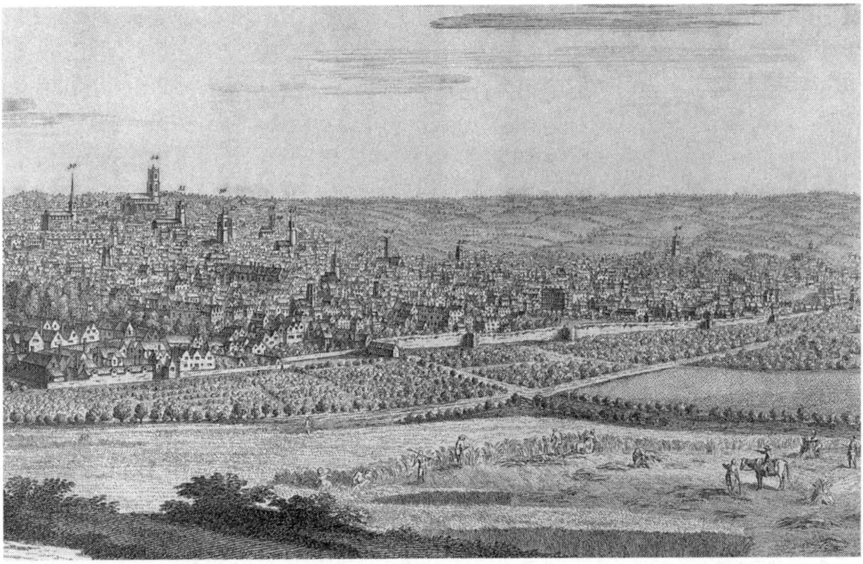

FIGURE 30. Detail from Samuel and Nathaniel Buck's north-east prospect of 1741 shows the continuing proximity of common land to the crowded northern parts of the city. (*Norfolk Heritage Centre, photograph by Terry Burchell*)

of fuel, building materials and grazing lands on Mousehold Heath and in Thorpe Wood, where both urban poor and rural commoners claimed traditional rights, in opposition to rural lords.[29] It is highly significant that, as a result, many of the conflicts in Norwich both involved and won the immediate sympathy of the commons of rural Norfolk. It did not require a giant leap of imagination to see the extension of rich men's houses over the humble plots of the urban poor as the equivalent of rural enclosure. Indeed, disputes over the city's common fields and the urban poor's claims to pasture and timber rights in Mousehold Heath and Thorpe Wood connected directly with the conflicts in the countryside, pitting the urban poor against some of the rural commoners' leading opponents: wealthy families such as the Corbets, Spencers and Pastons.

It was the market place that formed the prime everyday arena for confrontations between popular opinion and urban authority. Increases in the price of food inspired verbal and physical anger against market traders and civic officials, sometimes culminating in riot.[30] Throughout the reigns of Henry VIII and Edward VI, sudden increases in prices led the ruling elite to anticipate the possibility of serious insurrection. In 1526, for instance, the 'greate skarsenes of corne ... abowte Christmas' persuaded some of 'the comons of the cyttye to ... ryse upon the ryche men'.[31] In response, the corporation ensured that exemplary punishment of offenders (whipping minor rioters; branding, mutilating, flogging or otherwise humiliating those who articulated seditious speech; and even occasional hangings) was followed not only by close supervision of the movements and speech of the poor ('badging' paupers; listing those in receipt of alms; alerting the magisterial ear to the merest hint of sedition) but also by ostentatiously ameliorative action (lowering the price of food; seeing to the rigid regulation of the market; enforcing compulsory contributions to poor rates from substantial citizens in the interests of the 'comon weale').[32]

By the time of Kett's Rebellion, the governors of Norwich had therefore grown used to balancing the interests of rich against the anger of the poor. That balance was usually weighted in favour of the rich, but public clamour, especially when combined with paternalist impulses from central government, might tilt it in the other direction. In May 1549, at the height of the commotion time across southern England, and in the midst of Protector Somerset's social reforms, the city's governors established a compulsory levy for the poor, similar to that which they had instituted following the threat of insurrection in 1526.[33] It is difficult to see this action as anything other than a response to growing internal tensions. The ambiguous reaction of the civic oligarchy to the arrival of Kett's rebels on the outskirts of Norwich on 10 July 1549 should be understood as a manifestation of their periodic willingness to compromise with dangerous forces within their own gates. Used to maintaining such a balancing act, Mayor Codd underestimated the threat posed by Kett's rebels, treating them as though he were negotiating with an unruly urban crowd. This circumspection proved near-fatal, allowing the insurgents to exercise partial control over Norwich, until the denunciation of Kett by York Herald on 21 July forced Codd to acknowledge the Mousehold 'commotioners' as rebels and to close the city to them. The herald thus precipitated the first bloodshed of Kett's Rebellion, the rebels' attack on Bishopgate on the following day. Yet the significance of the Norwich oligarchy's flirtation with the rebels, and more broadly of the urban contribution to Kett's Rebellion, has received little attention.

This general understatement of the urban contribution to Kett's Rebellion grows from twentieth-century historians' over-dependence upon three well-known narrative accounts of the insurrection: that presented in Nicholas Sotherton's manuscript history of the rebellion; Alexander Neville's printed history of 1575; and the account offered in Raphael Holinshed's *Chronicles*. In contrast to Sir John Cheke's condemnation of the city's governors, written in the immediate aftermath of the rebellions, these Elizabethan narratives presented the rebellion as an essentially rural affair and obscured the equivocal conduct of the Norwich elite during the 'commotion time'.[34] Yet, although these accounts did their best to draw clear distinctions between the citizens and the 'rude countrymen' and 'rude and rusticall people' whom they presented as the key constituents of the rebel host, the authors of the Elizabethan narratives were none the less forced to recognise, by virtue of its significance, the depth of urban support for the 'commotion time'.[35] This bias flowed from the authors' social position: Sotherton was born into the civic oligarchy, while the opening paragraph of Neville's account provides an unambiguous statement of his loyalties. Neville wished that the rebellion 'had either never hapned, or (if it could be) the remembrance of [it] were utterly rooted out of the minds of all men'. But knowing that 'things past cannot be altered, or changed', he stated his intention to retell the story of the rebellion in order that 'this staine of treason, branded in the forehead of our countrey [county] ... can be utterly blotted out, or altogether taken away'. Once the authors of the widely read Holinshed's *Chronicles* had plagiarised Neville's history, his sanitised version established the template for future treatments of the subject: the influential eighteenth-century Norfolk historian Francis Blomefield, for instance, fulminated against Sir John Cheke's 'upbraiding' of the elite, insisting that 'the mayor, older men, and principal citizens, with the City clergy, behaved with the utmost allegiance to the King, and the greatest prudence, for the safeguard of their City and country'.[36] The reality, however, was more complicated.

The curious conduct of the governors of Norwich during the 'commotion time' is illuminated by three folios in a volume of the proceedings of the mayor's court.[37] These folios, which cover the events of 9 to 21 July 1549, provide some fascinating insights into the conduct of the ruling elite during the crucial period between the arrival of Kett's rebel host on the outskirts of the city, and their denunciation as traitors by York Herald. Significantly, they describe the rebels in surprisingly positive language. They also hint at collusion between the rebel leadership and the aldermanic bench. Taken together with the Elizabethan narrative accounts, the information they contain allows us to reconstruct the actions of the leading citizens during this crucial stage in the rebellion. The folios confirm Neville's claim that, on the evening of 10 July, Thomas Codd led the aldermen to the temporary rebel encampment at Eaton Wood. Hoping that the rebellion 'might be repressed in the beginning', he 'allured' the insurgents 'by money, and fairer promises'. Following his rejection, Codd returned to Norwich and convened the common council. Although some 'doubtfull opinions' were expressed at the meeting, others proposed an attack upon the rebels. Finally, Neville claims that the council refused the rebels' request to march through Norwich, and decided instead to 'fortifie the citie'.[38] Despite this apparently unequivocal response, the folios suggest that the city fathers adopted a rather less resolute stance. Although the records of the common council for 10 July do not survive, a note describing a meeting of aldermen on the same day shows that the rebels were in fact allowed to provision themselves from Norwich markets. Notably, although rebel representatives are described as being 'of the rebellyous campe', the word 'rebellyous' was clearly inserted into the manuscript at a later date. By Saturday 13 July, the clerk to the mayor's court was describing the Mousehold gathering as 'the pore comons campe', and recorded how the aldermen had allowed the rebels to imprison their gentry captives both within the city's gaol and, 'for asmuche as the said prison is full of prisoners sent from the said campe', in Norwich castle itself. Here the clerk made no attempt to conceal the fact that these decisions emerged from discussions 'betwyn Robert Kette of Wymondham and Mr Maior'. Two days later, the rebels demanded that their gentry captives be returned 'without any condicon', so that they could stand trial. The corporation seemingly acquiesced to this demand. A characteristic mood of indecision prevailed at a meeting of aldermen on 17 July, at which it was recorded that 'muche matter was moved reasoned and debated ... concernyng the sayd campe but nothing ... concluded'. Finally, the folios tell us how the Norwich authorities were finally moved to action by the arrival of York Herald on 20 July, who on the following day denounced Kett as a traitor.

This important contemporary evidence suggests a striking lack of resolve to confront the rebel host. The material weakness of the city's defences, although potentially crippling, fails to provide sufficient explanation for the continued association of the aldermen with the rebel leadership. Both before and after the insurgents stormed Norwich on 22 July, Thomas Codd and other leading oligarchs sat upon the rebel council. According to the Elizabethan narrative accounts, the rebels forced them to do so, while they in turn made virtue of necessity, hoping that they might moderate the rebels' behaviour. The narrators did their best to praise those leading aldermen, such as Henry Bacon and Augustine Steward, who helped Northampton's and Warwick's forces; but the effect was only to highlight the failure of the mayor and most of the governing classes to take such a lead.[39] It is perhaps not surprising, therefore, that when the earl of Warwick paused at Cambridge to gather further forces before marching to confront Kett, he was met by a group of aldermen and citizens from Norwich, 'upon their knees ... weeping' and protesting that they had had no part in the rebellion. Warwick's response highlights the suspicion that had fallen upon the Norwich elite: he first admonished their failure to deal effectively with the rebellion 'in the very beginning', and then ordered them to join his forces, wearing 'laces about their necks, to be discerned from the rest', in order that any treachery on their part could be observed.[40] Warwick's suspicion seems well founded. At best, the rulers of Norwich had demonstrated a collective lack of judgment; at worst, they had become complicit with rebellion.

In contrast to the inconsistency of their rulers, many of the labouring people of Norwich were strong supporters of the rebel cause. When Augustine Steward surrendered the city's authority to the marquis of Northampton on 31 July, he blamed the insurrection upon 'a great rowt of the lewd citisens [who] were partakers with the rebelles', but asked the marquis to note that 'the substantiall and honest citizens would never consent to their wicked doings'.[41] The Elizabethan accounts of the rebellion developed Steward's social analysis. In Holinshed's *Chronicles* the urban rebels were described as 'rascals and naughtie lewd persons'. To Neville, Kett's Norwich supporters were 'pestilent persons' and 'beastly men ... of the common people of the city'. Like animals, the urban poor were full of 'violent rage and fury'. For Sotherton, the urban rebels were but 'vagrand persons'.[42]

Urban support for the rebellion was premeditated: preceding the outbreak of the Wymondham insurrection, there was a series of 'secret meetings of men running hither and thither'. Clearly, the conspirators had run as far as Norwich; for on 9 July, the same day that Kett assumed leadership of the Wymondham rebels, new enclosures upon the common land on Town Close were destroyed by what Neville called 'the scum of the City'. The following day, when Kett's forces camped at Eaton Wood, near the western edge of the city, they were met by 'wretched conspirators' from Norwich. These 'conspirators' carried 'little boughs' as a prearranged mark of their involvement in the rising, which the rural rebels recognised as a sign that they should concentrate 'all their cursed companies ... together into one place'.[43] There was a close relationship between the social geography of mid Tudor Norwich and the twists and turns in rebel and royal military strategy. Rebels seemed to move with impunity through the poor northern parishes and thence south across the Wensum.[44] At the height of the fighting on 25 August, when he proposed the destruction of the bridges that linked the rich centre of the city to the northern fringes, the earl of Warwick recognised the rebels' easy control of this area. In the earliest military encounters, it looked as if the rebel presence might manifest itself anywhere within the walls. In the night before the first rebel attack, the aldermen decided 'that it was ... safest for the gentlemen [hitherto captives of the rebels] that had been let out of prison to be shut up again, least the rebels finding them abroad should murder them'. This decision was taken because 'certain of the citizens that favoured the rebels had let a great number of them into the city'.[45] Similarly, Northampton's forces were kept constantly confused as to rebel movements by continuous shouting from the darkened streets surrounding the market place. Concerned for the security of his troops, Northampton anxiously illuminated the market place and appointed watches. The effect of the rebels' successful mobilisation of their urban support was to deny the military initiative to Northampton. Neville identified the social basis of this urban support with some clarity: whereas 'the citizens' were kept 'easily in order', 'the unruly ... whom no good order could command' clamoured for Kett.[46]

In the aftermath of the rebellion, the governing elite of the near-ruined city of Norwich had reason to feel vengeful, grateful and guilty. This knot of unhappy emotions was expressed in three forms: in the prompt execution of defeated rebels in the public places of the city, and in the longer process of repression that followed; in excessive displays of loyalty and gratitude to the earl of Warwick; and in the immediate commemoration of the supression of Kett's Rebellion. On the day after his defeat of the rebels at Dussindale, Warwick attended a service of thanksgiving at the richest parish church in the city, St Peter Mancroft. Following this, the corporation funded an elaborate masque in his honour. The earl's arms, the bear and ragged staff, were mounted alongside the royal arms on the gates; especially enthusiastic members of the elite also displayed them outside their own houses. These men knew that they had much to live down after Kett's Rebellion; their displays of loyalty formed an ironic contrast to Warwick's earlier scepticism at Cambridge. As late as July 1552, one of the Paston family could still taunt the mayor of Norwich with the accusation 'That their was a Rebellion late at Norwich and that is not yet oute of Mr Mayors stomake nor a great many of them besides'.[47]

The governors of mid Tudor Norwich found the traumatic memory of Kett's Rebellion difficult to manage. No doubt, like Alexander Neville, they too wished that the uprising 'had either never hapned, or (if it could be) the remembrance of [it] were utterly rooted out of the minds of all men'. But (again like Neville), recognising that so large an event could not simply be forgotten, they instead set to reshaping its meaning. On 21 September 1550, the assembly decreed that the anniversary of the battle of Dussindale, 27 August, should 'from hensfurth for ever' be kept as a holiday, to be marked by the sounding of every parish church bell in the city, a memorial sermon at St Peter Mancroft, and the reflection of 'both man and woman and childe' on the sins of rebellion.[48] Like the Elizabethan histories of the rebellion that followed it, the city's celebration of 'Kett's Day' constructed a collective memory of the 'commotion time' around ruling class priorities. In this official memorialisation, Robert Kett appears as diabolically-inspired leader of senseless insurrection; his followers became 'country clownes', joined by a mere smattering of 'the scum of the city'; and the rulers and citizens of Norwich were firmly established as the victims of the story.

In contrast to their loss of control over their city in 1549, the governors of Norwich succeeded in perpetuating this hegemonic myth until the early nineteenth century. Like George Orwell, they knew that 'Who controls the past controls the future: who controls the present controls the past'.[49] But the assertion of power always engenders resistance. In the immediate aftermath of the 1549 rebellions, and for a long time afterwards, the official commemoration of Kett's Rebellion stimulated opposing memories of the insurrection. For generations afterwards, mention of Robert Kett's name could be a way both of defying official ideology and of hinting at the possibility of resistance. That struggle over the meaning of the rebellion began within weeks of the defeat at Dussindale: in November 1549, a Norwich man called Claxton was asked his opinion of recent events within his city. Claxton is said to have replied 'that he did well in keping in ketts campe and so he wolde saye'. Asked 'what he did think by Kette ... he sayed nothing but well that he knewe ... he trusted to se a newe day for suche men as I was'.[50] Claxton's defiant words (whether he spoke them or not) retain a resonance today. And so by virtue of its everyday setting, the image of Robert Kett and the rude boy in the Castle Mall mural represents both a victory and a historical retrieval: a victory over earlier, officially sponsored condemnations of Kett; a retrieval of the diversity of rebel ideology in 1549, and of the inversive, mocking fun that comes from cocking a snook (or baring an arse) at authority.

13

Sickness and Health

Carole Rawcliffe

> I hold not so narrow a conceit of this vertue, as to conceive that to give almes, is onely to be Charitable, or thinke a piece of Liberality can comprehend the Totall of Charity; Divinity hath wisely divided the acts thereof into many branches, and hath taught us in this narrow way, many pathes unto goodnesse; as many wayes as we may doe good, so many wayes we may bee Charitable; there are infirmities, not onely of body, but of soule, and fortunes, which do require the mercifull hand of our abilities. I cannot contemn a man for ignorance but behold him with as much pity as I doe Lazarus. It is no greater Charity to cloath his body, than apparell the nakednesse of his soule.
>
> Sir Thomas Browne, *Religio Medici*, 1642[1]

At some point in the early 1560s, Thomas Wynter, citizen and alderman of Norwich, and three of his friends made a sworn deposition before the civic authorities. It records an animated exchange over dinner at his town house, when another guest had seized the opportunity to beg the surgeon, Johannes Hesse, to operate upon his young son. Like so many other boys and men in the region, the child suffered from bladder stone, an agonising condition for which surgery offered the only sure hope of relief. But the risks were overwhelming, and Hesse demanded a substantial fee, well in excess of the annual wages of a master craftsman. Reluctantly, 'at the instaunce and desier of suche as were then present', he 'came downe from tenne poundes to eight poundes and at the laste to xxtie nobles (£6 67p.), and lesse he wulde not take'. Having prevailed upon the father, John Sympson, to accept, the assembled guests then brokered a deal whereby the money was to be paid when Hesse

> shulde delyver unto the same Sympson the stone whiche he shulde take out of the said childes bodye, without any maner of warrantise [guarantee] of life of the said childe otherwise then it shulde please God to graunte in that

> behalfe. And it was also agreed ... that, if it shulde please God to graunte the said childe his lyfe, that the same Hanse shulde make hym perfightly whoall, the same Sympson at his coste and charge [would further agree to] fyndyng and exhibiting unto the same Hanse and two persons more horse meate [fodder] and mans meate at tyme afforsaid.[2]

Since Norwich surgeons were later to gain an international reputation for their expertise as lithotomists, it seems appropriate to begin with an early example of their business acumen.[3] Wynter's deposition is of more than antiquarian interest, however, reflecting as it does the high rate of infant mortality and chronic disease which then seemed an inescapable consequence of the human condition. Such a detailed account of the tortuous negotiations which customarily preceded medical or surgical treatment is, moreover, a rare survival, even for the sixteenth century, although the events it describes were far from unusual. The high cost and dangers of surgery in an age before antisepsis, reliable anaesthesia and blood transfusion; the practitioner's anxiety to absolve himself in the event of accidental homicide; and a clear awareness that, in the last resort, God, not man, would decide the outcome of so perilous an undertaking, are as much the hallmarks of medieval as early modern medicine.[4] One of the most dramatic twelfth-century miracles recorded in the Foundation Book of St Bartholomew's Hospital in London concerns a Norwich man whose session with the phlebotomist had condemned him to years of suffering. Hagiographers were rarely disposed to speak kindly of the medical profession, but even allowing for the inevitable rivalry between them, the limitations of earthly therapeutics seemed all too apparent.[5]

To understand the symbiotic relationship between spiritual and physical healing, as manifest in Norwich before the sixteenth century, and appreciate the difficulties encountered by local practitioners, it is first necessary to examine some of the major hazards of urban life and their impact upon the population as a whole. Thanks to the remarkable wealth of archaeological as well as documentary evidence now available, we can embark upon such an exercise from a comparatively early date in the city's history. The excavation of a late Anglo-Saxon graveyard in the north-eastern bailey of Norwich castle, undertaken during the civic developments of the 1970s, provided a valuable insight into standards of living among the less affluent inhabitants at the time of the Norman Conquest. Palaeopathological analysis of the skeletal remains of approximately 130 individuals from this poor community suggests a rate of infant and child mortality of about 63 per cent, and an average age at death among surviving adults of around thirty for males and thirty-three for females.[6] Physical injury, through industrial accidents and RSI, as well as premeditated violence, posed a serious risk to men, while women faced the potentially debilitating, if not immediately fatal, consequences of repeated pregnancy and childbirth. Immigration from the countryside was often necessary to sustain the population of medieval cities.[7]

Evidence of this kind provides a valuable context for accounts of medieval miracles, such as those attributed to William of Norwich, the boy 'martyr', whose cult was assiduously fostered by the cathedral monks during the 1170s. Among the many tales of human misery presented by his hagiographer, Thomas of Monmouth, we find that of Gurwain the Tanner, who made a pilgrimage to the saint's tomb in the hope of saving the only one of his six sons to survive infancy.[8] At least two other miracles involved women mutilated during childbirth, while a third concerned a mother traumatised by a difficult delivery.[9] Although the protracted labour reputedly endured in 1144 by the wife of a Norwich cook was far from typical, her resort to the occult powers of sacred relics from William's shrine reflects widespread contemporary practice which persisted until the Reformation.[10]

As 'a field haunted by women', when the arrival of a male practitioner generally spelt death for the mother and dismemberment for the child, obstetrics relied heavily upon the invocation of protective saints through a variety of material objects. During the later middle ages many women wore metal badges acquired on antenatal pilgrimages to shrines, such as that of the Holy House at Walsingham, near King's Lynn, whose connection with the Incarnation was considered especially propitious.[11] The Norfolk mystic, Margery Kempe, by then the mother of fourteen children, travelled further afield to Cologne in 1433 to venerate a piece of 'owr Ladys smokke', which was likewise believed to assist women in childbirth. She probably returned with a badge similar to one fashioned into an ornate pendant, depicting the *sancta roba*, Virgin and Child, which was unearthed in the 1970s, along with four Walsingham badges, during excavations in Pottergate, Norwich.[12] Devices of this kind constituted powerful symbols of fertility in an age when the failure to produce a healthy heir stigmatised women of all social classes (Plate 20). But women did not have to travel far for solace. At St Leonard's, a cell of the cathedral priory to the east of Norwich, a number of sacred images, including one of the Virgin Mary decked with objects associated with parturition, drew many pilgrims of both sexes.[13] Similarly associated with procreation and childbirth, the cults of St Margaret, St Anne and the Holy Family enjoyed great popularity among the affluent bourgeoisie of late medieval Norwich (Plate 25).

Images, in paint, embroidery, plate, stained glass, stone and wood, were a focus of widespread devotion before their destruction by iconoclasts during the sixteenth and seventeenth centuries; some may, indeed, still be seen in the parish churches of St Helen and St Peter Mancroft, which boasted its own guild and chapel of St Anne (Plates 16 and 26).[14]

The remains of several of the late eleventh-century individuals exhumed from the north-east bailey reveal evidence of dietary deficiencies, manifest at their most extreme in rickets, orbital osteoporosis and osteomyelitis. An impoverished diet, apparent from the high rate of dental hypoplasia and periodontal disease, not only rendered the population more vulnerable to infection, but also inhibited recovery from childbirth, illness or trauma. Degenerative pathological conditions, most notably osteoarthritis, were a painful consequence of hard manual labour, aggravated in many cases by exposure to cold and damp.[15] Once again, palaeopathology helps to explain why ecclesiastical propaganda exercised such a pervasive hold over the medieval mind, and why so many people dragged themselves on crutches to St William's tomb when his cult was at its height.[16]

The late medieval cemetery of the parish church of St Margaret in Combusto, Magdalen Street (*c.* 1200–1468), has yielded similar information about another poor Norwich community weakened by sporadic food shortages, low levels of hygiene and endemic disease. No conclusive evidence of child mortality has emerged from this site, but it looks as if the high death rate among young adults (about two-fifths of a group of 413 predominantly male individuals died between the ages of nineteen and thirty) was not simply due to the proximity of the city's gallows. Once again, occupational accidents and traumatic stress appear to have been a constant scourge of the labouring classes: approximately one third of the adult skeletons showed signs of damage, notably to the feet and spine. Several individuals had sustained poorly healed fractures which would seriously have restricted their ability to work. Living conditions in English medieval towns provided an ideal environment for the transmission of tuberculosis, especially among the poor. At least four cases of infection sufficiently advanced to affect the spine and ribs were discovered, along with seven lepers and six victims of treponemal disease (yaws or syphilis).[17] Many sufferers would, moreover, have died long before they had deteriorated so far.

Did parishioners of St Margaret's seek the assistance of another local saint, whose shrine at Bawburgh, to the west of the city, attracted crippled agricultural workers and artisans 'sore vexed of bone ach[e]'? The cult of St Walstan, 'a petitioner for labourers', remained popular until the eve of the Dissolution, by which date it boasted an impressive catalogue of miracle cures, recounted in English for the benefit of the 'unlearned':

> Blind men made to see and looke on the sunne,
> Crooked both and lame right up for to goe,
> The deafe man perfectly his hearing hath wonne,
> Damned spirit cast out of man also,
> Leprosy, fevir, palsy, with many sicknesses more
> Be cured and healed in this holy place.[18]

Although conventional enough in its adherence to a standard biblical model, this list of cures reflects some of the major health problems encountered in medieval Norwich, of which leprosy, if not the most common, certainly came to be one of the most feared. Today regarded as a disease of the Third World, it was already endemic among the local populace at, or just before, the Norman Conquest.

Recent excavations at Timberhill, which then stood on the south-east boundary of the Anglo-Saxon city, have revealed a number of late eleventh-century skeletons (thirty-five out of 180, or about 20 per cent) which can be identified as leprous with reasonable certainty. Of these, no fewer than sixteen were suffering from lepromatous leprosy, the most virulent strain of the disease. Perhaps an informal leper colony had already been established nearby.[19] From the 1170s onwards, lepers were required by canon law to live apart, maintaining separate churches and cemeteries for their own use. Already by then Norwich boasted at least two *leprosaria*, one of which had reputedly been founded by Bishop Herbert de Losinga (d. 1119), and may thus not only have been the first of Norwich's many hospitals but perhaps also one of the earliest leper houses in England. Situated a mile from the city at Sprowston, and run under the aegis of the Benedictine monks, it followed a quasi-monastic regime, offering spiritual solace to the patients and a promise of salvation to patrons.[20] We should remember that for theologians, if not the populace at large, the leper had assumed Christ's mantle of suffering on earth, and was thus deemed worthy of honour as well as pity.

By the early fourteenth century, however, when medical ideas about the dissemination of disease had filtered down through society and attitudes towards the sick and indigent were hardening, the leper seemed more threatening than holy. No longer free to solicit alms within the city, suspects were regularly presented by the four leet courts, and ordered to withdraw beyond the walls or face a heavy fine.[21] But they remained an inescapable presence. The five civic leper houses, strategically situated just outside the gates, presented the inhabitants of Norwich with a constant reminder of the frailty of human life and their own impending decay (Map 14). Unlike Dives, the rich man who had driven the diseased beggar, Lazarus, from his door, the wealthy inhabitants took every step to advertise their collective compassion by building and maintaining extra mural *leprosaria.* Since support for these institutions flourished right up to the Dissolution, the corporation found it comparatively easy to integrate them into a more coherent scheme for assisting the sick and indigent poor. As leprosy began to disappear, they were used as general isolation hospitals for the 'sustentatcon, releeff and comfourte of the prysoners of almyghty God, vexed with suche sykenes and diseases that they of necessitee ar constreyned and compelled to eschewe and avoyde oute and from the company of all peopyll not being infected'.[22] Prominent among the men and women 'havyng no manere of lyveloode, helpe or socour to susteyn theire nedye and myserabyll lyffes', were victims of a new, virulent strain of treponemal disease (probably venereal syphilis), which assumed epidemic proportions in early sixteenth-century Europe, and prompted a radical reassessment of approaches to public health. Designed to remove noisome victims of 'the pox' from its streets to the security of hospitals, while also eliminating beggars and other undesirables, the Ypres scheme of poor relief (1525) helped to set an agenda for reform in Tudor England, and may have proved especially influential in Norwich because of the close links between East Anglia and the Low Countries.[23] By the 1540s, if not before, the corporation had actively begun to pursue such a policy, initiating a vigorous investigation into the management of its 'sykehouses', admission to which was, henceforward, subject to stringent controls.[24]

A significant proportion of the diseases contracted by the population of medieval Norwich have left little or no trace upon either the human skeleton or the surviving records. Whereas the upper and middling ranks of society were probably far cleaner than is generally supposed, the poor commanded few resources necessary to maintain a reasonable standard of personal hygiene. This was especially the case in the late thirteenth and early fourteenth centuries, when a dramatic population explosion was followed by years of famine and economic dislocation. Norwich, like many other English cities, had initially witnessed an influx of landless labourers and indigents already weakened by malnutrition and hardship. Coroners' inquests held during the early 1270s record several cases of death by exposure as a result of weakness, cold or exhaustion ('*ex debilitate corporis*'; '*propter frigiditatem*'), and such fatalities almost certainly increased over the following decades.[25] A sharp rise in the population from about 17,000 in 1311 to perhaps as many as 25,000 or more in 1333 put accommodation

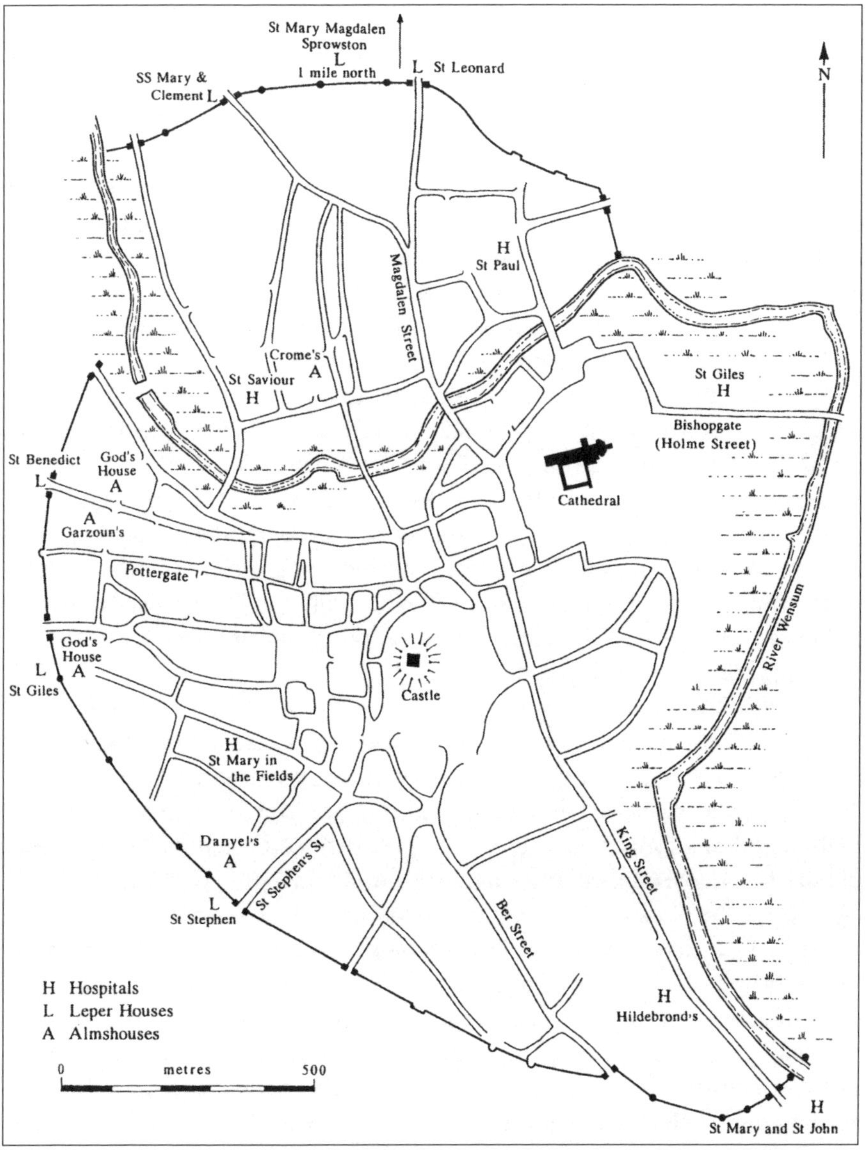

MAP 14. The hospitals, leper houses and almshouses of medieval Norwich. (*Phillip Judge*)

at a premium. Many newcomers lodged in rows of cottages built speculatively of clay and thatch on waste land around the city. Others crowded into existing dwellings in areas such as Upper Newport, where 112 adult males, along with an unrecorded number of women and children, are known to have occupied twenty-seven small properties in the early 1330s.[26] Since methods of sewage disposal were often rudimentary, the incidence of internal parasites, such as ringworm and tapeworm, must have been high. Trachoma, ulcerated eyes and conjunctivitis flourish in such conditions, being further aggravated by the dense smoke of open fires. In periods of dearth, the straw used for bedding and floor covering would be left rotting for long periods, and thus became infected with the vermin which spread epidemics, such as bubonic plague and typhus. Gastro-enteritis and dysentery ('the flux') remained endemic until the twentieth century, rising to serious levels in periods of high population density.[27]

A variety of factors, including diet, pregnancy, low standards of oral cleanliness, coarse bread and the use of teeth as tools for cutting, exacerbated dental problems among the poor. The notoriously sweet tooth of the upper classes made them vulnerable, too, and it is worth noting that the *ex voto* offerings at St Leonard's shrine included silver models of teeth as well as eyes.[28] Septicaemia was, moreover, common in a society without antibiotics. In 1253, for example, one Robert Winter died of infected stab wounds following a brawl. His attacker had, significantly, been bitten by a friend's dog running loose in St Stephen's.[29]

Urban life was hardly improved by the close proximity of livestock. In 1354, as a result of 'the great injuries and dangers' caused by 'boars, sows and pigs' roaming at large, the civic authorities decreed that, save on Saturday afternoons, when all domestic pigsties were to be cleansed, animals could no longer forage freely. The ordinance paints an alarming picture of 'children killed and eaten ... and others maimed' because of negligence on the part of owners. Stray dogs had likewise to be driven from the streets or killed on sight.[30] Fear that animals might spread infection, as well as leaving noxious waste, explains why legislation for the removal of pigs, ducks, cows, horses, dogs and 'other like bestes' so often coincided with epidemics.[31] Keeping a pigsty *outside* the boundaries of one's dwelling likewise constituted an offence, but since Norwich was celebrated for its gardens and orchards animals may have posed less of a health hazard than in more crowded urban environments, such as London.[32]

The problems of maintaining a clean water supply and effectively disposing of the large quantities of human, animal and industrial waste generated in a city the size of Norwich were formidable. Religious houses, such as St Giles's hospital and the Franciscan friary, enjoyed the benefits of piped water and culverted drains from an early date, but the majority of citizens were less fortunate.[33] During the 1260s and 1270s a number of women and children died while attempting to draw water from 'common pits' fed by underground streams. At least one poor creature killed herself in this way, overtaken *per morbum freneticum* (the disease of madness). Wells were another frequent cause of accidental death, and not simply by drowning; one man allegedly expired through the inhalation of corrupt air while he was examining a shaft.[34] Some city wells were impressively deep stone-lined structures built by masons at considerable expense; those sunk on private premises posed a far greater risk to health because of the seepage of toxic matter from the highly porous subsoil.[35] Irresponsible artisans, such as William the skinner, who was fined a considerable sum in 1289 for throwing the bodies of dead cats into one of the city's 'pits', constituted a further menace.[36] The River Wensum, which remained a principal source of water for domestic purposes until the nineteenth century, was even more dangerous. Open 'cockeys' or streams serving all too often as public gutters debouched into it, their contents joining the detritus from tanneries, potteries, cookshops, monastic slaughterhouses, breweries, smithies, fullers' 'holes', foundries, limepits, dyers' yards and all the other workshops which lay upriver to the north west of the city (Map 15).

As a hygienic measure, butchers were largely confined to the higher ground to the south and south west. It was thus possible to keep the Wensum free of entrails and carcasses as it flowed through the city, and thereby prevent a dangerous concentration of the noisome miasmas which were believed to transmit disease. But sizeable communities of leatherworkers congregated upriver in suburban Heigham, as well as within the walls in Coslany and Conesford, discharging their own poisonous waste (Map 9).[37] The Assembly Minute Book of 1510–1550 opens with a positive catalogue of fifty-five 'defects' and complaints, largely about the state of the Wensum. Tanners, such as Richard Skoles, who soaked 'rawe hydes in the ryuer', invited particular condemnation. Yet it was impossible to banish trades upon which the economy depended.[38] Pollution by noise and smell was such a hazard of urban life that physicians routinely asked their patients if they suffered the aggravation of 'an adjoining shop occupied by a carpenter, hammerer, tanner of hides, melter of tallow or by any persons who work with sulphur and the like'. The cacophony of smelting works and other manufacturing industries along Holme Street disturbed the calm of St Giles's hospital and the monastic cloister, prompting one exasperated Benedictine to copy a poem about 'swart, smoky smiths smirched with smoke' and the 'din of their dints' into a book of scientific texts.[39]

Although various city courts maintained a constant battle against the tradesmen, victuallers and private individuals who polluted the environment, even fining one barber surgeon in 1390 for 'throwing putrid blood into the king's highway in abominable offence', they faced an uphill struggle.[40] Public opinion none the less remained a powerful means of coercion, and belies some long-cherished assumptions about the squalor of medieval life. It also reflects an underlying belief that the community as a whole constituted a sentient being in need of protection against both physical and moral contagion.[41] As the Tudor polemicist Thomas Starkey (d. 1538) observed, every 'cyte or towne hathe hys commyn wele and most perfayt state, when fyrst the multytude of pepul and polytyke body ys helthy beutyful and strong ... then plentuously nuryschyd wyth abundance of al thyngys necessary ... and so thyrdly lyve togyddur in cyvyle ordur ... ychone lovyng other as partys of one body'.[42] Other contributors to this volume have stressed how comprehensively the ruling elite imposed order upon the residents of Norwich. It is important to note here that contemporary approaches to health were equally holistic, embracing ideas about self-discipline and personal conduct, as well as more predictable theories regarding diet, medication and exercise. A healthy city, like a healthy individual, depended upon the maintenance of a careful balance in which each limb and organ knew its place, and upon the elimination of any threats likely to disturb this prelapsarian state of equilibrium.[43] Although of considerable antiquity, such ideas were expressed with increasing forcefulness from the late fifteenth century onwards. One of the first measures taken by the corporation of Norwich in the aftermath of Kett's Rebellion in 1549 was to order a costly and systematic programme of street cleaning.[44] Such a step was clearly essential for the removal of accumulated filth and debris. But it also had powerful symbolic overtones: the connection between dirt and disobedience was striking. It is also worth noting that earlier regulations for 'for the dayly making and keaping cleane of the streetes' and cleansing the river were described at about this time as 'godly and goodly'.[45]

Complaints about 'noyous gutturs', 'castyng up of muk' and other nuisances were regularly heard in the local leet courts, as well as being examined by the assembly, which attempted from the later fourteenth century onwards to curtail the unauthorised removal of waste by riverboat, lest it result in further blockages and contamination. In 1380 draconian fines of 20s. for each offence, along with the loss of the freedom or expulsion from Norwich, were threatened for any breach of this regulation, although in practice a more realistic (but still heavy) sum of 6s. 8d. seems to have been the norm.[46] Nor were members of the elite exempt from censure. In 1468, for example, after renewed anxiety over the dumping of waste in the Wensum had prompted the appointment of a boatman to ferry it downstream

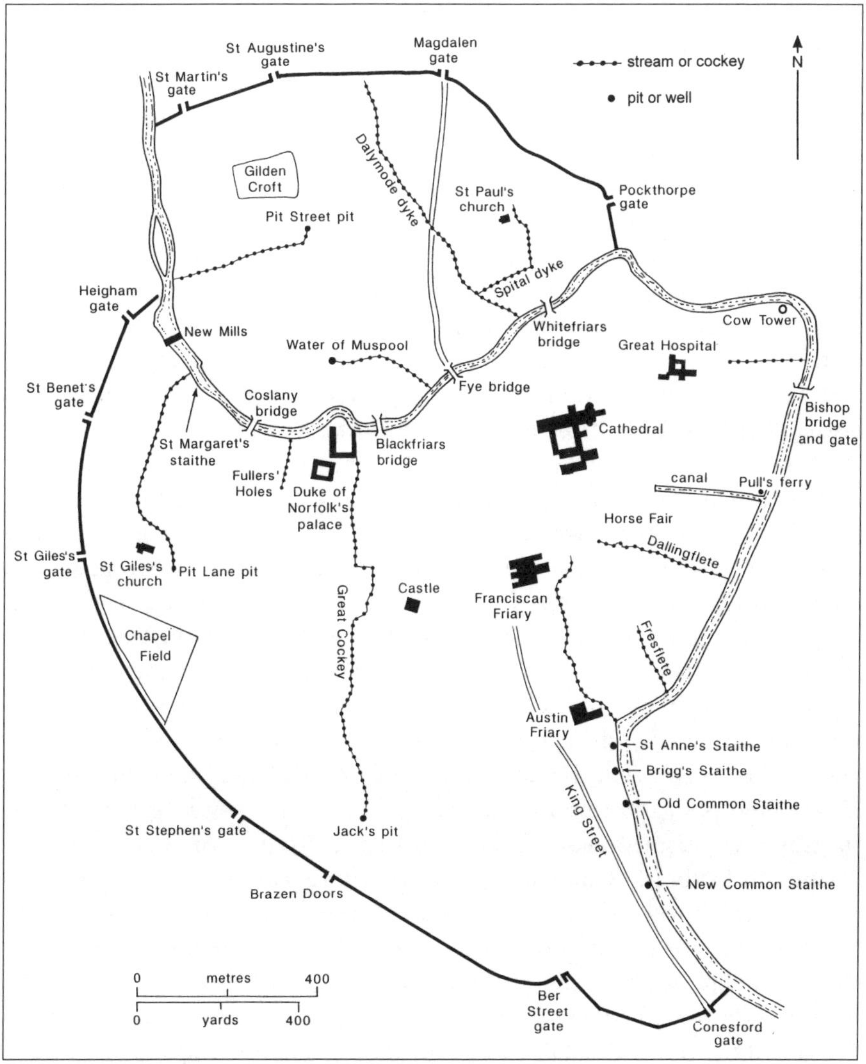

MAP 15. The streams, cockeys and watercourses of medieval and early modern Norwich. (*Phillip Judge*)

and the introduction of compulsory measures for street cleaning by householders, none other than the master of St Giles's hospital and the prior of Norwich were reported to the mayor as persistent and egregious offenders. Over £13 was then voted for clearing the river.[47] Initiatives of this kind tended to follow epidemics, which medical authorities attributed with faultless logic to the stench of foul air and brackish water. Without the infrastructure to sustain them, bouts of corporate vigilance thus proved sporadic, and private individuals were otherwise left to make their own arrangements for the removal of night-soil and rubbish.

During the population boom of the late thirteenth and early fourteenth centuries, when local farmers could barely meet the demand for produce, urban manure became a valuable commodity. The heavy cost of transportation by boat or cart could be recouped as food prices soared, but once the market began to contract so too did the need for intensive fertilisation. Rural landowners, such as the prior of Norwich and master of St Giles's, had arranged for the removal of dung in the empty carts which had brought in foodstuffs from their outlying manors, but the attendant shift from demesne farming to a scaled-down rentier economy dramatically curtailed such operations.[48] By 1517, when the cost of unblocking the Wensum had more than trebled, the authorities finally recognised that long-term official action would be necessary and levied a rate to provide a raker and two 'comon cartes for the avoiding of … filthie and vile mater' out of Norwich each week.[49] This step was not entirely unprecedented, for the scouring and repair of major sewers, which restricted the leakage of waste into neighbouring wells, had been financed from at least the early fifteenth century by the city treasurers and chamberlains in partnership with residents. Indeed, the latter could be heavily fined for failing to discharge their obligations in this regard.[50] Yet it was not until the 1670s, when measures were introduced for the regular collection of night-soil, that cesspits and rubbish heaps finally begin to disappear from the landscape.[51]

However slowly they may have moved towards a policy of corporate responsibility for schemes of urban improvement, individual members of the ruling elite took a keen personal interest in such matters. During the later middle ages changing ideas about the nature and purpose of charitable activity prompted wealthy merchants throughout England to regard public works as necessary measures which would not only secure their salvation and enduring fame, but also promote the health, wealth and reputation of the body politic.[52] Since it was during his mayoralty, in 1459, that the crown had insisted upon immediate action to remove 'mukke and fylth' from the Wensum, John Gilbert clearly recognised that he should lead the way by making a significant contribution towards the project, which his executors brought to completion at a total cost of £50.[53] The alderman, John Jowell (d. 1499), left over £30 in doles for the sick poor of Norwich, quantities of linen for 'bedred men and women' and £20 to repair the walls and river. No less mindful of the obligations of aldermanic office, Thomas Aldrich (d. 1529) instructed his executors to distribute £40 'in almes amonges pour people within the citie of Norwich', and devote a similar sum to 'common costes', such as paving the highways.[54] Clearly impressed by his visits to the capital, Edmund Wood (d. 1548) outdid his predecessors with bequests of £100 for street cleaning 'after the manner and custome of London', and £20 for improvements to the river.[55]

There was, nevertheless, no substitute for prompt collective action, especially in the aftermath of a natural disaster. With so many thatched roofs and inflammable buildings, Norwich, like other medieval towns, suffered from periodic fires, the worst of which, in March and June 1507, between them destroyed over 700 houses in sixteen city parishes. Seizing the opportunities for 'reformacion' thus offered, the mayor and corporation insisted that new buildings should be tiled rather than thatched, and pushed through additional schemes for laying drains and implementing other public works.[56] Such measures could, however, prompt resentment among poor or intransigent householders, who were powerless to resist wealthy neighbours bent on exploiting plans for urban renewal to their own advantage.[57] Even so, the process of rebuilding proved painfully slow in deprived areas blighted by economic stagnation. As late as 1535, a parliamentary Act 'for the re-edifienge of voyde groundes in the Citie of Norwich' reported that whole tracts of 'desolate and vacant groundes, many of theym nighe and adjoyninge to the highe stretes replenished with moche unclennes and filthe' still had to be cleared.[58]

Poor nutrition remained a cause of illness and disability across the social spectrum. Vitamin deficiencies accounted for the ubiquity of seasonal ophthalmia, whose victims so often appear in accounts of medieval miracles such as St Walstan's. The stone, which tormented John Sympson's son from childhood, was probably caused by the excessive consumption of cereals characteristic of an artisan's diet. Yet in times of real hardship, such as the famine years of the early fourteenth-century, all but the coarsest bread was a luxury beyond the means of the poor. Fear of unrest as much as philanthropic concern prompted the first official steps towards a regulated market. In 1308 the civic authorities sought to control both the quality and price of bread by subsidising some grain supplies and carefully supervising Norwich's bakers, 'that the people be not deceived, but rather … served rightly and faithfully without fraud'. Significantly, the comprehensive list of customs compiled at this time also included measures to prevent an influx of strangers into the city and to curtail the freedom of a potentially unruly band of indigent day labourers, desperate for food.[59] Not until 1522, however, when dramatically escalating grain prices and the recurrent threat of disorder obliged the mayor and aldermen to buy in stocks of wheat at their own expense, did the civic authorities again address a problem which from thenceforth became a matter of corporate action. Renewed fears 'that the commons of the city were ready to rise upon the rich men' lay behind efforts to peg prices in 1527; four years later another acute shortage prompted the assembly to protect those 'in gret jeoberdye of ffamysshing' by prohibiting the sale of grain to wholesalers.[60] Not all the inhabitants were, however, as appreciative as the authorities might have wished. In 1535 one William Thakker declared before the mayor's court that 'a cartlode of brede shall or cannot stop the mouthes of them that hath called Master Doctor Barret *apostata* and worse'.[61]

During the middle ages the distribution of aid had been largely consigned to the church in its dual capacity as relief agency and moral preceptor. Although he was never canonised, Bishop Walter Suffield enjoyed posthumous renown as a friend to malnourished beggars, whom he fed at his own table. In his will of 1256 he left over £375 for poor relief, as well as a bequest of £200 for the new hospital of St Giles, which he had built near the episcopal palace for the support of sick and indigent paupers. Like the older hospital of St Paul, founded by Bishop Everard (d. 1146) to the north of the city, it was pledged to feed anyone who solicited alms at the gates, especially in the difficult months before harvest. Additional help came from the nearby Benedictine community. During the hungry 1280s, the almoner of Norwich cathedral priory distributed an average of 274 loaves a day, as well as other food and clothing, among the poor. It was also then that at least four small hospitals, doubling as soup kitchens, were endowed by prosperous citizens in the poor area of Coslany, to the north west of the city.[62] The friaries must also have shouldered some of the burden, while preaching the virtues of Christian charity to their congregations. Prominent among the surviving stained glass panels in the merchants' church of St Peter Mancroft is a depiction of St Elizabeth of Hungary (a Franciscan tertiary) giving bread to a crowd of blind, lame and leprous beggars (Plate 27).[63]

Notwithstanding this powerful propaganda, late medieval economic and demographic vicissitudes, as well as mounting hostility towards outsiders, led many institutions sharply to curtail their philanthropic activities long before the Dissolution. Originally established in the early thirteenth century for 'poor people in want of lodging', Hildebrond's hospital in Conesford had, for example, already entered a period of decline by the time parliament attempted to criminalise vagrancy in the aftermath of the Peasants' Revolt of 1381.[64] Private individuals may well have defied the law by distributing food and clothing indiscriminately in their lifetimes, but most tended to make testamentary bequests in favour of the resident, deserving poor, whose intercessionary prayers seemed more pleasing to God. Fixed cash doles proved both convenient and attractive in periods of low population density when grain was relatively cheap. Characteristic of the generous, but specific, provision made by members of the ruling elite is a sum of £40 left by Alderman William Setman (d. 1429) for distribution in weekly handouts of 3d. among 'the poor, and especially the lame, the blind or the severely disabled *remaining continuously in Norwic*' over a period of three years.[65] Alderman John Cambridge's munificent bequest of one hundred coverlets, sixty pairs of sheets, sixty warm gowns and sixty matching hoods worth a total of £36 was specifically reserved 'to othir that arn *non comon beggeris*, as right pore folk that han many childeren'.[66] Whereas many testators felt their executors were best placed to determine cases of need, some, such as Walter Danyell (d. 1426), John Northalis (d. 1468), Hamon Claxton (d. 1501), John Brown (d. 1503) and Margery Dogett (d. 1516), singled out the 'bedred' and otherwise impoverished householders of designated city parishes, most notably their own.[67] Alderman Thomas Bewfeld's requirement, in his will of 1504, that a select group of paupers had to attend the parochial mass each day 'sittynge by the ffunte [font] to prey for my soule' before being paid, suggests that he shared these priorities.[68]

Ostentatious doles of food and clothing tended to be reserved for funerals and obits (anniversary services for the dead), when a square meal and perhaps also a warm gown rewarded the poor men and women whose presence served both to advertise the generosity of the deceased and also to speed his or her soul on its painful ascent through purgatory. Concern expressed by the alderman Richard Ferrour (d. 1501) that 'at the daye of my terment [burial] there dynne none other persons but suche as ben dwellers in [my] parishe' none the less confirms that, for him, too, charity began at home.[69] In Norwich, where parochial networks and loyalties were especially strong, the reputable poor, at least, could rely upon their neighbours for assistance. The miracles of St William include the case of a child, deformed from birth, who begged from door to door, supporting himself on his knees with a pair of crutches.[70] Skeletal evidence from the cemetery of St Margaret in Combusto certainly suggests that seriously disabled individuals incapable of work were helped in this way. Some of the more affluent citizens, such as Katherine, the widow of Walter de Norwich (d. 1329), budgeted for the cost of daily alms of bread and herring in their domestic accounts, but the extent to which such philanthropy constituted a safety net for the truly destitute is impossible to judge.[71]

Although the authorities of medieval Norwich regarded aid for the hungry as a matter for individual rather than collective action, they were neither unaware of, nor indifferent to, the dangers posed to the community by substandard food. A good diet, commonly recognised as 'the first instrument of medicine', was as necessary for the civic as the individual body. Because they could rarely afford lodgings with cooking facilities, let alone the necessary equipment, fuel and basic provisions for the preparation of hot meals, the urban poor were heavily dependent upon 'fast food' outlets, especially during periods of rapid population growth. Medieval cookshops were notoriously unappetising places. In 1287–88 alone local courts took steps, *inter alios*, against traders selling sausages and puddings made from 'measly pigs' and thus unfit for human consumption; others were indicted for offering 'putrid and badly salted meat' in the market and for passing off animals found dead in suspicious circumstances as sound; several cooks faced fines for reheating their wares; and vendors of shell fish were disciplined for mixing old stock in with the new.[72] Complaints voiced by the butchers of Norwich in 1373 that the city's cooks were undercutting their trade by feeding (and implicitly slaughtering) livestock in their own homes clearly sprang from commercial rather than hygienic concerns. The imposition of exemplary fines on any cook who kept oxen, pigs, calves, sheep or lambs on his premises must, none the less, have removed a major threat to health.[73] The mayor's court, too, amerced vendors of 'pokky pigges' and 'stynkyng makerelles', often insisting that corrupt meat and fish should be publicly burnt.[74] Some problems, however, defied the most assiduous efforts. As the climate grew wetter grain supplies were increasingly liable to infection by mould and fungus, which, in the case of rye, led to ergotism, or St Anthony's fire. At least one of the demoniacs described in dramatic detail by Thomas of Monmouth was probably suffering from this disease. His violent convulsions may well have been caused by poisoned rye, although to the observers gathered about St William's tomb in the cathedral, whence he was dragged screaming in chains, he gave every sign of being possessed by devils. Significantly, the cure followed a long period without food.[75]

Beyond the occasional mention of the violent insane in the *miracula* of St Walstan and the boy William, we know little of the way that the mentally sick were treated in medieval Norwich. The autobiography of the King's Lynn mystic Margery Kempe confirms the general supposition that those deemed capable of harming either themselves or others were forcibly restrained at home.[76] A few destitute but harmless individuals, such as William Hammond, 'ydiot', found refuge in the homes of more affluent neighbours. In her will of 1530, his protector, Margaret Yaxley, the widow of an influential Norwich lawyer, left £5 so that her son could continue supporting him in 'mete, drynke and clothyng duryng his naturall lyef, with other necessaries'. She also bequeathed quantities of bedding and apparel for his use.[77] The rich were, inevitably, assured of protection, if only by virtue of their status. In the case of a wealthy merchant, such as Edmund Reed, the crown would appoint 'nere frendes and allies' to act as keepers. Having been 'by the hande of All Myghty Gode ... sodenly striken yn to a grate diseas and sykenes of lunacye ... wherby the use of reason and discressyon ys and hathe byn thereby taken', Reed was deemed incapable of managing his own affairs at the start of the sixteenth century, but only after the escheator of Norfolk had examined him.[78]

No such courtesy was extended to 'mad Belle', a disruptive lunatic who was conveyed out of Norwich on the orders of the chamberlain in 1549, although he did receive 2d. 'in his purse' to see him on his way.[79] Attitudes may well have hardened in the recessionary years of Henry VIII's reign, when society looked even less kindly upon the mad, work shy or infectious. Writing in the aftermath of Kett's Rebellion, in 1549, one commentator compared the 'swarming of loitering vagabonds' to flies in plague time, adding ominously that, to preserve its health, the body politic sometimes needed 'desperate remedies'.[80] It is notable that, of the three major city hospitals set up in the twelfth and thirteenth centuries for the relief of the homeless poor, one had already become a retirement home for respectable women by the 1370s,[81] another was little more than a chantry chapel, and the third had been transformed into a magnificent liturgical centre with a modest almshouse attached. Such changes were an inevitable consequence of the economic and social upheavals following one of the grimmest chapters in the history of Norwich.

Chronic overcrowding, especially in the poorer areas of the city, helps to explain the devastating impact of bubonic plague, which first afflicted Norwich in 1349. Although subsequent claims that as many as 57,474 people died there in a single year are clearly implausible, the disaster must have seemed little short of apocalyptical.[82] When they came to depict the seven plague-bearing angels of the Book of Revelation in their cathedral cloister, the Norwich Benedictines, who lost approximately half their community at that time, actually showed a tonsured monk prostrate in a sea of blood (Plate 28).[83] Their terror is understandable. Despite its subsequent reputation as a *morbus pauperum* (disease of the poor), bubonic plague initially displayed scant respect for rank. Almost all the Norwich Dominicans died in the first epidemic; piles of filth lay uncollected in the streets as late as 1352; the state of the river, ditches and defences was still exercising the crown two decades later; and at least five parish churches eventually collapsed in ruins and were declared redundant. Having failed to let many of their stalls, the civic authorities surrendered part of the market to accommodate the rapidly expanding graveyard of St Peter Mancroft.[84] Death, at least, enjoyed a roaring trade. Initial hopes of recovery were undermined by a second national epidemic in 1361, which proved less virulent than the first but (as a local chronicler observed) took a heavy toll of children and adolescents throughout the region. A third, eight years later, and a fourth in 1383 reputedly had the same effect, with disastrous consequences for replacement rates.[85] The poll tax returns for 1377, which were supposed to record all individuals over the age of fourteen except for beggars and members of religious orders, list a mere 3952 names for Norwich. Even allowing for omissions and evasions, the entire population is then unlikely to have exceeded 8000, and was probably much lower. Although some decline may well have occurred before the late 1340s, the death or departure of as many as 17,000 inhabitants over the space of five decades was largely attributable to pestilence and the economic dislocation attendant upon it.[86]

Successive visitations of plague and other epidemics, such as dysentery, typhus and sweating sickness, caused regular disruption throughout the later middle ages and early modern period, culminating in the pestilence of 1579–80, when about 40 per cent of the population of Norwich succumbed.[87] It is, indeed, a testimony to the energy and enterprise of its residents that the city showed such economic resilience during the later fourteenth and fifteenth centuries. Yet familiarity with the Grim Reaper made his arrival no less terrible. If, as in other parts of Europe, the iconography of Death assumed an almost lugubrious humour (manifest in the one surviving panel of the Dance of Death series in the clerestory of St Andrew's church, opposite the Dominican friary), his potential victims still took every conceivable step to avoid the final confrontation (Plate 29). For wealthy landowners, such as the Clares and the Pastons, who fled Norwich in 1465 and 1471 because of 'vnyuersall dethe', escape to the country offered the only real hope of safety.[88] But sometimes there was nowhere left to run, as a letter sent by John Paston III from Norwich during the epidemic of 1479 reveals:

> Also, syr, I prey yow send me by the next man that comyth fro London ij pottys of tryacle of Jenne [Genoese theriac] – they shall cost xvjd; for I haue spent

> ought [everything] that I had wyth my yong wyff and my yong folkys and mysylff ... I prey yow lett it be sped. The pepyll dyeth sore in Norwyche, and specyally a-bought my house; but my wyff and my women come not ought, and fle ferther we can not, for at Sweynsthorp sythe my departyng thens they haue dyed and ben syke nye jn every house of the towne.[89]

Whereas theriac, an expensive and esoteric prophylactic, was shipped into London from Italy, nostrums to suit almost every pocket could be purchased locally. As Geoffrey Chaucer noted slyly in *The Canterbury Tales*, plague meant big business for the physicians and apothecaries who now catered for a nation of hypochondriacs.[90]

Few residents of Norwich would, however, have encountered anyone as learned, rich and successful as Chaucer's physician. University-trained practitioners were rare birds, who generally nested in London, at court and in baronial households, where they could enjoy the richest pickings. A small band of Cambridge graduates, such as Master Thomas Reed, who tended Isabella, Lady Morley, in Norwich at a cost of over 36s. in 1464, made the journey across the fens, but only in the service of wealthy patrons.[91] As in the case of Johannes Hesse, who requested board and lodging for himself and his assistants when he was treating John Sympson's son, leading practitioners expected to be housed in a befitting manner. This posed no problems for the cathedral monks, who probably enjoyed the highest standard of professional care then available in Norfolk, and employed a series of visiting *medici* in various capacities.[92] Others turned to more accessible and cheaper alternatives.

The expulsion of the Jews from England in 1290 deprived Norwich of at least one dynasty of resident physicians, whose knowledge of Hebrew as well as Latin placed them at the cutting edge of new theoretical developments. Their grasp of the emergent science of pharmacy must also have been considerable. A deed of 1266 refers to the herb garden (*herbarium*) of Solomon the physician, himself the son of a rabbi-physician named Isaac, which lay in the Jewish quarter south of Saddlegate.[93] From the 1280s onwards a number of individuals bearing the title leech, *mire* or *medicus* appear in the city records, almost invariably in the context of property transactions.[94] Resident and often married, these men offered a variety of services, including uroscopy and the casting of horoscopes, and would have treated the middling and upper ranks of Norwich society. Below them, an army of herbalists, wise-women, midwives, charmers and other empirics, who can rarely be documented let alone enumerated, catered for all but the destitute. Some sense of this bustling medical market place emerges later, in 1561, from the statutes of the reconstituted company of physicians and barber-surgeons, as submitted for approval to the Norwich assembly. Among those castigated as 'hauing neyther experience nor lernyng' were 'shomakers, hatmakers, dornyk wevers, smythes and worstedwevers, with others, and also dyverse and sundry women, geving over the good and profitable artes that they haue ben browght vpp with ... euen for lucars sake and ydelnes of lyfe, beyng unskylfull and utterly ingnorant of the nature and operacion of thos thinges that they do mynyster'.[95] That the civic authorities had long felt concern about the multiplicity of untrained and unregulated practitioners on the streets seems apparent from the decision to return Robert Harydaunce MD to the parliament of 1512. Harydaunce, who lived in Norwich and played an active part in its government, had read medicine at Cambridge and was only the second practising physician to sit in the House of Commons. Prominent on the legislative slate was a Bill for the licensing of physicians and surgeons, which obtained the royal consent and duly passed into law. Its preamble was incorporated, almost verbatim, into the Norwich regulations of 1561.[96]

Competition came from a variety of quarters. Ignoring the protests of qualified practitioners, apothecaries and spicers often seized the initiative, diagnosing, prescribing and selling drugs in response to popular demand. In a city such as Norwich, which presented limitless opportunities for medical entrepreneurs, apothecaries prospered, boasting their own quarter, the *forum unguentorum* or *apothecaria*, in the marketplace from an early date.[97] At least thirty-four apothecaries are documented between *c.* 1288 and *c.* 1348 alone, their trade in exotic spices exploiting a lucrative market at a time when food and medicine were deemed interchangeable. Successive outbreaks of plague engendered an insatiable demand for elixirs, fumigants, pomanders and other prophylactics, which promised to dispel the miasmas of disease while also stimulating the body's vital spirits. In 1542, for example, the chamberlain of Norwich paid 3s. 6d. 'for parfume to make the cownsell chambyr swete ageynst my lord of Norffolk's comyng to the cite, iij severall days: that ys to saye every day a parfume panne mad withe damask water and cloves'.[98] Whether produced at home or on the prescription of a society physician, most of the medication available in medieval and early modern England derived from herbs. As well as being grown in the city's many gardens, these were sold in the 'lekmarkette', where a number of herbalists plied their trade. At least one 'lekwoman' is mentioned in the local records, this being a field in which women were recognised for their expertise.[99]

Despite the potential rewards, it was far riskier for an apothecary or herbalist to attempt surgical procedures. In 1539 George Hill, 'potycarye', was committed to prison by the mayor's court, 'ffor that he hath used the science off Surgerye, not beyng experte theryn, nor yet admytted therunto accordyng to the lawe, and mynystred to dyuers persons within this citie'.[100] Expulsion from Norwich followed, along with a prohibition from practising until he had gained the necessary qualifications. Whereas the physicians of fifteenth- and sixteenth-century England failed to establish a monopoly even in the capital, surgeons and barbers were far better placed to assert themselves. As craftsmen, who drew their strength from the highly regulated and protectionist structures of the medieval guild system, they were more closely integrated into urban life and could rely upon the support of fellow townsmen. Their stock in trade of tooth drawing, bone-setting, dressing and concealing sores, bloodletting, treating operable conditions, such as hernias and haemorrhoids, and patching up the victims of accidents guaranteed a regular flow of custom. The early history of the Norwich guild is obscure, although the presence in the city of at least twenty-three barbers during the first half of the fourteenth century suggests that it predated the arrival of plague. By 1388 it boasted a minimum of twelve freemen members and three masters, who met annually at the Carnary chapel in the cathedral precinct to hear mass and present lights to the high altar.[101] All craft guilds observed a degree of religious ceremonial, but the understandable concern which practitioners felt about the dangers of accidental homicide probably intensified their devotion to a patron saint (John the Baptist) who was commonly invoked to prevent the loss of blood.

The practicalities of training and patient care would have been similar to those described in surviving ordinances for the surgeons of London and the barbers of York.[102] Two sets of general rules for the management of Norwich guilds, compiled in 1449 and 1543 respectively, suggest very close parallels: apprentices were to be indentured for seven years; the commercial freedom of outsiders was restricted to prevent competition; and a strict system of fines helped to maintain internal discipline.[103] Records of admissions to the freedom of Norwich provide sounder evidence of guild membership from 1350 onwards. Allowing for the fact that many barbers and barber-surgeons were reluctant to run a business or become liable for taxation, and thus remained unfree, a minimum of 112 new members are listed between then and 1550. Recruitment peaked in the 1440s and 1450s, when the city boasted at least fifteen master barbers: that is roughly one for every 530 head of population.[104] But, as was the case in Elizabethan and Stuart Norwich, most of these men had more than one occupation. Some invested their profits in smallholdings and animal husbandry, while others became involved in industries such as brewing, hat-making and wax-working.[105] The barbers and chandlers of Norwich marched together behind one banner in the annual *Corpus Christi* day procession, joined with the surgeons in performing the mystery play of 'the Baptysme of Criste', and occasionally shared a common guild. Since wax and animal fats were a basic component of the unguents which most practitioners made on their own premises, it seemed logical to ply both trades at once.[106] Wax was also essential in the embalming process, which called upon and helped to refine the anatomical skills of the barber-surgeon. Another aspect of the connection underscores the sometimes opportunistic relationship between physical and spiritual medicine. Chandlers derived a substantial income by selling *ex-voto* images of body parts for sick pilgrims to offer at shrines; if a barber failed to cure his patient, he might still exploit the attractions of a healing saint.[107]

Whereas most towns and cities of any size in late medieval western Europe employed physicians, surgeons and midwives to tend the sick poor, England lagged behind her wealthier continental neighbours.[108] Not until 1547, when they undertook to pay one of Norwich's leading barber-surgeons a handsome retainer of almost £7 a year to treat the inmates of God's House (as the radically reformed hospital of St Giles was now known), did the civic authorities provide subsidised medical treatment for paupers. Nor, before then, had any of the city's hospitals or *leprosaria* offered their patients much more than rudimentary nursing care.[109] Individual benefactors, such as Margaret Norman, who left 10s. in her will of 1516 to pay a surgeon for curing one of her poor dependents, clearly helped to provide *ad hoc* support, but we know little about this aspect of charitable effort.[110] Members of the city's many craft guilds and religious fraternities who experienced 'pouerte or secknesse or any other meschef be the sendyng of Crist', but certainly not through 'ryotous lyuyng' or criminality, could draw upon these mutual benefit societies, claiming at least a few pence a week in cases of hardship. Returns submitted to the parliament of 1388 by eighteen city guilds reveal that almost all made some such provision, thereby offering a degree of protection should illness, disability or a crippling industrial accident threaten reputable working men and women with destitution. The psychological and spiritual benefits of membership must also have been considerable in an age of high mortality. Masters and wardens were expected to visit each 'pore sikeman and woman' under their authority, offering consolation and, 'as charite requyreth', the promise of a Christian burial with full rites of commemoration.[111]

Still at less than half its pre-plague level in the early sixteenth century, a smaller and better nourished population encountered very different medical and social problems than those described at the start of this chapter. As the demand for soup kitchens and hostels declined, care of the elderly became a more pressing priority. Since food had been relatively cheap and plentiful for most of the previous century, those who survived epidemics tended to live longer, although life was by no means easy. Poverty, age and sickness formed a depressingly familiar trinity, revealed in Norwich's pioneering Census of the Poor of 1570. By then, and no doubt long before, between one third and one half of all the inhabitants over sixty were likely to be impoverished and at least one quarter of this significant group (approximately 14 per cent of the urban poor) faced serious disability as well.[112] Unlike York, however, where at least three out of a grand total of no fewer than eighteen late medieval almshouses were maintained by guilds, Norwich seems to have offered only modest institutional provision for the old and vulnerable.[113]

A few wealthy Norwich citizens with reserves of property are known to have established almshouses, perhaps for their own elderly dependents, but none lasted for long. Despite the apparent scale of their investment in an almshouse 'of new construction and ordinance' in St Stephen's parish, the brothers John and Walter Danyell failed to generate lasting support. Both men had served as mayor of Norwich, and clearly wished to found an institution which would redound to their lasting credit. Yet the project foundered within a few years of Walter's death in 1426.[114] Alice Crome's confident expectation that her seven dwellings near the church of St George Muspool 'shall remayne styll as almes howsys for euermore as they do at this present tyme' was apparently doomed to disappointment; the only reference to this generous endowment occurs in her will of 1519.[115] As in other late medieval towns and cities, such highly personal arrangements, which often proved short-lived, are hard to document and impossible to quantify. Even more elusive are the informal communities of religious women known to have sprung up in Norwich at the close of the middle ages. Two of them apparently made their homes in the neighbouring parishes of St Swithun and St Laurence, to the north west of the city, quite possibly continuing the work of a couple of obscure late thirteenth-century hospitals in caring for the local poor. Residents of the former are first mentioned in the late 1420s as '*quasi comversae*' or lay sisters, their appearance alongside the nuns of Carrow priory and the nurses of the hospitals of St Giles and St Paul in the wills of local testators reinforcing the assumption that they combined philanthropic and religious functions. It was at St Swithun's that the wealthy alderman Augustine Steward chose in his will of 1570 to establish an almshouse for respectable elderly women, which suggests a strong element of continuity.[116]

That Norwich, alone among English cities, possessed its own version of the Flemish beguinage reflects its close connections with the Low Countries, where such communities made an important contribution to charitable effort. Members of the mercantile elite, who travelled regularly across the North Sea, must have been impressed by the programmes of integrated relief they encountered in cities such as Bruges and Ypres. In Thomas Starkey's *Dialogue between Pole and Lupset*, written in about 1530, the latter draws some damning comparisons between England's declining towns and those he visited abroad. 'Me thought when I cam fyrst in to flaunders and france,' he recalls, 'I was translatyd as hyt had byn in to a nother world, the cytes and townys apperyd so gudly, so wel byldyd and so clene kept.'[117] Allowing for the author's rhetorical bent, this view was far from uncommon. In the Netherlands institutional provision for the sick and destitute developed alongside measures for civic improvement, subsidised food and free medical treatment. Yet the rulers of Norwich could themselves boast a long tradition of personal involvement in public works. As we have seen, they were far from supine when faced by death and disease, and had promoted a variety of schemes on both a collective and individual basis. Indeed, by the start of the sixteenth century, before the Protestant Reformation and the pioneering Census of the Poor, Norwich was gradually moving towards just such a continental model. The dissolution of religious houses enabled the corporation to integrate the city's two principal hospitals into a more comprehensive system of relief, which already regulated grain prices, attempted to monitor the quality of food on sale in local markets and sought to maintain basic standards of hygiene throughout the city. The foundation of this edifice none the less remained the medieval parish. Once the focus of a search for spiritual health on the part of affluent citizens who sought to avoid the pains of purgatory through good works, it became the principal agent for the enforcement of national and local legislation for the relief of poverty and elimination of vagrancy: twin goals which had, in fact, changed little for over two centuries.

Appendix

The Hospitals of Medieval Norwich

For Lepers

St Mary Magdalen, Sprowston: Reputedly founded by Bishop Herbert Losinga (d. 1119), about a mile to the north of Norwich at Sprowston, and run by the Benedictines of the cathedral priory as a religious foundation.

Brichtiu's: Described in the *vita* of William of Norwich as the scene of a healing miracle of about 1150 involving a woman with 'elephantiasis' or leprosy.

St Giles: Situated outside St Giles's gate, to the west of Norwich. By 1308 it comprised at least seven cottages 'where leprous people dwell'.

St Mary and St Clement: Founded by Margaret, countess of Lincoln (d. 1310), or an earlier namesake outside St Augustine's gate on the north-west approach to the city.

St Stephen: Lay just outside St Stephen's gate, to the south of Norwich. By 1315 there were four 'leper cottages' on the site, which later boasted a chapel.

St Leonard: Situated to the north of Norwich outside the Magdalen gate, it comprised a few wooden houses, which in 1335 needed repair. By the 1440s its chapel was being rebuilt.

St Benedict: Lay to the west of Norwich outside St Benedict's gate, where it owned sufficient property to warrant the acquisition of a seal.

Hospitals for the Sick Poor

St Paul (Norman's): Built on the northern margin of the city during the early twelfth century by the cathedral monks, with support from Bishop Everard (resigned 1145), who described himself as the founder. Initially offered facilities for 'the sick, infirm and child-bearing poor' of Norwich, temporary beds for needy travellers and a number of resident places for poor and aged brothers and sisters. In the aftermath of the Black Death it became an almshouse for respectable women, some on half-board.

St Mary and St John: Run by nuns 'in the fields of Norwich' and attached to a church of the same name by 1137. During the following decade the hospital apparently evolved into Carrow priory (see Chapter 4), and must therefore have stood outside the Conesford gate to south east of the city.

Hildebrand's (St Mary's or Ivy Hall): Founded, along with a detached chapel, by a Norwich mercer in about 1200 in King Street, Conesford, on the main thoroughfare into Norwich from the south east. Originally intended for pilgrims and poor travellers, perhaps to compensate for the loss of the hospital of St Mary and St John, it later declined into an underfunded almshouse.

St Mary in the Fields: Founded before 1248 by a Norwich priest on the south-western margins of the city, this hospital was quickly transformed into a college for secular clergy.

St Giles: The largest hospital in Norwich, founded in 1249 by Bishop Walter Suffield on the banks of the Wensum north of the cathedral. Maintained thirty beds for the sick poor and additional facilities for scholars and disabled priests. Doles of food were also distributed on a daily basis. Developed into a major liturgical centre; it was acquired by the city in 1547 and became known as the Great Hospital.

God's House (St Margaret): Founded by a Norwich merchant in 1292 as a refuge for the poor in Coslany, a deprived area to the north west of the city.

St Saviour: Another Coslany hospital, which Richard de Breccles set up in 1298 for the local poor. His executors lacked the funds to continue the project, which was abandoned by 1306.

Almshouses

God's House (St Giles): Founded before 1306 by John le Grant near St Giles's gate, and later brought under the patronage of the bishops of Norwich, perhaps in conjunction with the leper house near this site.

Garzoun's Almshouse: An obscure establishment founded during the early fourteenth century by a wealthy local merchant in Westwick, Coslany.

St Christopher: A small establishment to the north of the Wensum belonging to the hospital of the Blessed Mary of Rouncivalle, London, disbanded after 1369.

The Danyells' Almshouses: Founded by the brothers John and Walter Danyell on the southern margins of the city shortly before 1418. Despite the apparent scale of their investment, the almshouses did not function for long.

Crome's Almshouse: Seven dwellings to the north of the Wensum, in St George's parish, are described as almshouses in the will of Alice Crome (1519).

Further information about these institutions, along with full documentation, may be found in Rawcliffe, *Hospitals of Medieval Norwich*, and eadem, *Medicine for the Soul.*

Notes

Notes to Introduction

1. P. Browne, *The History of Norwich from the Earliest Records to the Present Time* (Norwich, 1814), pp. 98–9.
2. *RCN*, ii, p. 133.
3. See *History of Norwich*, ii, Chapter 7.
4. NRO, MS 79, typescript copy of Benjamin Mackerell, 'The History of the City of Norwich, both Ancient and Modern' (1737), p. 138.
5. For a discussion of this map, see R. Frostick, *The Printed Plans of Norwich, 1558–1840: A Carto-Bibliography* (Norwich, 2002), pp. 1–4. Cuningham described Norwich as 'an healthfull and pleasant Citye, hauinge a faire Riuer called Yareus, running thorow it': *Cosmographical Glasse*, p. 174.
6. G. Borrow, *Lavengro: the Scholar, the Gypsy, the Priest* (London, 1906), p. 89. The cathedral spire is late fifteenth-century not Norman, as he supposed.
7. See Chapter 12, above.
8. Discussed at length in P. Maddern, *Violence and Social Order: East Anglia, 1422–1442* (Oxford, 1992), pp. 175–205; B. McCree, 'Religious Guilds and Civic Order: The Case of Norwich in the Later Middle Ages', *Speculum*, lxvii (1992), pp. 69–97; idem, 'Peacemaking and its Limits in Late Medieval Norwich', *EHR*, cix (1994), pp. 831–66.
9. *RCN*, i, p. 109. The city had incurred a massive fine in 1266 for admitting rebels against Henry III, but its liberties were first taken into royal hands in 1285, after infringements of Edward I's prerogative (ibid., p. 32). The attack on the cathedral priory in 1272, discussed in Chapter 2, above, had done little to improve relations between city and monarch. There were further eruptions in 1377, in 1381, during the Peasants' Revolt, and again in 1415, this time fuelled by conflict between the 'commons' and the ruling elite: ibid., pp. 65–6, 94; R. B. Dobson, ed., *The Peasants' Revolt of 1381*(second edn, London 1983), part four.
10. *RCN*, i, pp. lxxix-lxxxvi, 114–22, 328–56; R. L. Storey, *The End of the House of Lancaster* (London, 1966), p. 225.
11. Thomas Tusser, *Five Hundreth Points of Good Husbandry* (London, 1573), Sig. Bb. ii, pp. 29–30. He was, however, helped by Dean Salisbury.
12. T. Park, ed., *Nugae antiquae* (2 vols, London, 1804), ii, p. 170.

13. *IJ*, 30 Oct. 1790.
14. From canto xx of *Poly-Olbion*, in R. Southey, ed., *Select Works of the British Poets* (London, 1831), p. 50. Alexander Neville's *Description of the Citie of Norwich*, appended to the 1623 edition of his *Norfolke Furies and their Foyle*, contains an even more fulsome eulogy to Norwich: 'So all sufficient in herselfe,/ And so complete is shee,/ That if neede were of all the Realme,/ The mistresse she might be.'
15. John Taylor, *A Late Weary, Merry Voyage and Journey* (London, 1650), pp. 17–18.
16. J. Freeman, ed., *The Worthies of England* (London, 1952), p. 419. He also emphasised the Dutch contribution to the city's strong horticultural traditions. His work must have been known to the anonymous author of *A Compleat History of the Famous City of Norwich* (London, 1728), whose description of the 'flowery, fragrant, fruitful and delicious gardens and orchards' and the 'lively verdure of the trees giving a delectable shade to the houses, making the whole appear like a city in a grove or a grove in a city', is even more effusive (ibid., p. 2).
17. *HMC, Thirteenth Report, Appendix II, Portland Manuscripts II* (London, 1893), pp. 269–70. Baskerville seems to have followed what had become the standard 'tour' for visitors, whose reactions are thus remarkably similar. See, for instance, the comments of the Dutch artist, William Schellinks: M. Exwood and H. L. Lehmann, eds, *The Journal of William Schellinks' Travels in England, 1661–1663* (Camden Society, fifth series, i, 1993), pp. 158–60.
18. John Evelyn (1671) cared no more than Baskerville for the duke of Norfolk's palace, which he pronounced 'an old wretched building', further marred by its proximity to the market place and the uninspiring Wensum. He pronounced the river 'a very narrow muddy one and without any extent': E. S. de Beer, ed., *The Diary of John Evelyn* (6 vols, Oxford, 1955), iii, pp. 592–5.
19. For a history of the market, see U. Priestley, *The Great Market: A Survey of Nine Hundred Years of Norwich Provision Market* (Norwich, 1987).
20. BL, Add. MS 71699A, fo. 37v.
21. C. Morris, ed., *The Journeys of Celia Fiennes* (London, 1949), pp. 146–50.
22. Daniel Defoe, *A Tour through England and Wales* (2 vols, London, 1927), i, p. 23.
23. As B. M. S. Campbell has shown in his study of dairy farming in Norfolk, the demand for meat, cheese, butter and hides shaped the pastoral economy of the region from the thirteenth century onwards: 'Commercial Dairy Production on Medieval English Demesnes: The Case of Norfolk', *Anthropozoologica*, xvi (1992), pp. 107–18. See also, idem, *English Seignorial Agriculture, 1250–1450* (Cambridge, 2000), pp. 148–50, 270–89.
24. N. Scarfe, ed., *A Frenchman's Year in Suffolk* (Suffolk Records Society, xxx,

1988), pp. 205–6; idem and R. G. Wilson, 'The Norwich Textile Industry in 1784', *Textile History*, xxiii (1992), pp. 113–20.

25. *The Norwich Directory: or Gentlemen and Tradesmen's Assistant* (Norwich, 1783; reprinted 1983), pp. iii–vi, presents a catalogue of 'Hints for Public Improvements', mostly directed against the medieval fabric.
26. J. Pound, 'Poverty and Public Health in Norwich, 1845–1880', in C. Barringer, ed., *Norwich in the Nineteenth Century* (Norwich, 1984), p. 51.
27. Although it cannot be described as a history of Norwich, Bartholomew Cotton's *Historia Anglicana* was compiled in the city, where the author lived as a Benedictine monk. Only part of the text is his own work, much being drawn from an earlier chronicle by William Hoo, the precentor of Norwich cathedral priory. Both authors took a lively interest in local affairs (not least the attack on the priory in 1272), and there are references to such events as the floods of 1289: A. Gransden, *Historical Writing in England*, i, *c. 550 – c. 1307* (London and New York, 1996), pp. 444–8; *HA*, pp. 146–53, 172.
28. William Worcester, *Itineraries*, ed. J. H. Harvey (Oxford, 1969), pp. 211, 234–9; A. Gransden, 'Antiquarian Studies in Fifteenth-Century England', *Antiquaries Journal*, lx (1980), pp. 75–97. John Kirkpatrick (d. 1728) dismissed the common belief that cracks then apparent in the structure of the castle were made 'by the earthquake which happened at the crucifixion of our Saviour', but accepted the rest of the legend of Gwyntelius and Caesar: J. Kirkpatrick, *A History of the Religious Orders and Communities of the Hospitals and Castle of Norwich, Written about the Year 1725*, ed. D. Turner (Yarmouth, 1845), pp. 242–5. For the persistence of these ideas see B. Ayers, 'Norwich: A City and its Image', in A. Longcroft and R. Joby, eds, *East Anglian Studies* (Norwich, 1995), pp. 1–10.
29. J. Caius, *A Boke, or Conseill against the Disease Commonly Called the Sweate, or Sweatyng Sicknesse* (London, 1552), introduction, sig. A, fo. 7r.
30. W. Hamper, ed., *The Life, Diary and Correspondence of Sir William Dugdale* (London, 1827), p. 353.
31. G. Keynes, ed., *The Works of Sir Thomas Browne*, iii (London, 1928), pp. 123–43. Discussed in G. Parry, *The Trophies of Time: English Antiquarians of the Seventeenth Century* (Oxford, 1995), pp. 259–60.
32. H. Smith and R. Virgoe, 'Norfolk', in C. R. J. Currie and C. P. Lewis, eds, *English County Histories: A Guide* (Stroud, 1994), pp. 282–3.
33. See note 4, above.
34. F. Johnson, 'John Kirkpatrick, Antiquary', *NA*, xxiii (1929), pp. 285–304. Some of Kirkpatrick's antiquarian notes survive as NRO, NCR, 21F. Extracts may be found in *RCN*, ii, pp. 404–13. Many were lost.
35. Notably *Leet Jurisdiction in the City of Norwich during the Thirteenth and Fourteenth Centuries* (Selden Society, v, 1891).

36. See A. Carter, 'The Anglo-Saxon Origins of Norwich', *Anglo- Saxon England*, vii (1978), pp. 178–9, for a discussion of this work.
37. 'Preface', *NA*, i (1847), p. xi. Not coincidentally, the inaugural meeting of the Archaeological Institute of Great Britain and Ireland was held in Norwich in July 1847. As president-elect, Bishop Stanley hosted the gathering, and drew attention in his address to 'the rapid growth of archaeological science' in the region: *Memoirs Illustrative of the History and Antiquities of Norfolk and the City of Norwich* (London, 1851), p. v.
38. See E. Darroch and B. Taylor, *A Bibliography of Norfolk History* (Norwich, 1975), for a list of these publications. Not all adhered to the highest standards of scholarship. The last word on Walter Rye (d. 1929), the most prolific – but not always the most reliable – of these authors, must go to A. Hassell Smith, who notes that he was 'a long-distance runner, which perhaps accounts for his haste, and a controversialist, which perhaps accounts for his inaccuracies': idem and Virgoe, 'Norfolk', p. 285.
39. Blomefield's work was completed to a less exacting standard by his friend, Charles Parkin, over the next eleven years, although publication was delayed until 1769–75. Contributors to *The History of Norwich* have used the London edition of 1805–10, which appeared in eleven volumes, of which Norwich comprises numbers three and four.
40. His struggle is recounted in D. Stoker, ed., *The Correspondence of the Reverend Francis Blomefield* (NRS, lv, 1992), pp. 15–56.
41. Blomefield, *Norfolk*, i, p. xvi.
42. Most recently, B. Ayers, *English Heritage Book of Norwich* (London, 1994; revised and enlarged in 2003 under the title *Norwich: A Fine City*); M. Atkin, *Norwich: A History and Guide* (Stroud, 1993); and F. Meeres, *A History of Norwich* (Chichester, 1998), each of which provide profusely illustrated and accessible introductions to the city's history based on a wide range of sources. A useful collection of essays may be found in Barringer, *Norwich in the Nineteenth Century*.
43. *RCN*, i, pp. xxxix–xxx, lvii, lxxix; ii, pp. cxxi, 254.
44. H. T. Riley, ed., *Munimenta Gildhallae Londonensis* (4 vols, London, 1859–62), i, pp. xviii–xix, 3–4; W. Kellaway, 'John Carpenter's *Liber Albus*', *Guildhall Studies*, iii (1978), pp. 67–84.
45. Edited by D. Palliser, Cambridge, 2000.
46. Although he still considered Kirkpatrick to be 'one of the most able, industrious, learned and useful antiquaries whom the county has produced': introduction to Kirkpatrick, *History of the Religious Orders*, p. vi.
47. F. Meeres, *Guide to the Records of Norwich Cathedral* (Norwich, 1998).
48. See the Bibliography at the end of each volume of *The History of Norwich* for a list of major publications.

49. One formerly crossed the castle dyke, and made a particular impression on Thomas Baskerville. There was, he reported, 'only one great and entire arch under it, and such vast breadth and height that it surpasses any of the bridges in Yorkshire': *HMC, Thirteenth Report, Appendix II, Portland Manuscripts II*, p. 269.
50. See Chapter 5, above.
51. For a broad survey of developments see B. Ayers, 'The Archaeology of Towns in Norfolk', in S. Margeson, B. Ayers and S. Heywood, eds, *A Festival of Norfolk Archaeology* (Norfolk and Norwich Archaeological Society, 1996), pp. 65–71.
52. B. Green and R. M. Young, *Norwich: The Growth of a City* (Norwich, 1963).
53. Carter, 'Anglo-Saxon Origins of Norwich', pp. 182–3.
54. A. Carter, 'The Norwich Survey. Excavations in Norwich – 1971: An Interim Report', *NA*, xxxv (1972), pp. 410–16.
55. S. Jennings, *Eighteen Centuries of Pottery from Norwich* (EAA, report 13, 1981); A. Carter, *Excavations in Norwich, 1971–1978: Part I* (EAA, report 15, 1982); M. W. Atkin, A. Carter and D. H. Evans, *Excavations in Norwich 1971–1978: Part II* (EAA, report 26, 1985); M. W. Atkin and D. H. Evans, *Excavations in Norwich 1971–1978: Part III* (EAA, report 100, 2002).
56. S. Margeson, *Norwich Households: Medieval and Post-Medieval Finds from Norwich Survey Excavations 1971–78* (EAA, report 58, 1993); U. M. Priestley, ed., *Men of Property: An Analysis of the Norwich Enrolled Deeeds 1285–1311* (Norwich, 1983). See also, Atkin, *Norwich History and Guide*, which draws upon his work for the Survey, and idem and S. Margeson, *Life on a Medieval Street* (Norwich, 1985).
57. J. Campbell, 'Norwich', in M. Lobel, ed., *Historic Towns*, ii (London, 1975).
58. B. Ayers, *A Waterfront Excavation at Whitefriars Street Car Park, Norwich, 1979* (EAA, report 17, 1983), pp. 1–60; idem, *Excavations within the North-East Bailey of Norwich Castle* (EAA, report 28, 1985); idem, *Excavations at St Martin-at-Palace Plain, Norwich, 1981* (EAA, report 37, 1987); *Excavations at Fishergate, Norwich, 1985* (EAA, report 68, 1994); O. Beazley, 'Excavations in St Martin-at-Palace Church, 1987', in idem and B. Ayers, *Two Medieval Churches in Norfolk* (EAA, report 96, 2001), pp. 1–63. For other reports in preparation, see Chapter 1, above.
59. B. Ayers, *Digging under the Doorstep: Recent Excavations in Norwich* (Norwich Museums Service, 1983); idem, *Digging Deeper: Recent Archaeology in Norwich* (Norwich Museums Service, 1987); idem, J. Bown and J. Reeve, *Digging Ditches: Archaeology and Development in Norwich* (Norfolk Museums Service, 1992).
60. M. J. Daunton, *Coal Metropolis: Cardiff 1870–1914* (Leicester, 1977); T. M. Devine and G. Jackson, eds, *Glasgow*, i, *Beginnings to 1830* (Manchester,

1995); W. H. Fraser and I. Maver, eds, *Glasgow*, ii, *1830 to 1912* (Manchester, 1996); J. Beckett, ed., *A Centenary History of Nottingham* (Manchester, 1997); C. Binfield and others, eds, *The History of the City of Sheffield, 1843–1993* (3 vols, Sheffield, 1993).

61. See Chapter 6, above.
62. H. C. Darby, *The Domesday Geography of Eastern England* (Cambridge, 1971), pp. 111, 139–40.
63. See Chapter 13, above, and P. Dunn, 'After the Black Death: Society and Economy in Late Fourteenth-Century Norwich' (UEA, Norwich, PhD, 2004), pp. 42–49, for a discussion of population figures.
64. C. Baswell, 'Aeneas in 1381', in R. Copland, D. Lawton and W. Scase, eds, *New Medieval Literatures* (Cambridge, 2002), p. 33.
65. T. Graham and A. G. Watson, *The Recovery of the Past in Early Elizabethan England* (Cambridge, Cambridge Bibliographical Society, 1998), pp. 20–21.
66. In his introduction to *The Tudor and Stuart Town: A Reader in Urban History* (London, 1990), pp. 22–3, for example, Jonathan Barry noted the general dearth of studies about health and the urban environment, urging an interdisciplinary approach to such issues as the impact of housing and water facilities.
67. See, for example, M. Pelling, *The Common Lot: Sickness, Medical Occupations and the Urban Poor in Early Modern England* (London, 1998).
68. De Beer, *Diary of John Evelyn*, iii, pp. 594–5.
69. Scarfe, *A Frenchman's Year*, pp. 209.
70. By Dr Victor Morgan, of the School of History, UEA. See idem, 'The Construction of Civic Memory in Early Modern Norwich', in M. Kwint, C. Breward and J. Aynsley, eds, *Material Memories: Design and Evocation* (Oxford, 1999), pp. 183–97; 'Perambulating and Consumable Emblems: The Norwich Evidence', in M. Bath and D. Russell, eds, *Deviceful Settings: The English Renaissance Emblem and its Contexts* (New York, 1999), pp. 167–202; and 'A Ceremonious Society – An Aspect of Power in Early Modern Norwich: The Aural Dimension', in A. Goldgar and R. Frost, eds, *The New Institutional History* (Leiden, forthcoming, 2004).
71. Recent projects concerned with market networks around medieval London and the way its people were fed provide a model that could profitably be adopted in the case of Norwich: J. A. Galloway and M. Murphy, 'Feeding the City: Medieval London and its Agrarian Hinterland', *London Journal*, xvi (1991), pp. 3–14; B. M. S. Campbell and others, *A Medieval Capital and its Grain Supply: Agrarian Production and Distribution in the London Region* (Historical Geography Research Series, xxx, 1993); J. A. Galloway and others, 'Fuelling the City: Production and Distribution of Firewood and Fuel in London's Region, 1290–1400', *EcHR*, xlix (1996), pp. 447–72. See also, articles

by Galloway and Murphy in M. Carlin and J. T. Rosenthal, eds, *Food and Eating in Medieval Europe* (London and Rio Grande, Ohio, 1998), pp. 87–100, 117–31, and P. Nightingale, 'Norwich, London and the Regional Integration of Norfolk's Economy in the First Half of the Fourteenth Century', in J. A. Galloway, ed., *Trade, Urban Hinterlands and Market Integration c. 1300 – 1600* (Centre for Metropolitan History, Working Papers, series three, 2000), pp. 83–101.

72. N. Pevsner, *The Buildings of England: North-East Norfolk and Norwich* (London, 1962), p. 204.
73. BL, Add. MS 71699A, fos 38r–39v.

Notes to Chapter 1: The Urban Landscape

1. N. Pevsner, *The Buildings of England: North-East Norfolk and Norwich* (London, 1962), p. 204.
2. I am grateful to my colleagues, Andy Hutcheson, John Schofield, Andy Shelley and Liz Shepherd Popescu, for their helpful and thoughtful comments on this paper, and also to my wife, Robina McNeil, for both ideas and encouragement.
3. B. Redhead, *Manchester: A Celebration* (London, 1993), p. 7.
4. J. Kirkpatrick, *The Streets and Lanes of the City of Norwich*, ed., W. Hudson (Norwich, 1889), pp. 99–103.
5. See *History of Norwich*, ii, Chapter 5. There are numerous references to cockeys in the medieval property deeds of the city. As an example, see D. Evans, 'Excavations on Botolph Street and St George's Street (Sites 170N, 281N and 284N)', in M. Atkin, A. Carter and D. Evans, *Excavations in Norwich, 1971–1978: Part II* (EAA, report 26, 1985), pp. 87 et seq., where part of a lost course of the *Dalymond* stream is evident from the documentation.
6. E. Shepherd Popescu, *Excavations at Norwich Castle, 1987–98* (EAA, forthcoming).
7. W. Hudson, *How the City of Norwich Grew into Shape* (Norwich, 1896), p. 49.
8. Hudson considered Norwich castle to be a foundation of the Angles, perhaps in the sixth century. Other English castles were frequently held to be of similar antiquity until the publication in 1912 of E. S. Armitage's *Early Norman Castles of the British Isles.*
9. C. Morris, ed., *The Illustrated Journeys of Celia Fiennes* (London, 1982), p. 137.
10. The most extensive recent work in this area was undertaken by the Norfolk Archaeological Unit ahead of the construction of the Norwich Southern Bypass. For the prehistoric material, see T. Ashwin and S. Bates, *Excavations on the Norwich Southern Bypass, 1989–91 Part I* (EAA, report 91, 2000), passim.

11. For Palace Street, see E. Shepherd, ed., *Norfolk Archaeological Unit Annual Review, 1999–2000* (Norwich, 2000), p. 14. For the Millennium Site, see D. Gurney and K. Penn, eds, 'Excavations and Surveys in Norfolk, 1999', *NA*, xliii (2000), p. 533.
12. The street-name is of interest. It derives from *berg* 'hill', with the suffix 'street' being extremely unusual in Norwich, perhaps itself indicative of Roman origin. See K. I. Sandred and B. Lindstrøm, *The Place-Names of Norfolk*, i, *The Place-Names of the City of Norwich* (English Place-Name Society, lxi, 1989), p. 88.
13. For a recent excavation of a similar Roman causeway at Nordelph in Norfolk, see H. Wallis, 'Roman Routeways in the Fens', *Britannia*, forthcoming.
14. A record of 1287 for the medieval river bridge at the southern end of Oak Street refers to the *duos pontes de Koslanye*, implying similar use of an island to assist bridging (Sandred and Lindstrøm, *Place-Names of the City of Norwich*, p. 15). Excavations by the Norfolk Archaeological Unit west of Oak Street in 1996 uncovered part of an arm of the river, subsequently infilled: B. S. Nenk, C. Haith and J. Bradley, 'Medieval Britain and Ireland in 1996', *Medieval Archaeology*, xli (1997), p. 13. See also *Current Archaeology*, clxx (2000), p. 51.
15. Personal communication from Barbara Green.
16. A Roman farmstead has been postulated on the north bank of the river following the discovery of a concentration of Roman finds in the area: M. Atkin and A. Carter, 'Excavations in Norwich – 1975/6. The Norwich Survey – Fifth Interim Report', *NA*, xxxvi (1976), p. 196.
17. B. S. Ayers, *Norwich* (London, 1994), p. 22.
18. Blomefield, *Norfolk*, iv, p. 326.
19. J. P. Roberts and M. Atkin, 'St Benedict's Church (Site 157N)', in A. Carter, ed., *Excavations in Norwich 1971–1978: Part I* (EAA, report 15, 1982), p. 11.
20. J. Campbell, 'Norwich' in M. Lobel, ed., *Historic Towns*, ii (London, 1975), p. 5.
21. Evidence for Middle Saxon activity has come from Barn Road, J. G. Hurst, 'Excavations at Barn Road, Norwich, 1954–55', *NA*, xxxiii (1963), pp. 131–79; the Cathedral Close, D. M. Wilson, 'Medieval Britain in 1956', *Medieval Archaeology*, i (1957), p. 148; Prince of Wales Road, P. Emery, *Norwich Greyfriars: Excavations at the Former Mann Egerton Site, Prince of Wales Road, Norwich, 1992–95* (EAA, forthcoming); and St Martin-at-Palace Plain. Stray finds of Middle Saxon pottery have also been unearthed on King Street (a personal communication from Andy Shelley). There is now also a suggestion that burials uncovered in Area 45 at Castle Mall – a non-riparian context – may be Middle Saxon in date (Shepherd Popescu, *Excavations at Norwich Castle*).

22. O. Beazley, 'Excavations in St Martin-at-Palace Church, 1987', in idem and B. Ayers, *Two Medieval Churches in Norfolk* (EAA, report 96, 2001), pp. 1–63.
23. A. Carter, 'The Anglo-Saxon Origins of Norwich: The Problems and Approaches', *Anglo-Saxon England*, vii (1978), pp. 175–204. Place-name evidence is provided by Sandred and Lindstrøm, *Place-Names of the City of Norwich*, p. 2.
24. B. S. Ayers, *Excavations at Fishergate, Norwich, 1985* (EAA, report 68, 1994), passim.
25. A silver penny of Athelstan showing the mint name NORVIC is illustrated in Ayers, *Norwich*, p. 29. See also C. R. Manning, 'On Saxon Coins Struck at Norwich, with the Moneyer's Name of Manning', *NA*, xiii (1896), pp. 93–9. A summary of recent discoveries is provided in B. Rushin, 'Making Money in the City – The Story of the Minting of Coins in Norwich', *Suffolk and Norfolk Life* (June, 1999), pp. 20–21.
26. E. O. Blake, ed., *Liber Eliensis* (Camden Society, third series, xcii, 1962), p. 20.
27. B. S. Ayers, *Excavations in the North-East Bailey of Norwich Castle, 1979* (EAA, report 28, 1985), p. 29 and figure 24; Shepherd Popescu, *Excavations at Norwich Castle.*
28. W. Hudson, 'On a Sculptured Stone Recently Removed from a House on the Site of the Church of St Vedast, Norwich', *NA*, xiii (1898), pp. 116–24.
29. B. S. Ayers, *Excavations at St Martin-at-Palace Plain, Norwich, 1981* (EAA, report 37, 1987), p. 63, figure 56 and plate xxxiv.
30. A. Borg, *Medieval Sculpture from Norwich Cathedral* (Norwich, 1980), p. 12 and plate 3. See also G. Zarnecki, *English Romanesque Art, 1066–1200* (London, 1984), p. 167.
31. Sandred and Lindstrøm, *Place-Names of the City of Norwich*, passim.
32. Sandred and Lindstrøm, *Place-Names of the City of Norwich*, pp. 8, 92.
33. R. Morris, *Churches in the Landscape* (London, 1980), pp. 175–6.
34. Campbell, 'Norwich', p. 4, n. 42. Terriers for St Clement of 1834 and 1845 list suburban garden ground of seventy acres, arable land of 110 acres and meadow and pasture of twenty acres. Payments continued to be made until 1925 (personal communication from Margot Tillyard).
35. A personal communication from the late Alan Carter.
36. Dr Barbara Crawford, in recent correspondence with the author, doubts whether the church is as early as 900, preferring an eleventh-century date and *imposition* of the church and its parish upon the urban area. Her ideas have some force and, for the moment, the matter must be left open pending her considered view in her forthcoming publication on churches dedicated to St Clement. It is also worth noting that churches dedicated jointly to both Saints Clement and Olaf can be rededications of earlier churches.
37. Evidence for the ditch was seen in Norwich Survey excavations at Alms Lane

in 1976 (Atkin, Carter and Evans, *Excavations in Norwich, 1971–1978: Part II*, p. 147) and, more extensively with traces of the rampart, at Calvert Street, which was excavated in 1989 by the Norfolk Archaeological Unit: D. Gaimster, S. Margeson and M. Hurley, 'Medieval Britain and Ireland in 1989', *Medieval Archaeology*, xxxiv (1990), p. 203; see also B. S. Ayers, J. Bown and J. Reeve, *Digging Ditches* (Norwich, 1992), pp. 7–9. Interestingly, further excavation in 1998, also on Calvert Street but south of the 1989 excavation, failed to locate either ditch or rampart, perhaps a result of early medieval quarrying: J. Bradley, M. Gaimster and C. Haith, 'Medieval Britain and Ireland 1998', *Medieval Archaeology*, xliii (1999), p. 269.

38. S. M. Youngs, J. Clark and T. Barry, 'Medieval Britain and Ireland in 1985', *Medieval Archaeology*, xxx (1986), p. 162.
39. W. Hudson, 'On an Ancient Timber Roadway across the River Wensum at Fye Bridge, Norwich', *NA*, xiii (1898), pp. 217–32. See also note 10 above.
40. J. Bradley and M. Gaimster, 'Medieval Britain and Ireland in 1999', *Medieval Archaeology*, xliv (2000), p. 295.
41. S. L. Dunmore, '171N. 22 Wensum Street', in J. P. Roberts, ed., 'Excavations in Norwich – 1974. The Norwich Survey – Fourth Interim Report', *NA*, xxxvi (1975), p. 101.
42. H. R. Loyn, 'Boroughs and Mints AD 900–1066', in R. H. M. Dolley, ed., *Anglo-Saxon Coins* (London, 1961), pp. 122–35.
43. Possibly an early market place. 'Stump Cross' refers to a stone cross for which, however, the earliest known documentary evidence is as late as 1500: see Kirkpatrick, *Streets and Lanes*, p. 83.
44. Again, probably a pre-conquest foundation. An All Saints church is mentioned in Domesday Book and probably refers to All Saints Fyebridgegate (Magdalen Street) but *may* be a reference to All Saints Westlegate south of the river. See P. Brown, ed., *Domesday Book: Norfolk* (Chichester, 1984), part one, pp. 61, 116b.
45. With the possible exception of a fragmentary post-hole structure (ref. A 01) located at Alms Lane in 1976 and dated to *c.* 1000–1050: see M. Atkin, 'Excavations on Alms Lane (Site 302N)', in Atkin, Carter and Evans, *Excavations in Norwich, 1971–1978: Part II*, pp. 145–6.
46. Initial foreshore consolidation off Oak Street appears to date from the late tenth or eleventh century but activity here seems mainly to have been industrial, specifically extracting iron ore from river gravels. Evidence for this was found close to the river in 1996: see above, note 16. Similar observations had been made at Alms Lane in 1976: Atkin, 'Excavations on Alms Lane', pp. 145 et seq.
47. A coin of Alfred dating from 887–9 has been recovered from excavations south of Prince of Wales Road. It was located within a post-hole of a sunken-

featured building: P. Emery, 'The Franciscan Friary', *Current Archaeology*, clxx (2000), p. 73.

48. A. Hutcheson, 'The French Borough', *Current Archaeology*, clxx (2000), pp. 64–8.
49. Sandred and Lindstrøm, *Place Names of the City of Norwich*, pp. 114–15.
50. All work by the Norfolk Archaeological Unit. See A. Shelley, 'King Street', *Current Archaeology*, clxx (2000), p. 81.
51. They are discussed in Campbell, 'Norwich', p. 3.
52. Brown, *Domesday Book: Norfolk*, part 1, p. 61.
53. B. S. Ayers, 'The Cathedral Site before 1066', *Norwich Cathedral*, pp. 59–72.
54. A. Shelley, 'King Street', pp. 84–5.
55. A. Shelley, 'Evaluation Excavations at Cannon Wharf, Norwich', Norfolk Archaeological Unit, upublished Client Report, 296. See also Shepherd, *Norfolk Archaeological Unit Annual Review, 1999–2000*, p. 47.
56. Ayers, 'Cathedral Site', p. 70.
57. The evaluation excavation by the Norfolk Archaeological Unit is reported in Bradley, Gaimster and Haith, 'Medieval Britain and Ireland 1998', p. 270, and a report of the main excavation by the Northamptonshire Archaeological Unit is currently in preparation.
58. Shepherd Popescu, *Excavations at Norwich Castle, 1987–98*.
59. M. Biddle, 'Towns', in D. M. Wilson ed., *The Archaeology of Anglo-Saxon England* (London, 1976), p. 136.
60. The bank south of the River Ouse survives in part. The northern defences were sectioned by excavation in 1997: see M. Gaimster, C. Haith and J. Bradley, 'Medieval Britain and Ireland in 1997', *Medieval Archaeology*, xlii (1998), p. 147. A longer summary may be found in E. Shepherd, ed., *Norfolk Archaeological Unit Annual Review, 1996–1997* (Norwich, 1997), p. 25.
61. Biddle, 'Towns', p. 136.
62. D. Whitelock with D. C. Douglas and S. I. Tucker, eds, *The Anglo-Saxon Chronicle: A Revised Translation* (corrected edn, London, 1962), p. 87.
63. Carter, 'Anglo-Saxon Origins of Norwch', figure 8d.
64. Shepherd Popescu, *Excavations at Norwich Castle*; Emery, *Norwich Greyfriars*.
65. Shepherd Popescu, *Excavations at Norwich Castle*; *Current Archaeology*, clxx (2000), pp. 54 and 74.
66. M. Atkin, B. S. Ayers and J. Jennings, 'Thetford-Type Ware Production in Norwich', in P. Wade-Martins, ed., *Waterfront Excavation and Thetford Ware Production, Norwich* (EAA, report 17, 1983), pp. 61–97.
67. It should, however, be noted that the discussion section of Atkin, Ayers and Jennings states that 'the perceived westward shift of the pottery industry may ... be an illusion with the industry merely surviving longer at its western extremity ... the late kiln at Lobster Lane ... cut earlier pits. These pits

contained waster sherds from an earlier kiln or kilns which may be of similar date to vessels located further to the east. Without more fieldwork ... the development of the industry, both spatially and technologically, cannot be adequately understood': Wade-Martins, *Waterfront Excavation*, p. 96.

68. Such as butchery at St Martin-at-Palace Plain, J. Cartledge, 'Mammal Bones', in Wade-Martins, *Waterfront Excavation*, pp. 30–32.
69. Ayers, *Norwich*, p. 40.
70. Ayers, *Excavations at St Martin-at-Palace Plain*, pp. 5–21, 165–7.
71. Infilling of the river margins is the most obvious such activity with good evidence now from Fishergate on the north bank of the Wensum and St Martin-at-Palace Plain and Quayside on the south bank.
72. J. Hillam, 'Wood', in Wade-Martins, *Waterfront Excavation*, p. 45.
73. T. Williamson, *The Origins of Norfolk* (Manchester, 1993), p. 114.
74. Ayers, *Excavations in the North-East Bailey of Norwich Castle*, p. 15.
75. C. Ahrens, 'Om "stavkirkeproblemet"', *Foreningen Til Norske Fortidsminnesmerkers Bevaring* (Særtrykk Fra Årbok, 1994) pp. 37–50, where the 'Norwich-type' is used in a discussion of the development of early stave churches.
76. B. S. Nenk, S. Margeson and M. Hurley, 'Medieval Britain and Ireland, 1994', *Medieval Archaeology*, xxxix (1995), pp. 233–4.
77. These and others are set out in B. S. Ayers, 'Anglo-Saxon, Medieval and Post-Medieval (Urban)', in J. Glazebrook ed., 'Research and Archaeology: A Framework for the Eastern Counties 2: Research Agenda and Strategy', *EAA, Occasional Paper*, viii (2000), pp. 27–32.
78. Brown, *Domesday Book: Norfolk*, part 1, pp. 63, 117b. Waleran seems to have held the fee farm for taxation purposes.
79. H. W. C. Davis, ed., *Regesta Regum Anglo-Normannorum, 1066–1154* (Oxford, 1913), p. 42.
80. Orderic Vitalis records that 'They pursued Ralph the Breton to his castle ... concentrating their forces they besieged and attacked Norwich ... harrying their besieged foes by continual assaults with every kind of engine of war. For three months they continued their relentless pressure': M. Chibnall, ed., *The Ecclesiastical History of Ordericus Vitalis* (6 vols, Oxford, 1969), ii, p. 317. The action subsequently occasioned Lanfranc to send the earliest recorded battle dispatch in English history: see Ayers, *Norwich*, p. 43.
81. Shepherd Popescu, *Excavations at Norwich Castle*, explores various ideas about phasing. See also, *Current Archaeology*, clxx (2000), pp. 52–9. Excavations by the Norfolk Archaeological Unit into the mound took place in 1999–2000. These revealed an early mound below the later stone keep with a chalk rampart to the north and east enclosing an area containing traces of timber buildings and hearths. Infilling above these structures created the larger mound which had a summit diameter of 127 yards.

82. For the second charter of Edward III, see *RCN*, i, pp. 23–7. The limits of the Castle Fee may have been marked by bronze plaques on posts: B. Green, 'Bronze Plaques from Norwich', *Medieval Archaeology*, ix (1965), pp. 163–4.
83. The area east and south of Norwich seems to have been particularly populous: 'In the eastern half of the county, the two most densely occupied areas were a) the island of the two Flegg hundreds, and b) the country to the south and south west of Norwich': H. C. Darby, *The Domesday Geography of Eastern England* (Cambridge, 1952), pp. 123.
84. T. A. Heslop, *Norwich Castle Keep: Romanesque Architecture and Social Context* (Norwich, 1994), p. 66.
85. Ayers, 'Cathedral Site', passim.
86. A riot in 1272 led to the destruction of claustral buildings and the firing of the cathedral church. Fire damage can still be seen, for instance, on the inner walls of the Ethelbert Gate (where fossilised late eleventh- and early twelfth-century masonry survives) and on the surviving piers of the infirmary. For a recent assessment of the riot, see N. Tanner, 'The Cathedral and the City', in *Norwich Cathedral*, pp. 253–280.
87. *RCN*, ii, facing p. cxxxviii.
88. Heslop, *Norwich Castle Keep*, pp. 11, 62.
89. S. Heywood, 'The Romanesque Building', in *Norwich Cathedral*, pp. 73–115.
90. As examples, sunken-featured buildings found at Castle Mall and Greyfriars are paralleled in York, R. Hall, *The Viking Dig* (London, 1984), p. 67; London, A. Vince, *Saxon London: An Archaeological Investigation* (London, 1990), p. 35; and Århus, E. Roesdahl, *Viking Age Denmark* (London, 1982), pp. 79–80.
91. Brown, *Domesday Book: Norfolk*, part one, pp. 66, 118a.
92. Its subsequent name of Mancroft probably derives from '(ge)mæne croft' meaning 'common enclosure' or 'common fields': Sandred and Lindstrøm, *Place Names of the City of Norwich*, p. 71.
93. F. Woodman, 'The Rebuilding of St Peter Mancroft', in A. Longcroft and R. Joby, eds, *East Anglian Studies* (Norwich, 1995), pp. 290–4. See also Chapter 3, above.
94. The St Peter's Street tenements were destroyed for the construction of City Hall. An aerial photograph of 1921 illustrates the pattern well: P. Wade-Martins, ed., *Norfolk from the Air*, ii (Norwich, 1999), p. 102.
95. Hutcheson, 'French Borough', pp. 66–7, and plan on p. 67.
96. Ayers, *Excavations at St Martin-at-Palace Plain*, p. 153, and figure 98.
97. Hutcheson, 'French Borough', p. 67.
98. Shelley, 'King Street', p. 82 and plan on p. 83.
99. I am grateful to Elizabeth Rutledge for this information. A report on excavations undertaken in 2000 by Northamptonshire Archaeological Unit is currently forthcoming.

100. Ayers, *Excavations at St Martin-at-Palace Plain*, pp. 28, et seq.
101. A review of the documentary evidence for stone buildings in Norwich by E. Rutledge is due to appear in D. Pitte and B. Ayers, eds, *La Maison Mediévale/The Medieval House* (Rouen, 2002), pp. 103–10.
102. R. Smith, 'The Music House', *Vernacular Architecture Group Conference Papers* (Norwich, 1997, unpaginated).
103. V. D. Lipman, *The Jews of Medieval Norwich* (London, 1967), p. vii.
104. Lipman, *Jews of Medieval Norwich*, figure 13.
105. C. Rawcliffe, *The Hospitals of Medieval Norwich* (Norwich, 1995), pp. 61–2.
106. The site has been excavated. The parish was always poor and the church ceased to exist after 1468. The graveyard was used for the burial of executed criminals (the church had an additional, topographically specific, suffix – *ubi sepeliuntur suspensi* – 'where those who have been hanged are buried'), many of whom were located in groups in pits: J. Bown and A. Stirland, *Criminals and Paupers: Excavations at the Church and Graveyard of St Margaret in Combusto, Norwich, 1987* (EAA, forthcoming). See also *Current Archaeology* cxxii (1990), pp. 56–9; and B. S. Ayers, *Digging Deeper* (Norwich, 1987), pp. 11–15.
107. Work at Cannon Wharf towards the southern end of the street in 1997: see Gaimster, Haith and Bradley, 'Medieval Britain and Ireland in 1997', p. 146; and Shelley, 'King Street' p. 170.
108. For example, that from Alms Lane: Atkin, 'Excavations on Alms Lane', p. 144.
109. Brown, *Domesday Book: Norfolk*, part one, pp. 66, 118a.
110. Lava fragments of quernstones from Germany have been recovered from sites throughout the city: for examples, see D. Smith and S. Margeson, 'Querns', in S. Margeson, ed., *Norwich Households: Medieval and Post-Medieval Finds from Norwich Survey Excavations, 1971–78* (EAA, report 58, 1993), p. 202. Other finds include ceramics from the Rhineland, the Low Countries, the Beauvais region of France and Gascony: see S. Jennings, *Eighteen Centuries of Pottery from Norwich* (EAA, report 13, 1981), pp. 26–35.
111. See above, Table 2.
112. See above, pp. 52–4.
113. See above, pp. 306–8.
114. E. P. L. Brock, 'On the Excavation of the Site of Carrow Abbey, Norwich, by J. J. Colman Esq., MP, in 1880–1881', *Journal of the British Archaeological Association*, xxxviii (1882), pp. 165–214.
115. Perhaps not all; the church of St Christopher burnt down in the reign of Henry III and was not rebuilt.
116. See Chapter 7 for a discussion of population and occupations.
117. There were numerous quarries within the urban area as well as immediately outside: see B. S. Ayers, 'Building a Fine City: The Provision of Flint, Mortar

and Freestone in Medieval Norwich', in D. Parsons, ed., *Stone: Quarrying and Building in England, AD 43–1525* (Chichester, 1990), pp. 217–27.

118. Dendrochronological analysis of timbers recovered at a depth of some thirteen feet behind the riverside wall gave a felling date of the summer of 1146: see B. S. Nenk, S. Margeson and M. Hurley, 'Medieval Britain and Ireland 1993', *Medieval Archaeology*, xxxviii (1994), pp. 235–6.
119. A. Carter and J. P. Roberts, 'Excavations in Norwich – 1972. The Norwich Survey – Second Interim Report', *NA*, xxxv (1973), pp. 457–62 (excavations at Westwick Street, North).
120. Ayers, Bown and Reeve, *Digging Ditches*, p. 31.
121. Kirkpatrick, *Streets and Lanes*, p. 69.
122. Houses on the site appear on Cuningham's plan of 1558: R. Frostick, *The Printed Plans of Norwich, 1558–1840: A Carto-Bibliography* (Norwich, 2002), pp. 1–4. The area is now occupied by a late nineteenth-century row of terraced houses. Fines for encroachments may, in practice, have constituted an unofficial type of building tax.
123. C. Rawcliffe, *Medicine for the Soul: The Life, Death and Resurrection of an English Medieval Hospital* (Stroud, 1999), p. 33.
124. H. Sutermeister, *The Norwich Blackfriars* (Norwich, 1977), passim.
125. The friars had to acquire land already owned by individual citizens. Many of the deeds survive and have been analysed and mapped: see M. Tillyard, 'The Acquisition by the Norwich Blackfriars of the Site for their Church *c.* 1310–1325', in eadem, S. Kelly and E. Rutledge, *Men of Property: An Analysis of the Norwich Enrolled Deeds, 1285–1311* (Norwich, 1983), pp. 5–11, and fold-out following p. 70.
126. As revealed by excavations by the Norfolk Archaeological Unit in 1991 in the cloister garth: B. S. Nenk, S. Margeson and M. Hurley, 'Medieval Britain and Ireland in 1991', *Medieval Archaeology*, xxxvi (1992), p. 253.
127. Bradley, Gaimster and Haith, 'Medieval Britain and Ireland in 1998', p. 269.
128. Blomefield, *Norfolk*, iii , pp. 144–9; *RCN*, i, pp. 348–53.
129. Blomefield, *Norfolk*, iii, p. 119.
130. *RCN*, ii, p. 220.
131. The excavated remains of the south face of the gate-tower of this structure remain visible.
132. Ayers 1990, 'Building a Fine City', p. 220.
133. B. S. Ayers, R. Smith and M. Tillyard, 'The Cow Tower, Norwich: A Detailed Survey and Partial Reinterpretation', *Medieval Archaeology*, xxxii (1988), p. 184–207.
134. Ayers, Smith and Tillyard, 'Cow Tower', p. 205.
135. Ayers, 'Building a Fine City', pp. 220–21.
136. The lime-kiln is illustrated in Hutcheson, 'French Borough', p. 68.

137. S. Kelly, 'The Economic Topography and Structure of Norwich, *c.* 1300', in eadem, Rutledge and Tillyard, *Men of Property*, p. 32. See also Chapter 7, above.
138. An evaluation excavation off Mountergate within the area of the Augustinian friary revealed deep infilling deposits: Bradley, Gaimster and Haith, 'Medieval Britain and Ireland in 1998', p. 269.
139. Kelly, 'Economic Topography', p. 32.
140. P. Cattermole, *Church Bells and Bell-Ringing: A Norfolk Profile* (London, 1990), pp. 141–2, 146, et seq. Bell-founding pits have been located off Timberhill at the Castle Mall excavations (Shepherd Popescu, *Excavations at Norwich Castle*) and at the site of the Franciscan Friary (Emery, 'Franciscan Friary', p. 78).
141. Atkin, Ayers and Jennings, 'Thetford-Type Ware', in Wade-Martins, *Waterfront Excavations*, p. 96.
142. Sandred and Lindstrøm, *Place Names of the City of Norwich*, passim.
143. Carter and Roberts, 'Excavations in Norwich – 1972', pp. 457–62.
144. *RCN*, ii, p. 224.
145. Ayers, *Norwich*, p. 78.
146. See also p. 229, above; and A. Shelley, *Dragon Hall: Excavations and Surveys of a Late Medieval Merchant's Hall* (EAA, forthcoming); idem, 'King Street', pp. 82–4.
147. Shelley, 'King Street', p. 84.
148. R. Smith and A. Carter, 'Function and Site: Aspects of Norwich Buildings before 1700', *Vernacular Architecture*, xiv (1983), pp. 5–18 and figure 3. The paper discusses undercrofts with close examination of the Bridewell and Dragon Hall as well as a third important surviving medieval building, that of Stranger's Hall.
149. A. Carter, J. P. Roberts and H. Sutermeister, 'Excavations in Norwich – 1973. The Norwich Survey – Third Interim Report', *NA*, xxxvi (1974), p. 56.
150. D. Evans and A. Carter, 'Excavations on 31–51 Pottergate (Site 149N)', in Atkin, Carter and Evans, *Excavations in Norwich, 1971–1978: Part II*, pp. 9–85.
151. Atkin, 'Excavations on Alms Lane', passim.
152. Summarised in M. W. Atkin, 'Medieval Clay-Walled Building in Norwich', *NA*, xli (1991), pp. 171–85. Atkin has also provided an overview of the work undertaken on buildings by the Norwich Survey in idem, 'The Norwich Survey, 1971–1985', in J. Gardiner, ed., *Flat Lands and Wetlands* (EAA, report ,50, 1993), pp. 127–43. A more recent study is in B. S. Ayers, 'Domestic Architecture in Norwich from the Twelfth to the Seventeenth Century', in *Lübecker Kolloquium zur Stadtarchäologie im Hanseraum*, iii (Lübeck, 2001), pp. 35–48.
153. A shingle was uncovered in a twelfth-century context at St Martin-at-Palace Plain: Ayers, *Excavations at St Martin-at-Palace Plain*, p. 108 and figure 85.

154. Ayers, *Norwich*, p. 33; Emery, *Norwich Greyfriars.*
155. A report by J. Percival on this work by the Norfolk Archaeological Unit is forthcoming.
156. Emery, 'Franciscan Friary', p. 77 and plan on p. 74.
157. See Chapter 3, above.
158. Ayers, Bown and Reeve, *Digging Ditches*, p. 32.
159. Sutermeister, *Norwich Blackfriars*, p. 3.
160. N. Spencer and A. Kent, *The Old Churches of Norwich* (Norwich, 1976), pp. 44–5.
161. H. Howard and D. Park, 'Oyster Shell Painter's Palette', forthcoming in Emery, *Norwich Greyfriars.*
162. H. Sutermeister, *The Norwich Guildhall* (Norwich, undated), pp. 9–12.
163. Evans and Carter, 'Excavations on 31–51 Pottergate', pp. 9–27.
164. Emery, *Norwich Greyfriars.*
165. Campbell, 'Norwich', pp. 23–4.
166. See T. R. Slater ed., *Towns in Decline AD 100–1600* (Aldershot, 2000), passim, for recent appraisals utilising much archaeological as well as historical data.
167. G. Astill, 'Archaeology and the Late Medieval Urban Decline', in Slater, *Towns in Decline*, pp. 217–19.
168. Astill, 'Archaeology', pp. 229–30.
169. See Chapter 11, above.
170. G. Borrow, *Lavengro* (London, 1896 edition), p. 96.

Notes to Chapter 2: Norwich before 1300

1. Cotton, *HA*, p. 148.
2. E. Rutledge, 'Immigration and Population Growth in Early Fourteenth-Century Norwich: Evidence from the Tithing Roll', *Urban History Yearbook* (1988), pp. 15–30, especially p. 271. The actual figure was maybe lower, or, indeed, higher. For other estimates, see *RCN*, ii, p. cxix; J. C. Russell, *British Medieval Population* (Albuquerque, New Mexico, 1948), pp. 285, 292–3; J. Campbell, 'Norwich', in M. Lobel, ed., *Historic Towns*, ii (London, 1975), p. 10. Rutledge's estimate is the highest and the most carefully supported.
3. A. Dyer, 'Ranking Lists of English Medieval Towns', in D. M. Palliser, ed., *The Cambridge Urban History of Britain*, i, *600–1540* (Cambridge, 2000), pp. 752–4; C. Stephenson, *A Study of Urban Origins in England* (Cambridge, Massachusetts, 1933), pp. 221–5.
4. N. E. S. A. Hamilton, ed., *De Gestis Pontificum* (RS, 1870), p. 151.
5. B. Ayers, *Norwich* (London, 1994), p. 63. The habitable area would have been to an extent limited by liability to flood.
6. Open spaces were an industrial resource for a cloth-producing city which

needed tenter grounds. The thirteenth-century gardens included the earliest private herb garden known in England: see above, p. 321.

7. H. C. Darby, 'Domesday England', in idem, ed., *A New Historical Geography of England before 1600* (Cambridge, 1976), p. 46.
8. J. Campbell, 'Domesday Herrings', in C. Harper-Bill, C. Rawcliffe and R. G. Wilson, eds, *East Anglia's History: Studies in Honour of Norman Scarfe* (Woodbridge, 2002), p. 11.
9. B. M. S. Campbell, 'Population Pressure, Inheritance and the Land Market in a Fourteenth-Century Peasant Community', in R. Smith, ed., *Land, Kinship and Life-Cycle* (Cambridge, 1984), pp. 87–134.
10. B. M. S. Campbell, 'Agricultural Progress in Medieval England: Some Evidence from Eastern Norfolk', *EconHR*, second series, xxxvi (1983), pp. 26–46.
11. T. Williamson, *The Norfolk Broads* (Manchester, 1997), pp. 12–15, 40–48.
12. D. Defoe, *Tour Through the Whole Island of Great Britain* (Everyman edn, 2 vols, London, 1962), i, p. 63.
13. Dyer, 'Ranking Lists', p. 755. For discussion of the Norwich and Yarmouth assessments, see R. E. Glasscock, ed., *The Lay Subsidy of 1334* (London, 1975), p. 192.
14. Campbell, 'Domesday Herrings', pp. 5–17.
15. *RCN*, ii, pp. lx.
16. J. M. Lambert, J. N. Jennings, C. Green, C. T. Smith and J. N. Hutchinson, *The Making of the Broads* (Royal Geographical Research Series, iii, London, 1960).
17. Lambert and others, *Making of the Broads*, p. 84.
18. Campbell, 'Domesday Herrings', pp. 9–10, 15–16.
19. R. Virgoe, 'The Estates of Norwich Cathedral Priory, 1101–1538', in *Norwich Cathedral*, pp. 339–59, especially p. 347.
20. C. Rawcliffe, *The Hospitals of Medieval Norwich* (Norwich, 1995), p. 118.
21. W. Hudson, 'Notes about Norwich before the Close of the Thirteenth Century', *NA*, xii (1895), pp. 66–70. See also R. McKinley, *Norfolk and Suffolk Surnames in the Middle Ages* (English Surnames Series, ii, Chichester, 1975), pp. 82, 83.
22. *RCN*, ii, pp. xxv–xxvii. Some of the references could have been to craft terms used as patronymics for those otherwise occupied.
23. S. Kelly, 'The Economic Topography and Structure of Norwich *c.* 1300', in S. Kelly, E. Rutledge, M. Tillyard and M. Priestley, *Men of Property: An Analysis of the Norwich Enrolled Deeds, 1285–1311* (Norwich, 1983), pp. 13–39, especially pp. 22–3. This evidence relates to a property-owning minority, and so is not necessarily a reliable indicator of the proportionate importance of the trades. For the leather trades see also Hudson, 'Notes about Norwich', pp. 59–61; and pp. 160–1, 165–6, above.

24. Kelly, 'Economic Topography', p. 24; Campbell, 'Norwich', p. 15.
25. J. Caley and W. Illingworth, eds, *Rotuli Hundredorum* (2 vols, Record Commission, London, 1812), i, p. 530.
26. D. M. Stenton, ed., *The Great Roll of the Pipe for the Fourth Year of King John* (Pipe Roll Society, new series, xv, London, 1937), p. 115. For the early Norwich textile trades in general, see Hudson, 'Notes about Norwich', pp. 61–6; and A. F. Sutton, 'The Early Linen and Worsted Industry of Norfolk and the Evolution of the London Mercers' Company', *NA*, xi (1989), pp. 201–5; and also pp. 178–9, above.
27. G. H. Orpen, *Ireland under the Normans* (4 vols, Oxford, 1920), iv, p. 274.
28. *RCN*, ii, pp. 209–12. The church of St John Maddermarket was already so called earlier in the thirteenth century: J. Kirkpatrick, *The Streets and Lanes of the City of Norwich*, ed., W. Hudson (Norwich, 1889), p. 58.
29. R. Frostick, *The Printed Plans of Norwich, 1558–1840: A Carto-Bibliography* (Norwich, 2002), pp. 1–4.
30. Thomas of Monmouth, *The Life and Miracles of St William of Norwich*, eds, A. Jessopp and M. R. James (Cambridge, 1896), pp. 152–3.
31. Kelly, 'Economic Topography', p. 27.
32. *RCN*, i, p. 189.
33. *RCN*, i, pp. 204–5.
34. Cotton, *HA*, p. 172. See also M. Atkin, 'Medieval Clay-Walled Building in Norwich', *NA*, xli (1991), pp. 171–85.
35. Rutledge, 'Immigration and Population Growth', pp. 26–7. For tithing men, see above, pp. 191–2.
36. Kelly, 'Economic Topography', p. 36, differs.
37. Kelly, 'Economic Topography', p. 19.
38. Kelly, 'Economic Topography', pp. 21, 32.
39. Illustrated in Kelly and others, *Men of Property*, p. 42.
40. E. Stone, 'Profit and Loss Accountancy at Norwich Cathedral Priory', *TRHS*, fifth series, xii (1962), pp. 25–48.
41. B. Dodwell, 'The Monastic Community', in *Norwich Cathedral*, pp. 248–9.
42. R. Virgoe, 'The Estates of Norwich Cathedral Priory, 1101–1538', in *Norwich Cathedral*, pp. 343, 349. At an earlier date the bishop and priory seem to have been able to tax the diocese.
43. Dodwell, 'Monastic Community', p. 232; H. W. Saunders, *An Introduction to the Obedientiary and Manor Rolls of Norwich Cathedral Priory* (Norwich, 1930), pp. 89–91, 162–3.
44. Campbell, 'Norwich', p. 8 n. 98.
45. Thomas of Monmouth, *Life and Miracles of St William*, pp. 16–19.
46. Campbell, 'Norwich', pp. 8–9.
47. *RCN*, ii, pp. xiii–xv; W. Rye, 'The Riot between the Monks and Citizens of

Norwich', *Norfolk Antiquarian Miscellany*, ii, part 1 (1883), pp. 17–89, especially pp. 17–19.

48. N. Tanner, 'The Cathedral and the City', in *Norwich Cathedral*, pp. 259–61, is the best modern account; Rye, 'Riot', publishes important documents and remains invaluable. The principal near contemporary accounts are Cotton, *HA*, pp. 146–53; T. Stapleton, ed., *Liber de antiquis legibus* (Camden Society, old series, xxxiv, 1846), pp. 145–8; J. Stevenson, ed., *Chronicon de Lanercost, 1201–1346* (Bannatyne Club, Edinburgh, 1839), pp. 103–4. An account in a fifteenth-century city collection may derive from inquest records: *RCN*, ii, pp. 269–71.
49. E. Fernie, *An Architectural History of Norwich Cathedral* (Oxford, 1993), pp. 163–81.
50. N. M. Trenholme, *The English Monastic Boroughs* (University of Missouri Studies, ii, number 3, 1927), especially pp. 1–30. An example is the Bury rising of 1264: F. M. Powicke, *King Henry III and the Lord Edward* (2 vols, Oxford, 1947), ii, pp. 449–50.
51. *RCN*, ii, p. 271; Stapleton, *Liber de antiquis legibus*, pp. 145–6.
52. Rye, 'Riot', p. 21. Gregory X's condemnatory bull shows that the priory held the city authorities to blame: Cotton, *HA*, p. 422.
53. Rye, 'Riot', pp. 21, 29–32 (some of Rye's details are flawed but his conclusions hold).
54. H. R. Luard, ed., *Chronicon Thomas Wykes: Annales Monastici*, iv (RS, 1869), p. 193; A. Gransden, ed., *The Chronicle of Bury St Edmunds* (London, 1964), p. 37.
55. Powicke, *Henry III and the Lord Edward*, ii, p. 450.
56. R. C. Johnston, ed., *Jordan Fantosme's Chronicle* (Oxford, 1981), pp. 66–7.
57. D. Carpenter, *The Minority of Henry III* (London, 1990), p. 25.
58. W. L. Warren, *Henry II* (London, 1973), pp. 66–7.
59. Stapleton, *Liber de antiquis legibus*, p. 145.
60. J. Schofield and G. Stell, 'The Built Environment 1300–1540', in Palliser, *Cambridge Urban History*, p. 382.
61. Rye, 'Riot', pp. 6–7.
62. W. Hudson, ed., *Leet Jurisdiction in the City of Norwich during the Thirteenth and Fourteenth Centuries* (Selden Society, v, 1892).
63. See above, p. 309.
64. Hudson, *Leet Jurisdiction*, pp. xxxix–xl.
65. S. Jenks, 'The Lay Subsidies and the State of the English Economy, 1275–1334', *Vierteljahrschrift für Sozial- und Wirtschaftgeschichte*, lxxxv (1998), p. 13.
66. V. D. Lipman, *The Jews of Medieval Norwich* (London, 1967), pp. 59–64.
67. M. McKisack, *The Parliamentary Representation of the English Boroughs during the Middle Ages* (Oxford, 1932), pp. 18–19.

68. The best account is still *RCN*, i, pp. iii–xliv.
69. The charter of Stephen to his son William, granting in specific terms (derived from Domesday) both Norwich boroughs, mentioned by Hudson (Thomas of Monmouth, *Life and Miracles of St William*, p. xlvi), does not appear to exist; Hudson was misled by Blomefield, *Norfolk*, iii, p. 25. However, the treaty of 1153 between King Stephen and the future Henry II confirms a grant made by Stephen to William of *castra et villas de Norwico*, and the plurals suggest the continued existence of a separate French borough: H. A. Cronne and R. H. C. Davis, eds, *Regesta Regum Anglo-Normannorum, 1066–1154*, iii (Oxford, 1968), no. 272, p. 98.
70. *RCN*, i, pp. 11–12.
71. *RCN*, i, pp. 12–14.
72. *RCN*, i, pp. xvi–xvii.
73. J. Campbell, 'Power and Authority, 600–1300', in Palliser, *Cambridge Urban History*, p. 61.
74. M. de W. Hemmeon, *Burgage Tenure in Mediaeval England* (Cambridge, Massachusetts, 1914), pp. 112, 138–43.
75. Hemmeon, *Burgage Tenure*, p. 90.
76. For example, E. Rutledge, 'Property Transfer and Enrolment in Norwich, 1285–1311', in Kelly and others, *Men of Property*, p. 52.
77. E. Rutledge, 'Property Transfer'; and eadem, 'Landlords and Tenants: Social Housing and the Rented Property Market in Early Fourteenth-Century Norwich', *Urban History*, xxii (1995), pp. 7–24.
78. *RCN*, i, pp. xxv–xxvii.
79. J. Tait, *The Medieval English Borough* (Manchester, 1936), p. 291 n. 5.
80. Hudson, *Leet Jurisdiction*, p. xv.
81. *RCN*, i, pp. 14–20, especially 16–18.
82. *RCN*, i, pp. 220–2. The city does not seem to have been at its most efficient in this affair. Although they hanged Eghe, they failed to kill him.
83. *RCN*, i, p. 17.
84. *RCN*, i, pp. 260–1 (where the relevant deed is misdated 1295).
85. J. Gillingham, *Richard the Lionheart* (London, 1978), pp. 243–4.
86. Gillingham, *Richard the Lionheart*, p. 241.
87. *RCN*, i, pp. 9–10: Twenty-five knights, twenty-five mounted men and twenty-five foot for forty days in late 1193 or 1194.
88. This was required by the Assize of Arms (1181): W. Stubbs, ed., *Select Charters and Other Illustrations of English Constitutional History*, revised by H. W. C. Davis (ninth edn, Oxford, 1951), pp. 183–4.
89. C. R. Young, *The English Borough and Royal Administration, 1130–1307* (Durham, North Carolina, 1961), p. 93.
90. *RCN*, i, pp. 390–403.

91. T. A. Heslop, *Norwich Castle Keep: Romanesque Architecture and Social Context* (Norwich, 1994), pp. 4, 58.
92. H. Clover and M. Gibson, eds, *The Letters of Lanfranc, Archbishop of Canterbury* (Oxford, 1979), no 35, pp. 124–7.
93. P. Brown, ed., *Domesday Book, Norfolk*, i (Chichester, 1984), item 1/61; and pp. 13–15, above.
94. Heslop, *Norwich Castle*, pp. 4–13, 59–60.
95. E. Fernie, *The Architecture of Norman England* (Oxford, 2000), pp. 279–80.
96. Stenton, *First Century*, pp. 192–217; Cronne and Davis, *Regesta Regum Anglo-Normannorum*, no. 757, p. 279; Heslop, *Norwich Castle*, p. 9.
97. Lipman, *Jews of Medieval Norwich*, p. 62.
98. C. Parker and S. Ward, eds, *Domesday Book, Nottinghamshire* (Chichester, 1977), items B/3, 9, 10; M. W. Beresford, *New Towns of the Middle Ages* (London, 1967), pp. 331–3.
99. Brown, *Domesday Book, Norfolk*, item 1/60.
100. *RCN*, ii, pp. 227–8.
101. Campbell, 'Norwich', p. 13 and n. 78.
102. Fernie, *Architectural History*, especially pp. 19–57; B. Dodwell, 'Herbert de Losinga and the Foundation', in *Norwich Cathedral*, pp. 36–43.
103. Fernie, *Architecture of Norman England*, pp. 284, 304.
104. Dodwell, 'Herbert de Losinga and the Foundation', p. 43.
105. H. Welldon Finn, *The Norman Conquest and its Effects on the Economy* (London, 1971), p. 35.
106. M. D. Lobel, *The Borough of Bury St Edmunds* (Oxford, 1935), pp. 11–15.
107. Thomas of Monmouth, *Life and Miracles of St William*, passim; Lipman, *Jews of Medieval Norwich*, pp. 49–57.
108. Lipman, *Jews of Medieval Norwich*, pp. 57–64; G. I. Langmuir, 'Thomas of Monmouth: Detector of Ritual Murder', *Speculum*, lvi (1984), pp. 820–56.
109. Lipman, *Jews of Medieval Norwich*, p. 38.
110. Lipman, *Jews of Medieval Norwich*, pp. 40, 95–112, 27–32; Ayers, *Norwich*, pp. 47–9.
111. Lipman, *Jews of Medieval Norwich*, pp. 65–94, especially p. 94.
112. Lipman, *Jews of Medieval Norwich*, pp. 113–41.
113. Campbell, 'Norwich', p. 3 n. 23.
114. Campbell, 'Norwich', p. 3. These churches presumably included three or four fairly recently found by excavation.
115. C. Hart, *The Danelaw* (London and Rio Grande, Ohio, 1992), pp. 91–2.
116. Campbell, 'Norwich', p. 5; Ayers, *Norwich*, p. 33.
117. E. O. Blake, ed., *Liber Eliensis* (Camden Society, third series, xcii, 1962), p. 100.
118. R. Fleming, 'Rural Elites and Urban Communities in Late Anglo-Saxon England', *Past and Present*, cxli (1993), pp. 3–37.

119. F. Barlow, *The English Church, 1000–1066* (London, 1963), p. 78.
120. Brown, *Domesday Book, Norfolk*, items 1, 4, 8, 9, 25, 31, 34. For Tokethorpe, see Campbell, 'Norwich', pp. 4–5; Ayers, *Norwich*, pp. 25–26.
121. Campbell, 'Norwich', pp. 7, 8.
122. Campbell, 'Norwich', p. 6; Ayers, *Norwich*, pp. 38–9; and above, p. 11–12. The 'Potter' of Potter Heigham suggests a ceramic involvement and first appears in 1182: K. I. Sandred, with others, *The Place-Names of Norfolk*, ii (English Place-Name Society, Nottingham, 1996), pp. 121–2. Was the industry moving nearer to its fuel, supposing that were peat?
123. Thomas of Monmouth, *Life and Miracles of St William*, p. 14: '*a parentibus traditur pellipariis arte pelliparia instruendus*'. The unfortunate William stands for many who for centuries to come (and perhaps for centuries before) came from a Norfolk village (William came from Haveringland or somewhere near) to Norwich, in the hope of a move up in life.
124. Ayers, *Norwich*, pp. 38–40.
125. M. Biddle, and others, *Object and Economy in Medieval Winchester* (2 vols, Oxford, 1990), i, pp. 42–73, especially p. 68.
126. Williamson, *Norfolk Broads*, especially pp. 12, 16–17, 40–42.
127. Campbell, 'Norwich', p. 7.
128. *NCR*, ii, pp. xiii, pp. 41, 207–9.
129. Thomas of Monmouth, *Life and Miracles of St William*, pp. 235–6.
130. NRO, DCN 45/40/55, charter of *c.* 1185–1200.
131. Campbell, 'Norwich', p. 6; Ayers, *Norwich*, pp. 24, 52.
132. Saunders, *Introduction to the Rolls*, p. 87.
133. Campbell, 'Norwich', p. 5.
134. See D. G. Russo, *Town Origins and Development in Early England, c. 400–950 AD* (Westport and London, 1998), pp. 137–192, for a survey.
135. M. Metcalf, 'Coins From *Wics*', in D. Hill and R. Cowie, eds, *Wics: The Early Medieval Trading Centres of Northern Europe* (Sheffield, 2001), pp. 50–53.
136. K. Ulmschneider, *Markets, Minsters and Metal-Detectors: The Archaeology of Middle Saxon Lincolnshire and the Isle of Wight Compared* (Oxford, 2000), passim.
137. E. Ekwall, 'Old English "wic" in Place-Names', *Nomina Germanica*, xiii (1964), passim.
138. A. Rumble, 'Notes on the Linguistic and Onomastic Characteristics of Old English *Wic*', in Hill and Cowie, *Wics*, p. 2.
139. Coins of Athelstan (924–39) bear Norwich as a mint signature; a single, and difficult, 'St Edmund memorial penny', which could be earlier, has been suggested to bear a Norwich signature: C. E. Blunt, 'The St Edmund Memorial Coinage', *Proceedings of the Suffolk Institute of Archaeology*, xxxi (1967–69),

pp. 245–6, plate xxx (8). This possibility is now thought discredited: M. Aitken, 'The Anglo-Saxon Urban Landscape of East Anglia', *Landscape History*, vii (1985), p. 32.

140. D. A. Hinton, 'The Large Towns 600–1300', in Palliser, *Cambridge Urban History*, pp. 221–2. There are possible indications, in particular finds of *sceattas*, that *Venta Icenorum* could have continued into the Middle Saxon period as a significant place: Aitken, 'Anglo-Saxon Urban Landscape', p. 30.
141. Ayers, *Norwich*, signals a number of areas inadequately explored: for example, pp. 47, 51–2, 58, 66, 67.
142. Campbell, 'Norwich', p. 2.
143. J. Campbell, 'What Is Not Known about the Reign of Edward the Elder', in N. J. Higham and D. H. Hill, eds, *Edward the Elder, 879–924* (London and New York, 2001), pp. 19–21.
144. Campbell, 'Norwich', pp. 5; Ayers, *Norwich*, pp. 25, 26–9.
145. Campbell, 'Norwich', p. 7; Ayers, *Norwich*, pp. 38, 103.
146. Ayers, *Norwich*, p. 103 (plate 83).
147. W. Hudson, 'On an Ancient Timber Roadway across the River Wensum at Fye Bridge, Norwich', *NA*, xiii (1898), pp. 217–32; Ayers, *Norwich*, p. 51. Such a causeway could have been constructed even in the early Saxon period. For comments on a causeway to Mersea island, Essex, see J. Hillam, 'An English Tree-Ring Chronology, AD 404–1216', *Medieval Archaeology*, xxv (1981), pp. 37, 42.
148. R. H. Britnell, *The Commercialisation of English Society, 1000–1500* (Cambridge, 1993), especially pp. 1–78.
149. Notably that of Professor Derek Keene and his colleagues at the Centre for Metropolitan History, and of Dr Pamela Nightingale, cited below.
150. McKinley, *Norfolk and Suffolk Surnames*, p. 78.
151. P. Nightingale, 'Norwich, London and the Regional Integration of Norfolk's Economy in the First Half of the Fourteenth Century', in J. A. Galloway, ed., *Trade, Urban Hinterlands and Market Integration* (Centre for Metropolitan History, Working Papers, series three, London, 2000), pp. 83–102.

Notes to Chapter 3: The Churches

1. NRO, DCN MC 1619/1 824X9, p. 62.
2. This paper has drawn on the unpublished archive of the Norwich Survey held at the Centre of East Anglian Studies (CEAS), UEA. The Survey team was established by the late Alan Carter, but the authors of individual reports are not recorded. I am grateful to the former Director of CEAS, Professor

Christopher Harper-Bill, for permission to use the archive. I have benefited from conversations with Kate Giles, Tim Pestell and Victoria Thompson, particularly regarding the early sections of this chapter.

3. See Chapters 1 and 2 above.
4. Probably the lost church at Fye bridge, which was combined with St Paul's parish in 1550, rather than that at Timberhill.
5. Currently thought to be the same foundation, probably situated around the north transept of the present cathedral.
6. Almost certainly St Martin-at-Palace, rather than one of the three other churches of the same name at Castle Gate, Ber Street and Oak Street.
7. St Mary-in-the Marsh: see B. S. Ayers, 'The Cathedral Site before 1096', in *Norwich Cathedral*, p. 66.
8. Demolished during the creation of the cathedral precinct after 1096: Ayers, 'Cathedral Site', p. 65.
9. Now known as St John de Sepulchre.
10. See above, pp. 5–6.
11. The dedication is also an early one: W. Hudson, 'On a Sculptured Stone Recently Removed from a House on the Site of St Vedast, Norwich', *NA*, xiii (1898), pp. 116–23; B. Ayers, *Norwich* (London, 1994), p. 29 and fig. 15.
12. Suggested in Ayers, 'Cathedral Site', p. 68.
13. R. Morris, 'Parish Churches', in J. Schofield and R. Leech, eds, *Urban Archaeology in Britain* (Council for British Archaeology Research Report, 61, 1987), p. 177.
14. R. Morris, *Churches in the Landscape* (London, 1989), pp. 222–5.
15. By the thirteenth century, London had a hundred churches, Norwich and Winchester about fifty-seven each, Lincoln forty-eight and York about forty: Morris, 'Parish Churches', p. 177. See also D. A. Hinton, 'The Large Towns 600–1300', in D. M. Palliser, ed., *The Cambridge Urban History of Britain*, i, *600–1540* (Cambridge, 2000), pp. 217–43.
16. B. Ayers, *Excavations within the North-East Bailey of Norwich Castle, 1979* (EAA, report 28, 1985).
17. Ayers, *Norwich*, pp. 37–8.
18. It was a *terminus post quem* of the tenth century: O. Beazley and B. Ayers, *Two Medieval Churches in Norfolk* (EAA, report 96, 2001), p. 55.
19. Beazley and Ayers, *Two Medieval Churches in Norfolk*, p. 55.
20. J. P. Roberts with M. Atkin, 'St Benedict's Church', in A. Carter, ed., *Excavations in Norwich, 1971–1978: Part I* (EAA, report, 15, 1982), pp. 11–29.
21. H. M. Taylor and J. Taylor, *Anglo-Saxon Architecture* (3 vols, Cambridge, 1965–78), i, p. 474.
22. Beazley and Ayers, *Two Medieval Churches in Norfolk*, p. 56; E. Fernie, *The Architecture of Norman England* (Oxford, 2000), p. 20.

23. Taylor and Taylor, *Anglo-Saxon Architecture*, i, p. 474; CEAS, Norwich Survey Report: St Mary Coslany.
24. Roberts with Atkin, 'St Benedict's Church', pp. 11–29.
25. The five known are St Mary Coslany, St Benedict's, St Julian's, St Etheldreda's and St Paul's, which was destroyed by bombs in 1942.
26. Fernie, *Norman Architecture*, p. 270. The windows have recently been described more confidently as Saxon: N. Pevsner and B. Wilson, *Norfolk*, i, *Norwich and North-East* (second edn, London, 1997) p. 241.
27. S. Heyward, 'The Round Towers of East Anglia', in J. Blair, ed., *Minsters and Parish Churches: The Local Church in Transition, 950–1200* (Oxford University Committee for Archaeology Monograph, xvii, 1988), pp. 169–78.
28. The chancel arch is nineteenth-century but preserves the late medieval position: CEAS, Norwich Survey Report: St Etheldreda.
29. Along with St Ethelbert's, St Helen's and Christchurch/Holy Trinity.
30. Now numbers 10–12, The Close: Ayers, *Norwich*, p. 56; R. Houlbrooke, 'Refoundation and Reformation, 1538–1628', in *Norwich Cathedral*, p. 529; I. Atherton, 'The Close', in ibid., p. 638.
31. NRO, DCN 127/11.
32. Heywood, 'Round Towers of East Anglia', passim.
33. J. Campbell, 'Norwich', in M. Lobel, ed., *Historic Towns*, ii (London, 1975), p. 4; see also above, p. 6.
34. Now in the Castle Museum, Norwich, as an unaccessioned loan. Significantly, the fourteenth-century design imitates an even earlier form.
35. Pevsner and Wilson, *Norfolk*, i, p. 237.
36. G. Zarnecki, J. Holt and T. Holland, *English Romanesque Art, 1066–1200* (London, 1984), p. 202.
37. T. Pestell, 'Monastic Foundation Strategies in the Early Norman Diocese of Norwich', *Anglo-Norman Studies*, xxiii (2000), p. 208.
38. Pestell, 'Monastic Foundation Strategies', p. 208.
39. Ayers, *Norwich*, p. 33.
40. J. Bown, 'Excavations on the North Side of Norwich Cathedral, 1987–88', *NA*, xlii (1998), pp. 428–52; Ayers, 'Cathedral Site', p. 66.
41. This includes a pair of triangular-headed arches linked by a third smaller arch, all composed of billet moulding; three large carved beasts' heads; a geometrically carved tympanum; and decorative bases to the blank arcading. Moreover, the only capital in the church with significant figural ornament and five of the six decorated colonnettes is to be found there: J. A. Franklin, 'The Romanesque Sculpture', in *Norwich Cathedral*, p. 119–22.
42. E. Fernie, *An Architectural History of Norwich Cathedral*, (Oxford, 1993), pp. 81–7; Pevsner and Wilson, *Norfolk*, i, p. 197; Franklin, 'Romanesque Sculpture', pp. 119–22.

43. It is worth noting, however, that the Norman palace was connected to the nave of the cathedral church at first floor level. Only in the fifteenth century were the later buildings of the palatial complex physically linked to the north transept.
44. The parishioners of St Margaret's Westminster attended services on the north side of the abbey. A carving of St Margaret and the dragon survives in the wall arcade of the abbey's thirteenth-century north transept: G. Rosser, 'The Cure of Souls in English Towns before 1000', in J. Blair and R. Sharpe, eds, *Pastoral Care before the Parish* (Leicester, 1992), p. 271.
45. Christchurch was owned by fifteen burgesses, which is indicative of early urban wealth and organisation.
46. Campbell, 'Norwich', p. 3.
47. F. Woodman, 'The Gothic Campaigns', in *Norwich Cathedral*, pp. 158–96; R. Fawcett, 'The Influence of the Gothic parts of the Cathedral on Church Building in Norfolk', in ibid., pp. 210–28.
48. CEAS, Norwich Survey Report: St John Maddermarket.
49. The original length of the chancel has been the topic of much speculation. Pevsner and Wilson, *Norfolk*, i, p. 240, suggest it might have been demolished in the sixteenth century, but the Norwich Survey report on the fabric is adamant that the chancel never spanned the lane to the east and has always been its current length: CEAS, Norwich Survey Report: St John Maddermarket.
50. CEAS, Norwich Survey: P. Cattermole, 'Some Norwich Churches as Seen in the Obedientiary Rolls of Norwich Cathedral Priory 1276–1536' (unpublished manuscript, 1985), pp. 4–8, 15, 37.
51. See R. Virgoe, 'The Estates of Norwich Cathedral Priory, 1101–1538', in *Norwich Cathedral*, pp. 339–59, for a discussion of its finances.
52. A. Watkin, *Inventory of Church Goods temp. Edward III* (2 vols, NRS, xix, 1947–48), ii, pp. 3–27.
53. In 1311, for example, three rural churches provided the almoner with a net income of just over £25, compared to that of only £5 15s. 1d. received by him from four city churches: Cattermole, 'Some Norwich Churches', p. 6.
54. P. G. Lindley, 'The "Arminghall Arch" and Contemporary Sculpture in Norwich', *NA*, xl (1987), pp. 19–43.
55. For Carrow priory and the friaries, see Chapter 4, below.
56. Ely was named in 1443 before the college was designed, and remained in charge until at least 1461: F. Woodman, *The Architectural History of King's College Chapel and its Place in the Development of Late Gothic Architecture in England and France* (London, 1986), pp. 84, 104.
57. Three essays on Erpingham's artistic and architectural patronage may be found in A. Curry, ed., *Agincourt 1415* (Stroud, 2000), pp. 78–110.

58. Only about eight churches apparently missed out on this building boom: P. Graves, *The Form and Fabric of Belief: An Archaeology of the Lay Experience of Religion in Medieval Norfolk and Devon* (British Archaeological Reports, British Series, 311, 2000), p. 60.
59. Robert de Dunston instructed his wife to give £5 to the tower in 1424; three bells were cast for it by Richard Baxter, who was active between 1416–24; the high stepped base-moulding was a form found in London *c.* 1396, and so was unlikely to reach Norwich before the fifteenth century: Blomefield, *Norfolk*, iv, p. 239; S. Cotton, 'Tradition and Authority in Church Building', *Norfolk Archaeological Research Group News*, xxvi (1981), pp. 8–13; CEAS, Norwich Survey Report: St Giles.
60. R. Fawcett, 'Later Gothic Architecture in Norfolk: An Examination of the Work of Some Individual Architects in the Fourteenth and Fifteenth Centuries' (UEA, Norwich, PhD thesis, 2 vols, 1975), ii, p. 305.
61. F. Woodman, 'The Rebuilding of St Peter Mancroft', in A. Longcroft and R. Joby, eds, *East Anglian Studies: Essays Presented to J. C. Barringer on his Retirement* (Norwich, 1995), pp. 290–91. See also Chapter 5, above.
62. See above, pp. 115–18.
63. This payment was followed in 1401 by one for the dedication of the altar: NRO, DCN 1/10/9, 11.
64. CEAS, Norwich Survey Report: St Gregory.
65. The upper levels of towers at St Mary Coslany and St Etheldreda were not accessible, which lends weight to the fact that St Gregory's tower may have been of a similar Saxo-Norman date: CEAS, Norwich Survey Report: St Gregory.
66. A. A. Nichols, *The Early Art of Norfolk* (Kalamazoo, Michigan, 2002), p. 197; E. A. Kent, 'A Mural Painting of St George in St Gregory's Church, Norwich', *NA*, xxv (1934), pp. 167–9; Pevsner and Wilson, *Norfolk*, i, p. 238; R. Marks and P. Williamson, eds, *Gothic Art for England 1400–1547* (London, 2003), pp. 408–9. Kent observes that a similar wall painting was once to be seen in the adjacent church of St John Maddermarket.
67. The vestry at St Andrew's seems to be an addition, since the Norwich antiquary, James Kirkpatrick (d. 1728), records the depiction of a man kneeling, with the arms of Calthorpe impaling Bullen on his garments, in the east window of the south aisle. He is not completely sure about the tinctures, since 'ye windows being blinded with ye vestry built against it 'tis not plainly to be seen'. The flushwork which is continued from the east end of the chancel onto the vestry, to the south, appears either to have been reset or is a poor imitation: NRO, MC 500/14 761x7 ('Notes on St Andrew's Church and St John Maddermarket', p. 69).
68. CEAS, Norwich Survey Report: St George Colegate.

69. CEAS, Norwich Survey Report: St George Colegate.
70. This type of tracery is described as 'using coupled tracery lights under an ogee over-arch, thus providing an asymmetrical base for the next tier' or 'an unresolved ogee motif with pairs enclosed within an ogee overarch'. There are four examples in York, five in the East Riding and five in the West Riding of Yorkshire, compared with thirty-five in Norfolk: Woodman, *Architectural History of King's College Chapel*, pp. 102–4 and appendix II.
71. Woodman, *Architectural History of King's College Chapel*, p. 104.
72. CEAS, Norwich Survey Report: St Michael Coslany.
73. The flushwork on the chancel was created as part of the nineteenth-century restoration: Fawcett, 'Later Gothic Architecture in Norfolk', ii, p. 468.
74. Fawcett, 'Later Gothic Architecture in Norfolk', ii, pp. 467–8.
75. CEAS, Norwich Survey Report: St Michael Coslany.
76. Norman Tanner identifies thirty-six perpetual chantries founded in Norwich between 1370–1547. Only eight (20 per cent) were in parish churches: three in St Peter Mancroft; three in St Stephen's; one in St Gregory's; and Thorp's in St Michael Coslany; Tanner, *CLMN*, Appendix 10, pp. 212–19. See also Chapter 6, above.
77. Estimated from testamentary bequests leaving money to images and altars: CEAS, Norwich Survey Report: St Michael Coslany.
78. Graves, *Form and Fabric of Belief*, pp. 58–66.
79. Cattermole, 'Some Norwich Churches', pp. 31–2; CEAS, Norwich Survey Report: St Peter Parmentergate.
80. An absence of cusping is almost exclusively confined to Norwich, though it is found in Canterbury *c.* 1470. The other roof with tie beams is at St Swithin's: CEAS, Norwich Survey Reports: St Peter Parmentergate and St Swithin.
81. NRO, DCN 1/10/32, 34.
82. NRO, NCC, reg. Wylby, fo. 29r (Robert Pert); Woodman, 'Rebuilding of St Peter Mancroft', p. 293.
83. Graves, *Form and Fabric of Belief*, p. 60.
84. Cattermole, 'Some Norwich Churches', pp. 54–5.
85. NRO, DCN 1/10/29.
86. NRO, NCC, reg. Norman, fo. 34r (Robert Cok); reg. Cage, fo. 82r (John Grys); reg. Hyll, fo. 57r (James Cootes).
87. The tower porch is of *c.* 1320 but much restored in the seventeenth and nineteenth centuries: CEAS, Norwich Survey Report: St Stephen's.
88. Cattermole, 'Some Norwich Churches', pp. 35–6.
89. J. Finch, *Church Monuments in Norfolk before 1850: An Archaeology of Commemoration* (British Archaeological Reports, British Series, 317, 2000), pp. 151–4.

90. Finch, *Church Monuments in Norfolk*, pp. 37–44; R. Greenwood and M. Norris, *The Brasses of Norfolk Churches* (Norwich, 1976).
91. N. Rogers, *Whigs and Cities: Popular Politics in the Age of Walpole and Pitt* (Oxford, 1989), p. 326.

Notes to Chapter 4: The Religious Houses

1. C. A. Sneyd, ed., *A Relation, or Rather a True Account, of the Island of England* (Camden Society, original series, xxxvii, 1847), p. 29.
2. N. Tanner, 'The Cathedral and the City', in *Norwich Cathedral*, pp. 255–80.
3. See above, pp. 325–6.
4. C. Harper-Bill, 'Searching for Salvation in Anglo-Norman East Anglia', in idem, C. Rawcliffe and R. G. Wilson, eds, *East Anglia's History: Studies in Honour of Norman Scarfe* (Woodbridge, 2002), pp. 19–39, especially pp. 26–32.
5. This brief survey is based on the medieval chapters of *Norwich Cathedral*, where more detailed references may be found.
6. N. Batcock, 'The Parish Church in Norfolk in the Eleventh and Twelfth Centuries', in J. Blair, ed., *Ministers and Parish Churches: The Local Church in Transition, 950–1200* (Oxford University Committee for Archaeology, Monograph 17, Oxford, 1988), p. 188.
7. For a summary architectural description, see *Norwich Cathedral*, chapters 4 to 11; and also E. Fernie, *An Architectural History of Norwich Cathedral* (Oxford, 1993).
8. C. N. L. Brooke, 'The Churches of Medieval Cambridge', in D. Beales and G. Best, eds, *History, Society and the Churches: Essays in Honour of Owen Chadwick* (Cambridge, 1985), p. 57.
9. D. Chadd, 'The Medieval Customary of the Cathedral Priory', *Norwich Cathedral*, pp. 314–24.
10. V. Sekules, 'The Gothic Sculpture', *Norwich Cathedral*, pp. 199–202.
11. Sekules, 'Gothic Sculpture', pp. 205–7.
12. For an interesting discussion of the landscape of the precinct, see C. Noble, 'Aspects of Life at Norwich Cathedral Priory in the Later Medieval Period' (UEA, Norwich, PhD thesis, 2001).
13. E. M. Carter, *Studies in Norwich Cathedral History* (Norwich, 1935), pp. 19–24.
14. F. Meeres, *Not of This World: Norfolk's Monastic Houses* (Norwich, 2001), p. 118.
15. M. Rose, *The Norwich Apocalypse* (Norwich, 1999).
16. For the bishops, see C. Harper-Bill, 'The Medieval Church and the Wider World', *Norwich Cathedral*, pp. 281–300.
17. A table of the *Valor* assessments of the various bishoprics appears in

D. Knowles and R. N. Hadcock, *Medieval Religious Houses: England and Wales* (second edn, London, 1971), p. 447.

18. F. M. Powicke and C. R. Cheney, eds, *Councils and Synods and other Documents Relating to the English Church*, ii, *1205–1313* (2 parts, Oxford, 1964), i, pp. 363–4.
19. Tanner, *CLMN*, p. 158.
20. C. Harper-Bill, ed., *English Episcopal Acta*, vi, *Norwich, 1070–1214* (British Academy, 1990), passim; idem, ed., *The Register of John Morton, Archbishop of Canterbury, 1486–1500* (Canterbury and York Society, lxxxix, 2000), no. 45.
21. N. P. Tanner, ed., *Heresy Trials in the Diocese of Norwich, 1428–1431* (Camden Society, fourth series, xx, 1977), passim.
22. P. R. Hyams, 'Deans and their Doings: The Norwich Inquiry of 1286', In S. Kuttner and K. Pennington, eds, *Proceedings of the Sixth International Congress of Medieval Canon Law* (Vatican City, 1985), pp. 619–46.
23. See, for example, R. M. Wunderli, *London Church Courts and Society on the Eve of the Reformation* (*Speculum* Anniversary Monograph, 7, 1991), passim.
24. Knowles and Hadcock, *Medieval Religious Houses*, p. 72.
25. See J. Greatrex, *Biographical Register of the English Cathedral Priories of the Province of Canterbury, c. 1066–1540* (Oxford, 1997), pp. 466–576, for details about individual monks.
26. Noble, 'Aspects of Life', pp. 230 et seq. and 260.
27. A. W. Saunders, *An Introduction to the Obedientiary and Manor Rolls of Norwich Cathedral Priory* (Norwich, 1930), pp. 162–3. For similar evidence from Westminster Abbey, see B. F. Harvey, *Living and Dying in England 1100–1540: The Monastic Experience* (Oxford, 1993), chapters 5 and 6.
28. C. Noble, ed., Norwich Cathedral Priory Gardeners' Accounts, 1329–1530', in eadem, C. Moreton and P. Rutledge, eds, *Farming and Gardening in Late Medieval Norfolk* (NRS, lxi, 1997), pp. 1–93.
29. Carter, *Studies in Norwich Cathedral History*, pp. 19–24.
30. C. R. Cheney, 'Norwich Cathedral Priory in the Fourteenth Century', *Bulletin of the John Rylands Library*, xx (1936), pp. 93–120.
31. A. Jessopp, ed., *Visitations of the Diocese of Norwich, 1492–1532* (Camden Society, new series, xliii, 1888), pp. 1–7 (1492), 71–8 (1514), 192–5 (1520), 196–206 (1526), 263–70 (1532).
32. Estate management is discussed at greater length in R. Virgoe, 'The Estates of Norwich Cathedral Priory, 1101–1538', *Norwich Cathedral*, pp. 339–59.
33. Knowles and Hadcock, *Medieval Religious Houses*, pp. 52, 55, 58.
34. For the involvement of the local laity in the endowment of monasteries, see Harper-Bill, 'Searching for Salvation', p. 21.
35. C. Johnson and H. A. Cronne, eds, *Regesta Regum Anglo-Normannorum*, ii, 1100–1135 (Oxford, 1956), nos 509, 548, 591, 762, 786, 946, 1955.

36. E. Stone, 'Profit and Loss Accountancy at Norwich Cathedral Priory', *TRHS*, fifth series, xii (1962), pp. 25–48. For the exploitation of the priory's estates, see B. M. S. Campbell, *English Seigniorial Agriculture, 1250–1450* (Cambridge, 2000), passim.
37. N. Tanner, 'The Cathedral and the City', *Norwich Cathedral*, pp. 255–69.
38. See above, p. 314.
39. For a full account of the rising, see P. C. Maddern, *Violence and Social Order: East Anglia, 1422–1442* (Oxford, 1992), pp. 175–200.
40. J. A. F. Thomson, 'Tithe Disputes in Later Medieval London', *EHR*, lxxviii (1963), pp. 1–17.
41. See above, pp. 153–4.
42. N. Vincent, *The Holy Blood: King Henry III and the Westminster Blood Relic* (Cambridge, 2001), pp. 69–71, 209–10; J. R. Shinners, 'The Veneration of Saints at Norwich Cathedral in the Fourteenth Century, *NA*, xl (1987–89), pp. 133–44.
43. Tanner, *CLMN*, pp. 88–90; Harper-Bill, 'Medieval Church', pp. 308–9.
44. W. A. Pantin, ed., *Documents Illustrating the Activities of the General and Provincial Chapters of the English Black Monks, 1215–1540* (3 vols, Camden Society, third series, xlv, xlvii, liv, 1931–37), iii, p. 28.
45. A. Gwynn, *The English Austin Friars in the Time of Wyclif* (Oxford, 1940), pp. 212–14.
46. J. J. Scarisbrick, *The Reformation and the English People* (Oxford, 1984), chapter 2.
47. Tanner, *CLMN*, pp. 67–82, 204–10.
48. Tanner, *CLMN*, pp. 113–40; idem, 'Cathedral and City', pp. 277–9.
49. J. Catto, 'Religious Change under Henry V', in G. L. Harriss, ed., *Henry V: The Practice of Kingship* (Oxford, 1985), pp. 97–115. This revival had a dramatic effect upon the fortunes of the cathedral's neighbour, St Giles's hospital: C. Rawcliffe, *Medicine for the Soul: The Life, Death and Resurrection of an English Medieval Hospital* (Stroud, 1999), chapter 4.
50. Tanner, 'Cathedral and City', p. 270.
51. Carrow priory and its relations with the city of Norwich have yet to receive the scholarly attention they deserve. Despite his assertion that the convent was 'never of any great importance', Walter Rye, *Carrow Abbey* (Norwich, 1889), offers a useful introduction to its history and records, which forms the basis of the brief survey in *VCH Norfolk*, ii, pp. 351–4. Its archaeology and topography are examined in R. Gilchrist and M. Oliva, *Religious Women in Medieval East Anglia* (Studies in East Anglian History, i, 1993), pp. 38, 40–42, 83–5. Oliva's more recent study, *The Convent and the Community in Late Medieval England* (Woodbridge, 1998), contains several references to the house, principally as a centre of female piety.

52. S. Thompson, *Women Religious: The Founding of English Nunneries after the Norman Conquest* (Oxford, 1991), pp. 49, 226. For subsequent confirmations, see NRO, NCR, 9B/6; 17B, Norwich Book of Customs, fo. 4v; *CChR, 1226–1257*, p. 91.
53. J. E. Sayers, ed., *Original Papal Documents in England and Wales from the Accession of Pope Innocent III to the Death of Pope Benedict XI* (Oxford, 1999), no. 155. This document has been consistently misdated by historians of Carrow as 1273.
54. Oliva, *Convent and Community*, p. 39; Jessopp, *Visitations*, p. 273.
55. Rawcliffe, *Medicine for the Soul*, pp. 95–8.
56. PRO, C171/7, unnumbered Carrow rent roll. We are grateful to Dr Claire Noble for this reference.
57. *VCH Norfolk*, ii, p. 352; Blomefield, *Norfolk*, iv, pp. 526–8.
58. Blomefield, *Norfolk*, iv, pp. 79–83, 130–34, 143–5.
59. T. D. Hardy, ed., *Rotuli chartarum in Turri Londinensi asservati* (London, 1837), p. 166; *CChR, 1257–1300*, p. 183. Some sources mistakenly give this date as 1199.
60. NRO, NCR, 17B, Norwich Domesday Book, fos 70r–70v; *RCN*, ii, pp. 254–8; W. Hudson, ed., *Leet Jurisdiction in Norwich during the Thirteenth and Fourteenth Centuries* (Selden Society, v, 1892), pp. 5, 8.
61. NRO, DCN 88/1–9.
62. NRO, NCR, 9B/6; 17B, Norwich Book of Pleas, fos 39v–41r; *RCN*, i, pp. lxxxi, 320; *CPR, 1416–1422*, p. 33.
63. J. Roskell, L. Clark and C. Rawcliffe, *The History of Parliament: The House of Commons, 1386–1421* (4 vols, Stroud, 1993), ii, pp. 243–4, 809–10; H. Le Strange, *Norfolk Official Lists* (Norwich, 1890), p. 130: NRO, NCR, 18A, Chamberlains' Account Book, 1384–1448, fo. 122v.
64. PRO, KB 27/621, rots 8r, 28r. Two sets of transcripts of the proceedings were likewise kept by the city (NRO, NCR, 9B/5; 17B, Norwich Book of Pleas, fos 38v–39r) and one by the cathedral chapter (NCP, 88/10). See also *RCN*, i, pp. lxxix-lxxx, 319. We owe the first of these references to Professor Philippa Maddern.
65. NRO, DCN 1/5/45. We are grateful to Professor Joan Greatrex for drawing our attention to this account.
66. *NCR*, ii, p. 62.
67. NRO, DCN 88/11–15.
68. T. Hawes, *An Index to Norwich City Officers, 1453–1835* (NRS, lii, 1986), p. 62. The alderman, who died in 1465, left Margaret 40s. and 10d. to each of the other sisters: NRO, NCC, reg. Brosyard, fos 350r–51r. From another brother, the rector of Heigham, near Norwich, she received a featherbed and a pewter bowl (ibid., fos 252r–52v).

69. NRO, NCC, reg. Haydon, fos 179r–79v; Rye, *Carrow Abbey*, p. 46.
70. Maddern, *Violence and Social Order*, pp. 175–200.
71. NRO, NCR, 16D, Assembly Proceedings, 1434–1491, fo. 4v.
72. *RCN*, i, p. 328.
73. *CPR, 1441–1446*, p. 366; NRO, NCC, reg. Wylby, fos 30v–32r; NRS, 26882 42 E8; Rye, *Carrow Abbey*, p. 7. Although Alice was allegedly sent to the nunnery at Bungay in disgrace, she did not resign until February 1445: NRO, DN reg. 5, book 10, fo. 58v.
74. L. J. Redstone, 'Three Carrow Account Rolls', *NA*, xxix (1946), pp. 43–4. St Giles's hospital, Norwich, was also obliged to accept lodgers: Rawcliffe, *Medicine for the Soul*, pp. 52–4, 60, 98, 152–3.
75. NRO, NRS, 26882 42 E8. Rye, *Carrow Abbey*, pp. 48–52, supplies a list of boarders, mostly female. For additional names, see also NRS, 26883 42 E8 and Hare MSS 5955–4 277X1. The number and monetary value of paying guests declined rapidly in the early sixteenth century, perhaps because of reforms following the critical episcopal visitation of 1492: Redstone, 'Three Carrow Account Rolls', p. 57.
76. Tanner, *CLMN*, pp. 155–6; NRO, NCR, 16D, Assembly Proceedings, 1434–1491, fos 132v, 137v; 17B, *Evidences Relating to the Town Close Estate, Norwich* (Norwich, 1887), pp. 50–52.
77. NRO, NRS, 26882 42 E8; Redstone, 'Three Carrow Account Rolls', pp. 59–63; Oliva, *Convent and Community*, pp. 126, 141.
78. Oliva, *Convent and Community*, p. 13; NRO, DCN, 1/13/2; Rawcliffe, *Medicine for the Soul*, p. 99. In 1434–35, the monks' net income stood at £1610, and their outgoings at £1960: NRO, DCN 1/13/2.
79. NRO, NRS, 26882 42 E8. Oliva, *Convent and Community*, p. 97, ignores this schedule in her rather optimistic survey of the house's finances, remarking that the cellaresses were 'able to collect receipts greater than their expenses', and were faced with no more than 'small but nagging debts'.
80. Rawcliffe, *Medicine for the Soul*, pp. 100–2; NRO, NRS, 26883 42 E8; Hare MS 5955.
81. Eileen Power's celebrated study, *Medieval English Nunneries, c. 1275 to 1535* (Cambridge, 1922), paints a gloomy view of the intellectual capacity and aspirations of these women, drawing much of its evidence from East Anglia. Oliva, *Convent and Community*, provides a useful corrective, but is highly selective in her choice of sources.
82. Jessopp, *Visitations*, pp. 15–17.
83. E. Powell, *The Rising in East Anglia in 1381* (Cambridge, 1896), p. 32.
84. Rye, *Carrow Abbey*, pp. 47–8 and appendix IX, provides a list of testators who left bequests to the house.
85. NRO, NCC, reg. Aleyn, fos 130v–32v.

86. NRO, NCC, reg. Platfoote, fo. 105r (1530). The image was a *pietà*: Elizabeth, Lady Morley, had given instructions to be buried before it in 1500, and William Aslak, who lived in the precinct, did likewise some thirty years later: reg. Cage, fo. 183v; Alpe, fos 195r–96v.
87. *Calendar of Papal Letters, 1362–1404*, p. 373.
88. T. Smith, L. T. Smith and L. Brentano, eds, *English Gilds* (Early English Text Society, xl, 1890), pp. 42–4. A lawsuit of 1290 over a right of way near the priory refers specifically to a processional route used by the nuns at festivals, so these events may have been common: *VCH Norfolk*, ii, p. 352.
89. E. P. L. Brock, 'On the Excavation of the Site of Carrow Abbey, Norwich, by J. J. Colman Esq., MP, in 1880–1881', *Journal of the British Archaeological Association*, xxxviii (1882), pp. 165–214.
90. Rye, *Carrow Abbey*, pp. 24–7; Gilchrist and Oliva, *Religious Women*, pp. 83–5; Blomefield, *Norfolk*, iv, p. 526. Suffield left the nuns a legacy of 66s. 8d.: NRO, NCR, 24B/2.
91. N. Bradley Warren, *Spiritual Economies: Female Monasticism in Later Medieval England* (Philadelphia, 2001), p. 184.
92. S. B. Meech and H. E. Allen, eds, *The Book of Margery Kempe* (Early English Text Society, ccxii, 1940), p. 43. See also Chapter 6, above.
93. NRO, NCC, reg. Surflete, fos 86r–88r (Baxstere); Wylby fos 30v–32r (Thomas Wetherby); Brosyard, fos 83r–84r (Margaret Wetherby), 133r (Bardolf); Multon, fos 89v–91r (Kerre).
94. M. C. Erler, *Women, Reading and Piety in Late Medieval England* (Cambridge, 2002), pp. 68–84, describes this remarkable group in detail.
95. D. N. Bell, *What Nuns Read: Books and Libraries in Medieval English Nunneries* (Cistercian Studies, clviii, 1995), pp. 126–8. Oliva, *Convent and Community*, p. 67, is, however, mistaken in asserting that the nuns 'marked their books with a Latin *ex libris* heading', which 'demonstrates the existence of a library'. She misreads the transcript made by Bishop Tanner from the house's lost cartulary, which he records as being taken '*ex libro* monasterii monalium de Carho', that is copied by him from *one single volume*: Rye, *Carrow Abbey*, appendix I.
96. Power, *English Nunneries*, pp. 305–9, 590–92.
97. J. Scattergood, ed., *John Skelton: The Complete English Poems* (New Haven and London, 1893), pp. 71–106, 405–17. Skelton knew Norwich well, and wrote a Latin poem about the fire of 1507: ibid., p. 521.
98. Tanner, *CLMN*, p. 164.
99. NRO, NCC, reg. Platfoote, fos 105v–6r. Elizabeth was the relict of John Yaxley, and thus a kinswoman of the pious Margaret Purdans, although not, as Erler, *Women, Reading, and Piety*, p. 178, suggests, her grand-daughter. Katherine Kerr likewise left smocks and petticoats to poor nuns: reg. Multon, fos 89v–91r.

100. NRO, NCC, reg. Brosyard, fos 159v, 206v. In 1457 alone, Isabel was left 6s. 8d. by Alderman John Harrowe, who may have been a kinsman (ibid., fos 84v–85v), and 2s. by Katherine Brasyer (ibid., fos 59r–59v).

101. Glichrist and Oliva, *Religious Women*, pp. 84–85; Rye, *Carrow Abbey*, pp. 28–32, and plate before p. 33.

102. Tanner, *CLMN*, p. 223; Rye, *Carrow Abbey*, appendix IX. One priest was buried in front of the chancel steps with vessels for the celebration of mass: M. W. Atkin and S. Margeson, 'A Fourteenth-Century Pewter Chalice and Paten from Carrow Priory, Norwich', *NA*, xxxviii (1983), pp. 374–80.

103. NRO, NCC, reg. Wymer, fo. 77r. Oliva, *Convent and Community*, p. 202, states that four of the Carrow nuns lived together in the Norwich parish of St Peter Hungate after 1536, but none of the sources cited, including this will (which she attributes to *two* different testators), refer to such a community.

104. Jessopp, *Visitations*, pp. 145, 208–9, 273–5; C. Harper-Bill, 'The Labourer Is Worthy of his Hire? Complaints about Diet in Late Medieval Monasteries', in idem and C. M. Barron, eds, *The Church in Pre-Reformation Society* (Woodbridge, 1985), pp. 95–108.

105. Rye, *Carrow Abbey*, p. 16. In 1539 the site and buildings (worth £145 in salvage) were awarded to Sir John Shelton: ibid., appendix VII.

106. For the most convenient introduction, see C. H. Lawrence, *The Friars: The Impact of the Early Mendicant Movement on Western Society* (Harlow, 1994); for England, the chapters on the friars in M. D. Knowles, *The Religious Orders in England* (3 vols, Cambridge, 1948–59). For their appeal to the young and the learned, see R. W. Southern, *Western Society and the Church in the Middle Ages* (Harmondsworth, 1970), pp. 272–99. Material relating to the Norwich houses may be found in J. L. W. Vinten Mattich, 'Friars and Society in Late Medieval East Anglia' (2 vols, University of Cambridge, PhD thesis, 1993), especially ii, pp. 305–32. For an older survey, see J. Kirkpatrick, *History of the Religious Orders and Communities ... of Norwich* (Yarmouth, 1845), which is valuable for the text of documents now lost, but almost comical in its rabid anti-Catholicism.

107. R. Brentano, *Two Churches: England and Italy in the Thirteenth Century* (second edn, Berkeley and London, 1988), pp. 223–4.

108. For the chronology of mendicant settlement in England, see Knowles and Hadcock, *Medieval Religious Houses*, pp. 212–50.

109. For an excellent survey, see P. R. Szittya, *The Anti-Fraternal Tradition in Medieval Literature* (Princeton, 1986).

110. For the establishment, subsequent development and moves of the Dominican convent, see *VCH Norfolk*, ii, pp. 428–30; C. F. R. Palmer, 'The Friar-Preachers, or Black Friars, of Norwich', *The Reliquary*, new series, ii (1888), pp. 151–70, 210–14; iii (1889), pp. 42–9, 98–103; W. A. Hinnebusch, *The Early*

English Friars Preachers (Rome, 1951), especially pp. 67–9, 94–5, 119–20; H. Sutermeister, *The Norwich Blackfriars* (Norwich, 1977).

111. For the foundation and subsequent expansion of the Franciscans, see *VCH Norfolk*, ii, p. 431; P. A. Emery, *The Greyfriars: Excavations at the Former Mann Egerton Site, Prince of Wales Road, Norwich, 1992–95* (EAA, forthcoming), especially chapter three, part 1.

112. A. G. Little, ed., *Fratris Thome vulgo dicti de Eccleston: tractatus de adventu fratum minorum in Anglia* (Manchester, 1951), p. 50.

113. Knowles and Hadcock, *Medieval Religious Houses*, pp. 248–9.

114. Lawrence, *Friars*, pp. 158–9.

115. *VCH Norfolk*, ii, pp. 431–2; K. J. Egan, 'The Establishment and Early Development of the Carmelite Order in England' (University of Cambridge, PhD thesis, 1965), pp. 278–80.

116. *VCH Norfolk*, ii, pp. 431–2; F. Roth, *The English Austin Friars, 1249–1538* (2 vols, New York, 1961–66), prints many of the relevant documents.

117. R. B. Brooke, *Early Franciscan Government* (Cambridge, 1959), pp. 187–209.

118. E. Jordan, ed., *Les registres de Clement IV, 1265–68* (2 vols, Paris, 1893–1912), i, no. 172. For a rare mendicant cartulary, revealing how one convent consolidated its site, see C. Harper-Bill, ed., *The Cartulary of the Augustinian Friars of Clare* (Suffolk Records Society, Charter Series, xi, 1991).

119. J. R. H. Moorman, *A History of the Franciscan Order from its Origins to the Year 1517* (Oxford, 1968), pp. 177–81.

120. Tanner, *CLMN*, p. 157.

121. For a discussion of these bulls, see Lawrence, *Friars*, pp. 159–61.

122. Sutermeister, *Norwich Blackfriars*, pp. 21–9. See N. Pevsner and B. Wilson, *Norfolk*, i, *Norwich and North-East* (second edn, London, 1997), pp. 265–9, for a discussion and plan of the remains.

123. J. H. Harvey, ed., *William of Worcester's Itineraries* (Oxford, 1969), p. 237.

124. Harvey, *Worcester's Itineraries*, pp. 324–7; A. Jotischky, *The Carmelites and Antiquity: Mendicants and their Pasts in the Middle Ages* (Oxford, 2002), pp. 20–21; P. G. Lindley, 'The "Arminghall Arch" and Contemporary Sculpture in Norwich', *NA*, xl (1987), pp. 19–43.

125. Roth, *Austin Friars*, i, p. 312; ii, no. 501.

126. Knowles and Hadcock, *Medieval Religious Houses*, pp. 218, 227, 236, 242 (mid fourteenth-century estimates), 492 (1500 estimates); for Dissolution dispensations, see Tanner, *CLMN*, p. 20.

127. Kirkpatrick, *Religious Orders*, pp. 113–15, 127.

128. Blomefield, *Norfolk*, iv, pp. 84–5.

129. See above, notes 44 and 45.

130. Vinten Mattich, 'Friars and Society', p. 315. For the background to his dispute, see Jotischky, *Carmelites*, pp. 20–21.

131. Palmer, 'Friar-Preachers', *The Reliquary*, new series, ii (1888), p. 169. At some point between 1479 and 1489, the Carmelite prior began litigation in chancery against the master of St Giles's hospital, who, he claimed, was wrongfully suing him for £33 in the court of the sheriff of Norwich. It was, he argued, impossible to secure a fair trial there because of the 'favour and gret asistens' shown to his adversary: PRO, C1/64/31. The master was, indeed, remarkably well connected, and would have pulled all the strings at his disposal: Rawcliffe, *Medicine for the Soul*, pp. 257–8.
132. For the wider context, see R. N. Swanson, 'The "Mendicant Problem" in the Later Middle Ages', in P. Biller and B. Dobson, eds, *The Medieval Church: Universities, Heresies and the Religious Life* (Studies in Church History, *Subsidia*, xi, 1999), pp. 217–38.
133. G. R. Owst, *Literature and Pulpit in Medieval England* (second edn, Oxford, 1961); B. Smalley, *English Friars and Antiquity in the Early Fourteenth Century* (Oxford, 1960), chapters 1–4. Almost certainly annotated by a Norwich friar, BL, Add. MS 27304, a text of Virgil's *Aeneid*, contains marginalia highlighting useful *exempla* for sermons designed to appeal to the citizens. It is apparent from many of his notes, which refer to trade, pestilence, married life and the events of 1381, that the friar had a close rapport with his congregation: C. Baswell, 'Aeneas in 1381', in R. Copeland, D. Lawton and W. Scase, eds, *New Medieval Literatures* (Oxford, 2002), pp. 23–30. We are most grateful to Professor Baswell for drawing this MS to our attention.
134. A. B. Emden, *A Biographical Register of the University of Cambridge to 1500* (Cambridge, 1963), pp. 541 (Somerton), 523 (Sloley).
135. Kirkpatrick, *Religious Orders*, pp. 123, 127.
136. N. Davis, ed., *Paston Letters and Papers of the Fifteenth Century* (2 vols, Oxford, 1971–76), i, pp. 1–12.
137. Emden, *Biographical Register, Cambridge*, p. 87.
138. Lawrence, *Friars*, pp. 84–7 (Dominicans), 127–51 (in general).
139. V. Doucet, 'Le *Studium* Franciscain de Norwich', *Archivum Franciscanum Historicum*, xlvi (1953), pp. 85–98. For Wodeham, see A. B. Emden, *Biographical Register of the University of Oxford to A. D. 1500* (3 vols, Oxford, 1957–59), iii, p. 2082; R. Wood, ed., *Adam de Wodeham, Lectura secunda in librum primum sententiarum* (St Bonaventura, New York, 1990), p. 6; for Assisi, Emden, *Biographical Register, Oxford*, i, p. 65; for Candia, ibid., pp. 345–6.
140. Moorman, *Franciscan Order*, p. 402.
141. Tanner, *CLMN*, appendix 5 (pp. 191–2).
142. *VCH Norfolk*, ii, 432; G. Keynes, ed., *The Letters of Sir Thomas Browne* (London, 1931), p. 338.
143. Tanner, *CLMN*, p. 120.
144. Vinten Mattich, 'Friars and Society', p. 327.

145. NRO, NCC, reg. Caston, fo. 237r. For a similar bequest to the Dominicans, see Tanner, *CLMN*, pp. 119–20.
146. NRO, NCC, reg. Ryxe, fo. 174r. Sir Thomas Brews, in his last testament of 1479 (proved in 1483), granted to Friar Thomas in the Carmelites four marks (53s. 4d.) a year to 'kepe and exercise his scole' for five years: NRO, DN reg. 7, book 12, fo. 242r.
147. See above, notes 46 and 47. For mendicant confraternities in Italy, see C. F. Black, *Italian Confraternities in the Sixteenth Century* (Cambridge, 1989), pp. 23–32.
148. For these confraternities, see Tanner, *CLMN*, p. 74, appendix 8 (pp. 205–10).
149. For comprehensive lists of altars, images and lights, compiled from various sources, see Vinten Mattich, 'Friars and Society', pp. 326–7 (Dominicans), 331 (Franciscans), 315–16 (Carmelites), 307 (Augustinians).
150. For the way Dominicans encouraged women to teach their children through the use of sacred images, see C. Dupeux, P. Jezler and J. Wirth, *Iconoclasme: vie et mort de l'image médievale* (Berne, 2001), pp. 39–40.
151. Tanner, *CLMN*, p. 12.
152. For lists of burials and benefactors, see Vinten Mattich, 'Friars and Society', pp. 305–6, 313–14, 323–5, 329–30.
153. K. B. McFarlane, *The Nobility of Later Medieval England* (Oxford, 1973), pp. 145–6; K. Mourin, 'Norwich, Norfolk and Sir Thomas Erpingham', in A. Curry, ed., *Agincourt 1415* (Stroud, 2000), p. 83. See also above, p. 125.
154. Vinten Mattich, 'Friars and Society', p. 327 (Skeet); Roth, *Austin Friars*, p. 328; Tanner, *CLMN*, pp. 216 (Kerdeston), 219 (Hobart).
155. W. E. Lunt, *Financial Relations of the Papacy with England, 1327–1534* (Cambridge, Massachusetts, 1962), p. 499.
156. R. N. Swanson, 'Mendicants and Confraternity in Late Medieval England', in J. M. Clark, ed., *The Religious Orders in Pre-Reformation England* (Woodbridge, 2002), pp. 121–44.
157. Lunt, *Financial Relations*, p. 521.
158. *VCH Norfolk*, ii, pp. 430–31.
159. Tanner, *CLMN*, p. 119.
160. Harper-Bill, *Register of John Morton*, pp. 33–115, passim.
161. Kirkpatrick, *Religious Orders*, pp. 7–8.
162. Tanner, *CLMN*, p. 14. For the rector of Bixley, see NRO, DN reg. 4, book 8, fo. 144v.
163. For a brief history, see *VCH Norfolk*, ii, pp. 455–7; and also Tanner, *CLMN*, index, under Norwich, colleges of secular priests.
164. Rawcliffe, *Medicine for the Soul*, p. 4.
165. S. Ayscough and J. Caley, eds, *Taxatio Ecclesiastica Angliae et Walliae auctoritate P. Nicholai IV* (Record Commission, 1831), p. 92; J. Caley and J. Hunter,

eds, *Valor Ecclesiasticus temp. Henry VIII* (6 vols, Record Commission, 1810–34), iii, pp. 289–90.

166. Tanner, *CLMN*, p. 30.
167. Emden, *Biographical Register, Oxford*, ii, pp. 1340–1.
168. Tanner, *CLMN*, p. 199.
169. For guilds, see Tanner, *CLMN*, pp. 76–8.
170. PRO, C43/47/291. For the popularity of this cult, see M. Rubin, *Corpus Christi* (Cambridge, 1990).
171. *RCN*, ii, p. 92.
172. For chantries, see Tanner, *CLMN*, pp. 95–7 and appendix 10 (pp. 212–19).
173. See Chapter 5, above.
174. PRO, C43/47/290; M. Grace, ed., *Records of the Gild of St George in Norwich, 1389–1547* (NRS, ix, 1937), pp. 6–8.
175. NRO, NCR, 17B, *Liber Albus*, p. 172.
176. See especially E. Duffy, *The Stripping of the Altars: Traditional Religion in England, 1400–1480* (New Haven and London, 1992).
177. R. Houlbrooke, 'Refoundation and Reformation, 1538–1628', in *Norwich Cathedral*, pp. 507–39.
178. Space does not permit a fuller discussion of the important part played by this institution in the religious life of the city, which is discussed at length in Rawcliffe, *Medicine for the Soul*, chapter 4. For the impact of the Dissolution see chapters 7 and 8.
179. N. Pevsner, *The Buildings of England: North-East Norfolk and Norwich*, (Harmondsworth, 1962), pp. 261, 286.
180. Emery, *Norwich Greyfriars*, chapter 3, part 11.
181. *VCH Norfolk*, ii, p. 433.
182. Sutermeister, *Norwich Blackfriars*, pp. 8–18.
183. Keynes, *Letters of Sir Thomas Browne*, p. 339.

Notes to Chapter 5: Glass-Painting

1. BL, Add. MS 17,462, fos 331r, 334r (Powell's Topographical Collections of Leicestershire, Lincolnshire and Norfolk).
2. R. Marks, *Stained Glass in England during the Middle Ages* (London, 1993), p. xxiv. This is the best general survey of English medieval glass. The standard work on Norwich glass is C. Woodforde, *The Norwich School of Glass-Painting in the Fifteenth Century* (London, New York and Toronto, 1950). For a wider perspective, see S. Brown and D. O'Connor, *Medieval Craftsmen: Glass-Painters* (London, 1991), and S. Brown, *Stained Glass: An Illustrated History* (London, 1994).
3. Between 1313 and 1513, the names of sixty-four glaziers are recorded at York;

in Norwich, at least seventy are known between 1280 and 1570: Marks, *Stained Glass*, p. 41.

4. I am most grateful to the Norfolk Archaeological Unit for permission to refer here to examples of excavated glass that have not yet been published.
5. V. D. Lipman, *The Jews of Medieval Norwich* (London, 1967), p. 262.
6. For Thetford, see D. B. Harden, 'Domestic Window Glass: Roman, Saxon and Medieval', in E. M. Jope, ed., *Studies in Building History* (London, 1961), pp. 46, 54. The Ely glass is unpublished. For the other places, see Marks, *Stained Glass*, pp. 109–12.
7. Marks, *Stained Glass*, p. 40.
8. The excavation, 777N, was carried out by the Norfolk Archaeological Unit.
9. T. A. Heslop, *Norwich Castle Keep: Romanesque Architecture and Social Context* (Norwich, 1994), p. 8.
10. Heslop, *Norwich Castle*, p. 12.
11. Marks, *Stained Glass*, p. 110.
12. I am grateful to Mr T. A. Heslop for this information.
13. F. Woodman, 'The Gothic Campaigns', *Norwich Cathedral*, pp. 158–61; Marks, *Stained Glass*, pp. 137–40; idem, 'Glazing in the Romanesque Parish Church', in F. Dell'Acqua and R. Silva, eds, *Il colore nel medioevo: arte, simbolo, tecnica* (Lucca, 2001), pp. 173–81. The medallions noted by Marks at Saxlingham Nethergate, south of Norwich, depicting St Edmund, another saint and two apostles, date from *c.* 1250. They are not from that church, but may have been made in the city. Recent excavations by the Norfolk Archaeological Unit on the site of the refectory have uncovered the remains of some thirteenth-century painted glass dating from between *c.* 1250 and *c.* 1280. One possibility is that they are part of the original glazing of the Lady chapel. Examination of the glass is under way at the time of writing. It includes much stiff-leaf grisaille, figure work and some canopies.
14. For Drayton, see N. Pevsner and B. Wilson, *Norfolk*, i, *Norwich and North East* (Harmondsworth, 1997), p. 448; Horsham St Faith's is unpublished. Stiff-leaf grisaille has been found at the site of the Norwich Greyfriars and at a site on Golden Ball Street (Norfolk Archaeological Unit excavation 26499): see the window glass report by the present writer in P. A. Emery, *The Greyfriars: Excavations at the Former Mann Egerton Site, Prince of Wales Road, Norwich, 1992–95* (EAA, forthcoming).
15. Woodforde, *Norwich School*, p. 9.
16. NRO, NCR, 1/4, m. 9r.
17. NRO, NCR, 1/1, m. 1r.
18. NRO, NCR, 1/1, mm. 2v, 3r; 1/2, mm. 5v, 25r, 34r, 43v, 50r; 1/3, mm. 2r, 7v, 8v; 1/4, mm. 30v, 35v; 1/5, mm. 7v, 8r, 19v.
19. See the previous chapter, pp. 102–9.

20. R. Marks, catalogue entry 226, in J. Alexander and P. Binski, eds, *Age of Chivalry* (London, 1987), p. 290.
21. Emery, *Norwich Greyfriars.*
22. D. J. King, 'Report on the Excavated Window Glass', in Emery, *Norwich Greyfriars.*
23. M. Archer, *English Stained Glass* (London, 1985), fig. 13; W. Wells, *Stained and Painted Glass: Burrell Collection* (Glasgow, 1965), catalogue entry 46.
24. Emery, *Norwich Greyfrairs.*
25. Norfolk Archaeological Unit excavation 35170N.
26. Blomefield, *Norfolk*, iv, p. 109. Over a thousand fragments of glass, mainly of the second half of the fourteenth century, have at the time of writing just been excavated from the site of the Carmelite friary in Norwich (Norfolk Archaeological Unit, Jarrold's Whitefriars Site 26598, on behalf of R. G. Carter Ltd). Preliminary analysis suggests that it includes royal heraldry and other motifs, possibly linked with the visit of John of Gaunt, duke of Lancaster, to Norwich in 1385–86. Walter de Dysse, the prior, was John of Gaunt's confessor. For the visit, see S. Walker, *The Lancastrian Affinity, 1361–1399* (Oxford, 1990), p. 184.
27. D. J. King, *Corpus Vitrearum Medii Aevi, Great Britain IV: The Medieval Stained Glass of St Peter Mancroft, Norwich* (Oxford, forthcoming).
28. Blomefield, *Norfolk*, iv, pp. 86–8. Erpingham was then old and childless, which may have prompted this lavish gesture: see K. Mourin, 'Norwich, Norfolk and Sir Thomas Erpingham', in A. Curry, ed., *Agincourt 1415* (Stroud, 2000), p. 83.
29. Norwich Castle Museum and Art Gallery, Todd Collection, 1954.138. Todd 6, Norwich, 282.
30. King, *St Peter Mancroft.*
31. R. W. Pfaff, *New Liturgical Feasts in Later Medieval England* (Oxford, 1970), pp. 62–3, identifies Norwich as a centre of this cult from the early fifteenth century.
32. D. J. King, 'A Glazier from the Bishopric of Utrecht in Fifteenth-Century Norwich', in E. de Bièvre, ed., *Utrecht: Britain and the Continent: Archaeology, Art and Architecture* (British Archaeological Association Transactions, xviii, 1996), pp. 216–25.
33. See P. Sheingorn, 'Appropriating the Holy Kinship: Gender and Family History', in K. Ashley and P. Sheingorn, eds, *Interpreting Cultural Symbols: Saint Anne in Late Medieval Society* (Athens and London, 1990), pp. 169–98.
34. See note 32.
35. See Chapter 3 above.
36. NRO, MC 500/16,761x7 (early eighteenth-century notebook of John Kirkpatrick), unpaginated; Blomefield, *Norfolk*, iv, p. 330.

37. The Four Doctors constituted a popular subject for East Anglian rood screens and pulpits: see E. A. Duffy, *The Stripping of the Altars: Traditional Religion in England, 1400–1580* (New Haven and London, 1992), p. 334.
38. Marks, *Stained Glass*, p. 79; A. E. Nichols, *Seeable Signs: The Iconography of the Seven Sacraments, 1350–1544* (Woodbridge, 1994), pp. 90–128.
39. Blomefield, *Norfolk*, iv, p. 330.
40. For All Saints' church, see Woodforde, *Norwich School*, pp. 172, 173, 179–80; for St John Maddermarket, A. V. Steward, *St John the Baptist, Maddermarket, Norwich* (Norwich, 1927), p. 6; and Pevsner and Wilson, *Norfolk*, i, p. 241; for St Swithun, Woodforde, *Norwich School*, p. 37; for St Laurence, Blomefield, *Norfolk*, iv, pp. 267–8, and Pevsner and Wilson, *Norfolk*, i, p. 242; for St Michael Coslany, ibid., p. 246.
41. For the glaziers mentioned below and others, see King, *St Peter Mancroft*.
42. R. Greenwood and M. Norris, *The Brasses of Norfolk Churches* (Holt, 1976), pp. 28–32.
43. For London, see Greenwood and Norris, *Brasses*, p. 32. In Norwich, John Alunday was both painter and glazier in the late fourteenth century (King, *St Peter Mancroft*), William Moundeford may have been both currier and glazier (King, 'A Glazier', pp. 216–17), and William Gylmyn, to whom John Wattok, glazier, was apprenticed, was left engraving tools in the will of a mason: J. Harvey, *English Medieval Architects* (Gloucester, 1984), p. 156.
44. For a fifteenth-century comparison, see S. Badham, 'London Standardisation and Provincial Idiosyncracy: The Organisation and Working Practices of Brass-Engraving Workshops in Pre-Reformation England', *Church Monuments*, v (1990), p. 11, and figs 4a and 4b; a sixteenth-century example is discussed in King, *St Peter Mancroft*, in the section on style (Elys-Garneys window).
45. The feast of the Transfiguration was introduced partially and in phases into late medieval England (Pfaff, *New Liturgical Feasts*, pp. 38–9). It is of note that, in the year after the commission from Heyward of the window with this subject, Edmund Ryx of Foulsham requested in his will that 'the boke of the service of the transfiguration of Christ be bought on my coste' (NRO, NCC, reg. Ryx, fo. 1). Nearer home, at St Giles's hospital, Norwich, the feast as celebrated from about 1500: C. Rawcliffe, *Medicine for the Soul: The Life, Death and Resurrection of an English Medieval Hospital* (Stroud, 1999), p. 128.
46. Blomefield, *Norfolk*, iv, p. 305; Pevsner, *Norfolk*, i, p. 231. For St Mary's, see the previous chapter, pp. 115–18.
47. The Dance of Death was a popular subject across western Europe at this time: see, for example, P. Binski, *Medieval Death* (London, 1996), pp. 153–9.

48. NRO, MC 500/14,761x7 (notebook of John Kirkpatrick), pp. 40–3; Blomefield, *Norfolk*, iv, pp. 304, 306, 311; G. A. King, 'The Pre-Reformation Painted Glass in St Andrew's Church, Norwich', *NA*, xvii (1914), pp. 283–94; King, *St Peter Mancroft*.
49. Blomefield, *Norfolk*, iv, pp. 150, 154, 155, 160; D. Harford, 'On the East Window of St Stephen's Church, Norwich', *NA*, xv (1904), pp. 335–48; King, *St Peter Mancroft*.
50. For an earlier case of continental influence, see note 29. On the subject of foreign glaziers working in England, see Marks, *Stained Glass*, pp. 205–28. For the glass at Shelton, see King, *St Peter Mancroft*.
51. I. Dunn and H. Sutermeister, *The Norwich Guildhall* (Norwich, 1978), pp. 2, 5, 6, 20; King, *St Peter Mancroft*.
52. Fuller's choice of St George probably derived from his membership of the prestigious guild of St George, whose members included the most influential citizens of Norwich. He appears in its records from 1524 to 1526: M. Grace, ed., *Records of the Gild of St George in Norwich, 1389–1547* (NRS, ix, 1937), pp. 124, 125. His will was registered in 1526 (PRO, PCC 11 Porch).
53. Blomefield, *Norfolk*, iv, p. 229.
54. Blomefield, *Norfolk*, iii, pp. 196–7; iv, p. 229; Tanner, 'Cathedral and City', pp. 267, 418, 463. The identification of the coat of arms of Ferrour now suggests that the resolution of the conflict in 1524–25, and the year of Ferrour's mayoralty, 1526–27, rather than Wolsey's visit in 1520, dates the cathedral glass. For Flemish 'justice pictures', see E. Panofsky, *Early Netherlandish Painting* (Harvard, 1971), p. 217; for the David paintings, see O. Pächt, *Early Netherlandish Painting from Rogier van der Weyden to Gerard David* (London, 1997), pp. 246–7, figs 181, 182.
55. Blomefield, *Norfolk*, iv, p. 229. This window may have influenced the artist who produced a posthumous portrait of Jannys (still hanging in Blackfriars Hall), as he is depicted with death as a tipstaff behind his right shoulder (Plate 21).
56. Blomefield, *Norfolk*, iv, p. 230.
57. NRO, MC 500/19 (loose notes by John Kirkpatrick).
58. For the Labours of the Months in Norwich glass, see Woodforde, *Norwich School*, pp. 149–60; for the Marsham Nine Worthies, see ibid., pp. 151–2 n. 1, and S. Lucas, 'On Some Wood Carvings and Glass Recently Discovered in Norfolk', in W. Rye, ed., *Norfolk Antiquarian Miscellany*, second series, i (1906), pp. 97–9.
59. A few fragments of the Caister glazing were found in the moat some years ago: H. D. Barnes and W. D. Simpson, 'Caister Castle', *Antiquaries Journal*, xxxii (1952), pp. 35–51. A panel showing a scene from the life of St Benedict,

now in the Victoria and Albert Museum, may be from the chapel rebuilt by Fastolf in the abbey of St Benet Holme, where he was buried in 1459: King, 'A Glazier', pp. 224–5.

60. A set of by-laws drawn up by the city in 1618 for the regulation of the Glaziers' craft specifically mentions rules governing the making of heraldic glass. See NRO, NCR, 10b, Norwich Glaziers' By-Laws 1618. For the nineteenth-century revival of glass-painting in Norfolk, see B. Haward, *Nineteenth-Century Norfolk Stained Glass* (Norwich, 1984).

Notes to Chapter 6: Religious Practice

1. E. Colledge and J. Walsh, eds, *A Book of Showings to the Anchoress Julian of Norwich* (2 vols, Toronto, 1978), long text, chapter 27, p. 405: 'alle shalle be wele, and alle shalle be wele, and alle maner of thynge shalle be wele'.
2. E. Rutledge, 'Immigration and Population Growth in Early Fourteenth-Century Norwich: Evidence from the Tithing Roll', *Urban History Yearbook* (1988), p. 27; J. Campbell, 'Norwich', in M. Lobel, ed., *Historic Towns II* (London, 1975), pp. 9, 16–17.
3. S. K. Cohn, *Death and Property in Siena, 1205–1800: Strategies for the Afterlife* (Baltimore, 1988); D. Waley, *Siena and the Sienese in the Thirteenth Century* (Cambridge, 1991); D. Norman, ed., *Siena, Florence and Padua: Art, Society and Religion, 1280–1400* (2 vols, New Haven, 1995).
4. Colledge and Walsh, *Book of Showings*, long text, chapter 27, p. 405.
5. C. Abbott, *Julian of Norwich: Autobiography and Theology* (Woodbridge, 1999), provides a good summary of modern scholarship on the remarkable anchoress. Its bibliography lists fifty books and articles about her and her *Revelations*, the large majority of them written since 1980.
6. Colledge and Walsh, *Book of Showings*; Julian of Norwich, *A Revelation of Love*, ed., M. Glasscoe (revised edn, Exeter, 1993); G. R. Crampton, ed., *The Shewings of Julian of Norwich* (Kalamazoo, Michigan, 1993).
7. R. Llewelyn, ed., *Enfolded in Love: Daily Readings with Julian of Norwich* (London, 1980 onwards), see back-cover of the latest reprint for sales.
8. Abbott, *Julian of Norwich*, pp. 22 (playful lover), 118 (heaven), 119 (transformation), 164–78 (pastoral concern).
9. S. B. Meech, ed., *The Book of Margery Kempe* (Early English Text Society, ccxii, 1940), pp. 42–3; Tanner, *CLMN*, pp. 58–64, 83, 90.
10. Abbott, *Julian of Norwich*, pp. xi–xiii, 1–2.
11. Tanner, *CLMN*, pp. 58–64.
12. The Scrope family was noted for its piety and connection with an eremitical revival in the north: see J. Hughes, *Pastors and Visionaries: Religion and Secular Life in Late Medieval Yorkshire* (Woodbridge, 1988).

13. John Bale, *Scriptorum illustrium maioris Brytannie catalogus* (Basel, 1557), pp. 334, 629–30; Tanner, *CLMN*, pp. 59–60.
14. E. Brown and S. Hopkins, 'Seven Centuries of Building Wages', in E. Carus-Wilson, ed., *Essays in Economic History* (2 vols, London, 1962), ii, p. 177.
15. NRO, NCC, reg. Surflete, fo. 86v (Baxter); reg. Jekkys, fos 15v–16r (Ferneys); Tanner, *CLMN*, pp. 60–2, 199, 202, 233–4.
16. Tanner, *CLMN*, pp. 130–1, 223.
17. Tanner, *CLMN*, pp. 64–6. See also pp. 323–4, above. The importance of the North Sea connection and, indeed, of the vibrant religious life of Norwich, is stressed by C. Baswell, 'Aeneas in 1381', in R. Copeland, D. Lawton and W. Scase, eds, *New Medieval Literatures* (Oxford, 2002), pp. 23–40.
18. For a discussion of religious life in late medieval English towns, see G. Rosser, 'Urban Culture and the Church 1300–1540', in D. M. Palliser, ed., *The Cambridge Urban History of Britain*, i, *600–1540* (Cambridge, 2000), pp. 335–69.
19. A. Farley and H. Ellis, eds, *Domesday Book* (4 vols, London, 1783–1816), ii, p. 117.
20. A total of 25,000 inhabitants for some fifty parish churches averages five hundred parishioners for each, not taking into account the cathedral and the churches of the friaries and the smaller religious houses and hospitals.
21. Tanner, *CLMN*, pp. 2–3.
22. Oxford, Bodleian Library, MS Tanner 100, fos 40r–42v, printed in Tanner, *CLMN*, pp. 179–88.
23. A. Watkin, ed., *Inventory of Church Goods temp. Edward III* (NRS, xix, in 2 vols, 1947–48), i, pp. 1–27; Tanner, *CLMN*, pp. 5, 8–9; W. H. St John Hope, 'Inventories of the Parish Church of St Peter Mancroft, Norwich', *NA*, xiv (1901), pp. 153–240.
24. Tanner, *CLMN*, pp. 126–9, 223.
25. J. Alexander and P. Binski, eds, *Age of Chivalry: Art in Plantagenet England, 1200–1400* (London, 1987), no. 711.
26. See especially, W. J. Courtenay, *Schools and Scholars in Fourteenth-Century England* (Princeton, 1987), chapters 2 to 4.
27. For the friaries, see Chapter 4, above. For schools in Norwich, see P. Cattermole, 'Schools in Medieval and Early Tudor Norwich', in idem and R. Harries, eds, *A History of Norwich School* (Norwich, 1991), pp. 1–22; J. Greatrex, 'The Almonry School of Norwich Cathedral Priory in the Thirteenth and Fourteenth Centuries', in D. Wood, ed., *The Church and Childhood* (Studies in Church History, xxx, 1994), pp. 169–81; Tanner, *CLMN*, pp. 32–5; N. Orme, *English Schools in the Middle Ages* (London, 1973), pp. 144, 230–31.
28. Tanner, *CLMN*, p. 34; *DNB*, Adam Easton.
29. Tanner, *CLMN*, pp. 28–30.

30. NRO, NCC, reg. Gylys, fos 181r–83v (Baker); Tanner, *CLMN*, pp. 35–7, 237–40.
31. Tanner, *CLMN*, pp. 37–42.
32. C. Rawcliffe, *Medicine for the Soul: The Life, Death and Resurrection of an English Medieval Hospital* (Stroud, 1999), chapter 4; Tanner, *CLMN*, pp. 111–12; M. C. Erler, *Women, Reading and Piety in Late Medieval England* (Cambridge, 2002), pp. 68–84.
33. Tanner, *CLMN*, pp. 92–104; Rawcliffe, *Medicine for the Soul*, pp. 119–26; R. Ward, 'The Foundation and Function of Perpetual Chantries in the Diocese of Norwich, 1250–1547' (University of Cambridge, PhD thesis, 1999), pp. 70–71, 101–19; C. Burgess, '"For the Increase of Divine Service": Chantries in the Parish in Late Medieval Bristol', *Journal of Ecclesiastical History*, xxxvi (1985), pp. 46–65.
34. Tanner, *CLMN*, pp. 27–8, 85–7, 101–2; G. Hay, 'Pilgrims and the Hospice', *The Venerabile*, xxi (1962), pp. 109–44.
35. Meech, *Book of Margery Kempe*, pp. 60, 102.
36. Tanner, *CLMN*, pp. 88–90, 231–2.
37. W. T. Bensly, 'St Leonard's, Norwich', *NA*, xii (1895), pp. 198–201; M. R. V. Heal, 'Veneration and Renovation at a Small Norfolk Priory: St Leonard's, Norwich in the Later Middle Ages', *Historical Research*, lxxvi (2003), pp. 431–9. For pilgrimage in Norfolk, see E. Duffy, 'The Dynamics of Pilgrimage in Late Medieval England', and C. Rawcliffe, 'Curing Bodies and Healing Souls: Pilgrimage and the Sick in Medieval East Anglia', both in C. Morris and R. Roberts, eds, *Pilgrimage: The English Experience from Becket to Bunyan* (Cambridge, 2002), pp. 164–77 and 108–40 respectively.
38. Tanner, *CLMN*, pp. 67–82, 204–20.
39. *RCN*, ii, p. 287; Tanner, *CLMN*, pp. 68–71.
40. N. Davis, ed., *Non-Cycle Plays and Fragments* (Early English Text Society, supplementary text 1, 1970), pp. xxii–xl, 8–18; Tanner, *CLMN*, pp. 71–3; see also G. M. Gibson, *The Theater of Devotion: East Anglian Drama and Society in the Late Middle Ages* (Chicago, 1989).
41. M. Q. Smith, 'The Roof Bosses in Norwich Cathedral and their Relation to Medieval Drama in the City', *NA*, xxxii (1961), pp. 12–26; M. D. Anderson, *Drama and Imagery in English Medieval Churches* (Cambridge, 1963), pp. 87–8.
42. M. Grace, ed., *Records of the Gild of St George in Norwich, 1389–1547* (NRS, ix, 1937); Tanner, *CLMN*, pp. 73–82; B. R. McRee, 'Charity and Gild Solidarity in Late Medieval England', *Journal of British Studies*, xxxii (1993), pp. 200, 214, 219–25; idem, 'Religious Gilds and Civic Order: The Case of Norwich in the Late Middle Ages', *Speculum*, lxvii (1992), pp. 69–97.
43. G. Unwin, *The Gilds and Companies of London* (fourth edn, London, 1963),

pp. 155–217, 367–70; B. Pullan, *Rich and Poor in Renaissance Venice* (Oxford, 1971), pp. 33–193.

44. See Chapter 13, above.
45. Tanner, *CLMN*, pp. 132–7; J. A. F. Thomson, 'Piety and Charity in Late Medieval London', *Journal of Ecclesiastical History*, xvi (1965), p. 187. Caistor may have had in mind the passage from *Corpus Iuris Canonici*, 'quicquid habent clerici pauperum est' (*Decretum Gratiani*, 2.16.1.68).
46. N. Tanner, ed., *Heresy Trials in the Diocese of Norwich, 1428–1431* (Camden Society, fourth series, xx, 1977), pp. 35–8, 43–50, 60, 195.
47. See p. 87, above.
48. R. Houlbrooke, 'Persecution of Heresy and Protestantism in the Diocese of Norwich under Henry VIII', *NA*, xxxv (1970–73), pp. 308–26; Tanner, *CLMN*, pp. 162–6; Bale, *Scriptorum illustrium Maioris Brytannie Catalogus*, part 1, p. 556; John Foxe, *Acts and Monuments*, ed. J. Pratt (8 vols, London, 1877), iv, pp. 620–1, 642–3, 652, 773, and after p. 778 'Documents Relating to Thomas Bilney'; Blomefield, *Norfolk*, iii, p. 199; ix, p. 461; Thomas More, 'Preface' to *The Confutation of Tyndale's Answer*, ed. L. A. Schuster and others, *The Complete Works of St Thomas More* (New Haven, 1963-), viii, p. 23.
49. Despenser, see Thomas Walsingham, *Historia Anglicana*, ed. H. T. Riley (2 vols, RS, 1863–4), ii, pp. 188–9. Wakeryng, see Foxe, *Acts*, iii, pp. 584–6, 848. Alnwick, see Tanner, *Heresy Trials*, pp. 8–9 and passim. Brown, see E. F. Jacob, 'Thomas Brouns, Bishop of Norwich, 1436–1445', in H. Trevor-Roper, ed., *Essays in British History Presented to Sir Keith Feiling* (London and New York, 1964), p. 66. Nykke, see Houlbrooke, 'Persecution of Heresy', pp. 309–13.
50. J. A. F. Thomson, *The Later Lollards, 1414–1520* (Oxford, 1965), chapter 5; Tanner, *Heresy Trials*, passim.
51. Tanner, *Heresy Trials*, pp. 8, 23.
52. Houlbrooke, 'Persecution of Heresy', pp. 322–3.
53. See *History of Norwich*, ii, Chapter 2.
54. See especially C. Haigh, *Reformation and Resistance in Tudor Lancashire* (Cambridge, 1975); idem, *English Reformations: Religion, Politics and Society under the Tudors* (Oxford, 1993); J. J. Scarisbrick, *The Reformation and the English People* (Oxford, 1984); E. Duffy, *The Stripping of the Altars: Traditional Religion in England, c. 1400-c. 1580* (New Haven, 1992).
55. For a fuller treatment of this argument, see N. Tanner, 'The Reformation and Regionalism: Further Reflections on the Church in Late Medieval Norwich', in J. A. F. Thomson, ed., *Towns and Townspeople in the Fifteenth Century* (Gloucester, 1988), pp. 129–47.
56. *Norwich Cathedral*, pp. 259–69. The circumstances of this display of civic antagonism (but not violence) towards the priory are discussed in C. Humphrey, *The Politics of Carnival* (Manchester, 2001), chapter 3.

57. Thomas of Monmouth, *The Life and Miracles of St William of Norwich*, eds, A. Jessop and M. R. James (Cambridge, 1896), passim; G. I. Langmuir, 'Thomas of Monmouth: Detector of Ritual Murder', *Speculum*, lvi (1984), pp. 820–56; A. L. Poole, *From Domesday Book to Magna Carta, 1087–1216* (Oxford, 1951), pp. 353–4.
58. Tanner, *CLMN*, pp. 5–10, 51–4; C. Harper-Bill, ed., *The Register of John Morton Archbishop of Canterbury, 1486–1500* (Canterbury and York Society, lxxxix, 2000), nos 276–81.
59. *Norwich Cathedral*, pp. 255–80, especially 270, 274, 280; Tanner, *CLMN*, pp. 5–10, 51–4; Langmuir, 'Thomas of Monmouth', pp. 838, 842–3.
60. Tanner, *CLMN*, pp. 18–21.
61. Tanner, *CLMN*, pp. 21–3.
62. Geoffrey Chaucer, *Canterbury Tales*, ed. L. D. Benson (Oxford, 1988), Prologue, lines 507–11, p. 31; William Langland, *Piers Plowman*, ed. J. A. Bennett (Oxford, 1972), B Text, Prologue, lines 83–6, p. 3.
63. Tanner, *CLMN*, pp. 24–8. For Norwich's nuns, see Chapter 4, above.

Notes to Chapter 7: Norwich before the Black Death

1. W. Rye, *Tourist's Guide to Norfolk* (London, 1892), p. 25.
2. E. Rutledge, 'Immigration and Population Growth in Early Fourteenth-Century Norwich: Evidence from the Tithing Roll', *Urban History Yearbook* (1988), pp. 15–30.
3. R. E. Glasscock, 'England *circa* 1334', in H. C. Darby, ed., *A New Historical Geography of England* (Cambridge, 1973), p. 141; B. M. S. Campbell, 'Population Pressure, Inheritance and the Land Market in a Fourteenth-Century Peasant Community', in R. M. Smith, ed., *Land, Kinship and Life-Cycle* (Cambridge, 1984), p. 92.
4. NRO, NCR, 5B, leet roll, 1300.
5. T. H. Hollingsworth, *Historical Demography* (London and Southampton, 1969), pp. 363–4, is working back from a doubtful Black Death mortality figure. He also suggests a 1311 population of 25,000, based on J. C. Russell's mistaken view that all the men in tithing were householders.
6. D. Nicholas, *Town and Countryside: Social, Economic and Political Tensions in Fourteenth-Century Flanders* (Bruges, 1971), p. 234.
7. A. Dyer, 'Appendix: Ranking Lists of English Medieval Towns', in D. M. Palliser, *The Cambridge Urban History of Britain*, i, *600–1540* (Cambridge, 2000), p. 754.
8. The following discussion develops the work done by S. Kelly in eadem, E. Rutledge and M. Tillyard, *Men of Property: An Analysis of the Norwich Enrolled Deeds, 1285–1311* (Norwich, 1983), pp. 13–39. I am grateful to the

British Academy for helping fund the preparation of the underlying database between 1990 and 1992. The major sources used are the series of Norwich enrolled deeds 1285–1340 (NRO, NCR, 1/1–13) and the Norwich leet rolls 1288–1313 (NRO, NCR, 5B). A brief calendar of the enrolled deeds is available in W. Rye, ed., *A Short Calendar of Deeds Relating to Norwich ... 1285–1306* (Norwich, 1903); and idem, *Calendar of Norwich Deeds Enrolled in the Court Rolls ... 1307–1341* (Norwich, 1915). Extracts from the leet rolls are published in W. Hudson, ed., *Leet Jurisdiction in the City of Norwich during the Thirteenth and Fourteenth Centuries* (Selden Society, v, 1892).

9. No one is counted more than once. A known merchant who exports wool, for instance, will only appear as a merchant.
10. D. Keene, 'Continuity and Development in Urban Trades: Problems of Concepts and the Evidence', in P. J. Corfield and idem, eds, *Work in Towns, 850–1850* (Leicester, London and New York, 1990), p. 7. His sixty-eight Norwich trades come from a single source, the Norwich enrolled deeds, between 1285 and 1311. Irrespective of population size, the number of occupations known for a town is dependent on the sources available, the timescale adopted and whether or not bynames are included.
11. Gundreda le Puddingwyf and Margery le Melewoman. Other superficially female forms such as brewster, bakster and combster were applied to men as well as women.
12. NRO, DCN 1/1/35. I am grateful to Dr Claire Noble for Norwich cathedral priory references.
13. Brewing would have been the primary occupation of some of those involved, but not of others. The recording of these offences is inconsistent; husbands and wives have been counted as one and only ten single men are included.
14. Hudson, *Leet Jurisdiction*, pp. 4–5. It should also be noted that agricultural activities less often gave rise to occupational titles in the later middle ages.
15. The skinners were furriers (dealers in skins).
16. See Chapter 13 for the problems of urban pollution.
17. J. Blair and N. Ramsay, eds, *English Medieval Industries* (London and Rio Grande, Ohio, 1991), pp. 93–5.
18. NRO, DCN 1/1/35, 38, fos 6v, 13v, 16v.
19. *CPR, 1292–1301*, p. 583.
20. Rutledge, 'Immigration and Population', p. 26.
21. Some of the general points suggested here are made in P. Nightingale, 'Norwich, London and the Regional Integration of Norfolk's Economy in the First Half of the Fourteenth Century', in J. A. Galloway, ed., *Trade, Urban Hinterlands and Market Integration c. 1300–1600* (Centre for Metropolitan History, series three, 2000), pp. 83–101. However, my analysis differs in a number of respects from that by Dr Nightingale who, *inter alia*, draws

conclusions from the references to trades in the Norwich enrolled deeds over five-year periods.

22. 1286–1305 and 1320–39 are the earliest and latest complete twenty-year periods covered by the Norwich enrolled deeds at this date. It was possible to be rich and not buy property, but the ability to purchase can be taken as a general indicator of wealth.
23. This drop is despite the fact that the proportion of trade ascriptions given in the Norwich enrolled deeds remains much the same between the two periods and the number of deeds enrolled increases.
24. PRO, E179/149/9, mm. 79–80. The numbers given here and in Table 2 for subsidy-payers are all minimum figures. It is sometimes impossible to tell which of two men, with the same name but different occupations, is intended.
25. For the suggestion that a high population density and a high ratio of single-adult households are indicated by cooks outnumbering bakers see M. Carlin, 'Fast Food and Urban Living Standards in Medieval England', in eadem and J. T. Rosenthal, eds, *Food and Eating in Medieval Europe* (London, 1998), pp. 50–1; *RCN*, i, p. 189.
26. H. Swanson, *Medieval Artisans* (Oxford, 1989), p. 89.
27. See Chapter 1 for these changes to the urban landscape.
28. C. W. and P. Cunnington, *Handbook of Medieval English Costume* (London, 1960), pp. 31, 60.
29. It is impossible, though, to determine how much Norwich property was passed on by inheritance. These impressions are based largely on evidence about men engaged in the land market.
30. M. Kowaleski, 'Town and Country in Late Medieval England: The Hide and Leather Trade', in Corfield and Keene, *Work in Towns*, pp. 66–7, 73 n. 53.
31. Swanson, *Medieval Artisans*, p. 55 n. 7. Nine Norwich cordwainers owned property in the outer parish of St Giles, where the tawyers were operating.
32. Kelly, Rutledge and Tillyard, *Men of Property*, pp. 24–5.
33. *RCN*, ii, p. lxiv.
34. *RCN*, ii, p. lxvi; NRO, NCR, 5C, Mancroft tithing roll, 1311–33, m. 3. For the dating of the roll, see Rutledge, 'Immigration and Population', p. 19.
35. See E. Rutledge, 'Landlords and Tenants: Housing and the Rented Property Market in Early Fourteenth-Century Norwich', *Urban History*, xxii (1995), pp. 7–24.
36. A. F. Butcher, 'Rent and the Urban Economy: Oxford and Canterbury in the Later Middle Ages', *Southern History*, i (1979), p. 18.
37. NRO, NCR, 5B, leet roll, 1289.
38. R. Britnell suggests that over 50 per cent of the working population of York, Winchester and Norwich were engaged in the supply of food, drink and clothing in the early fourteenth century, but this includes both cloth

production, omitted here on the assumption that most of the dyed cloth was exported from Norwich, and leather production: idem, 'The Economy of British Towns 600–1300', in Palliser, *Cambridge Urban History*, pp. 121–2.

39. The names, occupations and illicit trade practices mentioned in this paragraph are all documented in the city records, but the individual transactions are not.
40. *RCN*, i, p. 223.
41. NRO, Y/C4/63, m. 4d; DCN, 1/1/38, fo. 21v.
42. Although at York 'almost anyone sold fish', it appears to have been mainly a primary occupation at Norwich: H. Swanson, 'Artisans in the Urban Economy: The Documentary Evidence from York', in Corfield and Keene, *Work in Towns*, p. 47. In a bare dozen cases the supply of fish could have been secondary to another known Norwich trade. John Jaune, who cooked as well as selling both meat and fish, has been counted as a cook.
43. NRO, NCR, 5B, leet rolls, 1289, 1290, 1293.
44. *RCN*, i, p. 142.
45. Hudson, *Leet Jurisdiction*, pp. 14, 55; NRO, NCR, 5B, leet roll, 1296.
46. C. M. Woolgar, ed., *Household Accounts from Medieval England* (Records of Social and Economic History, new series, xvii–xviii, 1992–93), i, pp. 203–25.
47. *CPR, 1272–1281*, pp. 30, 61.
48. R. H. Hilton, *The Economic Development of Some Leicestershire Estates in the Fourteenth and Fifteenth Centuries* (Oxford, 1947), p. 32.
49. *CPR, 1313–1317*, p. 589.
50. Woolgar, *Household Accounts*, p. 227. A last contained 13,200 fish.
51. A. Saul, 'The Herring Industry at Great Yarmouth, *c.* 1280-*c.* 1400', *NA*, xxxviii (1981), pp. 37–8.
52. Norfolk demesnes stocked sheep at a density below the national average and it was not until the late fourteenth century that wool became more profitable than corn in the areas of sheep-corn husbandry: B. M. S. Campbell, *English Seignorial Agriculture, 1250–1450* (Cambridge 2000), pp. 154, 159. The high contribution made by Norfolk towards the wool tax of 1341 was based on the county's exceptional subsidy assessment and exacerbated by the low value of Norfolk wool: T. H. Lloyd, *The English Wool Trade in the Middle Ages* (Cambridge, 1977), p. 160.
53. Lloyd, *English Wool Trade*, table 12, p. 123.
54. Lloyd, *English Wool Trade*, passim; PRO, E122/148/1–3, 7, 8, 11, 14, 16–23, 28, 29, 32, 34, 36; 149/4; 216/4. Men are described as Norwich-based if they held property within the city.
55. Many exporting through Yarmouth also exported through Lynn, though they were not necessarily all Norwich men: Lloyd, *English Wool Trade*, p. 135. Only four Norwich men were apparently using Lynn for small exports of wool in

1322–3 (William Curzoun, John de Hale, Richard de Bytering and Hugh de Dunston): D. M. Owen, ed., *The Making of King's Lynn* (Records of Social and Economic History, new series, ix, 1984), pp. 337–41.

56. *CPR, 1338–1340*, pp. 292–3; *CCR, 1343–1346*, pp. 145, 155.
57. *CCR, 1307–1313*, p. 438.
58. Lloyd, *English Wool Trade*, p. 155.
59. M. Bailey, *A Marginal Economy? East Anglian Breckland in the Later Middle Ages* (Cambridge, 1989), p. 149 n. 148.
60. Based on Lloyd, *English Wool Trade*, p. 123.
61. For the early history of the linen and worsted industries see A. F. Sutton, 'The Early Linen and Worsted Industry of Norfolk and the Evolution of the London Mercers' Company', *NA*, xl (1989), pp. 201–25.
62. *RCN*, ii, p. 35.
63. Sutton, 'Early Linen and Worsted Industry', p. 202.
64. Table 2 shows when known individuals were active in Norwich rather than the dates their occupations were given.
65. Sutton, 'Early Linen and Worsted Industry', p. 209.
66. Sutton, 'Early Linen and Worsted Industry', pp. 205–7.
67. K. I. Sandred and B. Lindström, *The Place-Names of Norfolk*, i, *The Place-Names of the City of Norwich* (English Place-Name Society, lxi, 1989), p. 75.
68. Sandred and Lindström, *Place-Names of Norwich*, p. 77.
69. PRO, E372/177, m. 51v; 178, mm. 38v, 45r; E352/130, m. 39r.
70. *CCR, 1313–1318*, p. 489.
71. *CPR, 1317–1321*, p. 199.
72. *CCR, 1318–1323*, p. 333.
73. PRO, CP40/153, rots 63r, 63v, 78r, 105v, 111r, 116v, 276r, 290v. The sum involved was equivalent to the annual income of a member of the lesser baronage. It has been assumed that these cases refer to Robert de Holveston, draper, who is described as such from 1287 to 1308, rather than Robert de Holveston, weaver, who is only mentioned in 1292. They are probably not the same man. The weaver held property in the parish of St Andrew where the draper had no interests. There was also a contemporary, Robert son of Roger de Holviston, who was a tawyer.
74. *CCR, 1333–1337*, p. 125.
75. N. S. B. Gras, *The Early English Customs System* (Cambridge, 1918), pp. 425, 433.
76. Sutton, 'Early Linen and Worsted Industry', pp. 206–7.
77. Gras, *Customs System*, pp. 423–5, 431–3. There were five possible Norwich men out of a total of twenty-six exporters of worsted. This may be an underestimate, as there is a break in the Norwich enrolled deeds from 1340 and no one is described in the Yarmouth customs records as of Norwich, but the absence

of previously known Norwich men is striking. There is no indication of the origin of the other twenty-one exporters either. William Dunston alone handled over 12 per cent of the total.

78. B. Dodwell, 'William Bauchun and his Connection with the Cathedral Priory at Norwich', *NA*, xxxvi (1975), p. 115. For his activities as corn dealer see Nightingale, 'Regional Integration', p. 87.
79. NRO, DCN 1/1/38, fo. 3r.
80. *CCR, 1333–1337*, p. 125.
81. *Norwich Cathedral*, pp. 274–5.
82. *CCR, 1307–1313*, p. 312.
83. NRO, Y/C4/54, mm. 1–2.
84. B. Hanawalt, ed., *Crime in East Anglia in the Fourteenth Century: Norfolk Gaol Delivery Rolls, 1307–1316* (NRS, xliv, 1976), passim.
85. I am currently working on an article investigating the services provided by, and the status of, the clerks.
86. This is based on Blomefield, *Norfolk*, i–xi.
87. Woolgar, *Household Accounts*, i, pp. 177–8.
88. For both this reason, and because brewers are not included in Table 2, they make up only 3 per cent of the known trade population.
89. C. Rawcliffe, *Medicine for the Soul: The Life, Death and Resurrection of an English Medieval Hospital* (Stroud, 1999), pp. 169–171; NRO, NCR, 24A, Great Hospital Archive, general accounts, 1306–98.
90. Sandred and Lindström, *Place-Names of Norwich*, p. 122; for the lane's position, see NRO, MC, 146/52 684x5, plans 72–3,76; Hudson, *Leet Jurisdiction*, pp. 58–9.
91. H. Le Strange, *Norfolk Official Lists* (Norwich, 1890), pp. 92–3.
92. See Carlin, 'Fast Food and Urban Living Standards', pp. 42–3.
93. Sandred and Lindström, *Place-Names of Norwich*, p. 54.
94. In 1338: NRO, NCR, 17C, Old Free Book, fo. 31v.
95. The brewers specifically charged with this were all women: NRO, NCR, 5B, leet roll, 1300.
96. *CCR, 1341–1343*, p. 454.
97. M. Murphy, 'Feeding Medieval Cities: Some Historical Approaches', in Carlin and Rosenthal, *Food and Eating*, pp. 121, 125 n. 26.
98. B. M. S. Campbell, *English Seignorial Agriculture, 1250–1450* (Cambridge, 2000), pp. 149, 260–1, 268–9.
99. D. Dymond, 'Medieval and Later Markets', in P. Wade-Martins, ed., *An Historical Atlas of Norfolk* (Norwich, 1993), pp. 76–7.
100. W. Rye, ed., *A Short Calendar of the Feet of Fines for Norfolk* (2 parts, Norwich, 1885–86), passim. Only the men specifically described as of Norwich are included.

101. Twenty miles has been suggested as the usual sphere of influence of a prominent regional town: J. Masschaele, *Peasants, Merchants and Markets: Inland Trade in Medieval England, 1150–1350* (London, 1997), p. 82. The nearest substantial towns south and south west of Norwich were Ipswich (forty miles) and Bury St Edmunds (thirty-six miles).
102. Nightingale, 'Regional Integration', passim.
103. Rye, *Feet of Fines*, passim.
104. W. Hudson, 'Norwich and Yarmouth in 1332', *NA*, xvi (1907), pp. 179–80.
105. P. Rutledge, 'The Will of Oliver Wyth, 1291', in R. Houlbrooke, J. Key, P. Rutledge, R. Virgoe and R. Wilson, eds, *A Miscellany* (NRS, lvi, 1991), pp. 9–28.
106. *CPR, 1313–1317*, p. 589; *CPR, 1317–1321*, pp. 93, 199; *CPR, 1330–1334*, p. 503.
107. Nightingale, 'Regional Integration', pp. 88, 93–4.
108. *CCR, 1343–1346*, p. 569.
109. *CCR, 1296–1302*, p. 112.
110. *CCR, 1307–1313*, pp. 82, 348, 438; *CCR, 1313–1318*, p. 80; *CCR, 1333–1337*, p. 125.
111. Altogether 113 men served as bailiff during the period 1275–1348.
112. *RCN*, i, pp. 197–8.
113. *RCN*, i, pp. xxx–xxxii, 19; *CPR, 1281–1292*, p. 169.
114. *RCN*, i, pp. 132–3.
115. *RCN*, i, pp. 20, 23–6; ii, pp. 226–7.
116. *RCN*, i, p. 366.
117. *RCN*, i, pp. 148–9.
118. PRO, CP40/153, rots 179v, 195r, 216v, 312v, 313v, 351r. Widows at Norwich could claim dower in half of their husbands' former Norwich property.
119. In 1397 the landgable rent brought in £3 5s. 4d.: *RCN*, ii, pp. xviii, 35.
120. *CPR, 1324–1327*, p. 215.
121. *RCN*, ii, pp. 209–12; *CCR, 1313–1318*, p. 489.
122. *CCR, 1307–1313*, p. 82. Thomas le Fruyter appears as a foreign merchant in PRO, E122/148/9.
123. Lloyd, *English Wool Trade*, p. 123; Gras, *Customs System*, pp. 423–5.
124. *CCR, 1343–1346*, p. 569.
125. W. Hudson, 'Notes about Norwich before the Close of the Thirteenth Century', *NA*, xii (1895), p. 65; J. Aberth, 'A Medieval Norwich Feud: The Bitter Dispute between Richard Spynk and Thomas de Lisle, Bishop of Ely', *NA*, xli (1992), p. 296.
126. Tanner, *CLMN*, p. 34.
127. Based on a population of 25,000, a household size of five and 418 people paying subsidy.
128. Rutledge, 'Immigration and Population', p. 20.
129. H. Swinden, *The History and Antiquities of the Ancient Burgh of Great Yarmouth* (Norwich, 1772), p. 373.

130. See Chapter 13 for a discussion of urban poverty at this time.
131. Glasscock, 'England *circa* 1334', p. 184.

Notes to Chapter 8: Order and Disorder

1. P. Heath Barnum, ed., *Dives and Pauper* (Early English Text Society, cclxxv, 1976, and cclxxx, 1980), i, part 1, p. 328.
2. That is, players of dice, gamblers, adulterers, fornicators, burglars, bawds and house-breakers.
3. PRO, C1/33/56–9.
4. *RCN*, i, pp. 65–6, 94, 109; C. Baswell, 'Aeneas in 1381', in R. Copeland, D. Lawton and W. Scase, eds, *New Medieval Literatures* (Oxford, 2002), pp. 23–4.
5. PRO, C1/19/484 (28–31 Henry VI); NRO, NCR, 16A, Assembly Proceedings, 21 March 1437, fo. 2r; 9D/5, *c.* 1446.
6. *RCN*, i, pp. 137, 143.
7. *RCN*, ii, p. 81.
8. *RCN*, ii, pp. 90–91.
9. W. Hudson, ed., *Leet Jurisdiction in the City of Norwich during the Thirteenth and Fourteenth Centuries* (Selden Society, v, 1892), Introduction, especially pp. xviii–xxii and xxvi–xxxix, quote from p. xxxiv; E. Rutledge, 'Immigration and Population Growth in Early Fourteenth-Century Norwich: Evidence from the Tithing Roll', *Urban History* (1988), pp. 15–30, especially pp. 18–20.
10. Hudson, *Leet Jurisdiction*, pp. xxxiv–vii.
11. See, for example, Hudson, *Leet Jurisdiction*, pp. 3, 17, 58.
12. *RCN*, i, p. 261.
13. See the excellent summary of Norwich's late fourteenth-century governing institutions and personnel in B. R. McCree, 'Peacemaking and its Limits in Late Medieval Norwich', *EHR*, cix (1994), pp. 835–8.
14. J. Campbell, 'Norwich', in M. Lobel, ed., *Historic Towns*, ii (London, 1975), p. 18.
15. See, for example, PRO, JUST 3/207, mm. 1r–4r, 209, mm. 1r–11r, 218/6 (20 February 1422), 219/2 (20 July 1424), 219/3, mm. 205, 211, 218, 225–7, 239; JUST 3/220/3; JUST 3/50/12, especially m. 31r–31v, when Humphrey, duke of Gloucester, in East Anglia to head a general oyer and terminer, and his fellow justices held sessions of gaol delivery at Norwich.
16. See, for example, PRO, JUST 3/50/14 (11 August 1430). The sitting justices were John Cottesmore, John Fray, John Cambrigge (the mayor), and Robert Baxter and Thomas Wetherby, aldermen.
17. PRO, JUST 3/210, mm. 5r, 7v, 10r.
18. NRO, NCR, 16A/1, Mayor's Court Book, 1440–1456, fo. 17r.
19. PRO, KB 27/717, rot. 78v, 718, rot. 87v.

20. *RCN*, ii, p. 218.
21. R. Howlett, 'Norwich Artillery in the Fourteenth Century', *NA*, xvi (1907), pp. 46–75.
22. G. Rosser, 'Urban Culture and the Church 1300–1540', in D. M. Palliser, ed., *The Cambridge Urban History of Britain*, i, *600–1540* (Cambridge, 2000), pp. 343–4.
23. B. R. McRee, 'Unity or Division? The Social Meaning of Guild Ceremony in Urban Communities', in B. A. Hanawalt and K. L. Reyerson, eds, *City and Spectacle in Medieval Europe* (Minneapolis, 1994), pp. 189–207, especially p. 191. See also the guild's admission oath, in M. Grace, ed., *Records of the Gild of St George in Norwich, 1389–1547* (*NRS*, ix, 1937), pp. 29–30.
24. E. Toulmin Smith, L. Toulmin Smith and L. Brentano, eds, *English Gilds* (Early English Text Society, xl, 1870), pp. 443–60. The date of this copy is established by the list of members given at the end of the document; they include 'Johannes Cambridgge, Maior' and 'Rogerus Felbrigge'. John Cambridge achieved the mayoralty first in 1430: see B. Cozens-Hardy and E. A. Kent, *The Mayors of Norwich, 1403–1835* (Norwich, 1938), p. 22; Roger, son of Sir Simon Felbrigge, was dead by 1434, when the St George's guild surveyors' rolls give details of his funeral expenses: NRO, NCR, 8E/3. Another version, said to be earlier, but unfortunately undated, appears in Grace, *Records of the Gild of St George*, pp. 33–8. McCree argues that the regulations were originally compiled sometime in the 1420s: B. R. McCree, 'Religious Gilds and Civic Order: The Case of Norwich in the Late Middle Ages', *Speculum*, lxvii (1992), p. 77 n. 26.
25. Tanner, *CLMN*, appendix 8, pp. 208–10. I have not counted craft guilds which also maintained religious activities. Twelve of the English guild returns to the 1389 ordinance are printed in Smith, *English Gilds*, pp. 14–34. J. C. Tingey, 'The Hitherto Unpublished Certificates of Norwich Gilds', *NA*, xvi (1907), pp. 267–305, discusses and prints a further five which were in Latin. Clearly, however, not all guilds were active at all times during the later middle ages.
26. *RCN*, ii, p. 33.
27. Hudson, *Leet Jurisdiction*, p. 18, and also pp. 4, 36 (1287–88 and 1289–90), for the cases of Simon de Melton (Wymer), William Calf (Berstrete) and Seman the needler (Conesford); *RCN*, i, p. 269 (1372).
28. Hudson, *Leet Jurisdiction*, p. 39.
29. Rutledge, 'Immigration and Population Growth', pp. 18–21; Hudson, *Leet Jurisdiction*, pp. 3, 4, 6–8, 10–11, 14–19, 29, 33–4, 37–9, 42, 46–8, 50, 52–3, 56, 63, 65–6, 70.
30. *RCN*, i, p. 189 (chapter 43 of the city custumal).
31. See, for example, Hudson, *Leet Jurisdiction*, pp. 3, 11, 14, 15, 17, 22, 25–6.
32. Grace, *Records of the Gild of St George*, pp. 46–67; NRO, NCR, 8E, St George's

guild, surveyor's accounts, 12 Henry VI; *RCN*, ii, p. 269 (1372); McCree, 'Peacemaking and its Limits', p. 837.

33. Hudson, *Leet Jurisdiction*, pp. 24, 33–5, 37, 47, 52–3, 55, 67, 73–4.
34. Hudson, *Leet Jurisdiction*, pp. 5, 11, 66–7.
35. McCree, 'Peacemaking and its Limits', p. 840.
36. *Curia Regis Rolls of the Reign of Henry III ... 17 to 21 Henry III* (London, 1972), no. 1385, pp. 352–3.
37. The most complete account is still W. Rye, 'The Riot between the Monks and Citizens of Norwich in 1272', *Norfolk Antiquarian Miscellany*, ii (1883), pp. 17–89. Contemporaries give a range of figures; Rye counts 173. See also, N. Tanner, 'The Cathedral and the City', *Norwich Cathedral*, pp. 255–62.
38. McCree, 'Peacemaking and its Limits', pp. 843–4; B. Cornford and A. Reid, 'The Uprising of 1381', in P. Wade-Martins, ed., *An Historical Atlas of Norfolk* (second edn, Norwich, 1994), pp. 86–7.
39. PRO, KB 9/84/1, rots 3r–4r, 10r–13r; KB 27/728 Rex, rots 24r et seq., 729 Rex, rot. 64, rots 18r, 28r.
40. Rye, 'Riot', p. 32. See also P. C. Maddern, *Violence and Social Order: East Anglia, 1422–1442* (Oxford, 1992), pp. 198–204.
41. Rye, 'Riot', p. 74.
42. *Curia Regis Rolls of the Reign of Henry III ... 17 to 21 Henry III*, no. 477, p. 100.
43. *RCN*, i, p. 243; part of the fine was then delivered to the 'community of Norwich' as an item of public 'treasure'.
44. Hudson, *Leet Jurisdiction*, pp. 37, 42 (1290–1 and 1292–3).
45. *RCN*, ii, p. 84; Maddern, *Violence and Social Order*, p. 193.
46. *RCN*, i, pp. 320–21.
47. E. Powell, *The Rising in East Anglia in 1381* (Cambridge, 1896), p. 30; McCree, 'Peacemaking and its Limits', p. 844; Cornford and Reid, 'Uprising of 1381', pp. 86–7.
48. *RCN*, i, pp. 61–2.
49. *RCN*, i, pp. 66–94. For a fuller discussion of civic government at this time, see Chapter 10, below.
50. Maddern, *Violence and Social Order*, pp. 183–91, in which I argue that the allegation was probably partial and exaggerated.
51. Maddern, *Violence and Social Order*, p. 196.
52. McCree, 'Peacemaking and its Limits', pp. 831–66.
53. *RCN*, i, pp. 109–12.
54. NRO, NCR, 16A/1, Mayor's Court Book, 1440–1456, fos 75r, 78r–9r, 80r, and 99r. For examples in 1492, see *RCN*, ii, pp. 305–6 and also PRO, C1/73/91, for one unsatisfactory 'settlement' which led to a chancery petition.
55. *RCN*, i, pp. 304–5; PRO, JUST 3/50/14. For similar activities at other fifteenth-century gaol delivery sessions, see *RCN*, i, pp. 302–6.

56. NRO, NCR, 6H/12.
57. PRO, JUST 3/219/2/, m. 1r. See also *RCN*, ii, p. 66, for the 1427–28 accounts for wood for burning Pye, William White and William (or John) Waddon.
58. PRO, JUST 3/207, mm. 1r–3r.
59. Maddern, *Violence and Public Order*, pp. 101–2.
60. NRO, NCR, 8A/10.
61. NRO NCR, 8A/1, coroners' presentments, 1263–67.
62. Rutledge calculates that the 1311 population may have risen to 17,000 ('Immigration and Population Growth', p. 27), but presumably the numbers would be lower some forty years earlier; 10,000 is a conservative, but not impossible estimate.
63. Home Office, Criminal Statistics England and Wales, supplementary tables, 2000, iii, at http://www.homeoffice.gov.uk/rds/pdfs/crimstatvol3.pdf; National Statistics: Population Estimates for England and Wales, Table 8, p. 23, at http://www.statistics.gov.uk/downloads/theme population/PEN03/PEN03 v3.pdf; both consulted 22 Feb. 2002.
64. C. Hammer, 'Patterns of Homicide in a Medieval University Town: Fourteenth-Century Oxford', *Past and Present*, lxxviii (1978), pp. 10–11.
65. *Curia Regis Rolls of the Reign of Henry III ... 9 to 10 Henry III* (London, 1957), no. 1778; *21 to 26 Henry III* (London, 1979), nos 980 and 2655; *17 to 21 Henry III* (London, 1972), nos 475, 477, 1320, 1385 and 1729.
66. W. Rye, 'The Alleged Abduction and Circumcision of a Boy at Norwich in 1230', *Norfolk Antiquarian Miscellany*, i (1877), pp. 312–44. V. D. Lipman comes to the same conclusion in *The Jews of Medieval Norwich* (London, 1967), pp. 59–62.
67. See above, notes 39–54.
68. Figures in column 2 are derived from Maddern, *Violence and Public Order*, table 2.1, p. 28.
69. That is supporting quarrels between other parties, in the case of embracery through the bribery or intimidation of juries.
70. PRO, KB 27/717, rots 58v, 64v, 80v, 81v (twice) 91r–91v, 92v, 107r.
71. PRO, KB 27/717, Rex rot. 1r (Trinity term 1440): *Rex* v. *Gregory Draper and others*. Wymondham also preferred the same suit by bill in the same term: ibid., rot. 48r.
72. See Maddern, *Violence and Social Order*, pp. 46–7, for some examples.
73. PRO, KB 27/719, rot. 59v. This case reached the stage of calling a jury.
74. Rosser, 'Urban Culture and the Church 1300–1540', p. 341; R. Gilchrist, 'Medieval Bodies in the Material World: Gender, Stigma and the Body', in S. Kay and M. Rubin, eds, *Framing Medieval Bodies* (Manchester, 1994), pp. 46–9.
75. On late-medieval views of the household as polity, see my 'Interpreting Silence: Domestic Violence in the King's Courts in East Anglia, 1422–1442', in

E. Salisbury, G. Donavin, and M. Llewelyn Price, eds, *Domestic Violence in Medieval Texts* (Gainesville, Florida, 2002), pp. 31–56.

76. Sir John Fortescue, 'On the Nature of the Law of Nature', in S. Lockwood, ed., *On the Laws and Governance of England* (Cambridge, 1997), p. 132, and also pp. 20–21.
77. Fortescue, 'Nature of the Law', p. 20.
78. Fortescue, 'Nature of the Law', p. 20. See also Augustine, *The City of God Against the Pagans* (Loeb Classical Library, London, 1957–72), book 19, chapter 21, p. 207.
79. Augustine, *City of God*, books 13–14.
80. Augustine, *City of God*, book 13, chapter 13, p. 179.
81. P. Meredith and S. J. Kahrl, eds, *The N-Town Plays: A Facsimile of British Library MS Cotton Vespasian C VIII* (Ilkley, 1977), fo. 12r–12v. See also fos 14r–16v.
82. Meredith and Kahrl, *N-Town Plays*, fo. 16v.
83. Meredith and Kahrl, *N-Town Plays*, fos 136r–37v.
84. Heath Barnum, *Dives and Pauper*, i, part 1, p. 308.
85. Grace, *Records of the Gild of St George*, pp. 16–18, 31, 67; Maddern, *Violence and Social Order*, pp. 181–2, 202–3; *RCN*, ii, p. 230; McCree 'Religious Gilds', p. 79.
86. Grace, *Records of the Gild of St George*, pp. 39–43.
87. McCree, 'Religious Gilds', pp. 69–97, especially pp. 93–6.
88. *Curia Regis Rolls of the Reign of Henry III ... 17 to 21 Henry III*, no. 1385, pp. 352–3 ('*cum ignis esset appositus per duas vices domibus Judeorum*'); N. Tanner, *Heresy Trials in the Diocese of Norwich, 1428–3* (Camden Society, fourth series, xx, 1977), p. 8.
89. Tanner, *Heresy Trials*, pp. 7–8.
90. See Chapter 13, above.
91. H. N. MacCracken, ed., *The Minor Poems of John Lydgate* (Early English Text Society, cxcii, 1934; reprinted 1961), p. 706. See also F. J. Furnivall, ed., *The Babees Book* (Early English Text Society, original series, xxxii, 1868; reprinted 1969), 'Dietarium', p. 56.
92. Thomas Gaascoigne, *Loci e libro veritatum*, ed. J. E. Thorold Rogers (Oxford, 1881), p. 12.
93. C. Woodforde, *Norwich School of Glass-Painting in the Fifteenth Century* (Oxford, 1950), plate 41, facing p. 188.

Notes to Chapter 9: Trade

1. G. H. Martin, ed., *Knighton's Chronicle, 1337–1396* (Oxford, 1995), pp. 98–105.
2. See A. Dyer, *Decline and Growth in English Towns, 1400–1640* (Cambridge, 1995), pp. 4–11, for a useful summary of late medieval urban historiography.

3. NRO, NCR, 17C, Old Free Book, fo. 33. The same pattern can be observed in York: R. B. Dobson, 'Admissions to the Freedom of the City of York in the Later Middle Ages', *EconHR*, second series, xxvi (1973), pp. 17–18.
4. These were first generation freemen, not the sons of freemen who could enter without payment and consequently left no trace in the records. Sixty-three of the 120 men who entered in 1349–50 had locative surnames pertaining to places outside the city walls, such as Walter of Gressenhall, for example, which suggests they were immigrants who moved into Norwich after the plague had subsided.
5. The population figure of 8000 is based on the 1377 poll tax figure of 3952 taxpayers. See the discussion of population in P. Dunn, 'After the Black Death: Society and Economy in Late Medieval Norwich' (UEA, Norwich PhD thesis, 2004), pp. 42–9.
6. Many towns and cities experienced a 'boom' in the late fourteenth and early fifteenth centuries: M. Kowaleski, *Local Markets and Regional Trade in Medieval Exeter* (Cambridge, 1995), p. 89; R. Holt, 'Gloucester in the Century after the Black Death', *Transactions of the Bristol and Gloucestershire Archaeological Society*, ciii (1985), p. 149; E. Miller, 'Medieval York', in *VCH City of York*, pp. 84–5, 88–9; R. H. Britnell, *Growth and Decline in Colchester, 1300–1525* (Cambridge, 1986), pp. 149–50.
7. A. Dyer, 'Appendix: Ranking Lists of English Medieval Towns', in D. M. Palliser, ed., *The Cambridge Urban History of Britain*, i, *600–1540* (Cambridge, 2000), pp. 761, 765.
8. H. W. Fowler and F. G. Fowler, eds, *The Concise Oxford Dictionary of Current English* (Oxford, 1996), p. 265.
9. See pp. 238–42, above.
10. *RCN*, ii, p. 42.
11. *CPR, 1381–1385*, p. 593.
12. W. Hudson, ed., *Leet Jurisdiction in the City of Norwich during the Thirteenth and Fourteenth Centuries* (Selden Society, v, 1892), p. 65.
13. PRO, E122/149/22.
14. Evidently the Paston family held worsted cloth in high esteem: N. Davis, ed., *Paston Letters and Papers of the Fifteenth Century* (2 vols, Oxford, 1971–76), ii, p. 140.
15. The most important 'tenter-ground' in late fourteenth-century Norwich was situated in the parish of St Giles, where there was sufficient open space to accommodate the large drying frames: NRO, NCR, 1/14, mm. 18r, no. 7, 36v, no. 2; 1/15, m. 9, no. 5.
16. The spinning wheel arrived in England during the fourteenth century but, for several centuries, spinning with distaff and suspended spindle continued for combed wool: P. Walton, 'Textiles', in J. Blair and N. Ramsay, eds, *English*

Medieval Industries (London and Rio Grande, Ohio, 1991), pp. 325–6. Regrettably, there is no comprehensive study of the late medieval worsted industry to date.

17. The late fifteenth century probably saw the introduction of the practice of calendering worsteds in Norwich: L. F. Salzman, *English Industries of the Middle Ages* (Oxford, 1923), p. 237; K. J. Allison, 'The Norfolk Worsted Industry in the Sixteenth and Seventeenth Centuries', *Yorkshire Bulletin of Economic and Social Research*, xii (1960), p. 73.
18. See *History of Norwich*, ii, Chapter 9, for a discussion of why worsted production was restricted to Norwich and its neighbouring villages, and p. 166 above, for possible innovation from Flanders in the 1330s.
19. Worsted weavers are mentioned for the first time during the reign of Richard II.
20. See Table 2, above.
21. NRO, NCR, 5B/10 (1375–76) and 5B/11 (1390–91); J. L'Estrange, *Calendar of Norwich Freemen, 1317–1603*, ed. W. Rye (London, 1888); NRO, NCR, 1/14 (1377–90) and 1/15 (1390–99). Weavers were usually described as 'websters' or 'textors' but, occasionally, 'wullen websters' and 'irlondwebsters' are mentioned. The term 'Irlonder' was interchangeable with 'worsted-weaver' in the late-fourteenth and fifteenth centuries: *RCN*, ii, p. lxvii.
22. Weavers appear with increasing frequency in all the surviving late fourteenth-century sources, not just the Old Free Book, confirming that the increase in numbers did not simply occur because they were being included in the franchise for the first time. It should be noted, however, that sources for the reign of Edward III are patchy compared to those for Richard II: Dunn, 'After the Black Death'.
23. Broadcloth was certainly being finished, and probably woven, in Norwich in the first half of the fifteenth century because fullers were still entering the franchise. Furthermore, equipment for fulling, such as kettles and troughs (also used in dyeing), was then being imported from the Continent. It was not until the New Mills were constructed, in 1429, that Norwich acquired its own fulling mill: Walton, 'Textiles', p. 332.
24. There are references to the bailiffs' sealing irons for cloth as early as 1345.
25. Blomefield, *Norfolk*, iii, p. 113. The new regulations surrounding the 'worsted-seld' probably also introduced some system of search and quality control in the county; by the end of the fifteenth century Norwich had acquired rights of search over Norfolk, Suffolk and Cambridgeshire.
26. The individual rooms brought in rents of between 13s. 4d. and 26s. 8d. each *per annum*, when they were fully occupied in 1397: NRO, NCR, 17B, Norwich Domesday Book, fo. 36r.
27. *RCN*, i, pp. 74–5.

28. The farm of the 'worstedseld' fell sharply from £4 in the 1420s and 1430s to only 20s. by the late 1450s.
29. A. King, 'The Merchant Class and Borough Finances in Later Medieval Norwich' (University of Oxford, DPhil thesis, 1989), p. 152.
30. King, 'Merchant Class', table 5.3.
31. For York's changing fortunes see J. N. Bartlett, 'The Expansion and Decline of York in the Later Middle Ages', *Econ HR*, second series, xii (1959), p. 29; and Miller, 'Medieval York', pp. 89–91.
32. *CPR, 1391–1396*, p. 306. A sarplar is two sacks of wool. For medieval weights and measures, see W. Childs, ed., *The Customs Accounts of Hull, 1453–1490* (Yorkshire Archaeological Society, cxliv, 1986), pp. 253–7.
33. PRO, E122 and NRO, Y/C4, passim.
34. E. Carus-Wilson and O. Coleman, *England's Export Trade, 1275–1547* (Oxford, 1963), p. 47.
35. J. L. Bolton, *The Medieval English Economy, 1150–1500* (London, 1980), p. 193.
36. T. H. Lloyd, *The English Wool Trade in the Middle Ages* (Cambridge, 1977), pp. 205–8.
37. For yearly wool exports from Yarmouth, based on the central enrolled customs accounts, see Carus-Wilson and Coleman, *England's Export Trade*, pp. 47–74.
38. PRO, E122/149/17, 18. There were fifty-two cloves in one sack.
39. PRO, E122/149/14, 17–19, 21.
40. The staple was at Middelburg in Zeeland between 1383 and 1388, but 1391 saw a brief return to the home staples, including Norwich. Sixteen city merchants contributed funds to petition for the re-establishment of the Norwich staple in 1390–91: *RCN*, ii, pp. 50–51. In the event, their petition was not necessary, but the incident highlights the citizens' keen interest in safeguarding the supply of wool to the Norwich textile industry and their determination to dominate the market.
41. Lloyd, *English Wool Trade*, pp. 225–56.
42. N. S. B. Gras, *The Early English Customs System* (Cambridge, 1918), p. 433; E. Power and M. M. Postan, *Studies in English Trade in the Fifteenth Century* (London, 1966), p. 359 n. 1.
43. A. Saul, 'English Towns in the Late Middle Ages: The Case of Great Yarmouth', *Journal of Medieval History*, viii (1982), p. 80.
44. PRO, E122/149/22, 33, 34.
45. To this figure, of course, would be added any revenues raised through the sale of produce and stock, although many landowners had by then abandoned demesne farming altogether.
46. Hugh Holland, better known for his wool exports, stayed clear of worsted but did export fulled cloths: PRO, E122/149/22, 27; E122/150/1.

47. Allison, 'Norfolk Worsted Industry', p. 79.
48. H. L. Gray, 'English Trade from 1446 to 1482', in Power and Postan, *Studies in English Trade*, pp. 4, 361 n. 7. Worsteds were charged by the piece so it is impossible to know the size of single and double worsteds with any certainty: Childs, *Customs Accounts of Hull*, p. xxv.
49. G. V. Scammell, 'English Merchant Shipping at the End of the Middle Ages: Some East Coast Evidence', *EconHR*, second series, xiii (1961), p. 330.
50. Allison, 'Norfolk Worsted Industry', p. 79; Bolton, *Medieval English Economy*, p. 252; J. Campbell, 'Norwich', in M. Lobel, ed., *Historic Towns*, ii (London, 1975), p. 16.
51. Allison, 'Norfolk Worsted Industry', p. 78; N. J. M. Kerling, *Commercial Relations of Holland and Zeeland with England from the Late Thirteenth Century to the Close of the Middle Ages* (Leiden, 1954), pp. 84, 87.
52. E. M. Veale, *The English Fur Trade in the Later Middle Ages* (Oxford, 1966).
53. PRO, E122/149/22, 33; NRO, Y/C4/103, m. 12r. Sporle also had a sideline in the export of cheese.
54. PRO, E122/149/33, m. 4r.
55. PRO, E122/149/27, 33.
56. PRO, E122/152/11. For the decline of Yarmouth see Saul, 'English Towns'.
57. PRO, E122/149/22, m. 1v; NRO, Y/C4/99, m. 16v. Thomas Hulveston exported malt in 1386: Y/C4/97, m. 16r, as did William Bolour in 1388: Y/C4/100, m. 14r.
58. R. H. Britnell, 'The Pastons and their Norfolk', *Agricultural History Review*, xxxvi (1988), pp. 132–44.
59. PRO, E122/149/22. Thomas Hert paid customs on imports worth £519 15s. in that year; Hugh Holland £217 6s. 8d.; William Lomynour £162 16s. 8d.; Ralph Skeet £224 2s. and John Worlyk £202 3s. 4d.
60. Saul, 'English Towns', p. 81.
61. PRO, E122/149/28, mm. 3r, 4r.
62. Power and Postan, *Studies in English Trade*, p. 206.
63. In 1438, for example, Thomas Skowe of Norwich sold a Boston merchant madder to the value of £42, which was to be transported by cart: NRO, NCR, 16D, Assembly Proceedings, 1434–1491, fo. 8v.
64. Kerling, *Commercial Relations*, p. 123.
65. For soap see PRO, E122/149/33, 194/9; and ashes E122/149/27, m. 8r.
66. PRO, E122/149/28, m. 4r; 149/33, m. 5r, for the late fourteenth century, and E122/150/11 for 1475–76.
67. Robert Brasier brought in such a shipment in 1398: PRO, E122/149/14, m. 2v.
68. For example, PRO, E122/149/34.
69. See p. 177, above.
70. John Cambridge regularly imported building supplies: PRO, E122/149/27, 34, 36.

71. B. S. Ayers, 'Domestic Architecture in Norwich from the Twelfth to the Seventeenth Century', *Lübecker Kolloquium zur Stadtarchäologie im Hanseraum*, iii (2001), pp. 35–46.
72. For the dominance of London grocers in this trade see P. Nightingale, *A Medieval Mercantile Community: The Grocers' Company and the Politics and Trade of London, 1000–1485* (London and New Haven, 1995), pp. 194–555.
73. This would explain why the only mention of Norwich merchants' involvement in the salt trade comes from the record of their salt being weighed, and the fee of 'measurage' being paid, in the local customs accounts.
74. A wey was the equivalent of 320 gallons.
75. NRO, Y/C4/91. The merchants involved were Thomas Hert, William Lomynour, John Piking, Ralph Skeet and William Skorrel. The salt in question was probably black salt from the Loire region, but a better quality white 'zelle' was available, which was derived from peat in Holland and Zealand. See A. R. Bridbury, *England and the Salt Trade in the Later Middle Ages* (Oxford, 1955), pp. 102, 114; Kerling, *Commercial Relations*, pp. 98–103.
76. PRO, E122/149/22, m. 2r. Thomas Cok and William Clement were the individuals involved. A tun of wine contained about 250 gallons.
77. PRO, E122/194/9; Power and Postan, *Studies in English Trade*, p. 360.
78. NRO, Y/C4/104, m. 15v. John Bordekyn paid duty on wine from the Rhine specifically described as being intended for Norwich.
79. The range of imports to Norwich, although impressive, was not as extensive as the diversity of goods entering the port of London in the late middle ages: H. S. Cobb, ed., *The Overseas Trade of London: Exchequer Customs Accounts, 1480–81* (London Records Society, xxvii, 1990).
80. An archaeological survey of goods for domestic use in medieval Norwich can be found in S. Margeson, *Norwich Households: The Medieval and Post-Medieval Finds from Norwich Survey Excavations, 1971–1978* (EAA, report 58, 1993), especially pp. 73–142.
81. PRO, E122/149/27, m. 6r.
82. See C. Dyer, *Standards of Living in the Later Middle Ages: Social Change in England, c. 1200–1520* (Cambridge, 1989), pp. 188–210.
83. For example, carriers from the ports of Arnemuiden, Dordrecht, Middelburg, Veere and Zierikzee.
84. This fits into the wider history of relations between the Hanse and England: M. M. Postan, 'The Economic and Political Relations of England and the Hanse from 1400–1475', in Power and Postan, *Studies in English Trade*, pp. 91–155.
85. K. Koppman, ed., *Die Recesse und andere Akten der Hansetage, 1256–1430* (8 vols, Leipzig, 1875), iii, pp. 405–7.
86. G. Von der Ropp, ed., *Hanserecesse, 1431–76* (3 vols, Leipzig, 1878), ii, pp. 537-46.

87. H. J. Smit, ed., *Bronnen tot de Geschiedenis van den Handel met Engeland, Schotland en Ierland, 1150–1485* (2 vols, The Hague, 1928), i, no. 981, p. 607.
88. PRO, E122/149/22, m. 6r, ship 2.
89. For medieval ships see Kerling, *Commercial Relations*, p. 173.
90. Between November 1399 and October 1400 Outresson carried five shipments of Norwich-owned worsted cloth from Yarmouth: PRO, E122/150/1.
91. PRO, E122/149/22, m. 5v, ship 4.
92. PRO, E122/149/22, m. 6r, ship 2; m. 7r, ship 4.
93. PRO, E122/149/19.
94. NRO, NCR, 1/15, m. 10r, no. 3.
95. *RCN*, ii, pp. 79–84.
96. Petitions to the court of chancery frequently concern Norwich men as the victims of disorder on the seas, bad debt and wrongful imprisonment. See, for example, PRO, C1/7/53, 9/410, 31/33, 103, 37/14.
97. PRO, C1/29/318, 544.
98. PRO, KB/29/5, Memoranda Roll 1408 (9 Henry IV), Trinity rot. 5.
99. Smit, *Bronnen tot de Geschiedenis*, ii, no. 1418, pp. 906–7.
100. NRO, NCC, reg. Popy, fo. 258r.
101. PRO, C1/62/311.
102. PRO, C1/59/151. Hoste sent the goods from Barrow-in-Furness, in Cumbria, but a certain John Piers of Yarmouth confiscated them.
103. NRO, NCR, 8D, Assembly roll, 27 May 1426.
104. *CPR, 1429–1436*, p. 112.
105. NRO, NCR, 5B/10, 11; N. J. M. Kerling, 'Aliens in the Country of Norfolk, 1436–1485', *NA*, xxxii (1963), p. 205.
106. Hudson, *Leet Jurisdiction*, p. 64.
107. Thomas Hert, Hugh Holland, Henry and William Lomynour, Alice Skeet's husband Ralph and John Worlyk were all bailiffs of the city.
108. Thomas Elys, Richard Spurdance, Robert Toppes and Thomas Wetherby, to name but a few.
109. NRO, Y/C4/88, mm. 12v, 13r.
110. PRO, E122/152/17.
111. NRO, Y/C4/91. A last was usually twelve barrels.
112. NRO, NCR, 5B/10 (Conesford and Mancroft leets); NCR, 1/15, m. 16v, no. 6.
113. Kowaleski, *Local Markets and Regional Trade*, p. 225.
114. *CPR, 1374–1377*, p. 357; *1370–1374*, p. 48.
115. Scammell, 'English Merchant Shipping', p. 329.
116. See Chapter 2.
117. NRO, NCR, 17B, *Liber Albus*, fo. 185v.
118. NRO, NCR, 17B, Norwich Domesday Book, fo. 23r.

119. King, 'Merchant Class and Borough Finances', table 10.5, p. 375.
120. NRO, DCN 9/5.
121. PRO, SC6/1255/3, 1255/5.
122. Davis, *Paston Letters*, i, p. 440; PRO, PROB, 2/97; C. W. Foster, ed., *Lincoln Wills Registered in the District Probate Registry at Lincoln* (Lincoln Record Society, v, 1914), i, p. 17; C. Rawcliffe, *Medicine for the Soul: The Life, Death and Resurrection of an English Medieval Hospital* (Stroud, 1999), pp. 256–7.
123. Allison, 'Norfolk Worsted Industry', p. 78.
124. The close connection between Norwich and London dates back to the thirteenth century at the latest: A. F. Sutton, 'The Early Linen and Worsted Industry of Norfolk and the Evolution of the London Mercers' Company', *NA*, xl (1989), pp. 205–9.
125. For example, *CCR, 1381–1385*, p. 127; *CPR, 1374–1377*, p. 357.
126. PRO, E122/73/23.
127. NRO, NCC, reg. Heydon, fo. 27.
128. William, brother of Robert Toppes, was based in London: NRO, NCC, reg. Jekkys, fo. 97.
129. NRO, NCR, 1/18, m. 22v.
130. For Welles see J. S. Roskell, L. Clark and C. Rawcliffe, eds, *The History of Parliament: The House of Commons, 1386–1421* (4 vols, Stroud, 1992), iv, pp. 802–5; and Catteworth J. C. Wedgwood, ed., *History of Parliament Biographies of the Members of the Commons House, 1439–1509* (London, 1936), pp. 165–6.
131. Richard Broun and Richard Drewe came to Norwich from Lynn and Thomas Ingham originated in Yarmouth.
132. P. Wade-Martins, ed., *An Historical Atlas of Norfolk* (Norwich, 1993), pp. 78, 94–6.
133. King, 'Merchant Class and Borough Finances', pp. 149–51.
134. U. Priestley, *The Great Market: A Survey of Nine Hundred Years of Norwich Provision Market* (Norwich, 1987).
135. J. Kirkpatrick, *The Streets and Lanes of the City of Norwich*, ed. W. Hudson (Norwich, 1889), pp. 31–8.
136. NRO, NCR, 17B, Norwich Domesday Book, fo. 23.
137. *CPR, 1476–1485*, p. 326.
138. In contrast to the other major provincial cities, such as York, Bristol and Lincoln, only Norwich and Newcastle on-Tyne did not secure a substantial reduction in their farms during the fifteenth century on grounds of poverty. Norwich did gain a remission in 1444, during the political troubles, because it was not master of its own income at the time: *RCN*, ii, p. 69.
139. Ayers, *Norwich*, p. 79.
140. King, 'Merchant Class and Borough Finances', pp. 42–54.

141. R. B. Dobson, 'Admissions to the Freedom', p. 16; Miller, 'Medieval York', p. 108.
142. Hudson, *Leet Jurisdiction*, p. 63.
143. Hudson, *Leet Jurisdiction*, p. 65.
144. King, 'Merchant Class and Borough Finances', p. 394.

Notes to Chapter 10: The Urban Elite

1. *RCN*, i, p. 123.
2. M. McKisack, *The Parliamentary Representation of the English Boroughs during the Middle Ages* (Oxford, 1932), p. 163. My thanks to Drs Linda Clark and Charles Moreton of the History of Parliament Trust for letting me consult drafts of the Constituency Survey for Norwich, 1422–60, and of the biographies of Norwich MPs for the same period. Thanks also to Ms Faith Peyton of Okanagan University College for obtaining many interlibrary loans and to Dr Ben Nilson and Dr Barb Angel for their helpful comments. Much of this chapter derives from my doctoral dissertation, 'The Aldermen of Norwich, 1461–1509: A Study of a Civic Elite' (University of Cambridge, PhD thesis, 1996).
3. C. Rawcliffe, *The Hospitals of Medieval Norwich* (Norwich, 1995), pp. 24 and 31 n. 37.
4. A. King, 'The Merchant Class and Borough Finances in Later Medieval Norwich' (University of Oxford, DPhil thesis, 1989), pp. 393, 394.
5. K. J. Allison, 'The Norfolk Worsted Industry in the Sixteenth and Seventeenth Centuries, Part 1, The Traditional Industry', *Yorkshire Bulletin of Economic and Social Research*, xii, part 4 (November, 1960), p. 79; J. L. Bolton, *The Medieval English Economy* (London, 1980), p. 252.
6. A. Carter, J. P. Roberts and H. Sutermeister, 'Excavations in Norwich – 1973. The Norwich Survey – Third Interim Report', *NA*, xxxvi (1974), p. 48.
7. *RCN*, i, pp. xxv (government under four bailiffs), 12–14 (charter of Richard I), 31 (abstract of the royal charter of 1404); J. Campbell, 'Norwich', in M. Lobel, ed., *Historic Towns*, ii (London, 1975), pp. 12, 15; J. F. Pound, *Tudor and Stuart Norwich* (Chichester, 1988), p. 68. For a nineteenth-century interpretation of these developments, see A. S. Green, *Town Life in the Fifteenth Century* (2 vols, London, 1894), i, pp. 360–73.
8. Norwich loaned the substantial sum of 1000 marks (£666 13s. 4d.) to Henry IV in 1402: L. C. Attreed, 'The English Royal Government and its Relations with the Boroughs of Norwich, York, Exeter and Nottingham, 1377–1509' (Harvard, PhD thesis, 1984), p. 310; Blomefield, *Norfolk*, iii, 119.
9. H. Le Strange, *Norfolk Official Lists* (Norwich, 1890), pp. 96–8 (bailiffs) and 99–100 (sheriffs). Le Strange states that a mayor and sheriffs first held office

in 1403, which is puzzling as the charter establishing these offices was not granted until the following year.

10. *RCN*, i, p. 31; Pound, *Tudor and Stuart Norwich*, p. 68.
11. *RCN*, i, p. 31.
12. *RCN*, i, pp. 13–14 (charter of Richard I).
13. *RCN*, i, p. 129 (oath of citizens). Women were hardly ever granted the freedom in Norwich and rarely received it in other medieval English towns.
14. *RCN*, i, p. lxx.
15. *RCN*, i, pp. 64–6.
16. See the petition printed in *RCN*, i, pp. 64–6, and also pp. liv, xlviii-lviii; Campbell, 'Norwich', p. 15. All but six of the twenty-four men noted in 1367 either had been or were shortly to be elected as bailiffs: B. R. McRee, 'Peacemaking and its Limits in Late Medieval Norwich', *EHR*, cix (1994), pp. 837 and 840–41 regarding the petition of 1378.
17. Attreed, 'Royal Government and Boroughs', p. 14.
18. *RCN*, i, pp. lxiii, 66–77.
19. *RCN*, i, pp. 93–108.
20. *RCN*, i, pp. 97–8.
21. *RCN*, i, pp. lxix, 98–100.
22. *RCN*, i, pp. 94, 96, 97, 98–9, 103, 104.
23. *RCN*, i, p. 104.
24. An abstract of this charter appears in *RCN*, i, pp. 36–7. See also ibid., p. lxx; McRee, 'Peacemaking and its Limits', p. 852.
25. *RCN*, i, pp. 109–14.
26. *RCN*, i, p. 33. Lorraine Attreed has noted the use of symbols to convey the honour and dignity of office: 'The Politics of Welcome: Ceremonies and Constitutional Developments in Later Medieval English Towns', in B. Hanawalt and K. Reyerson, eds, *City and Spectacle in Medieval Europe* (Minneapolis, Minnesota, 1994), p. 210.
27. *RCN*, i, p. 102.
28. NRO, NCR, 16A, Mayor's Court Book, 1510–1532, Wednesday before the feast of St Martin the Bishop 4 Henry VIII (10 November 1512).
29. *RCN*, i, pp. 94–6. The selection process for the mayor altered somewhat over the course of the fifteenth century. After 1447 the councillors and twenty-four ward constables nominated the mayoral candidates, but in 1462 this system changed, and the citizens once again voiced their preferences. Occasional modification of the voting process also occurred: in 1471 and 1472, for example, the sheriffs cast votes along with the mayor and aldermen, but the voting ultimately reverted back to the mayor and aldermen alone. See *RCN*, i, p. cv; NRO, NCR, 16D, Assembly Proceedings, 1434–1491, fos 88(1)v, 91r, 128v.

30. *RCN*, i, p. 95.
31. *RCN*, ii, p. xxx.
32. R. B. Dobson, 'Admissions to the Freedom of the City of York in the Later Middle Ages', *EconHR*, second series, xxvi (1973), especially pp. 8 and 18.
33. For examples of fees, see *RCN*, ii, pp. xxxix, xlvi. For more on entrance to the freedom in general, ibid., pp. xlviii-liii.
34. The aldermen first elected to this office between 1461 and 1509 had waited an average of seventeen years since being admitted to the freedom: Frost, 'Aldermen of Norwich', pp. 15–16.
35. This was not unique to Norwich. For an examination of office-holding patterns in York, see A. Kulukundis, 'The *Cursus Honorum* in Fifteenth-Century York: The Rise to Power' (University of York, MA thesis, 1991).
36. NRO, NCR, 16D, Assembly Proceedings, 1491–1553, fos 60v, 61r. The craft ordinances of 1449 acknowledged that some able men might be prevented from holding office because they followed occupations that had never produced a mayor, alderman or sheriff. Henceforward they were permitted to change occupations: *RCN*, ii, 289–90.
37. This protest supports S. H. Rigby's observation that 'Urban political conflicts ... rarely challenged hierarchy in general. Social protests normally centred on the alleged failure of the rich to carry out their side of the social contract, rather than rejecting the social contract *per se*': 'Urban "Oligarchy" in Late Medieval England', in J. A. F. Thomson, ed., *Towns and Townspeople in the Fifteenth Century* (Gloucester, 1988), p. 68.
38. Frost, 'Aldermen of Norwich', p. 29.
39. PRO, PCC 4 Dogett (T. Wilkyns, 1492); 16 Bodfelde (T. Wilkyns the younger, 1523); 21 Bennett (T. Caus, 1509); 28 Hogen (R. Wilkyns, 1535). The Wilkyns family was related to the Clerks, another aldermanic clan: see PCC 28 Holder (G. Clerk, 1517); NRO, NCC, reg. Gyles, fo. 102 (Gregory Clerk III, 1518).
40. PRO, C1/64/70; PCC 12 Horne (Rose, 1497).
41. Frost, 'Aldermen of Norwich', p. 140.
42. J. I. Kermode, 'The Merchants of Three Northern English Towns', in C. H. Clough, ed., *Profession, Vocation and Culture in Later Medieval England* (Liverpool, 1982), pp. 17–19.
43. Carter, Roberts and Sutermeister, 'The Norwich Survey – Third Interim Report', p. 49.
44. No list of aldermen survives for 1451, but most of those who served in 1453 had probably been in office then. While the tax assessment may not provide an accurate picture of the wealth of those taxed, it reveals who the richest people may have been: R. Virgoe, 'A Norwich Taxation List of 1451', *NA*, xl (1988), p. 147.
45. PRO, E179/149/187; Frost, 'Aldermen of Norwich', p. 87.

46. S. Thrupp, *The Merchant Class of Medieval London, 1300–1500* (Chicago, 1948), p. 81.
47. J. Kermode, 'Obvious Observations on the Formation of Oligarchies in Late Medieval English Towns', in Thomson, *Towns and Townspeople*, pp. 96–7.
48. PRO, PCC, 9 Jankyn.
49. C. Dyer, *Standards of Living in the Later Middle Ages: Social Change in England, c. 1200–1520* (Cambridge, 1989), p. 193.
50. In the late 1400s, relatively few men of substance avoided office, although the type and frequency of exonerations changed between 1510 and 1530: Frost, 'Aldermen of Norwich', pp. 32–7.
51. B. H. Allen, 'The Administrative and Social Structure of the Norwich Merchant Class, 1485–1680' (Harvard, PhD thesis, 1951), p. 371.
52. Kermode notes Susan Reynolds's perceptive observation that 'oligarchies were not automatically assumed to be corrupt nor out of line with contemporary notions of natural justice in the middle ages': 'Obvious Observations', p. 87. See also, P. Fleming, 'Telling Tales of Oligarchy in the Late Medieval Town', *The Fifteenth Century*, ii (2001), pp. 177–93.
53. In 1487 regulations requiring attendance at assembly meetings were reiterated, and the penalties for absence were reaffirmed at 6d. for aldermen and 3d. for common councillors: NRO, NCR, 16D, Assembly Proceedings, 1434–1491, fo. 130r. Fines had been set at 6d. and 3d. in 1476: Assembly Proceedings 1434–1491, fo. 102v. Penalties for absence had existed at least since 1422, when they were set at 12d. for aldermen and 6d. for councillors: *RCN*, i, p. 278. In 1424 the tripartite indenture alluded to a fine of 6d. leviable on aldermen who missed meetings without a reasonable excuse: see *RCN*, i, 109.
54. PRO, C1/45/116.
55. PRO, C1/158/54.
56. Frost, 'Aldermen of Norwich', p. 50.
57. S. Reynolds, 'Medieval Urban History and the History of Political Thought', *Urban History Yearbook* (1982), p. 21. When a citizen assumed the freedom, he swore that he would serve in civic offices if called upon to do so: *RCN*, i, p. 129.
58. NRO, NCC, reg. Aleyn, fo. 184v. For a fuller discussion of charitable activity, see Chapter 13.
59. PRO, PCC 2 Moone. Jowell left £10 to be spent on the day of his death and £20 at his burial. In 1510 his executors gave £20 to rebuild the city's woolhouses: NRO, NCR, 16D, Assembly Proceedings, 1491–1553, fo. 66v.
60. NRO, NCC, reg. Jekkys, fo. 84 (Hoste); PRO, PCC 25 Horne (Brian). Brian made provision for additional expenditure on the repair of the walls if his estate sufficed.

61. NRO, NCC, reg. Ryxe, fo. 89v. See also the 1503 will of Agnes Thorp, widow of two aldermen: PRO, PCC 26 Blanyr.
62. Frost, 'Aldermen of Norwich', p. 218.
63. On 30 April 1480 the mayor, Thomas Bokenham, was twice disturbed by men breaking into his home in St Stephen's ward as a protest following his imprisonment of Thomas Hay of Claxton, Norfolk, and his wife: PRO, KB 9/353, m. 86. Other examples of violence or threats against office-holders may be found in KB 9/418, m. 43, and KB 9/377, m. 6. Such disruptions were usually dealt with swiftly and sternly.
64. Green, *Town Life in the Fifteenth Century*, ii, p. 397.
65. P. Maddern, *Violence and Social Order: East Anglia, 1422–1442* (Oxford, 1992), pp. 174–205; B. McRee, 'Religious Gilds and Civic Order: The Case of Norwich in the Late Middle Ages', *Speculum*, lxvii (1992), pp. 84–91.
66. McRee, 'Religious Gilds and Civic Order', pp. 88–9.
67. McRee, 'Religious Gilds and Civic Order', pp. 91–3.
68. McRee, 'Religious Gilds and Civic Order', pp. 95–7. See also L. Attreed, 'Arbitration and the Growth of Urban Liberties in Late Medieval England', *Journal of British Studies*, xxxi (1992), p. 224.
69. Attreed, 'Royal Government and Boroughs', p. 310.
70. Attreed, 'Royal Government and Boroughs', p. 310; eadem, *The King's Towns: Identity and Survival in Late Medieval English Boroughs* (New York, 2001), p. 157; Blomefield, *Norfolk*, iii, 119.
71. Attreed, *King's Towns*, pp. 156 and 176 n. 68; Blomefield, *Norfolk*, iii, p. 147.
72. Blomefield, *Norfolk*, iii, p. 147.
73. Blomefield notes that the city of London, other English towns, members of the royal court and private donors contributed to the rebuilding of the city: Blomefield, *Norfolk*, iii, p. 131; NRO, NCR, 16D, Assembly Proceedings, 1491–1553, fo. 62r.
74. Attreed, 'Royal Government and Boroughs', pp. 114–24.
75. Blomefield, *Norfolk*, iii, p. 174.
76. H. Harrod, 'Queen Elizabeth Woodville's Visit to Norwich in 1469', *NA*, v (1859), p. 35.
77. Attreed, 'Royal Government and Boroughs', pp. 119–20.
78. Attreed, *King's Towns*, p. 221.
79. A. J. Pollard, *Late Medieval England, 1399–1509* (Harlow, 2000), p. 29.
80. Attreed, 'Politics of Welcome', p. 212.
81. Attreed, 'Politics of Welcome', p. 212.
82. T. John, 'Sir Thomas Erpingham, East Anglian Society and the Dynastic Revolution of 1399', *NA*, xxxv (1970), p. 107; A. Curry, ed., *Agincourt 1415* (Stroud, 2000), pp. 78–110.
83. E. F. Jacob, ed., *The Register of Henry Chichele* (4 vols, Oxford, 1937), ii, p. 380.

84. Attreed, 'Royal Government and Boroughs', pp. 332–50.
85. Attreed, 'Royal Government and Boroughs', p. 345.
86. Attreed, 'Royal Government and Boroughs', p. 350.
87. Attreed, 'Royal Government and Boroughs', p. 351; NRO, NCR, 16D, Assembly Proceedings, 1434–1491, fo. 54r.
88. M. Jurkowski, 'Parliamentary and Prerogative Taxation in the Reign of Edward IV', *Parliamentary History*, xviii, part 3 (1999), p. 271.
89. NRO, NCR, 16D, Assembly Proceedings, 1434–1491, fo. 76v.
90. Jurkowski, 'Parliamentary and Prerogative Taxation', p. 283.
91. NRO, NCR, 16D, Assembly Proceedings, 1434–1491, fo. 111v; Jurkowski, 'Parliamentary and Prerogative Taxation', p. 285. The benevolence of 1481 was to finance an expedition against the Scots.
92. *RCN*, i, pp. lxi, 31.
93. *RCN*, i, p. 126.
94. *RCN*, i, p. cvii.
95. *RCN*, i, pp. cxxvii-cxxxiv.
96. *RCN*, i, pp. lxi, 32.
97. *RCN*, i, p. cxxx.
98. *RCN*, i, pp. xciv–xcix, 37–40.
99. *RCN*, i, pp. xciv–ix, 38; Blomefield, *Norfolk*, iii, p. 158. Hudson notes that this charter was instrumental in solidifying the aldermen's position and authority: *RCN*, i, p. xcix.
100. J. S. Roskell, L. Clark and C. Rawcliffe, eds, *The History of Parliament: The House of Commons, 1386–1421* (4 vols, Stroud, 1992), iv, p. 148.
101. Information provided by Dr L. S. Clark and Dr Charles Moreton of the History of Parliament Trust.
102. Information provided by L. S. Clark and Charles Moreton.
103. NRO, NCR, 16D, Assembly Proceedings, 1434–1491, fos 103r–3v, 126r, 137r; McKisack, *Parliamentary Representation*, p. 89.
104. NRO, NCR, 16D, Assembly Proceedings, 1434–1491, fo. 99r; McKisack, *Parliamentary Representation*, p. 88.
105. NRO, NCR, 16D, Assembly Proceedings, 1434–1491, fo. 103r–3v.
106. Much of the material discussed here and in the following paragraphs has been supplied by L. S. Clark and Charles Moreton.
107. Roskell, Clark and Rawcliffe, *House of Commons, 1386–1421*, i, pp. 524–5.
108. For Bixley, see Roskell, Clark and Rawcliffe, *House of Commons, 1386–1421*, ii, p. 243.
109. Roskell, Clark and Rawcliffe, *House of Commons, 1386–1421*, i, p. 527.
110. Roskell, Clark and Rawcliffe, *House of Commons, 1386–1421*, ii, pp. 31, 809.
111. J. Topham, P. Morant and T. Astle, eds, *Rotuli Parliamentorum* (6 vols, London, 1767–77), v, pp. 60–61 (1442), 105–6 (1444).

112. S. T. Bindoff, ed., *The History of Parliament: The House of Commons, 1509–1558* (3 vols, London, 1982), i, p. 653.
113. Blomefield, *Norfolk*, iii, p. 178; A. Luders and others, eds, *Statutes of the Realm* (11 vols, London, 1810–28), ii, 11 Henry VII cap. 11, 19 Henry VII cap. 17.
114. Attreed, *King's Towns*, p. 59.
115. The two men received over £28 for their work in this matter. In addition, Ingham was paid 9s. for examining evidence at the exchequer concerning the dispute. I am grateful to Dr L. S. Clark for this information.
116. McKisack, *Parliamentary Representation*, pp. 133–4.
117. Roskell, Clark and Rawcliffe, *House of Commons, 1386–1421*, ii, p. 149.
118. Attreed, *King's Towns*, concluding pages, especially p. 319.

Notes to Chapter 11: The Reformation

1. From epistle dedicatory by Robert Hill.
2. See Chapter 6, above.
3. Recent surveys of the English Reformation which assess the local effects of these major measures include C. Haigh, *English Reformations: Religion, Politics and Society under the Tudors* (Oxford, 1993); R. Rex, *Henry VIII and the English Reformation* (Basingstoke, 1993); and E. Duffy, *The Stripping of the Altars: Traditional Religion in England c. 1400-c. 1580* (New Haven and London, 1992).
4. R. A. Houlbrooke, 'Refoundation and Reformation, 1538–1628', in *Norwich Cathedral*, pp. 507–8; M. C. McClendon, *The Quiet Reformation: Magistrates and the Emergence of Protestantism in Tudor Norwich* (Stanford, 1999), pp. 72, 101–4, 119, 121–3; Blomefield, *Norfolk*, iii, pp. 220, 261; iv, pp. 72, 86, 109, 169–83, 339, 390–94, 421, 433–4; T. F. Barton, ed., *The Registrum Vagum of Anthony Harison* (2 vols, NRS, xxxii, xxxiii, 1963–4), i, pp. 124–6.
5. John Foxe, *Acts and Monuments*, ed. J. Pratt (8 vols, London, 1877), iv, pp. 621–2, 624–32, 635–6, 641–3.
6. McClendon, *Quiet Reformation*, pp. 73–81, 111–20, 123–42; Nicholas Sotherton, *The Commoyson in Norfolk 1549*, ed. S. Yaxley (Dereham, 1987), pp. 5, 15, 21; W. Rye, ed., *Depositions Taken before the Mayor and Aldermen of Norwich, 1549–1567; Extracts from the Court Books of the City of Norwich, 1666–1668* (Norfolk and Norwich Archaeological Society, Norwich, 1905), pp. 24–5; D. MacCulloch, ed., 'The *Vita Mariae Angliae Reginae* of Robert Wingfield of Brantham', *Camden Miscellany, 28* (Camden Society, fourth series, xxix, 1984), p. 253.
7. D. MacCulloch, 'A Reformation in the Balance: Power Struggles in the Diocese of Norwich, 1533–1553', in C. Rawcliffe, R. Virgoe and R. Wilson, eds, *Counties and Communities: Essays on East Anglian History Presented to Hassell*

Smith (Norwich, 1996), pp. 97–114; R. Houlbrooke, *Church Courts and the People during the English Reformation, 1520–1570* (Oxford, 1979), pp. 181–2, 218–19, 232–7; Foxe, *Acts and Monuments*, viii, pp. 380–81, 427–9.

8. N. L. Jones, *Faith by Statute: Parliament and the Settlement of Religion, 1559* (London, 1982), emphasised the influence of conservative opposition; D. MacCulloch, *Tudor Church Militant: Edward VI and the Protestant Reformation* (London, 2000), pp. 185–95, that of Elizabeth's own conservatism. P. Collinson, *The Elizabethan Puritan Movement* (London, 1967), is still the standard account of its subject; for origins, see ibid., pp. 21–55, 71–83.
9. R. A. Houlbrooke, ed., *The Letter Book of John Parkhurst Bishop of Norwich* (NRS, xliii, 1974 and 1975), especially pp. 25–32, 38, 42–7; A. H. Smith, *County and Court: Government and Politics in Norfolk, 1558–1603* (Oxford, 1974), pp. 21–44; Blomefield, *Norfolk*, iii, pp. 279–80.
10. W. J. C. Moens, *The Walloons and their Church at Norwich: Their History and Registers, 1565–1832* (Huguenot Society, i, 1887–8), especially pp. 21, 38; Blomefield, *Norfolk*, iii, pp. 292–4; J. Browne, *History of Congregationalism and Memorials of the Churches in Norfolk and Suffolk* (London, 1877), p. 37.
11. Smith, *County and Court*, pp. 47–8, 157, 201–28; Houlbrooke, *Letter Book of Parkhurst*, pp. 46–7, 49–53, 164–5, 231–6, 241–2, 245–7; D. MacCulloch, *Suffolk and the Tudors: Politics and Religion in an English County 1500–1600* (Oxford, 1986), pp. 97–100, 185–6.
12. Collinson, *Puritan Movement*, pp. 243–329; Smith, *County and Court*, pp. 62–3, 84, 185, 187, 225; MacCulloch, *Suffolk and the Tudors*, pp. 215, 217–8.
13. Barton, *Registrum Vagum*, i, p. 177; M. E. Simkins, 'Ecclesiastical History (From A. D. 1279)', *VCH Norfolk*, ii, p. 277 n. 1.
14. On the difficulties involved in interpreting early modern wills, see, for example, J. D. Alsop, 'Religious Preambles in Early Modern English Wills as Formulae,' *Journal of Ecclesiastical History*, xl (1989), pp. 19–27; Duffy, *Stripping of Altars*, chapter 15; C. Litzenberger, 'Local Responses to Religious Changes: Evidence from Gloucestershire Wills', in E. J. Carlson, ed., *Religion and the English People 1500–1640: New Voices/New Perspectives* (Kirksville, Missouri, 1998), pp. 245–70; M. Zell, 'The Use of Religious Preambles as a Measure of Religious Belief in the Sixteenth Century', *Bulletin of the Institute of Historical Research*, l (1977), pp. 241–53.
15. McClendon, *Quiet Reformation*, appendix 2.
16. McClendon, *Quiet Reformation*, pp. 130–32, appendix 3.
17. McClendon, *Quiet Reformation*, pp. 180–82, appendix 4.
18. George Leedes, George Gardiner and John Walker, discussed below, preached before the magistrates from 1561–62: NRO, NCR, 18A, Chamberlains' Accounts, 1551–1567, fos 228r, 260v, 272v, 305r, 335r, 336r, 360v. Chamberlains' accounts for the 1570s have not survived, but those that are extant from the

1580s show the frequent engagement of other puritan clergy, such as Thomas Roberts, John More, John Burgess and John Holden, also discussed below. See, for example, Chamberlains' Accounts, 1580–1589, fos 31r, 65r–5v, 97v, 109r, 197v, 267v; 1589–1602, fos 60r, 256r–57v, 292v.

19. PRO, PCC 6 Sheffield.
20. PRO, PCC 13 Lyon; Houlbrooke, *Letter Book of Parkhurst*, pp. 41, 53, 118.
21. PRO, PCC 49 Pyckeryng; 27 Tirwhite.
22. John Bale, *The Actes of English Votaryes* (1560; reprint, Amsterdam, 1979), part 2, sigs 03–05.
23. M. C. McClendon, '"Against God's Word": Government, Religion and the Crisis of Authority in Early Reformation Norwich', *Sixteenth-Century Journal*, xxv (1994), pp. 353–69.
24. NRO, NCR, 16A, Mayor's Court Book, 1549–1555, p. 295.
25. Robert Watson, *Aetiologia Roberti Watsoni* (n. p., 1556), sigs G3-G6.
26. *CLPFD*, xiii (part 2), no. 282; xv, no. 831 (72); C. Rawcliffe, *Medicine for the Soul: The Life, Death and Resurrection of an English Medieval Hospital* (Stroud, 1999), chapter 7.
27. For a fuller discussion of these issues, see McClendon, *Quiet Reformation*, chapter 3.
28. NRO, NCR, 16C, Assembly Minute Book, 1510–1550, fos 145v, 179v, 185r; *RCN*, ii pp. 120–21, 123–4.
29. D. Galloway, ed., *Records of Early English Drama: Norwich, 1540–1642* (Toronto, 1984), pp. 17, 340–41; NRO, NCR, 16A, Mayor's Court Book, 1540–1549, p. 218; 18A, Chamberlains' Accounts, 1537–1547, quoted in A. H. Nelson, *The Medieval English Stage: Corpus Christi Pageants and Plays* (Chicago, 1974), p. 125.
30. NRO, NCR, 16A, Assembly Proceedings, 1493–1553, fo. 239r; J. Cornwall, *Revolt of the Peasantry, 1549* (London, 1977), p. 224.
31. Galloway, *Norwich*, pp. 38–42, 392.
32. NRO, NCR, 16A, Mayor's Court Book, 1587–1595, p. 191; 16C, Assembly Minute Book, 1585–1613, fo. 51r; D. Cressey, *Bonfires and Bells: National Memory and the Protestant Calendar in Elizabethan and Stuart England* (Berkeley, 1989), p. 51. This service continued at least until the end of Elizabeth's reign: see Galloway, *Norwich*, pp. 95, 99, 101, 103, 105, 107, 114, 119, 122.
33. In 1546, Sir Roger directed the mayor's court to punish three men whom he had seen reading the Bible in Norwich cathedral, contrary to the statute of 34–35 Henry VIII, cap. l (1543): NRO, NCR, 16A, Mayor's Court Book, 1534–1549, fo. 51v; 1540–1549, p. 323.
34. On the development of the structure of Norwich's city government, see McClendon, *Quiet Reformation*, pp. 3–4.

35. NRO, NCR, 16A, Mayor's Court Book, 1534–1540, pp. 13–15.
36. NRO, NCR, 16A, Mayor's Court Book, 1534–1540, p. 21, and 1534–1549, fo. 8r, where the case is recorded again with minor variations. On Barret, see *DNB*, *sub nomine*; L. Fairfield, *John Bale: Mythmaker for the English Reformation* (West Lafayette, Indiana, 1976), pp. 39–40.
37. NRO, NCR, 16A, Mayor's Court Book, 1534–1549, fo. 222r.
38. NRO, NCR, 16A, Mayor's Court Book, 1540–1549, p. 374. Gilmyn had appeared before the court previously in 1536 for possessing 'bokes suspected'. He was 'sette at large' on 'truste of amendment' at that time also: ibid., p. 320.
39. NRO, NCR, 16A, Mayor's Court Book, 1540–1549, p. 454. For other outbursts against Rose see ibid., pp. 455, 467; 12A, Norwich Sessions Depositions, Book 1A, fos 108v–109r.
40. NRO, NCR, 16A, Mayor's Court Book, 1534–1549, fo. 63v.
41. NRO, NCR, 16A, Mayor's Court Book, 1549–1555, p. 192.
42. McClendon, *Quiet Reformation*, pp. 81–5. On London during this period, see S. Brigden, *London and the Reformation* (Oxford, 1989), pp. 320–40.
43. McClendon, *Quiet Reformation*, pp. 166–74.
44. Foxe, *Acts and Monuments*, viii, pp. 380–81.
45. Foxe, *Acts and Monuments*, viii, pp. 427–9.
46. On the aldermen who died in the epidemic, see McClendon, *Quiet Reformation*, pp. 194–8, appendix 5.
47. McClendon, *Quiet Reformation*, pp. 248–9.
48. McClendon, *Quiet Reformation*, chapter 6.
49. Blomefield, *Norfolk*, iv, pp. 52, 70, 78, 105–6, 116, 118, 121–2, 136–7, 144, 299–300, 439, 440, 443, 450, 475.
50. Barton, *Registrum Vagum*, i, p. 53; ii, pp. 322–3; Blomefield, *Norfolk*, iv, pp. 75, 186–8, 246–7, 249, 286, 300–1, 390–92; J. Caley and J. Hunter, eds, *Valor Ecclesiasticus temp. Henrici VIII, Auctoritate Regia Institutus* (6 vols, Record Commission, 1810–34), iii, pp. 284, 289, 293–4.
51. NRO, ANW/1/4 (see Norwich section of 1563 archdeaconry visitation record); J. F. Williams, ed., *Diocese of Norwich: Bishop Redman's Visitation, 1597* (NRS, xviii, 1946), pp. 29–36; T. Newhouse, *A Learned and Fruitfvll Sermon, Preached in Christs Church in Norwich* (London, 1612), epistle dedicatory by Robert Hill; Blomefield, *Norfolk*, iii, pp. 361–2.
52. *DNB*, iii, p. 278; Foxe, *Acts and Monuments*, viii, pp. 581–4; Blomefield, *Norfolk*, iii, p. 666; McClendon, *Quiet Reformation*, pp. 75–6, 118, 120, 133–4; NRO, NCR, 16A, Mayor's Court Book, 1534–1540, fo. 26v; F. W. Russell, *Kett's Rebellion in Norfolk* (London, 1859), pp. 62–6; Chapter 12, below, discusses the rebellion in greater detail.
53. G. R. Elton, *Policy and Police: The Enforcement of the Reformation in the Age of Thomas Cromwell* (Cambridge, 1972), pp. 138–9; NRO, NCR, 16A, Mayor's

Court Book, 1534–1540, fo. 152r; *CPR, Edward VII*, ii, *1548–1549*, p. 178; iv, *1550–1553*, p. 53; Sotherton, *Commoyson*, p. 7; Russell, *Kett's Rebellion*, pp. 37–8; McClendon, *Quiet Reformation*, pp. 140–42; NRO, DN/ACT 6/7a, fos 132r, 156v, 161v, 168v; DN/ACT 6/7b, fo. 102v.

54. McClendon, *Quiet Reformation*, pp. 163–4; Watson, *Aetiologia*, fos 10r–52r; NRO, DN/ACT 7/8, fo. 26r; Foxe, *Acts and Monuments*, viii, pp. 588–90; G. Baskerville, 'Married Clergy and Pensioned Religious in Norwich Diocese, 1555', *EHR*, xlviii (1933), pp. 49, 52–3; Blomefield, *Norfolk*, iii, pp. 618, 666.
55. *DNB*, xx, p. 412; lix, p. 72; McClendon, *Quiet Reformation*, pp. 198, 215; NRO, ANW/1/4; Cambridge, Corpus Christi College, MS 97, p. 198; PRO, SP 15/12/27.
56. *DNB*, xxxviii, p. 425; Houlbrooke, *Letter Book of Parkhurst*, p. 216; Blomefield dates More's presence at St Andrew's from 1571 (*Norfolk*, iv, p. 301); F. R. Beecheno, *Notes on the Church of St Andrew Norwich* (Norwich, 1883), p. 4, lists him under 1573.
57. Browne, *Congregationalism*, pp. 18–20; Collinson, *Puritan Movement*, pp. 127, 202–4, 213–14; A. Peel, ed., *The Seconde Parte of a Register* (2 vols, Cambridge, 1915), i, pp. 143–7; Houlbrooke, *Letter Book of Parkhurst*, pp. 38 n., 130, 254; Blomefield, *Norfolk*, iv, p. 458 (though Roberts clearly did not die in 1576).
58. A. H. Smith, G. M. Baker and R. W. Kenny, eds, *The Papers of Nathaniel Bacon of Stiffkey*, i, *1556–1577* (NRS, xlvi, 1978 and 1979), pp. 236–7; Peel, *Seconde Parte*, i, pp. 157–60; A. Peel, *The Brownists in Norwich and Norfolk about 1580* (Cambridge, 1920), pp. 6–7.
59. *DNB*, vii, pp. 58–9; Peel, *Brownists*, p. 17; Peel, *Seconde Parte*, i, pp. 223–4, 244; Collinson, *Puritan Movement*, pp. 263–6; S. B. Babbage, *Puritanism and Richard Bancroft* (London, 1962), pp. 166–74; Williams, *Redman's Visitation*, pp. 29–36; Blomefield, *Norfolk*, iv, pp. 188, 327.
60. *DNB*, viii, p. 17; Newhouse, *Learned and Fruitfvll Sermon*, epistle dedicatory; Blomefield, *Norfolk*, iv, pp. 301, 312.
61. NRO, ANW/1/4; A. H. Smith and G. M. Baker, eds, *The Papers of Nathaniel Bacon of Stiffkey*, iii, *1586–1595* (NRS, liii, 1987 and 1988), pp. 238–40; Babbage, *Puritanism and Bancroft*, pp. 205–6. These statements exclude those members of the cathedral chapter who did not occupy city benefices.
62. Williams, *Redman's Visitation*, pp. 29–36; Peel, *Seconde Parte*, ii, p. 155; Barton, *Registrum Vagum*, i, pp. 159–62.
63. Houlbrooke, 'Refoundation and Reformation', pp. 521–4; Blomefield, *Norfolk*, iii, pp. 662, 665, 668; iv, pp. 187–8; Houlbrooke, *Letter Book of Parkhurst*, p. 216.
64. Blomefield, *Norfolk*, iv, p. 354; Houlbrooke, *Letter Book of Parkhurst*, pp. 161–2; Peel, *Seconde Parte*, ii, p. 155; Williams, *Redman's Visitation*, p. 36.
65. Houlbrooke, *Letter Book of Parkhurst*, p. 212; Blomefield, *Norfolk*, iv,

pp. 150–65, 273–4; Caley and Hunter, *Valor Ecclesiasticus*, iii, p. 294; J. T. Evans, *Seventeenth-Century Norwich: Politics, Religion and Government, 1620–1690* (Oxford, 1979), pp. 174, 226; R. A. Houlbrooke, 'Church Courts and People in the Diocese of Norwich, 1519–1570' (University of Oxford, DPhil thesis, 1970), pp. 101–5. The tower of St Stephen's was rebuilt in 1601.

Notes to Chapter 12: Kett's Rebellion

1. Ralph Holinshed, *Chronicles of England, Scotland and Ireland* (6 vols, 1577; second edn, 1580, reprinted London, 1808), iii, p. 989. Others, such as James Stotter of Ranworth, near Norwich, took a different view of the rebellion. He was said to have remarked in 1551 that 'suche as were slayn and dyd [died] upon mushold in the comocyon tyme wer honest men ... that Robert Kette was an honest man': NRO, NCR, 12A/1(a), City Quarter Sessions, 1549–1553, fo. 31r.
2. I am grateful to John Arnold for reading an early draft of this chapter, and to Paul Griffiths, Andy Hopper and Carole Rawcliffe for many conversations about sixteenth-century Norwich.
3. For the shifting representation of Kett's Rebellion, see my *Insurrection and Popular Political Culture in Tudor England: The Rebellions of 1459* (Cambridge, forthcoming). For the history of the plaque on Norwich Castle, see NRO, MS 4265, MC4/HEN43/26, 40; MS 21525, MC4/HEN8.
4. Until very recently, accounts of Kett's Rebellion have treated the Norfolk rising in isolation from the other insurrections of 1549. For descriptions of the Norfolk rebellion, see S. K. Land, *Kett's Rebellion: The Norfolk Rising of 1549* (London, 1977); F. W. Russell, *Kett's Rebellion in Norfolk* (London, 1859); S. T. Bindoff, *Kett's Rebellion, 1549* (London, 1949); J. Cornwall, *Revolt of the Peasantry, 1549* (London, 1977), chapters 7, 9 and 12; B. L. Beer, *Rebellion and Riot: Popular Disorder in England during the Reign of Edward VI* (Kent, Ohio, 1982), chapters 4 and 5. The best of these accounts remains Russell's 1859 work. For introductory discussions of the 1549 rebellions, see A. Wood, *Riot, Rebellion and Popular Politics in Early Modern England* (Basingstoke, 2002), pp. 54–71, and A. Fletcher and D. MacCulloch, *Tudor Rebellions* (1968; fourth edn, Harlow, 1997), pp. 50–80.
5. Holinshed, *Chronicles*, iii, p. 963; R. Woods, *Norfolke Furies, and their Foyle, under Kett, their Accursed Captaine* (London, 1615; second edn, 1623), sig. B3r-v.
6. For these negotiations, see E. Shagan, 'Protector Somerset and the 1549 Rebellions: New Sources and New Perspectives', *EHR*, cxiv (1999), pp. 34–63.
7. The Neville/Woods narrative has provided the main basis for all subsequent histories of Kett's Rebellion. See A. Neville, *De furoribus Norfolciensium Ketto*

duce (London, 1575), translated in 1615 as Woods, *Norfolke Furies.* Holinshed's *Chronicles*, although derivative of Neville, also provide some new information: iii, pp. 963–84. At least two eyewitness accounts of Kett's Rebellion were written, neither of which saw contemporary publication. That by Nicholas Sotherton survives as BL, MS Harley 1576, fos 251r–9r, and has been edited: see B. L. Beer, ed., '"The Commoyson in Norfolk, 1549": A Narrative of Popular Rebellion in Sixteenth-Century England', *Journal of Medieval and Renaissance Studies*, vi (1976), pp. 73–99. The other eyewitness account, known as the Norwich Roll, had been lost by 1859: see Russell, *Kett's Rebellion in Norfolk*, p. 38. But hints of its contents are apparent from its use in earlier works, in particular Anon., *The History of Kett's Rebellion in the Reign of Edward the Sixth* (Norwich, *c.* 1843), and Blomefield, *Norfolk*, iii, pp. 223–60.

8. Woods, *Norfolke Furies*, sigs H4r-I1v. The king of arms had been subject to similar abuse from Kentish rebels in July 1549: BL, Microfilm M485/39, MS Salisbury, 150, fo. 117r–17v. Royal heralds were accustomed to greater respect. Discussing the suppression of the Lincolnshire rising in 1536, Henry VIII assumed that 'the presence of our coat [of arms] was a greate means to abashe' the rebels: PRO, SP1/108, fo. 67r.
9. For recent critiques of this dichotomy, see E. Duffy, *The Voices of Morebath: Reformation and Rebellion in an English Village* (New Haven, 2001), pp. 129–32; Wood, *Riot*, pp. 54–60.
10. BL, MS Harley 304, fos 75r–7v, reproduced in Fletcher and MacCulloch, *Tudor Rebellions*, pp. 144–6.
11. PRO, SP1/119, fo. 38r; NRO, NCR, 12A/1(a), City Quarter Sessions, 1549–1553, fos 8r–9r; 16A/4, Mayor's Court Book, 1534–1549, fo. 65r; 16A/6, Mayor's Court Book, 1549–1555, pp. 1–2; Blomefield, *Norfolk*, iii, p. 263.
12. A. Jones, '"Commotion Time": The English Risings of 1549' (University of Warwick, PhD thesis, 2003), provides a detailed narrative of the rebellions outside Norfolk, Devon and Cornwall. The essential discussion of the wider geographical context of Kett's Rebellion is D. MacCulloch, 'Kett's Rebellion in Context', *Past and Present*, lxxxiv (1979), pp. 36–59. For risings in Cornwall and Devon, see F. Rose-Troup, *The Western Rebellion of 1549* (London, 1913).
13. J. G. Nichols, ed., *Literary Remains of King Edward the Sixth* (2 vols, London, 1857), ii, pp. 226–7.
14. MacCulloch, 'Kett's Rebellion in Context', pp. 39–40.
15. D. MacCulloch, *Tudor Church Militant: Edward VI and the Protestant Reformation* (London, 1999), p. 49. For the council's criticism of Northampton's generalship, see N. Pocock, ed., *Troubles Connected with the Prayer Book of 1549* (Camden Society, new series, xxxvii, 1884), pp. 58–9.

16. For the beginnings of this critique, see PRO, SP10/8/4, 33.
17. A. Vere Woodman, 'The Buckinghamshire and Oxfordshire Rising of 1549', *Oxoniensia*, xxii (1957), pp. 78–84.
18. M. E. James, *Society, Politics and Culture: Studies in Early Modern England* (Cambridge, 1986), pp. 344–57.
19. Beer, '"The Commoyson"', pp. 90–1.
20. On events in Sussex, see L. Stone, 'Patriarchy and Paternalism in Tudor England: The Earl of Arundel and the Peasants' Revolt of 1549', *Journal of British Studies*, xiii (1974), pp. 19–23.
21. Woods, *Norfolke Furies*, sig. K3r.
22. R. J. Hammond, 'The Social and Economic Circumstances of Kett's Rebellion' (University of London, MA thesis, 1933), remains useful.
23. Hence, for example, the title of Cornwall's book: *Revolt of the Peasantry, 1549*. Broad surveys of European rebellions also tend to present it as an 'agrarian' insurrection. See, for instance, P. Zagorin, *Rebels and Rulers, 1500–1660*, i, *Society, States and Early Modern Revolution: Agrarian and Urban Rebellions* (Cambridge, 1982), pp. 208–14.
24. Quoting NRO, NCR, 16A/2, Mayor's Court Book, 1510–1532, fos 15r, 16r. For early Tudor popular criticism of urban authority, see, for instance, PRO, STAC2/21/151; NCR, 16A/2, fo. 16v, p. 276; 12A/1(a), City Quarter Sessions, 1549–1553, fo. 76r. For criticism of lay subsidies, see 16A/2, fos 36r–7r, pp. 16–18, 173; 16A/3, Mayor's Court Book, 1534–1540, pp. 9–10.
25. C. Rawcliffe, *Medicine for the Soul: The Life, Death and Resurrection of an English Medieval Hospital* (Stroud, 1999), pp. 215–19. For two defining statements of popular perceptions of the governors of Tudor Norwich, see NRO, NCR, 12A/1 (c), City Quarter Sessions, 1561–1567, fo. 55r; *HMC, Salisbury (Cecil) MSS, XIII, Addenda 1276–1597* (London, 1915), pp. 168–9.
26. See, for instance, NRO, NCR, 12A/1(a), City Quarter Sessions, 1549–1553, fos 11v–12r.
27. NRO, NCR, 16A/4, Mayor's Court Book, 1534–1549, fo. 61v.
28. PRO, STAC2/2/225–7; NRO, NCR, 12A/1 (c), City Quarter Sessions, 1561–1567, fos 18r–19v.
29. For disputes over the city's commons, Thorpe Wood and Mousehold Heath, see NRO, NCR, 12A/1(a), City Quarter Sessions, 1549–1553, fo. 123r; 12A/1 (c), City Quarter Sessions, 1561–1567, fo. 23r; PRO, REQ2/18/106.
30. See for instance, NRO, NCR, 16A/2, Mayor's Court Book, 1510–1532, p. 227; 16A/3, Mayor's Court Book, 1534–1540, p. 23.
31. NRO, NCR, 17A, *Liber Albus*, fo. 8v. For other examples of serious trouble over food supply in the market place, see Blomefield, *Norfolk*, iii, pp. 197–8; NCR, 16A/2, Mayor's Court Book, 1510–1532, pp. 268–9, 319–20.
32. Quoting NRO, NCR, 16A/2, Mayor's Court Book, 1510–1532, p. 204. See, for

instance, the response to the economic troubles of the 1520s: ibid., pp. 138, 160, 201–2, 204, 207, 208, 210, 243, 256, 258, 263, 265.

33. P. Slack, *Poverty and Policy in Tudor and Stuart England* (Harlow, 1988), p. 123.
34. Cheke's *Hurt of Sedition* is reproduced in Holinshed, *Chronicles*, iii, pp. 987–1011.
35. Woods, *Norfolke Furies*, sig. D3r–3v; Beer, '"The Commoyson"', p. 85.
36. Woods, *Norfolke Furies*, sig. B1r; Blomefield, *Norfolk*, iii, pp. 228–9. For Cheke's critique of the Norwich governors, see Holinshed, *Chronicles*, iii, pp. 997–8.
37. NRO, NCR, 6A/4, Mayor's Court Book, 1534–1549, fos 66r–7r. Significantly, the Minute Books and Proceedings of the municipal assembly were not deployed as an official record during the insurrection: NRO, NCR, 16C/2, Assembly Minute Books, 1540–1550; 16D/2, Assembly Proceedings, 1491–1553.
38. Woods, *Norfolk Furies*, sigs B4v-C1r.
39. Beer, '"The Commoyson"', pp. 82, 88; Woods, *Norfolke Furies*, sig. F2v.
40. Woods, *Norfolke Furies*, sig. H2r.
41. Holinshed, *Chronicles*, iii, p. 972.
42. Holinshed, *Chronicles*, iii, p. 965; Woods, *Norfolke Furies*, sigs B3v, E3r–4v; Beer, '"The Commoyson"', p. 81.
43. Woods, *Norfolke Furies*, sig. B4v-r; Holinshed, *Chronicles*, iii, p. 964.
44. Beer, '"The Commoyson"', p. 92.
45. Blomefield, *Norfolk*, iii, p. 235.
46. Woods, *Norfolke Furies*, sigs E4v, F2v, F4v, G1r.
47. NRO, NCR, 16A/6, Mayor's Court Book, 1549–1555, p. 198.
48. NRO, NCR, 16D/1, Proceedings of the Municipal Assembly, 1491–1553, fo. 239r. See, for example, BL, Add. MS, 17,002, fo. 6v, a fifteenth-century breviary belonging to Norwich cathedral, the calendar of which contains a note recording the new service of celebration.
49. G. Orwell, *1984: A Novel* (London, 1949), p. 199.
50. NRO, NCR, 16A/6, Mayor's Court Book, 1549–1555, p. 3.

Notes to Chapter 13: Sickness and Health

1. G. Keynes, ed., *The Works of Sir Thomas Browne* (4 vols, London, 1964), i, part 1, p. 74.
2. NRO, NCR, 12A/1c, City Quarter Sessions, Interrogations and Depositions, 1561–1567, fos 92r–92v.
3. A. Batty Shaw, 'The Norwich School of Lithotomy', *Medical History*, xiv (1970), pp. 221–59.
4. K. Park, 'Medicine and Society in Medieval Europe, 500–1500', in A. Wear,

ed., *Medicine in Society* (Cambridge, 1992), pp. 59–90, provides a useful background.

5. E. A. Webb, ed., *The Records of St Bartholomew's Priory* (2 vols, Oxford, 1921), i, no. 25.
6. A. Stirland, 'The Human Bones', in B. Ayers, ed., *Excavations within the North-East Bailey of Norwich Castle, 1979* (EAA, report 28, 1985), pp. 49–58.
7. B. A. Hanawalt, *Growing Up in Medieval London* (Oxford, 1993), pp. 55–67, stresses 'the fragile years of childhood'. See also Chapter 9, above, for evidence of immigration, C. Roberts and M. Cox, *Health and Disease in Britain: From Prehistory to the Present Day* (Stroud, 2003), chapter 5, for a general survey of the archaeological evidence from later medieval towns, and M. Lewis, *Urbanisation and Child Health in Medieval and Post-Medieval England* (British Archaeological Reports, British Series, 339, 2002), chapter 2.
8. Thomas of Monmouth, *The Life and Miracles of St William of Norwich*, eds A. Jessopp and M. R. James (Cambridge, 1896), p. 167.
9. Thomas of Monmouth, *Life and Miracles of St William*, pp. 133, 169–70, 206.
10. Thomas of Monmouth, *Life and Miracles of St William*, pp. 78–9. For a fuller discussion of the religious component of medieval obstetrics, see C. Rawcliffe, 'Women, Childbirth, and Religion in Later Medieval England', in D. Wood, ed. *Women and Religion in Medieval England* (Oxford, 2003), pp. 91–117.
11. C. Rawcliffe, 'Curing Bodies and Healing Souls: Pilgrimage and the Sick in Medieval East Anglia', in C. Morris and P. Roberts, eds, *Pilgrimage: The English Experience from Becket to Bunyan* (Cambridge, 2002), pp. 108–40.
12. S. B. Meech, ed., *The Book of Margery Kempe* (Early English Text Society, ccxii, 1940), pp. 237, 346–8; S. Margeson, ed., *Norwich Households* (EAA, report 58, 1993), pp. 6–8.
13. M. R. V. Heale, 'Veneration and Renovation at a Small Norfolk Priory: St Leonard's, Norwich in the Later Middle Ages', *Historical Research*, lxxvi (2003), pp. 431–9; W. T. Bensly, 'St Leonard's Priory, Norwich', *NA*, xii (1895), pp. 198–201, 214–17. The girdle of the Virgin, conspicuously displayed there, was probably loaned to women in labour, as was the medieval custom.
14. See above, p. 128; and also C. Rawcliffe, *Medicine for the Soul: The Life, Death and Resurrection of an English Medieval Hospital* (Stroud, 1999), pp. 118, 125, 130–31, plates 9 and 33; W. H. St John Hope, 'Inventories of the Parish Church of St Peter Mancroft, Norwich', *NA*, xiv (1901), pp. 153–240, at pp. 161, 170, 172, 196–7, 204, 218, 221; P. Lasko and N. J. Morgan, *Medieval Art in East Anglia, 1300–1520* (Norwich, 1973), pp. 40, 50, 56, 66–7; B. R. McRee, 'Unity or Division? The Social Meaning of Guild Ceremony in Urban Communities', in B. A. Hanawalt and K. L. Reyerson, eds, *City and Spectacle in Medieval Europe* (Minneapolis, Minnesota, and London, 1994), pp. 201–2.
15. Stirland, 'Human Bones', pp. 54–6.

16. Thomas of Monmouth, *Life and Miracles of St William*, pp. 242–4, 271.
17. J. Bown and A. Stirland, *Criminals and Paupers: Excavations on the Site of the Church and Graveyard of St Margaret in Combusto, Norwich, 1987* (EAA, forthcoming), chapter 2, passim; Roberts and Cox, *Health and Disease*, pp. 236–41, 272–3.
18. M. R. James, 'Lives of St Walstan', *NA*, xix (1917), p. 258.
19. S. Anderson, 'Leprosy in a Medieval Churchyard in Norwich', in eadem, ed., *Current and Recent Research in Osteoarchaeology* (Oxford, 1998), pp. 31–7.
20. C. Rawcliffe, *The Hospitals of Medieval Norwich* (Studies in East Anglian History, ii, 1995), pp. 41–7, 138–9. Norwich's medieval hospitals and *leprosaria* are listed in the Appendix at the end of this chapter.
21. W. Hudson, ed., *Leet Jurisdiction in Norwich during the Thirteenth and Fourteenth Centuries* (Selden Society, v, 1892), pp. 68, 71, 72; NRO, DCN 79/3–4 (Holme Street leets, 1440–43). Individuals of high status, such as cathedral monks, were examined by medical experts to determine if they were leprous: NRO, DCN 35/7.
22. NRO, DCN 39/1.
23. For the social implications of the epidemic see A. Wear, *Knowledge and Practice in English Medicine* (Cambridge, 2000), pp. 260–74; and J. Arrizabalaga, J. Henderson and R. French, *The Great Pox: The French Disease in Renaissance Europe* (New Haven and London, 1997), pp. 146–70; and for the influential Ypres scheme, F. R. Salter, ed., *Some Early Tracts on Poor Relief* (London, 1926), pp. 32–76.
24. Rawcliffe, *Medicine for the Soul*, pp. 203–4, 223.
25. NRO, NCR, 8A/2, rots 3r–3v. See B. M. S. Campbell, ed., *Before the Black Death: Studies in the Crisis of the Early Fourteenth Century* (Manchester, 1991), for a wider discussion of these problems.
26. E. Rutledge, 'Immigration and Population Growth in Early Fourteenth-Century Norwich: Evidence from the Tithing Roll', *Urban History Yearbook* (1988), pp. 25–7; eadem, 'Landlords and Tenants: Housing and the Rented Property Market in Early Fourteenth-Century Norwich', *Urban History*, xxii (1995), p. 13.
27. J. Schofield and A. Vince, *Medieval Towns* (Leicester, 1994), pp. 196–202; Blomefield, *Norfolk*, iii, p. 77.
28. Stirland, 'Human Bones', pp. 53–4; Bown and Stirland, *Criminals and Paupers*; Roberts and Cox, *Health and Disease*, pp. 256–65; Bensly, 'St Leonard's Priory', pp. 198–201.
29. *Calendar of Inquisitions Miscellaneous, 1219–1307*, no. 2083.
30. *RCN*, ii, pp. 205–6.
31. *RCN*, i, p. 88; NRO, NCR, 16D, Assembly Proceedings, 1434–1491, fo. 5r; 1491–1553, fo. 202r; 16C, Assembly Minute Book, 1510–1550, fo. 237r–37v.

Similar measures for public health were adopted across medieval England in cities such as Gloucester: *HMC, Twelfth Report, Appendix IX* (London, 1891), pp. 432–5. The thinking behind them is explained in M. S. R. Jenner, 'The Great Dog Massacre', in W. G. Naphy and P. Roberts, eds, *Fear in Early Modern Society* (Manchester, 1997), pp. 44–61.

32. Hudson, *Leet Jurisdiction*, p. 13; H. M. Chew and W. Kellaway, eds, *London Assize of Nuisance, 1301–1431* (London Record Society, x, 1974), nos 63, 263, 293, 332, 382–3, 524.
33. Rawcliffe, *Medicine for the Soul*, pp. 42–4, 46–9, 63–4; P. Emery, *The Greyfriars: Excavations at the Former Mann Egerton Site, Prince of Wales Road, Norwich, 1990–95* (EAA, forthcoming); B. Ayers, *Norwich* (London, 1994), p. 73. Piped water was not made available to the public until the late sixteenth century: *RCN*, ii, pp. 392–4. Contrast this with the measures adopted far earlier in the capital: D. Keene, 'Issues of Water in Medieval London to *c.* 1300', *Urban History*, xxviii (2001), pp. 161–79.
34. NRO, NCR, 8A/1, 2. Death by drowning, sometimes in open pools and cesspits, was sufficiently common to fall within the remit of the city coroners: *RCN*, i, pp. 142–3. See *History of Norwich*, ii, Chapter 5, for a discussion of these dangers.
35. J. Kirkpatrick, *The Streets and Lanes of the City of Norwich*, ed. W. Hudson (Norwich, 1889), p. 28 n. 9.
36. Hudson, *Leet Jurisdiction*, p. 29.
37. Hudson, *Leet Jurisdiction*, pp. 10, 52, 55–7, 67, 99–103; M. Atkin, A. Carter and D. H. Evans, *Excavations in Norwich, 1971–1978: Part II* (EAA, report 26, 1985), pp. 240–44; M. Atkin and D. H. Evans, *Excavations in Norwich, 1971–1978: Part III* (EAA, report 100, 2002), p. 234; Rawcliffe, *Medicine for the Soul*, pp. 39, 46; S. Kelly, 'The Economic Topography and Structure of Norwich, *c.* 1300', in eadem, E. Rutledge and M. Tillyard, *Men of Property: An Analysis of the Norwich Enrolled Deeds, 1285–1311* (Norwich, 1983), pp. 22–4.
38. NRO, NCR, 16C, Assembly Minute Book, 1510–1550, fo. 2r–2v. In 1532 a rate was agreed for cleansing the river, 'provided that barkers, dyers, calaundrers, parchmentmakers, tewers, sadelers, brewers, wasshers of shepe, and all suche gret noyers of the same river be ffurder charged than other persons . . .': *RCN*, ii, pp. 122–3.
39. C. Rawcliffe, *Medicine and Society in later Medieval England* (Stroud, 1995), p. 39; BL, MS Arundel 292, fo. 71v, edited in A. R. Myers, ed., *English Historical Documents*, iv, *1327–1485* (London, 1969), p. 1055.
40. Hudson, *Leet Jurisdiction*, p. 70.
41. G. Rosser, 'Urban Culture and the Church 1300–1540', in D. M. Palliser, ed., *The Cambridge Urban History of Britain*, i, *600–1540* (Cambridge, 2000), pp. 340–41.

42. Thomas Starkey, *A Dialogue between Pole and Lupset*, ed. T. F. Mayer (Camden Society, fourth series, xxxvij, 1989), p. 38.
43. P. Gil Sotres, 'The Regimens of Health', in M. D. Grmek, ed., *Western Medical Thought from Antiquity to the Middle Ages* (Cambridge, Massachusetts, 1998), pp. 291–318. For a valuable discussion of the religious dimension of urban health, see P. Horden, 'Ritual and Public Health in the Early Medieval City', in S. Sheard and H. Power, eds, *Body and City: Histories of Urban Public Health* (Aldershot, 2000), pp. 17–40.
44. NRO, NCR, 18A/7, fos 305r–6v.
45. *RCN*, ii, p. 127. See also P. J. P. Goldberg 'Pigs and Prostitutes: Streetwalking in Comparative Perspective', in K. J. Lewis and others, eds, *Young Medieval Women* (Stroud, 1999), pp. 173–93; and idem, 'Coventry's "Lollard" Programme of 1492 and the Making of Utopia', in R. Horrox and S. Rees-Jones, eds, *Pragmatic Utopias: Ideas and Communities, 1200–1630* (Cambridge, 2001), pp. 97–116. I am grateful to Ms Isla Fay for drawing my attention to these references.
46. Hudson, *Leet Jurisdiction*, passim; *RCN*, ii, pp. 84, 85, 88; NRO, NCR, 16D, Assembly Proceedings, 1434–1491, fos 22r, 42v; 16C, Assembly Minute Book, 1510–1550, fos 2r–2v. See also, D. J. Keene, 'Rubbish in Medieval Towns', in A. R. Hall and H. K. Kenward, eds, *Environmental Archaeology in the Urban Context* (Council for British Archaeology, Research Report, xliii, 1982), pp. 26–30.
47. *RCN*, ii, pp. 91, 96–8; NRO, NCR, 16D, Assembly Proceedings, 1434–1491, fos 70r, 75v–76r. In 1459 provision had been made for the removal by boat of 'mukke and fylth' lying on the river bank: ibid., fo. 41r.
48. B. M. S. Campbell, *English Seigniorial Agriculture, 1250–1450* (Cambridge, 2000), pp. 361–2; NRO, NCR, 24E, Journal of John Boys, Carter at the Lathes, 1428–29.
49. *NCR*, ii, pp. 109–10.
50. See, for instance, NRO, NCR, 7C, Treasurers' Accounts for 1406–7, 1408–9, 1410–11 (when 33s. 6d. was also spent cleansing public latrines), 1416–17, 1418–19, 1420–21; Hudson, *Leet Jurisdiction*, p. 56.
51. Aitkin, *Excavations in Norwich*, p. 96.
52. J. A. F. Thomson, 'Piety and Charity in Late Medieval London', *Journal of Ecclesiastical History*, xvi (1965), pp. 178–95, at pp. 187–8.
53. *CPR, 1452–1461*, p. 441; NRO, NCR, 16D, Assembly Proceedings, 1434–1491, fo. 41r; NCC, reg. Jekkys, fos 47v–49r; Rawcliffe, *Medicine for the Soul*, p. 36.
54. PRO, PCC 2 Moone (Jowell); 9 Jankyn (Aldryche).
55. PRO, PCC 19 Populwell.
56. Blomefield, *Norfolk*, iii, pp. 182–3; *RCN*, i, p. 107 (regulations about roofing materials were repeated in 1570, pp. 137–40). Precautions against fire were

taken long before then. In 1437 the assembly ruled that each ward should keep an accessible supply of ladders; and in 1474 two wells were constructed to provide water in case of conflagration: NRO, NCR, 16D, Assembly Proceedings, 1434–1491, fos 6r, 87r.

57. See, for example, charges laid against the under sheriff, Richard Cattlyn, in 1520: PRO, STAC 2/2/225–7.
58. A. Luders and others, eds, *Statutes of the Realm* (11 vols, London, 1810–28), iii, 26 Henry VIII, cap. 8. The assembly was still dealing with petitions for the award of 'grounde decaied by the ffyer' in 1538, the new occupants being obliged to enclose and develop their plots: *RCN*, ii, p. 122.
59. *RCN*, i, pp. 141–2, 174–6, 188–90.
60. NRO, NCR, 16A/2, Mayor's Court Book, 1510–1532, fo. 138r; *RCN*, ii, pp. xcvii, 116–18, 161, 163–5; G. Johnson, 'Chronological Memoranda Touching the City of Norwich', *NA*, i (1847), p. 144.
61. NRO, NCR, 16A/3, Mayor's Court Book, 1534–1540, fo. 21.
62. Rawcliffe, *Medicine for the Soul*, pp. 18–33; eadem, *Hospitals of Medieval Norwich*, pp. 83–4, 146–8, 165–6.
63. See above, p. 128.
64. Rawcliffe, *Hospitals of Medieval Norwich*, pp. 143–6, 154–6.
65. Tanner, *CLMN*, p. 243. See also the wills of John Gilbert (d. 1466) and Robert Jannys (d. 1530): NRO, NCC, reg. Jekkys, fo. 48; Tanner, *CLMN*, p. 248. A Norwich labourer then earned less than 2d. a day.
66. NRO, NCR, reg. Doke, fos 192r–95r (1442–43).
67. NRO, NCC, reg. Hyrning, fos 148v–50r (Danyell); Jekkys, fos 100r–1v (Northalis); Popy, fo. 258r (Claxton); PRO, PCC 31 Holgrave (Brown); Tanner, *CLMN*, p. 230 (Dogett).
68. NRO, NCC, reg. Popy, fo. 491v. Thomas Ridlond (d. 1466) likewise expected his almsmen to stay for mass at All Saints, Ber Street, before receiving their doles: NCR, 1C, roll 19B, rot. 1v. Such concerns were voiced throughout late medieval England: P. J. P. Goldberg, 'Performing the Word of God: Corpus Christi in the Northern Province', in D. Wood, ed., *Life and Thought in the Northern Church, c. 1100-c. 1700* (Studies in Church History, *subsidia*, xii, 1999), pp. 145–70.
69. PRO, PCC 7 Blanyr.
70. Thomas of Monmouth, *Life and Miracles of St William*, p. 270.
71. Bown and Stirland, *Criminals and Paupers*; C. M. Woolgar, ed., *Household Accounts from Medieval England* (Records of Economic and Social History, new series, xvii–viii, 1992–93), i, pp. 177–227.
72. M. Carlin, 'Fast Food and Urban Living Standards in Medieval England', in eadem and J. T. Rosenthal, eds, *Food and Eating in Medieval Europe* (London, 1998), pp. 27–51; Hudson, *Leet Jurisdiction*, pp. 6, 8–10, 13, 16. Since the very

poor would not have been able to afford better quality fare, their dependence on contaminated food would have been all the greater: see above, p. 164.

73. *RCN*, ii, p. 81.
74. *RCN*, ii, p. 72; NRO, NCR, 16D, Assembly Proceedings, 1491–1553, fo. 175v; 16A/2, Mayor's Court Book, 1510–1532, pp. 11, 48, 168, 169, 207.
75. Thomas of Monmouth, *Life and Miracles of St William*, pp. 203–5; B. Ward, *Miracles and the Medieval Mind* (Ashford, 1987), pp. 142–3.
76. Meech, *Book of Margery Kempe*, pp. 6–9, 177–9.
77. NRO, NCC, reg. Platfoote, fo. 105v.
78. PRO, C1/351/47–48.
79. NRO, NCR, 18A, Chamberlains' Account Book, 1541–1550, fo. 281r.
80. Raphael Holinshed, *Chronicles of England, Scotland and Ireland* (6 vols, New York, 1965), ii, pp. 1003–5.
81. Rawcliffe, *Hospitals of Medieval Norwich*, pp. 69–71. Some of the sisters of St Paul's (or Norman's) hospital appear to have followed a religious vocation, while others were the elderly dependents of influential citizens. In his will of 1442, for example, Alderman John Cambridge left 6s. 8d. to Dame Anneys, 'suster of Normanes, sumtyme servant to my wyf': NRO, NCC, reg. Doke, fos 192r–95v. In 1488, Margaret Skipwith promised the sisters who attended her funeral twice the amount offered to those who did not, thus confirming their status as deserving paupers: reg. Woolman, fo. 18v. See also DCN 69, fo. 64r (will of Leonard Telyoun, 1526).
82. This figure appears as one of the *memorabilia* recorded in the Mayor's Book of Norwich (begun in 1526), being written in the margin against an entry for the regnal year 23 Edward III. It may, as Hudson and Tingey argue, be an estimated total for the entire county, and certainly reflects the indelible impression left upon the collective memory by the first epidemic: *RCN*, ii, pp. cxx–xxi; Johnson, 'Chronological Memoranda', p. 141. Claims of plague deaths in Yarmouth were equally dramatic: P. Rutledge, 'A Fifteenth-Century Yarmouth Petition', *Great Yarmouth and District Archaeological Society Bulletin*, xlvi (1976), pp. 1–3.
83. M. Rose, *The Norwich Apocalypse* (Norwich, 1999), pp. 126–7. For a background to these ideas see R. Horrox, *The Black Death* (Manchester, 1995), part two, passim.
84. *CPR, 1350–1354*, pp. 283–4; *1377–1381*, p. 121; J. Campbell, 'Norwich', in M. Lobel, ed., *Historic Towns*, ii (London, 1975), p. 16; Kirkpatrick, *Streets and Lanes*, pp. 33, 96.
85. A. Gransden, 'A Fourteenth-Century Chronicle from the Grey Friars at Lynn', *EHR*, lxxii (1957), p. 275; V. H. Galbraith, ed., *The Anonimalle Chronicle 1333 to 1381* (Manchester, 1927), p. 58. The 1383 Norfolk plague appears to have struck 'only persons between the ages of seven and twenty-two': L. C. Hector

and B. Harvey, eds, *The Westminster Chronicle* (Oxford, 1982), pp. 44–5. See J. M. W. Bean, 'Plague, Population and Economic Decline in England in the Later Middle Ages', *EcHR*, second series, xv (1963), pp. 452–3, for a list of national and regional epidemics.

86. J. C. Russell, *British Medieval Population* (Albuquerque, New Mexico, 1948), pp. 142, 292–4; J. F. D. Shrewsbury, *A History of the Bubonic Plague in the British Isles* (Cambridge, 1970), pp. 96–7, dismisses claims for such a high death rate over this period, but correspondingly underestimates the pre-plague population of Norwich. The problems of interpreting the Norwich poll tax return are discussed in P. Dunn, 'After the Black Death: Society and Economy in Late Fourteenth-Century Norwich' (UEA, Norwich, PhD thesis, 2004), pp. 42–9.
87. See P. Slack, *The Impact of Plague on Tudor and Stuart England* (London, 1985), pp. 126–43, for a case study of Norwich in the sixteenth and seventeenth centuries.
88. N. Davis, ed., *Paston Letters and Papers of the Fifteenth Century* (2 vols, Oxford, 1971–76), i, pp. 315–16, 440–41.
89. Davis, *Paston Letters*, i, p. 616.
90. Rawcliffe, *Medicine and Society*, pp. 152–5, 161–5.
91. Woolgar, *Household Accounts*, ii, pp. 576, 578, 579.
92. C. Rawcliffe, 'On the Threshold of Eternity: Care for the Sick in East Anglian Monasteries', in eadem, C. Harper-Bill and R. G. Wilson, eds, *East Anglia's History: Studies in Honour of Norman Scarfe* (Woodbridge, 2002), pp. 41–72.
93. V. D. Lipman, *The Jews of Medieval Norwich* (London, 1967), pp. 117–18, 180, 183. Benedict the physician, whose son was reputedly abducted by the Jews of Norwich in 1231, was presumably a convert to Christianity: ibid., pp. 59–62.
94. Such as Geoffrey Arderne (1299), John Aylemer (1437), Edmund de Belaghe (1308), Alan de Bodham (1322), John Breton (1303), William atte Churche (1379), Roger Dyngle (1432), William de Felton (1333), Master Godfrey (1471), Master Hervey (1260), Simon Lokyer (1409), Robert Marche (1440), Alan le Mundrey (before 1293), Richard (*c.* 1280), John Shirburne (1452) and Roger Taylor (1434).
95. NRO, NCR, 16D, Assembly Proceedings, 1553–1583, fos 75v–76r. The company claimed, significantly, to be acting in the wider interests of the 'common welthe'.
96. S. T. Bindoff, ed., *The History of Parliament: The House of Commons, 1509–1558* (3 vols, London, 1982), ii, p. 313; J. R. Guy, 'The Episcopal Licensing of Physicians, Surgeons and Midwives', *Bulletin of the History of Medicine*, lvi (1982), pp. 528–42.
97. This was probably in the spicery: NRO, NCR, 1/12, mm. 7r, 7v; NPD, box 8,

parish of St Peter Mancroft, no. 144; Kirkpatrick, *Streets and Lanes*, pp. 32, 94–5.

98. NRO, NCR, 18A, Chamberlains' Account Book, 1541–1550, fo. 70v. Similar expenses are recorded in 1544: ibid., fos 174r–74v.
99. Kirkpatrick, *Streets and Lanes*, p. 38.
100. NRO, NCR, 16A/4, Mayor's Court Book, 1534–1549, fo. 33v.
101. T. Smith, L. T. Smith and L. Brentano, eds, *English Gilds* (Early English Text Society, xl, 1890), p. 27.
102. Rawcliffe, *Medicine and Society*, pp. 133–8.
103. *RCN*, ii, pp. 279–80, 296–310. It is interesting to note the problems faced by the Gascon surgeon-physician (*medicus sive cirurgus*), Leonard Telyoun, in gaining acceptance in Norwich, despite the award to him of royal letters of protection: NRO, NCR, 16A/2, Mayor's Court Book, 1510–1532, pp. 143–4, 151.
104. There were fourteen admissions between 1350–99; forty-one between 1400–49; twenty-five between 1450–99; and twenty-nine (plus three surgeons) between 1500–49: W. Rye, ed., *Calendar of the Freemen of Norwich, 1317–1603* (London, 1888).
105. NRO, NCR, 1/14, m. 21v (brewing); 16A/5, Mayor's Court Book, 1540–1549, p. 164 (wax-working), p. 179 (hat-making); NCC, reg. Betyns, fos 9r–9v (smallholding); reg. A. Caston, fos 81r–81v (farming). Pelling, *Common Lot*, pp. 203–29, discusses occupational diversity after 1550.
106. NRO, NCR, 16A/2, Mayor's Court Book, 1510–1532, p. 226; 17B, *Liber Albus*, p. 172; H. Harrod, 'A Few Particulars Concerning Early Norwich Pageants', *NA*, iii (1852), p. 9.
107. Rawcliffe, *Medicine and Society*, p. 22.
108. See, for example, D. Jacquart, *Le milieu médical en France de XIIe au XVe siècle* (Paris, 1981), pp. 131–7.
109. Rawcliffe, *Medicine for the Soul*, pp. 227–8. Although the city provided surgery for its soldiers 'who came home very sore hurte': NRO, NCR, 18A, Chamberlains' Book, 1541–1550, fo. 218r.
110. H. Harrod, 'Early Norfolk Wills', *NA*, i (1847), pp. 124–5.
111. Smith and others, *English Gilds*, pp. 14–44; PRO, C43/44/301, 303; C43/47/290–91, 293, 297, 299; *RCN*, ii, pp. 294, 303–4; B. R. McRee, 'Charity and Gild Solidarity in Late Medieval England', *Journal of British Studies*, xxxii (1993), pp. 195–225.
112. Pelling, *Common Lot*, pp. 68–75.
113. P. H. Cullum, '"For Pore People Harberles": What Was the Function of the Maisondieu?', in D. J. Clayton and others, eds, *Trade, Devotion and Governance: Papers in Later Medieval History* (Stroud, 1994), pp. 38–9, 44–5; K. Giles, *An Archaeology of Social Identity: Guildhalls in York, c. 1350–1360* (British Archaeological Reports, British Series, 315, 2000), pp. 67–73.

114. NRO, NCC, reg. Hyrning, fos 32v–33r, 148v–50r; Rawcliffe, *Hospitals of Medieval Norwich*, pp. 146–9.
115. NRO, NCC, reg. Gyles, fos 93r–94v. Alms House Lane, near this site, is not recorded before 1626, although the name may denote continuity of occupation: Kirkpatrick, *Streets and Lanes*, p. 79.
116. Tanner, *CLMN*, pp. 64–6; NRO, NCC, reg. Surflete, fos 86r–88r (Baxstere, 1432), 124v–25r (Setman, 1428); Wylby, fo. 30v (Wetherby, 1444); reg. Aleyn, fos 130v–32v (Blickling, 1452); PRO, PCC 43 Holney (Steward).
117. Starkey, *Dialogue*, p. 62.

Select Bibliography

Each chapter of this volume provides detailed references to books, articles, theses and manuscripts relating to specific aspects of Norwich's medieval and early Tudor past. The works listed here offer an introduction to the city and the major themes in its history.

The City

M. Atkin, *Norwich: A History and Guide* (Stroud, 1993).

B. Ayers, *English Heritage Book of Norwich* (London, 1994; revised as *Norwich: A Fine City* in 2003).

A. D. Bayne, *A Comprehensive History of Norwich* (London, 1869).

F. Blomefield, *An Essay towards a Topographical History of the County of Norfolk* (11 vols, London, 1805–10), volumes three and four.

P. Browne, *The History of Norwich from the Earliest Records to the Present Time* (Norwich, 1814).

J. Campbell, 'Norwich', in M. D. Lobel, ed., *Historic Towns II* (London, 1975).

R. Frostick, *The Printed Plans of Norwich: A Carto-Bibliography* (Norwich, 2002).

B. Green and R. M. Young, *Norwich: The Growth of a City* (Norwich, 1963).

W. H. Hudson and J. C. Tingey, eds, *The Records of the City of Norwich* (2 vols, Norwich, 1906 and 1910).

J. Kirkpatrick, *The Streets and Lanes of Norwich: A Memoir*, ed. W. Hudson (Norwich, 1889).

C. Mackie, *The Norfolk Annals* (2 vols, Norwich, 1901).

F. Meeres, *A History of Norwich* (Chichester, 1998).

N. Pevsner and B. Wilson, *Norfolk I: Norwich and North-East* (Penguin 1997).

J. Pound, *Tudor and Stuart Norwich* (Chichester, 1988).

Institutions, Charities and Churches

I. Atherton and others, eds, *Norwich Cathedral: Church, City and Diocese 1096–1996* (London, 1996).

R. H. Frost, 'The Aldermen of Norwich 1461–1509: A Study of a Civic Elite' (University of Cambridge, PhD thesis, 1996).

M. Grace, ed., *Records of the Gild of St George in Norwich, 1389–1547* (NRS, ix, 1937).

E. Griffiths and A. Hassell Smith, *Buxom to the Mayor: A History of the Norwich Freemen and the Town Close Estate* (Norwich, 1987).

R. Harries, P. Cattermole and P. Mackintosh, *A History of Norwich School* (Norwich, 1991).

T. A. Heslop, *Norwich Castle Keep: Romanesque Architecture and Social Context* (Norwich, 1994).

J. Hooper, *Norwich Charities: Short Sketches of Their Origins and History* (Norwich, 1898).

W. Hudson, *Leet Jursisdiction in the City of Norwich during the Thirteenth and Fourteenth Centuries* (Selden Society, v, 1891).

J. Kirkpatrick, *History of the Religious Orders and Communities, and of the Hospitals and Castle of Norwich*, ed. D. Turner (Yarmouth, 1845).

M. C. McClendon, *The Quiet Reformation: Magistrates and the Emergence of Protestantism in Tudor Norwich* (Stanford, 1999).

C. Noble, 'Aspects of Life at Norwich Cathedral Priory in the Later Medieval Period' (UEA, Norwich, PhD thesis, 2001).

M. Pelling, *The Common Lot: Sickness, Medical Occupations and the Urban Poor in Early Modern England* (London, 1998).

J. Pound, ed., *The Norwich Census of the Poor 1570* (NRS, xl, 1971).

C. Rawcliffe, *The Hospitals of Medieval Norwich* (Studies in East Anglian History, ii, 1995).

C. Rawcliffe, *Medicine for the Soul: The Life, Death and Resurrection of an English Medieval Hospital* (Stroud, 1999).

N. Tanner, *The Church in Late Medieval Norwich* (Toronto, 1984).

People, Politics and Pleasures

C. Abbott, *Julian of Norwich: Autobiography and Theology* (Cambridge, 1999).

B. Cozens-Hardy and E. A. Kent, *The Mayors of Norwich 1403 to 1835* (Norwich, 1938).

E. C. Fernie, *An Architectural History of Norwich Cathedral* (Oxford, 1993).

D. Galloway, *Records of Early English Drama: Norwich, 1540–1642* (Toronto, 1984).

F. L. Huntley, *Sir Thomas Browne: A Biographical and Critical Study* (Ann Arbor, Michigan, 1962).

G. Jantzen, *Julian of Norwich* (London, 1987).

V. D. Lipman, *The Jews of Medieval Norwich* (London, 1967).

P. C. Maddern, *Violence and Social Order: East Anglia 1422–1442* (Oxford, 1992).

H. W. Saunders, *A History of the Norwich Grammar School* (Norwich, 1932).

Thomas of Monmouth, *The Life and Miracles of St William of Norwich*, eds A. Jessopp and M. R. James (Cambridge, 1896).

W. Wicks, *Inns and Taverns of Old Norwich* (Norwich, 1925).

C. Woodforde, *The Norwich School of Glass-Painting* (Oxford, 1950).

The Economy

P. Dunn, 'After the Black Death: Society and Economy in Later Fourteenth-Century Norwich' (UEA, Norwich, PhD thesis, 2004).

A. King, 'The Merchant Class and Borough Finances in Late Medieval Norwich' (University of Oxford, DPhil thesis, 1989).

U. M. Priestley, ed., *Men of Property: An Analysis of the Norwich Enrolled Deeds 1285–1311* (Norwich, 1983).

U. M. Priestley, ed., *The Great Market: A Survey of Nine Hundred Years of Norwich Provision Market* (Norwich, 1987).

E. Rutledge, ed., *The Norwich Landgable Assessment 1568–70* (NRS, lxiii, 1999).

Index